Introduction to **BUSINESS MANAGEMENT**

Introduction to **BUSINESS MANAGEMENT**

SIXTH EDITION

Editors
Prof GJ de J Cronje
Prof GS du Toit
Dr MDC Motlatla (Consulting editor)
Prof A de K Marais

Authors
Prof JA Badenhorst
Prof MC Cant
Prof GJ de J Cronje
Prof GS du Toit
Prof BJ Erasmus
Prof PA Grobler
Prof LP Krüger
Mr R Machado
Prof A de K Marais
Prof J Marx
Prof JW Strydom
Prof R T Mpofu

OXFORD
UNIVERSITY PRESS

OXFORD
UNIVERSITY PRESS

Southern Africa

Oxford University Press Southern Africa (Pty) Ltd

Vasco Boulevard, Goodwood, Cape Town, Republic of South Africa
P O Box 12119, N1 City, 7463, Cape Town, Republic of South Africa

Oxford University Press Southern Africa (Pty) Ltd is a wholly-owned subsidiary of
Oxford University Press, Great Clarendon Street, Oxford OX2 6DP.

The Press, a department of the University of Oxford, furthers the University's objective of
excellence in research, scholarship, and education by publishing worldwide in

Oxford New York

Auckland Dar es Salaam Hong Kong Karachi
Kuala Lumpur Madrid Melbourne Mexico City Nairobi
New Delhi Shanghai Taipei Toronto

With offices in

Argentina Austria Brazil Chile Czech Republic France Greece
Guatemala Hungary Italy Japan Poland Portugal Singapore South Korea
Switzerland Turkey Ukraine Vietnam

Oxford is a registered trade mark of Oxford University Press
in the UK and in certain other countries

Published in South Africa
by Oxford University Press Southern Africa (Pty) Ltd, Cape Town

Introduction to Business Management

ISBN 978 0 19 578129 8

© Oxford University Press Southern Africa (Pty) Ltd 2006

The moral rights of the author have been asserted
Database right Oxford University Press Southern Africa (Pty) Ltd (maker)

Previously published by Southern Book Publishers (Pty) Ltd and by International
Thomson Publishing
First edition 1987, second edition 1990, third edition 1994,
fourth edition 1997, fifth edition 2000, sixth edition 2003

Tenth impression 2007

Commissioning editor: Marian Griffin
Senior editor: Annette de Villiers
Editor: Lynda Gilfillan
Indexer: Ethné Clarke
Designer: Christopher Davis

Set in 9pt on 12pt Stone Serif
Reproduction by Global Graphics
Cover reproduction by The Image Bureau
Imagesetting by Castle Graphics
Printed and bound by ABC Press, Cape Town

The authors and publishers gratefully acknowledge permission to reproduce
material in this book. Every effort has been made to trace copyright holders,
but where this has proved impossible, the publishers would be grateful for
information which would enable them to amend any omissions in future editions

Abridged table of contents

Contents

Preface

This book is about the management of business organisations in the South African business environment. It describes how managers should manage resources and activities in such a way that organisations can operate as profitably as possible, thereby increasing the wealth of society. This, in a nutshell, is what business management is all about.

Since the publication of the first edition nearly 20 years ago, almost half a million students at many universities and other institutions have used *Introduction to Business Management* in preparation for their careers in business. In this sixth edition the authors have endeavoured to retain all the elements that have contributed to the book's success. Comments by students and academics were continuously incorporated into the text. This edition also retains the pragmatic approach adopted in the previous editions; true theory of business management is illuminated with practical examples and case studies. In this way, theoretical principles and concepts are explained in the South African business context – a crucial feature obviously missing from imported texts. This approach also ensures that both students and business people will find the text eminently readable.

The book was written by a team of professors of the Department of Business Management at the University of South Africa, who were able to utilise the advantages of functional specialisation. The authors selected the content of the book in accordance with their approach to the teaching of management as well as years of exposure to typical South and Southern African students. In this revision the following guidelines, originally adopted for the book, are still adhered to:

- the contents must be relevant and useful;
- practical examples must be based on scientific research, actual management experience and as far as possible in an African context;
- learning outcomes must be clearly specified;
- the text must be readable.

The first part of the book introduces the reader to business management and describes the role of the entrepreneur and manager in the business world, the business organisation as the subject of study and the South African business environment. A new chapter on entrepreneurship has been added to fully describe the driving force behind the business organisation and the market economy. Part 2 contains an exposition of the management process and a survey of general management principles on which the functional management areas discussed in Part 3 are based. Part 3 deals with marketing management, financial management, operations management and purchasing management. In Part 4 a number of contemporary management issues, such as productivity, globalisation and knowledge management are briefly discussed.

The book has been subjected to didactic editing and great care has been taken to ensure that the text conforms to the scientific curriculum requirements demanded of a book that simultaneously keeps abreast of the needs of business people and meets the requirements of an introduction to the science of business management.

We are grateful to colleagues and students who have, over the years, contributed to the ideas expressed in this book. When revising the text for this sixth edition we also gratefully benefited from the intellectual inputs of colleagues at other universities, business schools and other institutions, whose contributions have helped to improve the book.

We continue to welcome constructive comments from colleagues at universities as well as from managers in business practice in an attempt to make future management education in South Africa even more relevant and meaningful.

The authors

PART 1

Introduction to business management

1

The business world and business management

The purpose of this chapter

This is the introductory chapter of a textbook that introduces the student to the science of business management. It discusses the role of business in society and explains how a business organisation in a market economy employs the various resources of a nation – its natural resources, human resources, financial resources and entrepreneurship — in order to satisfy the need for products and services. This chapter gives an overview of the prevailing economic systems in the world, and explains how the business organisation functions in a market economy.

It is against this background that the purpose and nature of business management is examined, particularly with regard to the task of business management, which involves studying the factors, methods and principles that enable a business to function as efficiently as possible. A classification of the study material of business management is also presented.

Learning outcomes

The content of this chapter will enable learners to:
- Understand the role of the business organisation in society
- Describe the needs of society and how the business organisation satisfies those needs in a market economy
- Distinguish between the three main economic systems in the world
- Explain the interface between the business organisation and a market economy
- Describe the nature and purpose of business management as a science, that is, to study the factors, methods and principles that enable a business to function efficiently
- Comment on the development of business management as a science
- Distinguish and comment on the different management functions

1.1 The role of business in society

The business world is a complex system of individuals and business organisations that, in a market economy, involves the activity of transforming resources into products and services in order to meet the needs of people. These products and services are offered to the market in exchange for a profit. This description of business emphasises four different elements.

Firstly, business activity involves human activities. Business organisations are managed by people. While businesses may own property, machines and

3

money, all of these are managed or operated by people. Secondly, business activity involves production, which is the transformation of certain resources into products and services as illustrated in figure 1.1. This may, for example, be the conversion of flour, sugar and butter into bread, or the conversion of bricks, sand, cement, wood and steel into a house. Indeed, even services are produced, for example, a hospital, where labour, beds and medicine are converted into a health service. Thirdly, business involves exchange. Businesses produce products and services, not for their own use, but to exchange them for money or for other products and services. Finally, business involves **profit**. Neither individuals nor business organisations could continue producing products and services without earning a profit. Profit is the reward for meeting the needs of people, and it enables businesses to pay for resources and to make a living.

Figure 1.1: The transformation of a nation's resources into products and services by entrepreneurs

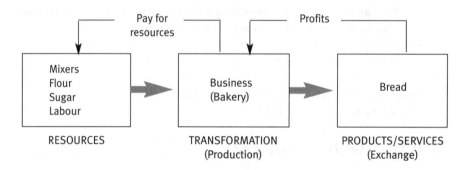

The business world is therefore a system of individuals and business organisations that produces products and services to meet people's needs. Some businesses produce tangible products such as cars, bread, houses or bicycles. Other businesses produce services such as transport, communication, television entertainment, insurance or lottery services. Business is the means by which society endeavours to satisfy its needs and improve its standard of living. At the heart of all business activity is the entrepreneur, who starts new ventures and thereby creates jobs, economic growth and, hopefully, prosperity. No one invented the business world. It is the result of activities related to meeting the needs of people in a market economy.

The most important characteristic of the business world in the developed countries of the West and Asia is the freedom of individuals to establish any business of their choice and to produce, within limits, any product or service the market requires. This system, in which individuals themselves decide what to produce, how to produce it, and at what price to sell their product, is called the market system or a market economy. This is the prevailing economic system in South Africa.

The market economy is a complex system comprising various types of small and large business organisations that collectively mobilise the resources of a country to satisfy the needs of its inhabitants. Figure 1.2 overleaf shows the composition of the South African business world in terms of large, medium and small businesses and their contribution to the economy. The business world or economic structure of South Africa resembles that of many industrialised countries. As figure 1.2 shows, large businesses (such as Eskom, Standard Bank, Daimler-Chrysler, Vodacom, Anglo American, Barlow World, and many other large public corporations, 680 of which are listed on the Johannesburg Securities Exchange (JSE)), are responsible for most of South Africa's economic activity.

Figure 1.2: The composition of the South African business world in terms of contribution to gross domestic product (GDP)

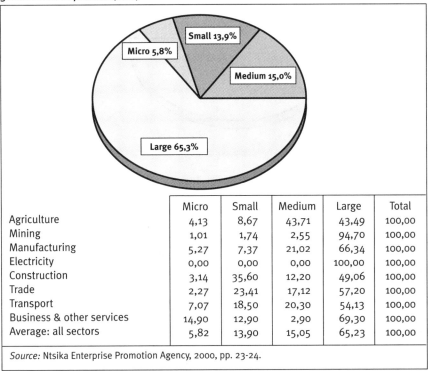

	Micro	Small	Medium	Large	Total
Agriculture	4,13	8,67	43,71	43,49	100,00
Mining	1,01	1,74	2,55	94,70	100,00
Manufacturing	5,27	7,37	21,02	66,34	100,00
Electricity	0,00	0,00	0,00	100,00	100,00
Construction	3,14	35,60	12,20	49,06	100,00
Trade	2,27	23,41	17,12	57,20	100,00
Transport	7,07	18,50	20,30	54,13	100,00
Business & other services	14,90	12,90	2,90	69,30	100,00
Average: all sectors	5,82	13,90	15,05	65,23	100,00

Source: Ntsika Enterprise Promotion Agency, 2000, pp. 23-24.

Large businesses contribute 65,2% to GDP, while small and medium-sized enterprises (SMEs), which are mostly family or individually owned, produce about 30% of products and services. Micro-enterprises consisting of one-person businesses contribute to 5,8% of economic activity. Strictly speaking, micro-enterprises (the informal sector) are not regarded as part of the formal economy because the people involved in these live primarily on a subsistence or survival basis. Moreover, such people put pressure on the infrastructure of inner city areas and contribute nothing in the form of income tax.

The variety of needs that a country has determines the complexity of its business environment. In first world countries businesses are the primary source of products, services and employment. Figure 1.3 (see p. 6) shows the importance of the South African business world in providing employment in this country.

Business creates wealth, is a catalyst for economic growth, and is credited with bringing about the high standard of living in developed countries.

Business also serves the community indirectly by means of technological innovation, research and development, and improvements to infrastructure. It plays a crucial role in supporting, in various ways, education, the development of human resources, the arts, conservation and sport, and other activities that improve the quality of life of a community.

Figure 1.3: The contribution of business to employment in South Africa

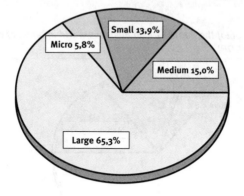

Source: Ntsika Enterprise Promotion Agency, 2000, p. 25.

The business world and society both depend on and influence each other. At the heart of the business world is the entrepreneur or businessperson. In the pursuit of profit, entrepreneurs constantly search for new ideas, new products and new technologies. In so doing, they initiate innovation and bring about change. Their decisions on investment, production and employment influence not only the state of the economy, but also the prosperity of whole communities. Consider, for example, the influence of the Enron and Worldcom accounting scandals on world economies in 2002. Because of such scandals caused by some of the most eminent entrepreneurs in the United States of America, stocks in New York fell to seven-year lows, thousands of employees lost their jobs, pensions evaporated, and investors lost confidence in corporate America. The scandals also had a ripple effect in Europe and Japan.

Conversely, society exerts its influence on business in a number of ways. If businesses fail to abide by the expectations and desires of the community, for instance by employing fraudulent or unethical practices, polluting or degrading the environment, or through profiteering and monopolistic exploitation, the community will often react by instituting regulations and legislation to curb such practices.

Moreover, the attitude of society towards the business world is by no means consistent, for in a changing environment the community will, at different times, have different expectations of the business world. If the business world fails to respond to the expectations of the community, the attitude of the latter towards the business world is likely to change. Consider, for example, the issue of equity in South African organisations. When the country became a democracy in 1994 businesses were obliged to include blacks in their organisations. Because of the slow rate of response to this call, however, society reacted through government by instituting legislation that forces the business world to transform its organisations so that blacks are included at all levels. The Employment Equity Act 55 of 1998 is society's response to the exclusion from business of blacks, women and persons who are physically challenged.

Most Western countries have, over the years, come to regard the business sector as a valuable social institution because it has helped to realise society's needs and also to raise the standard of living. In the closing decades of the last century, however, most Western nations decided that a high standard of living amid a deteriorating physical environment and inadequate social progress does not make sense. The business world is, thus, under continuous and often increasing pressure with regard to the following factors:

- **Social responsibility.** The social responsibility of business is a concept that originated in media revelations of malpractices by businesses and the resultant insistence of society on restricting such malpractices through regulation. Historically, social responsibility has been measured by the contribution of a business towards employment opportunities and its contribution to the economy. While profits and employment remain important, many other factors are today included in assessing the social performance of a business, namely equity or the empowerment of previously disadvantaged individuals, both economically and managerially, environmental awareness, the provision of housing and a responsible and safe workplace, concern about health issues, and involvement with community issues. Social responsibility will be discussed in more detail in chapter 4.
- **Business ethics.** As a concept, this is closely related to social responsibility[1], except that business ethics focuses specifically on the ethics or the ethical behaviour of managers and executives in the business world. Managers, in particular, are expected to maintain high ethical standards. At issue here is the integrity of entrepreneurs and managers, and the degree to which their decisions conform to the norms and values of society. Business ethics revolves around the trust that society places in people in business, and the obligations the latter have towards society. Factors such as greed, the exploitation of workers and consumers, and the abuse of positions of trust have often resulted in the business ethics of entrepreneurs being deplored.
- **Affirmative action or equity** regarding an organisation's workforce is aimed at creating equal employment opportunities for all by ensuring that workforces are composed in roughly the same proportions as the groups that make up the population as a whole. In South Africa, the Employment Equity Act became law in 1998. The stated intention of the Act is to eliminate unfair discrimination, ensure employment equity, and achieve a diverse workplace that is broadly representative of the country's demographic realities. The inclusion of blacks at management level is of crucial importance to South Africa's economy.

The economy can only grow at the much-needed growth level of 3% or higher if there are enough skilled managers to drive the economy. It is widely recognised that a moderate real economic growth rate of 2,7% per year will require an additional 100 000 managers each year for the foreseeable future. Since the traditional source of managers, namely white males, has been

The growth of black empowerment in the South African economy

The research group Empowerdex has examined a broad spectrum of empowerment issues. An important finding is that previously disadvantaged individuals now own a 9,25% share of the 115 largest companies quoted on the JSE. On 30 June 2002 this amounted to R143,4 billion. The following is an example of the share of black empowerment groups in some of the largest South African companies:

- Sasol   R16,2 billion
- Anglo American   R10,2 billion
- BHP Billiton   R8,97 billion
- M-Cell   R7,98 billion
- Standard Bank   R7,52 billion

The following are examples of large South African companies owned or controlled by empowerment groups (holdings as at 30 June 2002):

- Real Africa Holdings   R856 million
- Mvelaphanda Resources   R784 million
- ARM Gold   R2,7 billion
- Johnnic   R3,8 billion
- M-Cell   R7,9 billion

Source: *Sake Rapport*, 10 November 2002, p. 1.

exhausted, most of the managers required will have to come from the black population. Since 1994 there has been a steady increase in the number of blacks in management, yet despite this, whites, especially white males, remain over-represented in management. At the time of publication of this book, whites represented 57% of South African management. Moreover, white males comprise 41% of management, while white females comprise only 16%. Blacks comprise 27% of management, with black males comprising 20%, and black females a mere 7%.[2]

- **Environmental damage.** Citizens often form pressure groups to protect the environment. Businesses are frequently responsible for air, water and soil pollution, and for the resultant detrimental effects on fauna and flora. For example, because of pressure from the community, the construction of a new plant that Iscor had planned to establish at Saldanha was delayed for seventeen months. Iscor eventually had to build the plant eight kilometres away from the initial site, so as to avoid possible damage to the ecology.
- **Consumerism** is a further social force that protects consumers against unsafe products and malpractices by exerting moral and economic pressure on businesses. In South Africa the SA National Consumer Union acts as a watchdog for consumers.

Social pressure on businesses often results in increased government regulation to force compliance with social requirements and norms. Ultimately, the will of the community is seen to prevail.

The business world is so interconnected with society that it may be defined as **a process that uses the means of production of a country to produce**

products and services to satisfy the needs of the people. The primary purpose of business in a free-market system is to make a profit while satisfying the needs of the people. A brief overview of the needs of communities, and of the means of satisfying these needs, is given below to explain not only the purpose of business in a market system, but also the extent of the field of business management, which is the focus of this book.

1.2 Needs and need satisfaction

1.2.1 The multiplicity of human needs

The continued existence of humans depends upon the constant satisfaction of numerous needs, both physical and psychological. The work that every member of a community performs is directly or indirectly related to need satisfaction. There is, even in the most remote inhabited areas, a need for certain goods and services. These needs may be very simple and few, as in the case of a rural and underdeveloped community in which an individual or a family, with the help of nature, finds the resources necessary to satisfy a simple need structure. The traditional way of life of the Kalahari San people, for example, depends on the satisfaction of the most basic necessities for survival. However, in highly industrialised communities, needs may be numerous and may therefore require large and complex organisations to satisfy them.

A need may have a physical, psychological or social origin, but no matter what form it takes, it requires satisfaction. It is obvious, therefore, that the number of identifiable needs is infinite. Some needs, particularly those that are physiological, are related to absolutely basic necessities, such as the satisfaction of hunger and thirst, which have to be satisfied for the sake of survival. Others, particularly those that are psychological, involve needs merely to make life more pleasant – without their being essential to survival. Such needs include holidays, video machines, dishwashers, tennis courts, luxury cars, and innumerable products and services of a similar nature.

Basic physical and psychological needs may also overlap – for example, we do not wear clothes merely for warmth and protection, but also to be fashionable. We enjoy expensive delicacies, accompanied by fine wines, in a luxurious restaurant, and in this way we simultaneously satisfy survival needs and psychological needs.

Abraham H. Maslow (1908-1972) was an American clinical psychologist who explained variable and unlimited human needs by means of a sequence or hierarchy of needs. According to Maslow, human needs range in a definite order, from the most essential for survival to the least necessary. Figure 1.4 shows this hierarchy of needs.[3]

It is clear from this figure that the need hierarchy is composed in such a way that the order of importance ranges from basic physiological needs, such as hunger and thirst, that have to be satisfied for survival, to higher levels of the hierarchy, which are mainly concerned with psychological needs. Because humans are social beings who live in communities, they also have collective needs, such as protection and education. An individual, a family or a community first satisfies the most urgent needs, and then, when this has been done, moves up to the next level until the higher psychological levels are

Figure 1.4: The needs and resources of the community

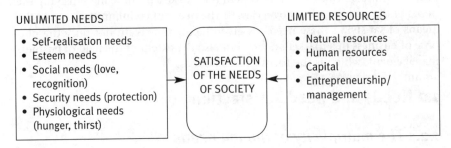

Source: Based on Maslow, A.H., "A theory of human motivation", as dealt with in Griffin, R.W., *Management*, Houghton Mifflin Co., Boston, 1990, p. 440.

reached. With changing circumstances, individuals not only desire more possessions, but also continually want still newer and better products and services. For example, radio offers entertainment, but black and white television is believed to offer better entertainment, and colour television better still. Once these have been acquired, however, the need arises for a video recorder or DVD, more television channels, and more and better programmes. And so it goes on. As society satisfies one need, a new one comes into existence, and there is no end to the constantly increasing number of human needs.

> Wealthy people apparently also have unlimited needs. When Henry Ford was asked how much money is necessary to satisfy all of one's needs, he replied: "Just a little bit more."

Table 1.1 indicates some of the needs people have. It is interesting to note that South African households spend 30,3% of their income on food, which satisfies one of the most basic needs.

Table 1.1: Expenditure patterns of South African households 2002

Product and service needs	Total expenditure %
Food, drink and tobacco	30,3
Clothing and shoes	5,1
Housing and household goods	21,2
Transport and communication	14,8
Medical	7,1
Education, recreation and relaxation	2,2
Other	19,3
Total expenditure	100,0

Source: Quarterly Bulletin, South African Reserve Bank, June 2001.

1.2.2 Society's limited resources

If one considers the multiple and **unlimited needs** of humans, especially in highly developed societies, it is clear that there are only **limited resources** available to satisfy all their needs. Although Western countries, most notably the USA, possess very impressive means of production, they do not have unlimited resources. A country has only a certain number of people in its workforce to operate a certain number of machines, and a certain number of factories, hospitals and offices to produce a certain quantity of products and services. In other words, the resources of any community are **scarce**, and can easily be exceeded by its needs. Resources are therefore the **basic** inputs in the production of products and services – they are also known as **production factors**. Figure 1.4 (see p. 10) shows those resources that society possesses in limited quantities only, and which it uses to satisfy its needs: **natural resources, human resources, capital and entrepreneurship:**

- **Natural resources**, often known as "land", include agricultural land, industrial sites, residential stands, minerals and metals, forests, water, and all such resources that nature puts at the disposal of mankind. The most important characteristic of natural resources is that their supply cannot be increased. In other words, the amount of natural resources any one country possesses is given, and therefore in most cases scarce. Moreover, human effort is usually necessary to process these resources into need-satisfying products, for example, the transformation of forests into timber and paper.
- **Human resources**, also known as the production factor of **labour**, include the physical and mental talents and skills of people employed to create products and services. People receive wages for their labours. The size of the labour force of any country, and therefore, in a sense, the availability of that production factor, is determined, inter alia, by the size of the population, the level of its education and training, the proportion of women in the labour force, and the retirement age. For the manufacturing processes of any country to be of any value, its labour force has to be trained for certain periods and to certain levels of skill to be able to produce the products and services required. The training of a petrol pump attendant, for example, will be considerably shorter than that for a brain surgeon. The combination of human skills is of particular importance, for without this natural resources and capital cannot be productively utilised.
- **Capital** is represented by the buildings, machinery, cash registers, computers, and other goods produced, not for **final** human consumption, but rather for making possible the further production of final consumer products. Capital products usually have a long working life, for example, office buildings, factories, machinery and other equipment that is used over and over again in the production process. The scarcity factor of capital is due to the fact that a community takes years to build up its stock of capital. Every year it spends a certain amount on roads, bridges, mineshafts, factories and shopping centres, and there is always a shortage of such things. The owners or suppliers of capital are usually remunerated in the form of interest or rent.
- **Entrepreneurship** is the fourth production factor. It refers to those individuals in the community who accept the risks involved in providing products and services for society. Entrepreneurs are rewarded with profits for

the risks they take and the initiative they show, but they suffer losses for errors in judgement. This production factor is also scarce in the sense that it is not everybody in a community who is prepared to take the risks that are inevitable when providing products or services, or who has the ability to manage an organisation successfully. Although the contemporary focus on entrepreneurship is mainly on small and medium businesses, entrepreneurs are not limited to these. The large or corporate business is also a place for entrepreneurship.

1.2.3 Need satisfaction: a cycle

To be able to satisfy the needs of the community, entrepreneurs have to utilise these scarce resources in certain combinations in order to produce products and services. Economic value is created in the course of the production process by combining production factors in such a way that final products are produced for consumers. It is clear that a nation's survival depends on the satisfaction of its people's needs, and that striving for need satisfaction with the limited resources available is an incentive for economic progress.

Given its unlimited needs but limited resources, society is confronted with a fundamental economic problem: how to ensure the highest possible satisfaction of needs with these scarce resources. This is also known as the **economic principle**.

Society cannot always get what it wants, so it must choose how it will use its scarce resources to the maximum effect in order to satisfy its needs. In short, it has to make a decision about solving the following fundamental economic problems:

- **Which products and services** should be produced, and in what quantities? What are the numbers and amounts of capital products, and what are the numbers and amounts of consumer products? Should railways or trucks, houses or flats be built? If flats are chosen, how many?
- **Who** should produce these goods? The state or private individuals?
- **How** should these products and services be produced and **what resources** should be used? There are various methods of production, and different

Example

The needs of society ultimately culminate in products or services that satisfy particular needs. A case in point is cell phones. People have a basic need to communicate, and where this is possible, to communicate with individuals over distance. During most of the last century the only way this could be done was by means of the telephone, where the caller first had to phone to a specific building (house or office) and then wait for the relevant person to be found by whoever answered the phone. The cell phone was, therefore, a response to the need to communicate immediately with a specific individual, without the inconvenience of having to locate the person first, or the frustration of dealing with inoperative telephone lines.

combinations of the production factors can be applied to create products and services.

- **For whom** are these products and services to be produced? For rich or poor people? Old or young people? Families or individuals?

The answers to the fundamental economic questions listed above are given by the community. The community decides which **institutions** should be responsible for the production and distribution of products and services, as well as the role that each institution has to play. Figure 1.5 shows how, against the background of its needs, and by means of its political process, the community determines the **economic system** in which the necessary **need-satisfying institutions are established**.

In a more or less free-market system, need-satisfying institutions, including business organisations, offer products and services on the market in return for profit. If the community is not satisfied with the way in which these organisations provide for its needs, it will change the economic system or choose a new

Figure 1.5: The cycle of need satisfaction in a community

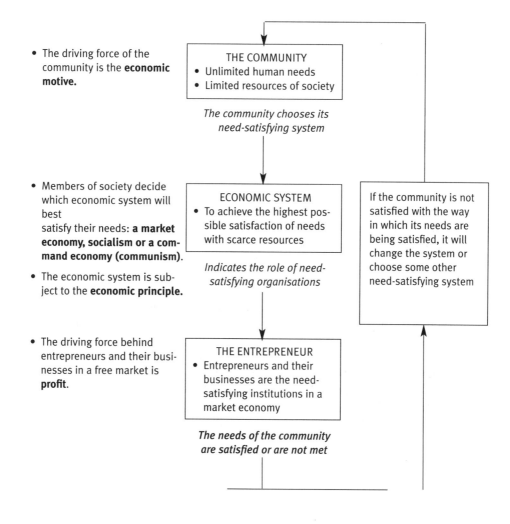

need-satisfying system. The appearance of new businesses and the disappearance of others are examples of this cycle of need satisfaction in the community. With the large-scale urbanisation of South African society and the participation of women in the labour market, especially during the late 1960s and 1970s, shopping hours increased to allow for Saturday afternoon and Sunday shopping. This proved extremely successful, because there was a communal demand for longer shopping hours. The community therefore got what it wanted!

Over the years, different communities have developed different approaches to the satisfaction of their needs, and different economic systems have been tried and tested.

Each of these systems, as chosen by various communities to satisfy specific needs, has its own approach to the fundamental economic problem of **what** products and services should be provided **by whom** and **for whom**. The study of these systems constitutes the field of economics as a social science, and examines the means used to satisfy innumerable human needs with limited resources. **Business management**, on the other hand, is concerned with the **institutions** that are created in the economic system to satisfy the needs of a community, and these are mainly business organisations.

To provide some necessary background to the study of business management and the role of business organisations in society, a brief overview of the different economic systems now follows.

1.3 The main economic systems

1.3.1 The community and its economic system

As stated earlier, every community is engaged in a struggle for survival, and that struggle originates in, and is necessitated by, scarcity. Therefore every community needs to have a complex mechanism that is constantly occupied with the complicated tasks of ensuring the production and distribution of products for the survival of the community. A country is therefore confronted with the fundamental economic problem, and it has to decide on some system to solve that problem. Which economic system should a country choose to solve the problem of what products should be produced and marketed by which producers for which consumers?

Over the years, countries and communities have approached need satisfaction in different ways. There are three main approaches that are still followed by present-day communities for the solution of their fundamental economic problems. They are the **free-market economy**, the **command economy** and **socialism**. While these economic systems are often incorrectly referred to as political ideologies, **they should rather be described as economic systems influenced by politics**. It is necessary to take a brief look at these systems to understand the origin and role of business organisations in society. As none of these economic systems is ever found in a pure form, the discussion that follows is merely an exposition of the basic premises of each system, and not a theoretical debate.

1.3.2 The free-market economy

One of the economic systems adopted by humans for the solution of their economic problems is the **market economy**, also known as the **free-market economy**. It is a system in which most products and services demanded by a community are supplied by private organisations seeking profits. It functions on the assumption that:

- Members of a community may possess assets and earn profits on these
- The allocation of resources is affected by free markets
- Members of the community have free choice of products, services, places of residence and careers
- The state keeps its interference in the system to a minimum

In the free-market economy, particular value is attached to **the right of individuals to possess property such as land, buildings, equipment or vehicles**, including the right to earn an income from them. This is also the driving force of the free-market economy: it stimulates individuals and entrepreneurs to acquire more and to make a profit through the productive utilisation of their assets or their capital. In seeking maximum profits, this **capital**, which is nothing other than the resources of the community, is applied as productively as possible. This aspect also affects the second basic premise of the free-market economy, namely the **distribution of resources through free markets**. The private possession of capital has an important influence on the manner in which resources are allocated or employed in a free-market economy. The decisions about **what products** should be produced by **which producers** therefore rest with those who own the resources.

This means that farmers, factory owners, industrialists and individuals are free to do what they like with their assets. In their decisions concerning production and marketing, however, they have to take account of the tastes, preferences and other demands of consumers if they want to make a profit. Thus, the question of **which consumers** (for whom?) is also solved. Such decisions in a **free-market** economy are not taken by some central body but by a system of free markets (market economy), which puts a price on every production factor or consumer product.

Free markets also imply the third characteristic of this system, namely **freedom of choice**. The producer is able to decide whether or not he or she can profitably produce their products at the price set by the market. This is the producer's **free choice**. Likewise, the consumer is free to choose whether to buy the product at that price. A system of free markets therefore necessarily entails freedom of choice. Private owners of property are free to own what they like, and to do with it as they please: whether to rent it out, sell it, exchange it, or even give it away. People with businesses are free to produce what they wish and to employ whoever they choose. Similarly, owners of the resource of labour, that is, workers, can use their resources as they choose. Consumers, again, are free to buy what they like, to live where they wish, to follow whatever career they choose. In this way, **competition** comes into operation in a system of free markets.

A free economy creates wealth

The fewer restrictions on economic activity, the wealthier a country's citizens. The Heritage Foundation/*Wall Street Journal's* 1998 Index of Economic Freedom measures how well 156 countries score on a list of ten broad economic factors. These factors include trade policy, taxation, government intervention in the economy, monetary policies, capital flows and foreign investment, banking and exchange controls, wage and price controls, property rights, regulation, and black market activities. Taken cumulatively, these factors offer an empirical snapshot of a country's level of economic freedom. The results demonstrate beyond doubt that countries with the highest levels of economic freedom also have the highest living standards.

The 1999 study rates South Africa a relatively poor 62nd, with a rating of 2,9 out of 5, where 5 represents absolute economic repression. This places South Africa on a par with Greece and Hungary, and ahead of some Eastern European and most African countries, but well below established industrial economies and certain Far East high-fliers.

Countries with high scores on the Economic Freedom Index (for example the USA) have an average per capita income of US $30 606, while those with lower scores, such as South Africa, earn a mere US $3 160 per capita. It is also quite clear that a country's level of economic freedom has a direct impact on its standard of living, as is clear from figure 1.6 below.

Figure 1.6: Rating of economic freedom (1998)

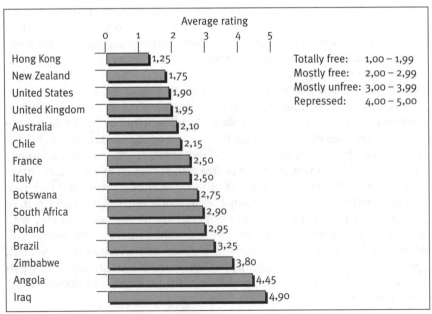

Source: Index of Economic Freedom, 1999. © The Heritage Foundation.

The final characteristic of a free-market economy is **minimum state interference** in markets. The assumption is that the state should merely ensure the proper maintenance of the system without excessive regulation of, or even participation in, the business world.

1.3.3 Command economy or centrally-directed economic system

The second type of economic system, adopted by some countries as an alternative to a free-market economy, is a command economy, which until recently was known as **communism**. Its main characteristic is that the state owns and controls the community's resources or factors of production.

In a command economy the state provides the answers to the fundamental economic questions. It is a system of **communal ownership** of the production factors of a country in which the individual owns no property, with the exception of private domestic assets. This means that individuals own no land, factories or equipment. The state assumes complete responsibility for the production and distribution of products and services, and as such all decisions about what should be produced, and how, by whom, and for whom it should be produced, rest with a central government.

The choices of products and services are therefore limited to what the state offers; they fall entirely outside the control of ordinary individuals. It is the state that decides what the needs of the community are, that determines how and where the goods desired will be obtainable, and in what quantities they may be used. In the absence of free consumer choice, the profit motive is also absent, as is the competition factor, because, as mentioned above, the state owns the organisations that produce the products and services.

The command economy failed in most countries that had adopted it because it robbed individuals of the initiative to produce goods and services, and prevented the creation of wealth. Proof that the system cannot create wealth has been the poverty and the collapse in the early 1990s of communism in the former Soviet Union and other East European countries. Command economies are, nevertheless, still officially adhered to in countries such as China, Cuba and some African states.

1.3.4 Socialism

Socialism may be taken as the third economic system proposed as a solution to a society's fundamental economic problems. Under this system, which may be regarded as a **compromise** between a pure market and a pure command economy, the state owns and controls the principal (generally strategic) industries and resources, such as manufacturers of steel, transportation, communications, health services and energy. Less important and smaller matters such as trade and construction, and the production of materials and services of lesser strategic importance, are left to private initiative. In socialism, the fundamental assumption is that strategic and basic resources should belong to every member of the community. For the rest, businesses and consumers operate within free markets in which they are at liberty to make decisions without restriction. Although consumers in a socialist economy have greater freedom of choice than those under a command economy, the provision of the basic products and services by the state is a limiting factor in the creation of wealth.

As mentioned earlier, none of the three main economic systems in use occurs in a pure form anywhere. They occur as mixed economies, with the dominant system incorporating certain characteristics of the other systems. Thus China, which officially has a command economy, employs private initiative, while growing state intervention in the major free-market economies of the world is no strange phenomenon.

Figure 1.7: Alternative economic systems

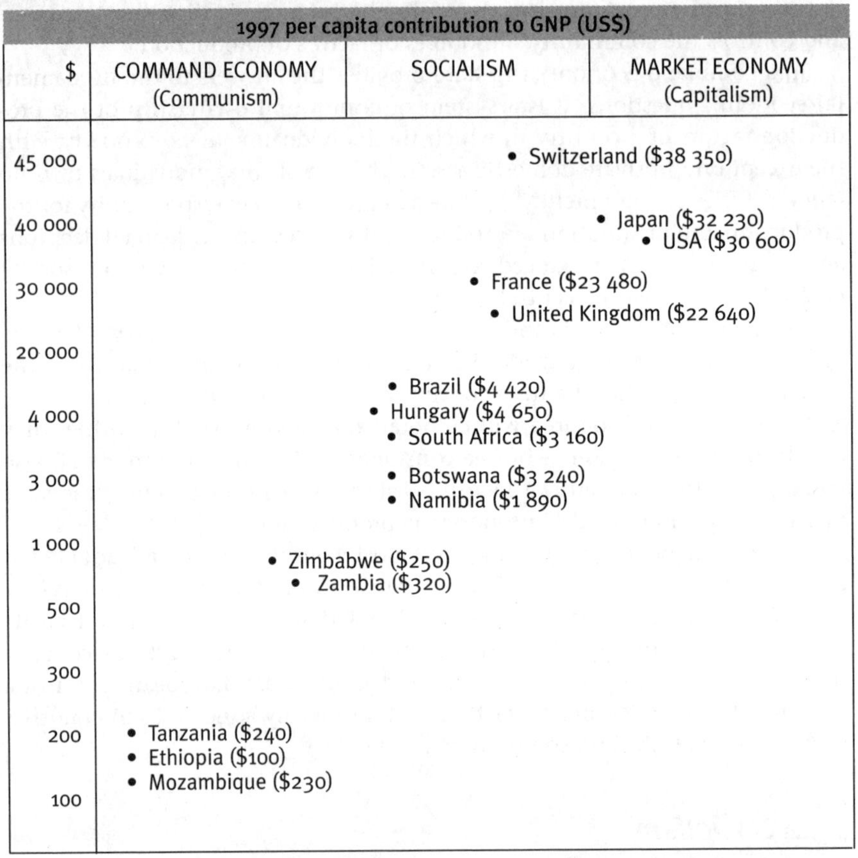

1997 per capita contribution to GNP (US$)		
$	COMMAND ECONOMY (Communism)	SOCIALISM	MARKET ECONOMY (Capitalism)
45 000			• Switzerland ($38 350)
40 000			• Japan ($32 230) • USA ($30 600)
30 000		• France ($23 480) • United Kingdom ($22 640)	
20 000			
4 000		• Brazil ($4 420) • Hungary ($4 650) • South Africa ($3 160)	
3 000		• Botswana ($3 240) • Namibia ($1 890)	
1 000		• Zimbabwe ($250) • Zambia ($320)	
500			
300			
200	• Tanzania ($240) • Ethiopia ($100) • Mozambique ($230)		
100			

Source: World Bank Development Report, 2000/2001. By permission of Copyright Clearance Center Inc.

Figure 1.7 shows the relative success of various countries with different economic systems. The gross national product (GNP) per capita of some of the world's poorest countries, namely Mozambique, Tanzania, Ethiopia, Zambia and Zimbabwe, is compared with that of some of the richest, namely Switzerland, Japan, Germany, the USA and the United Kingdom.

Countries such as South Africa, Brazil, Hungary, Namibia and Argentina, each of which has a unique economic system, rate about midway between the richest and poorest countries of the world. Several factors, including education, culture and work ethic, affect the prosperity of any particular country, but figure 1.7 shows that countries with free-market economies are wealthier than others.

1.3.5 The state and economic systems

The fact that under both the free-market system and socialism the state intervenes to help solve the economic problem does not mean that there is necessarily a tendency to move to the direction of a command or centrally-controlled economy. Any intervention by the state should be seen as necessary, to provide the essential collective products and services such as roads, education, water, power, health care and justice, on the one hand, and to maintain the economic system, on the other.

In particular, this means government intervention in market mechanisms and the so-called "freedom of entrepreneurs". Examples here are the protection of natural resources by preventing pollution, the restriction of monopolistic practices by ensuring competition, and the protection of consumers against false or misleading information and exploitation. The state also helps business by stimulating the economic system, through the promotion of exports, by encouraging the creation of small businesses, by assisting research, and by granting subsidies. Furthermore, through the application of its monetary and fiscal policies, the state creates a climate conducive to economic growth and productivity. In a nutshell, government intervention in the economic system aims at encouraging economic growth and stability by managing recession and inflation, and effecting greater equity in the distribution of incomes.[4]

A much debated form of government intervention takes place when the state does not limit itself to the above-mentioned activities, but acts as an entrepreneur in its own right, as it does in the areas of transport services, electricity supply, arms manufacture, broadcasting and television services, and many other industries in South Africa. The main reason usually advanced for government intervention in these spheres is that the free or private entrepreneur is not interested in these activities and, perhaps, is not even capable of carrying them out. This is because of the enormous scale of the businesses, for instance, power supply, transport and the production of arms, and the corresponding risks attached to them.

It is also argued that some government organisations are of such strategic importance to the community that they cannot be left to profit-seeking private entrepreneurs. However, these arguments do not entirely justify a regular and continuous entrepreneurial role by government. If any such intervention by the state is carried to excess, the result is a bureaucracy that affects national productivity adversely by limiting private competition.

The purpose of this overview has been to give a brief exposition of the basic economic systems and the role of government in them, rather than an evaluation of the divergent opinions about what the proper role of government in the economy of a country should be.

1.3.6 Final comments

Different communities use different economic systems to meet their needs with their available resources. Each system thus has its own peculiar characteristics (as can be seen from table 1.2 on p. 20), and each country arranges its economic system in such a way that it solves its wealth problem as effectively as possible in accordance with the wishes of its inhabitants. The free market is

Table 1.2: A comparison of the main economic systems

	Free-market economy	Socialism	Command economy
Main characteristics	Private ownership of production factors. Freedom of choice.	Basic industries owned by state. Freedom of choice.	State owns and controls all industries and agriculture.
Markets	Free competition.	Limited competition as a result of state industries.	No competition.
Driving force	Profit and reward according to individual ability.	Profit motive recognised. Employees' pay in state-owned concerns based on workers' needs.	Profit not allowed. Workers urged to work for the glory of the state.
Management	Management environment is private businesses. Free to choose career. Free to make decisions.	Management environment state-owned as well as private businesses. Decisions restricted to government policy in state-owned organisations.	Management environment is the state. No freedom of decision. Managers also party members.
Labour	Workers independent and free to choose job and employer. Free to join union and to strike.	Free to choose job and employer. Limited right to strike in state organisations.	Limited choice of job. State-controlled unions.
Consumers	Freedom of choice in free markets. Spending limited only by income.	Freedom of choice, except in respect of products of state organisations, the prices and quality of which have to be accepted.	Rationing of products. Very limited choice. Prices of goods and income levels set by state.
Advantages	Private initiative. Economic freedom.	Possibility of full employment. State stabilises economic fluctuations.	State can concentrate resources towards particular ends.
Disadvantages	Unstable environment. Cyclical fluctuations. High social costs.	Little incentive in state organisations. Unproductive state organisations.	Low productivity. Low standard of living. Planning difficult or impossible.

the current economic creed of South Africa, and decisions concerning **what, how, by whom** and **for whom** products should be produced, are largely left to the individual members of the community, and are effected through the operation of free markets. More precisely, the South African economic system can be defined as a **market-oriented economy with a high degree of government participation and control.**[5]

South African consumers thus enjoy a high degree of freedom to buy what they want and where. Consequently, the responsibility rests with the individual entrepreneur to judge which products and services the consumer wants, and then to offer them at a price the consumer is prepared and able to pay. A complex network of organisations evolves out of the interaction between needs and the entrepreneurs who satisfy these needs, and this network constitutes what is known in a free-market economy as the **business world**.

1.4 The need-satisfying institutions of the free market

1.4.1 Business organisations

From this discussion of contemporary economic systems it is clear that the economic systems of Western countries, with which South Africa associates itself, are combinations of a free-market economy and socialism. Despite the defects and shortcomings of the more or less free-market order in this country, most inhabitants believe that this economic system satisfies their needs better than any that might be based on pure socialism or a command economy.

The workings of a free-market economy are affected by the **need-satisfying institutions** created by the system, that is, the **private business organisations** which, for the most part, satisfy the needs of the community. The business world therefore consists of a complex system of interdependent organisations that mobilise the resources of a country to satisfy the country's needs **at the risk of a loss** and **in seeking profit**.

The emphasis is on the opportunity to make a profit as well as the risk of a loss. Such are the conditions under which a private business exists in a free-market economy. Under such a system, an organisation has to make a profit to be able to survive. This can happen only if it satisfies the needs or wishes of the consumer, and hence the community.

Business organisations therefore solve the fundamental economic problem, that is, which goods and services, how and for whom, should be produced, by meeting the wishes of the consumer.

Figure 1.8 shows how businesses, as the main need-satisfying institutions under this system, use the resources of society to produce products and services for consumers.

Consumers' needs culminate in the demand for consumer products and services offered, on the market (in department stores, boutiques, car salesrooms, pharmacies, and so on) by businesses. Therefore, consumer demand helps to determine **what**, and **for whom** products and services need to be provided. To be able to produce products and services, business organisations need resources, so a demand arises for production factors, which are offered in the factor market by the community. Business organisations pay salaries and wages to the community in exchange for production factors, and consumers in turn pay for their products and services with that money. Competition in both markets determines how the products and services are to be produced so that the entrepreneur can continue to make a profit.

In order to make a profit, the enterprise must therefore take the initiative and accept certain risks in mobilising the resources of the community before, for example, a single loaf of bread, or bicycle or house can be produced or

Figure 1.8:Goods and services offered in the free-market system

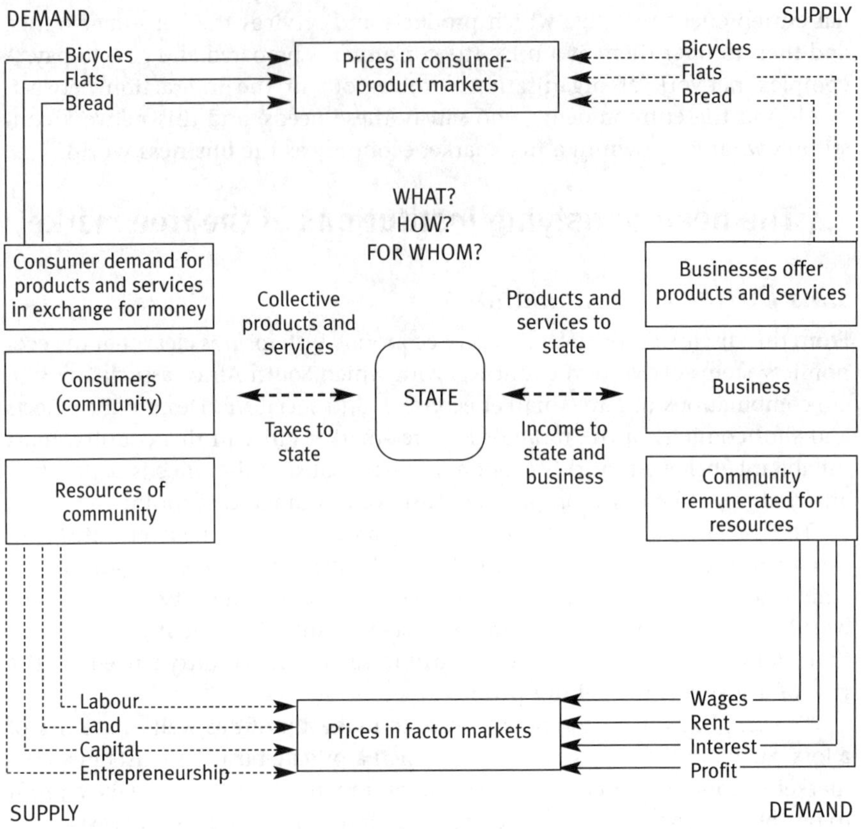

DEMAND SUPPLY

Bicycles → | Prices in consumer- | ← Bicycles
Flats → | product markets | ← Flats
Bread → | | ← Bread

WHAT?
HOW?
FOR WHOM?

| Consumer demand for products and services in exchange for money | Collective products and services | Products and services to state | Businesses offer products and services |

| Consumers (community) | ← - - - → | STATE | ← - - - → | Business |

Taxes to state | Income to state and business

| Resources of community | | Community remunerated for resources |

Labour → | | ← Wages
Land → | Prices in factor markets | ← Rent
Capital → | | ← Interest
Entrepreneurship → | | ← Profit

SUPPLY DEMAND

Note: All demand relationships are shown in black arrows and supply relationships in dotted arrows.

Source: Adapted from Samuelson, P., *Economics*, McGraw-Hill Company, 1980, p.41.

built. The owner of a bicycle factory, for example, has to erect or rent a building, install machinery, buy raw materials and components, and employ people to manufacture bicycles as productively as possible to satisfy the needs of consumers. The transport contractor has to transport goods to places where there is a need for them. The retailer has to present a range of products conforming to consumers' needs in as convenient a way as possible. A banker does not produce a physical article, but provides – also at a risk and in pursuit of profit – a service in the form of finance placed at the disposal of manufacturers, dealers and numerous other entrepreneurs and consumers. These are but a few examples of the innumerable activities carried out in the business world by such business organisations as Toyota, SABMiller, Pick 'n Pay, Standard Bank, and many others, large and small, local and multinational, that play an indispensable part in our society. Moreover, as will be discussed in greater detail in chapter 3, business organisations assume different forms: a sole-proprietorship, a partnership, a close corporation, a private company, or a public company.

The business organisations that we have examined may be defined as those **private need-satisfying institutions of a free-market economy that accept risks in pursuit of profit by offering products and services on the market to the consumer.** They constitute the main subject of the study of management and are therefore the major topic of research and study in business management. Businesses do not function in isolation, but in a business environment that influences their operation, and which is at the same time influenced by the business. Therefore an overview of certain aspects of the environment also falls within the field of study of management.

It should be clearly understood that when we speak of a business organisation we mean a **private enterprise** – that is, one owned by private entrepreneurs. This is because in a mixed market economy, there are state-owned and non-profit-seeking organisations in addition to the profit-seeking businesses that the community establishes as need-satisfying organisations. For the sake of completeness, a few observations about such organisations are made below.

1.4.2 Government organisations

In the discussion of the various economic systems, several principles of a free-market economy were identified, including the condition that government should intervene as little as possible with market mechanisms, and that when it does, it should confine itself to the protection and creation of collective non-profit-seeking facilities and services such as those concerned with health care, education, justice and defence. The government departments responsible for such state functions may themselves be regarded as need-satisfying organisations. Because the profit motive is absent and the services provided are collective, such institutions fall under the subject of Public Administration as an independent science.

It was also mentioned that the pure free-market economy exists only in theory, and that several mixed systems are in fact to be found, including the South African system, which was defined as a market-oriented economy with a high degree of state intervention. The intervention specifically indicates the large number of government organisations (also known as state-owned enterprises or SOEs, parastatals, or public corporations) in South Africa which – unlike the collective systems that produce products and services on a non-profit-seeking basis – offer products and services for profit, and sometimes in competition with other businesses in the market. Sometimes these **public corporations** may be regarded as business organisations, but with this difference: they are owned and controlled by the state and not by a private entrepreneur. Eskom, Transnet and Telkom are examples of such public corporations, and there are many others.

These public corporations may also be regarded as need-satisfying institutions through which the state creates products and services believed to be of strategic, economic or political importance to the community, especially as regards self-sufficiency in transport, energy, military equipment and armaments.

Although the productivity levels of government organisations are suspect, those that seek profits, and in which the state is the exclusive shareholder, also fall within the scope of business management.

1.4.3 Non-profit-seeking organisations

These organisations are the final group of need-satisfying institutions that offer services, and, to a lesser extent, products not provided by private enterprise, government organisations or the state. Examples are sports clubs, cultural associations and welfare organisations, and associations of organised business such as the National African Federated Chamber of Commerce (NAFCOC) and the South African Chamber of Business (SACOB). These organisations differ from other need-satisfying organisations in that they provide their services **without seeking profit**.

The continued existence of such organisations therefore depends on the financial support of those members of the community who require their services. Although such organisations do not set profit making as their primary objective, they often function on the same basis as a business organisation, seeking a surplus of income over expenditure, or at least a balance of income and expenditure. These organisations – especially the larger ones – therefore employ management principles. And despite their small share in the economy, the study of such organisations also falls within the field of business management.

Against the background of this exposition of the various economic systems, and in the light of various need-satisfying institutions, especially private businesses of the mixed market economy as found in South Africa and other countries, we will now examine the purpose and task of business management more closely.

1.5 The nature of business management

1.5.1 Economics and business management as related sciences

As explained earlier, human survival is closely linked to the problem of scarcity, that is, satisfying the unlimited needs of a community with limited resources. Moreover, a society is constantly faced with the problem of how to use these scarce resources so as to satisfy its needs as efficiently as possible. **Economics as a social science studies how humans and society exercise choices concerning different ways of using their scarce resources for products and services.** It is therefore a study of the economic problems and variables of the community as a whole, with the improved well-being of the community as its preconceived goal. The variables studied by economics as a science include prices, money, income and its distribution, taxes, productivity, government intervention, economic growth, as well as many other economic questions affecting the well-being of a country.

Business management as an applied science, on the other hand, **is concerned with the study of those institutions in a particular economic system that satisfies the needs of a community.** In a mixed market economy, as is found in South Africa, **private business organisations are therefore the main area of study.** Economics examines the **entire economic system of a country**, while business management limits its studies to one component of the economic system, namely the **individual organisation**, whether it be a private business, a government corporation or, to a lesser extent, a non-profit-seeking organisation. For example, economics examines the problem of inflation against the background of its implications for the national economy, while business management is more concerned with the effects of inflation on individual businesses. The main link between economics and business management as independent sciences is that one studies the economic system as a whole, while the other studies a single component of that system.

1.5.2 The purpose and task of business management

In discussing the cycle of need satisfaction it was indicated that the primary human endeavour is to achieve the highest possible satisfaction of needs with scarce resources. This endeavour is known as the **economic principle**, and every economic system is subject to it. That being the case, it follows that **any component of an economic system, including a business organisation, is also subject to the economic principle**. Where the individual business organisation is concerned, this entails achieving the highest possible output with the lowest possible input of means of production.[6] This is the **purpose** of business management, to produce the highest possible number or units of products and services, at the lowest possible costs.

The **task** of business management emerges from this, namely to determine how an organisation can achieve the highest possible output (products and services) with the least possible input (labour, capital, land). **More specifically, it entails an examination of the factors, methods and principles that enable a business to function as efficiently and productively as possible in order to maximise its profits.** In short, it is a study of those principles that have to be applied to make a business organisation as profitable as possible. It may also include a study of the environmental factors that could have an effect on the success of an organisation, its survival or its profitability.

The study of business management entails comprehensive and ongoing research and the examination of management problems, the testing of approaches and principles, experimentation with methods and techniques, and the continuous weighing up of environmental variables. The result is an applied science that indicates how business organisations can best be directed towards realising their objectives. Therefore, in the case of business organisations, the economic principle is defined as the endeavour to achieve the highest possible income in the market at the lowest possible cost, with profit as the favourable difference between the two.[7] This principle is also applicable to state-owned enterprises and non-profit-seeking organisations. The only difference is that in the case of state-owned enterprises and non-profit-seeking organisations, the difference between inputs and outputs is not measured in profit, but rather in terms of surplus, savings or higher productivity.

In a business organisation the economic principle and the profit motive coincide, making profits the driving force, and so the task of business management becomes one of maximising profits.[8] This does not, however, mean that the task of business management is to maximise profits at the cost of everything else, especially the well-being of society. In today's business environment the objective is rather to maximise profits through good man-

Examples of approaches, principles and methods studied by business management with the purpose of making an organisation function as productively as possible

- General approaches to management methods, tested over the years, include the following:
    - The **mechanistic approach,** introduced at the turn of the century, emphasises mass-production, especially under the management of engineers.
    - The **human relations management approach** originated in the 1930s, and puts emphasis on the motivation of workers.
    - The **contingency approach** of the 1950s argues that the management approach is prescribed by the prevailing situation.
    - **Strategic management,** the most recent approach, makes a special study of how management should act in an unstable environment.
    - Various supplementary approaches and developments, such as **organisation design, the management of change, information management, corporate culture** and the **management of diversity** are still being studied.
- In the field of marketing management, research into experimentation with approaches and methods has also contributed to the more productive operation of businesses. These include the following:
    - The **marketing concept** replaced the **production approach** in management philosophy to enable businesses to adjust their resources more effectively to the needs of consumers.
    - **Market research,** as an instrument of marketing philosophy, has developed many methods of studying the needs of consumers.
    - Methods of studying and determining consumer habits and segmenting markets, as well as strategic management aids, have also stimulated marketing management to higher productivity.
- **Financial management** as a area of business management has also tested many methods, especially financial ratios. The following are some examples:
    - The development of ratios to access the financial performance of businesses.
    - Capital budgets and capital budget techniques in particular to evaluate potential investment possibilities.
    - Approaches to dividend policy.
    - Approaches to and methods of financing growth and expansion as profitably as possible.
- In the same way, numerous methods, principles, approaches and problems in other areas of business management, such as production and operations, purchasing, human resources management, and external relations, have been researched and tested.

The sum total of this sustained study of, and experimentation with, management approaches and methods, and research on management problems, constitutes the **body of knowledge** known as business management.

agement **and** care of employees, customers, investors and society in general.

To summarise, the task of business management is to study those factors, principles and methods that will lead a business organisation, as a component of the prevailing economic system, to reach its objectives. In a mixed market economy this primarily – though not exclusively – means making a profit. Having clarified the field of study and the task of business management as an independent discipline, we will now discuss its development and its relationship to some other disciplines.

The purpose and task of business management

- The economic principle consists of the human endeavour to satisfy unlimited needs with limited resources. All economic systems are subject to it.
- In a mixed market economy, a business organisation as a need-satisfying institution, is a **component** of the economic system, and is therefore also subject to the economic principle.
- According to the economic principle, a business organisation always has to endeavour to obtain the highest possible output (product and services) at the least possible input (lowest cost). This is the **purpose** of business management.
- The business organisation is the subject studied by business management.
- The **task** of business management is to examine factors, methods and principles that enable a business organisation to maximise its profits and achieve its objectives.

1.6 The development of business management

1.6.1 The course of development of business management

In the previous sections we discussed the nature of business management and its role in the business world in detail, and also mentioned various interfaces between business management and other independent disciplines. Throughout, we defined business management as a science in its own right. It is probably not wrong to refer to business management as a science, but in an introductory work such as this, it is pertinent to pause and consider its status. Before deciding whether any given field of study is a science or not, we should look at its origins and history.

Although the origins of business management can be traced back to the age of mediaeval mercantilism or even earlier, it is not our intention to present a comprehensive historical survey of a subject that really developed into a science only in the last century. Nevertheless, the events leading up to the development of business management, as it now exists, deserve a brief mention.

Up to the Industrial Revolution, which was in full swing by the end of the 19th century, the economic systems of communities consisted of simple structures which aimed to satisfy the needs firstly of the individual, and secondly of the community. The early Middle Ages, from about the year AD 1 000, were characterised by subsistence economies that included craft, in a feudal and manorial system. A manor consisted of a number of families living in small villages or communities and working for the lord of the manor, with mere survival and shelter as their main objectives.

Example

Adam Smith, the father of capitalism, published his classic manifesto on the capitalist or market order in 1776, under the title *The wealth of nations*. In doing so, he gave form to what is now accepted as the free-market economy, and to economics as an independent science.

That period marks the beginning of the Industrial Revolution of the 18th and 19th centuries. The number of patents registered in the 18th century in Britain alone, and the rate at which they increased, show the expansion of technological innovation.

PERIOD	NUMBER OF PATENTS
1700–1730	149
1730–1760	230
1760–1790	976

This increase in technological innovation, together with the discovery of new sources of power and raw materials, and the invention of new means of communication and transport, provided the driving force of the Industrial Revolution.

Source: Viljoen, S., *Capitalism: a historical survey*, HAUM, Cape Town, n.d.

The voyages of the explorers in the time of the Renaissance stimulated trade and industry, and resulted in the birth of mercantilism during the later Middle Ages. The infant business era saw the rise of simple urban industries, territorial specialisation, and the development of banking and book-keeping, also known as accounting. The latter was probably the earliest management problem to be studied. Early capitalism followed the Renaissance and was characterised by the work of theorists such as Adam Smith, and the growth of cities, a middle class and world markets. It was during the Industrial Revolution that entrepreneurs first made their appearance. At that stage all economic activities took place on a small scale, both technically and financially. Business operations were carried out by individual entrepreneurs or one-man businesses.

Entrepreneurs risked their own money in ventures that they managed themselves. In other words, the business was financed almost exclusively by the owner, though supplemented by bank loans and, in the case of larger undertakings, by partners or members of the family. The one-man business was typical of how capitalism was organised, not only in commerce and industry, but also in mining, shipbuilding and banking. In this form of business the independent entrepreneur was the self-appointed manager who bore all the risks and to whom all profits accrued. The requirements for success were sound intelligence, common sense and an intimate knowledge of technical production. In a nutshell, experience, and not scientific management, was the prerequisite for a successful business.

Since the end of the 19th century, however, capitalism, or the free-market economy, has changed radically. The technological innovations of the

Industrial Revolution, which made mass production possible, not only gave rise to population growth and higher living standards but also created an almost insatiable demand for products. This convergence of factors then required a new form of organisation, much larger than that of the small entrepreneur, to make possible the extensive financing necessary for large-scale production. The company or corporation, with its great number of shareholders or suppliers of capital, now made its appearance. This form of business resulted in a dichotomy between suppliers of capital and management. The result was **suppliers of capital who did not manage, and managers who did not provide capital**.

From this unique convergence of circumstances in the market economies of the world there arose a need for professional management, for it soon became evident that the problems of management in the new form of organisation could not be solved by experience alone.[9] Following the demand for professional management, business management came into being as a discipline to examine how a business should best be managed. At the beginning of the last century the current stage of business management as a discipline was introduced. As a discipline, business management is therefore roughly 100 years old.

Since then it has followed a course of pragmatic empirical development, through which certain approaches, methods and functional areas have taken shape in conformity with practical needs. For example, during the early decades of the 1900s, **production management** was emphasised as a means of satisfying an almost insatiable mass demand for products. During the 1930s overproduction caused the emphasis to shift to **sales management** in an attempt to get rid of the excess. The **marketing concept** of the 1950s and 1960s followed. And in the 1970s and 1980s, a period marked by a turbulent business environment, the emphasis shifted to **strategic management**, and in the 1990s it moved again to the globalisation of business management as business activities across national boundaries increased. Coca-Cola, for example, is sold in 195 different countries and is a truly global product. Over 80% of Coca-Cola's annual profits come from international sales.

As the emphasis in management shifted from production to marketing to global management, different management theories were shaped. The existing knowledge of management, and perspectives on management, stems from a combination of sustained research and practical experience. These perspectives or theories on management are classified into different schools of thought, namely the **scientific school**, the **classical school**, the **human relations school**, and **contemporary management thinking** which includes downsizing, outsourcing, change management, the management of technology, total quality management, and the management of diversity. The latter is of special importance to South African managers. Over many decades business management developed a body of knowledge that is constantly improved by research, management education and training, mentoring and practical experience.

Against this background of the development of business management, we may now consider whether or not business management may be regarded as a science.

Business management education in South Africa

In South Africa it is estimated that some 12 000 students per year qualify for the various specialised BCom and BTech degrees, and some 1 600 advanced management education students per year complete the MBA/MBL degree. A feature of the MBA market in South Africa is its extraordinary growth. In 1997 the industry produced 689 MBA graduates from nine schools. A year later, there were twelve schools and they produced 909 graduates. The following year saw an increase of 38% to 1 254 graduates, and 2000 saw a 28% increase to 1 613 graduates from fifteen schools.

1.6.2 Is business management an independent science?

As mentioned, business management is a young subject, and its scientific basis is still the subject of lively debate. There are certain considerations that have to be met in order for a specific field of study, discipline or body of knowledge to be regarded as a science. There is no easy answer, because there are many diverse opinions as to what exactly constitutes a science.

The most common definitions of a science emphasise different characteristics. Business management is continually being tested in the light of these definitions to determine whether it merits the status of a science.

- Probably the most outstanding characteristic of an independent science is **a clearly distinguishable subject of study that forms the nucleus of a discipline.**[10] Business management completely satisfies this condition, particularly with regard to the business organisation, which, as a component of the free-market economy, is its subject of study.
- A fundamental characteristic of a science, which supplements the above-mentioned, is that it should be **independent of other sciences**. As already pointed out, business management has its own identifiable subject of study, and from this point of view may be regarded as a science. However, it should be clearly understood that a business organisation can be studied by other sciences for other reasons. People are social animals who organise themselves into groups to fulfil purposes that are too big or too complex for a single individual. As such, a business organisation comprises people who wish to attain certain personal and organisational goals. Business organisations may also therefore form a subject of study for sciences such as sociology, psychology and medicine. However, the way in which business management views an organisation is indicated by the purpose of the study, which is to examine those things that may guide businesses as effectively as possible towards their objective, which is primarily to make a profit. This essential characteristic also allows business management to qualify as a science because, unlike other sciences, it is concerned mainly with ways of maximising the **profitability** of a business.
- A third consideration is the definition of a science as a **uniform, systematised body of knowledge of facts and scientific laws,** and the existence of laws and principles that are constantly **tested in practice.**[11] In this regard business management encompasses a great deal of systematised knowledge found worldwide in the comprehensive literature on the sub-

ject. It also contains numerous rules and principles that may successfully be applied in practice, even though they are not as exact as in the natural sciences. This leads to the view that management is a normative science, which means that it constantly endeavours to establish norms or guidelines for management with a view to maximising profits.

- It is also said that the final purpose of a science should be to produce a **generally accepted theory**. In this regard, business management does not yet satisfy the requirements of an independent science. Because of the rapidly changing environment in which business organisations exist, it is doubtful whether this stage will ever be reached. It should also be borne in mind that the involvement of people in the management process, and the influence of uncontrollable variables make it difficult, if not impossible, to explain management problems with any single uniform theory.

Although we have not come to a perfectly clear conclusion as to whether business management can be regarded as an independent science, this examination at least provides an insight as to its nature. To summarise, we may say that business management is a young applied science that sets out to study the ways in which a business can achieve its prime objective, which is to make a profit. However, this does not mean that the application of management principles and approaches should always be done in a scientific way, nor does it require that the "feel" and experience of managers should be summarily dismissed. For this reason, successful management is often regarded as an art as well as a science.

1.6.3 The interfaces between business management and other sciences

Throughout the discussion of the scientific status of business management it was held that the business organisation, as the subject of study, is the most important entity. However, one should bear in mind that businesses are also studied by other disciplines for other reasons. In its task, namely the study and examination of those things that help a business to attain its goals as efficiently as possible, business management constitutes a young, developing science that frequently makes use of the knowledge gathered by other disciplines on the functioning of the business organisation, even though these disciplines may not be interested in the profitability of organisations. In short, business science takes from other disciplines what it can use to help businesses as much as possible to accomplish their goals.

Many current management concepts originated in other sciences and now form an integral part of the body of knowledge of business management. For example, the concept of strategy was borrowed from military principles; sociological knowledge and principles enable us to explain the behaviour of an organisation; engineering principles are applied to improve productivity in the manufacture of products; mathematical models and computer science are used to help management make decisions. Furthermore, in advertising, for example, psychology, the arts and communication principles and techniques are frequently used – all, of course, from the viewpoint of profitability. Table 1.3 (see p. 33) provides a self-explanatory exposition of the multidisciplinary nature of business management. In view of the constantly changing environment in which contemporary business operates, business management is likely to make more, rather than less, use of other sciences in future.

1.7 Classification of the study material of business management

Against the background of the above introductory discussion of the business world, the economic systems that people institute to solve their welfare problems, the business organisation as a component of the free-market economy, and the task of business management as a young science, we will now explain how the study material as well as the contents of this book have been organised.

In order to decide on appropriate study material as well as identify problems relating to business management – especially in view of its multidisciplinary character – a definite guideline must be followed. A business organisation, as a component of the economic system, is subject to the economic principle; therefore it can be said that all **internal or external phenomena that exert an influence on lower costs or increased profits can be viewed as questions within the field of business management**. This guideline not only creates a broad basis upon which knowledge of business management can be built, but also indicates the task of business management, which is to examine those things that will best improve the profitability of the business organisation.

In this endeavour certain activities in the organisation have to be carried out by management: markets must be researched to determine whether there is a need for a particular product; raw materials must be purchased to produce such products; staff and equipment must be acquired to manufacture the products; money has to be obtained to pay for the materials and the equipment, as well as to remunerate staff. Moreover, these often disparate activities have to be coordinated or managed. These different activities, which together make the business organisation work, constitute the field of business management. To give scientific direction to the study of these interrelated activities, the total field of business management is divided into seven functions. These functions, which are also known as management areas, comprise all aspects of a specific group of activities.

The main reason for dividing the field of study of business management into different functional areas of management is the need to systematise the large body of knowledge. The multidisciplinary nature of the subject also makes division necessary. The training and skills required for the various functions are highly diverse, and each function on occasion makes use of different disciplines to achieve its management purpose. As shown in table 1.3 (see p.33), financial management makes use of computer science, risk management and accountancy concepts, while human resources management uses a great deal of psychological knowledge and social theory.

Because of the broad basis of the body of knowledge, some degree of specialisation in a specific management area is necessary to make management as productive as possible. In this book, however, the functions are distinguished only for analytical purposes, to provide a better understanding of each and to explain its relation to the others. Ultimately, they form a synergistic whole to direct the business organisation towards its goal and objectives.

Table 1.3: Interfaces between business management and other sciences

Business management/ Other Sciences	General management	Marketing management	Financial management	Production and operations management	Purchasing management	Human resource management	Public relations management
Anthropology	• Cultural relationships and organisational behaviour • Management of diversity	• Cultural determinants of demand • Behavioural structures				• Employee behaviour • Diversity	• Behaviour of external groups
Economics	• Environmental scanning	• Market analysis of, for example, consumer expenditure	• Influence of financial strategy • Behaviour of financial markets	• Location problems	• Market analysis of availability and stockpiling • Evaluation of competition in the market	• Labour market analyses • Remuneration structures	• Economic influence of external groups
Engineering		• Product development		• Erection of factories • Factory outlay	• Value analysis	• Safety of employees	
Law (especially Mercantile law)	• Format of an organisation	• Misleading practices • Product safety • Packaging	• Takeovers • Mergers	• Pollution by factories	• Law of contracts • Representations	• Conditions of employment • Negotiation with unions • Labour laws	• Misleading messages • Sponsorship contracts
Computer science	• Information management • Planning models	• Marketing research • E-marketing	• Financial models	• Optimal outlays	• Materials requirement planning • Manufacturing resource planning	• Labour information systems • Labour research	• Public relations research
Accounting	• Control systems • Budgets	• Marketing audit • Sales and cost analyses	• Interpretation of financial statements	• Cost analysis	• Valuation of inventory • Cost analysis	• Human asset accounting	• Budgets
Psychology	• Leadership • Motivation • Negotiation	• Consumer behaviour • Communication			• Negotiation	• Testing • Performance analysis	• Communication • Persuasion
Sociology	• Organisational behaviour • Interfaces between the organisation and the environment	• Socio-demographic classification • Group influences			• Business ethics	• Organisational behaviour	• Group influences
Mathematics and statistics	• Decision models • Planning models	• Market research • Market forecasting • Market measuring	• Financial models • Deviations		• Inventory forecasting	• Human resource planning models	• Pre-and post-testing of programmes

The functional areas to be examined may be summarised as follows:

- The function of **general management**. This includes an examination of the management process as a whole: the planning that management has to do, the organisation that it has to establish to carry out its plans, the leadership to get things done and the control that has to be exercised over the whole process. This requires surveying the different management approaches that may be adopted. As shown in chapter 5, this embraces the overall function through which top management develops strategies for the **whole business**, and it cuts through all the other functions because such functions as planning and control are carried out not only at top level but also in each functional area. In chapter 5 we review the management process, developments in management theory and some of the approaches to management. Planning and organising, in chapters 6 and 7, form the starting point for the management process. In chapter 8, leadership is discussed, followed by chapters 9 and 10, which deal with people in the organisation. These chapters discuss the function of human resources, namely the appointment of the organisation's employees. The latter also includes chapter 11 on the legal environment of human resources. Chapter 12, which discusses control, is the final chapter of part 2. Part 3 examines the functional areas of business management.
- The **marketing function** is responsible for marketing the products or services of the business. This includes assessment of the market and the needs of consumers, as well as the development of a strategy to satisfy those needs profitably. Chapter 13 provides a brief overview of the marketing process. Chapter 14 deals with marketing instruments, while chapter 15 focuses on an integrated marketing strategy.
- The aim of the **public relations function** in a business organisation is to create a favourable and objective image of the business, and to promote good relations and goodwill between those businesses and external groups that are directly or indirectly involved in the business, its products or services. This is examined in chapter 16.
- The **financial function** includes the acquisition, utilisation and control of the money the business needs to finance its activities, raw materials and equipment in such a way that its profits are maximised without endangering its liquidity or solvency. Chapter 17 introduces financial management, while chapter 18 examines the management of investment. Chapter 19 discusses financing decisions.
- The **production** and **operational function** includes that group of activities concerned with the physical production of products, namely the establishment and layout of the production unit, the conversion of raw materials and semi-finished products into finished products and, scheduling services that are produced for the market. Chapter 20 provides an introduction to operations management, while chapter 21 focuses on operational management activities, techniques and methods.
- The **purchasing function** is responsible for the acquisition of all products and materials required by the business to function profitably, namely raw materials, components, tools, equipment and, in the case of wholesalers and retailers, the inventory to be purchased. Purchasing managers have to be in contact with suppliers, so that they are aware of new products and

know the prices at which goods can be bought; they also have to keep inventory up to date, to ensure continuity of functioning. Chapter 22 gives an overview of the purchasing and supply function, while chapter 23 focuses more specifically on sourcing activities.

Following on from the analysis of the functional areas in parts 2 and 3, part 4 deals with various contemporary management problems that accompany these functions, and briefly surveys some of the contemporary issues confronting business. Part 4 considers such matters as productivity, globalisation and knowledge management. These questions could not be discussed under each function because of limited space.

In completion of part 1 (the introduction to business management), chapter 2 discusses the entrepreneur, chapter 3 examines the establishment of the business organisation in greater detail, and chapter 4 examines the environment within which a business operates.

1.8 Summary

This chapter is the first of four that form the introduction to business management. We have explained the role of the business organisation in society, and we have considered the interaction between society and the organisation as a social process that transforms the means of production of a country, so that products and services can be produced that will satisfy the needs of society. This process was explained in greater detail in the discussion of a business organisation as a component of the economic system, where it was specifically shown how, as a need-satisfying institution of the free-market economy, it provides for the needs of people. In conclusion, we examined the task of business management.

References

1. Cowan, K.R. Business ethics in South Africa: an investigation of managerial perceptions and attitudes. Paper presented at the 4th Conference of the SA Institute of Business Scientists, Vista University, Bloemfontein, June 1992.
2. Smit, P.J. & Cronje, G.J. de J., *Management principles*, Juta, Cape Town, 2003, p. 19.
3. Based on Maslow, A.H., *A theory of human motivation*, as dealt with in Griffin, R.W., *Management*, Houghton Mifflin Co., Boston, 1987, p. 440.
4. Lombard J.A., Stadler J.J. & Haasbroek, P.J., *Die ekonomiese stelsel van Suid-Afrika*, HAUM, Pretoria, 1987, p. 34.
5. *Ibid.*, p. 17.
6. See also Rädel, F.E. & Reynders, H.J.J., (eds) *Inleiding tot die bedryfsekonomie*, J.L. van Schaik, Pretoria, 1980, p. 2.
7. Rädel, F.E. & Reynders, H.J.J., (eds), *op. cit.*, p. 4.
8. *Ibid.*, p. 5.
9. *Ibid.*, p. 3.
10. Lucas, G.H.G, et al., *Die taak van bemarkingsbestuurder*, J.L. van Schaik, Pretoria, 1979, p. 11.
11. Rädel, F.E. & Reynders, H.J.J., (eds), *op cit.*, p. 2. See also Marx, F.W. & Churr, E.G., *Grondbeginsels van die bedryfsekonomie*, HAUM, Pretoria, 1981, p. 24.

2 Entrepreneurship

The purpose of this chapter

This chapter examines entrepreneurship as the driving force behind the business organisation. It is basically the entrepreneur who decides what, how, by whom and for whom products and services should be produced to satisfy the needs of society. This chapter also examines the nature of entrepreneurship and the role of entrepreneurs and small businesses in the economy. In addition, it looks at the entrepreneurial process or the way in which one becomes an entrepreneur, as well as the different ways of entering the business world: by buying and growing an existing business, by entering into a franchise agreement or by starting a new business. Finally, aspects of new venture opportunities are discussed.

Learning outcomes

The content of this chapter will enable learners to:
- Explain the concept of entrepreneurship and the entrepreneurial process
- Define an entrepreneur
- Describe the roles of entrepreneurs and small businesses in the economy
- Describe how to become an entrepreneur
- Comment on the skills and resources required to become an entrepreneur
- Identify and describe the different ways of entering the business world
- Present recommendations on the choice of a business opportunity

2.1 Introduction

In the previous chapter our introductory discussion revolved around the role of the business organisation in society. We explained how business organisations, large and small, transform a nation's resources (land, labour, capital, entrepreneurship) into products and services to meet the needs of its people. We also explained that the purpose of business management as a science is to examine ways and means of improving the performance of a business organisation.

However, in order to understand how the business organisation satisfies the needs of a nation in a market economy, one needs to understand the driving force behind the business organisation, namely the entrepreneur. For it is basically the entrepreneur who decides what, how, by whom and for whom products and services should be produced. The entrepreneur is, moreover, one of the four main factors of production discussed in chapter 1: natural resources (land), human resources (labour), financial resources (capital) and **entrepreneurship**.

Entrepreneurship is the factor that mobilises the other three resources and harnesses them in different combinations to meet the needs of society. It is the fourth factor of production and includes those individuals in society who take the initiative and risk by harnessing the factors of production to produce products and services. The entrepreneur's reward for taking initiative and risk is profit. Loss is the punishment for taking the wrong decision. Entrepreneurship is, moreover, a scarce resource since not everyone in a country has the skills or is prepared to take risks in generating products and services. In South Africa, for example, only 3% of the population are entrepreneurs, compared to 17% in Canada.

By understanding what it is that drives the entrepreneur, how he or she identifies and assesses business opportunities and enters the business world, the student of business management will better understand how business organisations function. The entrepreneur is someone who starts a business and assumes the risk of losing all of his or her resources if the venture fails. This process of starting a new business, of sometimes failing and sometimes succeeding, is entrepreneurship. Entrepreneurs risk their resources to make a profit. Managers, in contrast, are not entrepreneurs for they assume relatively little risk for the success or failure of the business. However, managers play a key role in the success or failure of the business organisation, and need to know how the entrepreneurial process works. A brief overview of the rediscovery of entrepreneurship will help explain its nature and importance to society.

2.1.1 *The rediscovery of entrepreneurship*

Entrepreneurs throughout the world are stirring up a revolution that is revitalising economies, because the establishment of new businesses and the growth of existing ones are responsible for most of the products and services that are changing people's lives. These new products and services are generated by entrepreneurs. Furthermore, entrepreneurs create jobs. The traditional providers of job opportunities, namely large enterprises and government organisations, have been replaced by small businesses as the main provider of jobs. In the USA, the world's most successful economy, small and medium sized enterprises (SMEs) employ 85% of the workforce, and in Central and Eastern Europe millions of new entrepreneurs are endeavouring to reform and transform the liberated communist economies. Entrepreneurs are also transforming China and Cuba, the last bastions of communism.

Worldwide, countries are debating ways and means of addressing the problems of unemployment. Statistics show that the more flexible the labour market – in other words, the more free it is from government intervention – the lower the unemployment rate.

Slow growth of entrepreneurship in South Africa

Accentive Research and Insights researched the growth of entrepreneurship in 22 countries, including South Africa. A total of 880 top executives were interviewed. The following facts relating to South Africa emerged in the survey:

- More than 98% of the top executives are convinced that the only solution to creating wealth in South Africa is the promotion of entrepreneurship.
- More than 50% of the top executives believe that in South Africa a negative attitude exists towards entrepreneurship.
- South Africans are afraid to take risks, according to 85% of the interviewees.
- A new leadership style is necessary to create a national culture of entrepreneurship.
- Over 50% of the executives admit that their organisations lack entrepreneurial role models.

Source: http://www.accentur...\entre_home.xml&c=entrepreneurship&n=entrepreneurship&t=af, 5 November 2002.

In South Africa the unemployment situation is serious (see Figure 2.1 below).

Figure 2.1: The inability of the South African economy to accommodate job-seekers

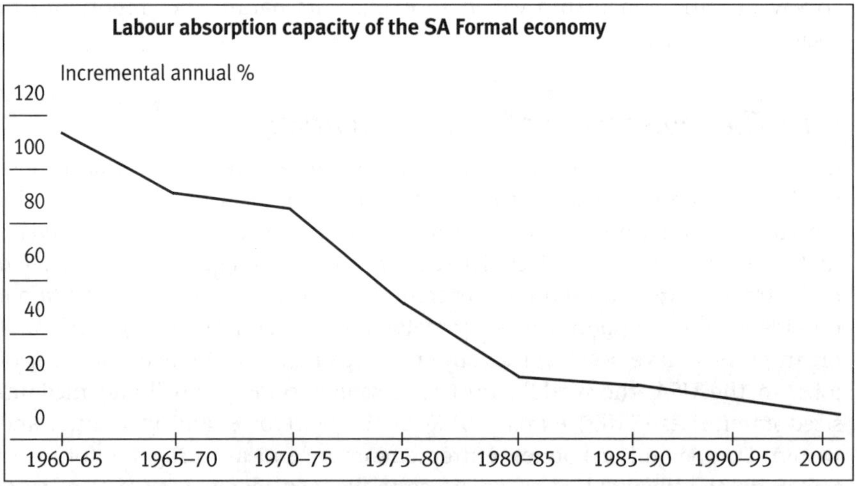

Source: Business Times, 21 June 1998, p. 1. © Sunday Times.

A study by the Development Bank of Southern Africa shows that the average absorption capacity of the economy (the percentage of the labour force that can annually be absorbed into the economy) is decreasing rapidly. This figure has deteriorated from 82,7% in 1974 to the present figure of less than 15%. This means that currently only one out of eight job-seekers in South Africa is likely to find a job. Over the past decade the South African economy has lost more than a million jobs. This is a serious situation because not even an economic growth rate of as high as 3% per year is likely to have much impact on the country's dire unemployment levels. An economic growth rate of about 12% per year is needed to achieve an employment growth of 3%.

There are many reasons for South Africa's high unemployment levels, in par-

The Centre for Small Business Promotion (CSBP) in the Department of Trade and Industry (DTI) has set up a website that is aimed particularly at providing information for small business. (On this website, BRAIN stands for Business Referral and Information Network. See www.brain.org.za)

ticular the labour laws, but one important reason is that South Africa does not have enough small business people to create employment. The current interest in the question of entrepreneurship is therefore only too clear, but various questions concerning the entrepreneur need to be answered. What is an entrepreneur? Is there a difference between an entrepreneur and a manager? Are entrepreneurs found only in the form of small business enterprises? The answers to these and other questions will not only help to clarify the nature of entrepreneurship, but also explain the interest that is being shown in it, and its importance. An examination of the concept of entrepreneurship is therefore important.

2.1.2 What is entrepreneurship?

The first question that arises in the quest for a scientifically based definition of the notion of "entrepreneur" is one of identity. Who or what is an entrepreneur? Is the owner of a suburban filling station, or an estate agent, or the local butcher, or the owner of a Fastfit or Nando's franchise an entrepreneur? Are there entrepreneurs in schools, government enterprises and large enterprises? There is no hard-and-fast rule here – nor is there a formal classification or register of entrepreneurs. Moreover, scientists have different views on who or what exactly an entrepreneur is.

- Economists subscribe to the view that entrepreneurs combine different resources in specific combinations to generate products and services at a profit. Entrepreneurs, to them, are people who are driven solely by the profit motive.
- Psychologists tend to see entrepreneurs (from the behavioural perspective) as achievement-oriented individuals to whom milestones offer specific challenges.
- Marxists regard entrepreneurs as exploiters.
- Corporate managers, on the other hand, see entrepreneurs as small operators who lack the potential to manage a large enterprise.
- Proponents of a market economy see entrepreneurs as the economic force responsible for the prosperity of a country.

Many more views may be added to the above list. Writers on management and entrepreneurship also have different views on the concept of entrepreneurship. This results in as many definitions of an entrepreneur as there are writers on the subject. **Entrepreneurs** have been described as persons who:

- Have innovative ideas, (because business involves new products, new processes, new markets, new materials and new ways of doing things)
- Identify opportunities (opportunities are created by the unlimited needs of people and trends that appear in the environment)
- Find resources (resources refer to capital, natural resources, human resources and entrepreneurship) to pursue these opportunities for personal gain (profit)

- Take a financial risk (the owner of a business runs the risk of potential loss or failure of the business)
- Bring about change, growth and wealth in the economy (winning nations have entrepreneur-driven economies)
- Re-energise economies and create jobs (South Africa desperately needs jobs)
- Manage small businesses (the owner of a business manages the business and re-allocates the business resources in such a way that the business makes a profit). In today's world it is important to remember that the word entrepreneur is associated with founding a new business or owning and managing a small one.

Against this background, two important definitions emerge. Firstly, **entrepreneurship** is the process of mobilising and risking resources (land, capital, human resources) to utilise a business opportunity or introduce an innovation in such a way that the needs of society for products and services are satisfied, jobs are created, and the owner of the venture profits from it. This process includes new as well as existing ventures, but the emphasis is usually on new products or services, and new businesses.

Secondly, an **entrepreneur** is a person who engages in entrepreneurship. He or she is usually a creative person with high achievement motivation who is willing to take a calculated risk, and who views new opportunities as a challenge. The fact that the word entrepreneur is associated with founding a new business or owning and managing a small one does not mean that entrepreneurs are not found in large corporations. In fact, most of South Africa's large corporations were started from small beginnings by men who went on to become illustrious entrepreneurs:

- Dr Anton Rupert, founder of Rembrandt
- Dr Malesela Motlatla, founder of Malesela Holdings
- Dr Bongani Khumalo, chairperson of Transnet
- Mr Patrice Motsepe of African Rainbow Minerals
- Mr Sol Kerzner, founder of Sun International
- Mr Herman Mashaba, founder of Black Like Me

However, these "captains" of South African business number but a few of the thousands of entrepreneurs, in large as well as small businesses, who drive the South African economy. A brief look at what they do will bring us closer to understanding entrepreneurship.

2.2 What entrepreneurs do and why they do it

2.2.1 The role of entrepreneurs in society

In chapter 1 we described how businesses, owned and driven by entrepreneurs, satisfy needs by mobilising a country's national, financial and human resources to produce much-needed products and services. In the process, wealth is created for society in the form of jobs, and wealth for the entrepreneur in the form of profits. Entrepreneurial activity is the essential source of economic growth and social development, and the key role played by this factor of production was underestimated for many decades. Entrepreneurship is the spark that brings the other factors of production into motion. On the other hand, it is also important to realise that entrepreneurship itself is, in turn, mobilised by the confidence, creativity, skills and expectations of individuals. If the entrepreneurial spirit is absent, the production machine does not go into action.

Persons with entrepreneurial talents and skills and leanings are able to achieve more than others in mobilising productive resources by starting enterprises that will grow. Persons with entrepreneurial qualities are **rare** and **valuable**. They constitute a resource that greatly contributes to, if not causes, the production of goods and services. They set in motion the creation of employment opportunities. Figure 2.2 illustrates that over 80% of businesses in the most successful economy in the world – that of the USA – have fewer than 100 employees. In fact, 50% of the businesses employ between one and four persons only.

Figure 2.2: Employment size of business in the USA

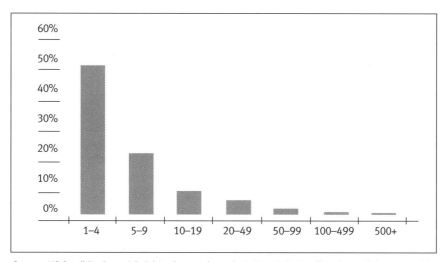

Source: US Small Business Administration, as shown in Hatten, T. S., *Small Business: Entrepreneurship and beyond*, Houghton Mifflin Company, 1997, p. 5.

The above brief overview of what entrepreneurs do, namely producing products and services and creating wealth in the form of economic growth, jobs and profits, sheds further light on the concept of entrepreneurship.

2.2.2 *Why do entrepreneurs do what they do?*

In endeavouring to explain the concept of entrepreneurship we have briefly examined what an entrepreneur is and what it is they do. A brief overview of **why** entrepreneurs enter the world of business will add to an understanding of this complex concept.

The question of why entrepreneurs do what they do has eluded researchers for many years. What is it about the entrepreneur that causes him or her to enter into the world of business? Comparative studies have indicated that roughly one-third of a nation's people enter into business, while the other two-thirds represent professionals, government employees, employees of businesses, and the unemployed.

The question as to why entrepreneurs initiate new ventures or have a desire to own and manage their own business is a complex one, and the decision to enter into business is influenced by many variables, which differ from country to country. Three broad categories of determinants or reasons why individuals initiate ventures are discussed in the sections below.

2.2.2.1 The influence of environmental variables

Some environments are more favourable to entrepreneurship than others. Environmental trends such as the fall of communism resulted in decreased employment by government organisations and more people entering the business world to make a living. The worldwide privatisation of government organisations also resulted in employees becoming entrepreneurs. This is especially true in the case of outsourcing, where government organisations and large businesses outsource many of the services and components they need. In this way they reduce personnel costs and gain access to special skills. Figure 2.3 illustrates the services that are most often outsourced. These environmental trends are only a few of the reasons why people become entrepreneurs.

Figure 2.3: Services most often outsourced

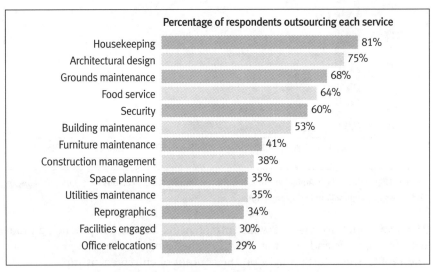

Source: International Facility Management, Research Report No 10, p. 6.

2.2.2.2 Experience in a particular industry or having particular skills

Some people can exploit certain opportunities more successfully than others. Skills and the quest for independence are among the most important reasons for people becoming entrepreneurs. Other reasons include events such as job termination, job dissatisfaction or an unexpected opportunity. In South Africa the experience of not having a job may trigger some people into becoming entrepreneurs.

2.2.2.3 Traits or psychological variables that distinguish some individuals as entrepreneurs

By examining what motivates people to become entrepreneurs, more people might be motivated to establish businesses. Consider the following:

- **Achievement motivation.** The most researched, and possibly the most important, trait of an entrepreneur is achievement motivation. In pioneer studies done by researchers such as McClelland, Murray and Gould, entrepreneurs are described as people with a higher need to achieve than people who are not entrepreneurs. Achievement motivation is characterised by actions of intense, prolonged and repeated effort to accomplish something that is difficult. The person with achievement motivation will also work single-mindedly towards his or her goal and will have the determination to win, do everything well and enjoy competition. Achievement motivation goes hand-in-hand with ambition and competitiveness. People with a high need to achieve are attracted to jobs that challenge their skills and their problem-solving abilities. They avoid goals that they think would be almost impossible to achieve or ones that would guarantee success. They prefer tasks in which the outcome depends upon their individual efforts. Entrepreneurs or would-be entrepreneurs are therefore not gamblers, but people who take calculated risks.

- **Locus of control.** The second important characteristic of an entrepreneur is a strong internal locus of control; the need of a person to be in charge of his or her own destiny. People with a strong internal locus of control believe that the outcome of an event is determined by their own actions. Luck or change of fate is therefore of little importance to an entrepreneurial personality. Those who start a new enterprise usually desire independence and do not want to be controlled by someone else.

- **Innovation and creativity.** Successful entrepreneurs and small business owners are innovative and creative. Innovation results from the ability to see, conceive, and create new and unique products, processes or services. Entrepreneurs see opportunities in the marketplace and visualise creative new ways to take advantage of them. Innovation, or the production of something new or original, is usually included in any definition of creativity.

- **Risk taking.** Most researchers agree that entrepreneurship behaviour involves the taking of risks in one way or another. In the business world there are variables such as interest rates and currency fluctuations, new laws, and so on, which are beyond production and control. The successful entrepreneur is an individual who correctly interprets the risk situation and then determines actions that will minimise the risk.

- **Other traits.** These include a high level of energy, confidence, orientation towards the future, optimism, the desire for feedback, high tolerance for ambiguity, flexibility/adaptability, and commitment.

The above brief overview of some of the most important reasons why people become entrepreneurs does not, however, cover the exhaustive list of traits that may be found in textbooks. The purpose of the overview is simply to help explain why certain people become entrepreneurs. It must also be remembered that small business owners and entrepreneurs come in every shape, size and colour, and from all backgrounds.

Figure 2.4 indicates the various reasons people in the USA have for going into business.

Figure 2.4: Reasons for going into business in the USA

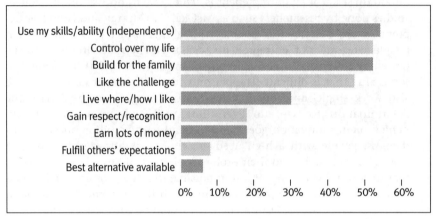

Source: Hatten, T. S., *Small business: Entrepreneurship and beyond*, Houghton Mifflin Company, p. 37.

2.2.3 The small business

Because of the fact that the concept of entrepreneurship is so strongly associated with the establishment of a small business or owning one, a few remarks about what is meant by small and medium enterprises (SMEs) is important at this stage.

2.2.3.1 Definition of a small business

It is difficult to formulate a universal definition of a small business, because the economies of countries differ and people adopt particular standards for specific purposes. Many of the enterprises we know of in our environment are typical examples of a small business – the local hairdressing salon, greengrocer, video shop and hardware store. A supermarket that we regard as big may actually be small in comparison with Pick 'n Pay. Likewise, medium and even large businesses in South Africa may be small in comparison with their overseas counterparts. In most countries it is therefore accepted practice to make use of quantitative and qualitative criteria when attempting to define a small business enterprise.

Examples of **quantitative** criteria in defining a small business are:

- Number of employees
- Sales volume
- Value of assets
- Market share

The most general quantitative measure for a small business is the number of people it employs. In countries such as Japan and the USA as well as some European countries, a small business may be defined as an enterprise with fewer than 500 employees.

From a **qualitative** point of view, a general criterion for a business to be classified as small is that **the owner must be part of the management of the business**.

A comprehensive definition of a small or medium enterprise (SME) in South Africa[1] is therefore any enterprise with one or more of the following characteristics:

- Fewer than 200 employees
- Annual turnover of less than R5 million
- Capital assets of less than R2 million
- Direct managerial involvement by owners

For the purposes of this discussion, it is not important to adhere to any particular definition. It is far more important to know that an enterprise that is not classified as large in South Africa is one which the owner owns and controls independently, and where he or she is directly involved in the management thereof. One should bear in mind that the concepts "small" and "large" may differ from one industry to the next.

2.2.3.2 The strategic role of small business in the economy

In advanced nations the entrepreneur is recognised as a key factor in the process of economic development. Entrepreneurs innovate, take risks and employ people. They create markets and serve consumers by combining materials, processes and new products in new ways. They initiate change, create wealth and develop new enterprises. More specifically, the strategic role of small business in any economy revolves around the following:

- **Producing products and services.** Small business combines the resources of society efficiently to produce products and services for the society in which it operates. Small businesses are less inhibited by large bureaucratic decision-making structures and are more flexible and productive than many large firms. In advanced economies they not only employ the majority of the workforce, but also produce most of the products and services.
- **Innovation.** Since the 1980s and 1990s small businesses have been responsible for most of the innovation that has taken place worldwide. Statistics show that many scientific breakthroughs in the USA originated with small organisations, and not in the laboratories of large businesses. The following are some examples of the twentieth century's new products that were created by small businesses:
  - Photocopiers
  - Jet engines
  - Insulin
  - Helicopters
  - Vacuum tubes
  - Colour film
  - Penicillin
  - Ballpoint pens
  - Zips
  - Personal computers
- **Aiding big business.** Any successful country needs large enterprises to be

able to function competitively in local and especially international markets. The Japanese mega-corporations, for example, compete internationally as world players and have conquered markets that earn them billions in foreign currency for domestic development. In the process, they provide millions of local suppliers with orders. It is the efficiency of the local suppliers, however, that enables the big corporations to compete internationally. Small businesses not only act as suppliers to large businesses, but also distribute their products and services.

- **Job creation.** As previously stated, small businesses provide many of the new job opportunities needed by a growing population. In fact, they create jobs whereas large corporations are shedding jobs.

Jobs for South Africa

If 400 000 additional small businesses could be established in South Africa, each employing ten people, unemployment could be wiped out, since the 4 million people who are currently unemployed would all have jobs.

The small enterprise is entrepreneurially driven. it is precisely this entrepreneurial spirit encountered in the smaller enterprise in particular that is the catalyst for economic development and job creation. Small businesses tend to stimulate competition and thereby improve productivity.

We have now clarified what an entrepreneur is, and we have discussed some of the reasons why people become entrepreneurs, including a brief overview of what a small business is, and its role in the economy. The entrepreneurial process may now be examined more closely.

2.3 The entrepreneurial process

Entrepreneurship is the process of identifying, creating or sensing an opportunity where others do not see it, and of finding and combining resources (often owned by someone else) to pursue the opportunity until it becomes a successful established business. Of the thousands of businesses ventures that entrepreneurs launch every year, many never get off the ground, while others may have a spectacular start. Much of the success in establishing a new business depends on how well the entrepreneur has done his or her homework. This is a difficult process because the range of problems and options confronting the entrepreneur is vast, and differs from one opportunity to the next. For example, although Holiday Inn and City Lodge compete in the same industry, they did not evolve in the same way. The options that are appropriate for one entrepreneurial venture may be completely inappropriate for another. Entrepreneurs must make a bewildering number of decisions – and they must make the right decisions, or perish.

By following a scientific decision-making framework as illustrated in figure 2.5 (on page 48), the entrepreneur has a better chance of success. This framework or entrepreneurial process of entering the business world follows a logical sequence and clarifies many of the questions the entrepreneur is faced

Figure 2.5: The entrepreneurial process: a framework for new venture decision making

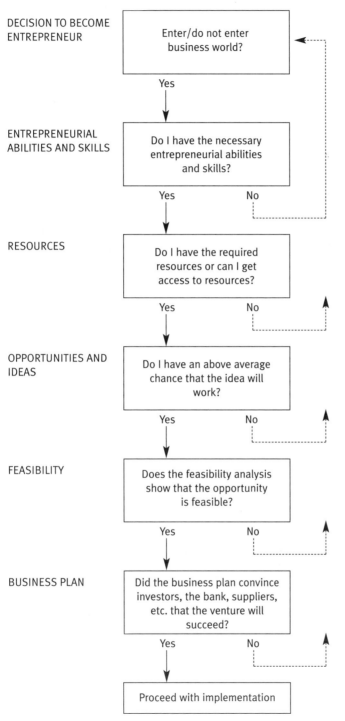

with. The entrepreneurial process involves the following phases or clusters of problems and questions which the entrepreneur must clarify and solve:

- **Abilities and skills.** The personal characteristics, abilities and skills of the new owner of a business have a profound influence on the success or failure of the new venture. Any potential entrepreneur should first clarify whether he or she has what it takes to enter the business world.
- **Access to resources.** Another key factor in new venture creation is the question of resources, or rather access to resources. Without capital or the other resources necessary for the establishment of a business, the new venture is doomed.
- **Opportunity.** A further important aspect of the entrepreneurial process is the assessment of the opportunity that the entrepreneur is pursuing.
- **Feasibility.** Once the opportunity has been identified and defined, the entrepreneur needs to find out if it can be turned into a successful venture. This calls for a feasibility study.
- **Business plan.** Once the entrepreneur has some certainty about the feasibility of the venture, he or she needs to compile a business plan.
- **Manage the business.** Once feasibility has been established and resources have been acquired, the entrepreneur launches and manages the new business.

The above phases of what is popularly called the entrepreneurial process can also be perceived as a framework for decision making. At each of the phases in the process the entrepreneur is faced with many questions that must be clarified before he or she can proceed to the next phase. The above framework does not guarantee that a new venture will be successful. Rather, it provides a logical sequence of steps or phases in the entrepreneurial process. In each phase there is a multiplicity of issues that need to be carefully assessed if the new idea is to be implemented successfully.

It is important to undertake a closer examination of the above phases of the entrepreneurial process.

2.3.1 Skills required for entrepreneurship

A skill is simply knowledge that is demonstrated through action. Potential entrepreneurs therefore need knowledge about the particular environments and industries in which they want to operate, plus considerable **management skills**, such as the following:

- **Strategy skills.** The ability to consider the business as a whole, to understand how it fits within its marketplace, how it can organise itself to deliver value to its customers, and the ways in which it does this better than its competitors.
- **Planning skills.** The ability to consider what the future might offer, how this will impact on the business, and what needs to be done now to prepare for it.
- **Marketing skills.** The ability to see past the firm's offerings and their features; to be able to see how these satisfy the customer's needs, and why the customer finds them attractive.
- **Financial skills.** The ability to manage money; to be able to keep track of

expenditure and to monitor cash flow, but also the ability to assess investments in terms of their potential and their risks.

- **Project management skills.** The ability to organise projects, to set specific objectives, to draw up schedules, and to ensure that the necessary resources are in the right place at the right time.
- **Human relations skills.** The ability to deal with people, which includes leadership skills, motivational skills and communication skills.

The above management skills are discussed in parts 2 and 3 of this book.

Figure 2.6 illustrates how entrepreneurial performance is influenced by a combination of industry knowledge, management skills, people skills and achievement motivation. The successful entrepreneur must learn these skills, that is, learn how to use them and learn from using them.

Figure 2.6: Factors influencing entrepreneurial performance

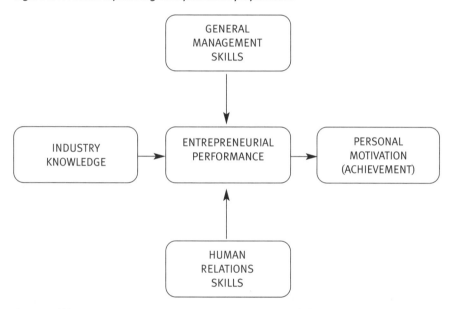

Source: Wickham, P., *Strategic entrepreneurship*, Pearson Education (UK), 1998, p. 43.

All these determinants of entrepreneurship are important, and the more favourably a person is endowed with these determinants, the greater the chances for success.

2.3.2 Resources needed to start a business

Any entrepreneur must have some resources to start a business. Alternatively, he or she must have access to resources to be able to enter into business. In many ventures entrepreneurs do not necessarily want to own the resources that will enable them to start a business, but they may seek control of the resources that they use. The emphasis is therefore not on what resources the entrepreneur owns, but rather what access to and control of resources he or she has.

It was stated in the introductory remarks that entrepreneurs acquire resources from the economy and transform these into need-satisfying products and services for the community. Resources are therefore the inputs that the business combines to create the outputs it delivers to its customers. In broad terms, there are three kinds of resources that entrepreneurs need to build their ventures, namely:

- **Financial resources.** An opportunity can only be exploited if the entrepreneur has money or has access to it. This can take the form of cash, a bank overdraft, loans, outstanding debtors or investment capital. Financial resources include basic resources that can readily be converted into cash.
- **Human resources.** Examples are the management team, lawyers, accountants, as well as technical and other consultants. Human resources basically include people with knowledge and skills that contribute to the success of the venture.
- **Operating resources or physical resources.** These refer to assets such as office or other equipment, a delivery vehicle, raw materials and, in the case of the larger small businesses, buildings, machinery and the plant.

Prospective entrepreneurs must realise that the acquisition of resources implies a risk, especially if the expected profits and return on investments do not materialise. Prospective entrepreneurs must know that investors always compare alternative investments to anticipated return on investment and the risks involved. The entrepreneur is the one who carries the risk, and who stands to lose personal savings or even the house he or she lives in, by acquiring resources for an unsuccessful venture.

Despite the fact that a prospective entrepreneur may have the right experience and the right personal traits to become an entrepreneur, he or she cannot successfully exploit an opportunity without the necessary resources, or without access to these resources. This is the most difficult hurdle to cross in becoming a small business owner.

2.3.3 New business opportunities

Establishing a new business usually involves an idea that the entrepreneur pursues enthusiastically. Finding a good idea is therefore a first step in converting an entrepreneur's creativity into a business opportunity. The danger, however, is that the importance of the idea is often overrated. In other words, having the best idea is by no means a guarantee of success. Unless the entrepreneur has the capacity and capability to transform the idea into a product or service that captures a significant share of the market, the idea is of little value.

But where do new ideas for a business start-up come from? Research in both the USA and other countries points to the fact that prior work experience, an understanding of the industry, and a knowledge of the market account for most new venture ideas.

However, the **scientific way** to search for ideas involves a thorough search of the business environment in which we find ourselves, for **ideas** and **patterns** that emerge from the various trends in the environment. The business environment is examined in more detail in chapter 4.

2.3.3.1 Searching for new venture ideas in the environment

The **environment** referred to includes everything that happens around us. Trends in the environment include economic, political and social trends, fashions that change over time, new ways in which goods are distributed, new services that are offered, and so on. In South Africa some of these trends include the following:

- **Economic trends.** The depreciation of the rand makes South Africa a very attractive tourist destination, and almost everything associated with tourism could provide entrepreneurial opportunities.
- **Social trends.** The high unemployment rate, as well as a police force that appears incapable of enforcing the law, makes violent crime the most prominent trend in South Africa. This trend threatens, for example, foreign investment and tourism, but offers many ideas and opportunities for protecting individuals and their property. Because of this trend, businesses that install burglar bars, security fences, security gates and alarm systems cannot cope with the demand. Changing social trends over the past decade include food consumption and distribution patterns, with the proliferation of fast-food outlets and pubs. Among the new services that have sprung up in the wake of privatisation are mail and courier services, as well as services which are outsourced by large organisations, such as garden services, cafeteria services, maintenance services, and so on.

In searching the environment for entrepreneurial ideas it must be remembered that industries, like fashions, go through various life cycle stages, as illustrated by figure 2.7 (see page 52). Virtually everything changes and goes through the stages of introduction, growth, maturity and decline. It is important to know in what life cycle stage a new venture idea falls, because each cycle needs a different strategy. Industries in the maturity stage are, for example, very competitive, and this requires high marketing costs. It is clear from the life cycle diagram that the car industry as a whole is very mature. Nonetheless, some of its segments are in a developing phase, for example, mini-vans, sports models, and upmarket imports. Convertibles are back in fashion, and in the suburbs young mothers drive around in 4 x 4s. Despite increasing traffic jams, people still drive, and the cars they drive reflect changing lifestyles.

Where can you find gaps in the life cycle diagram? Ideas can be generated at any point in the life cycle stages of industries. They may emerge even in those industries that fall into the decline category, as is evident from the revival of cigar smoking. There is even a magazine in South Africa that specifically targets cigar smokers!

South African industries also fall into the categories that appear in figure 2.7, but prospective entrepreneurs should take a close look at the following industries, which could, in the African landscape, be labelled **embryo** or **growth industries**:

- The government's main priority is to educate all South Africans. Proof of this is the fact that the budget for education comprises the largest portion of the annual budget. Because of the importance of education and the inability of the government to reach its educational objectives, there are

Figure 2.7: The life cycle stages of industries

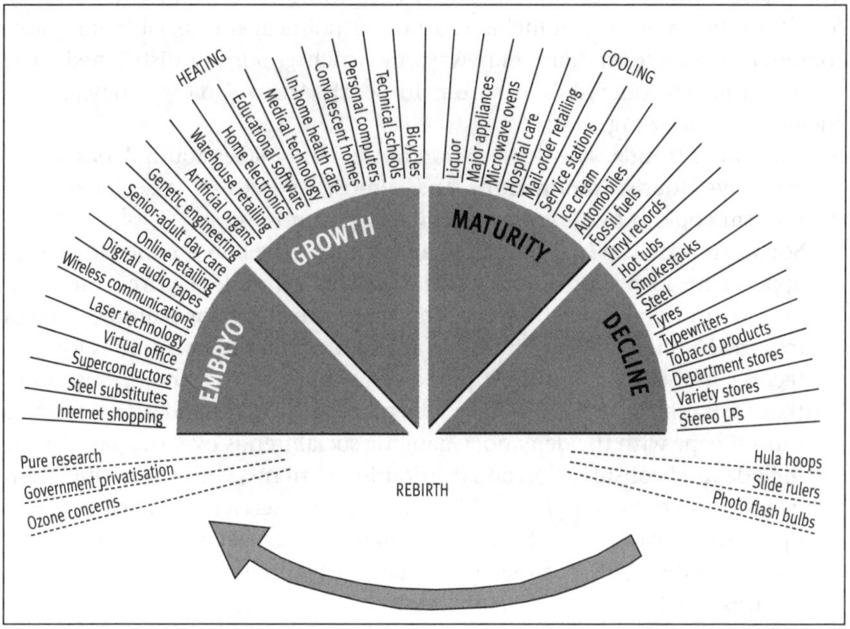

Source: Ryan, J. D., Ecked, L. A. & Ray, R. J., *Small Business*, South-Western Publishing, by permission of Thomson Learning, 1998, p. 29.

many opportunities in **private education**, from elementary education to technical and tertiary education.

- A second important industry in South Africa is **health care**. Because most government hospitals perform poorly, numerous opportunities exist for entrepreneurs to start health care ventures, especially home health care.
- A third important South African industry is **tourism**, which could provide thousands of new jobs. Very little start-up capital is needed, for example, to become a tour guide.
- The **privatisation** of government and semi-government services is another priority of the South African government. Many changes are currently taking place, since government services are being privatised worldwide. In many countries the government, for example, has been one of the principal markets in respect of programmes such as defence, energy, transport, cleaning services and building projects.

Other sources of ideas include advertisements, retailers, competitors, trade shows, industry associations, contracts, consultants, patents and research institutes. An important aspect in the generation of new ideas is the creative ability of the prospective entrepreneur. A truly creative person will find useful ideas in a variety of different ways and by various means.

Ideas, however, have to be transformed into opportunities if they are to result in the creation of small businesses.

2.3.3.2 Opportunities

Good ideas can be turned into successful new ventures. But a good idea is not necessarily the same thing as a good opportunity. It may, for example, be a good idea to freeze a swimming pool during the short South African winter to save pool chemicals and to provide a home ice-rink for children. But the idea cannot be transformed into a new venture opportunity because research has shown that South African pool owners do not find the idea persuasive (pool surfaces are too small); moreover, because of the costs involved, the idea is not feasible.

Experience shows that a good idea is not necessarily a good opportunity or a good **investment opportunity**. Many people tend to become infatuated with an idea and to underestimate the difficulty involved in developing it into a product or service that will be desirable to the market. Ultimately, the market determines whether an idea has potential as an investment opportunity. The following are some of the fundamental requirements for a good investment opportunity:

- There must be a clearly defined **market need** for the product. The most successful entrepreneurs and investors are **opportunity focused**; they start with what customers and the marketplace want, and they do not lose sight of this.
- The opportunity must be able to achieve a **sustainable competitive advantage**.
- The opportunity must have the **potential to grow**.
- The opportunity must be **rewarding** to the investor and/or the entrepreneur.
- The **timing** of the opportunity must be right. A **window of opportunity** must exist. The window of opportunity for delivery of a wedding cake, for example, closes on the Saturday of the wedding. If the wedding cake is delivered on the Monday morning after the wedding, it is worthless.

Good opportunities are therefore ones that satisfy a market need and also reward the entrepreneur. It is important that they be well-timed.

However, generating a good idea and starting a new venture from scratch is not the only way to enter the business world. Buying an existing business or procuring a franchise can reduce many of the uncertainties that must be faced when starting a business.

2.3.3.3 Buying an existing business

There are several advantages to buying an existing business when compared with other strategies for entering the business world. Since customers are used to doing business with the company at its present address, they are likely to continue doing so once it has been taken over by a new owner. If the business has been making money, the new owner will break even sooner than if he or she were to start the business from scratch. Planning for an ongoing business can be based on previous financial records, rather than having to rely on projections, as with a start-up. An inventory, equipment, and suppliers are already in place, and the business is managed by employees who know from experience how to keep the business going. In addition, it may be possible to obtain financing from the previous owner.

If the timing of the deal occurs when the entrepreneur is ready to buy a business and the owner needs to sell for a legitimate reason, this may be the best way of entering the business world. There may, however, be certain disadvantages in buying an existing business, as table 2.1 shows.

Table 2.1: Advantages and disadvantages of buying an existing business

ADVANTAGES	DISADVANTAGES
1. Customers familiar with location	1. Business location may be undesirable – or threatened with becoming undesirable
2. Established customer base at present location	2. Image difficult to change
3. Experienced employees	3. Employees are inherited rather than chosen
4. Planning can be based on known historical data	4. Possible difficulties in changing the way the business is run
5. Supplier relationships already in place	5. Potential liability for past business contracts
6. Inventory and equipment in place	6. Possible obsolete inventory and equipment
7. Possible owner financing	7. Financing costs could drain cash flow and threaten the survival of the business

One cannot simply buy an existing business in the hope that it is or will be an ongoing success. The business remains an **opportunity** for which a feasibility analysis will be necessary.

2.3.3.4 Franchising

A third way of entering the business world is through the acquisition of a franchise. The franchise concept gives an entrepreneur the opportunity of starting a business that has been proven in the marketplace. The entrepreneur then becomes a **franchisee**. The **franchisor** gives the franchisee the right to operate a business, using the franchise company's name, products and systems. In return, the franchisee pays the franchise company for this right on an ongoing basis.

Importance of franchising in South Africa

The importance of assisting the franchising sector is clear from its considerable contribution to the economy. Turnover generated by franchised systems during 2000 (excluding petroleum retail) is estimated at R58,97 billion. While the number of business units has increased annually by 17% since 1994, turnover increase for the same period, based on current prices, has been 28%. Furthermore, 293 000 people are directly employed in the franchise sector, of whom 20 995 are self-employed. In 2000 the contribution to GDP of the franchise sector was 6,75%. The contribution of the franchise sector to the economy is, thus, increasingly important.

Source: Bureau for Market Research, Unisa, 2001.

In South Africa most reputable franchises are registered with the Franchise Association of Southern Africa (FASA). The purpose of this organisation is to ensure that franchising in Southern Africa is a quality concept that can enable entrepreneurs to start new businesses. Fasa is an excellent source of information on franchises.

2.3.4 *The feasibility of the idea or opportunity*

Many small businesses result from an idea that has been converted into a useful application. Ideas have little value until they are converted into new products, services or processes. But, as discussed in previous sections, not all ideas can be converted into feasible ventures. An idea must therefore be subjected to a feasibility test to prove that it has value. Aspiring entrepreneurs often find that the idea has already been developed, or that competitors already exist. The same applies to any opportunities that entrepreneurs may recognise. The entrepreneur should therefore also do a feasibility analysis of any apparent opportunity.

Buying an existing business or recognising a franchise opportunity does not necessarily mean that the new or existing venture will be an instant success. No matter how promising the idea or opportunity may appear, the entrepreneur should as soon as possible determine whether it is feasible. Doing a feasibility analysis in good time may prevent the entrepreneur from losing valuable resources on an idea or opportunity that in fact offers little hope of success.

A **feasibility study** is the collection of data that helps forecast whether an idea, an opportunity, or a venture will survive. The feasibility study gives the entrepreneur an information profile that should enable him or her to take a definite decision on whether or not to go ahead with the venture. A feasibility study is not the same thing as a business plan. It precedes the business plan and consists mainly of gathering data to enable the entrepreneur to take a decision on whether to go ahead with the idea, opportunity or new venture. Once the feasibility of an idea has been assessed, the enterpreneur can commit to implementing the idea – or abandon the idea altogether, depending on the outcome.

Upon deciding that an idea appears feasible, and therefore to proceed with it, the entrepreneur has then to decide how to make the idea work. In other words, the entrepreneur must now decide how to translate the idea into reality. This stage entails the drawing up of a business plan. Because of its importance to the entrepreneurial process, the **business plan** will be discussed more fully in the following chapter.

2.4 Summary

In this chapter both the concept of entrepreneurship and the idea that the entrepreneur is the driving force behind the business organisation were dealt with. The role of entrepreneurs in the economy was examined, as were the reasons for people becoming entrepreneurs. Following this, the various aspects and phases of the entrepreneurial process were examined, including an assessment of the entrepreneur's unique abilities and skills, access to resources, the search for opportunities, the feasibility study, and, finally, the composition of the business plan. As stated, the business plan will be dealt with in detail in chapter 3, as will the professional management of the new venture.

Reference

1. Basson, E., The informal and SME sectors in the RSA economy, unpublished memorandum of the SBDC, pp. 4–5.

3 The establishment of a business

The purpose of this chapter

This chapter focuses on the different forms of legal ownership that are available to the entrepreneur. It includes the characteristics, advantages and disadvantages of the sole proprietorship, the partnership and the company. Each of these forms is discussed in order to enable learners to compare and make informed decisions. Once the entrepreneur knows what the available options are, he or she will be able draw up a business plan for the new business. The location factors are also discussed here.

Learning outcomes

The content of this chapter will enable learners to:
- Understand and discuss the key considerations that are applicable when a form of business has to be chosen
- Distinguish the different forms of ownership that are found in South Africa
- Explain the objectives, importance and need for a business plan
- Evaluate a business plan
- Give an overview of a business plan
- Identify the location factors of a business

3.1 Introduction

This chapter will focus on the different forms of ownership that are available to the entrepreneur. It will include the characteristics, advantages and disadvantages of the sole proprietorship, the close corporation, the partnership, and the company. Each of these forms will be discussed to enable you to compare and make an informed decision. When the entrepreneur knows what the available options are, he or she can put everything together by drawing up a business plan for the new business. This will also be discussed in this chapter.

The location factors of a business will also briefly be discussed.

3.2 The legal form of ownership

3.2.1 Introduction

Human resources – the people involved in the business – require a formal organisational structure in which to operate. Several options are available to the entrepreneur, but there are also many issues that should be considered when deciding on the form of ownership. To what extent does the entrepreneur want to be liable for financial and legal risk? Who will have a controlling interest in the business? How will the business be financed?

It is thus clear that one of the first issues to face any entrepreneur who wants to enter the business world, is choosing a form of ownership.

This decision can have a tremendous impact on almost every aspect of the business. Many factors influence the entrepreneur's decision about what form of business to use for the businesses. Some considerations are the size of the business, the proposed business activities, decisions about the shareholding, management structure and financial structure, the accountability of participants (partners or shareholders) and their needs, and tax and legal implications. This topic presents the issues that entrepreneurs must consider when choosing the form of ownership that is best suited to them. The key to choosing the "right" form of ownership is to understand how the characteristics of each ownership form influence an entrepreneur's specific business and personal circumstances. Although, generally speaking, there is no best form of ownership, there may well be one form that is best suited to each entrepreneur's circumstances.

3.2.2 Considerations in choosing a legal form of business

Businesses in South Africa usually take the form of sole proprietorships, partnerships, companies, close corporations or cooperatives. Cooperatives, which can be founded in South Africa under the Co-operatives Act 91 of 1981, are distinctive organisations with limited applications. Cooperatives attempt to achieve certain economic advantages for their members through joint action on the members' part. In South Africa cooperatives are found mainly in farming communities as organisations selling and/or supplying products or goods and services. Because of their distinctive features, cooperatives are not usually real alternatives to the forms of business mentioned, and they will therefore not be discussed any further.

When prospective entrepreneurs choose a form of business, they need to consider the following:

- The **legal personality** of the business. In other words, can the business, from a legal point of view, exist independently of its owner(s) and have its own assets and liabilities (possessions and obligations)?
- The **liability of the owner(s)**. This is linked to the first point. Are the owners liable for outstanding debts and claims against the business?
- The degree to which the owner(s) has/have **direct control and authority** over the activities of the business, the application or use of assets, and the distribution of the business profits.
- The **capital acquisition potential** of the business when it is first founded and in the event of expansion later on. Here, factors such as the number of owners permitted, their liability and their say in the management all play a role.
- The possibility of **change of ownership**, in other words, the ease with which an owner might transfer his or her interest in the business to someone else. Related to this is the **lifespan** or **continuity** of the business.
- The **legal requirements** regarding the establishment, management and dissolution of the business, and the **tax liability** of the business and its owner(s)[1].

In the paragraphs that follow we discuss the main characteristics of sole proprietorships, partnerships, close corporations, and companies in terms of these key considerations.

3.2.3 The sole proprietorship

The sole proprietorship is a business that is owned and managed by one individual. This is by far the most popular form of business. It is a simple form of business, and the least costly form of ownership for beginning your own business.

As stated, the sole proprietorship has a single, individual owner. It does not have an independent **legal personality**, and consequently cannot exist independently of the owner. The assets of the business belong to the owner alone, and the owner is also **personally liable** for all the debts and claims against the business. The owner could therefore lose all his or her personal possessions if the business is unable to meet its obligations.

The owner has direct control and authority over the activities of the business, and the entire profit of the business goes to him or her. The owner usually manages the business, and is free to take decisions concerning the running of the business. The business is therefore able to adjust readily to changes. On the other hand, a sole proprietorship can, depending on the circumstances, make exceptionally high demands on the management ability and personal freedom of the owner.

The **capital acquisition potential** of the sole proprietorship is limited to the owner's financial strength and creditworthiness. The available funds are thus often insufficient, particularly where the owner is considering expanding. On the other hand, too great a dependence on loan capital can result in the owner having to forfeit control, authority and freedom.

The **transfer of ownership** of the sole proprietorship is limited to the owner's financial strength and creditworthiness. The available funds are thus often insufficient, particularly where the owner is considering expanding. On the other hand, too great a dependence on loan capital can result in the owner having to forfeit control, authority and freedom.

The **transfer of ownership** of a sole proprietorship does not usually present many problems. The owner can decide at any time to sell the business (provided, of course, that a buyer can be found), to close down, or to transfer ownership to someone else. The **lifespan** (continuity) of the business is, furthermore, linked with the lifespan or the **legal capacity** of the owner. (The owner's legal capacity is his or her capacity to act under the law, for example to enter into contracts.) If the owner dies, becomes insolvent, or otherwise legally incapable, this usually means the end of the business.

Apart from the prescriptions (regulations) contained in the Business Names Act 27 of 1960 and the Licences Act 44 of 1962, and also in certain health regulations, there are no particular **legal prescriptions** with which a sole proprietorship has to comply regarding its founding or establishment, management or dissolution. As far as **tax liability** is concerned, we have already mentioned that the entire profit of the business belongs to the owner; accordingly, it is only taxable once it is in the hands of the owner as an individual. Depending on the owner's taxable income and the tax regulations at any given time, the sole proprietorship can therefore have greater tax advantages for the owner than any other form of business.

A sole proprietorship offers the following **advantages**:
- It is simple to create
- It is the least costly form in beginning a business
- The owner has total decision-making authority
- There are no special legal restrictions
- It is easy to discontinue

It also has the following **disadvantages**:
- Unlimited personal liability of owner
- Limited skills and capabilities
- Limited access to capital
- Lack of continuity

In the course of time, it has become evident that if two or more sole owners join forces, they are able to bring about a stronger unit, because their combined financial and other resources are then at their disposal. This has led to the development of the **partnership** as another form of business available to the entrepreneur. The partnership is possibly one of the oldest commercial institutions known to humankind. We discuss the partnership in the next paragraph.

3.2.4 The partnership

In many respects, a partnership is similar to a sole proprietorship, and many of the disadvantages of the sole proprietorship apply to partnerships as well. The partnership may be described as a contractual relationship between two or more – but usually not more than twenty – persons (called partners) who operate a legitimate business to which each contributes something, with the purpose of making a profit that is distributed among them. A partnership is a contractual relationship because the partners have a contract or agreement among themselves.

There are two forms of partnership: **ordinary partnerships**, and what are known as **extraordinary partnerships**. Here we focus on the ordinary partnership, since this is the most general form.

A partnership does not have a **legal personality**, and it is the partners in their personal capacity, rather than the partnership as such, who enter into all transactions, contracts or agreements. The partners are **jointly and severally liable** for all claims against the partnership, regardless of who was responsible for bringing about the claim. (In other words, they all take responsibility together for any claim made against the partnership.) The personal possessions of the partners are therefore not protected against any claim.

Unless they decide differently at the beginning, the partners have joint **control** and **authority** over the business. Obviously, this can lead to problems if the partners have different opinions, and in this respect the partnership is less adaptable to changing circumstances than is the sole proprietorship. On the other hand, this broader authority can mean improved management ability, because the business draws on the knowledge, experience and expertise of a greater number of people. It also allows for division of labour and specialisation, with the additional advantage that individual partners are exposed to less pressure than the owner of a sole proprietorship.

A partnership usually has better **capital acquisition potential** than a sole proprietorship because there are more people who can contribute and who can provide security for credit.

As far as **legal prescriptions** are concerned, there are few differences between a partnership and a sole proprietorship. The only real difference is a written partnership contract, which is highly desirable but not legally enforceable (that is, the partners cannot be forced by law to obey the contract). The partnership contract should comply with all the requirements for a valid contract. Thus, a partnership contract may not, for example, be in conflict with legislation, public policy or good morals.

There are no formal requirements for setting up a partnership. A valid partnership may therefore be concluded orally, in writing, or tacitly (that is, through certain behaviour). However it is customary and preferable for the contract to be in writing. The contract makes provision for matters such as the nature and goals of the business, capital contributions by individual partners, profit sharing, management and dissolution. As in the sole proprietorship, each partner is liable for **tax** on all income in his or her personal capacity. If, for example, a partner earns a salary plus profit from the partnership, the partnership as a business has no tax obligations.

In general, **transfer of ownership** is more complicated in partnerships that in sole proprietorships because more people are involved and because the stipulations or provisions of the partnership contract have to be complied with. However, it can be easier for a partner to sell his or her interest in a partnership than to sell a sole proprietorship. The reason for this lies in the advantages of a partnership, which a sole proprietorship cannot offer, namely better capital acquisition potential, better management skills, the potential for division of labour and specialisation, and less personal stress.

The most common methods of dissolving or terminating an existing partnership are the following:
- A mutual agreement between partners
- The withdrawal or death of one of the partners
- The entry of a new partner
- Insolvency (or any other legal incapacitation, that is, loss of legal capacity) of one of the partners, or insolvency of the partnership, which of course also causes the insolvency of the individual partners)

It is not always easy to choose the "right" partner for your business, and we often hear of so-called "business divorces" between partners who no longer get on. Based on studies of partners and partnerships, business therapists have compiled a list of 25 attributes the ideal partner should have:
- Is a good team player
- Does the job competently and skilfully
- Is a genuinely likeable person
- Is good at giving feedback to others
- Is a good listener

- Is open and receptive to feedback from others
- Treats people with dignity and respect
- Looks for "win-win" solutions to disagreements
- Is good at facing up to tough problems
- Is trustworthy
- Will "go to bat" (that is, stand in) for other people
- Gets along well with almost everybody
- Uses time efficiently and effectively
- Will admit it or apologise when wrong
- Has what it takes to be a good manager
- Is a good problem solver
- Speaks his or her mind, even if it is unpopular
- Is well-organised
- Treats people fairly and equitably
- Is good at giving compliments or positive feedback
- Is pleasant to be around
- Is open to other people's ideas and opinions
- Is level-headed, even under stress
- Presents ideas clearly and articulately
- Has good interpersonal skills

A partnership can sometimes be identified by the **name** of the business, for example, Drs Du Buisson and partners, Simey and Sons, Mohammed and Naicker, Smith and Brown Financial Advisers.

To summarise, the partnership offers the following **advantages**:
- Easy to establish
- Availability of complementary skills of partners
- Larger pool of capital available
- Little government regulation
- Flexibility

The partnership has the following **disadvantages**:
- Unlimited liability
- Difficulty in disposing of interest in partnership
- Potential for conflict – of personality and also about authority

3.2.5 The close corporation

The need for a smaller business entity with a separate legal personality arose as a result of the complexity of the Companies Act 61 of 1973 and the high costs of complying with its provisions. The Close Corporations Act 69 of 1984 provides for such a business. A close corporation has characteristics of both a partnership and a company and has the advantage of being a legal person that exists separately from its members.

The **legal prescriptions** with which the members of a close corporation must comply are not strict, and the corporation can be registered at very little cost. A close corporation is created by the registration of a founding statement, which contains details such as the proposed name of the corporation, the nature of the business, and the personal details of members and their interests in the corporation. The founding statement can be compared with the memorandum of association of a company. Although a founding statement is registered, nobody is considered as knowing anything about its contents. Unlike a company, a close corporation is not expected to appoint an auditor, but it does have to appoint an accountant. Financial statements must be drawn up within nine months of the corporation's year end, and must be approved and signed by all the members or on their behalf.

The **name** of a close corporation must end with the letters CC. In principle, a close corporation may only have natural persons (that is, individual people, not legal persons such as a company) as members, and the members are limited to ten. The core characteristic of the close corporation is that it is "closed" in the sense that the members both own and control the close corporation. The interest of a member is expressed as a percentage, and the total interest of members must always amount to 100%.

If the corporation has two or more members, they may enter into an **association agreement** that regulates the internal matters of the corporation in accordance with the provisions of the Act. For example, the members can state in this agreement that all members may actively participate in the operation of the corporation, and that authority is based on the percentage of each member's interest in the corporation. There are, however, certain matters which cannot be dealt with in the agreement, such as one or more members not becoming involved in the management of the corporation, and limitation on each member's right to call a meeting of the members. The law does not prescribe when or how meetings must be held, and simply states that each member may call a meeting by giving notice of it to every other member. A valid decision may also be made without holding a meeting, as long as all the members sign the decision.

Each person who becomes a member of the corporation on registration must make an initial contribution of money, property or services for the corporation to be formed and incorporated. The members' contributions and their interest in the corporation need not be in direct proportion to one another, as the following example shows.

Table 3.1: Example of members' contributions in a close corporation

	Member A	Member B	Member C	Total
Contribution	R50 000 (50%)	R30 000 (30%)	R20 000 (20%)	R100 000 (100%)
Percentage interest	35%	35%	30%	100%

Members of a close corporation have a fiduciary relationship with the corporation, which means that they are expected to carry out their duties honestly and in good faith, and not to exceed their powers. Usually, every member has the **authority** to bind the corporation to a transaction that falls within the corporation's scope of business. The close corporation is a **legal person**, and therefore the members are in general **not liable** for the debts of the corporation, but they may be liable jointly and severally with the corporation in circumstances specified by the Act. In addition, the Act makes provision for members to be held personally liable if they abuse the corporation by carrying on the business recklessly, fraudulently or with gross negligence. The close corporation has the same legal capacity as a natural person in matters such as concluding contracts and registering property in its name.

A close corporation may not make any payments to members in their capacity as members (for example, profit distribution or repayment of contributions) unless the following conditions are met:

- After the payment is made, the corporation's assets must still exceed its liabilities, based on a reasonable valuation.
- After the payment, the corporation must still be in a position to pay its debts in the normal course of business.

Because the close corporation has a legal personality, its continued **existence** is not influenced by the withdrawal or entry of members. An individual may become a member of an existing close corporation by acquiring the interest of an existing member, with the agreement of all the members. In other words, an existing member can transfer his or her part ownership in the close corporation to another individual, provided all the members give their approval. An existing member can also dispose of his or her interest in the corporation if the other members approve. The law also makes provision for a member to apply to the court to terminate his or her membership of a close corporation.

Close corporations are treated as companies for taxation purposes. The profit of the close corporation is therefore **taxed** at a fixed tariff. Distributed profit (dividends) is, however, not taxed again in the hands of the members.

In conclusion, the close corporation offers its members limited liability, it is relatively easy to form, it is continuous even if a member dies or leaves, and ownership is transferable.

To conclude this chapter, we discuss the two types of profit-making companies found in South Africa, namely the private company and the public company.

3.2.6 The company

The last form of ownership available to the entrepreneur is the company. The company (which functions in terms of the Companies Act 61 of 1973, as amended) developed to meet business people's need to obtain more capital than they could through a sole proprietorship or partnership, and also because the partnership still had certain deficiencies and undesirable features as a form of business. People eventually accepted the idea that, from a legal point of view, there could be a fictitious person having rights and duties, being able to participate in commercial life, and whose existence would not depend upon the life of a natural person or persons. Business people could obtain large sums of money through such a separate legal entity, so that they could undertake commercial ventures that individuals could not afford, to the benefit of the entire community.

A company is subject to many more **legal prescriptions** than the other forms of ownership, as the following shows:

- The company has to have a constitution, which has to be registered with the Registrar of Companies. The constitution is made up of two documents, namely the memorandum of association, which governs the external relationships of the company, and the articles of association, which govern the internal affairs of the company. These documents also contain the name, main objectives and internal management rules, among other things. They must be registered with the Registrar of Companies in Pretoria, and any person may be deemed or considered to have the right to know the contents of these documents.
- In terms of the Companies Act, a company acquires a legal personality only when the Registrar of Companies has issued a certificate of incorporation.
- The principal organs of the company are the annual general meeting of members, and the board of directors. The annual general meeting determines the general policy, while the board of directors attends to the administration of the company.
- A shareholder's interest in the company is represented by the number of shares he or she holds in the company. The share capital of a company is the amount that the shareholders contribute to the resources of the company. There are therefore certain rules aimed at maintaining the share capital. The money that makes up the contribution becomes the property of the company. The shareholder obtains certain rights against the company, for example, the right to receive dividends from its profits when such dividends have been properly declared.
- The company has to comply with requirements concerning accounting records, financial reporting, auditing, minutes, registers of shareholders, and so on.
- The Companies Act contains provisions regarding the rights, powers and duties of directors and other office bearers. The relevant provisions of the articles of association must also be adhered to.
- There are legal requirements concerning the dissolution or liquidation of a company.
- There is the matter of tax liability of a company and its shareholders. A company pays a fixed percentage of its net income before tax (for companies with financial years ending after 1 April 1994, this is currently 35%) as income tax. If the company declares a dividend, it pays secondary tax at 12,5% on all dividends declared after March 1996.

Table 3.2: Example of company tax

Description	Company A	Company B
Net income before tax	R500 000	R500 000
Dividend declared	Nil	R300 000
Income tax @ 35%	(R500 000 x 0,35) = R175 000	(R500 000 x 0,35) = R175 000
Secondary tax @ 12,5%	Nil	(R300 000 x 0,125) = R37 500
Total tax	R175 000	R212 500

A company has a **legal personality**, and the assets and liabilities of the company are therefore completely separate from those of the members or shareholders. The personal possessions of the shareholders are thus not involved when claims are instituted or made against a company. The **liability** of the shareholders is limited to paying up their share capital in the company in full.

As already stated, **control and authority** over the activities and assets of the company belong to two bodies – the board of directors and the annual general meeting.

The day-to-day management of the company is usually delegated to the board of directors by the company's articles of association, while the annual general meeting has the power to amend the articles of association, and in this way bring about a redistribution of power between the shareholders and the board of directors.

Directors are usually appointed by the annual general meeting, and their functions and powers are defined in the articles of association. These functions are jointly exercised by the directors (as the board of directors) by means of a majority vote. The board can, if it is empowered to do so by the articles of association or the annual general meeting, delegate some of its functions and powers to a managing director.

The only way in which the shareholders of a company can express their wishes regarding the business and management of the company is by voting at an annual general meeting, which must be held once a year. In principle, the voting right of shareholders is linked to the number of shares they hold in the company, and decisions at the annual general meeting are normally taken by means of a vote.

As in a partnership, the advantage of the broader authority usually found in a company is that more people know about and have experience in management. But this broader authority can also be a disadvantage if decision making is delayed because of a difference of opinion.

The company, and especially the public company, as a form of business has definite advantages over the sole proprietorship and the partnership as far as **capital acquisition potential** is concerned. This is because the general public can be invited to invest capital in a public company. They are usually willing to do so because of the legal personality that a company possesses, the limited liability the public accepts, and the strict legal regulations with which companies have to comply. For the same reasons, financial institutions are more willing to invest funds in a company than in a sole proprietorship or a partnership. The capital acquisition potential can be further enhanced if shareholders, particularly the directors, are prepared to provide additional loan security in their personal capacities. This often happens in practice.

In public companies the **transfer of ownership** takes place through the unlimited and free transfer of shares. Ownership is transferred through the private sale of shares or through selling shares on the stock exchange. The transfer of shares usually has no influence on the activities of the company, and the company therefore has an unlimited lifespan.

Shares in a private company are not freely transferable, and the method of transfer is laid down in the company's articles of association. Transfer is usually subject to the approval of the board of directors: a shareholder who wants to sell his or her shares therefore has to find a buyer who is acceptable to the board. In practice, this usually means relatives or friends, but it should not be difficult to find such a person if the company is profitable. The transfer of shares in a private company is also unlikely to influence its activities, or the continued existence of the business.

The Companies Act provides for the incorporation of two types of companies, namely companies with a share capital, and companies limited by guarantee as indicated by figure 3.1. Then there is also the incorporated association not for gain. This latter type of company does not have a share capital. It is a company limited by guarantee, and the liability of its members is limited by its memorandum of association. A company with a share capital can be either a public company or a private company. However, we will concentrate only on companies with share capital, and will now look at the main differences between the public company and the private company.

Figure 3.1: Types of companies

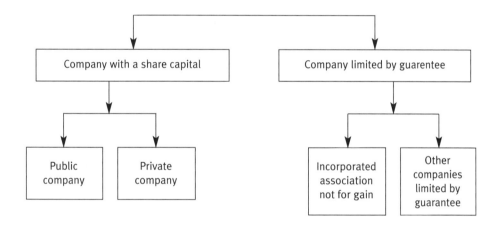

Source: Havenga, P.H., *General principles of commercial law*, 3rd edition, Juta Law, Cape Town, 1997.

3.2.7 Differences between the public company and the private company

The main **differences** between a private company and a public company are as follows:

- The number of members (**shareholders**) of a private company ranges from one to fifty people. The public company must have at least seven members, but there is no maximum, provided the authorised number of shares is not exceeded.
- The private company must have at least one **director**, and a public company must have at least two directors.
- The **general public cannot subscribe** to the shares of a private company, and shares may only be sold with the consent of the other shareholders. Public companies raise capital by issuing shares to the public. The public is invited to buy shares in the company by means of a prospectus. The shares are freely negotiable.

- The name of a private company must end with the words **(Pty) Ltd** or (Proprietary) Limited, for example, Maxi Removals (Pty) Ltd. There is also another type of private company, the incorporated company, whose name ends in the word Incorporated **(Inc.)**, for example, Andersons Incorporated. Certain professions allow their members to form this type of company instead of practising in a partnership. The name of a public company must end in Ltd or Limited, for example Moroko Traders Limited.
- Both types of company are subject to strict **legal regulations**, although a private company is not as strictly controlled.
- In both types of company, shareholders have **limited liability** – they are only liable for the amount that they invested in the company.
- In both, company profits are distributed as **dividends** declared on the number or value of shares held by each shareholder.
- The **life** of a company is indefinite, except when it is liquidated.

Applying the concept: types of companies

Complete the following table:

	PRIVATE COMPANY	PUBLIC COMPANY	PARTNERSHIP
Number of members			
Liability of members			
Name			
Division of profits			
Continuity of business			

3.2.8 Summary

Once entrepreneurs have identified their opportunity and evaluated it, they basically have three options for entering the business world (as discussed in chapter 2), namely entering into a franchise agreement, buying an existing business or establishing a business from scratch. In all these cases the entrepreneur's choice of a form of business is very important.

In choosing a form of ownership, entrepreneurs must remember that there is no single "best" form of ownership. Each form has its own advantages and disadvantages. An entrepreneur's choice must reflect his or her particular situation; there may be a business form that is best for the entrepreneur's individual circumstances. Understanding the forms of ownership, and the characteristics, advantages and disadvantages of each one, is the entrepreneur's key to selecting the form of ownership that best suits himself or herself.

In this section we have discussed the different forms of ownership available to the entrepreneur, and we have compared the characteristics, advantages and disadvantages of the sole proprietorship, the close corporation, the partnership and the company. Once the entrepreneur knows what the available options are, he or she can put everything together by drawing up the business plan for the new business.

3.3 Developing the business plan for the new business

In this section the development of the business plan for the new venture will be examined.

3.3.1 The objectives of a business plan

For the entrepreneur starting a new venture, a business plan is a written document that accomplishes certain basic objectives. The most important objective is to **identify and describe the nature of the business opportunity or the new venture.**

The second objective is to **present a written plan of how the entrepreneur plans to exploit the opportunity.** Here, the business plan explains the key variables for the success or failure of the new venture: it is a guideline to the things that must be done to establish and operate the new venture. It provides a large number of instruments such as the mission, goals, objectives, target markets, operating budgets, financial needs, and so on, which the entrepreneur and managers can draw on to lead the venture successfully. These instruments, which help managers to keep the venture on track, constitute the key components of the business plan. A business plan is therefore also a valuable managerial tool that helps the entrepreneur and his or her team to focus on charting a course for the new business.

A third objective of the business plan is to attract investors, or to persuade a bank or other institution or person who provides financial resources, to lend the entrepreneur the money he needs to establish the new business. Careful preparation can make the difference between success and failure when shopping in the capital market.

Apart from the above main objectives of a business plan, it provides many other benefits, such as the following:

- A systematic, realistic evaluation of the new venture's chances of success in the market
- A way of identifying the key variables that will determine the success of the new venture, as well as the primary risks that may lead to failure
- A game plan for managing the business successfully
- A management instrument for comparing actual results against targeted performance
- A primary tool for attracting money in the hunt for financial resources

3.3.2 Importance and necessity of the business plan

The overall importance of the business plan lies in its planning activities. Planning is the fundamental element of management that predetermines what the business organisation proposes to accomplish, and how this is to be accomplished. Planning, and thus the idea of a business plan, is hardly something new. Big businesses have long been turning out annual business plans by the thousands, especially for marketing new products, buying new businesses or expanding globally. What is new, however, is the growing use of such plans by small entrepreneurs. The latter are in many cases forced by financial institutions to draw up a business plan before any financial support will be considered.

The business plan is of importance not only to the entrepreneur, but also to his employees, potential investors, bankers, suppliers, customers, and so on. Each group of "stakeholders" in the business plan will study the plan from a different perspective. It is therefore clear that any business, but especially a new venture, needs to have a business plan to answer any questions that various stakeholders in the venture may raise.

There are eight reasons for writing a business plan:

- **To sell yourself to the business.** The most important stakeholders in any business are its founders. First and foremost, you need to convince yourself that starting the business is right for you – both from a personal point of view, and an investment viewpoint.

- **To obtain bank financing.** Up until the late 1980s, writing a business plan to obtain bank financing was an option left up to the entrepreneur. Bankers usually took the approach that a business plan helped the entrepreneur to make a better case, though it was not an essential component in the bank's decision-making process. Banks currently require entrepreneurs to include a written business plan with any request for loan funds. As a consequence, obtaining money from a bank is tougher than it has ever been, and a business plan is an essential component of any campaign to convince banks of your new business.

- **To obtain investment funds.** For many years now, the business plan has been the "ticket of admission" to the venture capital or "informal" capital from private investors.

- **To arrange strategic alliances.** Joint research, marketing, and other efforts between small and large companies have become increasingly common in recent years, and this requires a business plan.

- **To obtain large contracts.** When small companies seek substantial orders or ongoing service contracts from major corporations, the corporations often respond – perhaps somewhat arrogantly: "Everyone knows who we are. But no one knows who you are. How do we know you'll be around in three or five years to provide the parts or service we might require for our product?" It is for this reason that entrepreneurs are required to have a business plan.

- **To attract key employees.** One of the biggest obstacles that small, growing companies face in attracting key employees is convincing the best people to take the necessary risk – that the company will thrive and grow during the coming years.

- **To complete mergers and acquisitions.** No matter which side of the merger process you are on, a business plan can be very helpful if you want to sell your company to a large corporation.

- **To motivate and focus your management team.** As smaller companies grow and become more complex, a business plan becomes an important component in keeping everyone focused on the same goals.

3.3.3 Stakeholders in a business plan

There are both internal and external stakeholders, and each category is discussed in the sections that follow.

3.3.3.1 Internal stakeholders

- **New venture management.** A written business plan is essential for the systematic coverage of all the important features of a new business. It becomes a manual to the entrepreneur and his management team for establishing and operating the venture. The following are of primary importance to the entrepreneur and his or her team:
  - The vision which the entrepreneur has for the new business
  - The mission that defines the business
  - An overview of the key objectives, which is derived from the mission statement
  - A clear understanding of the overall strategy to accomplish the objectives, as well as a clear understanding of the functional strategies (marketing strategy, financial strategy, human resource strategy, etc.), which forms a substantial part of the business plan
- **Employees.** From the employees' point of view, there is also a need for a business plan. More specifically, employees also need to have a clear understanding of the venture's mission and objectives to be able to work towards attaining the objectives. A business plan also serves to improve communication between employees and to establish a corporate culture. A well-prepared plan provides employees with a focus for activities. The business plan also helps prospective employees to understand the emerging culture of the young business. It is important that managers and employees contribute to the development of the business plan to establish "ownership" of the plan among them.

3.3.3.2 External stakeholders

The business plan is even more important to outsiders, on whom the entrepreneur depends for the survival and success of the venture. Indeed, the importance of the business plan may be said to revolve around "selling" the new business to outsiders, who may include the following:

- **Customers.** When small businesses seek substantial orders or ongoing service contracts, major customers always want assurance that the business will still be around in three or five years' time to provide the parts or service they as customers might require for the product. Customers are almost always impressed by a business plan, since it proves to them that the entrepreneur has thought about the future.
- **Investors.** Almost anyone starting a business faces the task of raising financial resources to supplement their own resources (personal savings, investment in shares or property, etc.). And unless the entrepreneur has a wealthy relative who will supply funds, he or she will have to appeal to investors or bankers to obtain the necessary funds. Very few investors or financial institutions will consider financial assistance without a well-prepared business plan.

Investors have a different interest in the business plan to that of other stakeholders, and if the entrepreneur intends to use the business plan to raise capital, he or she must understand the investor's basic perspective. A prospective investor has a single goal: to earn a return on the investment, while at the same time minimising risk. While many factors may stimulate an investor's interest in the venture, certain basic elements of a business plan attract (or repel) any prospective investor interest more than others.

The following matrix presents an evaluation of business plans from the investor's point of view. Certain basic indicators only have been included.

Figure 3.2: Matrix for the evaluation of business plans

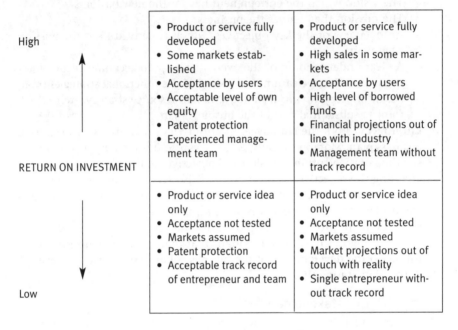

High

RETURN ON INVESTMENT

Low

• Product or service fully developed • Some markets established • Acceptance by users • Acceptable level of own equity • Patent protection • Experienced management team	• Product or service fully developed • High sales in some markets • Acceptance by users • High level of borrowed funds • Financial projections out of line with industry • Management team without track record
• Product or service idea only • Acceptance not tested • Markets assumed • Patent protection • Acceptable track record of entrepreneur and team	• Product or service idea only • Acceptance not tested • Markets assumed • Market projections out of touch with reality • Single entrepreneur without track record

- **Banks.** These are a common source of debt capital for small businesses. To improve the chance of obtaining bank loans or what is known in South Africa as overdraft facilities, the entrepreneur should know what it is that banks look for in evaluating an application for such a loan. Most banks look at the four Cs by which an application for a loan is evaluated, namely capital, collateral, character and conditions.
    - **Capital.** A small business must have a stable equity base of its own before a bank will grant a loan. The bank expects the small business to have an equity base of investment by the owner(s) before it will make a loan. South African banks generally insist on at least 50% equity.
    - **Collateral.** This includes any assets the owner pledges to a bank as security for repayment of the loan. Bankers view the owner's willingness to pledge collateral (personal or business assets) as an indication of the entrepreneur's dedication to making the venture a success.
    - **Character.** Aspects of the owner's character, such as honesty, competence, determination, ability and a good track record, plays a critical role in the bank's decision to grant a loan.
    - **Conditions.** The conditions surrounding a loan request also affect the bank's decision. Banks will consider factors relating to the business operation, such as potential market growth, competition, form of ownership, as well as the current state of the economy.

3.3.4 The scope of the business plan: how much planning is needed?

The level of commitment to the writing of a business plan varies greatly among entrepreneurs. Once the preparation of the business plan is under way, the question remains as to the level of effort to be given to the plan. Should it be one page long or should it be 100 pages long? Considerations that determine the amount of planning include the following:

- Management style and ability
- The preferences of the management team
- The complexity of the product or service and of the business
- The competitive environment
- The level of uncertainty

The depth and detail in the business plan therefore depends on the size and scope of the proposed new venture. An entrepreneur planning to market a new portable computer nationally will need a comprehensive business plan, largely because of the nature of the product and the market pursued. On the other hand, an entrepreneur who wants to manufacture burglar bars and steel gates for the local market will not need such a comprehensive plan. The difference in the scope of the business plan may depend on whether the new venture is a service, involves manufacturing, or is an industrial product or consumer goods. The size of the market, competition, and many other environmental factors may also affect the scope of the business plan.

3.3.5 Components of the business plan

While it is important that the primary components of a solid business plan be outlined, every small entrepreneur must recognise that such a plan should be tailor-made, emphasising the particular strengths of the new venture. Two issues are of primary concern when preparing the business plan, namely:

- The basic format of the written presentation
- The content or components of the business plan

3.3.5.1 The format of the business plan

The first question that comes to mind in writing the business plan is, Who should write the plan? Many small business managers employ the professional assistance of accountants, attorneys and marketing consultants. However, experts agree that the entrepreneur may consult with professionals, but should in the end write the plan himself or herself. To help determine whether to use a consultant, the entrepreneur may use table 3.3 (see p. 74) to make an objective assessment of his or her own skills.

Through such an assessment the entrepreneur can identify what skills are needed and who should be consulted to help prepare the business plan.

Regarding the format of the business plan, it should be pointed out that there are no rigid rules. But whatever format is eventually decided on, it should at all times be:

- Of a good appearance
- Concise

- Comprehensive
- Logical
- Easy to read and understand (that is, by the proposed reader or evaluator)
- Based on facts

Table 3.3: Skills assessment for writing a business plan

Skills	Excellent	Good	Fair	Poor
Planning				
Marketing research				
Forecasting sales				
Accounting charges				
Operational issues				
Labour law				
Management issues				
Product design				
Legal issues				

The length of the business plan will depend on the venture, but can vary from five to twenty pages, excluding annexures and substantiating documents.

3.3.5.2 The content of a business plan

As already mentioned, the business plan for each venture is unique. But while no single standard list of business plan components exists, there is considerable agreement as to what the content of the business plan should be. The following are the most important components of the business plan:

- The executive summary
- The general description of the venture
- The products and services plan
- The marketing plan
- The management plan
- The operating plan
- The financial plan
- Supporting materials

By now it may be assumed that you understand the value of a business plan and are ready to prepare one.

Apart from the fact that the business plan begins with the cover page, the huge amount of information that one has collected makes it difficult to decide what to include under the headings of the various business plan components listed above. The beginner needs a conceptual scheme to identify the important segments of a good business plan. Table 3.4 provides an overview of such a plan.

Table 3.4: Overview of a business plan

Executive summary	A one- to three-page overview of the total business plan. Written after the other sections are completed, it highlights their significant points and, ideally, creates enough excitement to motivate the reader to read on.
General company description	Explains the type of company and gives its history if it already exists. Tells whether it is a manufacturing, retail, service, or other type of business. Shows the type of legal organisation.
Products and services plan	Describes the product and/or service and points out any unique features. Explains why people will buy the product or service.
Marketing plan	Shows who will be your customers and what type of competition you will face. Outlines your marketing strategy and specifies what will give you a competitive edge.
Management plan	Identifies the "key players" – the active investors, management team, and directors. Cites the experience and competence they possess.
Operating plan	Explains the type of manufacturing or operating system you will use. Describes the facilities, labour, raw materials, and processing requirements.
Financial plan	Specifies financial needs and contemplated sources of financing. Presents projections of revenues, costs and profits.

Table 3.5 provides a more detailed outline for each section of a good business plan. Once each of these phases has been completed by the entrepreneur, he or she will have a simple but complete draft of a business plan.

Table 3.5: Outline of a simple business plan

General company description	Name and location Nature and primary product or service of the business Current status (startup, buyout, or expansion) and history (if applicable) Legal form of organisation
Products and/or services	Description of products and/or services Superior features of advantages relative to competing products or services Any available legal protection – patents, copyrights, trademarks Dangers of technical or style obsolescence

Marketing plan	Analysis of target market and profile of target customer How customers will be identified and attracted Selling approach, type of sales force, and distribution channels Types of sales promotion and advertising Credit and pricing policies
Management plan	Management-team members and their qualifications Other investors and/or directors and their qualifications Outside resource people and their qualifications Plans for recruiting and training employees
Operating plan	Operating or manufacturing methods used to produce the product or service Description of operating facilities (location, space, equipment) Quality-control methods to be used Procedures used to control inventory and operations Sources of supply and purchasing procedures
Financial plan	Revenue projections for three years Expense projections for three years Necessary financial resources Sources of financing

In developing a comprehensive plan, the above simple plan will be supplemented by an exhaustive set of questions that should be considered. The examination and consideration of each component of the comprehensive business plan will be discussed in more detail below.

3.3.6 Description of a new venture

With the introductory concepts of the business plan as well as an outline of the main components behind us, it may be said that step 1 of the business plan has been completed. More specifically, step 1 included an overview of the cover page and the preparation of the executive summary as well as the outline of the business plan.

Step 2 concerns a description of the venture and it is dealt with in this section. This step is actually an extension of the feasibility analysis that was discussed in chapter 2. The entrepreneur analysed the entrepreneurial environment to assess the new idea or venture as well as the factors that might improve his or her chances of success and factors that could work negatively against the proposed venture. The analysis of the environment assisted the entrepreneur in taking a rational decision whether to implement or abandon the idea. If the entrepreneur has decided to implement the idea, he or she must describe it in detail and prepare a business plan for the new idea or venture.

3.3.6.1 A general description of the new venture

Bearing in mind the needs and requirements of banks and investors for a successful business plan, namely that it should not be too long and that it should be concise and accurate, a brief but accurate description of the new venture is necessary.

The body of the business plan begins with a brief description of the new venture itself. If the business is already in existence, its history is included. By examining this section, the reader will know, for example, whether the business is engaged in tourism, retailing, construction, or some other line of business, and also where the business is located, and whether it is serves a local or international market. In many cases, issues noted in the legal plan – especially the form of organisation – are incorporated into this section of the plan. Some important questions to be addressed in this section of the plan may include the following:

- Is this a start-up, buyout, or expansion?
- Has this business begun operation?
- What is the firm's mission statement?
- When and where was this business started?
- What is the basic nature and activity of the business?
- What is its primary product or service?
- What customers are served?
- Is this business in manufacturing, retailing, service, or another type of industry?
- What is the current and projected state of this industry?
- What is the business stage of development, for example, Has it begun operations? Is it producing a full product line?
- What are its objectives?
- What is the history of this company?
- What achievements have been made to date?
- What changes have been made in the structure or ownership of the existing business?
- What is the firm's distinctive competence?

Again, there are no fixed questions that should be considered in the general description of the new venture. Some entrepreneurs may emphasise a successful history, while others may concentrate on the new venture's competitive advantage. The following, which is a sample of a general description, nevertheless highlights four critical aspects that should be included in the general description. The description is based on a case study, *Calabash Guided Tours and Transfers* (see p. 78).

3.3.7 Analysing the market

It must be remembered that certain activities that form the basis of the business plan take place simultaneously. Strictly speaking, the description of the new venture's strategy can only be finalised once the entrepreneur has completed a market analysis to find out if a market for the product exists, and if so, how he or she will exploit the market. In other words, once the entrepreneur is convinced that there is good market potential in a particular segment of the market, he or she will have to work out how the product will reach the market and what marketing strategy to adopt.

Case study: description of *Calabash Guided Tours and Transfers*

Name and location of the new venture

Calabash Guided Tours and Transfers is a proposed extension of a successful existing small venture called Tswane Airport Shuttle. Tswane Airport shuttle has been operating for three years, transferring mainly tourists from Johannesburg International Airport to Pretoria and back. It now wants to expand into guided tours to tourists. Calabash Guided Tours and Transfers will be a partnership between Mthombeni Mahlangu and Jacques du Toit. They can both be contacted at 444 Nicolson Street , Brooklyn, Pretoria, 0181, which is also the existing premises of Tswane Airport Shuttle. Tel. (012) 444-4444.

Nature and primary product or service of the business

During the past twelve months the two partners have studied trends in the transferring and transportation of tourists in mainly the Gauteng area of South Africa. They have identified a strong need by tourists for "safe" transfers, safe day-trips and longer tours in a crime-ridden South Africa, where tourists have come to be included in robbery and murder statistics. Because of their three years of experience in transferring tourists and business people from Johannesburg International Airport to Pretoria, offering guided transfers, trips and tours will form a natural extension of their existing small business. They expect to fully satisfy their customers by providing a safe and quality guided tour service in the upmarket segments of the tourism industry in Gauteng.

Current status

The new business, Calabash Guided Tours and Transfers, will be started at the beginning of the new year, assuming that adequate funding will be found in the next four months.

Legal form of organisation

The new business will begin operation as a partnership between Mthombeni Mahlangu and Jacques du Toit. Both partners agree to entering into a formal partnership agreement based on a 50-50 decision concerning workload, profits and responsibilities, and how the new venture is funded. Should the source of funding necessitate a closed corporation or a limited company, the two persons also agree to restructure the legal form of the new venture to accommodate any requirements a bank or private investor may have.

Entrepreneurs often run the risk of becoming infatuated with their product or service and consequently they simply **believe** or **hope** that there is a market for their product. This euphoria can be very costly, if not devastating, to the new venture with its limited resources. The analysis of the new venture's market and the development of a marketing strategy involve the following key activities:

- Marketing concepts
- The identification of a target market
- Researching and forecasting in the target market
- Preparing a marketing plan or strategy for the selected market segment(s)

Chapters 13 to 15 deal with these aspects in detail.

3.3.8 Determining the financial needs of the new venture

The entrepreneur or potential investors need answers to certain crucial financial questions to determine whether the new venture is not only attractive, but also feasible. The financial analysis constitutes a further crucial component of the business plan. The entrepreneur's projections of a new venture's profits, its required assets, and its financial requirements over the next one to five years should be supported by substantiated assumptions and explanations regarding how the costs, profits, and financial requirements are determined. In order to make the necessary financial projections, the entrepreneur must first have a good understanding of financial statements and how to interpret them.

The key issues in this section are therefore:
- An understanding of how financial statements work
- An understanding of how profitability is assessed
- An ability to determine a venture's financial requirements

Chapters 17 to 19 deal with these aspects in detail.

3.4 The location of the business

3.4.1 The choice of location

The choice of geographical location for premises is of extreme importance for all kinds of businesses, although for some it may be more important than for others. For certain businesses, this may be a crucial factor. Depending on the nature of the proposed product or service that is to be offered, the entrepreneur should, for example, decide whether the business needs to be located either near its market, or near its sources of raw materials, near to other competitors, in the city centre, in the suburbs, in a rural area, in existing industrial areas, or according to personal preference.

The location factors that have to be considered when making this choice are briefly analysed in the section below.[2]

3.4.2 Location factors

The most important location factors are the following:
- **Sources of raw materials.** Where, in what quantity and of what quality, and at what prices, can these materials be obtained?
- **Availability of labour.** Where, and at what cost, is the required labour available in terms of, say, quantities, levels of training, development potential and productivity?
- **Proximity of, and access to, the market.** This includes aspects such as the potential advantages over present competitors, the current extent and potential development of the market, the perishability of products, the needs of consumers and users regarding, for example, delivery, after-sales services and personal contact, as well as the possible entry of competitors into the market
- **Availability and cost of transport facilities.** This includes aspects such as

the availability of rail, air, road, and water transport facilities, the transport costs of raw materials in relation to finished products, and the possibility of using one's own transport (road links and limitations on private transport).

- **Availability and costs of power and water.** These must satisfy the needs of the prospective business.
- **Availability and costs of a site and buildings.** These comprise units of the required size and appearance, with the necessary facilities and expansion possibilities; consideration should also be given to accessibility for raw material suppliers, customers and employees.
- **Availability of capital.** This does not necessarily affect the choice of a specific location, but can still play a role where the suppliers of capital, say, set specific conditions or express certain preferences in this regard, or where capital is such a limiting factor that it necessitates the choice of the cheapest location.
- **Attitude, regulations and tariffs of local authorities.** These comprise, for example, the attitude of local authorities to industrial development, including possible concessions that encourage location, as well as health regulations, building regulations, property rates, water and electricity tariffs, and the availability and costs of other municipal services.
- **The existing business environment.** This could influence the establishment of the proposed business by, for example, the provision of repair and maintenance services, as well as the availability of spares and banking, postal and other communication facilities.
- **The social environment.** This concerns the provision of satisfactory housing and educational, medical, recreational and shopping facilities for employees of the proposed business.
- **Climate.** Some production processes require a particular type of climate, and also, climate can influence the acquisition, retention and productivity of personnel.
- **Central government policy.** This may encourage or discourage the establishment of certain types of businesses in specific areas in a direct or indirect manner through, for example, tax concessions.
- **Personal preferences.** This relates to the area or areas that entrepreneurs and their families prefer to live in.

3.5 Summary

In this chapter the legal forms of a business that are available to the entrepreneur were discussed. This included the characteristics, advantages and disadvantages of the sole proprietorship, the close corporation, the partnership and the company. In addition, the development of the business plan for a new venture was examined. The final section dealt with the most important location factors.

References

1. Havenga, P.H., *General principles of commercial law*, 3rd edition, Juta, Cape Town, 1997.
2. Cronje, G.J. de J., du Toit, G.S. & Motlatla, M.D.C., *Introduction to business management*, 5th edition, Oxford University Press, Cape Town 2000, p. 42.

4 The business environment

The purpose of this chapter

The purpose of this chapter is to introduce the student to the environment in which the business organisation functions, and to explain how the environment impacts on the business. It first introduces the student to the concept of environmental change and then explains the composition of the business environment. The impact of the different components that constitute the business environment, also called the environmental variables, are then examined, starting with the micro-environment and followed by the market environment and the macro-environment. The chapter is concluded with a brief discussion on how management should monitor the environment and how the business organisation can respond to the influences of the environment.

Learning outcomes

The content of this chapter will enable learners to:
- Understand the meaning of environmental change
- Explain the nature and composition of the business environment
- Discuss each of the components of the environmental paradigm (the environmental model), and the way scholars think about it
- Explain how each of the environmental variables can impact on an industry or an individual business
- Describe some ways in which management should respond to the influences of the environment

4.1 Introduction: The business organisation and its environment

In chapter 1 the interdependence between a business organisation and the environment within which it operates was briefly discussed. It was pointed out that society depends on business organisations for most of the products and services it needs, including the employment opportunities which businesses create. Conversely, business organisations depend on society for the resources they need. Business organisations are not self-sufficient, nor are they self-contained. They obtain resources from and are dependent upon the environment in which they operate. Business organisations and society, or, more specifically, the environment in which they function, therefore depend on each other. This mutual dependence entails a complex relationship between the two. This relationship increases in complexity when certain variables in the environment, such as technological innovation, economic events or political developments, bring about change in the environment which impacts in different ways on the business organisation.

The importance and influence of environmental change on the successful management of the organisation became apparent in the second half of the last century when environmental forces brought about unforeseen change. The 1970s were characterised by oil price and energy shocks. The 1980s experienced a shift from local to global business, and fierce competition from Japan and other Asian countries. And in the 1990s, new ways of communication, from fax machines to cell phones and the Internet, revolutionised the operations of business organisations. During the latter part of the 1990s Western countries enjoyed the longest ever economic boom, which ended on 11 September 2001 with the terrorist strike on the World Trade Centre in New York. This incident changed the world forever, introducing a new world order with new alliances and new enemies. These instabilities in the environment increased the need to stabilise the impact of environmental change on the business organisation. The result of this was a greater awareness of environmental influences on management decisions, and the development of an approach to investigate and monitor change in the environment.

In this chapter the concept of environmental change and its impact on the business organisation will be examined.

4.2 The organisation and environmental change

Change is a difficult concept to define. Expressed simply, it is any change in the status quo. This implies a change from a condition of stability to one of instability, a shift from the predictable to the unpredictable, or from the known to the unknown. It cannot be measured, and it causes insecurity. No single factor can be held responsible for it, and in particular places and communities it occurs in different ways and at a different rate. Moreover, the rate of change often has a greater effect on the environment than the direction of the change. Change is therefore a process of constant renewal and regeneration in every conceivable sphere of society.

Consider the following:

- The number of new inventions during the past 50 years has exceeded those of all previous centuries put together.
- The number of new inventions during the next ten years will probably exceed those of the past 50 years.
- Things that have already become indispensable to modern society, such as computers, the Internet, antibiotics, nuclear power, the fax machine, cell phones, and laser technology are products of the past twenty years.

Environmental variables that are constantly at work changing the environment in which business organisations operate include technological innovations like the fax machine, cell phones, the Internet and automated factories; economic fluctuations in emerging markets, which results in high interest rates and falling currencies; new laws, such as South Africa's labour laws; increased urbanisation; and changing social values. During the past decade the structure of South African society and its lifestyles, values and expectations have changed perceptibly, especially since 27 April 1994 when a new democratic South Africa was formally established.

For the first time in its history South Africa has a black government, and this has brought about drastic changes. Business organisations in particular are confronted with new demands from unions, the new labour laws and laws dealing with equity and preferential procurement, such as the Employment Equity Act 55 of 1998. The democratisation of South Africa normalised international relations, but at the same time exposed South African businesses to a borderless world in which they suddenly have to compete. Globalisation and the trend towards a borderless world affect businesses in new ways, and some have responded by taking their investments out of the country. In addition to this, accelerating urbanisation and increased poverty in Southern Africa, the influx of unskilled immigrants, the high crime rate, and the breakdown of law and order will increasingly affect the environment in which South Africans must do business and make decisions regarding their investments.

Business organisations, as the central component of the business environment, are naturally also subject to change. Worldwide, business organisations are restructuring, outsourcing and trimming workforces. Without these major changes, business organisations will not be able to align themselves with the realities of the changing external environment. And without adapting to these changes, they will not be fit to compete in the new global economy. Other changes that affect the business organisation include those in monetary and fiscal policy, which impact on financial management. Changing consumer habits, often the result of economic and technological change, make new demands on marketing management. Existing methods of production can change suddenly because of technological advances, and the introduction of new raw materials could cause established industries to disappear. Moreover, trade unions, through strikes and forced absenteeism, are making increasing demands on human resources management.

The interaction between the environment and a business organisation is an ongoing process that results in new problems and new opportunities. The consequence of this interaction is often a new environment, creating new problems and offering new opportunities. Management should align its organisation with the environment in which it operates in such a way that it can fully utilise the opportunities and deal with possible threats. To be able to do this, managers must first understand the composition and nature of the business environment.

The composition of the business environment will be discussed below.

Environmental change: some examples

- The rapid **technological innovation** in computers not only created a market for personal computers, but also caused revolutionary changes in many fields, from farming to manufacturing to the production of services. In fact, computers are radically changing the content of work and the workplace, as well as the way organisations are structured. Millions of households own personal computers, while the business world has jumped to the next step, with many small computers linked by a network. This is having a tremendous effect on marketing, advertising, communication, financial management, logistics management and also on many other fields.

- The **globalisation** of markets and manufacturing has vastly increased international competition. Production is also becoming globalised as manufacturers around the world locate manufacturing facilities where products can be cheaply produced. South Africa's labour legislation has impacted negatively on South Africa, as many manufacturers transfer their manufacturing to India and other Asian countries, where skilled labour produces sophisticated products for as little as US $4 per labourer per day (though such wages are widely regarded as exploitative).

- The **growth of poverty** and the increasing divide between rich and poor impacts on markets and governments. The world's richest 20% consume 86% of its products and services, over half its energy, and nearly half its meat and fish. Consumption in the poorest countries is too low to meet even the most basic needs of 1 billion people. Every year, Americans spend $8 billion on cosmetics, and Europeans $50 billion on cigarettes, yet the world cannot find the $9 billion that the UN estimates is needed annually to give all people access to clean drinking water and sanitation.

- The **collapse of emerging markets**. In 1997 many would have considered the Asian economic collapse unthinkable. This economic meltdown reached South Africa in June of 1998 and resulted in the August 1998 JSE crash, a 30% devaluation of the rand, and the prime interest rate going up to 26%. This happened at a time when economists had predicted that South African interest rates would decline from the previous high of 18% to about 15%. High interest rates devastated the economy, especially small businesses and home-owners, who could not afford the punitive rates. This process repeated itself in 2002 with the collapse of Argentina's economy.

- A **shift from manufacturing jobs to service jobs** is taking place in developed countries. Today, over two-thirds of the US workforce is employed in producing and delivering services such as travel, insurance, banking, teaching, cleaning and fast foods. This trend is likely to continue, and impacts on business, as new products are demanded and the new "knowledge" workers are developing new ways of managing organisations. The typical business of this century will be knowledge (and not labour) based. This will result in a growing emphasis on human capital – the knowledge, training, skills and expertise of an organisation's workers.

- Within 20-25 years, perhaps as many as half the **people who work for an organisation will not be employed by it on a full-time basis**. New ways of working with people at arm's length will become the central managerial issue of the next decade or two.

4.3 The composition of the business environment

4.3.1 The three sub-environments

The importance of environmental change to the effective management of the business organisation became apparent in the second half of the last century. This was partly the result of the systems approach to management, which argued that an organisation is an integral part of its environment, and that management should therefore adopt a policy of "organisational Darwinism" to ensure that its business does not become extinct in a rapidly changing world in which only the fittest can survive.

The 1950s and 1960s saw the beginning of a period of increasing instability in the environment that made it increasingly necessary to study environmental change and influences. The question was what exactly to look for in the environment, for it would have been hopelessly confusing to have to take every single factor into consideration. A variety of influences, ranging from spiritual and cultural values to purely natural influences, may be identified as determinant variables in the business environment.[1] The business environment is therefore defined as **all those factors or variables, both inside as well as outside the business organisation, which may influence the continued and successful existence of the business organisation**. In other words, the business environment refers to the internal as well as external factors that impact on the business organisation, and that largely determine its success.

In order to recognise the environmental variables that influence a business, a realistic classification is necessary. Classification makes it possible to identify distinct trends for further analysis in each group or sub-environment. Figure 4.1 (see p. 86) shows the composition of the business environment as it is usually presented in literature on the subject. It is a visual model of the interaction between a business organisation and its environment.

According to this model, the business environment consists of the following three distinct environments:

- The **microenvironment** consists of the business itself, over which management has complete control. This includes variables in this environment, such as the goals of the business organisation, the various functions of management, and the resources of the business, which are under the direct control of management. The decisions made by management will influence the market environment through the strategy that it employs to protect, maintain or increase its share of the market, for example, by applying a marketing strategy in which pricing and advertising can be applied to increase market share. The microenvironments of many business organisations all over the world have been subjected to changes relating to re-engineering, restructuring and trimming workforces. Without these major changes, businesses would no longer be able to align themselves with a changing environment.
- The **market environment** is encountered immediately outside the business organisation. In this environment all the variables depicted in figure 4.1 become relevant for every organisation, because they determine the nature and strength of competition in any industry. The key variables in this environment are: **consumers with a particular buying power** and

Figure 4.1: The composition of the business environment

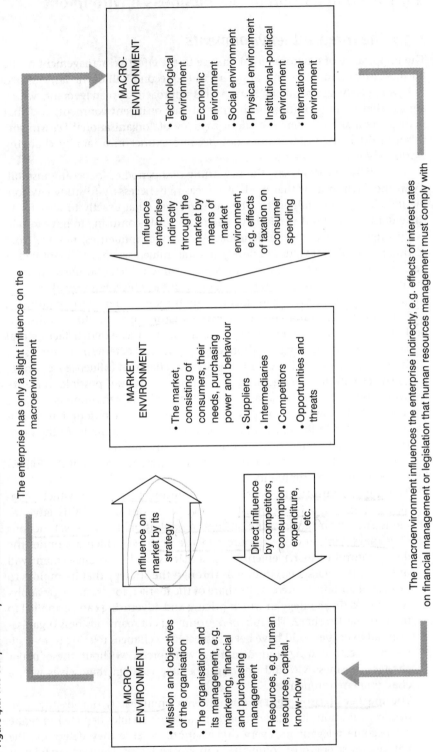

behaviour, who in turn determine the number of entrants to the market; competitors in the market, including new and potential competitors who want to maintain or improve their position; intermediaries who compete against each other to handle the business's product; suppliers who supply, or do not wish to supply, products, raw materials, services and financing to the business organisation.

All these variables give rise to particular opportunities and threats. It is in the market environment that management finds its most important tasks: to identify, assess, and take advantage of opportunities in the market, and to develop and adapt its strategies to meet competition. For these reasons the market environment is often called the task environment. Management has no control over the components of the market environment, although management may influence the variables concerned through its strategy. The market environment continually influences a business. For example, a new competitor with sufficient resources could start a price war, or a competitor could market a new product protected by patents. Similarly, conditions such as consumer buying power and consumer boycotts can affect a business. At the same time, the market environment, and therefore the microenvironment, are affected by developments in the **macroenvironment**, the third component of the business environment.

- The **macroenvironment** is external to both the organisation and the market environment, and consists of six distinct sub-environments: the **technological environment**, which continuously brings change and innovation; the **economic environment**, in which such factors as inflation, exchange rates, recessions, and monetary and fiscal policy influence the prosperity of the business organisation; the **social environment**, in which consumer lifestyles, habits and values, formed by culture, make certain demands on the business organisation, particularly through consumerism; the **physical environment**, which consists of natural resources such as mineral wealth, flora and fauna, and man-made improvements such as roads and bridges; the **institutional environment**, with the government and its political and legislative involvement as the main components; and lastly, the **international environment**, in which local and foreign political trends and events affect the business organisation (microenvironment) as well as the market environment. The individual business organisation has very little or no control over the macroenvironment, and its influence on these variables is negligible.

Each of these sub-environments – the microenvironment, the market environment and the macroenvironment – is characterised by an interplay of the components peculiar to the particular environment, while at the same time there is interaction between the various environments. These interactions will be elaborated on in the discussion of the various sub-environments. In the foregoing discussion we have described the **composition** of the business environment. We now examine the **characteristics** of the business environment.

4.3.2 Characteristics of the business environment

Before discussing the various sub-environments in greater detail, a brief survey of the most important characteristics of the business environment will help to show why it is necessary for management to continuously monitor the business environment.

The following are a few of the main characteristics of the business environment:

- **The environmental factors or variables are interrelated.** A change in one of the external factors may cause a change in the microenvironment and, similarly, a change in one external factor may cause a change in the other external factors. For example, the collapse of the emerging markets in 1998 caused a sharp decline in the value of the rand against foreign currencies, and this resulted in more economic change, including high interest rates, which reduced the purchasing power of consumers, and in turn led to depressed property and car sales. Export businesses benefited from this change in the macroenvironment.
- **Increasing instability.** One of the consequences of interdependence in the environment is increasing instability and change. Although the general rate of change in the environment accelerates, environmental fluctuation is greater for some industries than for others. For example, the rate of change in the pharmaceutical and electronics industries may be higher than in the automobile component and bakery industries.
- **Environmental uncertainty.** Uncertainty about the environment is, of course, a function of the amount of information about environmental variables, and of the confidence that management has in such information. If there is little information available, or if the value of the information is suspect, the uncertainty of management about the environment will increase, and vice versa.
- **The complexity of the environment.** This indicates the number of external variables to which a business organisation has to respond, as well as variations in the variables themselves. A bakery has fewer variables in its business environment to consider than a manufacturer of computers, and therefore has a less complex environment. It is one of the advantages of businesses with less complex environments that they need less environmental information to make decisions.

These few outstanding characteristics of the environment show how important it is for management to know and understand the environment within which the business organisation operates. With these facts in mind, we will now consider the various business sub-environments referred to above in greater detail.

4.4 The microenvironment

As explained, the microenvironment comprises the internal environment of the business. The microenvironment may be viewed as an environment with three sets of variables: the mission and goals of the business, its management, and its resources.[2] These variables are responsible for the outputs of the business, and they are under the direct control of management. Each of the variables in the microenvironment is linked to the external environment in some way.

The **mission** and **goals** of the enterprise are the reason for its existence. Without definite goals and objectives to strive for, there would be no need for an organisation. These goals are influenced by the external environment. For example, a property developer whose mission includes the development of luxury townhouses should reconsider its mission in an environment which is becoming poorer as a result of political, economic and social developments.

The different **areas of management or functions,** and the way in which an organisation is structured, that is, **its organisational structure**, constitute another set of variables in the microenvironment that has certain interfaces with the external environment. For example, marketing is that function of business which is in close contact with the market: marketing keeps an eye on consumers and their preferences as well as on the activities of competitors so that it can develop strategies to counter any influences from the market environment. Similarly, financial management keeps an eye on levels of taxation and rates of interest that could influence the financial position of the business.

Human resources management may influence the environment through its employment policy, just as trade unions, strikes, wage demands and new labour laws may affect its decisions. A business organisation should be structured in such a way that it is able to deal with influences from the environment and still operate productively within the environment, especially the market environment.

The resources of a business comprise the last set of internal variables that have certain interfaces with external environments. For example, an important resource, such as a particular production process, may be threatened by a new technology or some new invention. Alternatively, some special skills or knowledge can be employed to exploit an opportunity in the environment – for example, a business with knowledge and experience of exporting will take advantage of a devaluation in the local currency, making it a profitable opportunity.

The purpose of this brief survey of the microenvironment and its variables has been to indicate possible interfaces between the business organisation and its environment. It should, however, be remembered that the microenvironment varies from one business organisation to the next.

4.5 The market or task environment

The market environment is immediately outside the business organisation, as shown in figure 4.1 (see p. 86), and consists of the market, suppliers, intermediaries and competitors, who are sources of both opportunities and threats to a business. More precisely, this environment contains those variables that revolve around competition. In order to clearly understand the interaction between the enterprise and its market environment, it is necessary to examine the variables in the market environment more closely.

4.5.1 The market

Several meanings can be attached to the term market, and we discuss the subject more fully in chapter 13. Briefly, we can say that the market consists of people who have needs to satisfy and have the financial means to do so. In other words, the market, as a variable in the market environment, consists of people with particular demands who manifest certain forms of behaviour in satisfying those demands. If a business wants to achieve success with a strategy of influencing consumer decisions in its favour in a competitive environment, it follows that management needs to be fully informed on all aspects of consumer needs, purchasing power, and buying behaviour.

Management also has to understand that these conditions are directly influenced by variables in the macroenvironment. Therefore, demographic trends influence the number of consumers, economic factors such as high interest rates determine the buying power of consumers, and cultural values exert certain influences on the buying behaviour. Management should also understand that this continuous interaction between market variables and the variables in the macroenvironment give rise to changes in both environments.

The South African business operates in a complex market environment, characterised by a heterogeneous population. Table 4.1 illustrates certain features of the South African consumer market.

Table 4.1: Income features of South African consumers by area and population group, 2000

Population group and area	Household income	Income of earners			Income per person
		Male	Female	Total	
	R	R	R	R	R
ASIANS					
Durban	79 777	50 699	36 262	41 006	18 949
Gauteng	117 987	97 954	69 991	85 800	32 325
BLACKS					
Cape Peninsula	32 367	30 067	27 321	29 815	10 509
Durban	45 085	36 398	31 243	39 682	8 910
Gauteng – middle and upper class	119 525	79 760	57 529	69 146	25 984
Gauteng – all households	61 524	50 769	43 187	46 173	15 615
COLOUREDS					
Cape Peninsula	60 360	45 964	29 687	40 397	16 674
Gauteng	73 105	64 482	48 446	55 881	18 414
WHITES					
Cape Peninsula	107 351	101 000	58 652	85 267	36 390
Durban	164 443	128 219	61 476	105 818	53 916
Gauteng	137 456	122 301	71 261	100 200	48 230

Source: Research report no. 296, Bureau of Market Research, Unisa, Pretoria, 2001, p.3.

Besides the total number of consumers in a specific area or market segment analysed by management to determine the market for their market offering, the **buying power or purchasing power of consumers** is also a significant component of the consumer market. Buying power is represented specifically by consumers' **personal disposable income**. Personal disposable income is the portion of personal income that remains after direct taxes plus credit repayments (loans from banks, shops and other institutions) have been deducted, and that is available for buying consumer products and services.

Only two of the main characteristics of the consumer market, namely **number of consumers** and the **purchasing power** of consumers, were mentioned above. However, numerous other characteristics, such as language, age structure, gender distribution, marital status, size of family, and literacy, influence the **purchasing patterns** or buying behaviour of the consumer market. These factors are discussed in more detail in chapter 13.

The consumer market can further be subdivided into **durable products** (for example, furniture, domestic appliances and motorcars), **semi-durable products** (for example, food, tobacco) and **services** (for example, insurance, rental, communication). This classification enables management to analyse specific segments of the market.

Besides the market in consumer goods there are also **industrial markets** in which products and services are supplied by manufacturing enterprises for the production of further products and services. **Government markets** involve the purchase of products and services by the central government, provincial governments and local authorities. **International markets** relate to foreign buyers, including consumers, manufacturers, resellers and governments.

It is clear from the foregoing discussion of different markets why the market environment is of such importance to management. Without an ongoing assessment and analysis of this component, a business organisation cannot function successfully. Moreover, variables in the macroenvironment, such as economic factors, political trends and upheavals, as well as population growth and urbanisation, also influence the market environment and, eventually, the products and services which the business offers to the market.

4.5.2 Suppliers

According to the systems approach, a business organisation is regarded as a system that receives inputs from the environment and converts them into outputs in the form of products or services for sale in the market environment. The inputs required are mainly **materials**, including raw materials, equipment and energy, and **capital** and **labour**. Suppliers provide these items to businesses. If one considers that approximately 60 cents out of every rand spent goes into purchases from suppliers, the importance of suppliers in the market environment becomes clear. If a business cannot obtain the right inputs of the necessary quality, in the right quantity, and at the right price for the production of its products, then it

---

The importance of suppliers

Pick 'n Pay spends about 83 cents out of every rand on inputs from suppliers. This very high figure is typical of retail businesses.

In the case of Sasol, a producer in the chemicals industry, an average of 47 cents out of every rand goes to suppliers.

cannot achieve any success in a competitive market environment. The interaction between a business organisation and its supplier network is a good example of the influence of environmental variables on the business.

In the case of materials, practically every business, whether it is in manufacturing, trading or contracting, depends on regular supplies. The whole question of materials management, the scanning of the environment with regard to suppliers, and relations with suppliers as environmental variables is dealt with in chapters 22 and 23. A business organisation depends not only on suppliers of raw material, but also on suppliers of capital. Banks and shareholders are such suppliers. They are discussed in chapter 18. Small businesses in particular find it difficult to raise capital. Another supply which businesses needs is the provision of labour. Trade unions and other pressure groups can also be regarded as "suppliers" of labour with which enterprises, especially in the manufacturing and mining sectors, have complex relations.

The scanning of the environment, with particular regard to labour – or rather human resources problems – is discussed in greater detail in chapters 10 and 11.

4.5.3 Intermediaries

Apart from the consumers and competitors with whom market management has to deal in the market environment, intermediaries also play a decisive role in bridging the gap between the manufacturer and consumer. Intermediaries include wholesalers and retailers, agents and brokers, representatives and, in townships, spaza shops. They also include bankers, asset managers, and insurance brokers, who, from a financial perspective, are also involved in the transfer of products and services.

Decision making by management in respect of intermediaries is complicated by the following:
- **The dynamic and ever-changing nature of intermediaries.** New trends and markets are responsible for the development of new kinds of intermediaries. Contemporary trends in South Africa in this regard are, for example, extended shopping hours, the shift of power from the manufacturer to large retailers because of bar coding and own brand names, increased advertising by shopping centres themselves, the escalating importance of the black retailer in black residential areas, and the increase in the number of franchises and in spazas.[3]
- **Relationships with intermediaries.** This means entering into long-term agreements that, again, may have certain implications for marketing strategy. The power of large retailers also has certain implications for price and advertising decisions.

New trends among intermediaries provide management with certain opportunities, but also hold out the possibility of threats.

4.5.4 Competitors

Since the fall of communism, most business operates in market economies that are characterised by competition in a market environment. This means that every business that tries to sell a product or a service in a market environment is constantly up against competition, and that it is often competitors who determine how much of a given product can be sold, and what price can be asked for it.

Moreover, businesses compete for a share of the market and also compete with other businesses for labour, capital and materials. As a variable in the market environment, competition may be defined as **a situation in the market environment in which several businesses, offering more or less the same kind of product or service, compete for the patronage of the same consumers.** The result of competition is that the market mechanism keeps excessive profits in check, stimulates higher productivity, and encourages technological innovation. Although the consumer benefits from competition, the latter is, nevertheless, a variable that management has to take into account in its entry into, and operations in the market.

Countries with a competitive edge

The USA is the world's most competitive country, according to new rankings based on productivity and other factors. But the Finns, working through those long winter nights, run a close second.

1	USA	6	Denmark
2	Finland	7	Switzerland
3	Luxembourg	8	Canada
4	The Netherlands	9	Hong Kong
5	Singapore	10	Ireland

Source: Time, 13 May 2002.

In the assessment of competition, marketing management should bear in mind that the nature and intensity of competition in a particular industry are determined by the following five factors:

- The possibility of new entrants (or departures) N $B^2 E N S$
- The bargaining power of clients and consumers B
- The bargaining power of suppliers   B
- The availability or non-availability of substitute products or services S
- The number of existing competitors   E

Figure 4.2 (see p. 94) illustrates the five forces responsible for competition in a particular industry. The collective strength of these five forces determines the competitiveness in the industry and therefore the profitability of participants in the industry. Competition varies from intense, in industries such as tyres and retailing, to moderate in mining and cold-drinks. The weaker the five forces are, the better the chances are of survival and good performance. It is therefore an important task of management to find a position in the market where the business organisation can successfully defend itself against the forces of competition. The alternative would be to find a position where the business can influence the forces of competition in its favour.

Continuous monitoring of competition provides the basis for the development of a strategy. It emphasises the critical strengths and weaknesses of the business, gives an indication of the positioning strategy that should be fol-

Figure 4.2: The competitive forces in an industry

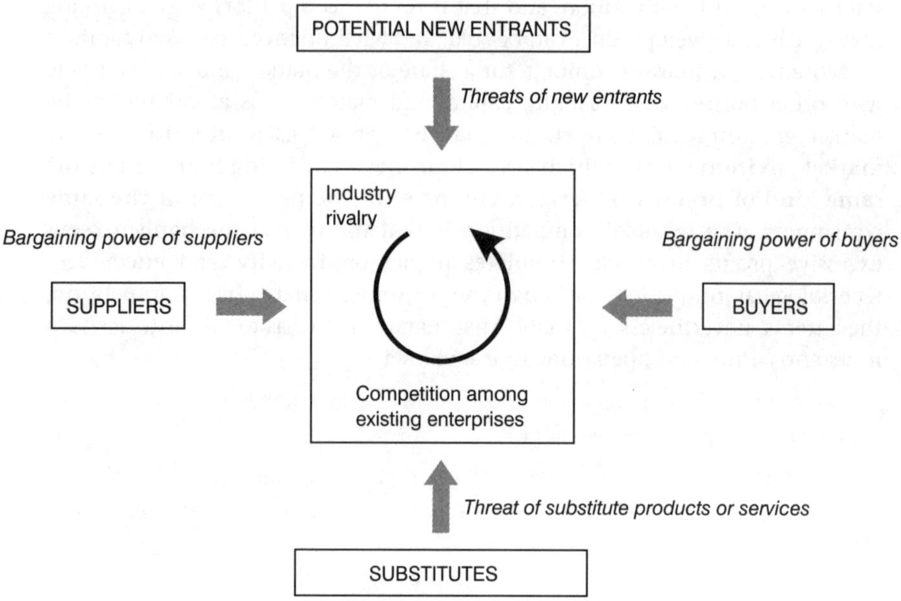

POTENTIAL NEW ENTRANTS

Threats of new entrants

Industry rivalry

Bargaining power of suppliers

SUPPLIERS

Competition among existing enterprises

Bargaining power of buyers

BUYERS

Threat of substitute products or services

SUBSTITUTES

Source: Griffin, R.W., *Management*, Houghton Mifflin Company, 1999, p. 87.

lowed, singles out areas in which strategy adjustments can contribute to higher returns, and focuses on industry trends in terms of opportunities and threats.

4.5.5 Opportunities and threats in the market environment

The changes brought about in the market environment by the respective variables and their interactions, and the trends that constantly develop in the macroenvironment, may be classified into two groups:
- Changes that offer an opportunity
- Changes that pose a threat

An **opportunity** may be defined as a favourable condition or trend in the market environment that can be exploited to advantage by a deliberate management effort. However, it should be clearly understood that the possibilities inherent in an opportunity always have to be assessed against the background of the organisation's resources and capabilities. Without the necessary capabilities and resources, an opportunity cannot be properly exploited. The success of a business in making good use of an opportunity therefore depends on its ability to satisfy the requirements for success in that particular market.

In contrast to an environmental opportunity, an environmental **threat** may be defined as an unfavourable condition or trend in the market environment that can, in the absence of a deliberate effort by management, lead to the failure of the business, its product or its service. In view of the constant changes in the market environment, it is the task of management to identify such threats, both actual and potential, and to develop a counter-strategy to meet them.

The scanning of the market environment for opportunities and threats entails an examination of such variables as the economy and technology in the macroenvironment, as well as trends in the variables within the market environment, namely those factors that influence consumer spending, suppliers and competition in the market.

4.5.6 Final comments

The market environment entails an interaction between a business and its suppliers, consumers, and competitors with alternative market offerings. This interaction can result in opportunities or threats to a business, and these require awareness on the part of management of trends in the market environment, so that management can exploit opportunities profitably and avoid threats in good time. Environmental scanning, market research and information management are the proper instruments to do this, as discussed elsewhere in this book.

4.6 The macroenvironment

4.6.1 The composition of the macroenvironment

Apart from the market environment, which has a direct influence on the fortunes of a business, a business also operates within a wider macroenvironment, with variables that directly or indirectly exert an influence on it and its market environment. These variables constitute the uncontrollable forces in the environment that are sometimes referred to as **megatrends**.

As can be seen from figure 4.1 (see p. 86), the contemporary literature on management divides the macroenvironment into six variables or sub-environments – technological, economic, social, physical, institutional or political, and international – which a business organisation has to observe and react to.

Macrovariables have an effect not only on the market environment and on decision-making by management, but also on one another, and this constantly causes change in the business environment. The community (which is also the consumer), with its particular culture and values, decides what government it wants, and gives it a mandate to form a certain political structure, which in turn determines the affairs of the community. Therefore, politics is interwoven with the economy and is influenced by the policies adopted and the economic measures taken to achieve political ends. The result is a certain standard of living for the community.

Stimulated by the needs of the community, and with the support of the economy and the government, technology is mainly responsible for the rate of change in the business environment, while social trends also influence politics and the economy, while the international environment acts as a considerable force for change in the other variables, and therefore in the total business environment. The result of this interaction is often a new business environment, with new opportunities and new threats.

The silent revolution in South Africa

- The so-called megatrends in South Africa may be regarded as a silent revolution in which political and social forces have irrevocably transformed society. The revolution or wave of change of recent years has been described as less bloody than the French or Russian revolutions: it has been more like the Industrial Revolution in England, which formed the basis of modern democracy.
- One component of the silent revolution is urbanisation. The level of urbanisation in South Africa now matches that of England in 1860, when the number of urban dwellers for the first time exceeded the number of rural dwellers.
- Another component of the silent revolution is education. By 2000, seven out of every ten matriculants were black. While in 1967 only 7% of university students in South Africa were black, by 2000 more than 40% were black.
- The implications of the silent revolution for the South African market are huge: 60% of all music sales are to black consumers, The *Sowetan* morning newspaper has the highest circulation figures in the country, and the black contribution to tourism in Durban grew from 4% in 1985 to 20% in 2000.

In studying the macroenvironment, the emphasis is on change caused by the uncontrollable macrovariables and the implications for management.

A rapidly changing macroenvironment

With the exception of a few basic products, most of the things bought and sold today came into existence in the last 60 years. Aeroplanes, radio, television and nuclear power were unknown in the time of Dingane, while Albert Luthuli never knew of antibiotics, personal computers, photostat machines or space flights. Steve Biko did not know of robot factories, ordinary citizens as space travellers or silicon protein molecules that have already made the silicon chip obsolete. And when president Nelson Mandela was inaugurated as State President, cell phones were not yet in operation. One reason for the constant rate of acceleration of technological innovation is the fact that 90% of all the scientists who have ever lived are alive today!

4.6.2 The technological environment

Change in the environment is generally a manifestation of technological innovation or the process through which human capabilities are enlarged. Technological innovation originates in research and development by business and government, and it results not only in new machinery or products, but also in new processes, methods, and even approaches to management, that bring about change in the environment. Technological innovation also affects other environmental variables. The economic growth rate is influenced by the number of new inventions. Social change, in which the appearance of a new product – such as satellite television, the Internet, or cell phones – brings about a revolution in people's way of life, is also partly the result of technology. Conversely, these variables influence technology, and so the process of innovation and change is repeated.

Technological breakthroughs such as cell phones, fibre optics and orthoscopic surgery, bullet trains, voice recognition computers, and the Internet result in new products and services for consumers, lower prices, and a higher standard of living. But technology can also make products obsolete, just as CDs wiped out the market for cassette tapes.

Every new facet of technology and every innovation create opportunities and threats in the environment. Television was a threat to films and newspapers, but at the same time it presented opportunities for instant meals, satellite communications, and advertising. The opportunities created by computers and the Internet in banking, manufacturing, transport, and practically every other industry are innumerable. Moreover, technological innovation often has unpredictable consequences. The contraceptive pill meant smaller families, more women at work, and therefore more money to spend on holidays and luxury articles that would previously not have been affordable. The most outstanding characteristic of technological innovation is probably the fact that it constantly accelerates the rate of change.

Technology and lifestyle

- Early in the 18th century, railroads opened up the hinterlands of America and England.
- In the 19th century, electricity revolutionised people's lifestyles. Today electricity supply in informal settlements in South Africa is changing people's lifestyles.
- Since the beginning of the previous century, the motorcar has brought radical changes to the development of cities and the workplace.
- The advent of the passenger jet in the 1950s transformed tourism within two decades into the world's major industry.
- People are now experiencing the impact of micro-electronics. What used to be a room-sized computer is now a pocket model. The effect of micro-electronics is that it results in ever-smaller units of production that nevertheless yield the same returns. Soon, consumption will be individualised, that is, consumers will be able to buy, almost instantaneously, a motorcar, jacket or article made to their own specifications.
- A telephone call is now 70 times cheaper and an airline ticket seven times cheaper than in 1930.
- Cell phones have revolutionised communication.

A further characteristic of technological innovation that impacts on management is the fact that inventions and innovations are unlimited. Table 4.2 (see p. 98) shows some possible innovations in the next century, with consequent opportunities and threats to businesses.

Technology influences the entire organisation. The most basic effect is probably **higher productivity**, which results in keener competition. The ability to produce more and better products threatens organisations with keener competition, compelling them to reassess factors such as mission, strategy, organisational structures, production methods, markets and other functional

Table 4.2: Actual and possible technological innovations in the 21st century

2000	New advances in genetics enable doctors to create more effective cancer treatments.	2016	Human beings land on Mars; a permanent colony is established on the planet around 2044.
2001	Well-mounted 1 m-long flat screens show television pro-grammes or videos, and when not in use display works of art.	2020	Flying wing aircraft are able to carry 1 000 passengers up to 9 000 km at average speeds of 900 km/h.
2003	Cellular phones with video cam-eras and screens enable people to watch films.	2022	Foetuses conceived in extra extra-uterine incubators are born with-out ever having been inside a human womb.
2005	Video postcards and postcard-sized film screens display ten sec-onds of holiday sights and sounds.	2025	Computers connected directly to the brain are able to recognise and respond to thoughts, obviat-ing the need for manual data input.
2006	The active contact lens, linked to the Internet, allows the wearer to read e-mail without even opening his or her eyes.	2030	Following on the development of artificial lungs, kidneys and livers, doctors now create artificial legs and fully functional artificial eyes.
2007	New cars are equipped with anti-collision radar and satellite posi-tioning systems.	2040	Cryogenics (human hibernation) is used for long-distance space travel.
2010	Robotic pets are programmed to recognise their owner's voice.	2050	Microscopic robots are capable of reproducing themselves.
2015	The genetic origins of all diseases are identified.	2500	From an average of 78 years (in the developed world), the human lifespan is extended to 140 years.

Source: Time, Summer, 1998, p. 26. © Time Inc, 1998.

strategies. Superior management of technology within the organisation can be an important source of competitive advantage. Continued assessment of the technological environment should include the following:
- The identification of important technological trends
- An analysis of potential change in important current and future technology
- An analysis of the competitive impact of important technologies
- An analysis of the organisation's technological strengths and weaknesses
- A list of priorities that should be included in a technology strategy for the organisation

In a developing country such as South Africa, managers should continually assess technology trends that revolve around:
- Water technology – South Africa's water resources can sustain only 80 million people
- Mineral technology – to improve the processing of our mineral treasures
- Marine technology – to utilise our vast coastal and oceanic resources
- Agricultural and veterinary technology – to preserve Africa's wildlife and tourism

- Medical technology – to prevent epidemics and to support the sports industry
- Transport technology – to provide transport for the people
- Power technology – to harness cheaper forms of power, such as solar power

Technological progress therefore affects the business as a whole, including its products, life-cycle, the supply of materials, production process, and even its approach to management. These influences all require that management be increasingly on the alert for technological change.

4.6.3 The economic environment

After technology, which is primarily responsible for change in the environment, there is the economy, which is influenced by technology, politics and the social and international environments, while itself asserting some influence on these variables. These cross-influences continuously cause changes in, for example, the economic growth rate, levels of employment, consumer income, the rate of inflation, interest rates, and the exchange rate. Ultimately, these economic forces have certain implications for management.

The economic well-being of a country, or its economic growth rate, is measured by the range and number of products and services produced. Expressed in monetary terms, this standard is known as the gross domestic product (GDP) – in other words, the total value of all goods and services finally produced within the borders of a country in a particular period (usually one year).[4] A high economic growth rate of around 7-8% per year in real terms signals an economy which grows fast enough to create jobs for its people, one which exports more products than it imports to sustain a positive trade balance and a stable currency, and one which can provide its people with an improved standard of living. A low economic growth rate, on the other hand, especially one that is below the population growth rate, usually lowers the peoples' standard of living. South Africa needs a growth rate of over 7% per year in real terms to provide jobs for the millions in the unemployment queue and the hundreds of thousands that join it annually. Unfortunately, as table 4.3 (see p. 100) shows, South Africa's growth rate hovers around 3% per year and is predicted to be only 2,7% in 2003. This figure is not sufficient to provide employment for the unemployed, to alleviate poverty, and to improve the living standards of all South Africans.

Impoverishment of the consumer, 1987-1997

- Current income (mainly salaries and wages) rose by 390%
  minus direct personal income tax, which rose by 549%
  = income after tax rises by 372%
  minus inflation, which rose by 214,6%
  = income after tax and inflation rise of 14,3%
- Factor in a population increase of roughly 25%
- The end result is a per capita income decline, after tax and inflation, of roughly 10%

Source: Quarterly Bulletin of the South African Reserve Bank, various editions.
South African Reserve Bank statistics: http://www.resbank,co.za/Economics/stats.html
http://www.resbank.co.za/Economics/qbu/698/kbp/kbp7.zip

Table 4.3: Predicted economic growth (GDP growth) in 2002 and 2003

Percentage predicted	2002 responses (%)	2003 responses (%)
Lower than 1,5%	6,0	1,2
1,5% – 1,9%	10,8	7,2
2,0% – 2,4%	37,3	22,9
2,5% – 2,9%	36,1	24,1
3,0% – 3,4%	7,2	33,7
3,5% +	2,4	10,8
	100,0	100,0

Source: Predicted GDP growth rate by the executives of 90 top South African companies, Bureau of Market Research, Unisa, Pretoria, Research Report 293, 2002, p. 12.

It is important to realise that when a country's standard of living is declining, consumers will experience a drop in their purchasing power, which can, in turn, give rise to changes in spending behaviour as well as changes in the type of products or services purchased. Management must take note of structural changes in the incomes of different consumer groups and adjust its strategies accordingly. In addition to the economic growth rate, management must also monitor the business cycle very carefully. The correct assessment of upswing and downswing phases in the economy is essential to the strategy of any business. If management expects a recession, it can, for example, reduce its exposure by decreasing inventory, thereby avoiding high interest costs. Any plans for expansion can also be deferred. In an upswing (or boom period) the right strategy may be to build up sufficient inventory in good time and to carry out whatever expansion is necessary.

Inflation, like economic growth, is an economic variable that affects the decisions that management has to make. During the 1960s South Africa had a very low inflation rate, but from the mid-1970s double-digit inflation became a regular phenomenon. From 1974-1992 the average annual rate of consumer price increases amounted to 13,8%. Since 1993, however, single-digit price increases, comparable to those of the early 1970s, have again been recorded. This is because of improved monetary discipline.

Although South Africa is experiencing its lowest consumer inflation rate in 25 years, the costs and effects of inflation on a business need to be analysed and managed on a permanent basis. Inflation increases costs for exporting industries and also local industries competing against imported goods. When a country's inflation rate is higher than that of its major trading partners and international competitors, there is a reduction in its international competitiveness. This is still the case with South Africa today, because its inflation rate is still higher than most of the world's important trading countries.

Another economic variable affecting a business and its market environment is the government's **monetary policy**. This affects or influences the

Facts regarding inflation in South Africa

- From 1946-1997 the average level of consumer prices rose by 4 638% over the entire period, or an average rate of 8,7% per annum.
- This means that an item that cost R100 in 1946 cost R4 638 in 1997.
- Expressed in terms of purchasing power, one rand in 1997 could therefore only purchase about one-fiftieth of the goods and services that it could buy in 1946.
- The average inflation rate in 1998 of 6,9% was the lowest since 1973, when it was 6.5%.
- The average consumer price inflation from 1953-1968 was 2,9% – at this rate it would have taken 29 years for consumer prices to double.
- The average annual rate of consumer price increases from 1974-1992 was 13,8% – at this rate, prices have doubled every five years.

Source: Quarterly Bulletin of the South African Reserve Bank, September 1998.
South African Reserve Bank statistics: http://www.resbank.co.za/Economics/stats.html
http://www.resbank.co.za/Economics/qbu/698/kbp/kbp7.zip

money supply, interest rates, and the strength of the currency, and therefore has certain important implications for management. High interest rates result in the high cost of credit and a subsequent decline in consumer spending and fixed investment. The government's **fiscal policy**, on the other hand, affects both businesses and consumers through taxation and tax reforms. Individuals now carry more of the tax burden than ever before, whereas revenue from company tax has seen little change.

The economies of surrounding countries also affect the economic variables of a country. The South African economy operates in a region where most of the world's poor people live on less than US $1 per day. Of Africa's 49 states, 24 are numbered among the poorest in the world. In addition, Africa has 11% of the world's population, but produces only 0,5% of world GDP.

The economic trends discussed above demand constant examination by management and regular consideration of the influences of economic variables.

Africa: A profile (2002)

- Manhattan has more telephone lines than all of Africa (International Telecommunication Union).
- To halve poverty by 2015, African economies will need to grow at 7% a year (World Bank Development Indicators, 2002).
- In 2001 Africa's average GDP growth was 4,3%, one of the highest rates in the world (Economic Report on Africa, 2002, UN Economic Commission for Africa).
- Africa received less than 1% (US $9,1bn) of foreign direct investment (FDI) in 2000 (World Investment Report, 2001, UN Conference on Trade & Development).
- South Africa is the continent's most important source of FDI, totalling 43% of all flows in 2000 (World Investment Report, 2001, UNCTAD).
- Post-colonial Africa has the world's most rapid educational expansion and the highest rate of skilled migration.

Source: Financial Mail, 3 May 2002, p. 35.

4.6.4 The social environment

The environmental variable that is probably most subject to the influence of other variables – especially technology and the economy – is the socio-cultural dimension of a nation. This affects management indirectly in the form of consumers, and directly in the form of employees.

Humans are largely products of their society. As members of a particular society, they accept and assimilate its language, values, faith, expectations, laws and customs. A culture, or the way of life of a group of people, influences the individual's way of life, and so, consumption cannot be explained solely in economic terms, since it is also a function of culture and social change. However, a culture is not static. Over time, a society's values, expectations, habits and way of life change.

Our changing language

In Shakespeare's time only 250 000 of the 450 000 words that are now part of the English language existed. If he were alive today, he would understand only five words out of nine.

We will now briefly examine the influence of certain observable social trends:

- **Demographic change**, that is, change in the growth and composition of populations, is probably the social variable that causes the most change in the market. It does so by altering people's way of life. Societies in **the developed world** are characterised by falling population growth rates and shrinking families, with the emphasis on smaller consumer units. There are growing numbers of one-person households, and consequently there is a growing demand for services. There is also a growing population of ageing, and more affluent, persons and families over the age of 65, who create special marketing opportunities. Affluent people of that age, for example, like to travel. South Africa should target these markets internationally by presenting our country as an attractive tourist destination.

  Internationally, the question of population growth and poverty in developing countries is causing great concern to politicians and environmentalists. Figure 4.3 (see p. 103) illustrates world population growth, from 200 million in the year AD 1 to 500 million in 1650, 1 billion in 1850, 4 billion in 1975 and currently 6,3 billion people.

  The concerns surrounding high population growth rates in developing countries revolve around poverty, pollution and degradation of the environment, as well as illness and famine. A third of the world (2 billion people) is in danger of starving. All of these questions have a profound effect on business, especially in Africa where 55 million people (including a large percentage of workers) are expected to die of Aids by 2020.

  The total population of South Africa is expected to increase at 1,5% per annum, from 45,3 million in 2001 to 52 million in 2021. The proportion of blacks, which was 69,5% in 1951, will increase to 79,6% in 2021, while that of whites, at 19,1% in 1951, will decrease to 9,7% in 2021. The number of illegal immigrants in South Africa is a controversial issue. Figures as high as 12 million have been quoted.

Table 4.4 indicates the projected growth rates of the various population groups in South Africa from 1996-2021.

Figure 4.3: World population growth, AD 1-2000

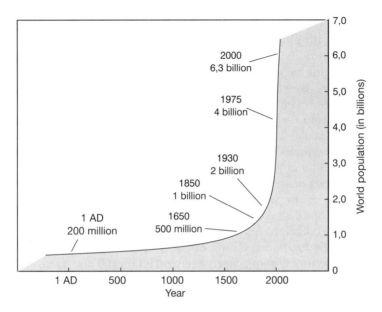

It is clear from table 4.4 that the growth rates of all four groups are due to decline, with the rate of decline greatest among whites, followed by Asians, coloureds and blacks. At 0,18% annual growth, the white population will be

Table 4.4: Projected South African population by population group and sex (1996 – 2021)

Year		Blacks	Asian	Coloured	White	Total population
1996	Female	16 300 130	543 110	1 819 110	2 595 740	21 249 090
	Male	15 944 970	521 640	1 727 010	2 577 800	20 771 420
	Total	32 245 100	1 055 750	3 546 120	5 173 540	42 020 510
2001	Female	17 885 480	564 710	1 955 530	2 637 510	23 043 230
	Male	17 299 450	548 510	1 853 280	2 604 990	22 306 230
	Total	35 184 930	1 113 220	3 808 810	5 242 500	45 349 460
2006	Female	19 273 100	589 590	2 072 870	2 657 410	24 592 970
	Male	18 375 170	570 100	1 955 500	2 607 610	23 508 380
	Total	37 648 270	1 159 690	4 028 370	5 265 020	48 101 350
2011	Female	20 208 320	605 550	2 160 240	2 650 250	25 624 360
	Male	19 010 880	583 250	2 022 770	2 581 920	24 198 820
	Total	39 219 200	1 188 800	4 183 010	5 232 170	49 823 180
2016	Female	20 800 110	611 760	2 216 710	2 624 080	26 252 660
	Male	19 453 770	587 730	2 064 910	2 538 310	24 644 720
	Total	40 253 880	1 199 490	4 281 620	5 162 390	50 897 380
2021	Female	21 401 380	614 440	2 255 690	2 580 910	26 852 420
	Male	20 005 930	588 740	2 094 660	2 479 160	25 168 490
	Total	41 407 310	1 203 180	4 350 350	5 060 070	52 020 910

Source: Bureau for Market Research, Unisa. Report No. 270; 1999.

approaching zero population growth by the year 2011. This has many implications for producers of products and services for traditionally white market segments.

Changes in population growth patterns, as well as age and composition patterns, have an effect on the needs, income and behaviour of consumers, and also on employment patterns. This will be discussed further under the section dealing with Aids below.

- **Urbanisation.** Following on from changes in population growth patterns are changing trends in the geographical distribution and mobility of the population. The movement of people towards cities is known as urbanisation. Estimates of the future spread of urbanisation are based on the observation that in Europe and the USA, the urban share of the total population has stabilised at approximately 75%. If the rest of the world follows this path, it is expected that in the next decade an extra 100 million people will join the cities of Africa. By 2030 nearly two-thirds of the world's population will be urban. Urbanisation therefore affects businesses in many ways, especially in the areas of housing, sanitation, slum-control, and health services. Informal settlements constitute need-specific market segments.

- **Level of education.** Another social trend that will greatly affect management is the level of education of the population. This will influence the level of skills of both managers and workers on the one hand, and books, magazines and newspapers on the other, as higher education will result in new demands for quality literature and articles. This trend will also influence the tourism industry.

  Furthermore, better education and training will mean a more sophisticated consumer, with definite demands being made on management regarding quality of goods, advertisements and working conditions. In South Africa, the educational level of all consumers is rising, with the number of successful black matriculants having increased sixfold from 35 000 in 1980 to 219 000 in the year 2000. While 80% of all those who passed their matriculation examinations in 1970 were white, by the year 2000 white matriculants represented less than 20% of all matriculants.

- **Changing role of women.** Another social variable with clear implications for management is the changing role of women in developed societies. As recently as 15 years ago, 60% of American women believed that a woman's place was in the home. Now only 22% are of that opinion.

  The proportion of economically active white South African women increased from 19% in 1960 to the present 36,7%. Similarly, the proportion of coloured women now stands at 34,6%. The involvement of Asian women in economic activities also increased sharply, from one in every 20 in 1960 to about one in every four at present. The proportion of economically active black women has nearly doubled to the present 27,3%. Today, only 17% of black managers are women, but this percentage is expected to show a marked rise. Figure 4.4 (see p. 105) illustrates the involvement of women in the labour forces of developed countries.

Figure 4.4: Working women as a percentage of the total labour force, 1960-1996

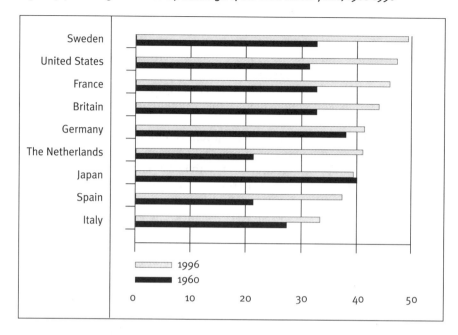

Source: A survey of women and work, *The Economist*, 18 July 1998, p. 4.

- **Consumerism.** A further social trend that has to be considered is consumerism – the social force that protects the consumer by exerting legal, moral, economic and even political pressure on management. This movement is a natural consequence of a better educated public that resists such things as misleading advertisements, unsafe products, profiteering and other objectionable trade practices, and presses for the so-called rights of the consumer. In a market system, these rights are generally recognised as the following:
  - **The right to safety.** This entails protection against products that may be dangerous or detrimental to life or health.
  - **The right to be informed.** This means the provision of objective information to enable the consumer to make rational choices.
  - **The right to freedom of choice.** This entails giving the consumer access to competitive products or substitutes, and it is, as such, a protection against monopolies.
  - **The right to be heard.** This means that consumers are given the assurance that their interests will receive attention from government and related parties.

The South African Consumer Union endeavours to protect the consumer, to act as a watchdog, and to be in direct contact with manufacturers, suppliers and distributors of consumer goods wherever this may be in the consumer's best interests. The Union also monitors legislation that may affect the consumer and, where necessary, campaigns for the amendment of existing laws, or advocates for new legislation to protect the consumer.

- **Social responsibility and business ethics.** Another important aspect of the social environment is the pressure that society exerts on business organisations, forcing them to be socially responsible. This means that business organisations should constantly consider the consequences of their decisions and actions. In most instances criticism of such aspects as misleading advertising, dangerous products, pollution of the environment and exploitation of the consumer is levelled against management.

  While profits and employment remain important, many other factors are today included in assessing the social performance of a business, namely equity or empowering designated groups economically and managerially, housing, responding to environmental concerns, providing a responsible and safe workplace, caring about health issues, and involving itself with community issues. Some businesses perform an annual social audit to measure their social performance. Based on the results of the social audit, a business can review its social responsibility. The crux of social responsibility is, however, the insistence of the community that business should in every respect be a "good corporate citizen", one that produces profit for owners and investors, but simultaneously markets safe products, combats pollution, respects the rights of employees and consumers, and assists the disadvantaged. In short, businesses are expected to promote the interests of society. Though South African business spends millions on social investment, it remains under pressure to uplift the disadvantaged. In future, in South Africa and elsewhere, pressure will intensify and may even give rise to a more regulatory environment.

  Table 4.5 (see p. 107) shows the various aspects according to which society judges the social performance of a business.

  As a concept, **business ethics** is closely related to social responsibility, except that business ethics has specifically to do with the ethics or the ethical behaviour of managers and executives in the business world. Managers, in particular, are expected to maintain high ethical standards. At issue here is the integrity of entrepreneurs and managers, and the degree to which their decisions conform to the norms and values of society. Business ethics revolves around the trust that society places in people in business, and the obligations they have towards society.

  Greed, the exploitation of workers and consumers, and the abuse of positions of trust have caused the business ethics of entrepreneurs and managers to be deplored. We have already mentioned the accounting scandals of Enron and Worldcom executives and their auditors in the USA, and the outcry from investors for increased regulatory measures. In South Africa, recent examples of unethical and corrupt conduct by executives include the controversial arms deal, the Saambou affair, and the misuse of funds at LeisureNet. Corporate governance was institutionalised by the publication of the King Report on Corporate Governance in November 1994, which has since been superceded by the King Code of 2002. The purpose of the Code of Corporate Practices and Conduct contained in the King Report is to promote the highest standards of corporate governance, and therefore business ethics, in South Africa.

Table 4.5: The social responsibility of business

Area of social responsibility	Issues in social responsibility	Laws/regulations pertaining to social responsibility issues
SOCIAL RESPONSIBILITY TO EMPLOYEES (Workplace responsibility)	• Equal employment opportunities • Developing a quality workforce (training and the skills levy) • Gender inclusion • Access for disabled persons • Sexual harassment awareness • Respect for diversity • Safe working conditions	• Employment Equity Act 55 of 1998 • Skills Development Act 97 of 1998 • Gender Equality Act 39 of 1996 • Health and Safety Act 29 of 1996
SOCIAL RESPONSIBILITY TO THE CONSUMER AND CUSTOMERS	• Safe products and services • No misleading advertising and communication • Proper information about products and services	• Consumer Protection Measures Act 95 of 1998
RESPONSIBILITY TO THE INVESTOR AND FINANCIAL COMMUNITY	• No deceptive accounting reports • Accuracy of financial reporting • No insider trading • No bribes to customs or other government officials	• South African Statement of Generally Accepted Accounting Practice (GAAP) as approved by the Accounting Practice Board • The King Code, i.e. the Code of Corporate Practices representing the principles of good governance as set out in the King Report 2 of 2002, which supercedes the King Report of 1994
SOCIAL RESPONSIBILITY TO THE GENERAL PUBLIC	• Natural environment issues, including conservation and the preservation of the ecology, and pollution control • Public health issues such as HIV/Aids • Housing for the poor • Philanthropic donations • Social welfare • Avoiding unlawful competition	• World Heritage Convention Act 49 of 1999 • Housing Act 107 of 1997 • Welfare Laws Amendment Act 106 of 1996

Losing faith in corporate America

After the Enron, Worldcom and Xerox scandals in the USA, with their huge bank-ruptcies, handcuffed executives, horrified investors, and the criminal conviction of accounting firm Arthur Andersen, society started asking questions such as, Can capitalism survive? The whole debacle of crooked accountants and executives drove confidence to ever-lower levels, as illustrated by the following graph:

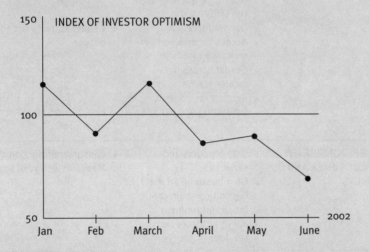

INDEX OF INVESTOR OPTIMISM

Source: Time, 8 July 2002, p. 26.

As society's doubt in corporate integrity increased, the lawmakers began to crack down on business fraud. Within hours of President George Bush signing these laws, the executives of Worldcom were arrested, handcuffed and taken to prison where, after the court hearings, they may remain an example of the way in which society puts pressure on issues that affect it negatively.

- **HIV/Aids.** A particular social problem that concerns and influences all South African (and other African) businesses is the curse of HIV/Aids. In sub-Saharan Africa it is devastating families and communities and destroying hope. So far, 17 million people have died of Aids. At least 25 million may follow in the next few years. South Africa now has the largest number of people living with HIV/Aids in the world, about 20% of its adult population, up from 13% in 1997. Table 4.6 (see p. 109) illustrates the frightening statistics of HIV prevalence, both around the globe and in South Africa.

  The concerns that potential investors, and especially human resource managers have about the epidemic, revolves around the fact that organisations will soon have to deal with a workforce where one-third is infected by HIV/Aids, and where an organisation could lose key people as well as 25% to 50% of its workforce. Because organisations are legally obliged to support HIV/Aids positive employees, few investors are interested in entering labour intensive industries such as transport, mining and manufacturing.

Table 4.6: HIV prevalence around the globe and in South Africa

HIV prevalence globally	Millions
Sub-Saharan Africa	25 300 000
South and South-East Asia	5 800 000
Latin America	1 400 000
North America	920 000
Eastern Europe	700 000
East Asia	640 000
Western Europe	540 000
Australia/New Zealand	15 000

HIV Women in South Africa	Percentage
1990	0,73%
1994	7,6%
1995	14,2%
1998	22,8%
2000	24,5%

Source: *Aids and Business*, unpublished report, Pretoria, 2002, p. 4.

The total cost to the South African economy could soon be a reduction in the economic growth rate of between 0,3%–0,4%, at a cost of R167 billion per year. To individual businesses, the cost of Aids includes absenteeism, lost productivity, hospitalisation, and replacing workers at enormous cost. This is presently costing businesses between 2% and 6% of salaries a year. Management urgently needs to develop strategies and programmes to deal adequately with HIV/Aids in the workplace.

- **Culture** is another social variable that influences organisations in a number of ways. In South Africa new cultural values are emerging among young urban blacks, for example, the extended family living under one roof is viewed with disfavour, women have become more independent, and negative attitudes towards marriage and large families are frequently expressed. The shape of the market, the influence of the culture that currently enjoys political power, and the attitude of the workforce are only a few of the numerous ways in which culture can affect an organisation.

Social problems such as the HIV/Aids epidemic and poverty bring about developments that in turn effect change in the environment. Management cannot afford to ignore these social influences.

4.6.5 The physical environment

The physical environment refers to the physical resources that people (and businesses) need to support life and development, such as water, air, climate, the oceans, rivers, forests, and so on. Environmentalists warn that if the biomass, which maintains a destructible balance in sustaining life, is damaged beyond repair, planet earth will simply shake us off, as it has shaken off countless species before us. With approximately 6,3 billion people relying on the resources of the same planet, government and business are now beginning to realise that the plundering of physical resources may endanger countries and even continents.

Currently, the numbers of domestic stock we keep are too high, and the amount of crops and other biomaterial that we extract from the earth each year exceeds by an estimated 20% what the planet can replace. The issues of most concern to environmentalists regarding the physical environment are the following:[5]

- **Population and health patterns.** Despite a slow-down in population growth, the number of people on earth is still rising. In poor countries, mostly in Asia and Africa, population growth leads to land degradation, pollution, malnutrition and illness.
- **Food.** Two billion people – a third of the planet's population – are in danger of starving.
- **Water.** Within the next 25 years, two thirds of humanity may live in countries that are running short of water. Only 2,5% of the earth's water is fresh, and only a fraction of that is accessible, despite the fact that each person needs 50 litres per day for drinking, cooking, bathing and other needs. At present, 1,1 billion people lack access to clean drinking water, and 2,4 billion lack adequate sanitation.
- **Energy and climate.** About 2,5 billion people have no access to modern energy sources, and the burning of fossil fuels such as oil and coal results in heavy air pollution, which promotes global warning and climate disruptions.
- **Biodiversity.** More than 11 000 known species of animals and plants are threatened with extinction. Many vanishing species provide humans with both food and medicine.

Table 4.7: Forest destruction causes the worst extinctions since dinosaurs were wiped out

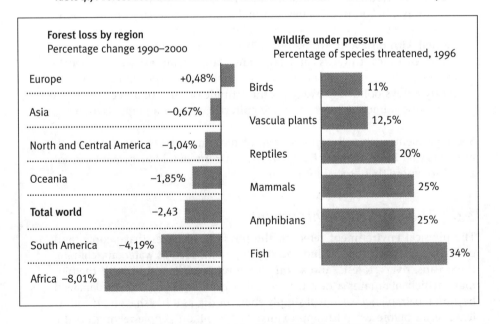

The physical environment influences business simply because it is the environment from which business obtains its physical resources. It is also the environment into which business discharges its waste. The following interfaces with the physical environment present opportunities as well as threats to the business organisation:

- **The cost of energy.** The increasing cost of energy has a direct bearing on the environment, with consequent threats to, and opportunities for, business. Research on solar power, wind power and nuclear power has been intensified, and offers many opportunities to entrepreneurs.
- **The growing cost of pollution.** Pollution costs the community a great deal in terms of destroyed living space, as well as expenses related to the prevention and remedying of pollution and complying with laws designed to minimise it. Here, opportunities present themselves, for example, in the form of new methods of producing and packaging goods to keep pollution to the minimum.
- **Environmentalism.** Many opportunities for entrepreneurs exist in the fields of conservation and ecotourism.
- **Scarce resources.** A broad range of resources that are becoming increasingly scarce, such as raw materials, energy and foodstuffs, are a matter of concern to entrepreneurs. Shortages affect the supply of products and can cause severe price rises. However, shortages also create opportunities, since they often necessitate different methods of production or substitute products.

Destruction of forests in South Africa

- Roughly 11 million tons of firewood are used every year in South Africa – more than all the wood commercially harvested in the same period. At least 12 million people, a third of the population, still rely on firewood as their main source of energy. This not only has far-reaching consequences for the environment, but the daily gathering of wood is uneconomical and time consuming.
- It is mainly indigenous and natural vegetation that is destroyed in this way, and such vegetation is not regenerated.
- The destruction of the natural habitat has had dire consequences all over South Africa. Soil erosion is one of the most visible results of the over-exploitation of natural resources.

Business should respond to the vulnerability of the physical environment by taking timeous steps to limit any harmful effects on the community. If management does not show clear signs of a sense of social and environmental responsibility, it should not be surprised if hostile relations develop that may threaten the survival of the business. The packaging industry is responding by developing containers to minimise pollution, the soap industry is carrying out research on less harmful chemicals, and the motor industry is being compelled by legislation to design emission systems that will minimise pollution.

4.6.6 The politico-governmental environment

Management decisions are continually affected by the course of politics, especially the political pressures exerted by the ruling administration and its institutions. As a component of the macroenvironment, government affects the business environment and business enterprise in a regulating capacity, as explained in chapter 1. The government intervenes in the macroenvironment on a large scale and influences it by means of legislation, the annual budget, taxation, import control (or a lack of it), promotion of exports, import tariffs to protect certain industries against excessive foreign competition, price controls for certain goods and services, health regulations, incentives to encourage development in a specific direction, and so on.

Furthermore, the government influences the market through government expenditure. Whenever the government acts as a producer, as in the case of numerous businesses, for example Eskom, it competes with private enterprise for labour, materials and capital. To an increasing extent, it is the task of management to study the numerous and often complex activities of government, as well as legislation and political developments, to determine their influence on the profitable survival of the business. The new political dispensation in South Africa, with its new form and philosophy of government, will undoubtedly result in new power bases, with far-reaching consequences for the South African business environment. The new labour laws and the Employment Equity Act 55 of 1998 are examples of how the government influences the management of businesses.

4.6.7 The international environment

While each of the factors so far discussed exerts – to a greater or lesser extent – an influence on the business environment, the situation is rendered even more complex, with even more opportunities and threats, if an international dimension is added to each. Businesses that operate internationally find themselves in a far more complex global business environment because every country has its own peculiar environmental factors, with its own technology, economy, culture, laws, politics, markets, and competitiveness, and each is different from those of every other country. International and multinational organisations are susceptible to all kinds of international currents and trends.

The new economic order that is taking shape worldwide is indicative of the increasing globalisation of the world economy. Globalisation and the trend towards a borderless world continually affect businesses in new ways. However, globalisation does not only present opportunities – it also poses threats. Management must therefore constantly assess possible global threats to their markets and product.

Applying the concept: environmental influences

Toyota South Africa is one of the country's largest car manufacturers. It is exposed to influences from the environment on a daily basis. Internally, management has to deal with problems ranging from its mission and objectives to marketing strategies, internal conflict and retrenchments.

It is directly affected by the market environment through the needs, preferences and purchasing power of consumers, and consequently has to produce vehicles to satisfy these demands. The access segment of the market, which developed during the past decade, is an example of a shift in consumer needs. The Toyota Tazz was developed for this market segment. Management also have to take into account suppliers of components, particularly with regard to their availability, quality and cost. In addition, management must keep an eye on competition to ensure Toyota leadership in the market.

Indirect factors, or, more specifically, variables in the macroenvironment such as technological innovation in production processes, inflation, or high interest rates, can also create an opportunity or a threat for Toyota South Africa. Toyota is also influenced by the new labour laws, including the Employment Equity Act 55 of 1998.

1. What other variables in the market environment could influence Toyota's management?
2. Name any further variables in the macroenvironment that might influence Toyota's management.

4.6.8 *Final comments*

Under the free-market system, a business exists in a dynamic environment in which technological innovation, economic fluctuations, changing ways of life, and political trends are continually altering the environment. Insight into trends and events in the environment, and an ability to foresee how these will affect decision making, are now assuming great importance for management, for, in a rapidly changing environment, experience of the past is often of little help in solving the latest problems. Extrapolation from previous experience is therefore futile and counterproductive. Knowledge of trends in the environment, and the identification of those issues that largely determine the course of development of a business are also necessary to make the decisions that will maximise profitability. For this, scanning the environment is a necessary management task. It enables management to identify threats and demands from the environment and, wherever possible, to turn these into opportunities.

4.7 **Environmental scanning**

The degree to which the environment influences the management of a business depends largely on the type of business and the goals and objectives of its management. Moreover, environmental influences differ from one management area to the next, and even at different levels of management. This means that the importance, scope and method of scanning – that is, the process of measurement, projection and evaluation of change in the different environmental variables – differs from one organisation to the next.

The importance of environmental scanning may be summarised as follows:[6]
- The environment is continually changing – therefore purposeful monitoring is necessary to keep abreast of change.
- Scanning is necessary to determine what factors and patterns in the environment pose threats to the present strategy of a business.
- Scanning is also necessary to determine what factors in the environment present opportunities for the more effective attainment of the goals and objectives of a business.
- Businesses that systematically scan the environment are more successful than those that do not.
- In the 50 years between 1920-1970 almost half of the 100 largest organisations in the USA failed because they did not scan the environment adequately and adapt themselves to change accordingly.

The scope of environmental scanning is determined by the following factors:
- The nature of the environment within which a business operates, and the demands made by the environment on a business. The more unstable the environment, and the more sensitive the business is to change, the more comprehensive the scanning has to be. Increasing instability usually means greater risk.
- The basic relationship between a business and its environment
- The source and extent of change. The impact of change is rarely so compartmentalised that it affects only one or two areas of an organisation. Change has an interactive and dynamic effect on several aspects of a business.

The best method of environmental scanning is a much-debated subject. It will in any case be determined by the importance that the business attaches to the environment, and the amount of scanning required. The following are a few guidelines that may be followed:
- The most elementary form of scanning is to update relevant secondary or published information which is obtainable from a wealth of sources such as the media, the organisation's own data, professional publications, financial journals, statistics, associates in other organisations, banks, research institutions, records in the organisation's own filing system, and even employees.
- A more advanced form of scanning is the addition of primary information, or special investigations on particular aspects of the environment. Such investigations can be carried out by members of the organisation's own staff or by outside consultants.
- Scanning at a much more advanced level could mean the establishment of a scanning unit within the business with its own staff, who monitor a broad range of environmental variables and make forecasts about certain of these. Economic predictions by economists using a number of models, assessments of the market and of competition by market researchers, and technological predictions by industrial analysts, are only a few examples. Such a scanning unit is usually located in management's planning department.

The question that arises is how all the collected information can be brought to the attention of the relevant manager. There are many different opinions about this, the most common being that information about the environment forms the basis of strategic planning, which is the responsibility of top management. This will be discussed in greater detail in chapter 6.

4.8 Summary

A business and the environment in which it operates, including the community that it serves, depend on each other for survival. Together they form a complex dynamic business environment where change in the environmental variables continually determines the success or failure of a business. Because these variables are often beyond the control of management, it is management's task to adapt the organisation to change in the environment. At times, management acts proactively by anticipating events, thereby also accelerating change. Knowledge of a changing environment by means of sustained environmental scanning is a prerequisite for taking advantage of opportunities as well as averting threats.

References

1. Van Wyk, R.J., Environmental change and the task of the human resource manager, *SA Journal of Business Management*, 16(2), 1985, p. 72.
2. See also Hodge, B.J. & Anthony, W. P., *Organization theory*, Allyn & Bacon, 1984, chapter 3.
3. Bureau for Market Research, The Advertising and Marketing Environment in the New South Africa, UNISA, Research Report no. 213, 1994, p. 2.
4. Mohr, P.J., Fourie, L.J., & Associates, *Economics for South African students*, J.L. van Schaik, Pretoria, 1995, p. 91.
5. *Time*, Special report: How to save the earth, 2 September 2002, pp. 18-22.
6. Glueck, W.F., *Business policy and strategy management*, McGraw-Hill, Tokyo, 1980, pp. 89-93.

2 Summary

PART 2

General management principles

5 Introduction to general management

The purpose of this chapter

Entrepreneurs identify opportunities and establish businesses to produce the products and services that the market needs. They are the driving force behind the venture, but not necessarily the only key success factor. Businesses or the ideas and new ventures of entrepreneurs, need to be managed. That is, the resources that are deployed in the business, such as people, money, equipment and knowledge, must be managed in such a way that the business reaches its profit and other goals. This means that the resources must be planned, organised, led and controlled in such a way that the business maximises its profits.

This chapter describes the role of management in the business organisation and examines the four fundamental management tasks of the management process, namely planning, organising, leading and control. It also explains the different levels and kinds of management in the business and gives an overview of the development of management theory.

Learning outcomes

The content of this chapter will enable learners to:
- Give an overview of the role of management in businesses
- Describe the four fundamental management tasks, namely planning, organising, leading and control
- Explain the management process
- Comment on the different levels and kinds of management in the business organisation
- Describe the various schools of thought in management

5.1 Introduction

In chapter 3 we discussed the entrepreneur who initiates new ventures and establishes new business organisations. We also examined the different types of business organisations, such as a partnership, a closed corporation, a private company, and so on. These different organisations, like the many other kinds of organisations such as hospitals, schools and sport clubs, which serve society, need to be managed. The purpose of this chapter is to examine the general principles involved in the management of a business.

5.2 The role of management

An organisation may be described as consisting of people and resources, and certain goals that have to be reached. These predetermined goals, which may differ from one organisation to the next, constitute the purpose of an organisation, because humans, as social beings, arrange themselves in groups to achieve goals that would be too difficult or too complex for an individual to achieve alone. For this reason, a squash club endeavours to get to the top of the league, a hospital tries to make its services as productive and efficient as possible, a political party tries to win an election, and a business endeavours to make a profit and achieve its goals, to mention but a few examples.

However, organisations do not achieve their goals automatically. In addition to the people, physical resources, financial resources and knowledge in an organisation, there is a further element that is necessary to direct all these resources and activities effectively toward goals. That indispensable element is **management**. Without this, no purposeful action is possible. All members of the organisation would pursue their own ends in their own way, and the result would be a waste of time and valuable resources, and the organisation would ultimately fail.

One of the commonest causes of failure in a business, especially a small one, is poor management. Table 5.1 indicates the main causes.

Table 5.1: Causes of business failure

Percentage of business failure	Cause of failure	Explanation
40%	Managerial incompetence	Inability to run the business, either physically, morally or intellectually
30%	Lack of leadership	Inability to think strategically and to bring about change in the organisation
20%	Lack of managerial experience	Little, if any, experience managing employees and other resources before going into business
10%	No industry experience	Little, if any, experience in the product or service before going into business

It is becoming more and more widely recognised and accepted that the performance and success of an organisation, whether large or small, profit-making or non-profit-making, private or public, depends on the quality of its management. Management is therefore indispensable to any business for the following reasons:

- **Management directs a business towards its goals.** Without the input of managers, the resources of the business would not be channelled towards reaching its goals, and in a market economy few businesses are able to reach their profit objectives without managers. No business can survive if it cannot make a profit. In short, a business cannot maintain the purpose for its existence without effective management.

Typical management tasks

- Who decides where the next Standard Bank branch will be established? Management.
- In a modest restaurant, who sees that there are adequate funds, equipment, raw materials and staff available to perform the various functions? Management, even when the manager is also the owner of the business.
- Who decides whether South African Airways will increase or reduce the number of its flights to London? Management

- **Management sets and keeps the operations of the business on a balanced course.** In the microenvironment – that is, within the business itself – a balance must be maintained between the goals of the business, the resources it needs to realise those objectives, the personal goals of the employees, and the interests of the owners. Table 5.2 shows four basic kinds of resources found in organisations, namely human resources, financial resources, physical resources such as equipment and raw materials, and information or knowledge resources. Management is necessary to combine and direct the resources of different organisations so that each can achieve its goals as efficiently or productively as possible.

Table 5.2: The basic resources used by an organisation

Organisation	Human resources	Financial resources	Physical resources	Information resources
Sasol	Managers, engineers, technical and administrative staff	Profits, shareholders' equity, loans	Refineries, coalfields, plant	Forecasts, market information
University of South Africa	Teaching and administrative staff	State subsidies, contributions from the private sector	Buildings, libraries, computers	Research reports, annual reports, calendars
City of Tshwane (Pretoria)	Engineers, lawyers, doctors, technicians, administrative staff	Municipal rates and taxes, fines	Buildings, cleaning services, waterworks	Various population statistics, annual reports, budgets
Joe's Café	Owner-manager, members of family, worker	Profits, owner's equity	Counters, shelves, tills	Price-lists, newspaper advertisements

Source: Griffin, R.W., *Management*, Houghton Mifflin Company, 1990.

To Sasol, the primary goal may be a certain profit margin or return on investment, while the management of the University of South Africa will see its goals as improving its teaching through more student support, and better research and service to the community. The management of the City of Tshwane may have as its goal making Pretoria a safer and cleaner city, while the owner-manager of a small corner shop may be in business to maintain a standard of living for his or her family. For these goals to be reached, management has to strike a proper balance between resources, interests and goals.

- **Management keeps the organisation in equilibrium with its environment.** On the one hand, management adapts the organisation to environmental change, for example, by aligning its employment policy with the requirements of the Employment Equity Act 55 of 1998, or increasing advertising in African languages to communicate with the increased number of black consumers in the market. On the other hand, management may try to achieve a better equilibrium with the environment by trying to change the environment itself, in an attempt to reach its objectives.
- **Management is necessary to reach the goals of the organisation at the highest possible level of productivity.** In chapter 1 we indicated that the economic principle, namely to ensure the greatest possible output with the least possible input, is the reason for the existence of business management.

Thus far, we have shown that management is an indispensable component in the successful functioning of an organisation, especially the business organisation. We now provide a more comprehensive overview of the task of management.

5.3 A definition of management

Management can, quite simply, be defined as the process followed by managers to accomplish a business's goals and objectives. More precisely, it may be said that management is a **process** of activities that are carried out to enable a business to accomplish its **goals** by employing **human, financial and physical resources** for that purpose. Therefore management may be formally defined as **the process whereby human, financial, physical and information resources are employed in order to reach the goals of an organisation**.

Much has been said about the goals and resources of a business, and the fact that management directs the resources to reach the goals. But how does this process manifest itself? What form and sequence does the process or activities assume for the accomplishment of business goals?

Although there is general agreement that management is necessary to direct a business toward its goals, the many definitions offered in the literature on management demonstrate the wide differences of opinion among writers and experts about exactly what the activities of management should be. Most experts, however, single out four fundamental activities as the most important tasks of the management process.

Management does four things: it decides **what** has to be done; it decides **how** this should be done; it **orders** that it be done; and, finally, it **checks** that its orders have been carried out. The management terms used to define these fundamental tasks are planning, organising, leading and control. These are the basic tasks of a manager, and they are linked in the sequence shown in figure 5.1 (see p. 123). It would not make sense to perform them in any other sequence, for managers cannot decide to do something unless they know what should be

Figure 5.1: Basic tasks of management

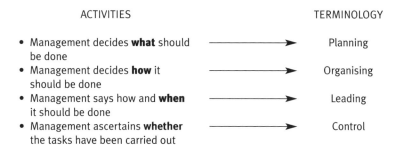

ACTIVITIES		TERMINOLOGY
• Management decides **what** should be done	⟶	Planning
• Management decides **how** it should be done	⟶	Organising
• Management says how and **when** it should be done	⟶	Leading
• Management ascertains **whether** the tasks have been carried out	⟶	Control

done; they cannot order a task to be done until they have decided how it should be done, and they cannot check the results before the orders have been given.

It should be clear at this stage that the fundamental management activities and the resources of a business, as well as its goals, should not be viewed as separate entities, but rather as an integrated process which has to do with the following: planning the goals and the resources to accomplish them, organising the resources and people, leading the people, and, lastly, controlling the resources and the activities of the people.

Figure 5.2 shows management as being an integrated process.

Figure 5.2: The four fundamental management tasks represented as a process

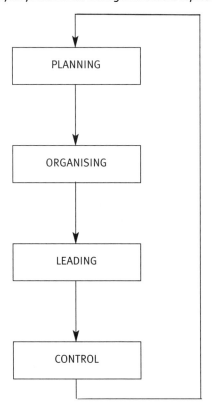

The following brief description of the fundamental management activities elucidates the concept of management and the management process:

- **Planning** determines the mission and goals of the business, including the ways in which the goals are to be reached in the long term, and the resources needed for this task. It includes determining the future position of the business, and guidelines or plans on how that position is to be reached.

- **Organising** is the second step in the management process. After goals and plans have been determined, the human, financial and physical resources of the business have to be allocated by management to the relevant departments or persons, duties must be defined, and procedures fixed, to enable the business to reach its goals. Organising therefore includes developing a framework or organisational structure to indicate how people, equipment and materials should be employed to reach the predetermined goals. Because the goals and resources of different businesses differ greatly, it makes sense that each must have an organisational structure suited to its own peculiar needs.

- **Leading** entails directing the human resources of the business and motivating them. Leaders align the actions of subordinates with the predetermined goals and plans. The part played by leadership in getting and keeping things going, in motivating and influencing staff through good communication and relations between management and staff, and among staff, has a decisive effect on the culture prevailing in a business. Managers do not only give orders. As leaders, they collaborate with their superiors, equals and subordinates, as well as with individuals and groups, to reach the goals of the business.

- **Control** means that managers should constantly establish whether the business is on a proper course towards the accomplishment of its goals. At the same time, it forces management to ensure that activities and performance conform to the plans for reaching predetermined goals. Control also enables management to detect any deviations from the plans and to correct them. It also obliges management to constantly reconsider its goals and plans.

Figure 5.2 illustrates the management process as a logical sequence of actions. It is, however, important to realise that the functions of management do not occur in a tidy, step-by-step order. Managers do not plan on a Monday, organise on a Tuesday, lead on Wednesday and control on Friday. At any given time a manager is likely to be engaged in several management activities simultaneously.

The management process and the four elements that it comprises are encountered at all levels and in all departments of the business. These are now examined more closely.

Applying the concept: the tasks of management

George Mahlangu completed his BCom at Unisa and was working for a local authority as a clerk in the electricity department. He was frustrated because his supervisor told him that his degree would not be of any advantage since there were no positions available to which he could be promoted. Moreover, he had been in his present position for the past six years.

So, when George's aunt asked him to come and help her build up the very successful little knitting factory she had started three years earlier, he was interested. His aunt told him that since Malome (his uncle) had died the previous year, it had become very difficult for her to keep the staff together and to process the many orders they received for jerseys. Despite the demand for their quality products at a very reasonable price, they were unable to keep things running as smoothly as before.

George accepted the position as assistant manager and joined the business at the beginning of March – when the first deliveries of orders for winter stock needed to be made. George found the little factory in disarray: no-one knew what objectives to achieve, who to turn to for advice and authority, what quantities to deliver, or what standards to adhere to. He observed that they were not planning what needed to be done, that resource allocation was haphazard, that no one was taking leadership, and that there was virtually no control over any activities. He decided that the most important problem was the lack of a proper management process, and that such a process should be implemented immediately.

If you were in George's position, how would you explain the basic tasks of a manager to his aunt?

5.4 The different levels and types of management in businesses

Managers are found not only at the top of a business hierarchy, but at all its levels. Thus, each manager is in charge of a number of managers under him or her and they, in turn, are in charge of a number of subordinates. A business also has different types of managers, each responsible for the management of a more or less specialised group of activities. Figure 5.3 (see p. 126) indicates the integrated management process.

5.4.1 The different levels of management

As shown in figure 5.4 (see p. 126), several levels of management may be identified. For the sake of convenience and ease of explanation, however, only three levels are represented, namely top, middle and lower management.

Figure 5.3: The integrated management process

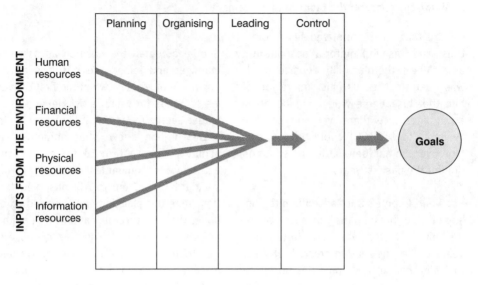

Source: Griffin, R.W., *Management*, Houghton Mifflin Company, 1990, p.7.

Top management comprises the relatively small group of executives who control the business and in whom the final authority and responsibility for the execution of the management process rests, for example, the board of directors, the partners, the managing director and the chief executive, as well as any

Figure 5.4: Different levels and types of management in a business or organisation

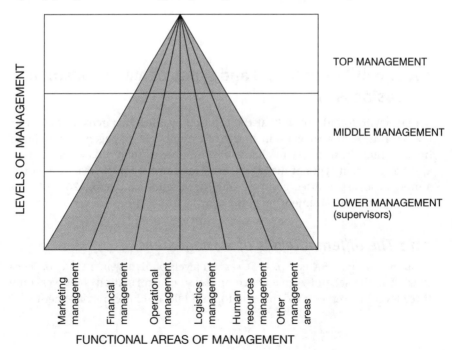

management committees consisting mainly of members of top management. Top management is normally responsible for the business as a whole and for determining its mission and goals. It is concerned mainly with long-term planning, with organising insofar as the broad business structure is concerned, and with providing leadership and controlling the business by means of reports and audits. Top management also monitors the environment within which the organisation operates.

Middle management is responsible for certain functional areas of the business, and is primarily accountable for executing the policies, plans and strategies determined by top management. Normally, middle management consists of functional heads, such as the marketing manager, the purchasing manager, the personnel manager, and so on. Middle management is therefore responsible for medium- and long-term planning and organising within its own functional areas, as well as for control of its management activities. It should at all times also monitor environmental influences that may affect its sphere of operations.

Lower management, also referred to as supervisory management, is responsible for still smaller segments of the business, for example, the various subsections that form part of a department. For instance, the marketing department may have a product manager, a promotions manager or a sales manager for certain areas. Supervisors and foremen are included in lower management. Their duties mainly involve the day-to-day activities and tasks of a particular section, short-term planning, and implementing the plans of middle management. Lower management supervises the finer details of organising, such as allocating tasks on a daily basis. They guide staff in their own subsections and keep close control over their activities. Lower management is often called line management; it is the first management level to which subordinates from operational ranks are promoted. They then devote most of their time to supervising their subordinates.

For the sake of simplicity and convenience, we have distinguished only three levels of management, but in practice the number of levels is determined largely, though not exclusively, by the size of the organisation. The main reason for this is a limit to the number of people whom one person can manage effectively. A one-person business, for example, has only one level of management, in which the functions of upper, middle and lower management are combined in the person of the owner. A very large business employing thousands of workers may well comprise far more than three levels.

In chapter 7 we will discuss this question further in our examination of organisational structures.

5.4.2 The different types of managers in a business organisation

Figure 5.4 showed the different levels of management and the different types, or functional areas, of management that may be distinguished, irrespective of level. **Functional management** refers to specialised managers who are necessary for the different functions of the business. Functional managers are only responsible for the specific management activities of their functions or departments.

Marketing management, for example, is responsible for the following:

- **Planning** the activities of the marketing department. This means that marketing objectives, for example a 10% increase in market share by 2005, are carried out in accordance with the goals and objectives of the business as a whole, and plans are devised to reach those goals.
- **Organising** marketing activities, such as the allocation of tasks to persons so that certain objectives can be attained
- The assumption of **leadership** of marketing activities. This entails motivating and giving orders to marketing staff in order to accomplish the goals and objectives, and also, where necessary, providing guidelines.
- **Controlling** marketing activities, for example, measuring the results and costs of a campaign against its objectives

In the same way, financial management, human resources management, logistics management, and other functional managements plan, organise, lead and control their departments. Many organisational functions may be identified, depending on the required number of specialist areas that a business may need. In practice, the number and importance of these specialised areas vary from business to business. There is, however, only one organisational function, that of general management, that is universally encountered, and that has a definite part to play in every organisation. Some examples of management levels are given in the accompanying box.

Management levels: some examples

- The Roman Catholic Church, an organisation with millions of members, has only four levels between Pope and priest.
- Sears and Mitsukoshi, the largest retailers in the world, are generally considered remarkable for their limited number of management levels.
- There are seven distinct levels of management in the USA armed forces.

Source: Mescon M.H., *Management*, Harper & Row, New York, 1985, p. 20.

5.4.3 The function of general management

One function not shown vertically in figure 5.4, but which is nevertheless identified as a separate function in the literature, and occurs in every business, is that of **general management**. General management differs from other specialised functions in that it integrates all the others. It deals particularly with the activities of top management, while at the same time manifesting itself in other functions, as in the case of marketing management. General management is therefore the overriding function that controls the management process and the general principles of management as applied by top management.

The same elements of the management process and the general principles of management also affect the other functions, however. This means that all managers in the business should have a thorough knowledge of the management process and its general principles in order to be able to manage their own specialised functions more efficiently. For this reason, general management is discussed as an introduction to the other functions in this chapter, and again in chapters 6, 7, 8 and 12.

A question that may justifiably be asked is whether there is any difference between business management as a subject of study and the management process. The answer is, decidedly, yes. Business management is the science that examines all the things that affect the productive and profitable operations of a business. It considers not only the management process, but also the external environmental factors that can influence it, as well as the specialised management areas and various disciplines and techniques. In contrast, the study of the actual management process of a business is only one component of business management. It only examines the management process and the general management principles that enable the business to accomplish its goals and objectives as effectively as possible.

We have described the management process, the levels of management, the functions in which the management process takes place, as well as the unique position and nature of general management. The skills required of managers in executing the management process, and the roles they play in the business, will now be considered in greater detail.

5.5 Skills needed at different managerial levels

Although management is found at all levels and in all functions of a business, the personal skills needed to do the job differ at each level. Figure 5.5 depicts the different skills.

Figure 5.5: The skills needed at various managerial levels

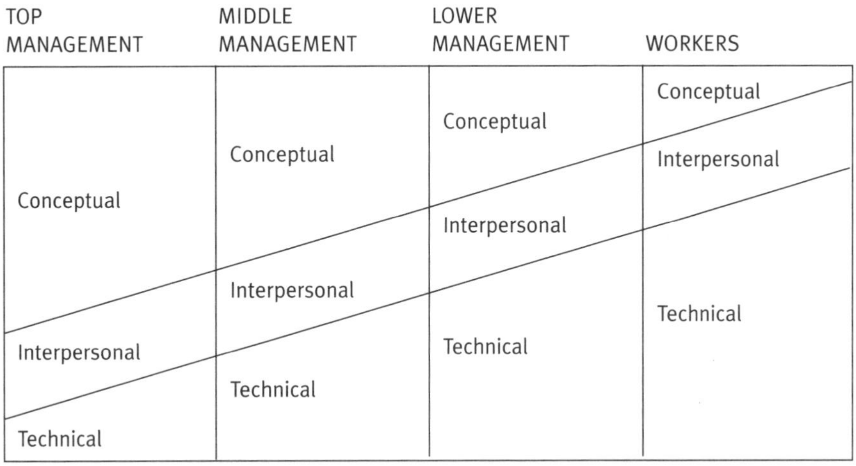

The skills and abilities necessary for top management to carry out the functions of general management are different from those required by lower management. Three key skills are identified as prerequisites for sound management:[1]

- **Conceptual skills,** that is, the mental capacity to view the business and its parts in a holistic manner. Conceptual skills involve the manager's thinking and planning abilities.

- **Interpersonal skills**, or the ability to work with other people. Since management is about dealing with people approximately 60% of the time, it is obvious that a manager should be able to communicate with and motivate groups as well as individuals.[2]
- **Technical skills**, that is, the ability to use the knowledge or techniques of a particular discipline. A knowledge of accountancy, or engineering, or economics, is an example of a technical skill that is required to perform a specific task. Managers at lower levels, in particular, should have sufficient knowledge of the technical activities they have to supervise. However, the time spent on technical activities decreases as managers move up the managerial ladder, where **conceptual and analytical skills** assume more importance.

Where do managers acquire these skills? One source is **management education at schools, technikons and universities**. Some businesses also provide their own management training. In the USA there is currently a strong tendency to consider formal academic education in management as a prerequisite for success in business.

Another source of managerial competence is **practical experience**. A natural aptitude for management, as well as self-motivation and ambition play a considerable part in the development of managerial skills.

5.6 The role of managers

Every manager must fulfil a specific role, irrespective of the managerial level or area occupied. A manager, after all, performs certain functions, meets certain needs and assumes certain responsibilities for the business. Mintzberg studied the behaviour of a group of managers and concluded that they fulfil about ten different roles.[3]

Figure 5.6: The overlapping roles of managers

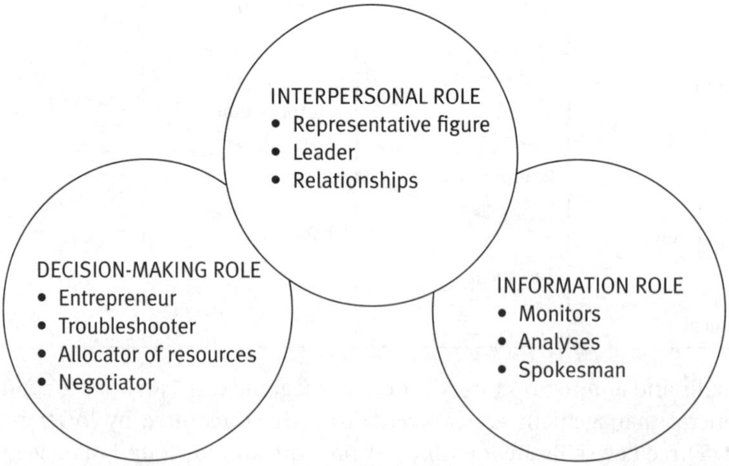

INTERPERSONAL ROLE
- Representative figure
- Leader
- Relationships

DECISION-MAKING ROLE
- Entrepreneur
- Troubleshooter
- Allocator of resources
- Negotiator

INFORMATION ROLE
- Monitors
- Analyses
- Spokesman

As figure 5.6 shows, these roles can be placed in three overlapping groups, namely interpersonal, information and decision-making roles:

- Three groups of activities constitute the **interpersonal role** of managers:

- Acting as the **representative figure** who takes visitors out to dine, attends a colleague's wedding, or opens a new factory
- **Leading** in the appointment, training, performance, promotion, and motivation of subordinates
- **Maintaining good relations** within the organisation and with its public (this role can occupy up to 50% of a manager's time): internal relations involve other managers and individuals; external relations involve suppliers, banks customers, and so on.

- The **information role** enables managers to obtain information from colleagues, subordinates, superiors and people outside the business, to help them make decisions. This role focuses on monitoring or gathering information about change, opportunities or threats that may affect their department. Managers analyse this information and pass relevant data on to colleagues, superiors and subordinates. In this way, they constitute an important link in the business's communication process. The information role also demands that managers act as a spokesperson in their department or business, both internally as well as with the outside world.

- The **decision-making role** involves the gathering and analysis of information. In this respect, managers may be regarded as entrepreneurs who use the information at their disposal to achieve positive change in the form of a new product or idea, or the restructuring of their business.

  They also have to deal with and solve problems such as strikes, shortages and equipment breakdowns. Managers have to decide how to allocate the resources of the business. These include funds, human resources and equipment, and their allocation is often a critical management decision. In their role as negotiators, managers regularly interact with individuals, other departments or businesses to negotiate goals, performance standards, resources and trade union agreements.

By viewing managers from a perspective of the different roles they play in a business organisation, insight is gained into the manager's **tasks**. This is important for the following reasons:[4]

- The concept of **a manager's roles** creates an awareness of what a manager does, and hence what skills are required.
- A manager's seniority in the business largely determines his or her role, and how much time is spent on each activity.
- The concept of role distribution explains why managers cannot systematically move from planning to organising to leading and eventually, to control. The complexity and turbulence of their environment requires a more flexible approach.

The above discussion regarding the management skills required for different management activities, and the role of managers, aims at explaining how management works, and should not be viewed as an exact exposition of a management process, because the variables differ from one business to the next. In addition, the four management tasks discussed in 5.3 above are supplemented by various other activities that also have to be performed by management, again depending on the nature of the business. Besides a knowledge of, and skills in, the four fundamental management elements, management also requires a basic knowledge of supporting management activities.

Although many activities may be identified, four main **supplementary or supporting management activities** are normally distinguished, namely the **gathering and processing of information** to make decisions possible, **decision making, communication and negotiation**. These supplementary activities are not grouped under any of the four management elements because they occur in each element – for example, information is necessary not only for planning but also for organising, and even more so for control. Similarly, management communicates while planning and organising. Communication is an essential component of leadership. In chapter 8 these activities are examined in greater depth.

The nature of management may further be explained by examining the evolution of management thought in the past few decades. This will also help to explain the present status of management and the approach followed in this book.

5.7 Development of management theory

Because management experience and knowledge of the past are important both to present and future management success, it is necessary to provide a brief overview of the development of management theory over the past century. In chapter 1 we briefly outlined the development of business management as a science. The emphasis here was mainly on business management in past centuries, when the entrepreneur both **owned** and **managed** his or her business. In contrast to this, the last century saw the emergence of the professional manager who is paid by the owners to manage the business. The manager's level of remuneration often depends on his or her success in managing the business profitably. Table 5.3 gives an exposition of the state of management in previous centuries as opposed to management in the last century.

Table 5.3: The development of management theory

State of management in previous centuries	State of management during the last century
• A few large organisations, but no mega-organisations	• Many huge and powerful organisations in both the private and public sector
• Comparatively few managers – no middle management	• Many managers – a comparatively large middle management group
• Managerial activities not clearly distinguished from the activities of owners	• Well-defined managerial activities clearly separated from non-managerial activities
• Succession to top management based primarily on birth	• Promotion to top management on a basis of qualifications, competence and performance
• Few decision makers	• Many decision makers
• Emphasis on command and intuition	• Emphasis on leadership, teamwork and rationality

Source: Mescon, M.H., *Management*, Pearson Education Inc.

The concept of the professional manager resulted, among other things, in a number of theories or approaches to management. Management scholars as well as practitioners researched management issues, postulated theories about how best to manage a business organisation, and published their theories or approaches to management.

Although professional management as we know it today is a product of the past century, during its early years there was much uncertainty about what the activities and elements of management actually were. It was only in 1911, with the publication of F.W. Taylor's *Principles of scientific management*, that management was at last placed on a scientific footing.[5] Since then, theories and approaches to management have developed unevenly, with a good deal of overlapping at times. This fitful progress is no doubt attributable to the uneven development of such supplementary disciplines as psychology, sociology and mathematics. With each wave of development in these subjects, new developments and theories in management evolved, which were in turn followed by more knowledge about the factors that determine the success of a business. At the same time, changes in the business environment resulted in the development of new perspectives on existing management theories.

Most of the approaches to management in the literature of even the recent past reveal a great deal of diversity and overlapping of the views of writers and scholars about what can properly be regarded as managerial activities. The inadequacy of academic research during the formative years of management has in recent decades been amply compensated for by an abundance of research and literature. Scholars are all too ready to put forward a wide range of opinions about management. Behaviourists, for example, inspired by the human relations approach of the 1930s, see management as a complex system of interpersonal relations, and psychology as the basis of management theory. Others, again, see sociology as the basis. Some maintain that the essence of management is decision making, with mathematics playing a central role, while others argue that accounting should be the basis of all management principles and theories. The different viewpoints and approaches towards a theory of management are a reflection of the political, economic, social, technological and environmental issues of the time.

It is often asked whether the various theories and viewpoints of the past have any relevance for the contemporary organisation. Among the many theories about how to improve the performance of the organisation, some aspects of each have survived and, indeed, contributed to contemporary theories on management. In this way, the legacy of past successes and failures become part of present and future management approaches. A brief examination of the different theories on management is therefore necessary.

5.7.1 The main schools of thought on management

The existing body of knowledge on management theory or management approaches has emerged from a combination of ongoing research on management issues and the practical experience of certain management scholars. The management theories that have evolved over many decades are referred to as **schools of thought** or **approaches to management**, and are grouped into a number of schools of thought. Each school believed at some stage that it had found the key to management success in terms of productivity and profitability. Later assessments of the various approaches to management, however, demonstrated that these so-called answers to the problems of management were at best only partially correct. Yet, each has made some contribution to the theoretical body of knowledge on management.

The theories of management can be classified into two main schools of thought, namely the **classical approaches** (+ 1910-1950) and the **contemporary approaches** (+1960-present). Figure 5.7 illustrates the development path of management.

Figure 5.7 The evolution of management theory

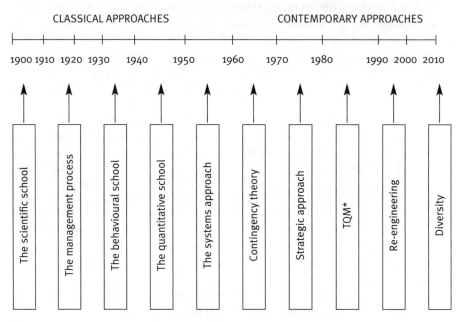

CLASSICAL APPROACHES   CONTEMPORARY APPROACHES

1900 1910 1920 1930   1940   1950   1960   1970   1980   1990 2000 2010

The scientific school · The management process · The behavioural school · The quantitative school · The systems approach · Contingency theory · Strategic approach · TQM* · Re-engineering · Diversity

* Total quality management

- The contribution of the **scientific school** is especially associated with the work of F.W. Taylor (1856-1915). He was an engineer at a steelworks in Philadelphia, and believed that a scientific approach to any task would greatly increase the productivity with which it was carried out. Through the scientific application of observation, job analysis, job measurement, the redesigning of jobs, and financial incentives (by paying workers according to their output), he and his colleagues proved that the productivity of a business could indeed be increased. Although research was confined to workers and lower management levels, this school made a valuable conceptual contribution in that managers and academics became convinced that scientific approaches and methods could be applied in productive ways to attain the goals of an organisation.

- The **management process school**, by contrast, concentrated on top management. Its method was to identify the most important functions in a business and the most important elements of management, so that universal principles of management could be developed for each function and element. The theory was that the application of universal management principles would take any business towards its goals. Henri Fayol (1841-1925) was the originator of this approach. His personal contribution included the identification of six functions of a business: the technical (production-operational management) function, the commercial function (purchasing and marketing), the financial function, an accountancy function, a security function (protection of property) and the function of general management. This functional approach, albeit in a modified form, still receives wide support and offers the following advantages:
  - It systematises the great variety of activities and problems in a business.
  - It facilitates the internal organisation of a business by classifying activities into departments according to their functions.
  - It facilitates management by making it possible to appoint people with the right qualifications to the various functional departments.
  - It makes the study of management science considerably easier by grouping similar problems. (This book, for example, is classified functionally.)

  Fayol also identified the following fundamental elements of the management process: planning, organising, leading, coordinating and control. This description of the management process is still accepted today.
- The **human relations or behavioural school** came into being because of the failure of the scientific and classical management process schools to make an adequate study of the human element as an important factor in the effective accomplishment of the goals and objectives of a business. Elton Mayo (1880-1949) found that increased productivity was not always attributable, as the scientific school believed, to a well-designed task and sufficiently high wages. It could also be attributed to such factors as the relationship between people in the business – between management and workers, and between workers themselves in a particular group. The basic premise of this school is that psychological and sociological factors are no less important than physical factors in the attainment of the goals of a business. Research into social interaction, motivation, power relations, organisational design and communications forms the basis for the contributions by this school, which are particularly valuable in the area of personnel management.
- The **quantitative school** sees management primarily as a system of mathematical models and processes. It is largely composed of operational researchers or decision experts who believe that if management or any elements of it are at all a logical process, then this should be expressible as mathematical relations. The contribution of this school, particularly in the development of models for the running of complex processes, is important, but should be regarded as an aid to management rather than as a separate school of management theory.

- The **systems approach** to management developed in the 1950s. This approach compensated for the main limitations of the previous approaches, namely that they ignored the relationship between the organisation and its external environment, and secondly, that they focused on only one aspect of the organisation at the expense of other areas. Some managers would, for example, focus only on financial aspects and neglect the organisation's market and customers. To overcome these shortcomings, management scholars developed systems theory, which views the organisation as a group of interrelated parts with a single purpose, where the actions of one part influence the other parts.

  Managers cannot therefore manage the separate parts independently, but should rather do so as an integrated whole. This approach was the forerunner of the concept of strategic management.

- The **contingency approach** seeks to eliminate the defects of other theories. Like the systems approach, it attempts to integrate the ideas of the different schools. The basic premise of the contingency approach is that the application of management principles depends essentially on a particular situation confronting management at a particular moment. In a given situation, management will decide to apply the principles of the functional, quantitative or behaviourist school, or combinations of these. In other words, the contingency approach attempts to adapt the available techniques and principles provided by the various management approaches to a given situation, so as to reach the objectives of the business as productively as possible. It may be said that this approach does not really recognise the existence of universal principles of management, but instead concentrates on whatever means are available to solve problems.

5.7.2 Some contemporary approaches to management

During the second half of the last century the environment in which business organisations operated began to change at an increasing rate, as explained in chapter 4. Because of the rapidly changing environment, new issues and challenges emerged, and so, too, did new approaches to management. The contemporary schools of thought were ushered in by the concept of strategic management, followed by a number of contemporary approaches:

- **Strategic management** as an approach to organisational success evolved from the turbulent environments of the 1960s and 1970s. The pace of technological change, the emergence of Japan and other new post-World War II economies, demographic change, as well as other political and social trends, forced management to align the goals and objectives of their organisations with trends in the business environment. By focusing on the threats and opportunities in the environment, and evaluating its strengths and weaknesses in order to overcome the threats and exploit the opportunities, the organisation builds a distinct competence in a particular market. During the early years of the strategic management approach, large organisations had to make big strategic planning decisions. Since the 1980s, however, many of these decisions have been abandoned because today every manager in the organisation is required to think and act strategically. Today, businesses involve managers from all levels of the organisation in the strategic planning process.

- **Total quality management (TQM).** One of the contemporary management approaches that evolved during the late 1980s and the 1990s revolves around the matter of quality. American managers examined the success of their German and Japanese counterparts in the American market, and found that the latter were obsessed with quality. What further inspired management scholars was the fact that Japanese and German managers not only delivered top quality products and services, but did so at a higher rate of productivity.

- The management theories that evolved in the 1990s relate to the concepts of the **learning organisation** and the **re-engineering** of businesses. The **learning organisation** is a management approach that requires learning individuals. The inability to learn can cripple an organisation. **Re-engineering** is a management approach

> "Learning disabilities are tragic in children, but they are fatal in organisations. Because of this, few organisations live even half as long as a person."
>
> *PETER SENGE*

that forces the organisation to focus on its core business and to outsource those activities that do not relate to the core business. Since the 1990s, most organisations have reduced the size of their workforce by outsourcing activities such as the company cafeteria, garden services, maintenance, and a host of activities that are unrelated to the organisation's core business.

- **Diversity management** is another important challenge to contemporary management. In South Africa, the management of diversity is partly enforced by the Employment Equity Act 55 of 1998. Management in Africa will, in due course, develop a management approach with a body of knowledge that is peculiar to the needs and cultural diversity of the continent.

Ubuntu: an African perspective

The upbringing and socialisation of individuals in African society have always emphasised interpersonal, informational and decision-making roles. Interpersonal roles are subsumed in the notion of **ubuntu** in Zulu and Xhosa, **unhu** in Shona, **botho** in Tswana, **broederbond** in Afrikaans, **bunhu** in Tsonga, **vhuthu** in Venda, and **brotherhood** in English. Thus, **ubuntu** is a literal translation of the notion of collective personhood and collective morality.

Therefore, a leader (**mutungamiri** in Shona, and **umukhokheli** in Zulu) guided by the **ubuntu** philosophy is expected to inform and communicate with his or her own group and to be their mouthpiece in external communication. Decision making is the hallmark of leadership, which involves analysis of the situation at hand, in consultation with others, and guiding the process until a course of action is selected.

Source: Mbigi, L., *Ubuntu: the African dream in management*, Knowledge Resources, Randburg.

Management approaches and theories are important instruments in broadening knowledge about management. The student of management will, accordingly, be equipped to take a critical view of new ideas and new approaches to management.

Management in the new millennium

Businesses today are exposed to a number of revolutionary forces: technological change, global competition, demographic change and trends towards a service society and the information age. Forces like these have changed the playing field on which businesses must compete. In particular, they have dramatically increased the need for businesses to be responsive, flexible and capable of competing in a global market. To be able to do this, management experts have predicted that the "new organisation" will have the following characteristics:

- The average business will be smaller and employ fewer people.
- The traditional pyramid-shaped business will give way to new organisational structures. In the boundaryless business, employees will no longer identify with separate departments, but instead interact with whoever they need to in order to get the job done.
- Employees at all levels will be called on to make more and more decisions.
- "Flatter" organisations will be the norm.
- Work will be organised around teams and processes, rather than specialised functional sections.
- The basis of power will change. Competency and knowledge, not titles, will be the basis of power.
- The new business will be knowledge based.
- Management will empower employees.
- Managers will have to become agents of change.

Source: Dessler, G., *Managing organisations*, The Dryden Press, Fort Worth, 1995, pp. 16-18.

5.7.3 Conclusion

The above examination of how management theory has evolved and contributed to the broader body of knowledge on management clearly shows that there is no single uniform and consistent theory of management that may be universally accepted and applied. However, understanding the historical context provides us with a broad perspective of the vastness of the body of knowledge, particularly with regard to the research, principles, problems and approaches to management, which managers can draw on.

We have adopted the process paradigm in this chapter because it offers a conceptual framework for the study of management, it simplifies the subject, and it favours the development of a universal theory of management.

5.8 Summary

This is the first of eight chapters dealing with general principles of management. We have learned that management is an indispensable component of any organisation without which its resources cannot be properly utilised to reach its goals and objectives. In addition, we have defined management as a process that consists of four fundamental elements or management activities: planning, organising, leading and controlling.

Management – that is, the process of planning, organising, leading and controlling – also represents a distinct function, namely **general management**, which, at the top level, predominates, and also coordinates other management areas. At middle and lower management levels the management process is evident in every business function. Each level of management requires certain skills, and the roles played by managers differ from one level to the next.

Our examination of the evolution of management theory and the various approaches to it has shown how the different schools of thought have contributed to the vast body of management knowledge. The process approach, which distinguishes four elements of management and seven functions within a business, forms the basis of this book. In the next seven chapters the various elements of the management process will be examined more closely.

References

1. Griffin, R.W., *Management*, Houghton Mifflen Co., Boston, 1990, pp. 18-23.
2. *Ibid.*, p. 19.
3. Mintzberg, H., The nature of managerial work, as quoted in Donnely, J. H., Gibson, J. C. & Ivancevich, J. M., *Fundamentals of management*, Business Publications, Plano, Texas, 1987, p. 28.
4. Griffin, R. W., *op. cit.*, p. 18.
5. Mescon, M. H., *Management*, Harper & Row, New York, 1985, p. 43.

6 The basic elements of planning

The purpose of this chapter

This chapter gives an overview of the first fundamental element of the management process. In fact, planning predetermines what the business proposes to accomplish (the development of the mission and goals), and determines how this will be achieved by making and implementing various plans. Chapter 6 covers the importance of planning, the planning process, goals and the development of goals, as well as the development of plans. The different types of plans, from long term or strategic plans to functional and operational plans, are examined. Some elementary strategies are also explained.

Learning outcomes

The content of this chapter will enable learners to:
- Explain the nature of planning as a management task
- Describe the importance of planning as the first step in the management process
- Describe the planning process
- Interpret meaningfully the importance of goals
- Describe the different organisational goals
- Depict the hierarchy of goals
- Differentiate between strategic, functional and operational planning
- Recommend different strategies to accomplish different goals

6.1 Introduction to planning

In chapter 5 we identified **planning** as the starting point of the management process. This is the fundamental element of management that predetermines what the business proposes to accomplish and how it intends realising its goals. In other words, planning involves those activities of management that determine the mission and goals of an organisation, the ways in which these are to be accomplished, and the deployment of the necessary resources to realise them. In short, planning entails a systematic and intelligent exposition of the direction a business organisation must follow to accomplish predetermined goals. Planning encapsulates the following three dimensions:
- **The determination dimension.** The business must determine what it wants to achieve by a specific date in the future. This means that goals have to be formulated that will serve as guidelines for the business and its various departments and sub-departments.

- **The decision-making dimension.** The goals determine the actions that are necessary, or the way in which they might be accomplished. In other words, management has to decide what resources (human, financial, knowledge) should be deployed in order to reach these goals, in what combinations, and over what period. This primarily means a choice between alternative ways of accomplishing the goals.
- **The future dimension.** A goal is something to be accomplished in the future. Planning establishes a connection between the things that have to be done now to bring about a certain situation in the future. This future dimension of planning is also intended to cope with change in the business environment. This dimension enables the organisation to be proactive in its interaction with its external environment.

As a fundamental element of management, planning is not only the starting point of the management process, but in a sense also the point around which management activities revolve. The goals and the plans determine the type of organisation needed, the leadership required, and the control to be exercised to steer the business as productively as possible towards its goals.

6.2 The importance of planning

It is clear that planning forms the basis of all the tasks of management, because it gives the business its direction and determines the actions of management. Without planning, organising would be haphazard, and it would be extremely difficult to lead subordinates and explain clearly where the business is heading. Moreover, any control measures would only be subjective, as there would be no norms or standards against which to judge actual performance. Planning is indispensable for the following reasons:

- **Planning gives direction.** Probably the most important contribution that planning makes to the managerial process is that it gives direction to the organisation in the form of goals, on the one hand, and in the form of plans indicating how to set about achieving them, on the other. At the same time, it clarifies the goals and determines their feasibility. In short, planning shows whether the business is doing the right thing. In the process, it eliminates all uncertainties and guesswork, thereby reducing risks.

Getting it right

Many businesses impress with their ability to turn out large quantities of products at a low unit cost and in a short time. That is, they do the thing right. Yet it is often these very businesses that fail to show a profit – probably because they are not in fact doing the right thing, although they are perfectly capable of getting it right.

- **Planning promotes coordination** between the various departments and people in the business. Once goals have been clearly formulated and plans have been developed, tasks and resources can be allocated so that everybody involved is able to contribute effectively to the realisation of the goals. Scarce resources can be channelled and utilised rationally, which is absolutely necessary for the productivity and ultimate profitability of the business.

- **Planning compels managers to look to the future.** It eliminates crisis management by obliging future-oriented management to anticipate threats in the environment, and to take steps in time to avert them. By looking back over the past and forward to the future, management can organise the present so that the future will be as prosperous as possible.

Looking to the future

Too many managers are so obsessed with the present that they spend too little time contemplating the future. They are like a woodcutter who has no time to sharpen his axe because he is too busy cutting down trees.

- **Planning ensures that businesses keep abreast of technology.** The influence of modern technology on contemporary businesses, especially in the development of complex products using complicated processes, makes heavy demands on planning. It takes about ten years to develop a supersonic aircraft or a military helicopter. It is very expensive in both time and money to launch such a project, and proper planning is critical to its success.
- **Planning ensures cohesion.** The increasing complexity of businesses and the interdependence of various functional management areas such as marketing, finance and production, where decisions cannot be made in isolation, also emphasise the necessity of planning. Planning enables top management to see the business as a total system in which the objectives of different functions are reconcilable with one another as well as with the primary endeavours and objectives of the business as a whole.
- **Planning promotes stability.** Probably the most important single factor – even in smaller or less complex businesses – that makes planning indispensable is rapid change in the business environment. Indeed, strategic planning has its origins in the very instability that has been one of the main characteristics of the business environment since the 1960s. Planning, therefore, encourages proactive management. In other words, management plays an active part in the future of the business.

Stressing the importance of planning as the point of departure in the management process helps to explain its nature. We will now consider it as a process.

6.3 The planning process

A goal or objective is a desirable state of affairs that a business aims to achieve at some point in the future. A plan is the means by which the goal is to be realised. Planning is therefore a complex process consisting of various activities.

As a process in its own right, planning may be seen as the identification and formulation of the goal of a business, followed by decision making to choose the right plan to achieve the goals, and then the implementation of the selected plan. Implementation of the plan means putting it into operation by organising tasks and departments for the purpose, taking the lead to set the plan in motion, and, finally, exercising control. In short, implementation means the execution of the plan throughout the management process. Figure 6.1 below illustrates the planning process.

What has to be clearly understood is that, although planning is a process in its own right, it does not take place in isolation, but rather in close relation to the other elements of the management process. Consider the following:

- Without planning, the next step in the management process, **organising**, cannot be taken. This is because without definite goals and plans to reach the goals, the human and physical resources of the business cannot be deployed in the most effective way to produce its products or services as profitably as possible.
- **Effective leadership** is also not possible unless the necessary planning has been done, for without goals and plans to accomplish them, people cannot be instructed and encouraged to carry out their tasks as productively as possible.
- **Control**, the last element in the management process, is closely related to planning. A good plan can achieve nothing by itself, and depends not only on effective organisation and leadership in order to be carried out, but also on effective control. If there is deviation from the plan, control will reveal this, and then reactive planning is necessary – that is, the goal and the resources required have to be reconsidered. Planning is therefore intimately bound up with organising, leading and controlling, though there is a particularly close connection between planning and control.

Figure 6.1: The planning process

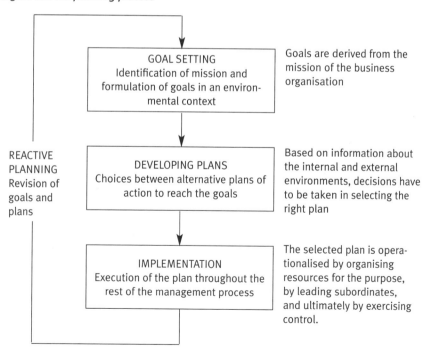

Planning does not take place in isolation; it is a dynamic process in which the deployment of the resources of the business and the influences of the business environment are constantly scrutinised. It is important to know that all organisations engage in a planning process, but no two organisations plan in the same way. Figure 6.1 represents the planning process that most organisations follow. Against this background, the planning process can now be examined at greater length. We will begin with the setting of the mission and goals of the business organisation.

6.4 Organisational goals

6.4.1 The importance of goals

An organisational goal may be defined as a particular future state of things to be achieved by the business. Goals serve various important purposes. Firstly, they provide direction for everyone in the organisation. Goals can help everyone understand where the organisation is going. A university or bank or clothing manufacturer that does not know where it wants to be in three or five years will not be able to formulate any plan to get there. Secondly, goals affect other aspects of planning in the organisation. A strong growth goal, for example, encourages marketing management to look for new marketing opportunities. Thirdly, goals serve as motivation for people to achieve, especially if they are rewarded when they achieve the goals for which they are responsible. Finally, goals provide a benchmark for performance measurement and control purposes. It is not possible to measure goal achievement if no goals have been set or if the goals are not clear.

6.4.2 The formulation of goals

Goals are not set in isolation, but in relation to the four factors that form the basis of planning, namely the **mission** of the organisation (which describes the organisation's purpose), the **environment** in which the organisation operates, the **values** held by management, and the experience that management has gained. These four factors are relevant in setting realistic organisational goals. A change in any of them influences the organisation's goals.

- The **mission** of an organisation is a statement made by the owners and managers of the organisation that defines the purpose of the organisation in terms of the product or service it produces, the market it serves and the technology it applies in serving the market. The mission therefore describes those characteristics of the business that set it apart from other business organisations. The mission gives direction to the activities of the business and is a concise organisational outline of who it is, what it does and where it is heading. Sun International's mission stresses its superior entertainment facilities as the factor that sets it apart from City Lodge, which focuses instead on a "no frills" concept and tariffs that are below those of full-service hotels. It is clear that any goal that is set should be derived from the mission.
- The **business environment**, as discussed in chapter 4, impacts in various ways on organisations, and therefore on the goals that organisations set.

The current focus of society on gender equality has forced many South African organisations to reconsider their employment goals. Although it has no control over the environment, an organisation nevertheless has to assess environmental trends carefully in order to plan realistically, and this obviously includes periodically revising its mission and goals in terms of changes in the environment. Anticipating change in the environment results in proactive planning.

- Managerial **values** have an important influence on the formulation of goals. The values of management may vary from the ethical standards held, to how the organisation treats its employees, to its position on social welfare. The mission statements of Sun International and City Lodge reflect divergent managerial values. Whereas the management of Sun International sees gambling as an important facility it offers its customers, City Lodge does not pursue this line of business. Values therefore have a profound effect on the goals of an organisation.
- The **experience** of management is a further factor that influences the formulation of goals is. The experience that management has of a specific market or industry will affect the formulation of goals relating to that market.

With the above factors in mind, management can now formulate goals for the organisation. It is, however, important to know that organisations establish different kinds of goals. These goals vary according to organisational level and time frame.

6.4.3 The different organisational goals

There are basically two sets of goals in any organisation. The one set of goals may be described as organisational goals that include the mission, long-term strategic goals, as well as tactical and operational goals. These goals form the basis of organisational planning and direct the organisation towards the accomplishment of its mission. However, the organisation consists of people who have their own private aspirations and personal goals. Although personal goals in an organisation are of no direct concern to management, they nevertheless have an enormous influence on the accomplishment of the organisational goals, and management should be aware of this.

Organisational goals should flow directly from the mission statement of an organisation. If, for example, the mission statement or overall strategic goal of a hospital is to offer a full range of medical services to the eastern suburbs of Pretoria within six years, the following goals would be appropriate:

- To increase the number of beds by 180 within the next three years
- To increase operational productivity by 20% over the next two years
- To install surgery units, which will include a full range of heart surgery, within five years

More specific short-term goals should then be formulated to accomplish the above longer term goals. Figure 6.2 (see p. 146) depicts the different kinds of goals and the levels at which they are encountered in the organisation.

Figure 6.2: Different organisational goals and the levels at which they occur

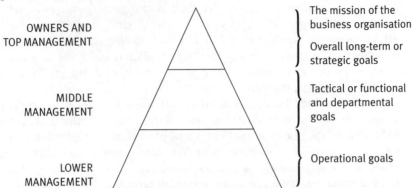

According to figure 6.2 the following kinds of goals are encountered at various levels in the organisation:

- The **mission** of the business organisation is formulated by the owners and top management. The mission or overarching goal defines the organisation in terms of its unique combination of products, markets and technology, which sets it apart from other organisations operating in the same industry. Long-term strategic goals are derived from the mission and are formulated by the top management. These long-term goals are more specific than the broad guidelines implicit in the mission. For example, the mission of a hotel group may be to make a profit for the owners by providing economical accommodation in key urban areas. From this, more precise and detailed long-term goals are derived, for example, to expand its share of the market over the next five years from 15% to 25%, or to raise its return on investment from 8% to 12%. Table 6.1 gives examples of such long-term goals. In considering long-term or strategic plans, top management usually includes goals in such critical areas as profitability, productivity, competitive position, human resources development, human relations, technological leadership, and social responsibility. The strategic goals must be clear, since the tactical goals are derived from them.

- **Functional or tactical goals.** These refer particularly to those set at middle management level and by managers in each functional area. Tactical goals focus on how to carry out tasks necessary to the achievement of strategic goals. They are, by their very nature, medium-term or short-term goals derived from the long-term objectives, for example: in order to increase market share from 10% to 20% over the next four years, sales will have to be increased in urban areas by 18% a year, present production facilities will have to be expanded by 30%, and additional staff will have to be appointed.

- **Operational goals.** Operational goals are set by lower level management. These are short-term goals concerning such matters as sales for a particular month or quarter, or additional temporary workers to cope with the Christmas holiday period.

Table 6.1 Examples of missions and long-term (strategic), functional (tactical) and operational goals

Kind of goal	The Lodge hotel group	Hospital	University
Mission	• To provide affordable accommodation in urban areas	• To provide a complete range of medical services to patients	• To provide academic tuition and research to serve the needs of the community
Long-term (strategic or overall) goals (5-10 years)	• Offer investors returns of 15% over the next 10 years • Expand market share from 15% to 25% over the next five years • Improve image of affordable accommodation	• Achieve return on total capital of 16% p.a. • Establish image as best provider of medical services	• Create facilities to accommodate growth of 6% p.a. over next five years • Raise contributions by private sector by 10% p.a. over next six years
Tactical or functional goals (1-3 years)	• Raise room occupancy by 15% over next two years (marketing objective) • Increase restaurant turnover by 10% over next two years • Reduce staff turnover by 3% over next three years (human resources objective)	• Increase number of beds by 175 over next two years (production objective) • Limit increase in patient costs to 5% next year • Repay expensive loan over next 18 months (financial objective)	• Raise teaching productivity by 3% p.a. over next three years • Establish image of academic excellence over next 36 months • Build up research fund to R50m over next two years
Operational short-term goals (1 year at most)	• Launch 6-month advertising campaign aimed at December holiday-makers • Take on 200 additional employees for December • Extend restaurant hours over Easter weekend	• Take on additional temporary nursing staff for Easter weekend • Increase supply of blood plasma by 30% for Christmas weekend	• Keep library open until 10 p.m. during October • Next January provide additional student guidance during registration

The second set of objectives within the business comprises the **personal goals of employees,** that is, the goals that employees hope to accomplish as a result of their activities and involvement in the business. Examples are a basic salary and a particular status or opportunity for self-development. Conflict may arise if organisational and personal goals cannot be reconciled. Employees working for financial benefits, and who realise that it is possible to achieve a higher income if the business is successful, will work harder to meet organisational objectives so that their personal goals can be accomplished.

With these different objectives in mind, we will now briefly consider the setting of goals.

6.5 Setting goals

In formulating goals for the business organisation or a department or a particular project, management first has to satisfy the following requirements:

- Management must clearly understand the importance of goals because:
  - Goals provide **guidance and unanimity**. They spell out to everyone the direction of the business and the importance of achieving goals. Without goals, a business is like a ship without a rudder.
  - Setting realistic goals facilitates planning.
  - Goals can inspire and motivate subordinates, especially if their achievement is linked to remuneration.
  - Goals provide an effective means of evaluation and control.
- Goals should accurately represent the details of what is being pursued. This means that goals have to be **measurable**, so that managers can check whether they are being accomplished when comparing results with predetermined goals. This is especially true for tactical and functional goals. To say, for example, that market share should be increased is too vague and not measurable, whereas to say that market share should be increased by 10% over the next two years in Gauteng is precise and measurable.

> "If you do not know where you're going, any road will take you there."
>
> *THEODORE LEVITT*

- Not only should goals be precise, but the **responsibility** for reaching them should be clearly assigned to specific individuals. Each manager, however, generally has responsibilities for setting goals at his or her level in the organisation. This means that the relation between the expected results and the persons responsible for them should be clearly stated, so that managers fully understand the aims and goals and are in no doubt about what they have to do to achieve them.
- Goals should be set **consistently**, that is, not in conflict with one another. **Horizontal consistency** refers to the compatibility of the objectives of various departments with one another. If, for example, the marketing department proposes to extend its line of products, the costs of production will increase, and therefore the production division will find it difficult to embark on cost cutting as one of its goals. **Vertical consistency** means that departmental goals are compatible with those of subsections. For example, an increase of 8% in sales set by marketing has to be compatible with the sales objectives set for certain geographical markets of the business – in other words, the total increase in sales for the particular regions should add up to 8%.
- Goal setting must be integrated with **the remuneration system** of the business to provide subordinates with a means of realising both business and personal goals. Employees who realise that their personal goals, for example, a higher income or more status and power, can only be achieved if the business's goals are achieved, will set more realistic goals and work much harder to achieve them.
- Management must ensure that **subordinates accept the goals** and are willing to cooperate in achieving them. People who share in formulating goals more readily associate themselves with their achievement.

There is some argument about the way in which management should ensure the effective setting of goals. There are two basic approaches: the hierarchical or top-down approach, and the management by objectives or bottom-up approach.

The **hierarchical approach** is one in which managers at upper levels determine the goals to be worked for by their subordinates. Figure 6.3 shows this schematically. The advocates of this approach argue that it is the proper and obvious way because top management knows exactly the direction the business should take to achieve its long-term goals, due to their involvement in formulating its mission. The problem with this approach, however, is that top management does not always possess the information required by the lower ranks to perform a particular task.

Bottom-up or the well-known **management by objectives** is the second approach. This technique is sometimes referred to as a distinct management approach because it facilitates the setting of goals and the planning and controlling that follows from this. Management by objectives[1] entails the setting of goals and objectives that are considered jointly by superiors and subordinates. This method may be used at any level of management, and the goals set for employees can be linked to a given remuneration for their achievement. The advantage of this method lies mainly in its motivation of employees – they tend to work harder and more purposefully when they have had a part in the formulation of objectives. It also makes performance management possible.

Figure 6.3: The hierarchy of goals and objectives for The Lodge hotel group

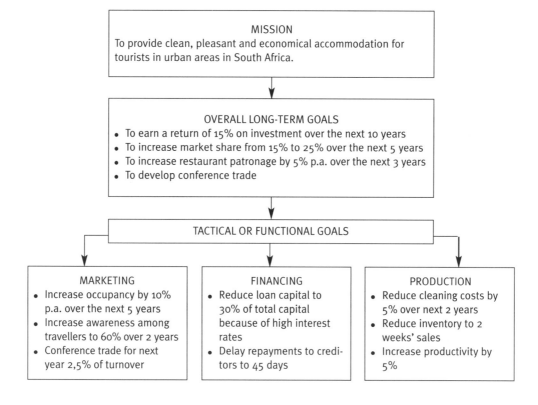

The choice of a particular approach, however, is limited by such factors as the size of the business, its organisational structure, its corporate culture, the prevailing situation, and the leadership style of top management.

Management has to take into account the personal objectives of individuals, and coordinate and integrate them in such a way that the purpose and mission of the business are fulfilled as productively as possible. The next step in planning, namely the developing of actual plans, will now be considered.

Applying the concept: setting goals

John du Toit, a senior civil servant, was offered an early retirement package in 1998. He accepted the offer. A few weeks into retirement, however, he felt that he was too young to simply stop working, so he started looking for a small business to invest in.

With property prices all over South Africa in a slump because of high interest rates resulting from the 1998 Asian crisis, John was able to buy a well-located bed and breakfast outfit. He decided to reposition it as an upmarket guest house, but for this he needed to know more about management, especially planning and the setting of goals.

Beginning with the mission, what kinds of goals would you advise John to set?

6.6 Developing plans: the choice of alternatives

Planning has already been defined as the fundamental element of management that determines what a business proposes to achieve and how it should go about it. The importance of goals and goal formulation discussed in the previous section indicates what the business organisation intends to achieve, and, to an extent, how this should be done. In other words, the goals themselves implicitly indicate the combination of resources – people, equipment and money – that need to be employed, as well as the ways of realising, or plans to be followed, in achieving the goals. In planning, it should also be made clear who is to do what, and when. In a nutshell, the second phase of planning includes the consideration of several alternative plans of action, and ultimately the selection of that alternative or plan that will lead to the achievement of the predetermined goals.

If an existing plan of action does not succeed in accomplishing the predetermined goals, or if some new goal is established, then management has to develop alternative plans from which a new plan can be selected. In developing such alternative plans, management must constantly bear in mind the following:

- The influence of **external factors** – such as market factors, legislation or economic trends – on the business environment for the achievement of goals, and hence the level of action. Such environmental influences occur in the form of opportunities that may be exploited or threats that must be averted and should be considered in the development of alternatives. Environmental scanning was discussed in chapter 4.
- The **strong and weak points** of the business. When alternative plans of action to achieve some purpose are being developed, the strong points – for instance, a particular skill, a patent, possession of a raw material source or a marketing channel, capital, or even the image of the business – should

always be taken into account. At the same time, alternative plans should not expose the weak points of the business to threats.

- In choosing an alternative plan of action, the **costs** of each alternative should be weighed against the advantages offered by it. In this way, a more or less rational plan of action may be developed. **Rational decision making** plays a vital role in the choice of an optimal plan of action – or the plan of action – that has evolved against the backdrop of environmental influences and been assessed in accordance with costs and benefits, and that will stand the best chance of achieving its purpose.

This process of devising plans, in which several alternatives are developed and an optimal plan decided on, indicates that different kinds of plans may be developed to make the accomplishment of different kinds of goals possible. An overview of the types of plans originating at different levels of management makes the planning process clearer.

6.6.1 Types of plans: the levels and time frames of planning

Just as different kinds of goals and objectives are encountered at each level of a business, so different kinds of plans originate on different levels of management (see figure 6.2 on p. 146). It follows that certain objectives can be attained only by means of specific actions or plans. For this reason, particular plans have to be formulated at the different levels to achieve the different objectives. Figure 6.4 shows the kinds of plans encountered at various levels. Each merits a brief overview.

Figure 6.4: The levels and time frames of different kinds of plans

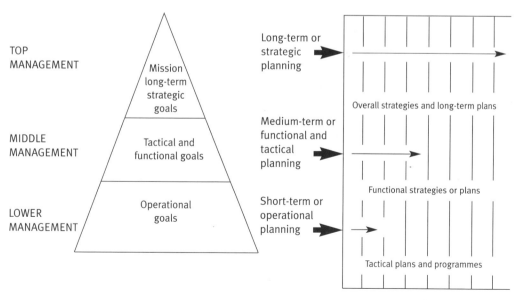

6.6.1.1 Strategic planning

Strategic planning, or long-term planning as it is sometimes called, is the development of a broad long-term overall strategy to realise the mission of the business. In figure 6.4 the following characteristics of strategic planning are apparent:

- It is carried out by top management, which normally devotes most of its time to strategic or long-term planning.
- It has a time frame of three to ten years or more.
- It is focused on the business as a whole.
- It is future-oriented, and is at all times on the lookout for changes in the environment.
- It includes constant adaptation to the environment.
- A long-term or strategic plan is not concerned with details, but is in the form of broad general guidelines to keep the business on its course.
- Management constantly endeavours to use it to deploy the resources and skills of the business among the opportunities and risks in the business environment, and to steer the business as profitably as possible towards its mission.

These characteristics distinguish strategic planning from functional and operational planning (also known as conventional planning), in which the emphasis falls more on short-term and comprehensive plans for particular departments.

The first half of the last century was characterised by stable business environments with low and stable rates of interest, few raw material shortages, a slow and steady rate of technological innovation, and a general economy in which inflation was practically unknown. In such a stable environment businesses were able to sell their products or services without being too concerned about the future. It was assumed that future environments would be more or less the same as prevailing ones, so that a mere extension or projection of old plans was perfectly adequate to ensure profitable survival.

However, since the 1950s, as discussed in some detail in chapters 4 and 5, the business environment has been changing at an unprecedented rate, and management has had to look for new approaches, because old ones, such as budgeting, management by objectives, and policy formulation, proved to be of little use in an unstable environment. At the same time, businesses have become larger and more complex. In these circumstances, long-term planning came into being during the late 1950s in an attempt to take countermeasures against instability in the business environment. In the 1960s and 1970s especially, the general concept of strategic planning was deployed to try to keep abreast of change in the business environment, and various concepts were developed to enable managers to develop long-term or strategic plans.

Strategic planning therefore gives long-term direction to a business, with its mission as the ultimate aim to be achieved. Various long-term strategies can be devised to accomplish the mission. The following are typical examples:[2]

- A **concentration strategy**. This is the most popular long-term strategy, and normally entails a business directing all its resources and skills to the profitable growth of a single product in a single market – in short, concentrating all that it has on what it does best to realise its mission. In the case of Avis, for example, the business concentrated on car hire and got rid of businesses for which it did not have the necessary expertise and skills.

Example

In the 1970s, Avis, the multinational car rental organisation, was a conglomerate with businesses involved in car rental, motels, hotels, travel agencies and tourism. For many years it operated at a loss, until Robert Townsend was appointed chief executive and gave it a much-needed sense of direction. He formulated Avis's mission as follows: "We want to be the fastest growing organisation with the highest profit margins in the business of renting cars without drivers." Three years later, Avis was number two in the industry. To achieve this, Townsend had to develop and implement various strategies, including selling off related but money-losing businesses. But most importantly, he focused on the core business of Avis, namely renting out cars.

- **Market development.** This means that existing markets for the present products of the business are developed more intensively, or else new markets are developed for existing products. In the latter case, new regions or even an export market can be considered.
- **Product development.** This type of strategy is closely related to market development, and involves new products being developed for existing markets, or existing products being modified to win greater approval among consumers. For example, in the 1990s, Castle Lite was introduced to the existing market by South African Breweries to satisfy the needs of beer drinkers who preferred a light beer.
- **Innovation** is a long-term strategy that entails constantly changing and improving products to take advantage of the initial high profitability of a new improved product in order to achieve the mission. This strategy is especially popular in the motor vehicle industry, with the underlying idea of creating a new life cycle for the product with each innovation, and so making competitive products obsolete. It is also effective in other markets: Polaroid, for example, markets each new camera intensively until competitors have caught up with it technologically. By that stage, they usually have an advanced new product ready for the market.
- **Horizontal integration** is a long-term growth strategy in which similar businesses are taken over. This strategy gives access to new markets, on the one hand, and gets rid of competition, on the other.
- **Vertical integration** occurs when the business's strategy is to take over suppliers, such as those providing raw materials, or businesses that buy from it. It can be used to ensure a source of supply, or a distribution channel to ensure an outlet.
- A **joint venture** is a strategy for two or more firms to embark on some project that is too big for one to tackle on its own. The advantage of such a strategy lies mainly in the pooling of resources and skills.
- **Diversification.** This strategy represents a positive departure from existing activities by the takeover of other firms, or the setting up of a completely new entity by the business itself. The objectives of such a strategy include distribution of risk, synergy, a more rapid rate of growth, or higher profits.
- **Rationalisation.** In difficult times businesses may find that their profits decline and they are compelled to drastically cut costs by terminating

unprofitable products, getting rid of unprofitable assets, and, in particular, by improving ineffective management.

- **Divestiture.** This is closely related to the foregoing strategy, and may lead to selling off a business or parts of it to make it possible for it to fulfil its mission.
- **Liquidation.** This is a final strategy, and amounts to the discontinuation of the whole business, because it cannot be successfully sustained.

Table 6.2: Choice of alternative strategies

Strategic options						
	1	2	3	4	5	6
Opportunities in the business environment	Western Cape markets offer little competition		Present market sensitive to prices		Business offers too narrow a range of products	
Long-term goals derived from mission						
• Average investment over five years	15%	19%	13%	17%	23%	19%
• Sales over five years	+50%	+40%	+20%	+0%	+35%	+25%
Overall strategy	Horizontal integration	Market development	Concentration	Selective retrenchment	Product development	Concentration

The question that now arises is how a business should decide on one of these strategies. Several advanced techniques have been developed for this purpose, such as the well-known PIMS (profit impact of market share) studies, the BCG (Boston Consulting Group) portfolio matrix, the GE (General Electric) matrix, and many others. Table 6.2 shows a simple matrix which management can use to make use of opportunities in the environment for the accomplishment of its mission and long-term goals.

Strategic planning – that is, the development of a mission and long-term goals in a business and the choice of one or more long-term strategies to realise them – depends on functional planning or the development of functional plans to put the overall or grand strategy into effect.

6.6.1.2 Functional planning

As shown in figure 6.4 (see p. 151), functional and tactical planning refers to medium-term planning carried out by middle management (in cooperation with top management) for the various functional departments to realise their goals (which are themselves derived from the long-term strategic goals). Table 6.3 provides examples of functional strategies or functional plans. Functional plans may sometimes be of a long-term nature, although they are normally designed for the medium term, and are therefore more tactical than strategic. Most medium-term plans are components of long-term strategies and plans.

Because long-term strategies and plans are exposed to many uncertainties and changes in the business environment, medium-term planning, especially in very turbulent environments, forms the nucleus of the planning activities of some businesses.

Table 6.3: Functional strategies and plans

Functional management area	Key aspects to be considered
Marketing	Product line, market position, distribution channels, marketing communication, prices
Finance	Policy on debtors, dividends, asset management, capital structure
Production and operations	Improvement of productivity, locational problems, legislation
Human resources	Labour relations, labour turnover, training of human resources, equity considerations
Purchasing	Suppliers, policy on creditors, sources of raw materials

6.6.1.3 Short-term planning

Short-term planning, also referred to as operational planning, is done for periods of not longer than a year. It is developed by lower management to achieve operational objectives (which are derived from the functional and tactical goals), and may therefore be regarded as a component of functional plans. Short-term plans are concerned with the day-to-day performance of tasks and the allocation of resources to particular persons in accordance with particular programmes, schedules or budgets to fulfil certain aims. Budgeting is the main method used by management in planning the allocation of resources to alternative plans of action. Moreover, planning is carried out in accordance with a particular policy or set of procedures that gives direction to routine activities, thereby facilitating plans.

Many factors may disturb the planning process: unrealistic objectives, environmental influences, financial constraints, and a host of others. Management can take various actions to overcome these disturbances, but should start by setting realistic objectives that are precise, clear and achievable. Top management should take responsibility for planning and allied activities. Communication with subordinates and gaining their participation promotes good planning. People who are informed and share in decision making are likely to cooperate in making the plans succeed. Management should also realise that planning is subject to certain limitations, and should be revised from time to time.

6.6.2 Implementation of the selected plan

During the first two phases of the planning process – while objectives are being formulated and plans devised – management must decide who is to be responsible for the activities to be carried out, and what means or resources are to be used in doing so. Obviously, therefore, even at the planning stage attention is given to some aspects of the other three elements of management, namely organising, leading and control. This confirms, once again, the interdependence of the four fundamental elements of management, and reminds us that none of them can be carried out in isolation. The implementation of the chosen plan therefore involves the development of a framework for its execution, leadership to set the plan in motion, and the exercising of control to determine whether the performance of the activities is going according to plan. In short, the third phase of planning, that is, the implementation of the plan, forms part of the other three elements of the management process.

6.7 Summary

Planning is the starting point of the management process – it determines what an organisation proposes to achieve and how it is to be done. The "what" refers to the various goals to be formulated prior to different strategies and plans being devised so as to realise them. The "how" is the plan, which describes how the goals should be achieved. The plan can be strategic, tactical or operational. To implement the plans the tasks and activities must be organised and leadership must be applied to achieve the goals. Plans are finally controlled to establish if the goals have been achieved.

The development of an organisational structure is the second fundamental task of the management process which needs to be examined.

References

1. Drucker, P., *The practice of management,* Harper & Row, New York, 1954, p. 62.
2. Pearce, J.A. & Robinson, R.B., *op. cit.,* pp. 189-203.

7 Organising management activities

The purpose of this chapter

Once management has devised a plan to achieve the organisation's goals, it must deploy resources such as people, equipment, money and raw materials. In addition, it must design jobs, assign tasks, duties and responsibilities to people, coordinate activities, and establish lines of reporting and communication. This is called organising. This chapter examines organising as the second fundamental task of management. An overview of the importance of organising is provided, followed by an examination of the fundamentals of organising. An exposition is given of how an organisation evolves from a one-man business to a large business organisation with many departments. Authority relationships as well as reporting relationships are explained, and thereafter coordination is discussed. A brief overview of the informal organisation is also given. Finally, the factors influencing the design of an organisation's structure are discussed, and it is emphasised that such a structure must enable the people concerned to work effectively towards the organisation's mission and goals.

Learning outcomes

The content of this chapter will enable learners to:
- Explain the concepts of organising and organisational structure
- Describe the importance of organising
- Discuss the fundamentals of organising
- Explain how an organisation evolves from a single-entrepreneur organisation to a large one
- Present viewpoints regarding the factors that influence organising

7.1 Introduction to organising

Planning, the first fundamental element of the management process, is defined as the setting of goals and the development of a plan of action to achieve the goals as productively as possible. Planning, however, is only one component of the management process, and it alone cannot guarantee that the goals of the business organisation will be accomplished. Once the plan to achieve certain goals has been selected, management must combine human and other resources, such as money, machines, raw materials and information or knowledge, in the best possible way to achieve the organisation's goals. The most important of these is the task of grouping people into teams or departments to **perform** the activities that will convert the plan into accomplished goals. The structured grouping and combining of people and other resources, and coordinating them to achieve organisational goals, constitute the second fundamental element of management, namely **organising**.

Organising means that management has to develop **mechanisms** in order to implement the strategy or plan. Arrangements have to be made to determine what **activities** will be carried out, what **resources** will be employed, and **who** will perform the various activities. This involves the distribution of tasks among employees, the allocation of resources to persons and departments, and giving the necessary authority to certain people to ensure that the tasks are in fact carried out. Above all, there must be communication, cooperation and coordination between the people and the departments or sections performing the tasks.

The business's organisational structure therefore indicates the work to be done and the connections between various positions and tasks. Organising, or the design of a framework of how the work must be done to accomplish the goals, is an indispensable step in the management process of any business, whether existing or new.

In a newly established business, decisions have to be taken regarding equipment, supplies, processes to be followed, and the people who must perform the tasks. In addition, the structure indicating the distribution of tasks among departments and individuals has to be drawn up, indicating the responsibilities and lines of authority and communication. In an existing business, organising has to be constantly reviewed and adapted to accommodate new products and new processes or any organisational changes which affect the activities. In line with the strategy or plan, management still arranges what needs to be done so as to reach the objectives.

Organising the activities that must be performed to achieve the goals is like building a toy castle. Imagine giving a child a pile of coloured wooden blocks of different shapes and asking him or her to build a castle. The child then selects some square blocks, some round blocks, some red blocks and a combination of other wooden blocks, and builds a castle. Ask another child to do the same, and a different selection of shapes and colours will be combined differently and will produce a different castle. Choosing certain combinations of blocks and putting them together in unique ways is, in a sense, like trying to organise or choose certain combinations of resources and people and putting them together in unique ways. Just as children select different building blocks to build a castle, managers choose the building blocks of an organisation. And no two teams of managers will put the same organisational structure together. Managers can use various basic building blocks to construct an organisation, such as **job design**, the **grouping of jobs**, also called departmentalisation, establishing **chains of command**, assigning **authority**, and establishing **coordination** mechanisms to link activities between jobs. Before we examine the building blocks of an organisation, a few comments on the importance of organising are necessary to help clarify the nature of the second fundamental element of management.

7.2 The importance of organising

Organising, like planning, is an integral and indispensable component of the management process. Without it, the successful implementation of plans and strategies is out of the question because of the absence of a systematic allocation of resources and people to execute the plans. Leadership and control are not possible if the activities of management and subordinates are not organised, or if the business does not clearly designate the individuals responsible for specific tasks.

More specifically, organising is important for the following reasons:[1]

- Organising entails a detailed analysis of work to be done and resources to be used to accomplish the aims of the business. It is through organising that tasks and resources, and methods or procedures, can be systematised. Everyone should know their duties, authority and responsibility, the procedures they must follow or the methods they have to adopt, and the resources they can use. Proper organising ensures that the joint and coordinated efforts of management have a much greater and more effective result than the sum of individual efforts.
- Organising divides the total workload into activities that can comfortably be performed by an individual or a group. Tasks are allocated according to the abilities or qualifications of individuals, thus ensuring that nobody in the business has either too much or too little to do. The ultimate result is higher productivity.
- Organising promotes the productive deployment and utilisation of resources.
- The related activities and tasks of individuals are grouped together rationally in specialised departments such as marketing, personnel or finance departments, in which experts in their particular fields carry out their given duties.
- The development of an organisational structure results in a mechanism that coordinates the activities of the whole business into complete, uniform, harmonious units.

Successful organising, then, makes it possible for a business to achieve its goals. It coordinates the activities of managers and subordinates to avoid the unnecessary duplication of tasks, and it obviates possible conflicts. It also reduces the chances of doubts and misunderstandings, enabling the business to reach its goals efficiently. Against this background, we will now examine the building blocks or the fundamentals of organising.

7.3 The fundamentals of organising

Building an organisational structure revolves around the building blocks or the fundamentals of organising, namely:
- Designing jobs for employees
- Grouping employees into teams or departments based on commonalities
- Assigning authority
- Establishing a command structure
- Establishing coordinating mechanisms

7.3.1 *Designing jobs*

Job design is the determination of an employee's responsibilities in the organisation and the compilation of a job specification that explains what he or she must do and what performance standards are expected. The job design and description of a bricklayer in a construction company, for example, would give a detailed exposition of what it is that he must do with the bricks and mortar, and the performance standard would include the number of bricks that must be laid per day or per week.

The point of departure of designing jobs for employees is to determine the level of specialisation or the degree to which the overall task of the organisation is broken down into smaller, more specialised tasks. **Specialisation** is the way in which a task is broken up into smaller units to take advantage of specialised knowledge or skills to improve productivity. The best example of specialisation or division of labour is still the **assembly line**, a production method usually attributed to the inventive mind of Henry Ford. His pioneering work opened the way to mass production, which, in the early decades of this century, had a profound effect on Western societies. The division of a task into smaller units, however, means that the various units have to be coordinated. Coordination is therefore an indispensable part of organising.

Specialisation

The principle of specialisation or the division of labour is generally ascribed to Adam Smith. In his famous work, an enquiry into the wealth of nations, he describes how specialisation is applied in a pin factory so as to increase productivity. One man unrolls the wire, another straightens it, a third cuts it, a fourth sharpens the tip, and so on. In that way, says Smith, ten men could produce 48 000 pins a day, while one man on his own could make only 20 a day!

Source: Smith, A., *The wealth of nations*, J.M. Dent & Sons, New York, 1960, p. 5.

The way in which the principle of work specialisation operates may be illustrated by means of the hypothetical example in figure 7.1 (see p. 161).

Suppose an amateur inventor designs a machine in his garage. First of all, he builds it at home, sells it himself, keeps a set of accounts himself, and also buys the parts required. If he is successful, the business will soon become too big for him to do all these things by himself. At this stage, as phase 2 in the figure shows, he has a small business with a part-time bookkeeper who relieves him of part of the total workload. Therefore, in phase 2 he is beginning to specialise. As the business grows, he is compelled, in phase 3, to get help with the production of the machine. At the same time, he employs somebody else to help him sell it, and the part-time bookkeeper is appointed on a full-time basis so that the inventor can devote more of his time to the general management of his business. Eventually he arrives at phase 4, at which point he is becoming a large business.

Figure 7.1 The evolution of specialisation

PHASE 1: THE SINGLE ENTREPRENEUR

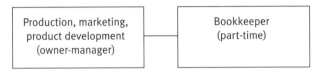

PHASE 2: THE SMALL BUSINESS

PHASE 3: THE GROWING BUSINESS

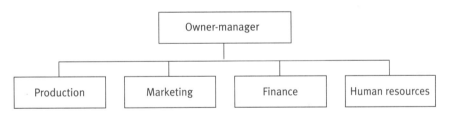

PHASE 4: THE LARGE BUSINESS

The growth of the business, as depicted in this model, is characterised by two developments in particular:
- The growing total task of the business
- Constant pressure to split the total task into smaller units

Put differently, the growing business is continually compelled to apply specialisation or the division of labour. Besides this evolutionary pressure, there are other reasons that justify specialisation, including the following:
- **Individual ability.** If individuals concentrate on some simple small task, they acquire a certain degree of skill in that area, and can perform the task as a specialist quicker and better than anybody else, with obvious advantages for the business.
- **Reduced transfer time.** Workers who do several jobs lose time when they switch from one job to another. Specialisation eliminates such non-productive transfer time.

- **Specialised equipment.** Specialisation leads to the development of specialised equipment, which increases the productivity of each worker.
- **Reduced training costs.** Division of labour reduces the costs of training, because workers are trained in a particular part of the total task.

The main purpose of specialisation is to increase productivity. Although it has traditionally been applicable mostly at the operational level, it is increasingly being applied at managerial levels also. However, one should not lose sight of the fact that excessive specialisation may have a negative effect on productivity.

The main criticism of specialisation is that workers who perform highly specialised jobs may become bored and demotivated. Managers should be sensitive to overspecialisation and also consider such approaches as **job enrichment, job enlargement** and **job rotation** to counter the negative effects of specialisation.

7.3.2 Departmentalisation

A second principle underlying organising is the **formation of departments.** While this is a result of specialisation, it also promotes specialisation, since it is necessitated by the logical grouping of activities that belong together. The reasons for departmentalisation are therefore inherent in the advantages of specialisation and the pressure in a growing business to split the total task of management into smaller units. As soon as a business has reached a given size, say phase 4 in figure 7.1, it becomes impossible for the owner-manager to supervise all the employees, and so it becomes necessary to create new managerial positions according to departments based on a logical grouping, in manageable sizes, of the activities that belong together.

The various departments created constitute the organisational structure of the business as they appear on the organisation chart. Depending on such factors as the size and kind of business, and the nature of its activities, various organisational structures may be developed through departmentalisation. We will now discuss some basic forms of organisation:

- The **functional organisational structure**, as shown in figure 7.2, is the most basic type. Here, activities belonging to each management function are grouped together. Activities such as advertising, market research, and sales, for example, belong together under the marketing function, while those concerned with the production of goods are grouped under operations.

Figure 7.2: A functional organisational structure

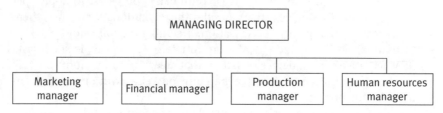

- **Product departmentalisation** is illustrated in figure 7.3. Departments are designed so that all activities concerned with the manufacturing of a product or group of products are grouped together in product sections, where all the specialists associated with the particular products are grouped. The rationale for this structure is that the marketing, financing and personnel needs for the production of, say, diesel engines, differ considerably from those in the manufacture of cigarettes. This is a logical structure for large businesses providing a wide range of products or services. The advantages of this structure are that the specialised knowledge of employees is used to maximum effect, decisions can be made quickly within a section, and the performance of each group can easily be measured. The disadvantages are that the managers in each section concentrate their attention almost exclusively on their products, and tend to lose sight of those of the rest of the business. Moreover, administrative costs increase, because each section has to have its own functional specialists, such as market researchers and financial experts.

Figure 7.3: Departmentalisation according to product

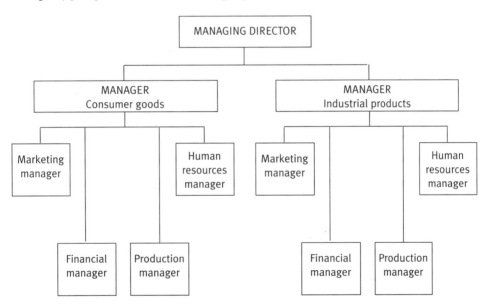

- **Location departmentalisation** is illustrated in figure 7.4 (see p. 164). This is a logical structure for a business that manufactures and sells its goods in different geographical regions, for example, SABMiller, which operates and markets its range of products all over the country and as well as internationally. This structure gives autonomy to area managements, which is necessary to facilitate decentralised decision making and adjustment to local business environments. This structure is also suitable for a multinational business.

Figure 7.4 Departmentalisation according to location

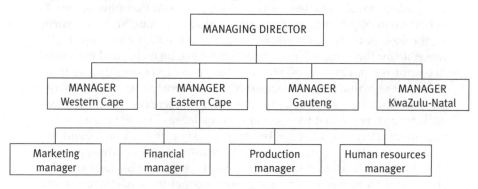

- **Customer departmentalisation** is adopted particularly where a business concentrates on some special segment of the market or group of consumers or, in the case of industrial products, where it sells its wares to a limited group of users. Figure 7.5 illustrates this structure. The structure has the same advantages and disadvantages as departmentalisation according to product and location or geographical area.

Figure 7.5: Departmentalisation according to customer

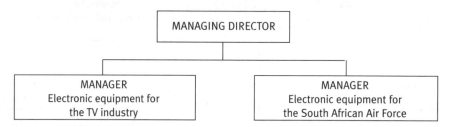

Unlike a functional structure in which activities are grouped according to knowledge, skills, experience or training, a section based on product, location or customers resembles, in some respects, a small privately owned business. It is more or less autonomous, and is accountable for its profits or losses. However, unlike an independent small business, it is still subject to the goals and strategies set by top management for the business as a whole.
- The **matrix organisational structure** is important because no organisational structure, whether designed according to function, product, location or customer, will necessarily meet all the organisational needs of a particular business. Where departments are formed according to function, there is sophisticated specialisation, but coordination remains a problem. If they are formed according to product, location or customer, certain products or regions may be successful, but the rest of the business does not reap the benefits of good organisation.

To overcome these problems, which mainly occur in large businesses and in those handling specific projects, the matrix organisational structure has been created to incorporate the advantages of both structures discussed earlier. As indicated in figure 7.6, horizontal (staff) and vertical (line) authority lines occur in the same structure so that project managers (horizontal) and functional managers (vertical) both have authority.

Figure 7.6: The matrix organisational structure

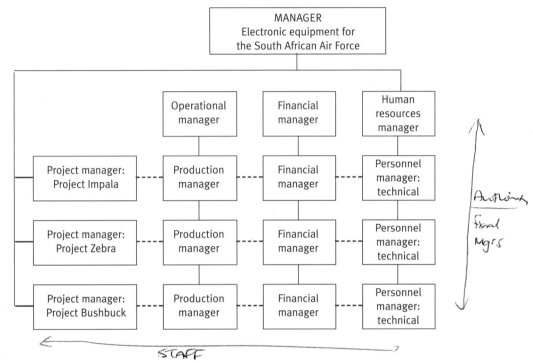

This organisational structure is particularly suited to ad hoc and complex projects requiring specialised skills. For example, IBM created a matrix structure for the development of its personal computer, and disbanded the team when the product had successfully been launched. However, in other businesses the matrix structure may be permanent, for example, a car manufacturer that continually develops certain models as projects. The major advantage of the matrix structure is that specialist project managers can help manage complex projects while the advantages of functional specialisation are retained. The disadvantage is divided authority. Both project leader and departmental head can exercise authority over the same subordinates. The unit of command is therefore affected, and there is a serious risk of soured relations between the project and functional executives. In addition, the position of subordinates may be difficult in the case of having to satisfy two bosses.

7.3.3 *Authority relations*

In the previous section we discussed the process of task distribution, which, as we stated, includes the breaking up of the total task of the business into smaller specialised units, and the allocation of these units to certain departments and persons. However, this is not the end point of organising. The assignment of tasks to sections and members of staff also entails the assignment of **responsibility** and **authority** to each post in an organisational structure. This further entails the creation of organisational relations, that is, stipulating the persons from whom subordinates receive instructions, to whom they report, and to whom and for what they are responsible.

Responsibility is a particular **obligation** or commitment on the part of managers (especially at middle or lower level) and, to a more limited degree, their subordinates, to carry out tasks in accordance with instructions they have received. This also means that subordinates should be able to account for what they have done.

Authority, on the other hand, is the right to command or to give orders. Authority is power that has been legitimised by the organisation. It also includes the right to take action to compel the performance of duties and to punish default or negligence. In the formal business structure, several examples of which have been discussed, the owners of the business possess the final authority. They appoint directors and give them authority, and these in turn appoint managers, who assign a certain authority to subordinates, and in this way authority flows down the line.

On 14 July 1789, after the storming of the Bastille, the French people refused to accept the authority of their king, Louis XVI, any longer. This was the start of the French Revolution.

This formal authority passed down from above is known as **delegation of authority**. Delegation can be viewed as the main source of authority. On the other hand, according to the acceptance theory of authority, authority originates from lower levels, because no one has any authority unless subordinates accept instructions and carry them out. Other sources of authority are, or may be, the personality of the manager, or his or her style of leadership or exceptional knowledge of some particular job or situation.

Responsibility and authority go hand in hand. No one can take responsibility without the authority necessary to enable him or her to compel action. The centralisation of authority means the concentration of power in the hands of top management, with little delegation to middle and lower managements, as is the case with decentralisation of authority.

Responsibility and authority

The pilot of an aircraft flying the President may decide, on the authority of personal specialised knowledge, to alter the course for Cape Town International Airport before returning to Johannesburg International Airport, in the event of a problem arising. In such a case, personal competence overrides all other authority.

In our discussion of authority, the terms line and staff authority require some clarification.

- **Line authority** is authority delegated down through the line of command. In figure 7.7 (see p. 167), the managing director has line authority over the financial, human resources and marketing managers, while the marketing manager has line authority over the advertising manager, and so on, down the line of command. The managers in this line are directly responsible for achieving the goals of the organisation.

Figure 7.7: Line and staff authority in the organisational structure

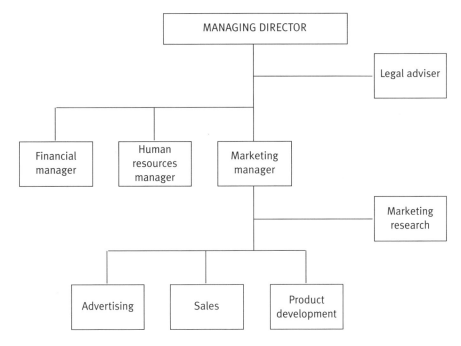

- **Staff authority** is an indirect and supplementary authority. Individuals or sections with staff authority, for example, the legal adviser and the marketing research section shown in figure 7.7, assist, advise and recommend. Their source of authority is usually their special knowledge of a particular field.

Once the distribution of tasks and authority has been completed, management has to design an organisational structure that will enable the various jobs to be done in a coordinated fashion.

7.3.4 *Reporting relationships*

A further fundamental element of organising is the establishment of reporting lines among departments and positions in departments. For example, will the marketing manager report to the operations manager, or will the operations manager report to the marketing manager? Or should both report to the general manager?

The first step in establishing reporting lines is to determine who reports to whom. Clear and precise reporting lines are important, so that everybody knows who is in charge of what activities. This is called the **chain of command**. The second part of establishing reporting lines is to determine the **span**

of management, that is, the number of subordinates who report directly to a manager. Figure 7.8 illustrates this concept schematically.

Figure 7.8: The span of management

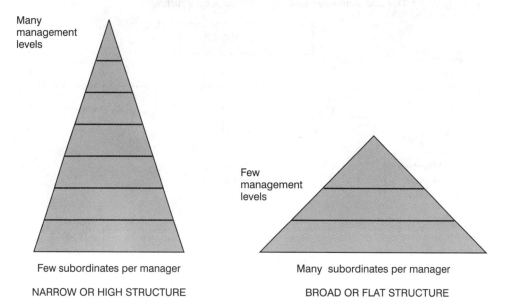

Many management levels

Few management levels

Few subordinates per manager

Many subordinates per manager

NARROW OR HIGH STRUCTURE

BROAD OR FLAT STRUCTURE

A narrow or high structure may mean that managers are being under-utilised, and that there is excessive control over subordinates. At the same time, it may be difficult to coordinate the tasks of a large number of managers. The converse is true of a broad or flat structure, in which management has little time to spare for individuals. The ideal span of management, however, exists only in theory. In practice, factors such as the complexity of the business and the degree of supervision and planning that are necessary determine the span. However, the trend is that structures are becoming flatter as re-engineering and outsourcing result in the need for fewer middle managers, and, consequently, the emergence of leaner organisational structures.

Managers should understand the variables that affect the span of management, as well as the implications of a taller or flatter organisation.

7.3.5 Coordination

Yet another fundamental element of organising is coordination.

Organisation means dividing up the total task of the business into smaller units so as to take advantage of specialisation and achieve the goals of the business as productively as possible. However, this division of work into smaller jobs immediately raises the problem of cooperation, or the coordination of divided tasks and various departments into an integrated whole to achieve the goals of the business.

The key to keeping each department focused on the organisation's goals is coordination or the process of **linking** the activities of the various departments in the organisation into a single integrated unit. The primary reason for coordination is that departments and groups are interdependent. They depend on each other for resources in order to be able to perform their activities. The greater the interdependence between the departments, the more coordination the organisation acquires.

Without coordination, individuals and departments lose sight of the organisations' primary goals and of their part in that effort. Coordination is the synthesis of separate parts into a unity, and as such it is the binding factor in the managerial process. It means the integration of goals and tasks at all levels and also of all departments and functions to enable the business to work as a whole. In addition, an element of timing is necessary, because various smaller tasks have to be scheduled to mesh with one another.

Hence, coordination is an endeavour by management to develop congruence, or harmony of goals, through organising. Other mechanisms that promote coordination are the organisation chart, the budget, a committee, the broad policy and procedures in accordance with which tasks are carried out, and the information system of the business.

Once management has deployed all the building blocks of the organisation, it can finalise the formal structure of the organisation. Besides the formal organisation of a business, there is also an informal organisation that often supplements it and helps it to run smoothly.

7.4 The informal organisation

So far, only the formal organisation has been considered. However, relations within a particular business are not confined to those prescribed by the formal organisation chart. Alongside the formal structure there is also an informal organisation, which may be defined as the interpersonal relations between people in a business that are not defined by the formal organisational structure.

Because there is regular interaction between people, social relations are established that assume a definite form. This interaction is achieved by informal communication, also known as "the grapevine". Moreover, these relations exist not only between individuals, but also between groups – though on an informal basis. If sound, these relations can support the formal structure, but if not, they may include activities that are not in harmony with those envisaged in the formal structure. Rather than trying to suppress the informal structure, management should encourage it, for the following reasons:

- Informal communication takes place much more rapidly than formal, and therefore decision-making could be expedited.
- The informal organisation promotes teamwork within departments, as well as cooperation between departments.
- The informal organisation supports the formal organisation.

Having considered the basis of the task of organising, we will now examine some of the factors that may influence the organisational structure.

7.5 Factors that influence organising (organisation design)

Organising can be effectively carried out only if the organisational structure has been developed to optimise the execution of strategies and plans. In other words, plans can be successfully implemented only if the organisational structure makes this possible. Planning, leading and control are facilitated if management has an effective and dynamic organisational structure. This raises the question: Which organisational structure is the best? There is no definitive answer, and a business must choose a structure that is best suited to its particular activities or may be adapted to its strategy and requirements.

Organising is carried out in a context where many different factors need to be taken into account, each of which may provide input in the designing of the organisational structure.

Some experts believe that the environment in which a business operates is a decisive factor. Others emphasise the connection between strategy and structure. Obviously, the size and complexity of the business, the competence of its employees, and the nature of the product and the market all play important parts. Moreover, the organisational climate or corporate culture should not be ignored in designing the structure and in forming departments and distributing tasks. Above all, according to modern management theory, whatever structure is designed should be adaptable to changes in the business environment. We will now briefly examine the above factors as we finalise our study of organising.

7.5.1 The environment in which a business operates

The environment in which a business operates may be taken as a basis for designing an organisational structure, since it is the starting point for the development of strategy, on the one hand, and because the organisational structure is the mechanism that should keep the business in touch with its environment, on the other. As we have already said, a business has to adapt to its environment to survive. There are various types of environment, including the following:

- A **stable environment** is one that does not change much or is not subject to unexpected change. Here, product changes are the exception rather than the rule and, when a change does occur, plans can be made to cope with it in good time. Demand for the product is regular, with only slight fluctuations. New technological changes are small or unlikely. A foundry manufacturing manhole covers and a workshop making violins operate in stable environments.

  In a stable environment the functional structure is suitable, because there is little in the way of innovation and no great need for coordination and cooperation between departments. Similarly, businesses with fewer competing markets, that are under less pressure regarding product development to satisfy consumers' needs (for example, a manufacturer of nuts and bolts), will have a functional structure with few specialists such as market researchers and advertising experts. Decision making takes place mainly at the top level.

- A **turbulent environment** is one in which changes are the norm rather than the exception: competitors unexpectedly bring out new products, and technological innovations cause revolutionary changes in the manufacturing process or the product itself. The pharmaceutical industry is an example of such an environment, which necessitates many specialists for market research, product development and production, and close coordination and communication between them. In such a business, departmentalisation according to product is especially suitable, as this speeds up decision making. More decisions are made in the separate departments than by top management. Businesses in stable environments are less differentiated in structure than those in turbulent environments.
- In a **technologically dominated environment** – that is, when a particular technology forms the basis for a business's product – organisational design will be influenced by the level of technological sophistication. Technologically complex firms tend to have more managers and more levels of management because specialised technicians work in small groups with a narrow span. Technology, and especially technological innovation, requires an adaptable organisational structure that is based on one or other form of departmentalisation.

7.5.2 The relationship between strategy and structure

The close relationship between the strategy of a business and its organisational structure is well known. The implication is that the strategy provides a direct input in the design of the organisational structure, and that the structure cannot be separated from the strategy.

7.5.3 The size of the business

It is equally obvious that the structure also depends on the number of employees and managers to be coordinated. An increase in the size of the business also creates a need for greater specialisation, more departments, and more levels of management. The danger of bureaucratic management, as a result of detailed procedures, strict job demarcation and, consequently, less emphasis on initiative and regeneration, is always present in large businesses.

7.5.4 Staff employed by the business

There is also a close relationship between an organisational structure and the competence and role of staff, whether this competence is a result of training or experience, availability or attitude. In management, especially in top management, the structure influences both the choice of strategy and the preferences as to how things should be done. Most managers have a personal preference for a particular organisational structure, for the type of relations with subordinates, and also attitudes to formality and authority. As to the latter two, some experts maintain that the tendency is to move away from the strictly formal bureaucratic structure.

7.5.5 *The organisational culture*

The final factor that plays an important part in organisational design is organisational culture. This so-called culture is a concept that may be defined as the beliefs and values shared by people in a business. It is the "personality" of the business. Unless management analyses this concept correctly, it will never know why employees do, or do not do, certain things. Corporate culture comprises basic values that are reflected not only in organisational behavioural patterns, but also in aspects such as the business's architecture, office decor, dress regulations, and the general way things are done.

The type of structure that leads to the successful implementation of tasks also depends on the culture of the business. The structure of a business with a formal culture will differ from one with a more informal culture.

The above are some of the considerations that may influence the design of an organisational structure. They are, however, no more than guidelines for organising. It should, moreover, be understood that the organising process is not only used for a new structure. Any existing organisational structure should be revised whenever its strategy or plans are changed.

7.6 Summary

The setting in motion of the planned activities is part of the organising task of management. Organising is the development of a structure or framework within which the tasks to be performed for the accomplishment of goals, and the resources necessary for this, are allocated to particular individuals and departments. This division of labour may be done in various ways, and ultimately coordinated to make concerted action possible. Someone, however, has to take the lead in setting in motion the activities involved in the various phases of planning, organising and control. We will deal with the third fundamental element of management in chapter 8.

Reference

1. Stoner, J.A.F. & Freeman, R., *Management*, Prentice Hall, Englewood Cliffs, New Jersey, 1992, p. 312.

8 Leadership: leading people in the organisation

The purpose of this chapter

If organisations consisted solely of machines that could implement plans predictably and with precision, only the planning and organising tasks of management would be necessary in order to reach the organisation's goals. But organisations are made up of machines **and** people. And people are the most complex resource of the organisation. It therefore follows that an equally complex management task, namely leading, is required to direct people towards reaching the organisation's goals. Guiding or leading the employees of an organisation towards accomplishing its goals is called leadership. This chapter deals with the nature of leadership, the difference between leadership and management, and the concepts of authority, power, influence, the delegation of responsibility, and motivation. Various leadership models are briefly examined, including leadership characteristics and the importance of motivation and communication. The characteristics of groups are also examined.

Learning outcomes

The content of this chapter will enable learners to:
- Explain the concept of leadership as a fundamental management task
- Differentiate between leadership and management
- Describe the concepts of authority, power, influence, delegation, responsibility and motivation
- Give a superficial exposition of some leadership models
- Describe a simple communication model
- Discuss the characteristics of groups in the organisation

8.1 Introduction

In the introductory discussion of general management in chapter 5, it was said that organisations consist of resources such as money, machines, raw materials, information and, most important of all, **people**. People are undoubtedly the most complex resource in the organisation, because they are unpredictable and unique. Each individual in an organisation has a different combination of interests, capabilities, habits, beliefs and personal objectives, and each is differently motivated. This third and complex element of the management process is called **leadership**. Leadership is that element of management that sets activities in motion and keeps the activities moving until the goals have been accomplished. It deals with the relationship between leaders and followers, and the behaviour of followers. It is for this reason that the next set of chapters deal with the human dimension of management. Chapter 9 deals with attracting people to the organisation, chapter 10 with motivating and managing human resources, and chapter 11 with the legal environment of human resources.

An examination of the nature and importance of leadership is necessary to an explanation of leadership as the third element of the management process.

8.2 The nature of leadership

Leadership, one of the four fundamental management functions, is one of the most researched as well as most controversial subjects in management. If an organisation is to reach its goals, someone must set certain activities in motion and keep them going. In the preceding chapters, the first two of the four fundamental management functions were discussed, namely planning and organising. These two functions set the wheels of the management process in motion, but the process is by no means complete, since the plans formulated to achieve the goals must still become a reality. Thus, the management activities that are **set in motion** must also be **kept in motion** if the goals are to be accomplished. It is here that the third fundamental function of management comes into play, namely the initiative that management takes to set the organisation's activities in motion. In leading, management also gives **direction** to the organisation's activities so that all its resources are deployed as effectively as possible.

Leadership is therefore the process of directing the behaviour of others towards the accomplishment of predetermined goals. It involves taking the lead to bridge the gap between formulating plans and reaching goals, in other words translating plans into reality. Leadership is a somewhat elusive concept and is difficult to define precisely. It involves elements such as influencing people, giving orders, motivating people, either as individuals or in groups, managing conflict, and communicating with subordinates. It is that element of management that injects energy into the business to activate employees to get things moving and to keep them moving. Leadership also means passing on information to subordinates, explaining the mission, goals and plans of the business, allocating tasks and giving instructions, consulting with staff and supervising their work, taking whatever steps are necessary to raise production, as well as disciplining staff and handling conflict.[1] In its simplest form, it is the relation between superior and subordinate. From the point of view of management, **leadership may be defined as the influencing and directing of the behaviour of subordinates in such a way that they willingly strive to accomplish the goals or objectives of the business.**

To exercise leadership, that is, to influence and direct the behaviour and actions of people in some particular direction, management has to understand the most important components of its leadership role. Figure 8.1 (see p. 175) gives an exposition of the main components of the leadership task of management.

Figure 8.1: The components of the leadership task of management

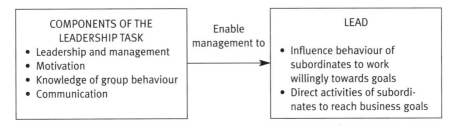

Leadership is often defined as the management function that activates people to willingly do things. This means that leaders must know how to **motivate** their followers.

The leader will find that he or she also has **groups** as followers in the organisation. Groups are the basis for much of the work that gets done, and may consist of a task group, a functional group or an informal group. These groups, such as unions, the legal section, the purchasing department, the accountants, or salesmen must also be guided towards reaching the goals and objectives. In many cases the leader will need to build **teams** to perform certain tasks. As such, the leader must also understand how groups and teams behave, and why individuals join groups.

Leaders finally have to communicate their vision, plans, problems and expectations to followers, and must also listen to the ambitions and aspirations of followers.

An examination of each of these components of leadership will promote an understanding of leadership as a fundamental element of management.

8.2.1 Leadership and management

Whenever an organisation finds itself in trouble, the problem is usually leadership. Ask employees about their jobs, and chances are that they will complain about leadership. Study large corporations, and one will discover that the biggest barrier to change is leadership. And wherever managers underperform, it is likely that their leadership abilities are weak. Moreover, the increasingly fast-changing and competitive business environment demands more and better leadership from more people to make organisations work. Without leadership organisations stagnate, lose their way and eventually become irrelevant and close down.

The performance of any business, whether large or small, is therefore in direct proportion to the quality of its leadership. It is not the only ingredient of success, but it is certainly an important one. Indeed, in the world of business there are innumerable examples of success or failure that can be attributed to a particular leader. Dr Anton Rupert built the Rembrandt Group into an international business empire. In less than 25 years, Raymond Ackerman established Pick 'n Pay as the largest retail business in South Africa. Dr Albert Wessels was already 55 when he founded Toyota South Africa, now the largest motor manufacturer in the country. Within a few years of the dismantling of apartheid, Dr Nthato Motlana developed the Metlife Group into a business giant, while business leaders such as Tokyo Sexwale of Trans Hex and Don Ncube of Real Africa Infolink have had similar success. The success of these businesses is ascribed not necessarily to the managerial abilities of these persons, but to the excellence of their leadership.

It is striking that leadership is often highlighted as the primary management activity. A survey in the USA on the need for expertise in the different functional areas of management revealed that the greatest need is in the area of leadership, as shown in table 8.1.

Importance of leadership

Survey results have revealed that academics and practitioners alike agree that leadership is the most important topic within the realm of organisational behaviour. According to a leadership study of more than 25 000 employees, 69% of employee job satisfaction stems from the leadership skills of the employee's manager. The major reason for employee failure is poor leadership. Management experts believe that leadership could be the number one strategic concern of businesses in the 21st century.

Source: Lusier, R.L., *Management*, South-Western, 1997, p. 390.

Table 8.1: The need for expertise in different fields of management

Management area	Greatest needs
Leadership	53%
Operations management	28%
Marketing	27%
Finance	13%
Organisational behaviour	11%
Accounting	3%

(Numbers do not add up to 100% because of multiple responses.)

Source: Fortune, 24 August 1992, p. 85. © Time Inc.

In less successful businesses there is likewise a connection between performance and quality of leadership. The lesson to be learned is that good managers can lead their businesses to even greater heights of achievement, productivity, and ultimate profitability if, besides being good managers, they are also good leaders. For this reason, business management needs to learn more about leadership as a component of the management task, and to establish how it may be utilised to accomplish the goals of the business as effectively as possible.

To clarify the term leadership, some remarks about the difference between management and leadership are necessary. **Managers** are the bearers of authority allocated to them by the organisation – that is, they have the **authority to enforce, order and direct the activities of others**. This includes issuing orders and being responsible for their execution. **Leaders** have the authority, but **get results without having to use force.**[2] They are leaders by virtue of certain personal qualities that they possess, including the ability to consult followers and motivate them, and to enlist their cooperation of their own free will.

This, precisely, is the importance of leadership in management. Good managers are not necessarily good leaders, and vice versa. To make the business more successful it is, of course, desirable that all managers also be leaders, and for this reason people who are both managers and leaders are sought and trained, as shown in figure 8.2. The underlying reason for studying leadership is therefore to make leaders of managers, so as to enable them ultimately to become better managers. An extensive body of knowledge about leadership is already available that might profitably be used to improve the performance of managers.

Figure 8.2: The integration of leadership and management

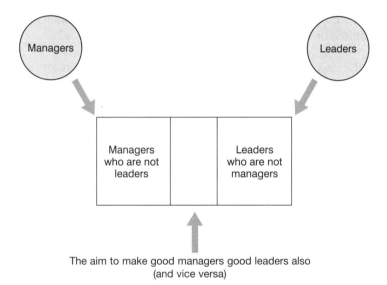

As an element of the management process, leadership may now be defined as **the ability to influence and direct the behaviour of individuals and groups, and to induce them to work willingly for the accomplishment of the business's predetermined goals.** Because the influence exerted by leaders on subordinates has such an important effect on the performance of a business, several attempts have been made to determine precisely what it is that enables leaders to influence their followers in this way. We will now consider certain aspects of leadership.

8.2.2 Aspects of leadership

Against the background of this general discussion, leadership is clearly seen to be a complex management activity. The definition of leadership given above is merely an attempt to find direction in the clutter of views relating to it. In order to appreciate the complex process of leadership, one has to understand the aspects of authority, power, influence, delegation, responsibility, and accountability:

- **Authority** denotes the right of a leader to give commands to, and demand actions from, subordinates.
- **Power** denotes the ability of a leader to influence the behaviour of others without necessarily using authority.
- **Influence** refers to the ability to use authority and power to move subordinates to action. In this way, leaders move soldiers, for example, to kill enemy troops; in businesses, subordinates are often influenced or moved to make personal sacrifices for the good of the business.
- **Delegation** occurs when a leader transfers authority to a subordinate. It involves splitting up the task and entrusting part of it, together with the necessary authority, to a subordinate for execution on the leader's behalf.
- **Responsibility** rests on a leader carrying out a given task in accordance with instructions, and being held accountable for the execution of all tasks by himself or herself and subordinates.

Of all these aspects, **authority** and **power** are probably the most important and therefore deserve a few further remarks, which will help to explain how leadership works.

The challenge facing South African leaders

One of the biggest challenges facing South African leaders, however, is within the organisation. It is clear from the survey mentioned earlier that many corporations in South Africa today are over-managed and under-led. The real challenge is to combine strong leadership and strong management and use the one to balance the other. While management is about coping with complexity, leadership is about coping with change. Major changes are increasingly necessary to survive and compete effectively in this new environment. This boils down to a real democratisation of the workplace with a simultaneous flattening of the hierarchy, the devolution of power and authority, the opening up of existing communication channels and the recreation of new ones. The leadership will thus no longer focus on power but on achievement. This requires the meaningful participation of all players as well as ongoing consultation.

Source: Grobler, P.A., Leadership challenges facing companies in the new South Africa, Unpublished professorial inaugural speech, UNISA, 22 February 1996.

8.2.2.1 Authority

Leaders, no matter to which managerial level they belong, are, on occasion, also managers responsible for ensuring that subordinates work together to achieve the business's goals. Without authority they are unable to manage, initiate or sustain the management process. Authority therefore revolves around obtaining the right to perform certain actions (within specified guidelines), to decide who does what, to compel the execution of tasks, and to punish those who fail to do what is expected of them.[3] In short, this means the right to demand action from subordinates, which may also be seen as the right to take action.

Final authority rests with the owners or shareholders who transfer or delegate it to the board; the board in turn delegates it to top management; top management to middle management, and so on, to the lowest levels. Hence, authority flows out of delegation, but management in turn delegates authority to subordinates to enable them to execute tasks and compel action. For example, certain bank officials have the authority to enter the bank's vault; certain managers have the authority to sign cheques in the business's name; and others have the authority to negotiate and conclude contracts on behalf of the business. The business confers this authority on them, and it primarily constitutes **formal authority**.

The clearest manifestations of formal authority are seen in the army, where those with specific powers wear insignia to indicate their authority or rank: captains have authority over lieutenants, lieutenants over sergeants, and so on. Although civilian managers do not wear insignia, authority is conferred in the same way on a specific position or rank in the business. However, the right to expect action from others is conferred on a manager not only by the business, but also by members of a group if they regard the person as competent to act as their leader.

Authority is therefore closely related to leadership, and it is granted by the business to particular managers. In contrast to authority, power is not granted to a manager. It is acquired in various ways, as we explain in the next section. This difference between authority and power is important, because in practice, many people to whom authority is delegated, but who lack power – which is earned or achieved – fail to exercise that authority effectively. Let us now consider power as an aspect of leadership.

8.2.2.2 Power

Worthy leaders influence their subordinates because they possess power of one kind or another, and therefore exercise their authority effectively. Without power, it is believed, a leader would not be able to influence subordinates sufficiently to induce them to direct their activities voluntarily toward the productive accomplishment of business goals. Power, or the ability to influence the behaviour of others, has nothing to do with the position occupied by a manager in the hierarchy, and it is not acquired through a title or an entry in an organisational diagram. It has to be earned. A person who holds both authority and power, that is, a manager with power, is far more effective than a manager who possesses only authority.

Leadership and management

- Leadership is the ability to influence others to cooperate willingly.
- Management requires leadership as well as other elements of management such as planning, organising and controlling.

Management scholars[4] have identified the following kinds of power:
- **Legitimate power.** This refers to the authority granted in a business to a particular position. Accordingly, a manager has the right to insist on the execution of certain duties by subordinates, and the right to dismiss them if they fail to comply. Legitimate power is therefore the same as authority. However, even though managers may possess legitimate power, this in itself does not necessarily make them good leaders.

- **The power of reward.** This concerns the power to give or withhold rewards. Such rewards include, for example, salary raises, bonuses, recognition, and the allocation of interesting assignments. The larger the number of rewards conferred by a manager, and the more important these rewards are to employees, the greater the reward power will be.
- **Coercive power.** This is the power to enforce compliance through fear, whether psychological, emotional or physical. Gangsters often make use of such power through physical force or violence. Physical force is not a consideration in modern business, but the psychological or emotional fear of being retrenched, or of social exclusion from a group, constitutes a form of power that may be exercised by managers to put pressure on employees.
- **Referent power.** This refers to **personal power** and is a somewhat abstract concept. Subordinates obey leaders simply because they like or respect them, and identify with them. In other words, the leaders' personal characteristics make them attractive to others. Such leaders are said to have charisma.
- **Expert power.** This is derived from expertise, knowledge and professional ability. A leader who possesses it has power, particularly over those who need that knowledge or information. The more important the information, and the fewer the people who possess it, the greater will be the power of the person who commands it.

A manager who commands all five kinds of power is a strong leader. But it is not only managers, or rather leaders, who possess power – employees possess

Table 8.2: Uses and outcomes of power

Source of leader influence	Type of outcome		
	Commitment	**Compliance**	**Resistance**
Referent power	*Likely* If request is believed to be important to leader	*Possible* If request is perceived to be unimportant to leader	*Possible* If request is for something that will bring harm to leader
Expert power	*Likely* If request is persuasive and subordinates share leader's task goals	*Possible* If request is persuasive but subordinates are apathetic about leader's task goals	*Possible* If leader is arrogant and insulting, or subordinates oppose task goals
Legitimate power	*Possible* If request is polite and highly appropriate	*Likely* If request or order is seen as legitimate	*Possible* If arrogant demands are made or request does not appear proper
Reward power	*Possible* If used in a subtle, very personal way	*Likely* If used in a mechanical, impersonal way	*Possible* If used in a manipulative, arrogant way
Coercive power	*Very unlikely*	*Possible* If used in a helpful, non-punitive way	*Likely* If used in a hostile or manipulative way

Source: Griffin, R.W. & Moorhead, G., *Organisational behaviour*, Houghton Mifflin Company, 2001, p. 370.

it occasionally too, for instance when a manager is dependent on them for information, or the social influence of one of them over others is needed for the group's cooperation, or one of them has the ability to carry out a specific task. Managers should therefore understand that their subordinates also possess power, and that they should use their own power judiciously, and only to the extent necessary to accomplish their goals. Table 8.2 provides a useful perspective on how power may be wielded.

Effective managers use their leadership, or their command of power, in such a way that a healthy balance between their own power and that of subordinates is maintained. Figure 8.3 illustrates such a balance.

Figure 8.3: Equilibrium between the power of management and that of subordinates

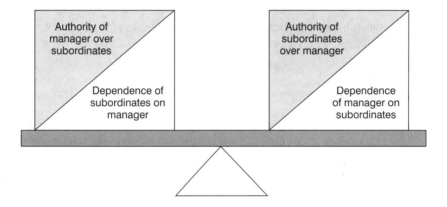

This brief discussion of certain aspects of leadership has elucidated its nature. The characteristics of a good leader will now receive attention.

8.2.2.3 Leadership models

The discussion above of aspects of leadership clearly shows its complexity and why so much research has been undertaken into what makes a person a good leader. However, the belief is still prevalent that good leaders are born, not made a – belief that is not, however, shared by most researchers.

In order to analyse the term leadership and identify the influences that produce a great leader, various leadership models have been researched, developed and tested to determine the key characteristics and behaviour patterns of a good leader. The research was based on the assumption that identifying or distilling the characteristics that make certain people excellent leaders would increase the effectiveness of both organisations and communities in their selection of leaders. In this way, only true leaders would be chosen, with the advantage that both the organisation and the community would function more effectively.

Research into leadership and the development of leadership models was driven by the assumption that certain personality traits and behaviour patterns are crucial to a leader's success. Consequently, the research encompassed everything from leadership qualities and the behaviour of leaders to various approaches and theories of leadership, including a few contemporary perspectives. A brief review of the research that led to specific leadership models, theories and perspectives will help to elucidate leadership in management.

As far as **leadership characteristics** are concerned, the research conducted was unsuccessful in pinpointing a definite set of characteristics. Most studies found that effective leadership does not depend on a particular set of characteristics, but rather on how well the leader's own personal characteristics fit the needs of a given situation.

Leadership characteristics

- One study found that characteristics such as intelligence, initiative and self-confidence are closely related to managerial proficiency, while another rated very highly the ability to supervise.
- The most recent studies have found that women are less likely than men to emerge as leaders but that, when they do, they are as effective as men.
- Subordinates regard women in managerial positions as no less competent leaders than men.

Source: Stoner, J.A.F. et al., *Management*, Prentice-Hall, Englewood Cliffs, N.J., 1995, p. 472.

The **behaviour patterns** of leaders, that is, the styles that they display, have also been thoroughly examined. Among the several styles of leadership that have been identified are the following:
- Autocratic or task-oriented leaders, who are dominating and make all decisions themselves
- Democratic or relationship-oriented leaders, who believe in teamwork
- Theory-X leaders, who believe that most people are lazy and have to be forced to work
- Theory-Y leaders, who believe that most people like to work and accept responsibility willingly

Of course, each leadership style has its strengths and weaknesses, but none can be regarded as the "best" style or model, for that depends entirely on the situation.

Situational leadership models have therefore been proposed to determine a style of leadership that will be most effective in any given situation. The basic idea is that if managers can be trained to be more flexible and ready to adapt their style of leadership to a particular situation, they will be able to perform more effectively as leaders in a variety of situations.

Contemporary research focuses on investigating leadership as a **dynamic interaction** between leaders and followers. Business scientists, for example, are examining the concept of transformation leadership, that is, the ability of a leader to inspire followers to function on a level higher than they had previously managed, for instance by thinking and acting in novel ways. The transformational or charismatic leadership style also refers to leaders who are able not only to change things successfully, but to manage competently in times of change. Another contemporary leadership theory, called the contribution theory, holds that leaders find out why their followers act in a certain way, and then adjust their own behaviour so that they are able to provide appropriate leadership.

As women move into higher positions in organisations, they bring a different leadership style to organisations. **Female leadership** is very effective in today's turbulent corporate environment. Although women also possess assertiveness, initiative and aggressiveness, they tend to engage in leadership behaviour that may be called interactive. **Interactive leadership** is concerned with consensus building, is open and inclusive, encourages participation by others, and is more caring in nature than the leadership style of many males. Interactive leaders are not, of course, found exclusively among women. Anyone can develop these qualities, especially because they are consistent with the trend towards participation and empowerment.

It is evident from the above that leadership is a complex concept and that the wide range of models developed and researched has not really succeeded in identifying the supposedly "best" characteristics or indicating the "best" style of leadership. Effective leadership may be ascribed to a variety of factors, as figure 8.4 shows. Leadership, however, is not the only instrument involved in management's task of getting things done by other people. Motivation also plays an important part in good leadership.

Figure 8.4: Factors influencing effective leadership

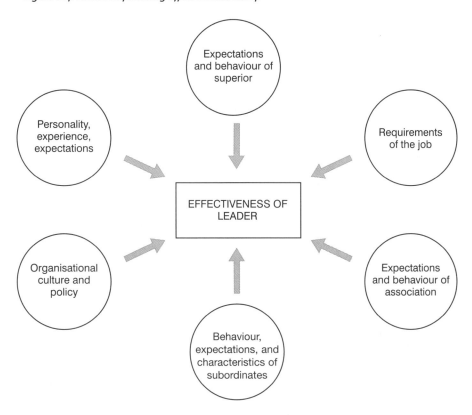

Source: Stoner, J.A.F. et al., *Management*, Pearson Education (UK), 1995, p. 481.

8.2.3 Motivation

Motivation is the second component of leading that may be used to influence the behaviour and performance of subordinates. Motivation is closely linked with leadership.

Managers work with and through people to attain the objectives of a business. But people are complex and often irrational in their behaviour. Their motives are not always easy to assess or to understand. Therefore, the better managers understand the motives behind behaviour, the better they are able to influence employees' behaviour in the best interests of the business. Productivity, and therefore profitability, is a function of the behaviour of employees of the business, and it follows that successful influencing of that behaviour is the key to higher productivity. A brief overview of what constitutes motivation now follows.

8.2.3.1 A basic model of motivation

A motive is an inner drive, stimulus or incentive to satisfy a human need of some kind. It is the behavioural determinant that makes people aware of their needs and drives them to respond to such needs. A motive is therefore a symptom of a need, and it activates the need-satisfying process in the direction of a preconceived goal. In other words, it motivates a person to satisfy a need in a particular manner. Figure 8.5 shows the basic motivation process.

Figure 8.5: A fundamental motivation model

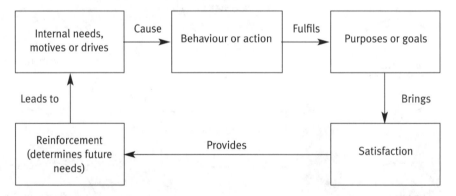

The process is cyclical in character, beginning with internal motives or drives that stimulate people towards a particular form of action or behaviour to achieve the ends they think will satisfy their inner needs. After achieving these goals, they will consciously or unconsciously judge whether the effort has been worthwhile, that is, what level of satisfaction was obtained from it. That decision will reinforce or modify their behaviour when they next have needs, and they will act either in the same way or in some other way. From the point of view of business management, being able to motivate subordinates implies that managers should have knowledge of the inner needs of subordinates, and of the way to satisfy those needs and so influence their behaviour in a way that accomplishes the attainment of the business's goals.

It must also be understood that people differ from one another, and that no two people have the same needs, desires, expectations, goals or ambitions. Moreover, needs and goals alter over time. From management's point of view, there are many reasons for people to work. Whatever the reason, however, work remains one of the most important human activities and the focal point of human life. People do not work merely to earn enough money to live on – their work also plays an important part in the development of their self-realisation and identity.

In every community it is the work people do that largely determines who and what they are. Work determines status, where they live, what school their children go to, and the people with whom they associate. Others judge them by the work they do and, more importantly, they judge themselves by the same standard. Work, therefore, satisfies a number of needs, and for this reason, managers can use motivation as a valuable instrument to improve the performance of employees. To motivate subordinates, managers need to be able to answer two fundamental questions: **what are the subordinates' needs**, and **how can they as managers satisfy these within the context of the business?** Decades of research have produced many theories of motivation, of which Maslow's is probably the most familiar and widely accepted.

8.2.3.2 Maslow's hierarchy of needs

Maslow[5] proposes that people have five kinds of needs, and that these occur in a certain hierarchy, as seen in figure 8.6. People endeavour to satisfy the first group (basic needs) first, then the second, followed by the third, and so on.

Figure 8.6: Maslow's hierarchy of needs

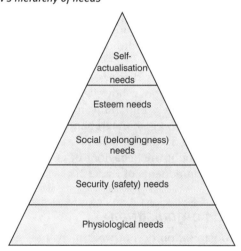

Based on Griffin, R.W., *Management*, Houghton Mifflin Company, 1999, p.47

At the very bottom of the hierarchy we find basic needs such as those for food, clothing and shelter. Once these have been satisfied, they have a diminishing influence on people's behaviour, and the next level assumes a larger role in directing behaviour. The five groups are:
- **Physiological needs** such as food, clothing and shelter. These are neces-

sary for survival. The remuneration of employees is normally adequate to satisfy these needs.

- **Security needs,** which include, for example, protection against danger. Employees need insurance policies against possible losses, as well as medical insurance and pension schemes to make provision for sickness and old age. (Many employers offer such benefits as medical aid and pension schemes to provide for some of the security needs of their employees. It is unlikely that people would change their jobs simply because they were offered a better pension or medical scheme elsewhere. However, if the business made no provision for security needs, it is conceivable that its employees would change jobs to receive such benefits.)
- **Social needs,** which include friendship, love and social acceptance. These play an important role in the informal organisational structure discussed in the previous chapter. Teamwork and team building are also important in the motivation of employees.
- **Esteem or respect needs,** also known as egoistic needs. These arise after social needs, such as those for membership of a group, have been satisfied. These needs include success, status, a sense of value and dignity, and appreciation of performance. Cars, especially the make and model, are important motivating instruments for this kind of need, because they are associated with a particular status.
- **Self-actualisation,** which needs include the urge towards self-expression or the need to be one's true self and "do one's own thing". In developing countries only about 10% of people actively strive to satisfy these needs because they are usually striving to satisfy those needs upon which their basic survival depends. In the work context, self-actualisation needs are probably the most difficult category of needs to satisfy. Assignments that present challenges and the opportunity for participation in decision making can do much to motivate subordinates in this area.

There are, in addition to Maslow's theories, many other theories on motivation.[6] The foregoing discussion does, however, give some idea of a complex instrument that can be extremely important in achieving the goals of a business. Leadership and motivation go hand in hand in inducing subordinates to reach goals productively. To do this with some measure of success, managers should know something about the behaviour of groups and also about communication. These two components of leadership will now be examined.

8.2.4 Groups in an organisation

Subordinates in an organisation do not work merely as individuals with certain needs and personal goals to provide for those needs, but also as members of groups that may on occasion influence the behaviour of other individuals. In fact, a business may be regarded as a group consisting of separate groups.

A group consists of two or more individuals who regularly interact with one another and who work for a common purpose. As in the case of a business, the goals that the group strives for constitute the reason for its existence. Groups in the working place come into being for various reasons, though these are usually related to the needs of individual members. According to

Maslow's hierarchy of needs, it can be said that groups are formed for the following reasons:

- **Basic needs.** To satisfy basic needs, individuals may join a group that demands higher pay, for example.
- **Security needs.** When an individual has insufficient power to bring about change, he or she tends to form a group along with other individuals in the same situation. For example, the trade union movement came into existence because individual employees felt themselves exploited and at the mercy of employers. The trade union, as a group, offers protection (and therefore security) to the individual who wishes to protest, complain, etc. about conditions that threaten his or her personal security.
- **Social needs.** These needs occur to some extent in any group. The group itself is a social phenomenon, that is, it satisfies a deep-rooted need in people to be involved with others, to feel that they belong. Indeed, one of the severest punishments that can be inflicted on people is to ignore or isolate them. The results of many research programmes indicate that employees (even those in small groups) who are separated from one another because of the factory layout, find their work less satisfying than those who can freely associate with others.
- **Esteem needs.** Some people aspire to join a group or occupy a position that, in their opinion, carries social prestige. There are, for example, certain social and sports clubs that are highly selective in admitting new members. Applicants are rigorously scrutinised before being accepted, and membership is a valued status symbol.
- **Self-actualisation needs.** It is sometimes difficult to distinguish between groups formed to satisfy the need for esteem and those formed for the purpose of self-actualisation. Groups are often formed to promote communication between members of the same profession, and a sense of personal development and competence is consolidated by the "shop-talk" and professional jargon bandied about in such associations.

Group membership

Edgar Schein refers to the unusually low number of attempts at escape made by American prisoners of war in Korea. He suggests that one reason for this was the manner in which they were treated.

The North Koreans made sure that no social groups were allowed to form or to continue if they did. Officers were separated from other ranks, groups were systematically broken up, and prisoners were regularly transferred from one camp to another.

The fact that social groups were constantly repressed may perhaps explain the low escape figure. The prisoners were unable to develop the organisation necessary for devising plans of escape. Moreover, they could not develop the necessary trust and confidence in one another that was indispensable for any attempt at escape. Without mutual trust they were deprived of the ability to plan, and their morale was generally very low as a result.

Source: Schein, E., The Chinese indoctrination program for prisoners of war, in *Psychiatry*, Vol. 19, May 1956, pp. 149-72.

Clearly, membership of a group does not satisfy one particular set of needs alone. In many cases, all five of the identified needs are satisfied to some extent by belonging to a group. However, leaders need to know and understand why groups are formed so that they can enable them to function more successfully.

We will now consider the kinds of groups encountered in a business:[7]

- **Functional groups** are set up by management when arranging the activities of the business, for instance the marketing department.
- **Task groups**, such as committees, are created by management to carry out particular duties.
- An **interest group**, in contrast to the previous two, which are formally established by management, is an informal association whose objectives may be either the same as those of the business, or in opposition to them. For example, there may be lunch-time meetings to discuss improving productivity (relevant and desirable), ways to embezzle money (relevant but highly undesirable), or politics and sport (irrelevant to the business).

Informal groups can have an important influence on the operation of a business. The advantages of informal groups are that they satisfy social needs, facilitate communication, maintain social and cultural values, and can solve problems. However, they can also have disadvantages, for example, a group with a negative attitude may frustrate an individual who wishes to progress, or their goals may conflict with those of the business, or they may start or spread gossip and backbiting that is harmful to the morale of employees, or they may set up resistance to change.

8.2.4.1 The characteristics of groups

To further explain how groups operate, and their significance to management, particularly in its task of leading, their salient characteristics will now briefly be surveyed.

- **A leader.** A group will always have a leader, and its success will depend on the leadership qualities he or she possesses. In an informal group it is important that the leader should align his or her objectives with those of the business.
- **Followers or members.** The success of the leader depends on whether group members are willing to accept his or her leadership. It is therefore important that managers and supervisors should also be good leaders.
- **Norms and standards.** The interaction between members of a group will eventually create group norms or generally accepted standards of behaviour, which every member is expected to maintain. Members of the group may reject these norms, conform to them, or accept only the most important. Group pressure, however, will tend to ensure that individual behaviour conforms with group norms. Group pressure may have both positive and negative effects. It promotes teamwork and protects the interests of the group. On the other hand, it can discourage new ideas and creativity. Management can do very little about group pressure, since it is inevitable. The best it can do is to channel it in constructive directions.
- **Group solidarity.** This is the degree of influence that the group is able to exert on individual members. Groups with a strong sense of solidarity usu-

ally display less tension, misunderstanding and conflict among members than those with a weak sense of solidarity. However, a strong sense of solidarity may cause trouble in situations where cooperation between groups is important, for example, where different functional managers are engaged in strategic planning.

- **Interdependence.** Groups are also interdependent – they compete and conflict with one another. Management should understand that the nature of relations between groups will have a direct effect on success in the business.

Good workers and leadership

It is often the best artisans who are made supervisors. Yet it does not necessarily follow that such people make good leaders. A mediocre worker with qualities of leadership may well make a better supervisor than an excellent one who lacks those qualities.

In the work situation, cooperation between individual group members is of vital importance. The better workers in a section function as a group, the greater is the possibility of their fulfilling common goals, and therefore those of the business. The leader's task is to ensure that group members work for the goals of the business within the context of the group.

8.2.5 Communication

It is evident from the foregoing that good leadership depends on constant communication between leaders and subordinates. Good communication is conducive to good relations, not only between management and employees and within groups, but also, ultimately, between the business and its environment. It results in greater work satisfaction and higher productivity. A considerable proportion of a leader's time is devoted to communication, for without it the management process could not be carried out.

Communication is the transfer of information or messages from one person to another. Figure 8.7 illustrates a simple communication model.

Figure 8.7: A basic communication model

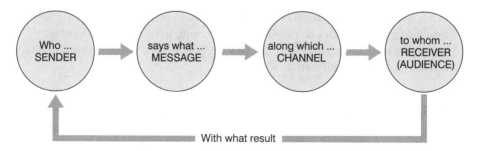

Senders are the source of messages, and to communicate effectively they have to know what they wish to transmit. They should take care with their choice of words and their meaning, and encourage two-way communication; they need to have some insight into the receiver's perceptions.

The **message** may consist of ideas, opinions, plans, orders, or explanations to be conveyed. In the interests of effective communication, the message should be simple and clear.

The **communications channel** is the manner in which the message reaches the receiver. It may assume any form that is perceptible to any of the recipient's senses, as long as it is comprehensible. Spoken language can be heard, gestures can be seen or felt, and the written word can be read.

Receivers of messages should absorb them and facilitate effective communication by showing that they have been received and understood.

Effective communication entails the sender's message being received unimpeded by the recipient, in other words, the recipient grasps the message in accordance with the sender's intentions. Because effective communication is so important in leadership, management should be careful to remove all hindrances to clarity, such as obscure messages, language differences, erroneous perceptions, doubts about the source or sender, and all possible ambiguities. It should also promote effective communication by encouraging feedback, by using face-to-face communication wherever practicable, and by using simple language (which is repeated if necessary), as well as by being aware of any symbolic content in communication.

> **Non-verbal communication**
>
> A touch of the hand may convey a message ranging from sympathy to menace. A wave may carry quite different messages, depending on the number of fingers extended. A letter redolent of the sender's perfume can say a great deal to the recipient.
>
> Non-verbal messages are a very important form of communication, for they are often more forthright than oral or written messages. For example, a manager who greets a latecomer with a frown when saying "Good morning" conveys more than a mere polite greeting might imply.

Communication, the process through which people share opinions and intentions by means of messages, is an essential component of leadership, for without it leaders and subordinates cannot understand one another, and the management process cannot be carried out. Therefore, in order to be good leaders, managers need to be able to communicate intelligibly, thereby encouraging effective communication in others.

8.3 Summary

Leading an organisation towards its goals is a critical management task because it is that element of the management process which translates plans into goals. Leadership, which is defined as the ability of a leader to influence individuals and groups to work willingly towards the accomplishment of the organisation's goals, is a necessary skill for all managers, and the reason for studying leadership is to improve the leadership skills of managers. To be good leaders, managers must understand the nature of leadership, how to motivate subordinates, how groups behave, and how to communicate effectively with individuals and groups.

References

1. Reynders, H.J.J., *Die taak van die bedryfsleier*, J.L. van Schaik, Pretoria, 1975, p. 100.
2. Reynders, H.J.J., *op.cit.*, p. 47.
3. Reynders, H.J.J., *op.cit.*, pp. 78–9.
4. See also French, R. P., & Raven, B., The basis of social power, in Griffin, R.W., *Management*, Houghton Mifflin, Boston, 1990, p. 421.
5. Based on Griffin, R.W., *op. cit.*, p. 440.
6. See also Griffin, R.W., *op. cit.*, pp. 394–7.
7. Griffin, R.W., *op. cit.*, pp. 454–6.

9 Meeting human resource requirements and developing effectiveness in HR

The purpose of this chapter

Successful human resource management is the key to the prevention and solution of many of the problems currently facing South African business organisations and government institutions. Issues that come to mind are the dismantling of discriminatory labour practices, equity and comparable worth, and the social responsibility of organisations towards their employees. Most important of all, perhaps, is respect for the human dignity of every employee or worker as an individual in his or her own right. Here, too, effective and sound human resource management practices can enhance the success of private organisations and public institutions alike. This chapter provides a framework within which managers can achieve these goals by correctly applying the various available human resource management practices.

Learning outcomes

The content of this chapter will enable learners to:
- Describe the basic steps involved in human resource planning
- Explain how companies use recruiting to find qualified job applicants
- Describe the selection techniques and procedures that companies use when deciding which applicants should receive job offers
- Describe how to determine training needs and select the appropriate training methods
- Discuss how to use performance appraisal to give meaningful performance feedback
- Describe basic compensation strategies and how they affect human resource practice

9.1 Introduction

Internationally renowned HR consultant Jeffrey Pfeffer contends in *Competitive advantage through people*[1] that what separates top performing companies from their competitors is the way they treat their workforces. He goes on to argue that companies that invest in their employees create long-lasting competitive advantages that are difficult for other companies to duplicate. However, the process of finding, developing and keeping the right people to form a qualified workforce remains one of the most difficult and important of all management tasks.[2] To assist in this regard, this chapter is structured around the four parts of the human resource management process shown in figure 9.1: determining human resource needs, and finding, developing and keeping a qualified workforce.

Figure 9.1: The HR cone

Accordingly, this chapter begins by reviewing how human resource planning determines human resource needs, such as the kind and number of employees a company requires to meet its strategic plans and objectives. Next, we explore how companies use recruiting and selection techniques to find and hire qualified employees to fulfil those needs. The following section reviews how training and performance appraisal can develop the knowledge, skills and abilities of the workforce, while the last part concludes with a review of compensation, that is, how companies can keep their best workers through effective compensation practices.[3] However, before we look at each of these aspects in detail, it is necessary to find out who will take responsibility for these tasks.

9.2 The relationship between line management and the HR department

It is important to understand that managing people is every manager's business.[4] However, successful organisations are those that combine the experience of line managers with the expertise of HR specialists to develop and utilise the talents of employees to their greatest potential. Addressing HR issues is thus rarely the exclusive responsibility of HR departments acting alone.[5] Instead, HR managers work side by side with line managers to address the people-related issues of the organisation. Although line managers and HR managers need to work together, their responsibilities are different, as are their competencies and expertise. According to Bohlander, Snell and Sherman,[6] the major activities for which an HR manager is typically responsible are the following:

- **Advise and counsel.** The HR manager often serves as an in-house consultant to supervisors, managers and executives on issues such as HR policies, labour agreements, past practices and the needs of employees.
- **Service.** HR managers also engage in a host of service activities such as HR planning, recruiting, selecting, conducting training programmes and compensation.
- **Policy formulation and implementation.** HR managers generally propose and draft new policies or revise existing ones to cover recurring problems or prevent anticipated ones.
- **Employee advocacy.** Another HR responsibility is being an employee advocate, that is, listening to employees' concerns and representing their needs to managers.

Applying the concept: the role of a human resource manager

Are HR managers responsible for the motivation and utilisation of employees in a business?

No. It is not the responsibility of human resource managers to motivate employees in a business (except for their own immediate subordinates in the HR department). Their responsibility is to assess the level of productivity and motivation in the various departments and to advise line managers of methods to improve these.

To successfully execute these roles, HR managers must assume a broader role within the organisation and acquire a complementary set of competencies as shown in figure 9.2 (see p. 195).[7]

Thus, by helping their organisations build a sustained competitive advantage, and by learning to manage many activities well, HR professionals can become full business partners. The first step towards making this process a reality is to establish a company's human resource needs.

9.3 Human resource planning

Human resource planning is the process of using an organisation's goals and strategy to forecast the organisation's human resource needs in terms of finding, developing and keeping a qualified workforce. HR planning can be divided into three specific steps:

- **Step 1:** Identify the work being done in the business at present (job analysis and job description).
- **Step 2:** Identify the type of employees needed to do the work (job specification).
- **Step 3:** Identify the number of employees who will be needed in the future (human resource forecasting and planning).

Figure 9.2: Human resource competency model

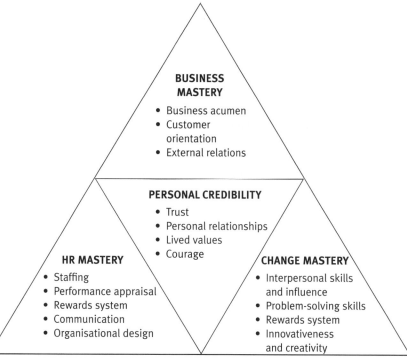

BUSINESS MASTERY
- Business acumen
- Customer orientation
- External relations

PERSONAL CREDIBILITY
- Trust
- Personal relationships
- Lived values
- Courage

HR MASTERY
- Staffing
- Performance appraisal
- Rewards system
- Communication
- Organisational design

CHANGE MASTERY
- Interpersonal skills and influence
- Problem-solving skills
- Rewards system
- Innovativeness and creativity

KEY
- **Business mastery.** HR professionals need to know the business of their organisation thoroughly.
- **HR mastery.** HR professionals should develop competencies that keep them abreast of changes in the different HR activities.
- **Change mastery.** HR professionals must be able to manage change processes so that HR activities are effectively merged with the business needs.
- **Personal credibility.** HR professionals must establish personal credibility in the eyes of their internal and external customers.

Source: Yeung, A., Brockbank, W. & Ulrich, D., Lower cost, higher value: human resource function in transformation, in Bohlander, G., Snell, S. & Sherman, A., *Managing human resources*, 12th edition, South-Western Publishing, by permission of Thomson Learning, 2001, p. 30.

9.3.1 Job analysis

The first step in HR planning is to determine the nature of the work being done. Job analysis is the **process of describing and recording information about job behaviours and activities**[8]. The following questions might be asked when undertaking a job analysis:
- What is the employee responsible for?
- What tasks are performed?
- What decisions are made?
- What information is needed to enable the work to be done?
- Under what conditions is the job performed?

There are various ways in which this information can be collected. One method is **observation** by a qualified job analyst. The job analyst observes the employee working, and records all the relevant information. Observation may also include videotaping, audiotaping and electronic monitoring. This method is especially suited to manual labour, where it is easy to see exactly what the employee is doing. However, administrative work is more difficult to observe.

The method generally followed for administrative work is **interviewing**, where the job analyst interviews an employee and asks for a description of responsibilities and tasks.

Questionnaires may also be used. Here the employee (and sometimes his or her immediate superior) answers a number of specific questions about the tasks and responsibilities of the job. Questionnaires may be developed for specific circumstances, or standardised questionnaires (which are more economical) may be purchased from external vendors.

Applying the concept: job analysis

Is it possible for the HR manager to appoint suitable candidates without an indication of what it is they will be doing?

No. Job analysis involves collecting informa-tion on a specific job, and a job description is the recording of that information. As such, the two activities go hand-in-hand and are therefore vital before the recruiting process can start.

9.3.2 Job description

Whatever method of data collection is used for job analysis, the information is put in writing in a certain format – a **job description** – so that other people, who are not involved in the job analysis, can nevertheless gain thorough insight into the contents of the job.

A job description does not merely list a number of facts. It is usually prepared in a predetermined format so that it is easily readable. It generally starts with a summary of the job, followed by a brief description of each main task, with more detail and practical examples as subdivisions. A description of the kind of decisions that need to be taken by the employee may follow.[9]

The job description format generally differs from business to business. The important point, however, is that the content of jobs must be put on record in an understandable way.

9.3.3 Job specification

The personal qualifications an employee must possess in order to perform the duties and responsibilities depicted in the job description are contained in the job **specification**.[10] Typically, job specifications detail the knowledge, skills and abilities relevant to a job, including the education, experience, specialised training, personal traits and manual dexterity of the person doing the job. At times, an organisation may also include the physical demands the job places on an employee. These might include the amount of walking, standing, reaching, or lifting that is required of the employee.[11]

Applying the concept: job specification

Will the qualifications of the present job incumbent help the HR manager to appoint suitable candidates to the position in the future?

No. The present employee's qualifications are not under discussion. The person cur-rently occupying the job might meet all the requirements or even surpass them – or might not meet all the requirements. It is in fact the job specification that indicates what the qualifications and experience of an employee ought to be.

9.3.4 Human resource forecasting

A further step in human resource planning is to conduct regular forecasts of the quantity and quality of employees that the business is going to need in the future. As indicated in figure 9.3 (see p. 198), the purpose of the process is to balance human resource supply and demand. Demand is affected by business objectives – the number of people needed to obtain the objectives – while supply is affected by the HR programmes providing the human resources. Factors to be kept in mind during forecasting are:

- **Economic growth.** This involves forecasting the expected growth (or shrinkage) of the business in view of probable economic developments. For example, will there be a recession or growth in the near or distant future?
- **New developments in the business.** These include planned physical extensions, the establishment of new branches, and technological changes (especially those that will affect staff, such as computerised machinery, which might create a greater need for technically skilled employees).
- **The labour market.** Important questions in this regard are the following: Are there sufficient opportunities in the labour market, or is there a high level of unemployment? What will the nature and scope of labour turnover in the future be? Will there be a shortage of a certain type of skilled employee? Will employees be readily available?

9.3.5 The human resource plan

Using the information obtained thus far, the HR manager can compile an HR plan, the final step in the process. The purpose of this plan is to provide concrete guidelines and steps that indicate how the business's short, medium and long-term human resource requirements can be provided for. In other words, it answers the question, What must we do today to be prepared for tomorrow? The HR plan should dovetail with the strategic plan of the business, as mentioned earlier.

Such an HR plan might, for example, make provision for an active recruiting campaign, emphasise the need for intensive training programmes – or even make a strong recommendation to automate because of a possible shortage of human resources.

Figure 9.3: A procedure for estimating the human resource shortage or surplus for a job or occupational category

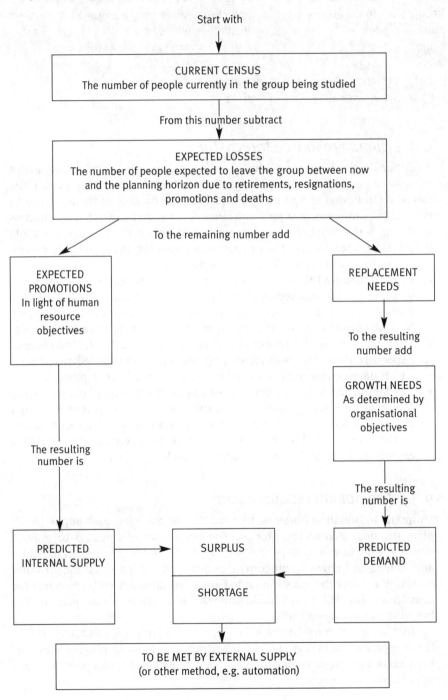

Source: Anthony, W.P., Kacmar, K.M., & Perrewé, P.L., *Human resource management: a strategic approach*, 4th edition, South-Western Publishing, by permission of Thomson Learning, 2002, p. 127.

Applying the concept: human resource planning

Will the HR manager be able to supply a sufficient number of people to the business without proper HR planning?

No. If proper provision is not made for determining the number and types of employees required by the business, now as well as in the future, the business will not survive.

This stage concludes the process of HR planning. The next activity in the process is finding qualified workers.

9.4 Finding qualified workers

9.4.1 Recruiting

The express purpose of recruitment is to ensure that a sufficient number of applicants apply for the various jobs in the business as and when required. Therefore, as soon as vacancies occur, the HR manager must decide from where suitable candidates for the job will be obtained. There are two basic sources from which potential employees can be recruited: from inside the business or from external sources.

9.4.1.1 Recruitment from inside

Recruitment from inside means trying as far as possible to fill vacant positions with existing staff members, except for jobs on the lowest levels. In practice, it means that people from outside are appointed only at the lowest level, and that all more senior jobs in the hierarchy are filled by means of promotion (or sometimes lateral transfers) of existing staff. Where a job at a very senior level becomes vacant, this leads to a whole series of promotions. Whatever a business decides, it will also have to take into account labour legislation such as the Employment Equity Act 55 of 1998 and the Labour Relations Act 66 of 1995.[12] These issues will be discussed more fully in later chapters.

An example of recruitment from inside the business

If the marketing manager resigned, the assistant marketing manager would probably be promoted. His or her job might then be filled by a regional sales manager, whose job, in turn, would be filled by a sales manager. The sales manager's job would then be filled by promoting one of the salespeople, and it is only at this point that a new salesperson would be recruited from outside.

The **advantages** of a policy of recruiting from inside are the following:
- Career planning becomes possible, in that individual employees see a future for themselves in the business. This, again, has a positive effect on morale.
- Assessment of applicants is easier because the business already has considerable information on the possible candidates' abilities, work performance and potential.

- The cost of recruitment is low because advertising, travel, and board and lodging expenses are largely eliminated.

However, there are also three **disadvantages** connected with such a policy:
- The business tends to stagnate because staff members often think like their predecessors. There are therefore no new ideas.
- Staff appointed at lower levels do not necessarily have the potential to fill senior management posts. If people with high potential are appointed at the lowest levels, they might not be prepared to wait long for promotion opportunities.
- There can be a lot of personal competition among colleagues, to the detriment of cooperation among them.

9.4.1.2 Recruitment from outside

Recruitment from outside means looking for suitable applicants outside the business when a post becomes vacant.

This has the following two **advantages**:
- An active effort is made to obtain the right person for the job, that is, someone with the most suitable qualifications and experience.
- The opportunity is created for bringing in new ideas, schools of thought and approaches, which considerably increase the possibility for innovation in the business.

However, the **disadvantages** must also be taken into consideration:
- Recruitment costs are considerably higher for items such as advertising and travelling expenses to enable applicants to come from elsewhere for the interview, and the reimbursement of successful applicants' moving costs.
- It is risky because the assessment of applicants can never be perfect. The possibility therefore exists that the successful applicant will not be successful **in the job**.
- The morale of existing personnel can be negatively influenced. Employees with high potential will not be prepared to stay indefinitely at the same level, and might consider resigning.

It is especially for the last reason that most businesses do not follow a policy of recruitment only from outside. Most businesses apply both approaches in one of two ways:
- Some businesses first **look inside** – and only when they cannot find a suitable candidate do they recruit outside.
- Some businesses **advertise all jobs** above a certain level, but encourage existing personnel to apply. In this way, management tries to find the most suitable candidate, regardless of whether the person comes from inside or outside.

9.4.1.3 The recruiting procedure

If a business recruits from inside, the HR manager must ensure that an efficient HR record system exists. Such a record system – which is now available in computerised form known as a human resources information system (HRIS)[13] – should contain information on each employee's qualifications, training and experience, as well as an assessment of achievements and interests. When a job becomes vacant, the HR manager should be in a position to identify the most suitable candidates.

Recruitment from outside is much more complex, and it is important that the HR manager should know exactly **whom** to recruit, **where** to recruit from, and **how** the people should be recruited. Successful recruitment does not only mean that enough people apply for a job. If too many applicants apply for a job, selection will be a very time-consuming process. The ideal is therefore that only those suitable for the job apply.

To begin with, recruitment from outside requires a thorough **labour market analysis**. A labour market can be defined as the social or **geographical area** from which a business draws its employees. Certain mines in South Africa draw most of their staff from neighbouring countries. Their labour market is, for example, Lesotho or Malawi (that is, a geographical area). Other businesses, again, might employ mainly women who want to work half-days. This market can be regarded as a **social area**.

Every labour market has unique characteristics. A characteristic of the South African labour market is that the relationship between skilled and unskilled workers is relatively unbalanced. Obtaining unskilled labour does not appear to be a big problem, whereas this is not the case for skilled and professional people, who are exceptionally scarce. Human resource managers must therefore know the composition of their company's labour market as well as that of the South African labour market as a whole, if they are to recruit effectively.

9.4.1.4 Recruiting techniques

The HR manager can employ various recruiting techniques:[14]

- **Recruitment through advertisements**. This is probably the most common form of recruiting, in spite of its high cost. The compiling and placing of an advertisement is a specialised task and because it can cost thousands of rands, some companies use professional advertisement compilers. With the implementation of the Labour Relations Act 66 of 1995, as well as the Employment Equity Act 55 of 1998, it is crucial that the advertisement be neutrally worded. If a requirement is set which may preclude one of the disadvantaged groups, then it must be a genuine prerequisite for the performance of the job. It has been found that the more specifically the responsibilities for the job are defined, the better the chances are of drawing the "right" applicants. Qualifying requirements, such as a certain academic qualification, or language ability, must be included to limit unsuitable applications to a minimum. An indication of the remuneration offered is also important, firstly to draw the right applicants and secondly to eliminate potential applicants who already earn more. General requirements in the advertisement, such as "loyalty", "initiative", "sense of responsibility" and "drive" are totally superfluous, because they never deter a person from applying for a job. Advertisements may be placed in journals and newspapers or on bulletin boards.
- **Recruitment through consultants and labour agencies.** This approach is becoming increasingly prevalent in South Africa. The use of HR consultants is especially suitable for smaller businesses for which the services of a

full-time HR manager cannot be justified. Such businesses inform a consulting firm of their needs, and the latter undertakes all the recruitment, including preliminary selection and recruitment administration for the business. In most cases (depending on the job level), the consultant recommends two or three applicants to the business, which must then make the final choice.

- **Recruitment through existing employees.** Existing employees are asked to recruit friends or acquaintances for the business. The rationale of this approach is that if members of staff feel positively about their work, they will more easily persuade others to apply. This method obviates the necessity for advertisements.

- **Recruitment through personal approach.** Using this method (often called head-hunting), an individual personally known to the management of a business or consulting firm is approached and offered a job. This saves a lot of recruiting costs but has the disadvantage that the person cannot be weighed objectively against other applicants. This means that the selection process takes place before the recruitment process, in that the business first decides to appoint an individual to a specific job, and then asks him or her to consider the appointment.

- **Recruitment through radio, TV and the Internet.** Using this type of media is costly, and still in its infancy in South Africa. However, looking at international trends, the approach should become more popular in the future, especially via the Internet.

- **Sundry recruiting strategies.** Visits to schools, technikons and universities to draw students' attention to employment opportunities are often used by businesses – not so much to recruit for specific jobs, but with long-term objectives in mind. The allocation of study bursaries with a compulsory period of service linked to them is a further method of drawing candidates with high academic potential. Participation in career exhibits and the distribution of general recruitment brochures are other techniques available to the HR manager to ensure a sufficient flow of suitable applicants from whom appointments to the business can be made.

Applying the concept: recruitment

Is it likely that the HR manager will be able to obtain the services of enough people for the running of the business?

Yes. Not only can the HR manager recruit internally, but vast external sources for recruiting suitable candidates are also available through the use of various techniques.

After applicants have been recruited, the next step is to select the best candidates.

9.4.2 Selection

The selection process can vary from a very short interview, to obtain a general impression of the applicant, to an intensive assessment process. However, this differs from business to business and depends especially on the level of the appointment.[15] In figure 9.4 (see p. 203), nine steps in a typical selection process are depicted.

Figure 9.4: Steps in a typical selection process

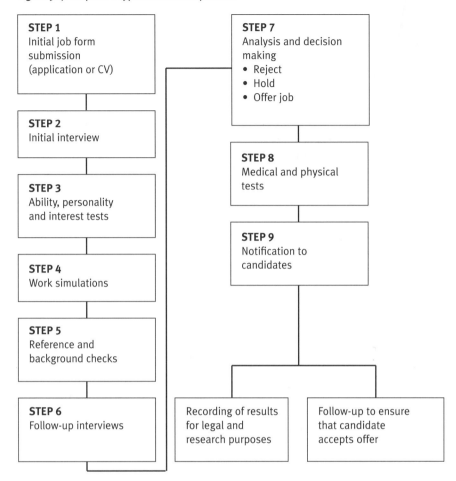

STEP 1
Initial job form submission (application or CV)

STEP 2
Initial interview

STEP 3
Ability, personality and interest tests

STEP 4
Work simulations

STEP 5
Reference and background checks

STEP 6
Follow-up interviews

STEP 7
Analysis and decision making
- Reject
- Hold
- Offer job

STEP 8
Medical and physical tests

STEP 9
Notification to candidates

Recording of results for legal and research purposes

Follow-up to ensure that candidate accepts offer

Source: Adapted from Jackson, S.E. & Schuler, R.S., *Managing human resources: a partnership approach*, 7th edition, South-Western Publishing, by permission of Thomson Learning, 2000, p. 315.

The process described below, however, is the more intensive approach followed in the selection of applicants for senior management posts. For this reason, not all the steps indicated in figure 9.4 are followed in this discussion. The selection process to be used for senior management posts can be divided into the following three phases:
- Preliminary screening
- Intensive assessment
- Final selection

With the implementation of the Labour Relations Act and the Employment Equity Act, a number of important components of the selection process, that is, the application form, the interview and the tests used, have been affected. For example, the application form must not contain discriminatory questions such as, Are you married, divorced, single? Moreover, these types of questions may not be asked during the interview, and the various tests used must not be culturally biased.

9.4.2.1 Preliminary screening

The most efficient method for separating undesirable candidates from potential applicants is to compare the application with the job specification (step 1 in figure 9.4).

A great deal of information can be included on the application form. What is asked depends largely on the needs of the specific business and the nature of the selection process. Information that is usually requested on an application form is **personal detail** (for example, name, address, educational qualifications) and **work history** (for example, jobs held in the past, reasons for resignation, and salary progress). Also, references are usually requested, that is, persons or institutions are approached to support the information given on the form (step 5 in figure 9.4).

Questions can also be asked about the applicant's significant achievements, disappointments, career expectations and communal and leisure-time activities. What is important is that the application form should serve as a preliminary selection instrument. In this preliminary selection, the HR manager should learn the following:

Does the applicant comply with the minimum requirements as given in the job specification?

- What types of jobs did the applicant hold in the past?
- How quickly did he or she progress?
- How often has he or she changed jobs?

After the above activities have been completed, the next step is to have a short interview with the applicants who are, according to information in the application form, suitable candidates (step 2 in figure 9.4). This **interview** provides the HR manager with the opportunity to form a general opinion of the applicant, based on appearance, articulateness and self-confidence. It also gives the applicant the opportunity to obtain more information about the business and the specific job.

A preliminary interview is usually not practical for applicants who would have to travel far, and they would instead be invited to report for a more intensive assessment.

9.4.2.2 Intensive assessment

Intensive assessment basically involves two steps, namely **psychological testing** and **diagnostic interviewing**. Although medical selection usually forms part of the final selection process (step 8 in figure 9.4), it is advisable to have the applicant first assessed medically if the job has stringent physical requirements, for example, in the case of an airline pilot. However, the use of general medical tests in South Africa could have legal implications for the business, depending on the results of the medical examination, and any hint of discrimination in their interpretation or use. Businesses therefore need to act with caution in this regard.

- **Psychological testing** can provide valuable information on an applicant. Tests usually involve a measurement of the applicant's personality, abilities and management skills (steps 3 and 4 in figure 9.4). An important aspect here is to take care that the tests used are not culturally biased, as mentioned earlier. Some HR managers have the required qualifications for doing testing themselves, while others have the testing done by professionals. The important point to remember is that a test can never predict accurately whether an applicant will be successful or unsuccessful. Test results give only a general indication that must be considered together with other factors.

- A **diagnostic interview** is used to obtain information that was not highlighted in the tests or on the application form (step 6 in figure 9.4). A good interviewer looks for certain characteristics by asking specific questions about the applicant's past performance. For instance, an applicant's initiative can be assessed by asking about new projects that he or she may have initiated in previous jobs. The interview also gives the HR manager a chance to delve deeper into possible shortcomings indicated by tests. If, for example, the interviewer suspects that the applicant does not always have good relationships with other people, more can be asked about interpersonal relationships. However, as mentioned previously, questions of a discriminatory nature must be avoided, such as about the person's religious convictions or sexual preferences.

The key to good interviewing is to ask questions that give no indication of what answer is expected.

Some HR managers prefer to do diagnostic interviews alone, without involving the line functionaries under whom the applicant will work. Others, however, find it useful to include line functionaries at this stage, and sometimes even to have them take part in the interview.

9.4.2.3 Final selection

At this stage there is usually enough information available about the applicants to compile a **shortlist** of, at most, three persons.

Before the applicants on the shortlist are finally weighed against each other, the HR manager must consult their **references** to confirm the information they have provided. (In figure 9.4 this was done before the diagnostic interview. However, there is no right or wrong stage at which to consult references.) Some HR managers do not attach much value to references because applicants would not refer HR managers to people who do not have a high regard for them. Therefore it is not, in fact, worth very much simply to ask referees for an opinion about the applicant's suitability. However, if the referees are asked to confirm information (whether positive or negative) obtained in the intensive assessment phase, they can make a very valuable contribution to the selection process.

In the final **comparison of applicants** it may be useful to interview all three (or two) again briefly. What is essential, however, is to record the strengths and weaknesses of each of the final applicants in writing before the final decision is made (step 7 in figure 9.4). These documents must be kept for record purposes should a problem arise in the future.

An example of a final selection decision

Recently, an HR consultant recommended three applicants for the job of general manager of an agricultural cooperative. In the directors' discussion after final interviews with all three, opinion was divided between applicant A and applicant B because both showed certain outstanding characteristics. However, they both also had several shortcomings, and after the strengths and weaknesses of all three applicants had been written down, the directors decided unanimously on applicant C.

After the most suitable applicant has been decided on, the person concerned is offered the job (step 9 in figure 9.4). This is the time to explain what is expected of the person in the job and to advise what the conditions of employment are. The applicant can then decide whether to accept the job or not.

If the job is accepted, the applicant usually has to be **medically examined** to ensure that there are no serious health problems.

Applying the concept: selection

Is it possible for the HR manager to make a correct decision when appointing a candidate?

Yes. By making use of a formal selection process and using various inputs obtained from tests, interviews and references, it is possible that the appointment made is the most suitable one at the time. Additional inputs from line managers can also be obtained. However, even though everything possible may be done to retain the new employee, it is a reality that good people resign and accept jobs at other businesses.

9.4.2.4 Placement and induction

Once the job offer has been accepted, the new employee must report for duty as soon as possible. With the placement of the person in the job a number of outstanding matters can be finalised. For example, in some cases arrangements must be made for the transport of furniture, provision of temporary housing, collection of missing information (for example, copies of education certificates) and the completion of forms authorising tax and medical aid contribution deductions.

The new employee must also go through a process of induction (also known as **orientation** or **socialisation**). Experience has shown that when employees do not do this, it takes much longer for them to start working productively.

An induction programme will achieve the following:[16]

- Introduce new employees to their colleagues and facilitate and expedite the socialising process
- Explain to them the business's policy, procedures and rules, so that they are aware of the environment in which they will work
- Inform new employees about the business's history, products and services, as well as its reputation in the market, not only to fix their attention on their futures, but also to make them aware of the contribution they might make to the realisation of the business's objectives
- Inform employees about practical arrangements, for example, about pay-

ment procedures, overtime payment, incentive systems, eating arrangements and leave benefits
- Inform them about the organisational structure of the business and show them where they fit in and which communication channels are available to them

Applying the concept: induction

Will the HR manager be able to get the newly-appointed employee to become productive as soon as possible?

Yes. With the help of information sessions held by the HR manager, as well as by the employee's immediate supervisor, the new appointee will be able to function efficiently within a relatively short time.

Once employees have been recruited, selected and placed in their jobs, the next step is training. This involves providing them with the skills, knowledge and abilities necessary to successfully perform their jobs.

9.5 Developing qualified workers

9.5.1 Human resource development (HRD)

It is the task of the human resource manager not only to ensure that the company employs sufficient staff but also to create **opportunities** for the employees to make themselves more valuable to the company. This activity can be subdivided in several ways, but a good method is to distinguish firstly between **training** and **development**, and secondly between **technical** and **management training**.

Training typically involves providing employees with the knowledge and skills needed to do a particular task or job, although attitude change may also be attempted (for example, in sexual harassment awareness training). **Developmental** activities, in contrast, have a longer-term focus on preparing for future work responsibilities, while at the same time increasing the capacities of employees to perform their current jobs.[17]

While the methods used for training and development are basically the same, the **purpose** differs. Thus, one person may attend a course on marketing because he or she currently fills a marketing post, whereas another person may be sent to the same course because management wants him or her to fill a marketing post at some future point. Similarly, a superior may spend time teaching a subordinate how to do his or her work correctly, but may also spend time teaching the subordinate to do the superior's work with a view to future promotion.

For our purposes, we will speak of **development** as the overall concept, with the understanding that it includes both training and development in the narrower sense of the word. We can thus define **human resource development** as a set of systematic and planned activities designed by an organisation to provide its members with the opportunities to learn necessary skills to meet current and future job demands. Consequently, learning is at the core of all human resource development activities.[18]

The word **technical** means not so much tasks performed in a workshop, but any task that has to be performed physically. Accordingly, the keeping of journals is just as technical as the repair of a machine. In its wider sense, we use the word technical to refer to all non-management tasks. By **management work** we mean tasks like planning, organising, controlling, and especially managing people.

HRD activities should begin when an employee joins an organisation; and continue throughout his or her career, regardless of whether that employee is an executive or a worker on an assembly line. HRD programmes must respond to job changes and integrate the long-term plans and strategies of the organisation to ensure the efficient and effective use of resources. The HR manager does not have to train other employees personally (usually there are HRD professionals to do this) but he or she is primarily responsible for providing development facilities and courses. The HR manager must ensure that the employees are given an opportunity for training and development and that they are encouraged to develop to higher levels of competence.

9.5.2 *Development methods*

The development activities can be executed in four basic ways, namely:[19]
- Informally within the work situation
- Formally within the work situation
- Informally outside the work situation
- Formally outside the work situation

9.5.2.1 Informal development inside the work situation

In this situation the employee does not follow an official training programme. He or she is put to work immediately and expected to **learn in due course**. It might also happen that a newcomer works with an experienced employee for a while to give him or her time to "find his feet".

Informal development within the work situation can also occur through coaching by the employee's immediate superior. The latter, for example, may give his or her subordinate certain responsibilities and show the employee how to perform certain tasks.

Another common form of informal internal development is **job rotation**. This means that a staff member is moved to a new job as soon as he or she knows the current job well. The rotation could be short-term, for example, two weeks in every job, or long-term, for example, one year in every job. The latter usually applies to more senior management jobs and is often preparation for a general management position. What is important, however, is that **the development does not take place at random**. The HR manager can make an important contribution in this regard by:
- Keeping a careful record of each employee's development progress
- Encouraging line managers to establish this type of development (the HR manager does not usually have the official authority to enforce the development described)
- Discussing the progress and prospects of individual staff members with those individuals themselves

It often happens that when an employee resigns he or she is informed for the first time of all the development plans that the company had for the person. In most cases, however, it is then too late. The HR manager can, indeed, prevent many resignations by ensuring that individuals are kept informed of the career path planned for them in the enterprise.

9.5.2.2 Formal development within the work situation

By formal development we mean a training process in which the employee receives a formal qualification. The most common form of this type of development is a learnership. The subordinate is allocated to a qualified artisan and so provided with the necessary practical training. From time to time, the subordinate must attend a few block courses, usually at a technical institution. After a certain period (the time varies according to the nature of the training) the subordinate receives a certificate if he or she has passed the compulsory examination. Other examples of this type of training are the qualifying exams for promotion in the South African National Defence Force and banking exams. The purpose of this type of training is not only to equip employees for their present jobs, but also to give them a wider perspective and background on the work situation in which they find themselves.

9.5.2.3 Informal development outside the work situation

In this sort of training an employee does not receive a qualification as such, although a certificate is sometimes issued to indicate that he or she has attended a particular training programme.

Probably the most common form of this type of development is a **training course** offered inside the company. Many companies (especially the larger ones) have training centres where staff members receive training in a variety of subjects, for example, interpersonal relationships, sales techniques, secretarial skills, supervising techniques, communication techniques, and planning techniques.

An **induction course** would also fall into this category. These courses are sometimes presented by the HR manager or by a HRD manager specially appointed for the job. They can also be presented by outsiders who specialise in presenting this type of course.

The advantage of courses presented within a company is that the training material is aimed specifically at the circumstances and operations of that particular company. This type of course is not only meant for workers at the lowest level of the company, but also for managers.

There are many courses in which managers can learn skills for handling and motivating subordinates. By arranging for managers in the company to attend such training programmes, the HR manager can make a big contribution towards line managers' optimal utilisation of employees.

Another form of informal development outside the work situation is the public seminar presented by an outside institution (for example, a consultant or professional institution). Such courses are normally attended by a variety of employees from various companies. This type of course is valuable especially to smaller companies that want to expose only a few staff members to this type of training and can therefore not present the course within the organisation. The disadvantage here is that training material becomes generalised because it must apply to a number of widely divergent companies.

The abovementioned courses normally last a few days or weeks, on a full-time basis. However, staff members might also attend a training session one morning a week, for example, and such a programme can last for a number of months.

Some companies use **programmed instruction** (PI) as a training method. Here, the instructional material is broken down into frames and programmed for the computer. Each frame represents a small component of the entire subject to be learned, and each frame must be successfully completed before the next one can be tackled. An advantage of PI is that large numbers of employees can be trained simultaneously, with each learner free to explore the material at his or her own pace. In addition, PI includes immediate and individualised feedback. A disadvantage is that development costs are high, especially for computerised PI.[20]

Another form of informal development is a fixed **reading programme**. For example, an employee may undertake to study certain books before a certain date, or to become a regular subscriber to a professional journal. If such a programme is agreed on, the HR manager must follow it up regularly, otherwise it is likely to peter out in the course of time.

9.5.2.4 Formal development outside the work situation

By this we mean formal study programmes presented by educational institutions, for example, universities, technikons and colleges. What mainly contributes to the employee's general development is extensive and general training, rather than equipping the person for the specific job he or she is currently doing. Many companies encourage their employees to attempt this type of development and even offer to pay the fees if the employee is successful in his or her studies.

9.5.3 The danger of the "shotgun" approach to development

As is clear from the above, there are many development possibilities that the HR manager can use. However, the problem is that many HR managers are of the opinion that "any training is valuable". They therefore encourage employees to attempt extramural studies, and arrange for a certain number of employees to attend some training programmes every year. They aim, as if with a shotgun, in a general direction, and hope to hit something.

The successful HR manager, however, attempts to obtain as much value as possible from development programmes. He or she will therefore first make a thorough analysis of the **development needs** that exist within the company, and then choose training programmes on the basis of how specific programmes comply with these needs. Secondly, he or she will ensure that training money is spent only on members of staff who show a potential for further development. The HR manager will then make plans with the immediate superior of the employee concerned to utilise the new skills or insight in the work situation. Lastly, the HR manager must undertake follow-up studies to determine whether the training programmes have had the desired results.

Applying the concept: development

Why do companies spend so much time and money on developing their employees?

According to the American Society for Training and Development, an investment in training increases productivity by an average of 17%, reduces employee turnover, and makes companies more profitable.[21]

We have focused thus far in this chapter on some of the most effective methods available to managers for finding and developing top-notch employees. However, having talented employees is not enough – successful organisations are particularly adept at engaging their workforce to achieve goals that benefit the organisation as well as the individual. One of the most helpful tools a company can use to maintain and enhance productivity and facilitate progress towards strategic goals, is performance appraisal programmes.[22]

9.5.4 Performance appraisal

The purpose of a performance appraisal is to determine in which aspects the employee:

- Performed exceptionally well (that is, surpassed the requirements for the job)
- Complied with the requirements for the job
- Did not comply with the requirements for the job

Such appraisal has also been called **employee rating, employee evaluation, performance review, performance evaluation** and **results appraisal**.[23] **Performance appraisal** can be done by anyone who is familiar with the performance of individual employees, including supervisors who rate their employees, employees who rate their superiors, team members who rate each other, employee self-appraisal, or outside sources.

The more **objective** this appraisal, the more successful it is likely to be, and it is therefore important for the HR manager to ensure that there are objective criteria against which the performance of the individual or team can be measured. Thus, an ideal performance appraisal involves the comparison of work results with quantitative objectives.[24] For example, a salesman's actual sales are compared with a sales target, a truck driver can be appraised, inter alia, against the maintenance costs of his truck, and a teller's performance may be measured against the number of times he or she did not achieve a balance.

Some performance appraisal methods also provide for the assessment of an employee's **characteristics**, such as attitude, enthusiasm, initiative and neatness. However, this type of assessment is much more subjective than the comparison of results with objectives because it depends mainly on the opinion of the immediate superior.

The least effective form of performance appraisal is where employees are compared with each other in general. In this approach the employee is assessed mainly on the basis of the **impression** the superior has of him or her – and the risk of prejudice (positive or negative) is much greater.

As a result of the numerous problems that arise out of traditional performance appraisal methods, a new approach, namely the **360° system**, was developed some years ago. This multi-source rating recognises that the manager is no longer the sole source of performance appraisal information. Instead, feedback from various colleagues and constituencies is obtained and given to the manager, who then interprets the feedback from the various sources.[25]

In practice, and for a number of reasons, formal performance appraisal programmes sometimes yield disappointing results. Primary causes include a lack of top-management information and support, unclear performance standards, rater bias, too many forms to complete, and the use of the programmes for conflicting purposes.[26] The **results** of a performance appraisal can be used for three basic purposes, namely:

- To provide a basis for financial rewards
- To determine whether the employee should be promoted to a higher level of work
- To provide the employee with feedback on how well he or she is doing

Since it is not possible for the HR manager to do the performance appraisal himself (except where employees – that is, the HR officers – fall directly under his or her control), the HR manager must ensure that it is done by the line managers and help them to do it, especially by providing them with suitable instruments for doing appraisals.

A critical aspect in performance appraisal is **feedback** to the individual or team concerned. In order to be effective, feedback should possess characteristics other than timeliness – for example, it must be concise (not too lengthy), specific (examples must be provided), relevant (it must be job related) and supportive (offer suggestions for positive change).[27]

Applying the concept: performance appraisal

Should performance appraisal in a company be seen merely as a once-off activity?

No. The best performance appraisal systems are those in which the supervisor or manager makes an **ongoing effort to coach and monitor** employees, instead of leaving evaluation to the last minute.

Rewarding those employees whose performance appraisals are excellent is important and necessary. However, organisations also use compensation to attract the quality and quantity of employees needed, retain those employees, and motivate them towards organisational goal achievement. In the following section, the important role played by compensation within an organisation will be discussed.

9.6 Keeping qualified workers

9.6.1 Compensation of employees

Compensation refers to all forms of financial returns and tangible services and benefits employees receive as part of an employment relationship.[28] It is one of the most important factors that motivates an individual to seek employment with a specific company. The other is the nature of the work. If an employee is dissatisfied with his or her compensation, there is a good chance that the employee will not remain with the company for long. The HR manager must therefore ensure that the **compensation policy** does not lead to a high staff turnover.

Thus, the establishment of a compensation policy is an absolute necessity.[29] Although the HR manager, in most companies, does not have the final say in the compensation policy, it must nevertheless be initiated by him or her. Regarding this policy, it must in the first place be decided how the company's compensation in general should compare with that of the labour market. Will it be the same? A little higher? Considerably higher? Or a little lower? What form should the compensation take? How much will be in the form of direct financial compensation? And how much in the form of fringe benefits? The fringe benefits of some companies do not involve more than 30-40% of the total compensation, while those of others are as high as 50%. Secondly, a policy must be determined on a cost-of-living adjustment. Does every employee automatically receive an increase that corresponds with the Consumer Price Index (CPI), or do they receive a larger or smaller increase? Thirdly, the compensation policy must determine what form rewards will take. Most companies reward by means of salary increases. Other companies, however, only give salary increases in accordance with the rise in the cost of living, and then give cash bonuses to reward good work performance.

9.6.2 Types of compensation

Compensation can be regarded as the output an employee receives for the input (work) he or she produces. **Direct compensation** is the basic salary or wage an employee receives, while **indirect compensation** refers to the fringe benefits an employee receives, such as leave, medical aid and pension scheme.[30] The other aspect of compensation is **reward**, that is, the recognition of good work performance.

9.6.2.1 Direct compensation

Most employees' salaries or wages (a person who is paid monthly receives a salary, whereas someone who is paid daily or weekly receives a wage) are based on the period of time they have worked for the company, measured by days, weeks or months. Thus, there is no direct relationship between the compensation they receive and the amount of work that they perform. Such a system is simple to administer, but has the disadvantage that, for remuneration purposes (in the short term, at any rate) there is no distinction between productive and unproductive workers. To overcome this problem, some companies use a **piece wage** system. Here, the employee is compensated for the amount of work he or she performs, regardless of the time used to perform the work. For example, a vegetable farmer in Kwa-Zulu Natal, pays his labourers R30 per day (that is, time wages) but at harvesting time he pays them R6,00 for every bag of peas they pick (that is, piece wages). If they pick only three bags a day, they receive R18,00 for the day's work. If they pick eight bags, they receive R48,00 for the day's work.

9.6.2.2 Indirect compensation

The benefits an employee receives from his or her membership in an organisation are called **fringe benefits**. These increase in size and scope as the employee moves to higher levels in the organisation.

Fringe benefits that are generally provided are:

- **Leave**, for holidays, illness, studies, etc.
- **Insurance**, for example, against medical costs, injury, and unemployment; this also includes life coverage and pension benefits
- **Housing**, in the form of free housing, housing at a low rental, or loan subsidies for buying a house
- **Car**, which can vary from a free car with all expenses paid, to financial assistance in buying a car

In addition to these, there are other types of fringe benefits, which differ from company to company. The important point, however, is that this is a form of compensation linked to the hierarchical level of the employee. For example, only staff members above a certain status level enjoy cars as a fringe benefit, and the higher the level, the more expensive the car.

9.6.2.3 Reward

In most cases, neither direct nor indirect compensation is linked to an individual's work performance, and both forms of compensation are therefore regarded as "rights" by most employees. They therefore have very little influence on the motivation of employees. The fact that an employee receives a Christmas bonus (often equivalent to a month's salary) will not cause him or her to work twice as hard to merit this in future.

The HR manager must therefore ensure that there are other ways of rewarding an individual's work performance. Such a reward can take various forms, a few of which are mentioned below:

- The most common form of reward is a **salary increase** based on the individual's work performance (that is, a merit award). A distinction must be made here between the **cost-of-living adjustment** (given to all employees to adjust to the inflation rate) and **merit increases** that are given in recognition of the individual's achievement.
- Some companies give **financial bonuses** to those employees who have performed exceptionally well.
- Other companies reward outstanding employees with a **paid holiday** or an **overseas trip** with all expenses paid.

To summarise: compensation is part of an agreement and is given to the employee for satisfactory performance. It can therefore correctly be regarded as a **right** because the company is **committed** to paying it. A **reward**, however, is not a commitment on the part of the company – it is, instead, the company's **voluntary** acknowledgement of an individual's good work performance.

9.6.3 The size of compensation

The question that now arises is how much a specific staff member should be paid by way of compensation (salary and fringe benefits). We know that a factory manager will probably earn more than a machine operator, but how large ought the difference to be, and how much should each receive?

The first step in deciding on compensation is to make an **external comparison**. How much do factory managers at other companies earn? What is the nature and scope of their fringe benefits? The HR manager must do a **salary survey** to obtain this information. He or she might, for example, find that the average salary of a factory manager is R20 000 per month, while in the HR manager's own company the salary is only R12 000 per month. There is, clearly, a risk here that the factory manager will not stay in the company very long. However, if he or she earns R30 000 per month, the company may be paying too much.

Salary surveys are undertaken countrywide by different institutions, and the HR manager may choose to use such surveys rather than do his or her own survey. However, it is important in such a survey that equivalent jobs be compared with each other. The mere fact that two people have the job title "factory manager" does not necessarily mean that they do the same type of work. So, for example, a person in control of a small workshop where hand-made chairs are manufactured by three artisans might carry the title "factory manager", but it is obvious that this job is not equivalent to that of a factory manager in a large motor manufacturing plant.

The second step is to make an **internal comparison**.[31] This means that the value of jobs must be compared with each other in terms of the demands that they make on the employee. Accordingly, it may be said that the demands made on an accountant are higher than the demands made on an accounting clerk.

This internal comparison is known as **job evaluation**[32], and there are various methods of undertaking it. One method is to **rank** all jobs in the company in terms of their "value". This ranking system is usually used in small to medium sized companies, and the assessment is made by a panel of senior managers.

A second general method of job evaluation is the **factor comparison method**, in which jobs are compared according to the demands they make on the employee with regard to factors such as knowledge, communication skills, level of responsibility and, especially, decision-making skill. Points are awarded to each factor (also known as compensable factors) and the total points indicate into which **job grade** a specific job falls. The information about the jobs can be obtained from the **job description**. Job descriptions therefore have a twofold purpose. They form the basis for a **job specification**, with a view to recruitment, selection, and training. Secondly, they provide a basis for job comparison, with a view to job evaluation. It is important to remember that in job evaluation, only the job is assessed, and not the job incumbent. The value of the job has nothing to do with how well or how badly the present incumbent carries it out.

Job evaluation in itself cannot tell us exactly how much a specific staff member ought to earn. The HR manager can only determine, in light of the findings of the external comparison, what the broad salary range of an accountant, for instance, ought to be.

The decision as to what a specific employee ought to earn once he or she is employed will depend on years of experience, qualifications, what other employees on the same level earn, and other similar considerations. The question can be decided by the HR manager in conjunction with the line manager. However, the HR manager cannot decide on an individual staff member's reward. That decision can only be made by the staff member's immediate superior. Nevertheless, the HR manager can make an important contribution by ensuring that line managers have suitable instruments for assessing their subordinates' performance, as mentioned earlier.

Applying the concept: compensation

Must companies have only one pay structure?

It is not mandatory that companies should have only one pay structure for their staff. Since the pay structure must match the over-all business strategy and market forces, management may choose to fit the various systems chosen to the specific needs of a business segment.

9.7 Conclusion

The primary function of the HR manager is to help other managers in the company to utilise their employees fully. How well the HR manager does this is not easily measurable, and there are, furthermore, big differences in the views of HR managers regarding their task. One HR manager may regard his or her task mainly as HR administration, and to such a person, as long as the HR records are kept up to date and salaries are paid regularly, the task is done. Yet another will concentrate on the full range of tasks discussed in this chapter. No matter how he or she regards the task, however, it is clear that the HR manager can make a unique and very important contribution to the efficiency and effectiveness of a company, and therefore also to its overall profitability and competitiveness.

References

1. Pfeffer, J., *Competitive advantage through people*, Harvard Business School Press, Boston, Mass., 1994.
2. Williams, C., *Management*, South-Western College Publishing, Cincinnati, 2000, p. 546.
3. *Ibid.*, p. 546.
4. Bohlander, G., Snell, S. & Sherman, A., *Managing human resources*, 12th edition, South-Western College Publishing, Cincinnati, 2001, p. 28.
5. *Ibid.*, p. 28.
6. *Ibid.*, p. 28.
7. *Ibid.*, p. 30.
8. Jackson, S.E. & Schuler, R.S., *Managing human resources: a partnership perspective*, 7th edition, South-Western College Publishing, Cincinnati, 2000, p. 220.
9. Grobler, P.A., Wärnich, S., Carrell, M.R., Elbert, N.F. & Hatfield, R.D., *Human resource management in South Africa*, 2nd edition, Thomson Learning, London, 2002, p. 95.
10. Anthony, W.P., Kacmar, K.M. & Perrewé, P.L., *Human resource management: a strategic approach*, 4th edition, Harcourt College Publishers, Orlando, 2002, p. 221.
11. *Ibid.*, p. 221.
12. Grobler, P.A., et al., *op. cit.*, p. 157.
13. Dessler, G., *Human resource management*, 8th edition, Prentice Hall, Upper Saddle River, N.J., 2000, p. 645.

14. Mello, J.A., *Strategic human resource management*, South Western College Publishing, Cincinnati, 2002, pp. 242-245.
15. Williams, C., *op. cit.*, p. 565.
16. Grobler, P.A., et al., *op. cit.*, p. 217.
17. Desimone, R.L., Werner, J.M. & Harris, D.M., *Human resource development*, 3rd edition, Harcourt College Publishers, Orlando, 2002, p. 10.
18. Desimone, R.L., et al., *op. cit.*, p. 3.
19. Jackson, S.E. & Schuler, R.S, *op. cit.*, p. 367.
20. *Ibid.* p. 371.
21. Livingston, S., Gerdel, T.W., Hill, M., Yerak, B., Melvin, C. & Lubinger, B., Ohio's strongest companies all agree that training is vital to their success, *Plain Dealer*, Vol. 21, 1997, p. 305.
22. Bohlander, G., et al., *op. cit.*, p. 318.
23. Mathis, R.L. & Jackson, J.H., *Human resource management: essential perspectives*, 2nd edition, South-Western, Cincinnati, 2002, p. 93.
24. Williams, R.S., *Performance management: perspectives on employee performance*, International Thomson Business Press, Filey, North Yorkshire, 1998, pp. 84-85.
25. Mathis, R.L. & Jackson, J.H., *op. cit.*, p. 96.
26. Bohlander, G., et al., *op. cit.*, p. 320.
27. Williams, R.S., *op. cit.*, p. 152.
28. Milkovich, G.T. & Newman, J.M., *Compensation*, 7th edition, McGraw-Hill, New York, 2002, p. 7.
29. Dessler, G., *op. cit.*, p. 399.
30. Mathis, R.L. & Jackson, J.H., *op. cit.*, p. 104.
31. Milkovich, G.T. & Newman, J.M., *op. cit.*, p. 89.
32. Bohlander, G., et al., *op. cit.*, p. 372.

10 Motivating and managing human resources

The purpose of this chapter

In this chapter theories on the motivation of human resources and aspects relating to managing human resources are discussed. In addition, the role of the human resources function, as well as human resources management and organisational effectiveness are briefly explained. Theories relating to employee motivation constitute the bulk of the chapter, and are provided with the aim of exposing students to the basic principles of various motivational theories.

Learning outcomes

The content of this chapter will enable learners to:
- Describe the role of the human resource function in organisations
- Explain the contribution human resource management can make to organisation effectiveness
- Provide an outline of who is responsible for human resource management
- List and explain the different content theories of motivation
- Discuss the process theories of motivation
- Evaluate the different motivation strategies

10.1 Introduction

In today's society notions such as "people make up a business", "people are an organisation's greatest assets", "managing human resources is fundamental to organisational success", and "motivated employees make a difference" are in general use, and are crucial to organisational success. The emphasis has shifted from endeavouring to solve people-related problems in organisations in an ad hoc fashion, to a more professional approach where the overall organisational philosophy, culture and tone reflect this belief. While certain aspects of human resource (HR) management were discussed in chapter 9, this chapter will focus on the broader issues related to HR management, with particular emphasis on motivation and the theories that underpin them.

10.2 The role of human resource management in the organisation

Before continuing with a discussion on employee motivation as a crucial element in organisational success, we will briefly discuss certain aspects of human resource management in organisations, such as the role of the human resource function, human resource management and organisational effectiveness, and, finally, we will look at the person who performs the human resource function in organisations.

10.2.1 *The role of the human resource function*

Today, human resource management strategies should be integrated with organisational plans and be in line with the broad organisational strategy. The human resource function is concerned with much more than filing, routine administration actions, and record-keeping activities. Its main role should be that of strategic partner, and human resource strategies should clearly demonstrate the organisational strategy regarding people, profit and overall effectiveness. In the South African context, a crucial role of the HR manager is to improve the skills base of employees and to contribute to the profitability of the organisation. The human resource function must be accountable for its actions and should operate as a "profit centre" (see box below). The emphasis on accountability is even more important if one considers the legal environment in which human resource-related decisions have to be taken (see chapter 11), and the very negative consequences for the organisation if the right decisions are not made, for example, if the correct procedures as prescribed by the Labour Relations Act 66 of 1995 are not followed in the event of a retrenchment.

Every manager in the organisation should realise the importance of recruitment, selection, training, developing, rewarding, assisting and motivating employees (see section 10.2.3), though to achieve organisational success both locally and internationally, the focus should be on integration and teamwork among employees.

Links between HR strategies and profits: research by PriceWaterhouseCoopers (PWC)

PWC launched a global human capital survey in 2002-2003, and the survey's participants represented 1 056 organisations in 47 countries, with a combined workforce of more than 6 million employees. South Africa was represented by 25 organisations, eleven of which are from the financial services sector, and nine of which are from the products sector. The results are briefly reported below.

Businesses with a documented HR strategy are more profitable, and typically benefit from 35% higher revenue per employee. This is one of the key findings to emerge from a global human capital survey by PWC.

Although the majority of South Africa's human resource leaders are members of their organisation's highest-ranking leadership team, they generally do not have an officially documented human resource strategy.

Furthermore, only around half of those with a strategy in place claim close integration of that strategy with the overall business strategy.

There is powerful evidence that good people management has a positive effect on a range of issues, from increased employee productivity and reduced absenteeism to improved profitability. To reap the benefits in terms of business performance, organisations need to address three important issues:

- An HR strategy that is documented and also integrated into the business strategy
- Effective people policies and practices that deliver the strategy across the business
- An HR function that can implement policy and strategy, and also influence the business

Highlights of the comparison of South African organisations with the global benchmarks include the following:

- The top business issue for South African organisations is revenue growth; global participants report cost reduction as their top issue, perhaps suggesting that the South African economy is in a growth phase. Leadership development is an important business issue, and it is the top HR issue in South Africa and globally.
- HR functions do not report on many of the business and HR issues they identify as most important to their organisation. Even the traditional measures of headcount, staff turnover and training are only reported by around 60% of organisations. Two-thirds of participants do not track absence from work, and yet the survey indicates that there is a clear link between reduced absenteeism and increased profit margins per employee.
- The ratio of full-time HR specialists to employees is lower in South Africa than in all other regions (50 employees per HR specialist against a global average of 62 employees).
- South Africa employs more females than most other countries, pointing to the likelihood that legislation has made a difference to gender diversity. Whereas regulatory compliance does not feature in the top five business issues globally, South African participants believe it is as important as leadership development, and nearly 50% of participants believe that regulatory compliance is an area where HR has clearly and measurably improved business performance.
- South African organisations provide an average of five days' training per employee per year, compared with the global average of three days – further evidence, perhaps, of the positive impact of skills development legislation. In the South African services sector this average was even higher – with seven days' training per employee per year.
- Among the minority of HR leaders who do have an officially documented HR strategy, only 62% (compared to a global result of 96%) report having an HR strategy that is closely integrated with the overall business strategy.

Source: PriceWaterhouseCoopers, Global Human Capital Benchmarking Survey 2002/03, South African Survey Findings, Media Release, 5 February 2003.

10.2.2 Human resource management and organisational effectiveness

Among the things that organisations need in order to be effective are a mission and strategy, an organisational structure, and human resources. It is people in organisations who create the ideas and allow the organisation to prosper, and even in the most capital-intensive organisation, people are needed to run the organisation. Human resources in organisations either limit or enhance the strength or weaknesses of organisations, and a problem that managers experience in organisations is how to put a monetary value to people in organisations. While it is easy to evaluate other resources in terms of their monetary value, for example machines and equipment, putting a monetary value to people is very difficult. Various research projects have been launched to put a monetary value to people, for example, human resource accounting practices, but a conclusive methodology and process have not yet been established.

For organisations to be really effective, top managers should treat human resources as the key element of effectiveness. The contribution of human resources to organisational effectiveness includes the following:[1]

- Assisting everybody in the organisation to reach stated goals
- Employing the skills and abilities of the workforce efficiently
- Providing the organisation with well-trained and motivated employees
- Assisting in the attainment of the employee's job satisfaction and self-actualisation (see 10.3.4.1)
- Maintaining and developing a quality of work life that makes employment in the organisation desirable
- Assisting with the maintenance of ethical policies and socially responsible behaviour
- Managing change to the mutual advantage of individuals, groups, the organisation and the public
- Executing human resource functional activities in a professional manner

10.2.3 Who performs the human resource function?

As soon as a new person (employee) is recruited and appointed in an organisation, management's main concern must be to get that person to do his or her work as well as possible. In this process (see chapter 9) certain functions have to be performed by the human resource specialist, who would normally be situated in a human resource department, as well as by line managers and direct supervisors. Line managers are those people in other departments, such as operations, marketing and finances, who have the responsibility to optimally utilise all the resources at their disposal.

The human resource is a unique resource because if it is not properly managed effectiveness can decline drastically. For this reason, it is essential to understand why people work in organisations, and why some people want to perform better than other people. In South Africa, where we have high unemployment, having a job has become an important goal, and people compete fiercely for jobs. It is thus important for managers to take note of the complex issues motivating employees and to manage these. In most organisations – apart from capital-intensive organisations – the investment in people has more effect on organisational success than investment in other resources, for example, materials, equipment or capital.

In large organisations the human resources function is mainly coordinated by the human resource department. In smaller organisations which do not have a human resource department, the main human resource functions, such as recruitment and selection, scheduling work, performance management, compensation, training and development and labour relations (see chapter 11), are performed by line managers over and above their normal duties. As the organisation grows and increases in size, the line manager's job is divided up, and some aspects, such as recruitment and selection, become more specialised. These duties are then dealt with by a human resource specialist.

Depending on the nature of the organisation, a human resource specialist is normally employed in organisations with approximately 50 to 150 employees. In South Africa, the ratio of full-time human resource specialists to employees is 50, while the global average is about 62 (see box on p. 219–220). A human resource department or section is typically created when the number of employees reaches a figure of between 200 to 500 employees.

From the above discussion on the role of the human resource manager, it is clear that without a well-trained and motivated workforce, organisations cannot be successful. Both human resource specialists as well as line managers are responsible for managing the people talent in organisations, and one aspect that can make a difference in achieving organisational success is the level of employee motivation, which is dealt with in the section below.

10.3 Employee motivation

10.3.1 Introduction

People are complex beings, and are motivated by different kinds of needs. Certain basic needs first have to be satisfied, such as for food, clothing, shelter and security, but there are also other needs that have to be satisfied, such as the need to be accepted, and the need for recognition and self-esteem. People are also motivated by different needs at different times of their lives, for example, children have different needs to those of adults.

In the workplace, motivation is what makes people want to work. Motivation may broadly be defined as the reason people want to work.[2] It is the internal drive that encourages people to achieve a particular goal.[3] To be successful in any organisation, employees and managers should understand what causes different motivational levels, because the achievement of both personal and organisational goals is important. Motivation in a work setting may be driven not only by internal rewards, but also by external factors. Motivation is therefore two-dimensional, with an internal dimension and/or an external dimension.

- **Internal motivation.** This motivation originates from the satisfaction that occurs when a task is executed or a duty is performed. If a teacher enjoys teaching children, the activity is in itself rewarding, and the teacher will be self-motivated. The intrinsic rewards of the job motivate some people more than external influences such as money and trophies do. Hertzberg's theory on motivation emphasises that jobs should be enriched to provide opportunities for growth and more responsibility (see section 10.3.4.3).

- **External motivation.** In contrast to internal motivation, external motivation usually involves action taken by a third party. Here, a person is motivated because it is in anticipation that a reward of some kind, for example, money, awards or feedback regarding performance, will be given. Incentives such as profit sharing, bonuses and awards are used by organisations to instil certain work habits that are beneficial both for the organisation and the individual. Unfortunately, external rewards are not enough to motivate people in the long term. Organisations should therefore focus on a combination of both internal and external rewards by allowing job satisfaction by means of challenging jobs and an appropriate number of external awards.

See also chapter 8, section 8.2.3, where the same aspects are discussed.

10.3.2 Motivation in the workplace: a basic understanding

Managers must motivate a diverse and complex group of people in organisations. Employee performance in organisations is mainly determined by three things, namely a desire to the job (motivation), the capability to do the job (ability), and the resources to do the job (work environment). If an employee cannot do the job, he or she can be trained or replaced (see chapter 11 on the requirements laid down by the Labour Relations Act), and if more resources are required, the manager can rectify the problem. The problem becomes more challenging if the employee is not motivated to do the job.[4] Because of the complex nature of human beings, managers may not fully understand the problems experienced by employees and their effect on individual performance. The level of motivation thus has a direct influence on performance, and it is important to understand how motivation takes place.

In terms of the basic motivational model (figure 10.1), we see that the motivation process begins when people experience a need or a deficiency, for example, a need for food or the need for recognition or for more pay. The employee will, in response, direct his or her behaviour in a direction, or **set goals to satisfy the need**, for example, to work harder, to impress the boss, or to buy gifts. This is followed by taking **action** and doing what is planned, for example, working harder. Once the action has been taken by the employee, he or she then **evaluates the behaviour**, the result of which will be some type of **reward or punishment**. If the employee is successful and, for example, obtains recognition, he or she will feel good and be **satisfied** and keep on working hard. If the result is negative, however, the person will be **unsatisfied** and choose another course of action. The cycle may then be repeated as explained.

Figure 10.1: Basic motivational model

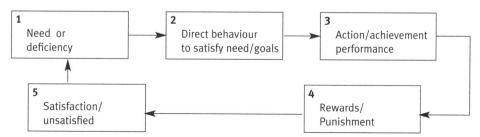

10.3.3 Characteristics of motives

Motivators or motives prompt people to act in a certain way. According to Reece and Brandt,[5] an understanding of the following characteristics of motives may help a manager to understand employee motivation:

- **Motives are individualistic.** Each individual is unique and has different needs. What may satisfy one person may not satisfy another, for example, one person may be highly motivated to win a sales contest while another person may want to work in a team. It is important that colleagues understand each others' motives, for, if they fail to, this could lead to counterproductive actions and a loss of productivity.
- **Motives change.** It has been mentioned that motives change constantly, and what motivates one early in one's career may not be a motivator later on. For example, a job with a high salary without security might motivate a young person but be unacceptable to someone in his forties where job security is more important. Similarly, more vacation time may be desired near retirement age than earlier in life.
- **Motives may be unconscious.** Most people are not fully aware of the inner needs and drives that influence their behaviour. The desire of an employee, for example, to win the "salesperson of the month" trophy may be due to an unconscious feeling of inadequacy, and that this would be a way of proving herself.
- **Motives are often inferred.** However closely one may observe the behaviour of a colleague, it is only possible to draw conclusions (infer) as to what motives actually caused the behaviour. It is sometimes very difficult to understand the real motives underlying certain behaviour. For this reason it is important that managers discuss with employees the things that motivate them so that suggestions can be made in order to meet the needs of employees more adequately.
- **Motives are hierarchical.** The motives that employees display in their behaviour vary according to their levels of importance. The most important (strongest) motive usually guides behaviour, for example, a person might leave a secure job for a more risky job with higher pay.

There are two basic approaches to motivational theories, namely a content approach and a process approach. These two approaches will be discussed in the following section.

10.3.4 Content approaches to motivation

The content theories of motivation emphasise the factors within individuals that guide behaviour. These theories are: Maslow's hierarchy of needs, Alderfer's ERG theory, Herzberg's two factor theory, and McClelland's learned needs theory.

10.3.4.1 Maslow's hierarchy of needs

One of the best-known theories of motivation is Abraham Maslow's theory of a hierarchy of needs. The crux of Maslow's theory is that needs are arranged in a hierarchy where the lowest-level needs are physiological needs and the highest-level needs are self-actualisation needs.

Figure 10.2: Maslow's hierarchy of needs (see also chapter 8, section 8.2.3.2)

HIGH- LEVEL NEEDS	Maximum use of own abilities, skills and potential	Self-actualisation needs
	Self-esteem and esteem for others	Esteem needs
	Friendship, belonging	Affiliation needs
	Protection from physical and emotional harm	Safety needs
LOW-LEVEL NEEDS	Food, drink, relief of pain	Physiological needs

At the bottom of the hierarchy are the **physiological needs**, which include food, drink, sex and air – the basic ingredients for survival and for biological functioning. In an organisation these needs of employers are satisfied by providing aspects such as a salary, rest rooms, a cafeteria, heating and adequate lighting. The next level in the hierarchy is **safety and security needs**, which include protection from physical and emotional harm. They also include the desire for clothing, job security, pension plans, structures in the organisation to deal with grievances, and employee assistance programmes. **Affiliation needs** include friendships, love and affection, and the need to be accepted by peers. Family and, to some extent, office parties, for example, in the workplace, satisfy this level of need. **Esteem** needs include the need for a positive self-image and self-respect, and the need for recognition from others. In organisations this need can be satisfied by means of compliments to employees, access to information, job titles, and challenging job assignments.

At the top of the hierarchy are **self-actualisation** needs, which involve realising one's potential through growth and development. In an organisational context the focus here is on providing development opportunities, challenging assignments, and decision-making opportunities.

Maslow's theory assumes that a person attempts to satisfy the more basic needs before progressing to satisfy higher-level needs. A further assumption is that people strive to move up the hierarchy in terms of need satisfaction, and that a specific need ceases to motivate an employee once it has been satisfied. Unsatisfied needs cause stress, frustration and conflict within an individual and also between individuals. Management can help employees to satisfy needs at various levels by promoting a culture wherein, for example, self-esteem and self-actualisation needs can be satisfied. The opportunity of participation in decision making about work and the provision of learning opportunities are examples of self-actualisation opportunities. Some research, however, suggests that not all levels of needs as identified by Maslow are always present, and that certain cultures may have different need categories and hierarchies.

Shosholoza: does this song motivate?

Shosholoza is the song that black South Africans, especially long-term convicts engaged in hard labour, have traditionally sung in conditions of hardship. *Shosholoza* is like a child with no parents, however. Nobody knows when or where it originated from, but what everyone does know is that when there is some kind of deep-rooted ache in the heart, the first sound to rise from the lips will be *Shosholoza*. It is a song with no beginning and no end, as old as misery itself.

Shosholoza	Shosholoza
Ku lezontaba	You are meandering on those mountains
Stimela si qhamuka e South Africa	The train is from South Africa
Wen u ya baleka	You accelerate
Wen u ya baleka	You accelerate
Ku lezontaba	On those mountains
Stimela si qhamuka South Africa	The train is from South Africa

Here are the lyrics as recorded by Ladysmith Black Mambazo:

Chorus

Shosholoza	*Wena u ya baleka*
Ku lezontaba	*Wena u ya baleka*
Stimela si qhamuka e South Africa	*Ku lezontaba*
Shosholoza	*Stimela si qhamuka South Africa*
Stimela si qhamuka e South Africa	

Verse 1	**Verse 2**
Shosholoza	*Shosholoza*
Work, work, working in the sun	Push, push, pushing on and on
We will work as one	There's much to be done
Shosholoza	*Shosholoza*
Work, work, working in the rain	Push, push, pushing in the sun
'Til there's sun again	We will push as one

Sithwele kanzima, sithwele kanzima (ooh, aah!)
Sithwele kanzima, sithwele kanzima (ooh, aah!)
Sithwele kanzima, sithwele kanzima (ooh, aah!)
Sithwele kanzima, sithwele kanzima (ooh, aah!)
Sithwele kanzima, sithwele kanzima (ooh, aah!)

Etshe!
Shosholoza
Repeat chorus
Repeat verse 1
Repeat chorus

Source: http://www.geocities.com/rembrandt/Lyrics/S/Shosholoza.html

10.3.4.2 Alderfer's ERG theory

Alderfer's theory represents a refinement of Maslow's five-level hierarchy in that, according to Alderfer, there are three core needs, namely "Existence", "Relatedness" and "Growth" (ERG). These needs are summarised as follows:[6]

- **Existence needs.** These needs relate to a person's basic material, existence needs – the same as Maslow's physiological and safety needs.
- **Relatedness needs.** These needs relate to a person's desire for interpersonal relationships and interaction – similar to Maslow's affiliation/social needs and the external aspect of Maslow's esteem needs.
- **Growth needs.** These relate to the desire of an individual to make a creative or productive contribution – similar to Maslow's esteem and self-actualisation needs.

The ERG theory does not subscribe to a rigid hierarchy of needs, whereas Maslow maintains that a lower-level need must first be satisfied before a higher-level need will be entertained. According to the ERG theory, two or even all three need categories can influence behaviour simultaneously. The ERG theory also suggests that if a person is continually frustrated in his or her attempts to satisfy **growth** needs, **relatedness** needs re-emerge as a major motivating force, and this may force the person to redirect efforts towards satisfying a lower-order need category.

10.3.4.3 Herzberg's two-factor theory

Frederick Herzberg proposed a motivational model called the two-factor model, which consists of **maintenance** and **motivational** factors.

The **maintenance** (hygiene) **factors** do not act as motivational factors, but if they are absent in an organisation this could have a negative affect on employee morale. The maintenance factors are those aspects people consider essential to do any job, for example, organisational policy and administration, equipment, supervision, interpersonal relationships with colleagues and supervisors, salary, status, working conditions, and work security.[7]

Motivational factors, also called growth factors, are focused on the content of the job, and include aspects such as achievement (successful completion of tasks); recognition for what has been achieved; the job itself (meaningfulness and challenge); progress and growth; responsibility and feedback. Motivational factors are benefits over and above the normal job to be done, which tend to increase employee satisfaction because employees get more out of the normal job they do. When motivational factors are present they are likely to motivate employees to achieve higher productivity, to be more committed to their jobs, and to find creative ways of accomplishing both personal and organisational goals.[8]

Herzberg's theory can be linked to Maslow's hierarchy of needs. The maintenance (hygiene) factors are similar to the lower-level needs in the hierarchy, while the motivators are the same as the higher-level needs.

According to Herzberg's theory, job satisfaction lies in the task itself, but critics of Herzberg have pointed out that he assumes that most people are motivated only by higher-order needs such as responsibility and recognition. Herzberg's theory does not acknowledge the fact that some people may prefer a routine and a predictable job, and may be motivated more by security than the prospect of job advancement.

Figure 10.3: Comparison of the theories of Herzberg and Maslow

	Herzberg	Maslow
Maintenance factors	Social network Supervision	Social/belongingness
	Policy/Administrative	Safety/Security
	Job security Salary Working conditions	Physiological
Motivational factors	Recognition Status Advancement	Esteem needs
	Work itself Responsibility	Self-actualisation

10.3.4.4 McClelland's theory of needs

This theory of needs focuses on three needs that explain motivation, namely:[9]

- **Need for achievement (nAch).** This is a need to excel, to be successful or to exceed a set standard.
- **Need for power (nPow).** This is a need to be influential, to control others, or to make others behave in a way they would not otherwise behave.
- **Need for affiliation (nAff).** This is the need for warm and close interpersonal relationships, and to be liked and accepted by others.

Given the above needs of employees, managers have the challenge of determining the dominant need of their subordinates, and of offering opportunities whereby the individual needs can be met. For example, research has found that employees with a high need for power (nPow) and a low need for affiliation (nAff) make good managers, and that people with a high need for achievement (nAch) generally make successful entrepreneurs.

10.3.4.5 Summary

The four content theories discussed above attempt to explain behaviour from different perspectives. Each of the theories has its strengths and limitations, and managers should consider this when they endeavour to understand their employees' behaviour. Good managers will evaluate all these approaches so as to gain insight when solving problems in the workplace.

10.3.5 Process approaches to motivation

Process perspectives on motivation focus mainly on **why people choose certain behavioural options** to satisfy their needs, and **how they evaluate their satisfaction** after they have achieved the goals.[10] The content theories dis-

Applying the concept: Pick 'n Pay

Research has shown that customer service begins inside an organisation, with the way employees are treated, valued, respected, empowered and rewarded. For this reason, the emphasis on adding value and delivering good results is increasingly being linked to the way organisations manage and motivate their people. As Tom Peters explains in *In search of excellence*, "Business success today rests on quick action, service to customers, practical innovation, and the fact that you can't get any of these without virtually everyone's commitment."

No one knows this better than Pick 'n Pay CEO Sean Summers. He has been widely praised for *Vuselela*, a staff motivational campaign that involves extensive training, for example, trips for staff at all levels to courses at Disneyworld in the USA. In stark contrast to the knee-jerk antics of many panicky SA retailers, Summers is backing a long-term strategy aimed at creating a climate in which Pick 'n Pay employees are able to realise their own potential. He is reportedly a firm believer that motivated employees keep the tills ringing.

And the results speak for themselves. Pick 'n Pay came out tops in the retail sector of the *Financial Mail's* recent *Top Companies Survey*, and ranked 76th in the top 250. In a recent interview in the *IMM Journal of Marketing*, Summers cited dignity and respect as two commodities essential to growth. He also confirmed his belief that if you can't deliver a good experience for employees within the workplace, you are highly unlikely to deliver a positive experience for customers.

Yet, despite the clear need for staff motivation, there is very little of it to be found in the adult world of work. Why is it that the innovative spirit we are born with seems to get stamped out, and fear or passivity sets in?

Source: Burton, L., *Managing motivation*, People Dynamics, 2001.

cussed above, however, focus more on the **needs** and **incentives** that cause behaviour. Three process theories are discussed below, namely the expectancy theory, equity theory and goal-setting theory.

10.3.5.1 Expectancy theory

According to Vroom's expectancy theory, motivation depends on two aspects, namely how much we want something, and how likely we think we are to get it. There are four assumptions upon which the expectancy theory rests. Firstly, behaviour is a combination of forces controlled by the individual and the environment. Secondly, it is assumed people make decisions about their own behaviour in organisations. Thirdly, different people have different needs, goals and desires, and finally, people will act in a certain way, and the tendency to act in a certain way depends on the strength of the expectation that the action will be followed by a given outcome, and the degree to which the person desires the outcome.[11] Three key concepts in the theory are valence, instrumentality and expectancy. Each is briefly discussed below:[12]

- **Valence** (desirability) refers to the attractiveness of a specific outcome to an individual. An outcome is positive valence when it is preferred, and negative valence when it is avoided. For example, a person might prefer relocation to a new site (positive valence) to a 5% increase in salary (negative valence).

- **Instrumentality** refers to the strength of a person's belief that a certain performance will lead to a desired outcome. But first, two types of outcomes require clarification: if an outcome is associated with the job itself (for example, productivity and absenteeism), it is called a first-level outcome, while second-level outcomes are those events (rewards or punishments) that the first-level outcomes are likely to produce, for example, group rejection or acceptance, or promotion. Instrumentality can be **negative** if a first-level outcome (for example, promotion) has occurred but it is likely that a second-level outcome will occur (for example, group acceptance). It is **positive** when the second-level outcome (for example, group acceptance) is likely if the first-level outcome has already occurred (for example, promotion).
- **Expectancy** refers to a person's belief that a certain level of effort will lead to a particular outcome. In the workplace, employees hold an effort-performance expectancy, for example, employees may have the expectancy that if they work hard they will get a day off. If an employee has zero expectancy that an effort will lead to performance, the employee will not put in an effort. Factors such as a person's self-esteem, previous success, support from others, and access to information will influence a person's expectancy perceptions.

Managers should take note of this theory. Some of its implications are as follows:
- Attainable standards should be set for employees, supported by the necessary training and development
- Rewards should be linked to performance standards
- An attempt should be made to link personal goals to organisational goals

10.3.5.2 Equity theory

The crux of the equity theory advanced by Stacey Adams is that employees compare their efforts and rewards with those of other employees in similar situations. This motivational theory is based on the assumption that people are motivated by the desire to be equitably treated in the marketplace. A state of equity exists when one employee's input-outcome ratio compared with that of another employee in a similar position is equal. On the other hand, if input-outcome ratios are unequal, inequity is said to exist, with the result that the person will perceive the situation as unfair and therefore be motivated to do something else. Various means can be used to restore equity after equity tension has been experienced, including the following:[13]
- The employee will change inputs.
- The employee will change outputs.
- The employee will change his or her attitude.
- The employee will change the person he or she compares herself with.
- The employee will leave the job.

For most employees, motivation is influenced by relative monetary rewards as well as absolute monetary rewards. Despite the research that supports this theory, certain aspects remain unclear, for example, how do employees deal with conflicting equity signals, and how are inputs and outputs defined? Equity theory does, however, provide an important insight into employee motivation, and every manager should take note of its implications.

10.3.5.3 Goal-setting theory

Goal-setting theory is built on the assumption that, all things being equal, people will perform better if they strive towards a definite goal. By setting specific goals, it is possible to further motivated behaviour since the employee will know what needs to be done and how much effort is likely to be required.

Vague goals such as "you have to perform better" are unhelpful, while specific goals such as "you have to obtain 80% for the Business Management I examination" are clear and therefore useful. Obviously, when setting goals, the person concerned must be capable of achieving those goals. The thrust of goal-setting theory is that the more difficult the goal, the higher the level of performance. Other factors also play a role, for example,[14] employees will perform better if they receive feedback. This theory presupposes that an employee is committed to a goal, and that a negotiated goal between an employee and the organisation has the likelihood of legitimacy and commitment.

10.3.6 Managerial implications

While other theories of motivation, such as the cognitive dissonance theory, McGregor's theory X and Y, and reinforcement theory have not been discussed, these also contribute to the body of knowledge related to motivation. These may briefly be defined as follows:

- **McGregor's theory X and Y.** According to this theory, a manager's view of human nature is based on certain assumptions, for example, theory X assumes that employees dislike work and responsibility, are lazy, and must be forced to perform, while the assumptions of theory Y are that employees like work, want responsibility, are creative, and can exercise self-direction.
- **Cognitive dissonance theory.** This theory presumes that if a person has performed poorly in a number of tasks, he or she will perform poorly again, even though the person might be able to do better.
- **Reinforcement theory.** This is in contrast with goal-setting theory, which is a cognitive theory (see 10.3.5.3). Instead, reinforcement theory is a behavioural approach in that behaviour is a function of its consequences. This theory ignores the inner state of the individual and concentrates solely on what happens when a person performs the same action again.

As stated earlier, managers need to be actively involved in the motivation of employees. In doing so, managers should be aware of subordinates' needs, intentions, preferences, comparisons and goals. Managers can also play a significant role in creating an atmosphere that supports improvement, in showing sensitivity towards employees' abilities and preferences, and in offering jobs that provide a challenge and are also diverse. It has been suggested that, on the basis of the motivational theories currently available, the following actions might be taken to manage people effectively:[15]

- Set specific goals for employees.
- Goals should be realistic and attainable.
- The job must suit the employee's personality.
- Respect and recognise individual differences.
- Provide immediate feedback to employees on their performance.

- Because employees have different needs, rewards should be individualised to make provision for different motivational levels.
- Link rewards to performance.
- Honour the principle of internal equity in the organisation's reward system.
- Although great emphasis has been placed on intrinsic motivators it should not be forgotten that people work for money, and an organisation's reward system should, accordingly, receive due status.
- Motivational theories are culture bound, and should be recognised as such.

10.4 Employee motivational strategies

Employees need to be better motivated not only to improve organisational effectiveness, but also to provide a better quality of life for all employees. Possible broad motivational strategies to improve employee motivation are briefly discussed below, but may include aspects already mentioned in paragraph 10.3.6, which focused more on specific motivational aspects:[16]

- **Job design.** Employees place a high value on jobs that provide satisfaction, are challenging, provide growth, and will allow adequate achievement opportunities. Jobs can be redesigned to make them more challenging by using job rotation, job enlargement or job enrichment. **Job rotation** allows employees to move through a variety of jobs, functions or departments. **Job enlargement** focuses on expanding an employee's duties and/or responsibilities, and **job enrichment** allows jobs to become more desirable and challenging by including new and more difficult tasks and granting an employee more accountability. Other aspects to consider are variable work schedules, flexible work schedules, job sharing and telecommuting.
- **Intrapreneurial incentives.** New ideas from employees can be developed within organisations with the financial support of the organisation. Such programmes are known as intrapreneurship, which encourages employees to come up with new suggestions and ideas.
- **Training and education.** Learning opportunities can be a strong motivational force since they are critical to individual growth and opportunity. Organisations that invest in the training and development of employees are generally more successful (see box on p. 229). In South Africa, opportunities to invest in the training and development of employees have been created by means of the Skills Development Act 97 of 1998 and the Skills Development Levies Act 9 of 1999 (see chapter 11).
- **Incentives.** Incentives and rewards for above average work performance are widely used to drive results in organisations, and they vary from cash, shares, profit sharing, overseas visits and bonuses, to trophies and certificates.
- **Empowerment and participation.** Empowerment and participation are two important methods of enhancing employee motivation.[17] Empowerment is the process of enabling employees to set their own goals, make decisions, and solve problems within their sphere of responsibility and authority. Participation is the process of giving employees a voice in making decisions about their own work (see the influence of content theories in 10.3.4, and expectancy theory in 10.3.5.1 above).

Ten rules for workplace motivation

1. Build self-respect
2. Don't be neurotic
3. Show respect
4. Live with integrity
5. Be fair
6. Value and reinforce ideas
7. Provide unique rewards – everyone is different
8. Provide immediate feedback
9. Reinforce the right things
10. Serve others

- **Devising reward systems.** A basic management tool to motivate employees is the organisation's reward system. A reward system is directly related to the expectancy theory of motivation, and the effect of the reward system on attitudes and employee behaviour should be fully investigated.
- **Career management.** Career management and development is the path that an employee identifies and follows in order to achieve his or her aspirations. Employees will be better motivated if they are personally involved in decision making about possible career options open to them. This leads to a better motivated workforce, and employees will have been empowered in being assisted by an organisational career management team to face challenges and make decisions that benefit both the individual and the organisation (see McClelland's theory of needs in 10.3.4.4).
- **Create a culture of change.** It has been suggested that motivating people to work in the 21st century by employing motivational theories conceived in the 1800s and early 1900s is unlikely to be wholly effective.[18] The focus for the new century is on quality, customer service and the capacity of the workforce to change.

Any organisation that still uses functional/vertical hierarchies instead of self-directed work teams that are truly empowered to make changes is not ready for change. True change will only come about when organisations motivate people to work by using the formula: Effective change = F (friendship, work, respect).

10.5 Summary

This chapter has focused mainly on the importance of motivation in the workplace. It began, however, with a brief description of the role of human resource management in organisations, with particular emphasis on human resource management and organisational effectiveness, and the responsibility area of the human resource function. It was clearly demonstrated that employee motivation is an important part of the task not only of human resource practitioners, but also of any manager in an organisation.

The section on motivation highlighted both the content theories of motivation and the process theories. Each approach endeavours to organise and explain the major variables associated with the relevant theory. Since the various theories were only briefly discussed, it is suggested that more specialised publications be consulted to obtain more detail about the theories.

References

1. Reece, B.L. & Brandt, R., *Effective human relations*, 6th edition, Houghton Mifflin Company, New York, 1996, p. 152.
2. Invancevich, J.M., *Human resource management*, 7th edition, McGraw-Hill, Boston, 1998, p. 9.
3. Robbins, S.P., *Organisational behaviour: concepts, controversies, application*, 8th edition, Prentice Hall, Upper Saddle River, N.J., 1998, p. 168.
4. Moorhead, G. & Griffin, R.W., *Organisational behaviour: managing people and organisations*, 6th edition, Houghton Mifflin, Boston, 2000.
5. Reece, B.L. & Brand, R., *op. cit.*, p. 155.
6. Swanepoel, B., Erasmus, B., Van Wyk, M. & Schenk, H., *South African human resource management: theory and practice*, 3rd edition, Oxford University Press, Cape Town, 2003, p. 357.
7. Nel, P.S., Gerber, P.D., Van Dyk, P.S., Haasbroek, G.D., Schultz, H.B., Seno, T. & Werner, A., *Human resource management*, 5th edition, Oxford University Press, Cape Town, 2001, p. 331.
8. Reece, B.L. & Brandt, R., *op cit*, p. 162.
9. Robbins, S.P., *op. cit.*, p. 175.
10. Moorhead, G. & Griffin, R., *op. cit.*, p. 490.
11. Moorhead, G. & Griffin, R., *op. cit.*, p. 492.
12. Nel, P.S., et al., *op. cit.*, p. 336.
13. Invancevich, J.M. & Matteson, M.T., *Organizational behaviour and management*, 4th edition, Irwin, Boston, 1996, p. 171.
14. Swanepoel, B., et al., *op. cit.*, p. 361.
15. Swanepoel, B., et al., *op. cit.*, p. 369.
16. Reece, B.L. & Brandt, R., *op. cit.*, p. 166.
17. Moorhead, G. & Griffin, R., *op. cit.*, p. 499.
18. Reis, D. & Pena, L., Reengineering the motivation to work, *Management Decision*, Vol. 39, No. 8, p. 675.

Websites: www.accel-team.com/motivation
         www.workplaceissues.com/motivate

11 The legal environment and human resources

The purpose of this chapter

This chapter provides a brief overview of the most important labour laws applicable to the workplace and which influence human resources in organisations. It commences with a discussion on the Constitution of South Africa, followed by an explanation of the Labour Relations Act; Basic Conditions of Employment Act; Skills Development Act; Skills Development Levies Act; South African Qualifications Authority Act; Employment Equity Act; Occupational Health and Safety Act; Compensation for Occupational Injuries and Diseases Act; and the Unemployment Insurance Act.

Learning outcomes

The content of this chapter will enable learners to:
- Understand the importance of the Constitution of South Africa
- Describe and analyse the impact of the following Acts on the management of human resources in organisations:
  - The Labour Relations Act 66 of 1995
  - The Basic Conditions of Employment Act 75 of 1997
  - The Skills Development Act 97 of 1998
  - The Skills Development Levies Act 9 of 1999
  - The Employment Equity Act 55 of 1998
  - The Occupational Health and Safety Act 85 of 1993
  - The Compensation for Occupational Injuries and Diseases Act 130 of 1993
  - The Unemployment Insurance Act 63 of 2001

11.1 Introduction

Several different environmental factors influence the way an organisation's human resources are managed. One such factor is the legal environment, and, in particular, those laws that are applicable to people in organisations. Legal issues affect almost all aspects of human resource management, whether discharge, retrenchment or retirement. The impact of legal issues is so complex that line managers and human resource professionals should have a good understanding of these laws. At times, legal expertise is required to solve workplace problems or to take legal aspects further, but in most cases, legal matters can be solved independently by line managers and/or human resource professionals.

In this chapter the South African Constitution will briefly be examined, and, following this, those labour laws that affect employees in organisations directly, and therefore also the management of employees, will be discussed. The management of human resources is, however, a more complex matter than the simple application of various laws (see chapter 9), but without a basic knowledge of the most important labour laws, organisations may find themselves with more people problems than anticipated.

11.2 The Constitution of South Africa, Act 108 of 1996

The Constitution of the Republic of South Africa, Act 108 of 1996, is the highest law of the land, and is seen as a bastion against racism and any infringement of individual rights. No law or decree in South Africa may supersede the Constitution. It provides for a federal state, governed by a central government and nine provincial governments. The Constitution includes a Bill of Rights (chapter 2) that binds private persons and the state and addresses social issues. Section 23 of the Constitution guarantees a number of extensive labour rights as fundamental rights, for example: the right to fair labour practices; the right of workers to form and join a trade union; the right of employers to form and join an employers organisation; the right to engage in collective bargaining, and the right to strike. Certain administrative law rights are also protected as fundamental rights (section 23), as are the following:

- The right to equality (section 9)
- The right to privacy (section 14)
- The right to religion, belief and opinion (section 15)
- The right to freedom of expression (section 16)
- The rights of assembly, demonstration, picket and petition (section 17)
- The right to freely choose a trade, occupation and profession (section 22)

Some of the values underlying the Constitution and the Bill of Rights are human dignity, the achievement of equality; the advancement of human rights and freedom, non-racism, non-sexism, and the rule of law (sections 1 and 7(1)). The Constitutional Court is the highest court in all constitutional matters and consists of eleven members. It should therefore be understood that all human resource management practices in organisations should be in line with the Constitution, and that the various laws regulating the employment relationship are subordinate to the Constitution.

11.3 Laws affecting business activity

Before focusing on the specific labour laws that regulate human resources, the laws affecting business activities more generally must briefly be attended to. To be a successful businessperson in South Africa requires, among other things, that businesses adhere to the laws of the land. The regulation of commercial activity in South Africa is on a par with that of the major economic powers in the world, and covers aspects such as intellectual property, disputes, copyright and labour relations. The most important laws that affect business activities in South Africa are shown in the box overleaf.

Important laws affecting businesses in South Africa

Insolvency Act 24 of 1936
Merchandise Marks Act 17 of 1941
Pension Funds Act 24 of 1956
Business Names Act 27 of 1960
Income Tax Act 58 of 1962 as amended
Capital Gains Tax (Section 26A of the Income Tax Act)
Sales and Service Matters Act 25 of 1964
Usury Act 73 of 1968
Companies Act 61 of 1973
Patents Act 57 of 1978
Copyright Act 98 of 1978
Protection of Business Act 99 of 1978
Credit Agreement Act 75 of 1980
Close Corporations Act 69 of 1984
Consumer Affairs (Unfair Business Practices) Act 71 of 1988
Banks Act 94 of 1990
Value Added Tax Act 89 of 1991
Aliens Control Act 96 of 1991
Trade Marks Act 194 of 1993
Designs Act 195 of 1993
National Road Traffic Act 93 of 1996
National Small Business Act 102 of 1996
Counterfeit Goods Act 37 of 1997
Non-profit Organisation Act 71 of 1997
Competition Act 89 of 1998
National Environmental Management Act 107 of 1998
Promotion of Access to Information Act 2 of 2000
Promotion of Equality and Prevention of Unfair Discrimination Act 4 of 2000
Protection Disclosures Act 26 of 2000 (Whistle-blowers)
Electronic Communications and Transactions Act 25 of 2002

The legal environment influencing human resources management in organisations includes the following Acts:

- Occupational Health and Safety Act 85 of 1993
- Compensation for Occupational Injuries and Diseases Act 130 of 1993
- South African Qualifications Authority Act 58 of 1995
- Labour Relations Act 66 of 1995
- Basic Conditions of Employment Act 75 of 1997
- Employment Equity Act 55 of 1998
- Skills Development Act 97 of 1998
- Skills Development Levies Act 9 of 1999
- Unemployment Insurance Act 63 of 2001

The Acts mentioned above will be briefly discussed in the sections that follow. If further information is required concerning these Acts, it is suggested that the entire Act be studied. Copies may be obtained from the Government Printer.[1]

11.4 Labour Relations Act (LRA) 66 of 1995

11.4.1 Introduction

Since the first democratic election in 1994 in South Africa, the labour dispensation has changed significantly, and organised labour has played an important role in South Africa's transformation process. Not only do workers, through their trade unions, play a key role in the redistribution of wealth through collective bargaining over wages, but they are also instrumental in the broader socio-political struggle to transform South African society. Consequently, the labour field in South Africa has seen tremendous changes. For example, a new Labour Relations Act was introduced in 1995, and a new Basic Conditions of Employment Act and Employment Equity Act were introduced in 1997 and 1998, respectively.

The implementation of sound labour relations in businesses not only ensures fair labour practices, but also contributes to organisational success. Labour relations, from a business management point of view, may be described as **a complex system of individual and collective actions as well as formal and informal relationships that exists between the state, employers, employees and related institutions concerning all aspects of the employment relationship.**

Relationships in a business are considered to be a crucial element in labour relations, and in the next section more attention is given to the different parties in the labour relationship.

The parties involved in the labour relationship are the employer and employee as primary parties, and the state as a secondary role player. The state's role is to create, by means of legislation, a framework within which the primary parties can conduct their relationship. Figure 11.1 illustrates this tripartite relationship. Basically, employees in managerial positions represent the interests of the owners of businesses in the workplace. In the private sector this essentially means safeguarding and improving the profitability of businesses. The state's primary role is, as stated, to create the framework or infrastructure within which labour and management can conduct their relationship.

Figure 11.1: Participants in labour relations

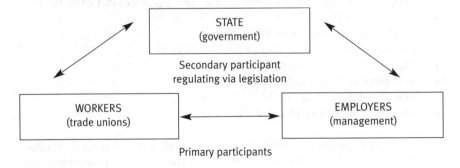

A trade union, on the other hand, is a continuous, permanent organisation created by workers to protect themselves at work, to improve their working conditions through collective bargaining, to better their quality of life, and to provide a means of expressing their views on issues in society.

11.4.2 A brief overview of South Africa's statutory labour relations system

South Africa's statutory labour relations system is mainly regulated by the Labour Relations Act 66 of 1995.[2] Certain categories of people are excluded from the Act: members of the South African National Defence Force, the National Intelligence Agency, and the South African Secret Service. The purpose of the Act is to advance economic development, social justice, labour peace, and the democratisation of the workplace. The Act covers various important aspects, which are briefly discussed below.

11.4.2.1 Freedom of association

Workers have the right to form and join trade unions, and employers enjoy a similar right to form employers' organisations. These rights form the cornerstone of the notion of collectivism, and are enshrined in the international labour standards of the International Labour Organisation (ILO). They are a recognised freedom in most modern labour relations systems, and are generally referred to as the right to freedom of association.

11.4.2.2 Organisational rights

The LRA also provides for trade union access to the workplace. An office bearer or union official is entitled to enter an employer's premises in order to recruit members or to communicate with trade union members. A union may also hold meetings on an employer's premises, as long as these take place outside working hours. The interest of the employer is, however, also protected. Trade union rights are subject to whatever conditions regarding time and place that may be necessary, namely "to safeguard life or property or to prevent the undue disruption of work". Any employee who is a member of a trade union may also authorise the employer in writing to deduct subscriptions or levies payable to that trade union, from the employee's wages.

11.4.2.3 Bargaining councils

Bargaining councils are bargaining and dispute resolution structures introduced by the Act centralised at sectoral level. One or more registered trade unions and one or more employers' organisations may form a bargaining council. The powers and functions of bargaining councils include the following:
- To conclude collective agreements
- To enforce collective agreements
- To prevent and resolve labour disputes
- To perform dispute functions set out in the Act
- To establish and administer a fund to be used for resolving disputes
- To promote and establish training and education schemes
- To establish and administer funds related to pension, provident, medical aid, sick pay, holiday, unemployment schemes, or other schemes or funds

for the benefit of one or more of the parties to the bargaining council or their members
- To determine, by collective agreement, the matters which may not be an issue in dispute for the purpose of a strike or lock-out at the workplace
- To consider workplace forums or additional matters for consultation

11.4.2.4 Statutory councils

A representative trade union (or more than one, combining forces), with members who constitute at least 30% of the employees in a sector, or one or more employers organisations, may apply to the Registrar (Department of Labour) for the establishment of a statutory council in a sector or area in which no bargaining council is registered.

11.4.2.5 Commission for Conciliation, Mediation and Arbitration (CCMA)

The CCMA has a director and commissioners who carry out its functions. It is independent of the state, and of any political party or any other organisation. Its functions are to attempt to resolve, through conciliation, any dispute referred to it in terms of the LRA; to arbitrate any dispute that remains unresolved by these means, if the LRA requires arbitration and any party to the dispute requests arbitration, and if all the parties consent to arbitration under the auspices of the Commission; to assist in the establishment of workplace forums; to compile and publish statistics concerning its activities. The Commission may, if asked:
- Advise a party to a dispute about the appropriate dispute resolution process
- Assist a party to a dispute to obtain legal advice
- Subsidise accredited councils or agencies
- Conduct, oversee or scrutinise any election or ballot of a registered trade union or registered employers' organisation
- Publish guidelines in relation to any matter dealt with in the Act
- Conduct and publish research

11.4.2.6 Labour Court and Labour Appeal Court

The Labour Court has authority, inherent powers and standing in relation to matters under its jurisdiction equal to those of a court of a provincial division of the High Court. It consists of a Judge President, a Deputy Judge President and as many judges as the President may consider necessary. The Court is constituted before a single judge and may sit in as many courts as the available judges may allow. The Court has various functions, which are stipulated in the Act.

The Labour Appeal Court has the jurisdiction:
- To hear and rule on all appeals against final judgements or final orders of the Labour Court
- To rule on any questions arising from proceedings in the Labour Court

11.4.2.7 Strikes and lock-outs

The LRA defines a strike as "the partial or complete concerted refusal to work, or the retardation or obstruction of work, by persons who are or have been employed by the same employer or by different employers, for the purpose of remedying a grievance or resolving a dispute in respect of any matter of mutual interest between employer and employee, and every reference to 'work' in this definition includes overtime work, whether it is voluntary or compulsory". This definition is broad, in that it covers any refusal to work overtime, whether compulsory or voluntary.

If a strike or lock-out does not comply with the provisions of the LRA, the Labour Court has exclusive jurisdiction to grant an interdict or order to restrain any person from participating in or furthering such action, and also to order the payment of just and equitable remuneration of any loss attributable to the strike or lock-out.

The LRA also makes provision for protest action, and includes stipulations regarding replacement labour during strikes, picketing, essential and maintenance services, and lock-outs.

11.4.2.8 Collective agreements

The aim of collective bargaining is to reach agreements. The purpose of the LRA is to provide mechanisms through which the parties can achieve this. Although disputes or industrial action may form part of the process of negotiation, the ultimate goal is to conclude collective agreements.

There are two types of collective agreements: procedural agreements and substantive agreements. Recognition agreements (procedural) regulate how the parties will conduct the relationship, and substantive agreements deal with the content of the relationship and conditions of services.

11.4.2.9 Agency shop and closed shop agreements

A representative trade union whose members are in a majority in a workplace may conclude with the employer an agency shop agreement requiring the employer to deduct an agreed agency shop fee from the wages of its employees who are not members of the trade union and to whom the agreement applies.

Alternatively, a representative trade union whose members are a majority in a workplace may conclude with the employer a closed shop agreement requiring all employees in respect of whom the agreement applies, to be members of the trade union.

11.4.2.10 Workplace forums

Workplace forums are designed to facilitate a shift at the workplace from an adversarial relationship between trade unions and employees to a joint problem-solving and participatory relationship on certain subjects. These forums are also designed to foster cooperative relations through dialogue, information sharing, consultations and joint decision making, which is not possible through collective bargaining processes. The focus is on non-wage matters, such as restructuring, the introduction of new technologies, changes in work scheduling, physical conditions of work, and health and safety, and also those issues that can best be resolved at workplace level.

The **functions** of a workplace forum are to promote the interests of all employees in the workplace, irrespective of whether or not they are union members, and to enhance efficiency in the workplace.

A workplace forum may be established in the workplace of any employer with more than 100 employees. Only representative trade unions may apply to the CCMA for the establishment of a workplace forum. Workplace forums employ a consultative approach and a joint decision-making approach.

11.4.2.11 Automatically unfair dismissals

The LRA specifically recognises the right of an employee not to be unfairly dismissed and has introduced certain stipulations to indicate automatically unfair dismissals, such as:

- Dismissal on account of participation in protected strike action
- Dismissal on account of a refusal to do the work of another employee who is participating in protected strike action, unless that work is necessary to prevent actual danger to life, personal safety or health
- Dismissal in order to compel the employee to accept a demand in respect of any matter of mutual interest between the employer and employee
- Dismissal related to the employee's pregnancy
- Dismissal as a result of unfair discrimination, whether directly or indirectly, on any arbitrary ground

Applying the concept: unfair dismissal

Mary, a young married woman, had been working for four months as a typist, and had recently been informed by her supervisor that her permanent appointment had been confirmed. According to the supervisor she was such an excellent typist that the business could not afford to lose her services. The business grew rapidly during the next two months and Mary felt that there was too much typing for only one person. She decided, however, that she would rather stay on and work overtime. But some time later, Mary informed her supervisor that she was pregnant and that she would therefore only be available for the next two months, but that she would return after the birth of her child. The next morning Mary was given a letter by her supervisor informing her that for unforeseen reasons her services had to be terminated and she did not have to return to work after her child was born.

Was Mary unfairly dismissed?

Apparently, yes. According to the LRA, it is automatically unfair to dismiss Mary on the grounds of her pregnancy. However, there may have been other reasons for Mary's dismissal, for example, restructuring of the business or a take-over by another business. Mary should therefore take the matter up with her bargaining council or the CCMA, and if no valid reasons for the dismissal are found, she would be entitled to reinstatement or to compensation.

11.4.3 Communication: grievances and disciplinary aspects

Communication has a tremendous influence on the quality of labour relations in any organisation. It is therefore recommended that all possible structures and avenues be put in place to ensure constructive relations between management and workers. There are various ways of enhancing the quality of communication between the parties in the employment relationship, including one-on-one "chat sessions", performance appraisals, departmental meetings, safety and health committees, briefing sessions, workplace forums, and coaching sessions. Two communication procedures of paramount importance that are not part of the LRA are grievance and disciplinary procedures.

11.4.3.1 The grievance procedure

In the context of labour relations, a grievance is an employee's response to a real, perceived, or alleged breach of the terms of the employment contract, for example, one-sided changes to the employee's conditions of employment, or being insulted by a supervisor. An effective grievance handling procedure has many advantages:

- It is a safety valve that will release the tension and dissipate the latent aggression inherent in all businesses
- It allows the raising and settlement of a grievance by a worker without fear of retribution or victimisation
- It makes for an open and honest relationship between manager and worker
- It allows managers to identify and remove legitimate causes of dissatisfaction or conflict

11.4.3.2 The disciplinary procedure

Discipline can be described as **any action or behaviour on the part of authority (the employer) in a social system that is aimed at stopping member behaviour that threatens to disrupt the functioning of the system**. It is therefore a normal and inherent part of any business's actions and responsibilities.

Discipline should not be aimed at punishment for the transgression of rules, but rather at rectifying unacceptable behaviour. The principles underlying the disciplinary procedure are:

- The right of management to take appropriate disciplinary steps against any worker who acts in a manner that conflicts with the interests of the business (see box below)
- The right of workers to a fair procedure

Dismissals from organisations should be conducted substantively and procedurally.

Dismissals

"Dismissal is unfair if the employer fails to prove that the **reason** for dismissal is a fair reason:
(i) related to the employee's conduct or capacity; or
(ii) based on the employer's operational requirements; and
that the dismissal was effected in accordance with a fair **procedure.**

Any person considering whether or not the reason for dismissal is a fair reason or whether or not the dismissal was effected in accordance with a fair procedure, must take into account any relevant code of good practice issues in terms of this Act."

Source: LRA, section 188

11.5 Basic Conditions of Employment Act 75 of 1997

11.5.1 Introduction and application

The overall purpose the Act is to advance economic development and social justice in South Africa by enforcing basic conditions of employment (section 2). All employees and employers **except** members of the South African National Defence Force, National Intelligence Agency, South African Secret Service, and unpaid charitable workers fall under the Act.

The basic conditions of employment as prescribed by the Act should form part of every contract of employment unless more favourable terms of employment have been negotiated with an employer. This Act[3] covers a wide variety of topics such as working time, leave, remuneration and obligations. Only a few important aspects will be discussed in this section.

11.5.2 Working time

Employees' working time must be arranged so as not to endanger their health and safety, and with due regard to their family responsibilities. The maximum number of ordinary weekly hours for all employees is 45. The maximum daily hours an employee may work are nine for employees who work on five days or fewer a week, and eight for employees who work six days a week. **Overtime** may only be worked by agreement and is paid at one and a half times the employee's normal wage, or, by arrangement, by giving the employee paid leave equal to the value of the overtime payment. An employee must have a **meal interval** of at least 60 minutes after five hours of continuous work. This may be reduced to 30 minutes by agreement. An employee must have a **daily rest period** of at least twelve consecutive hours between ending work and commencing work the following day. Every employee must have a rest period of at least 36 consecutive hours each week. The rest period must include a Sunday, unless otherwise agreed. An employee may agree in writing to rather have a longer rest period of 60 consecutive hours every two weeks.

Night work is defined as work performed between 18h00 and 06h00. Employees must be compensated by the payment of an allowance or by a reduction of working hours. Transport must be available for employees who work at night. Employers must also inform employees who "regularly" work between 23h00 and 06h00 of the health and safety hazards of night work, and, on request, provide employees with a free medical assessment. The limits on ordinary and overtime working hours, and the requirements for meal intervals and rest periods do not prevent the performance of **emergency work**.

The limits in hours of work and overtime do not apply to senior managers, travelling sales personnel and employees working less than 24 hours a month. The Minister of Labour may exclude or vary the provisions in respect of limits on hours of work and overtime to employees earning more than a certain amount.

11.5.3 Leave

Employees are entitled to 21 **consecutive** days fully paid **annual leave** after every twelve months of continuous employment. An employer may not pay an employee instead of granting annual leave. However, an employee whose employment is terminated must be paid out leave pay due for leave that he or she has not taken. An employee is entitled to six weeks' paid **sick leave** for every 36 months of continuous employment. However, during the first six months of employment an employee is entitled to only one day's paid sick leave for every 26 days worked. An employer may require a medical certificate for absence of more than two consecutive days from an employee who is regularly away from work, before paying the employee for sick leave. Sick leave may not run concurrently with annual leave or notice to terminate services.

A pregnant employee is entitled to a four consecutive months **maternity leave**. This leave may begin up to four weeks before the expected date of birth, unless otherwise agreed or if the employee is required to take the leave earlier for medical reasons. An employer may not require an employee to return to work for six weeks after the birth of a child. An employee may, however, elect to do so if a medical doctor or midwife certifies that she is fit to return to work. Maternity leave is unpaid leave, although an employee is entitled to claim maternity benefits in terms of the Unemployment Insurance Act. It is also possible that the employer may pay maternity leave. An employee who has worked for at least four months is entitled to three days paid **family responsibility** leave per leave cycle. This only applies to employees who work on four or more days in a week, however. The employee may take this leave in the event of the birth of a child, if the child is sick, or if a member of the employee's immediate family dies. An employer may require reasonable proof of the purpose for which this leave is taken before paying the employee. Unused days do not accrue.

11.5.4 Remuneration, deductions and notice of termination

An employer must pay an employee according to arrangements made between them. An employer may deduct money from an employee's pay only if permitted or required to do so by law, collective agreement, court order, or arbitration award. A deduction for loss or damage caused by the employee in the course of employment may only be made by agreement and after the employer has established by a fair procedure that the employee was at fault. An employee may agree in writing to an employer deducting a debt specified in the agreement.

During the **first six months** of employment, an employment contract may be **terminated** on **one week's** notice. The notice period during the remainder of the first year of employment is **two weeks**, while for employees with more than a year's service it is **four weeks**.

The notice period for a **farm worker** or **domestic worker** who has worked for more than four weeks is one month. The notice period may be altered by a joint agreement, but only for employees who have been employed for a year or more. This may, however, be reduced to not less than two weeks.

Notice must be given in writing, and if the recipient cannot understand the notice, it must be explained to the employee in a language he or she can understand. An employer may pay the employee the remuneration for the notice period instead of giving notice. An employee who occupies accommodation situated on the employer's premises or supplied by the employer may elect to remain in the accommodation for the duration of the notice period.

Termination of employment by an employer on notice in terms of the Act does not prevent the employee from challenging the **fairness** of the dismissal in terms of the Labour Relations Act.

On termination of employment an employee must be paid:

- For any paid time off that he or she is entitled to, which he or she has not taken, for example, time off for overtime or Sunday work
- Remuneration for any period of annual leave due and not taken
- In respect of annual leave entitlement during an incomplete annual leave cycle, either one day's remuneration in respect of every seventeen days on which the employee worked or was entitled to be paid, or remuneration calculated on any other basis, whichever is the most favourable to the employee (this applies only if the employee has been in employment longer than four months).

Where an employee's services are terminated because of the **operational requirements** of the employer, severance pay has to be paid (in addition to other payments due to the employee). The minimum amount of severance pay required by the Act is the equivalent of one week's remuneration for each completed year of continuous service. Employees who unreasonably refuse to accept an offer of alternative employment with the same or any other employer, forfeit the entitlement to severance pay.

11.5.5 *Administrative obligations*

The employer must:

- Provide the employee with written particulars of employment when the employee starts employment. These particulars include the employee's ordinary hours of work, the employee's wage, rate of pay for overtime work and leave
- Keep these particulars of employment for three years after the end of the contract of employment
- Give an employee information concerning remuneration, deductions and time worked with regard to his or her pay
- Keep a record of the time worked by each employee as well as of their remuneration
- Display at the workplace a statement of employees' rights under the Act

Upon termination of employment, an employee is entitled to a certificate of service. Simplified provisions apply to employers who have less than five employees and to employers of domestic workers.

11.5.6 Prohibition of the employment of children and forced labour

No person may employ a child under fifteen years of age, and the Minister of Labour may make regulations prohibiting or placing conditions on the employment of children over fifteen years of age.

Basic conditions of employment may be varied by collective agreements (concluded in bargaining councils or outside them), individual agreements, determinations by the minister, or sectoral determinations.

11.5.7 Sectoral determinations

The Minister of Labour may make sectoral determinations establishing basic conditions of employment for employees in unorganised sectors. Two important determinations have been made, namely **domestic sector** workers (see box below) and for the **farm work sector.** Minimum wages and other conditions have been regulated. The Minister of Labour must direct a person in the public service to investigate conditions of employment in any sector or area in which it is proposed to make a sectoral determination.

Sectoral determination for domestic workers: pay slips

Details on pay slips should include:
- The employer's name and address
- The domestic worker's name and occupation
- The period in respect of which payment is made
- The domestic worker's wage rate and overtime rate
- The number of ordinary hours worked by the domestic worker during that period
- The number of overtime hours worked by the domestic worker during that period
- The number of hours worked by the domestic worker on a public holiday or on a Sunday
- The domestic worker's full wage
- Details of any other pay arising out of the domestic worker's employment
- Details of any deductions made
- The actual amount paid to the domestic worker

11.5.8 Employment Conditions Commission

The Employment Conditions Commission was established to advise the Minister of Labour on the making of sectoral determinations, the effect of government policies on employment, and any matters arising out of the application of the Act.

The Minister of Labour may appoint labour inspectors who perform functions such as to promote, monitor or enforce compliance with employment laws. Labour inspectors must advise employees and employers on their rights and obligations in terms of employment laws. They may also conduct inspections, investigate complaints and secure compliance with an employment law.

11.6 Skills Development Act 97 of 1998 (SDA)[4]

To improve the low skills base of people in South Africa, the government has promulgated three important Acts, namely the Skills Development Act, the Skills Development Levies Act (see 11.7) and the South African Qualifications Authority Act (see 11.8). These Acts form part of the national skills development strategy, a new approach that aims, among other things, to link learning to the demands of the world of work, to develop the skills of existing workers, and to enable employers to become more productive and competitive.[5]

It must, however, be noted that there is clear link between the different training legislation and the Employment Equity Act (see 11.9). The principles of equity, access and redress underpin the transformation of the legislation.[6] The linkages might be explained as follows: The South African Qualifications Authority Act (SAQA) creates the National Qualifications Framework (NQF), an integrated framework where all knowledge and skills outcomes can be registered as unit standards. The Skills Development Act introduces a strategic approach to skills development by creating 25 Sector Educational and Training Authorities (SETAs), learnerships and skills programmes that are to be assessed against NQF standards and qualifications. The Skills Development Levies Act imposes a skills development levy on employers, and the Employment Equity Act requires all employers to eliminate unfair discrimination and promote greater representation of black people (that is, Africans, coloureds and Indians), women and people with disabilities. The General and Further Education and Training Quality Assurance Act 58 of 2001 (not discussed in this chapter) transforms the governance and funding of technical colleges.

11.6.1 Purposes of the Act

Section 2 of the Skills Development Act sets out the various purposes of the Act, namely:
- To develop the skills of the South African workforce
- To increase the levels of investment in education and training in the labour market and to improve the return on investment;
- To use the workplace as an active learning environment, to provide employees with the opportunities to acquire new skills, and to provide opportunities for new entrants to the labour market to gain work experience
- To employ persons who find it difficult to be employed
- To encourage workers to participate in leadership and other training programmes
- To improve the employment prospects of persons previously disadvantaged by unfair discrimination and to redress those disadvantages through training and education
- To ensure the quality of education and training in and for the workplace
- To assist work-seekers to find work, retrenched workers to re-enter the labour market, and employers to find qualified employees
- To provide and regulate employment services

The following institutions are established by the Act, namely:
- The National Skills Authority
- The National Skills Fund

- A skills development levy grant scheme as stipulated in the Skills Development Levies Act
- Sector Educational and Training Authorities (SETAs)
- Labour centres
- A Skills Development Planning Unit

11.6.2 National Skills Authority

The main functions of the National Skills Authority are as follows (Section 5 of the Act):
- To advise the Minister of Labour on a national skills development policy and strategy; guidelines on the implementation of the national skills development strategy; the allocation of subsidies from the National Skills Fund; and any regulations to be made
- To liaise with SETAs and the national skills development policy, and the national skills development strategy
- To report to the Minister on the progress made in the implementation of the national skills development strategy
- To conduct investigations on any matter arising out of the application of the SDA

11.6.3 Sector education and training authorities (SETAs)

The establishment of Sector Educational and Training authorities is described in chapter 3 of the Act, and the Minister of Labour may establish a SETA with a constitution for any national economic sector.

The Minister of Labour must, however, take the following into account:
- The education and training needs of employers and employees
- Technologies
- The potential of the proposed sector for coherent occupational structures and career pathing
- The scope of any national strategies for economic growth and development
- The organisational structures of the trade unions, employer organisations and government in closely related sectors
- Any consensus that there may be between organised labour, organised employers and relevant government departments as to the definition of any sector, and the financial and organisational ability of the proposed sector to support a SETA

SETAs have various functions, of which the most important are:
- To develop a sector skills plan within the framework of the national skills development strategy
- To implement its sector skills plan by establishing leaderships; approving workplace skills plans; allocating grants in the prescribed manner to employers, education and training providers and workers; and monitoring education and training in the sector
- To promote leaderships by identifying workplaces for practical work experience; supporting the development of learning materials; improving the facilitation of learning; and assisting in the conclusion of leadership agreements

- To register learnership agreements
- Within a week from its establishment, to apply to the South African Qualifications Authority for accreditation as a body
- To collect and disburse the skills development levies in its sector

11.6.4 Learnerships

Learnerships are described in chapter 4 of the Act, and a SETA may establish a learnership if, firstly, the learnership consists of a structured learning component; secondly, if the learnership includes practical work experience of a specified nature and duration; thirdly, if the learnership leads to a qualification registered by SAQA and is related to an occupation; and, finally, if the intended learnership is registered with the director-general in the prescribed manner.

Learnership agreements are agreements entered into for a specified period between a learner, an employer or a group of employers, and a training provider. The employer has the responsibility to:

- Employ the learner for the period specified in the agreement
- Provide specified practical work experience
- Release the learner to attend the education and training specified in the agreement

The learner has the responsibility to work for the employer and to attend the specified education and training. The training provider must provide the education and training specified in the agreement as well as the learner support specified in the agreement.

The Act also makes provision (in chapter 6) for the establishment of the Skills Development Planning Unit.

Labour centres are to provide employment services for workers, employers and training providers.

11.6.5 Financing skills development

The National Skills Fund (chapter 7 of the Act) must be credited with, firstly, 20% of the skills development levies as stipulated in the Skills Development Levies Act; secondly, with the skills development levies collected and transferred to the Fund; thirdly, with money appropriated by parliament for the Fund; fourthly, with donations to the Fund; and lastly, with money received from any other source.

11.7 Skills Development Levies Act 9 of 1999

The purpose of the Skills Development Levies Act 9 of 1999 is to provide for the imposition of a skills development levy. The most important aspects of the Act[7] will be outlined below.

11.7.1 Levy to be paid

According to section 3 of the Act, every employer must pay a skills development levy, and the South African Revenue services will be the national collection agency.

Every employer must pay a levy at a rate of 1% of an employee's total remuneration. Pensions, superannuations or retiring allowances are, for example, excluded according to section 2(5) of the Act.

Employers who are liable to pay the levy must apply to the commissioner of the South African Revenue Services to be registered, and indicate the jurisdiction of the SETA within which they belong. The employer must also register with the relevant SETA.

11.7.2 Payment of levy to Commissioner and refund

An employer must pay the levy to the Commissioner of Inland Revenue Services not later than seven days after the end of each month.

The National Skills Fund will receive 20% of the levy, and organisations will be able to claim for financing for up to 80% of the levy, less the set-up and running costs of the SETA.

11.8 South African Qualifications Authority Act 58 of 1995 (SAQA)

11.8.1 Introduction

After the publication in 1994 of the National Training Strategy Initiative document and the debate on it, the government's White Paper on Education and Training was published in 1995, and the South African Qualifications Authority Act 58 of 1995[8] (SAQA) was passed on 4 October 1995. The objective of SAQA is to provide for the development and implementation of the NQF and to establish the South African Qualifications Authority. The SAQA board has 29 members representing different sectors, for example, education and training providers, non-governmental organisations, trade unions, and industry. It is responsible for establishing the NQF.

11.8.2 The South African National Qualifications Framework (NQF)

The NQF is based on a credit system for achieving learning outcomes. A learning outcome is, in essence, an ability developed by the learner that reflects an integration of knowledge and skill that can be transferred to different contexts. Qualifications can be obtained by means of full-time study, part-time study, distance education, work-based learning, or a combination of these, together with an assessment of previous learning experiences and general experience.

The NQF is a totally new approach to education and training in South Africa, and figure 11.2 (see p. 252) shows that the NQF consists of a framework with eight levels and three identified bands. The first or lowest band is general education and training (GET), with two sub-sectors, namely formal schooling and adult basic education and training (ABET), culminating in level 1. This qualification represents nine years of compulsory schooling and is equivalent to the present grade 9 at school.

The second band, further education and training (FET), comprises levels 2 to 4. Here a large number of sectors can provide education and training. Level

4 is equivalent to grade 12 (formerly standard 10) at school. The third band is higher education and training, and comprises levels 5 to 8. Moving from the ways of the past to those of the future requires a new mind-set (or paradigm shift) among education and training providers. It also affects the way in which learners at schools and higher educational institutions, as well as employees in the workplace, learn and continue to learn. The concept of lifelong learning is introduced, in the sense that different forms of learning, for example, part time, full time, in-company training, and also experience, are recognised, and credits are awarded and registered with the NQF. The NQF is the foundation for people wishing to achieve national qualifications through formal and informal learning, and in the process contributes to the government's aims of equality, quality, access to opportunities, and the redress of past inequalities.

Figure 11.2: Structure of the NQF

NGF level	Band	Type of qualification and certificates		Locations of learning for units and qualifications		
8	Higher education and training	Doctorates Further research degrees		Tertiary/Research/Professional institutions		
7		Higher degrees Professional qualifications		Tertiary/Research/Professional institutions		
6		First degrees Higher diplomas		Universities/Technikons/Colleges/Private and professional institutions/Workplace/etc.		
5		Diplomas Occupational certificates		Universities/Technikons/Colleges/Private and professional institutions/Workplace/etc.		
Further education and training certificate						
4	Further education and training	School/College/Training certificates/Mix of units from all		Formal high schools/ Private/ State schools	Technical/ Community/ Police/ Nursing/ Private colleges	RDP and labour market schemes/ Industry Training Boards/Unions/ Workplaces/etc.
3		School/College/Training certificates/Mix of units from all				
2		School/College/Training certificates/Mix of units from all				
General education and training certificate						
1	General education and training	Senior phase	ABET Level 4	Formal schools (Urban/Rural/ Farm/Special)	Occupation/ Work-based training/ RDP/Labour market schemes/ Upliftment pro- grammes/ Community programmes	NGOs/ Churches/ Night schools/ ABET programmes/ Private providers/ Industry train- ing boards/ Unions/ Workplace/etc.
		Intermediate phase	ABET Level 3			
		Foundation phase	ABET Level 2			
		Pre-school	ABET Level 1			

11.9 Employment Equity Act 55 of 1998 (EEA)[9]

11.9.1 Introduction

The main aim of this Act is to do away with all forms of discrimination in employment in South Africa by promoting equity and non-discrimination in the employment sector. The overall purpose of the Act is to achieve equity in the workplace, chiefly through the following two main elements:

- The prohibition of unfair discrimination, which applies to all employers
- Affirmative action measures, which apply only to "designated" employers

The most important provisions of the Act are as follows:

- All employers are required to take steps to end unfair discrimination in their employment policies and practices.
- Unfair discrimination against employees or job applicants on the grounds of race, gender, sex, pregnancy, marital status, family responsibility, ethnic or social origin, colour, sexual orientation, age, disability, HIV status, religion, conscience, belief, political opinion, culture, language and birth is prohibited.
- Medical and psychometric testing of employees is prohibited unless properly justified.
- Designated employers must prepare and implement employment equity plans after conducting a workforce analysis and consulting with unions and employees.
- Employment equity plans must contain specific affirmative action measures to achieve the equitable representation of people from designated groups in all occupational categories and levels in the workforce.
- Designated employers must take measures to progressively reduce disproportionate income differentials.
- Designated employers must report to the Department of Labour on their implementation of employment equity.
- A Commission of Employment Equity should be established.
- The Labour Inspectorate and the Director-General of the Department of Labour are responsible for enforcing equity obligations.
- Any employer who intends to contract with the state must comply with its employment equity obligations.
- An employee is protected from victimisation for exercising rights conferred by the Act.

11.9.2 Scope of application of the EEA

Chapter 2 of the Act, which deals with unfair discrimination, applies to all employees and employers. Chapter 3, which covers affirmative action, applies to "designated employers" and people from "designated groups" only.

A **designated employer** is:

- One who employs 50 or more employees
- One who employs fewer than 50 employees, but with a total annual turnover that is equal to or above the applicable annual turnover of a small business in terms of Schedule 4 of the Act

- A municipality
- An organ of state, but excluding local spheres of government, the National Defence Force, the National Intelligence Agency, and the South African Secret Service
- An employer who, in terms of a collective agreement, becomes a designated employer to the extent provided for in the collective agreement

Designated groups are:
- Black people (used broadly to include Africans, coloureds and Indians)
- Women
- People with disabilities

Medical testing as part of the employment process is also prohibited, unless it is justifiable in the light of medical facts, employment conditions, fair distribution of employee benefits or the inherent requirements of the job.

11.9.3 Affirmative action

The Act introduces a duty to apply affirmative action and a process of ensuring that over time, progress is made towards employment equity. The main focus of the Act is on getting employers to prepare plans to achieve progress towards employment equity, and on the assessment of the plans by the Department of Labour. However, the eventual burden of the EEA on employers will to a large extent depend on how the Department of Labour applies the Act, and its approach to the employment equity plans submitted by employers.

The main duties of the employer are to:
- Implement affirmative action measures
- Consult with employees
- Conduct an analysis or audit
- Prepare an employment equity plan
- Report to the Director-General (annually or bi-annually)

The enforcement of the affirmative action provisions is part of a process that

Employment Equity Plan

Designated employers must prepare and implement an employment equity plan in order to bring about reasonable progress towards employment equity in their workforce. The information to be contained in such a plan is set out in the Code of Good Practice: Employment Equity Plan. It must contain at least the measures for affirmative action that the employer has instituted, the numerical goals required to achieve reasonable representation, and the time within which the goals must be achieved if the designated groups are under-represented in the employer's workforce. Monitoring and dispute resolution procedures must also be clearly stated. It is very important to set the numerical goals, which must be established with reference to the factors that the Director General takes into account when he or she revises an employment equity plan. The plan must be valid for a period of from one to five years.

starts with a labour inspector and might end up in the Labour Court. The labour inspector may, for instance, issue a compliance order to an employer who refuses to give a written undertaking to comply with the Act, or an employer who fails to comply with such an undertaking.

If an employer fails to comply with the administrative duties in the Act, the Labour Court may impose a hefty fine, ranging from R500 000 for the first offence to R900 000 for four offences. Fines cannot be imposed for not achieving targets, although the Labour Court may make any appropriate order to ensure compliance with the Act if an employer makes no bona fide effort to achieve the targets.

However, given South Africa's history, employers should be extremely sensitive as to how they manage employment relationships, particularly because there are so many possible discrimination traps that employers could fall into.

11.10 Occupational Health and Safety Act 85 of 1993

11.10.1 Introduction

The main purpose of this Act[10] is the protection of employees by providing a healthy and safe work environment. The origin of the Act can be found in the late 1800s and early 1900s, when mining operations presented many dangers to workers, and poor working conditions led not only to various illnesses but also, at times, to death.

The Act has a wide application and covers all workers, though there are the following exceptions:

- A mine, a mining area or any works as defined in the Minerals Act 50 of 1991, except insofar as the Act provides otherwise
- Certain vessels as defined in the Merchant Shipping Act 57 of 1957
- The Minister may grant exemptions from any or all of the provisions of the Act
- Labour brokers are not considered to be employers in terms of this Act
- The Act provides for an Advisory Council for Occupational Health and Safety with certain functions as stipulated in the Act.

11.10.2 Duties of employers and employees

The general duties of employers to their employees are to:

- Provide and maintain a working environment that is safe and without risk to the health of employees
- Take whatever steps are necessary to eliminate any hazard or potential hazard to the safety or health of employees
- Provide any information, instructions, training and supervision as may be necessary to ensure the health and safety of all employees
- Take all necessary steps to ensure that the requirements of this Act are complied with
- Enforce any measures that may be necessary in the interests of health and safety
- Ensure that the work is performed and that this is done under the general supervision of a trained person
- Keep employees informed at all times

The general duties of employees at work are to:
- Take reasonable care for their own health and safety and also that of others
- Cooperate with their employer regarding this Act and its provisions
- Carry out lawful orders and obey health and safety rules and procedures
- Report any situation that is unsafe or unhealthy
- Report any accident they may have been part of

11.10.3 *Representatives and committees*

Any employer with more than twenty employees must appoint one or more **safety representatives**, after consultation with the workers.
Their functions include the following:
- Functions that may be performed:
  - Review the effectiveness of health and safety measures
  - Identify potential hazards
  - Examine causes of incidents in collaboration with employer
  - Investigate complaints by employees
  - Make representations to the employer and inspector
  - Inspect the workplace
  - Participate in consultations with inspectors
  - Receive information from inspectors
  - Attend meetings of the health and safety committee
- Functions that **must** be performed:
  - Visit the site of an accident at all reasonable times and attend any inspection *in loco*
  - Attend any investigation or formal inquiry in terms of this Act
  - Inspect any document which the employer is required to keep
  - Accompany an inspector on any inspection
  - With the approval of the employer, be accompanied by a technical advisor
  - Participate in any internal health and safety audit
- An employer shall provide such facilities, assistance and training as the representative may require.
- A health and safety representative shall not incur any civil liability by reason of the fact that he or she failed to do anything the representative was required to do in terms of this Act.

Functions of **health and safety committees** include the following:
- Recommendations may be made to the employer or inspector
- Any incident that led to a person's death or illness must be discussed and a report may be sent to an inspector
- A record must be kept of all recommendations

The Minister appoints inspectors, and a certificate is issued as proof of their appointment. Their duties include general functions to ensure that the provisions of the Act are complied with – and here they have special powers relating to health and safety – and also functions with regard to incidents at the workplace.

11.11 Compensation for Occupational Injuries and Diseases Act 130 of 1993[11]

11.11.1 Introduction

In terms of the common law, an employee had no recourse if injured in the course of performing his or her duties. The only way to claim compensation was if intent or negligence on the side of his or her employer could be proved.

The first Act to give some form of protection to the employee was the Workmen's Compensation Act of 1941, which provided for payment of compensation even if intent or negligence on the side of an employer could not be proved. In terms of this Act, compensation will be paid if an injury has been caused by an accident "arising out of and in the course of the employee's employment".

The following persons are excluded:

- Persons performing military service or undergoing military training who are not Permanent Force members
- Permanent members of the South African National Defence Force and South African Police Services while acting in defence of the country
- Domestic workers in private households
- Persons who contract for the carrying out of work, and themselves engage other persons to perform the work

The Act provides for the establishment of a Compensation Board, whose main function is to advise the Minister on various matters concerning the application of this Act and its provisions.

11.11.2 Duties of an employer

An employer must register and furnish the Commissioner with details about his or her business. He or she must keep records of all employees, wages paid and time worked, for a period of four years. Such a record must be sent each year to the Commissioner. The Commissioner will then determine the amount of money that has to be paid by the employer to the Compensation Fund, and the employer must comply within 30 days. The state, parliament, provincial governments, exempted local authorities, and employers who have obtained an insurance policy for the extent of their potential liability, are exempted from giving the required details and paying the determined sum of money.

11.11.3 Procedure to claim compensation

The employee must, as soon as is reasonably possible, notify his or her employer of the accident, as well as his or her intention to instigate a claim. The employer will then notify the Commissioner within seven days. A claim for compensation must be lodged within twelve months of the date of the accident or the date of death.

There are, however, certain requirements that must be met before an employee qualifies for compensation:

- An employer-employee relationship must exist, and the employee must be an employee as defined in this Act.

- Injuries or death must have been caused by an accident.
- The accident must have happened in the scope of the employee's employment; this would be if the accident happened in the nature of the employee's
  duties and in the course of his or her service.

11.12 Unemployment Insurance Act 63 of 2001 (UIA)

This Act[12] provides for the payment of benefits for a limited period to people
who are ready and willing to work, but are unable to get work for whatever
reason. In terms of the UIA, some employees (those who qualify as contributors in terms of section 2 of the UIA) contribute monthly to the
Unemployment Insurance Fund (UIF), which is administered by the
Department of Labour. Employers also pay in a certain amount for every contributor (employee) that they employ. An employee who is out of work can
claim benefits from the Fund. The UIA also provides for sickness benefits,
benefits to dependents if an employee – referred to as a contributor – dies, and
for maternity and adoption benefits.

The UIA should be read in conjunction with the regulations in terms of
section 54 of the Act (Government Gazette, No. 23283, of 28 March 2002) and
the Unemployment Insurance Contributions Act 4 of 2002.

11.12.1 *The scope of the Act*

With the exception of the following categories of people, most employees are
covered by the Act. The following people are not covered:

- Employees employed for less than 24 hours a month with a particular
  employer, and their employers
- Employees who receive remuneration under a learnership agreement registered in terms of the Skills Development Act 97 of 1998, and their employers
- Employers and employees in the national and provincial spheres of
  government
- Those in the Republic on a contract, apprenticeship or learnership, if the
  employer is required to repatriate the employee, or if the employee is
  required to leave the Republic at the end of the contract.

The Act provides for the institution of an Unemployment Insurance Board to
assist the Minister of Labour.

11.12.2 *Duties of employers*

In terms of the Act, employers have certain duties. Every employer is obliged
to do the following:

- As soon as commencing activities as an employer, the business must
  provide the following information regarding its employees to the
  Commissioner, irrespective of the earnings of such employees:
  - The street address of the business, and of its branches
  - The particulars of the authorised person who is required to carry out the
    duties of the employer in terms of this Act if the employer is not resi-
    dent in the Republic, or is a body corporate not registered in the
    Republic

- The names, identification numbers and monthly remuneration of each of its employees, stating the address at which the employee is employed
- Before the seventh day of each month, inform the Commissioner of any change during the previous month in any information furnished
- Pay into the Fund the required amount from the employer and every contributor in his or her employ. (Both the employer and the contributor must pay in an amount equivalent to 1% of the contributor's earnings – a total contribution of 2%. The employee's contribution can be deducted from his or her wages. Employers must make monthly payments into the Fund within seven days of the end of the month.)

11.12.3 Benefits and allowances

Contributors who lose their jobs are entitled (as are their dependants) to the following:

- **Unemployment benefits** for any period of unemployment lasting more than fourteen days if the reason for the unemployment is the termination of a contract, dismissal, or insolvency; the contributor is registered as a work-seeker with a labour centre established under the Skills Development Act and is capable of and available for work.
- **Illness benefits** if the contributor is unable to perform work on account of illness, and fulfils any prescribed requirements in respect of any specified illness. The period of illness should be fourteen days or more.
- **Maternity or adoption benefits.** The contributor will be paid the difference between any maternity or adoption benefit received in terms of any other law or any collective agreement or contract of employment, and the maximum benefit payable in terms of this Act.
- **Dependant's benefits** for a surviving spouse or dependent child, if an application is made within six months after the contributor's death.

In all instances, application should be made in accordance with the prescribed requirements.

11.13 Conclusion

In this chapter a brief overview was provided on the legal environment that influences human resource managers in an organisation. The importance of the Constitution as the supreme law of the land was highlighted, followed by a brief overview of the most important labour laws that line managers and human resource practitioners should take note of in the workplace. The Labour Relations Act, which is the focal point of matters concerning labour relations in organisations, was explained. This was followed by a brief outline of the Basic Conditions of Employment Act (stipulating minimum employment conditions), the Skills Development Act, the Skills Development Levies Act, the South African Qualifications Authority Act (which regulates, inter alia, learnerships and the skills levy payable by employers) the Employment Equity Act (prohibiting unfair discrimination and regulating affirmative action, among other things), the Occupational Health and Safety Act (focusing on a safe and healthy work environment), the Compensation for Occupational Injuries and Diseases Act, and, finally, the Unemployment Insurance Act.

References

1. While effort has been made to provide an accurate summary of the various acts in this chapter, the editors, publishers and printers take no responsibility for any loss or damage suffered by any person as a result of reliance upon the information contained therein.
2. Based on the Labour Relations Act 66 of 1995, *Government Gazette*, Vol. 366, No. 17516, Government Printer, Pretoria.
3. Based on the Basic Conditions of Employment Act 75 of 1997, *Government Gazette*, Vol. 390, No. 18491, December, Government Printer, Pretoria.
4. Based on the Skills Development Act 97 of 1998, *Government Gazette*, Vol. 401, No. 19420, November, Government Printer, Pretoria.
5. Mercorio, G. & Mercorio, C., *An employer's guide to the Skills Development Act*, SEIFSA, 2000, p. 1.
6. *Ibid*, p. 5.
7. Based on the Skills Development Levies Act 9 of 1999, *Government Gazette*, Vol. 406, No. 19984, April, Government Printer, Pretoria.
8. Based on the South African Qualifications Act 58 of 1995, *Government Gazette*, Vol. 364, No. 1521 Government Printer, Pretoria.
9. Based on the Employment Equity Act 55 of 1998, *Government Gazette*, Vol. 400, No. 19370, Government Printer, Pretoria.
10. Based on the Occupational Health and Safety Act 85 of 1993, *Government Gazette*, Vol. 337, No. 14918, July, Government Printer, Pretoria.
11. Based on the Compensation for Occupational Injuries and Diseases Act 130 of 1993, *Government Gazette*, Vol. 340, No. 15158, October, Government Printer, Pretoria.
12. Based on the Unemployment Insurance Act 63 of 2001, *Government Gazette*, Vol. 439, No. 23064, January, Government Printer, Pretoria.

Websites: www.acts.co.za
         www.labour,gov.za
         www.gov.za
         www.ccma.org.za

12 Controlling the management process

The purpose of this chapter

Control is the last of the four fundamental tasks of management. It is the final step in the management process, where the assessment of actual performance against planned performance initiates a new cycle of planning, organising, leading and control. This chapter deals with the nature of control and examines how the control process works. It also examines the areas of control that management should focus on, such as the control of physical resources, quality, control, financial control, budgetary control, the control of information, and the control of human resources. The characteristics of an effective control system are also briefly examined.

Learning outcomes

The content of this chapter will enable learners to:
- Understand the management process
- Give an overview of the importance of control
- Describe how a control process should function
- Explain the key areas of control in the organisation
- Discuss the characteristics of an effective control system
- Describe how the control process provides feedback for the revision of planning

12.1 Introduction

Organisations use control procedures to ensure that they are progressing towards their goals and that their resources are being used properly and productively. This chapter examines the final component of the management process, namely controlling. Although it is the final step in the management process, it forms the basis for a new cycle of management activities because it gives feedback to and influences the first step in the management process, namely planning. Without any knowledge of how successfully the plans were implemented or how effectively the goals were achieved, managers would not be able to start the next management cycle of planning, organising, leading, and ultimately controlling.

Controlling is the final step in the management process and it is, as stated, an important part of the management cycle. Brilliant plans may be formulated, impressive organisational structures may be created, and good leadership may be applied, but none of this ensures that the activities will proceed according to plan or that the goals and carefully laid plans will in fact be realised.

An effective manager is therefore someone who follows up on planned activities, and sees to it that the things that need to be done are in fact carried out, and that the predetermined goals are reached. It is for this reason that managers at all levels and in all departments should be involved in the process of control. Until the activities of individuals, departments or units are evaluated, that is, until actual performance is compared with the standard required, management will not know whether activities have been executed according to plan and will be unable to identify weaknesses in their plans. Controlling means narrowing the gap between what was planned and the actual achievement of management, and ensuring that all activities are carried out as they should be.

Controlling blunders

- In 2001/2002 Saambou did not properly control the share dealing activities of its executives, and rumours had it that the bank was insolvent. A run on the bank resulted in the bank being placed under the curatorship of KPMG, even though the bank was in fact solvent. Poor governance control resulted in hundreds of thousands of depositors waiting to get their money back.
- Enron, the biggest US utility company, exercised poor control over its financial systems and in 2002 the liquidation of this giant corporation resulted in millions of dollars in losses by employees and shareholders.

The management process takes place between planning and control, and successful management is often dependent on sound planning and effective control. The preceding introductory remarks have already partly indicated the importance of control. A few additional remarks are now necessary.

12.2 The importance of control

An organisation needs a control process because the best of plans may go wrong. A control process is necessary in an organisation for the following reasons:

- **The nature of the management process itself and, in particular, the task of planning.** Control is intimately linked with planning, organising and leading. Planning is the first step in control, and without control it is pointless. Again, control without planning is not possible.
- **The constantly increasing size of businesses.** As a business grows, more people are employed, new products are developed, new equipment is bought, new industries are entered, and branch offices are opened as the activities of the business expand into different geographical regions. Over time, the business becomes an extensive network of activities that include production, finance, administration, staff and marketing. Without an effective system of control it would be extremely difficult to spot weak points in a highly complicated network and rectify them timeously.
- **Managers and subordinates are capable of making poor decisions and committing errors.** An effective control system should detect such errors before they become critical.
- **The delegation of tasks to a subordinate does not mean that the job of**

Low ratings for South African management

A global productivity survey by Proudfoot Consulting placed South African managerial efficiency last out of seven countries. The consultants point out that the main reason for such a low rating is inadequate and insufficient **planning and control.**

This is the first time South Africa has been included in Proudfoot Consulting's global productivity survey, which examined global productivity among 1 300 managers and workers of large companies. The survey found that local businesses waste 122 working days a year, resulting in a productivity level of 46%. Germany delivered the most favourable result: a productivity level of 63%. The US and Austria followed with 62% each.

South Africa's productivity was found to be hampered by insufficient planning and control, inadequate management, inappropriately qualified personnel, ineffectual communication, information technology (IT) related problems and poor working morale.

Proudfoot says a well-managed business should be able to achieve a productivity level of 85% without major capital investment.

Source: Business Times, 13 October 2002, p. 5. © Sunday Times.

management has been completed. Management always has to check whether subordinates are doing their job properly. Without an adequate control system this task cannot be carried out.

- Control enables management to **cope with change and uncertainty**. If an organisation is to reach its goals according to plan, control is necessary. Because of the variables in the turbulent contemporary business environment, an organisation is seldom able to realise its goals strictly according to plan. Raw materials may not be delivered on time, labour unrest or defective machinery may delay the organisation's operations, unexpectedly high interest rates may affect the cost structure, and so on. Without control the impact of environmental change on the organisation will be difficult to detect.
- **Competition** is a significant factor. In chapter 1 we briefly discussed the disintegration of centrally directed economic systems and showed how a market economy is better able to satisfy the needs of people. A successful market economy, however, also gives rise to more active competition. This in turn necessitates stricter cost and quality control if the organisation is to remain competitive. Globalisation is responsible for the fierce competition in international markets.
- Control is applied to ensure that the organisation's **resources are deployed** in such a way that it reaches its goals. If there is no control, the organisation's resources could be wasted or misapplied.
- Control usually results in better **quality**.

An overview of the control process will further elucidate the importance of control.

12.3 The control process

As mentioned in the introduction, control is the process whereby management ensures that the organisation's goals are accomplished or that actual performance compares favourably with the predetermined standards. This process comprises four steps, which figure 12.1 illustrates. The process includes setting standards against which actual performance can be measured, measuring actual performance, evaluating any deviations that might occur, and taking steps to rectify deviations. Each of these steps will now briefly be discussed.

Figure 12.1: The control process

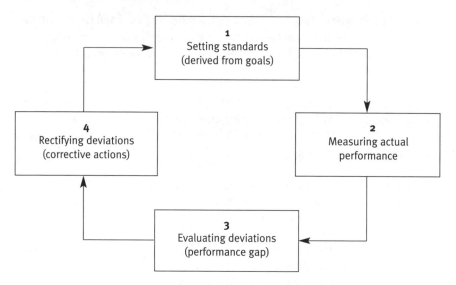

12.3.1 *Step 1: Establish standards*

The first step in control is to establish performance standards at strategic points. Because of the close relationship between planning and control, it may be said that control in fact begins at the planning stage. It is often difficult to distinguish between these two tasks of management, because, in a sense, control means revised planning and the revised allocation of resources. The control system should therefore be a mirror image of planning, as the plans indicate the goals and setting of standards or norms necessary for control.

A **performance or control standard** is a planned target against which the actual performance will be compared. A building project which has to be completed on a certain date will have control standards at strategic stages, such as completion of foundations by 31 March, completion of concrete structure by 30 June, completion of roof by 15 June, and so on.

To make the control process possible and worthwhile, the performance standard should be relevant, realistic, attainable and measurable, so that there can be no doubt whether the actual performance meets the standard or not.

Although it is difficult to make generalisations about suitable performance standards for different businesses, it should be possible in any particular business to convert strategy into comprehensive plans and goals. From these appropriate performance standards others can be developed, for example:

- **Profit standards** indicate how much profit the business expects to make over a given period.
- **Market share standards** indicate what share of the total market the business is aiming to conquer.
- **Productivity standards** are indicated by expressing inputs and outputs in relation to one another as ratios. Such ratios indicate the relative productivity with which tasks are performed.
- **Staff development standards** indicate the effectiveness of training programmes for staff.

Standards are a function of the goals that are set in the planning phase. Performance standards, of which the above examples are only a few, enable management to distinguish between acceptable and unacceptable performance. They also enable management to monitor strategies and goals. To be effective, these standards should be the responsibility of a particular individual at some strategic point.

12.3.2 Step 2: Measure actual performance

The collection of information and reporting on actual performance are continuous activities. As in the case with performance standards, it is also important for the activities to be **quantifiable** before any valid comparisons can be made. Another important requirement regarding the measurement of actual achievement is that the reports be **absolutely reliable**. Unless they are totally accurate, control will not be effective. Moreover, observation and measurement must be carried out at the necessary strategic points and according to the standards determined by the control system.

Important considerations in the measurement and reporting of activities are **what information** and **how much** should be fed back, and **to whom**. In a small business or at the lower management levels of a fairly large business, operational management is more or less fully informed, and this is not of vital importance. But as a business increases in size, and information about activities has to be transmitted to higher levels, the question of control becomes more important. It is at that point that the principle of **control by exception** is applied. This means that only important or exceptional disparities between real and planned achievement are reported to top management, and that less important deviations are dealt with by subordinates.

Management information is presented to indicate the disparities between performance standards and actual performance, and to enable management to concentrate on deviations or problem areas. For example, management might be highly satisfied with a report indicating that sales are 10% higher than in the previous year, but they are likely to feel less complacent about the fact that sales of its market leader have shown a drop of 10%. The lapse of time between performance and measurement must be kept to the minimum so that deviations may be spotted as early as possible.

12.3.3 Step 3: Evaluate deviations

This step comprises the determination of the performance gap between the performance standard and actual performance. It is important to know why a standard has only been matched, and not exceeded, or even why performance has been much better than the standard. This could, for example, be the result of a new trend in the business environment, which might then be exploited more effectively. The nature and scope of the deviations responsible for the so-called performance gap may have various causes. In some cases the causes may be fairly obvious, while in others they may be so obscured that it becomes difficult to identify them. It is therefore impossible to make generalisations about the causes of disparities between actual performance and standards.

Firstly, it is necessary to make sure that the disparities are genuine, that is, that both the performance standard and the actual performance have been objectively set and measured. If the standard is set too high, further examination of apparent deviations may be a waste of time.

Secondly, it must be determined whether the deviations are large enough to justify further investigation. Upper and lower limits should be set for each deviation, and only those that exceed the limits should be subjected to further examination.

Thirdly, all the reasons and activities responsible for the deviation should be identified.

At this point, decisions about corrective action, the last step in control, are needed.

12.3.4 Step 4: Take corrective action

The final step in the control process is to determine the need for corrective action and to ensure that deviations do not recur. If actual achievements match the standards, then of course no corrective action is needed, provided that standards have been objectively set. If not, management has a choice of three possible actions:

- Actual performance can be improved to reach the standards.
- Strategies can be revised to accomplish the standards.
- Performance standards can be lowered or raised to make them more realistic in the light of prevailing conditions.

This completes the cycle of the control process, and corrective action is in a sense, as stated, the point of departure of the next cycle in the management process. However, the term control has different meanings for different people. It often has a negative connotation for those who feel that their freedom and initiative are being restricted. It is therefore important to maintain a balance between control measures and control of people. It should also be borne in mind that on consideration of costs alone, there are limits to the time and money that can be spent on control. Moreover, control should be continually adapted to changing circumstances.

12.4 The focus of control

In the preceding introductory discussion of control, the importance of control as a fundamental function of management was emphasised. But the question now is, what, in fact is it that should be controlled? The important point is that organisations control activities and processes in a number of different **areas (areas of control)**, and at different **levels (strategic points)** in the organisation.

In the preceding section we mentioned that the organisation's activities should be controlled at strategic points. The issues surrounding the design of a control system may be complex and depend on a variety of factors, including the nature of the organisation, its activities, its size, and its structure. As a rule, management should identify the key areas to be controlled. These are the areas responsible for the effectiveness of the entire organisation. For example, the production department of a manufacturing organisation is a key area, as is the purchasing department of a chain store. Generally, a small percentage of the activities, events or individuals in a given process are responsible for a large part of the process. Thus, 10% of a manufacturing organisation's products may be responsible for 60% of its sales, or 2% of an organisation's personnel may be responsible for 80% of its grievances. By concentrating on these strategic points, for example, the organisation's main activities are exposed to control.

Most organisations define areas of control in terms of the four basic types of resources they use. In chapter 5 we defined management as the process in which the organisation's human, financial, physical and information resources are deployed to accomplish specific goals, especially those revolving around profitability. The implication here is that control should focus on the effective management of these resources. Figure 12.2 illustrates the focal points or key areas of control, namely:

- **Physical resources.** This entails factors such as inventory control, quality control and control of equipment.
- **Human resources.** This involves orderly selection and placement, control over training and personnel development, performance appraisal and remuneration levels.
- **Information sources.** This relates to accurate market forecasting, adequate environmental scanning, and economic forecasting.
- **Financial resources.** In figure 12.2 financial resources are situated at the centre of the other three resources not only because they are controlled in their own right (for example, cash-flow or debtor control), but also because most control measures or techniques (such as budgets, sales, production costs, market share, and various other magnitudes) are quantified in financial terms.

Figure 12.2: Key areas of control

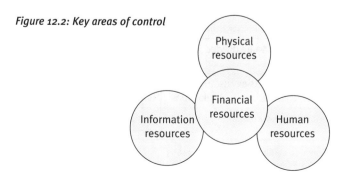

Each of the focal points of control will now be discussed in greater detail.

12.4.1 The control of physical resources

An organisation's physical resources are its tangible assets, such as buildings, office equipment and furniture, vehicles, manufacturing machinery and equipment, trading stock, raw materials, work in process, and finished products. Various control systems of an administrative nature can be established to control physical resources – in particular office furniture, equipment and vehicles – which normally appear on an asset register. Control systems for these resources involve usage procedures, periodic inspections and stocktaking, which often fall within the ambit of the internal audit. The control systems for inventories, raw materials and finished products are inventory control and quality control. Although inventory control falls within the field of purchasing and logistics management, it is necessary to make a few remarks about it here.

12.4.1.1 Inventory

Inventory refers to the reserves of resources held in readiness to produce products and services, as well as the end products that are kept in stock to satisfy consumers' and customers' needs. It normally refers to the four basic kinds of inventory, such as raw materials, work-in-process, components, and finished products, but it need not only have to do with manufacturing. For an airline, a seat on an aircraft is inventory, and an unsold seat on a flight is a loss. By the same token, money in a safe in a bank is inventory that can be lent to clients at a certain interest rate, and an empty bed in a hospital ward is ître trading stockî. Organisations keep inventories – and here the word is used in a wide sense – mainly for the following purposes:
- To satisfy the needs of customers and consumers
- In the case of raw materials and components, to keep uncertainties regarding delivery and availability to a minimum, so that the manufacturing process is not interrupted
- As a hedge during times of high inflation

There are, as table 12.1 shows, a number of reasons[1] why organisations keep inventories, but, as the above emphasises, there is one especially important reason, namely the cost of inventories and the need to control that cost.

Table 12.1: Types of inventory, purpose and sources of control

Type	Purpose	Source of control
Raw materials	Provide the materials needed to make the product	Purchasing models and systems
Work-in-process	Enables overall production to be divided into stages of a manageable size	Shop-floor control systems
Finished goods	Provide ready supply of products on customer demand, and enable long, efficient production runs	High-level production scheduling systems, in conjunction with marketing
In-transit (pipeline)	Distributes products to customers	Transportation and distribution control systems

Source: Griffin, R.W., *Management*, Houghton Mifflin Company, 1999, p. 663.

It is estimated that it costs an organisation 20 to 25 cents per R1.00 of inventory per annum to keep inventories. These costs refer mainly to interest, space and risk factors. The most expensive cost is the price of money, or interest, to finance inventories, followed by storage costs, insurance, and risk. Because of the high cost of inventories, it stands to reason that organisations, especially in times when interest rates are high, will try to keep inventory levels as low as possible. Inventory control is introduced to keep inventory, and the costs involved, as low as possible without causing shortages that may delay the manufacturing process or other transactions. The following three control systems are relevant here:

- The concept of economic ordering quantity (EOQ), in use as early as 1915, is based on replenishing inventory levels by ordering the most economic quantity. The disadvantage of this control system is that inventory must be kept, regardless of the needs of the manufacturing department or customer, for particular raw materials, components or finished products. This means that items must be kept in stock for indefinite periods in spite of efforts to keep inventory costs as low as possible.
- The materials requirements planning (MRP) system was developed in the 1960s to eliminate the shortcomings of the EOQ control system. With this system, an estimate is made of the demand for raw materials and the components necessary to create a finished product. Inventories are ordered only when they are needed, and the costs of maintaining inventory levels over extended periods of time are thus eliminated.
- The just-in-time (JIT) system is a refinement of the MRP system and originated in Japan, where it was developed by Toyota in the 1970s.[2] The JIT philosophy is the same as MRP in the sense that organisations endeavour to manufacture products without incurring significant inventory costs. However, in contrast to MRP, where the need for raw materials and components is estimated and they are ordered according to demand, JIT is based on the premise that actual orders for finished products are converted into orders for raw materials and components, which arrive just in time for the manufacturing process. A manager applying the JIT principle orders materials and components more often in smaller quantities, thereby reducing risk and investment in both storage and actual inventory.

Toyota and JIT: the origin of the JIT system

The JIT production method, although recent in origin, has become the backbone of Japanese manufacturing. JIT production was developed in the mid-1970s by the Toyota Motor Company in response to the energy crisis. Faced with increasing energy and production costs, Toyota had to find a way to make its products more competitive in the international market.

One way was to cut inventory costs. Rather than producing finished goods destined for storage as stock, Toyota decided to produce cars just in time to be sold. It fabricated parts just in time to be assembled into subcomponents and materials just in time for fabrication. By using the JIT programme system, Toyota was able to use all materials promptly, incurring no carrying or ordering costs.

Source: Chung, K.H., *Management: critical success factors,* Allyn & Bacon, p. 607.

The success of this complex inventory control system depends largely, however, on reliable deliveries of flawless components, stable relationships with outside suppliers, and a reliable labour force.

This discussion of inventory control systems is extremely superficial, since the aim is merely to introduce the field of application and the complexity of control systems relating to physical resources.

We will now examine an element that is closely intertwined with inventory control, namely quality control.

12.4.1.2 Quality control

Quality and productivity have become increasingly important issues in management, especially in the USA where business organisations are continually searching for ways of countering the success of foreign competitors in American markets. The management approach, which emphasises the management of quality, is known as **total quality management** (TQM). Because of its importance, particularly in competitive international markets, it is necessary to give a brief overview of quality control.

Japanese products were once regarded as cheap goods. Today, however, the quality of Japanese products is acknowledged globally. Because of the success of Japanese products, especially in the USA, Western managers are realising increasingly that access to international markets depends not only on mass production, but also on quality. Whereas quality control was formerly the responsibility of a single department or section, TQM means that quality is the responsibility of everyone in the organisation,[3] from the chairman of the board of directors, down to clerks, purchasing managers, engineers, and selling and manufacturing personnel. Figure 12.3 illustrates the major factors involved in improving quality.

Figure 12.3: Managing quality

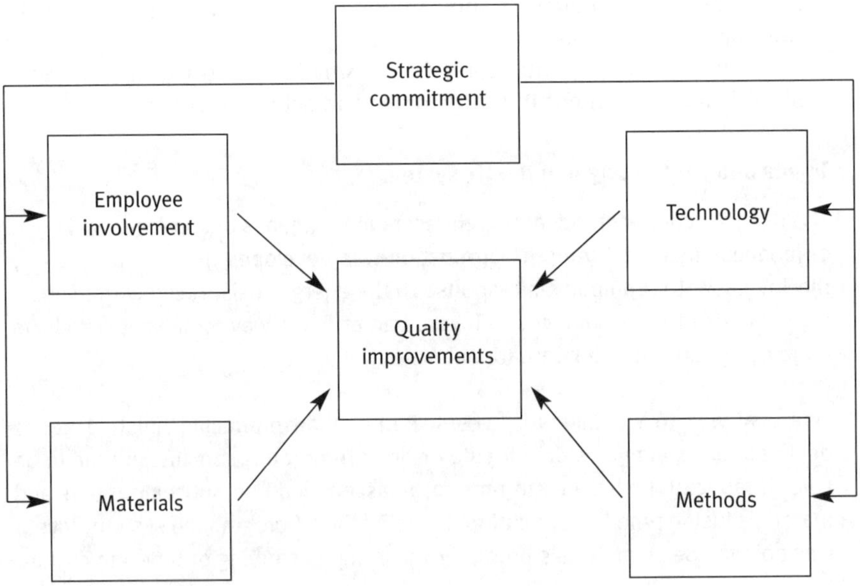

Source: Based on Griffin, R.W., *Management,* Houghton Mifflin Company, 1999, p. 644.

A strategic commitment on the part of top management will ensure that quality is included in the mission statement of the organisation and transmitted to operational levels. The ultimate test of product quality is in the marketplace, where it becomes evident whether or not the product satisfies consumers' needs.

Quality control refers to the activities that management performs to ensure a level of quality that will satisfy the consumer, on the one hand, and have certain benefits for the organisation, on the other. It usually comprises the following steps:

- The first step in quality control is the **definition of quality goals or standards**. This entails setting standards as prescribed by purchasers, chosen by consumers and necessitated by competition. However, quality means different things to different people. Some might perceive it as value for money, and others simply as the durability of the product. In setting quality standards, management should focus on both qualitative product characteristics, such as reliability, durability, design, style and colour, and quantitative characteristics such as length, height and mass.
- The second step in quality control is **measuring quality**. This entails the use of the following: **benchmarking**, or the process of learning how other businesses do things exceptionally well; **statistical control methods** to analyse product data with a view to quality; **variation measurement**, that is, measuring variations in materials, processes, equipment and the final product; and the determination of whether or not **specification limits** have been met or exceeded.
- Thirdly, quality control entails rectifying deviations and solving quality problems in an effort to keep the **cost of quality** as low as possible. This refers to the cost of control as well as the cost of failures, or the cost of poor quality. To be able to decide which products or product processes should be improved, management should conduct quality cost studies. These analyses indicate the cost-quality ratio of the organisation's products and services. Another technique that can be applied to improve quality is **quality circles**. These are forums of employees who get together to identify aspects of their jobs that impede, prevent or promote quality, and who endeavour, on the strength of their expertise, to find solutions. The influence of quality circles in improving quality is felt not so much in direct savings, but in the positive motivational effect that participative problem solving has on employees.

The discussion above of the control of the organisation's physical resources, though somewhat cursory, points not only to the complexity of controlling physical resources, but also to the importance of control in the success of the organisation. Aspects of control are expressed mainly in financial magnitudes. Control of the organisation's financial resources is the next topic of discussion.

12.4.2 The control of financial resources

An organisation's financial resources is the second group of resources that management must control. Financial resources and abilities are vital to the success of the organisation and are at the heart of the control process, as indicated in figure 12.2 (see p. 267). While financial resources are a group of resources in their own right, the control of financial resources is central to the control of other resources of the organisation. Financial control is concerned with the following: resources as they **flow into** the organisation (revenue returns on investments); financial resources that are **held** by the organisation (working capital, cash); and financial resources **flowing out** of the organisation (salaries, expenses).

Each of these categories of financial resources is controlled so that revenues are sufficient to cover expenses and show a profit. Incoming funds, which normally represent revenue in the form of electronic transfers, cheques and cash, must be controlled rigorously because this is an area where fraud is often experienced. Funds that are held by the organisation, such as working capital, should not be tied up in areas such as outstanding debtors or slow moving inventory. Of equal importance is the control of outgoing funds such as salaries and expenses, which are also areas where fraud and serious errors might be found.

Financial management principles that deal with cash flows, cash management, investment returns, and so on, can also be regarded as financial control measures, but it is beyond the scope of this chapter to deal with that in detail. However, since financial control is pivotal to the control process, we will examine two instruments of financial control, namely budgetary control and financial analysis.

12.4.2.1 The budget

As part of the planning process, management allocates financial resources to different departments of the organisation in order to enable them to accomplish certain goals, and by allocating funds to specific activities management can implement certain strategic plans. This allocation of financial resources is done by means of the **budget**. From the point of view of control, management wants to know how the financial resources are applied. The budget is therefore used as an instrument of control.

A budget is a formal plan, expressed in financial terms, that indicates how resources are to be allocated to different activities, departments or sub-departments of an organisation. At the same time, it forms the basis for controlling the financial resources, a process known as budgetary control. Budgets are usually expressed in financial magnitudes, but can also be expressed in other units such as sales volumes, units of production, or even time. It is precisely because of the quantitative nature of budgets that they provide the foundation for control systems – they provide benchmarks or standards for measuring performance and making comparisons between departments, levels and periods. More specifically, the contribution of a budget to financial control is as follows:

- It supports management in coordinating resources, departments and projects.
- It provides guidelines on the application of the organisation's resources.
- It defines or sets standards that are vital to the control process.
- It makes possible the evaluation of resource allocation, departments or units.

Table 12.2: Types of budgets

Type of budget	Focus	Examples
Financial budgets	Focus on cash flow Focus on capital expenditure	• Cash-flow budget • Capital budget
Operational budgets	Revenue Focus on the operational aspects of the organisation	• Sales budgets, contract budgets • Sales budget • Income budget • Expenditure budget
Non-financial budgets	Focus on diverse aspects of the organisation not expressed in financial terms	• Production budgets in units • Sales volumes in units • Time projections of projects

Various kinds of budgets, a few examples of which are provided in table 12.2, can be used to make financial control possible across the financial spectrum.

Budgets were traditionally developed in a top-down fashion, where top management would develop the budget and impose it on the rest of the organisation. However, the way budgets are set today, especially in larger organisations, is to involve all managers of operating units, from the bottom to the top, in the budget process. A great deal of interaction takes place between heads of operating units (supervisory management) dimensional heads (middle management) and top management. The budget is usually set by a budget committee consisting of top managers, and it is here that top management also implement their strategies, which they do by allocating financial resources to the areas or divisions which must lead the organisation's strategy.

Budgets have a number of strengths as well as weaknesses. The most important advantage of a budget is that it facilitates effective control by placing a money value on operations, and in doing so enables managers to pinpoint problems. Budgets also facilitate coordination between departments and maintain records of organisational performance. But on the negative side, budgets may sometimes limit flexibility.

Budgets are not the only instrument that management uses to apply financial control, however. To complement the budget, management can use financial analysis, also known as ratio analysis, to apply financial control. This will be discussed in chapter 17.

12.4.3 The control of information resources

All the tasks of management, namely planning, organising, leading and controlling, are dependent on supporting information in order to function effectively. However, it is the relevant and timely information that is made available to management during the management process that is vital in monitoring how well the goals are accomplished. Only with accurate and timely information can management implement plans and determine on a continuous basis whether everything is proceeding according to plan, and whether adjustments need to be made. The faster managers receive feedback on what is going smoothly or badly in the course of the management process, the more effectively the organisation's control systems function.

12.4.4 *The control of human resources*

Although the control task of management focuses mainly on financial and physical resources, this does not mean that the performance of one of the organisation's main resources, namely people, is exempt from control. The management of people, that is, the control of human resources, also falls within the ambit of human resources management. A few remarks will be sufficient to emphasise the scope of control of human resources throughout the organisation.

The main instrument used to control an organisation's human resources is **performance measurement**. This entails evaluating employees and managers in the performance of the organisation. More specifically, from a control point of view, the performance of individuals and groups is assessed and compared with predetermined standards. Tasks are subdivided into components, and the importance of each subtask is determined so that criteria and measuring instruments can be developed. Performance standards must then be developed, for example, 40 production units per hour, an accuracy level of 98% in tuning machines, or a quality level of at least 93%. Actual performance can be measured against these standards for feedback to and action by management.

Other human resources control instruments include specific ratio analyses that can be applied in respect of **labour turnover, absenteeism** and the **composition of the labour force**.

The preceding discussion of the control of an organisation's resources mainly emphasises the formal control systems developed by management. As far as informal control systems are concerned, however, people in the organisation play a decisive role in social control mechanisms. This refers specifically to group behaviour. When a group of people work together on a regular basis, they develop norms that lay down guidelines for the behaviour of the group. These norms, which may include the quality of products, speed of production, and reliability, are usually not written down, and have nothing to do with the formal organisational structure. Nevertheless, they still have a profound influence on the behaviour of groups when it comes to control or social control. Members of the group subject themselves to the norms of the group because, if they do not, they may be punished by the group in ways that may range from light-hearted teasing to outright rejection. Compensation by the group for group cohesiveness and control consists of approval of action, emotional support, and the assignment of a leadership role to the leader of the group.

The above discussion of the areas of control provides an overview firstly of the control process as it applies to the organisation's different resources, and secondly of some of the instruments that enable management to control resources.

12.5 Characteristics of an effective control system

The following are characteristics of an effective control system:
- **Integration.** A control system is more effective when it is integrated with planning, and when it is flexible, accurate, objective, timely and not unnecessarily complex. The interface between control and planning is dis-

cussed in the introduction to this chapter. Control complements planning, because deviations highlight the need to review plans and even goals. In this way, control provides valuable inputs to planning. The closer the links between control and planning, the better the eventual control system will be. This is why provision should be made at the planning stage to make control possible, for example, by formulating goals in such a manner that they can be converted into or applied as control standards. This means setting quantifiable goals. Figure 12.4 shows how planning and control should be integrated.

Figure 12.4: Integration of planning and control

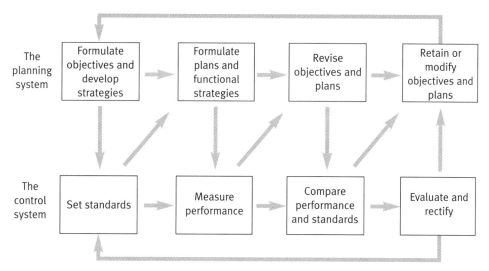

* **Flexibility.** The second characteristic of an effective control system is flexibility. This means that it should be able to accommodate change. Timeous adjustments in objectives or plans should not be regarded as deviations, but as revised objectives or plans, and the control system should be able to adjust to such revisions, within limits, without management having to develop and implement an expensive new control system.
* **Accuracy.** A control system should be designed in such a way that it provides an objective and accurate picture of the situation. Errors or deviations should not be concealed in the data. A total amount expressed in rand certainly does not show a profit, nor does it indicate which products sell better than others. Similarly, production management can conceal indirect costs to make production performance look good. Inaccurate information leads to incorrect modifications of new plans based on unreliable control data.
* **Timeliness.** Timely control data are not obtained by means of hasty, makeshift measurement; control data should be supplied regularly, as needed. A sensible approach is one based on the principle of timeliness.
* **Unnecessary complexity.** Unnecessarily complex control systems are often an obstacle because they can have a negative influence on the sound judgment of competent managers. If managers are hampered by red tape, they may leave the system to keep things going, and in so doing lose their

personal involvement and motivation to see to it that things proceed according to plan. Unnecessary control is equally demotivating for personnel, and leads to resistance to control systems.

It should be realised that too much information, especially if it is irrelevant, makes great demands on the time and attention of management, which means that the control process becomes too expensive. The unwritten rule of effective control is that control should not become so complex that the implementation of the control system becomes more expensive than the benefits derived from it. At the same time, a system should not be oversimplified to the extent that the essence of control is lost.

12.6 Conclusion

Control is one of the four fundamental management functions. It is the final step in the management process, and the starting point for planning and strategic development. The control process narrows the gap between planned performance and actual performance by setting performance standards in the right places, against which the performance of management, subordinates and resources can be measured, and deviations rectified, if necessary. Control focuses on virtually every activity or group of activities in the organisation, but normally aims at physical, financial, information and human resources. Effective control systems are characterised by the extent to which planning and control are integrated, as well as the flexibility, accuracy and timeliness of the system. Management information plays an important role here.

However, too much information, especially irrelevant information, demands too much time and attention from management, which makes it too expensive. This ties in with the unwritten rule pertaining to control, namely that the application of the control system should not become so complex that it costs more than it saves. At the same time, the system should not be oversimplified to the point of losing its significance.

12.7 Summary

This discussion of control as the final fundamental element of management completes the examination of the management process, and with it, part 2 of this book. It should be clearly understood, however, that the general principles forming the subject of this section are also relevant in part 3, which deals with the specialised or functional areas of management. Less detail from this section is provided when discussing, say, financial planning or marketing control, where the emphasis in the treatment of different business functions falls mainly on the activities peculiar to a particular functional area.

References

1. Griffin, R.W., *Management*, Houghton Mifflin, New York, 1999, p. 663.
2. See also Chung, K.H., *Management: critical success factors*, Allyn & Bacon, p. 607.
3. See also Oakland, J.S., *Total quality management: text with cases*, Butterworth-Heinemann, Oxford, 1995, pp. 27–9.

PART 3

The functional management of the organisation

13 The marketing process

The purpose of this chapter

The purpose of this chapter is to give an overview of the evolution of marketing thought and to define marketing and what it entails. At the same time, the various components of the marketing process are discussed, with an emphasis on the way these components interact. In the total process, marketing research forms a crucial part of the process of gathering information and evaluating it. This information is used in understanding the behaviour of customers and also to segment the market and to position the company and its products in the marketplace.

Learning outcomes

The content of this chapter will enable learners to:
- Define marketing as part of the management process
- Describe the origin and evolution of marketing thought
- Describe the market offering
- Indicate how marketing research can be used in scanning the environment
- Describe the behaviour patterns of consumers
- Explain how the consumer market can be segmented in order to select a target market

13.1 Introduction[1]

In the introductory chapters, the business world, and, more specifically, a business organisation, is described as an institution of the free-market (capitalist) system, which, in striving to make a profit, attempts to meet the needs of society. A business is also described as a system that converts inputs in the form of, say, raw materials, into outputs (products and services) for society. The marketing function is that aspect of the business involved in the marketing process, which is the transfer of products (or services) to the market.

The marketing process broadly involves the following:
- Environmental scanning (by means of marketing research) in order to collect pertinent information on which marketing management can base sound decisions
- The development of a market offering, consisting of a tangible product or an intangible service offered at a specific price at a convenient place and about which the consumer has received adequate information

In this process, marketing management, which is also responsible for the marketing process, must monitor competitors and develop strategies to exploit opportunities in the environment and to counter threats, while taking into account the strengths and weaknesses of the business. As mentioned previously, the realisation of long-term profit maximisation in a free-market system is the basis of these activities.

Marketing is the bridge between a business and its environment, bringing into contact the business and its market, providing input in the development of the business's mission and strategies, and helping to correlate the resources of the business with the demands of the market. It can be said that the activities of the business begin with and revolve around the marketing function, because top management must first determine what can be achieved in the marketplace before considering production facilities, employing labour, purchasing raw materials, and financing all these activities. Marketing is therefore regarded as the logical point of departure for investigating the specialised management functions of a business.

In this chapter the evolution of marketing thought is discussed, marketing is properly defined, and the components of the marketing process are examined.

13.2 Evolution of marketing thought

The importance of marketing has filtered through to management over time. Initially management believed that contact with consumers was unimportant. However, this approach has changed drastically over the years. This is especially because of pressure from consumers and an increase in competition.

Before the Industrial Revolution, households were mainly self-sufficient. Many cottage industries produced goods that were made available for barter or sale. Trade had already developed to the extent that money was regarded as acceptable tender in exchange for products. This made trade and bartering much easier, but as distances increased between producers and their markets, intermediaries were needed to provide services to facilitate the bartering process. Hawkers were the link, since they purchased a variety of products, which were then offered for sale; they often used donkeys and camels to transport their wares. In South Africa in the 17th and 18th centuries, hawkers used to visit farms in donkey carts. The farmer's wife would then barter farm produce for consumer goods such as fabric to be made into dresses, shirts or sheets. This whole process was market driven. What could not be sold was not produced.

The technical advances of the Industrial Revolution created machinery capable of mass manufacturing of consumer products in a relatively short time. Large factories built to house the new machines necessitated some form of management. Over the years, management approaches to the marketing function gradually changed, with different aspects being emphasised. These approaches will now be discussed in more detail:

- **Operation-oriented management.** Initially, the operation process demanded all of management's attention. Top management was interested mainly in encouraging production and in solving operation problems. The marketing of manufactured goods did not create many problems because consumers were largely unsophisticated and not accustomed to the consumer products that the factories and newly developed modern machinery produced in mass. Moreover, it was hardly necessary to encourage these unsophisticated consumers to buy the new products – they found them extremely desirable. Thus, marketing as a management function was undervalued.

- **Sales-oriented management.** The situation gradually changed as top management succeeded in solving the most pressing operation problems. The new machines worked steadily, and stocks began to pile up. During the period 1930-1950, selling mass-produced products became problematic. Misleading advertising and unethical sales methods were employed. The objective was to sell products at any cost. Management had to get rid of overproduced stock and did not care if customers were exploited in the process. This led to excessive promotion and hence high advertising and sales costs. Management was compelled, in the face of increasing competition, to look for more productive marketing methods. This gave rise to the idea that products should be marketed instead of merely sold.
- **Marketing-oriented management.** Marketing orientation means that not only the sales message and the price of the product have to be considered, but also the quality of the product, the packaging, the choice of distribution channels, and the methods of informing potential consumers about the market offering. After 1950 the use of advertising became increasingly important. Management now realised that advertising was a very good method of transmitting information to a mass market. Top management focused its attention on the internal organisation of the marketing function. It also realised that all functional departments must join forces to ensure the successful marketing of the business's products.
- **Consumer-oriented management.** As increasingly competitive consumer products became available and the financial position of consumers improved, consumer demands also started changing. The importance of consumer demand now became clear to management, which realised that decisions about a product's attributes and quality, its packaging, the choice of the brand, the type of distribution outlet (store), the price and marketing communication methods, should all be based on consumers' needs, demands and preferences. There is no sense in producing a product if there is no demand for it. A business that is market driven is also consumer oriented, and applies a strategic approach to marketing.
- **The strategic approach to marketing.** This is a more recent development in marketing thought. Because of continual changes in the marketing environment and the need for the survival and growth of the business, attention is focused on strategic long-term issues and environmental scanning. Scanning identifies environmental changes such as technological innovation, economic influences, cyclical movements (growth periods followed by recessions), political factors, increasing competition, demographic aspects and changing consumer preferences. It became clear that maintaining close relationships, both internally and externally, was of increasing importance in a changing environment. This led to relationship marketing.
- **Relationship marketing.** In order to survive in a changing environment it became necessary for marketing management to maintain long-term relationships with persons and institutions in the environment in which the

marketing task was to be performed. A long-term relationship with customers leads to loyalty and the repeated purchase of need-satisfying products. A long-term relationship with suppliers ensures the availability of raw materials and inventory. This is especially important in retailing, where out-of-stock situations can inconvenience customers. Marketing managers are not responsible for negotiations with suppliers, but in the light of the close contact between buyers and sellers, marketing management should help establish long-term relationships through mutual cooperation. In the same way, a long-term relationship between producer and intermediaries such as retailers can ensure the availability of products at the right place and time.

In order to establish a favourable corporate image, the goodwill of society towards the business and its products must be fostered. Here, marketing managers can also make a considerable contribution because of their close contact with the general public. Through internal marketing, all personnel (not only those in the marketing department) become involved in marketing objectives and plans. Everyone must realise that customer satisfaction and success in the market will be reflected in their own career opportunities and remuneration. Relationship marketing is used to good effect by market-driven businesses.

This historical review of the evolution of marketing does not only point to developments in the past. Even today, there are many businesses that are still operation or sales oriented. They are not market driven at all, and cannot hope to achieve sustainable success.

The marketing task in a market-driven business must be performed according to an ethical code or philosophy. This is closely related to the long-term objective of corporate management. The marketing process itself often provides many opportunities for exploitation, with one participant in a transaction being enriched by taking unfair advantage of another. Many such incidents occur daily. Salespeople often make promises they cannot keep, and persuade naïve people to buy their products or to invest money in dubious schemes. Soon afterwards, the salesperson (or institution) suddenly disappears with the money, without delivering the promised product, high interest, or sudden wealth. In such cases the marketing task is not performed according to an ethical code of conduct. In fact, these examples are not marketing at all, but rather fraud. A swindle has only a short-term objective, is mainly sales-oriented, and has no chance at all of long-term survival.

Because an ethical code according to which the marketing task ought to be performed is regarded as the basis of all marketing activities and decisions, it is necessary to describe it in more detail. This ethical code is known as the marketing concept, and is discussed in chapter 15 as part of social responsibility and business ethics.

Against this background, we will now provide a full definition of marketing.

13.3 Defining marketing

Many people, including managers, see marketing as sales or advertising. However, these are only a part of marketing. A definition of marketing is given overleaf.

Definition

Marketing consists of management tasks and decisions directed at successfully meeting opportunities and threats in a dynamic environment, by effectively developing and transferring a need-satisfying market offering to consumers in such a way that the objectives of the business, the consumer and society will be achieved.

Table 13.1 gives an explanation of the key concepts.

Table 13.1: Key words in the definition of marketing

Management tasks	Planning, organising, leading, control
Decisions	Product distribution, marketing communication methods and price
Opportunities	Favourable circumstances in the marketing environment which must be utilised by marketing management
Threats	Unfavourable conditions which marketing management must endeavour to change into opportunities
Dynamic environment	Continually changing environmental variables which necessitate appropriate reaction from marketing management
Development	Creating a need-satisfying product or service
Transferring	Effectively bridging the gap between the producer and consumer
Need-satisfying	Properties of a product based on what the consumer wants
Market offering	Product, price, distribution, marketing communication and service
Attainment of objectives • The enterprise • The consumer • Society	Maximisation of profitability in the long term Need satisfaction within the limits of the resources and capacities of the enterprise Ensuring the well-being of society in the longer term

13.4 The components of the marketing process

In its simplest form, the marketing process entails the transfer of a product or service from one person to another, and is as old as humankind itself. Even in primitive societies people performed marketing activities of one kind or another. One primitive marketing process involved bartering, where, for example, people would barter meat, of which they had a surplus, for grain that another person could spare. Initially, only useful products may have been bartered. It may sometimes have happened, however, that one participant in a bartering transaction would use force to compel the other to participate in the exchange process.

In business management, marketing entails the transfer of a product from business to consumer. The fundamentals of the marketing process can be described as needs, and a transaction or exchange that leads to the satisfaction of those needs. Every time people attempt to satisfy their needs by means of an exchange, marketing is involved. However, in contrast to primitive bartering, where force was sometimes used to compel people to participate, nowadays, in a free-market society, consumers are free to decide which products best satisfy their needs, and also how much they are prepared to spend.

Consumers cannot be compelled to sacrifice money for the product offered by the marketer, and while they are free, on the one hand, to decide for themselves, marketers, on the other hand, use marketing strategies to persuade consumers to accept their products. Hence, in its simplest form, the marketing process involves a transaction between at least two separate parties, the one being the marketer (or business) attempting to realise certain objectives, and the other being consumers attempting to satisfy their needs. Figure 13.1 illustrates this process. More details are given about the components in the following discussion, which should be followed by referring to the figure.

Figure 13.1: The marketing process

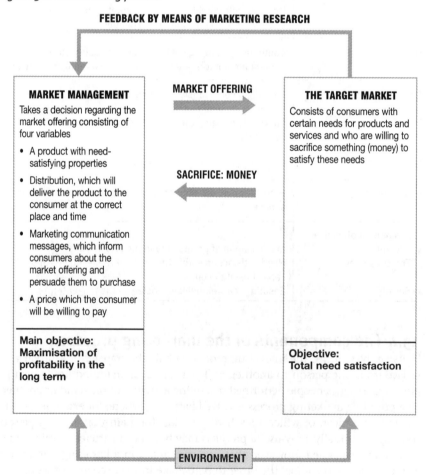

FEEDBACK BY MEANS OF MARKETING RESEARCH

MARKET MANAGEMENT

Takes a decision regarding the market offering consisting of four variables

- A product with need-satisfying properties

- Distribution, which will deliver the product to the consumer at the correct place and time

- Marketing communication messages, which inform consumers about the market offering and persuade them to purchase

- A price which the consumer will be willing to pay

Main objective: Maximisation of profitability in the long term

MARKET OFFERING

SACRIFICE: MONEY

THE TARGET MARKET

Consists of consumers with certain needs for products and services and who are willing to sacrifice something (money) to satisfy these needs

Objective: Total need satisfaction

ENVIRONMENT

Marketing management uses four variables for decision making:

- The product itself
- The place where it is offered for sale (distribution of the product)
- The marketing communication methods used to inform consumers about the product
- The price that reflects the product's value to consumers

These four variables, which are known as marketing instruments, combine to form the **market offering** which consumers purchase to satisfy their needs. Since the 1960s, they have been known as the 4 Ps of the marketing mix (product, place, promotion, price). Decisions about the use of the 4 Ps result in the **marketing strategy**, which is directed at specific consumers in a specific environment.

The market offering to consumers comprises a basic product with need-satisfying attributes. The price of this product, its easy availability, and the information in the marketing communication message (advertisements) all contribute to the product's value or utility. A specific market offering is not supposed to satisfy the needs of one individual only, but rather a whole group of consumers or **market segments**. The larger the market segment, the more the business will benefit. In a market segment, members share common characteristics and preferences. They also have similar consumption patterns and make similar product choices. From all the many different market segments, the marketer carefully selects a **target market**, or several target markets. The market offering is often changed very slightly to meet the demands of different target markets. It seldom happens that a business only has a single target market.

The four decision-making variables are discussed at length in chapter 14, while **market segmentation** and **target market selection** are explained in this chapter.

As stated in chapter 1, it is not possible for people to completely satisfy all their needs, because needs are unlimited, (even though resources for satisfying them are not). This means that the marketer can never fully meet consumer needs, especially those that are unrealistic, such as demanding a Mercedes Benz at the price of a Golf! **The behaviour patterns of consumers** when attempting to satisfy unique needs, demands and preferences are discussed in section 13.6.

Profit seeking has already been mentioned. Profit is the reason for the existence of any profit-seeking business. The marketing management of such a business must therefore strive towards this objective. This can be done by combining the four marketing instruments in an integrated marketing strategy so as to maximise profits. Profitability in the long term is necessary for a business to survive and grow. Where the main focus is on short-term profit only, there is a tendency to mislead or exploit consumers. To show any degree of long-term profitable growth, marketing management must maintain close contact with the market at all times and conduct regular marketing research. Sometimes consumer preferences in the target market change, or new competitors enter the market. Marketing management should be aware of every change that occurs, carefully consider the implications, and then decide what to do about it.

In the business environment there are often opportunities that can be utilised to the business's advantage. There are also threats that have to be countered. By making timely changes to the four marketing instruments, marketing managers are able to react appropriately to opportunities and threats. **Marketing research** (see section 13.5) is used to obtain relevant information on the market, competitors and other environmental changes. By means of marketing research, management receives feedback from the market and the environment.

Look at figure 13.1 again, and note the relationship between the different components of the marketing process. Note the direction of the arrows from the environment to marketing management and the target market. Both are influenced by environmental changes. In order to take effective decisions, marketing management needs feedback from the target market and the ever-changing environment.

The marketing process indicates a market-driven approach to marketing management, one that is a distinctive characteristic of a successful modern business. All the activities and decisions of marketing management are focused on the demands of the market. This is why marketing research is important.

Applying the concept: marketing

Cell phones are used by virtually everyone today. Major suppliers such as Ericssons and Nokia are located in Europe, where manufacturing takes place. People all over the world, including South Africa, buy these products. By means of marketing, the product arrives in South Africa, where it is then locally marketed. Owing to the need for more and better features, constant product development takes place to meet the demands of the market. A wide range of cell phones thus becomes available. It is clear, thus, that a broad range of activities are involved in this process, all of which form part of the marketing process.

13.5 Marketing research

13.5.1 The necessity of information

The components of the marketing environment in which the marketing task is performed are discussed in chapter 4, where it is shown that continuous scanning of the microenvironment, the market environment and the macroenvironment is necessary to effectively evaluate internal strong and weak points and external opportunities and threats (SWOT analysis), before managerial decisions can be taken. The following section deals with the way in which marketing research is used to obtain internal and external information.

Marketing opportunities can be identified and measured only if the marketing environment is scanned or monitored on a continuous basis. Marketing managers purposefully gather information on external environmental variables and on internal resources in the form of reports on, among others, current prices, sales figures, market trends, technological changes, changes in market share, consumer preferences, new legislation, production schedules, and internal financial problems. This information is then systematised and classified in a way that is easily accessible to marketing management.

It is important to remember that all marketing decisions are based on information received on the microenvironment, market environment and macro-environment. If a problem occurs, existing information sources are consulted. Sometimes, however, there are problems about which there is little or no information available. This means that marketing management must look for information before decisions can be taken. This is done by means of marketing research.

13.5.2 Marketing research methodology

In this section a method used to obtain primary marketing information is discussed step by step. External ad hoc marketing research is undertaken to obtain information on a specific problem in the external market environment, while internal ad hoc research is undertaken to obtain information on a problem in the internal (micro) environment.

Definition

Marketing research is the systematic gathering, analysis and interpretation of information on all types of marketing problems by utilising recognised scientific methods for the accumulation of information to facilitate marketing management's decision making.

The definition of marketing research refers to the use of recognised scientific methods for obtaining market data. One of the most common methods is the **survey method**. There are other research methods that can be used, but only the survey method is described here. It is a good example of an ad hoc research project where the information collected concerns a specific problem in the external or internal environment.

In the survey method, a questionnaire is used and questions are put to respondents either personally by specially trained field workers, or telephonically or through the mail. The personal method of questioning is the most time-consuming and expensive, because field workers have to conduct a door-to-door survey, but it is also the best and most reliable method. The results of the survey can be subjected to statistical analysis to enable the researcher to draw meaningful conclusions. If the research has been conducted in a scientific manner, the results may point to the solution of the problem. We will now discuss the steps in conducting a survey. Please refer to the practical examples presented throughout the text.

- **Step 1: Definition of the problem to be investigated.** The research results will be useless unless the problem has been carefully defined.
- **Step 2: Formulation of probable explanations and causes for the defined problem.** The reasons provided are known as hypotheses. A hypothesis is a proposed explanation for the problem.

Example

Assume that the problem is that sales for a specific product have suddenly declined. There may be many reasons for this state of affairs (the problem), for example, quality changes in the product itself, changes in consumer preferences, or the introduction of a new and improved competitive product. These reasons (hypotheses) now need to be investigated to determine the real reason for the decline in sales.

- **Step 3: Investigation of all the hypotheses in order to eliminate the less likely ones and find a solution to the problem.** Secondary information sources are consulted first of all, for example, internal reports, marketing literature, articles in trade journals or on the Internet. Investigation of existing secondary sources of information is known as desk research.

Example

Suppose the secondary investigation (desk research) reveals that a drop in quality is probably the main reason for the decline in sales. The problem can be resolved by asking the production department to maintain the quality standards that have been laid down. A primary investigation is therefore unnecessary. However, if the problem has not been solved, a survey may provide the answer.

- **Step 4: Compilation of a questionnaire.** The compilation of a questionnaire requires skill. Each question has to be formulated carefully (involving the entire research department – often experts and consultants are called in to assist) so that the answers clarify the problem. Questions on the sex, age, place of residence and language of each respondent should be included for classification purposes.

Example

Suppose that one of the hypotheses regarding the problem of declining sales is that there has been a change in consumer preferences. This assumption now needs to be tested by means of relevant questions. Such questions would concern respondents' **perceptions** (do they know that the product exists?), **purchasing patterns** (have they ever purchased the product?), **experiences** (were they satisfied with the product – if not, why not?), and **purchasing intentions** (do they intend to purchase the product in future?).

- **Step 5: Testing the questionnaire.** The questions should be put to about ten respondents if the answers obtained are to be meaningful. Errors can be eliminated and mistakes rectified if the answers are meaningless or ambiguous.
- **Step 6: Choosing the respondents to whom the questions are to be put.** This is known as drawing a sample. It is obviously a very important step,

because a biased sample leads to unreliable and invalid results. A representative sample should be drawn so that every person in the market has an equal chance of being included. Suppose housewives are the respondents – then all housewives should have an equal chance of being selected. A list of all names and addresses of housewives should be available to the marketer (researcher), who then randomly draws as many respondents as the size of the sample dictates. Only these housewives are to be questioned, and the field worker has to obtain permission to substitute one name for another not included in the original sample. If field workers are allowed to pick and choose, they may select only those who seem friendly, those who are about their own age or those whom they know personally. The answers given by such respondents will obviously not be representative of those of all housewives. As a rule, it is difficult and expensive to draw a representative sample, although the results of such a project are reliable. Usually a sample is drawn according to the judgement of the researcher, who describes the number of respondents in each group to be questioned.

- **Step 7: The training of fieldworkers.** Fieldwork is a laborious task requiring thorough training. Fieldworkers should put the questions exactly as formulated in the questionnaire and should enter the responses correctly. They may not prompt respondents, and obviously have to be reliable. Unreliable fieldworkers could succumb to the temptation of completing questionnaires themselves, without even bothering to visit the respondents. It is important to control fieldworkers and the completed questionnaires. The head of the marketing research department can do this by telephoning a few respondents to check whether the questionnaires have in fact been completed properly. Statistical techniques can also be used to "catch out" fieldworkers, as an analysis of results will show any deviations from the pattern. Fieldworkers are paid anything from R20 to R200 and even more for each completed questionnaire. It is obvious that very large samples dramatically increase the cost of a research project.

- **Step 8: The processing and analysis of the information contained in the questionnaires.** A computer is normally used for this. Statistical methods can be used to facilitate the processing and interpretation of the results. These methods include averages, percentages, confidence intervals, regression and variance analysis.

- **Step 9: The interpretation of results.** The researcher must decide what data to include in the research report. In the above example, the information given must point to the reasons for the decline in sales. The initial hypothesis must be proved or disproved. The researcher interprets the reasons and draws meaningful conclusions.

- **Step 10: The compilation of a research report and the making of recommendations based on the conclusions.** The research report "tells the story" of the research project and presents the collected information in the form of tables, graphs or figures. Presenting the completed report to marketing management concludes the task of the research team.

Example

Suppose the research results prove that 70% of respondents drew a negative comparison between the product of the business and that of its main competitor, and 80% of respondents indicated that they did not intend buying the product again. It is easy to draw the conclusion that something is drastically wrong with the product compared to its competitor. However, it is more difficult to make a recommendation. Should the product be withdrawn completely or should it rather be improved? If it is improved, who is to say that the improvement will be to consumers' liking? If the questionnaire has been properly compiled, the analysis will also provide answers to these questions.

- **Step 11: Marketing management (and top management too, perhaps) study the report and make decisions.** They must either accept or reject the recommendations.

Example

Suppose that marketing management has considered the research report and decided to accept a recommendation that the product should be improved. The purchasing and operation departments have to be informed of the proposed improvement (for example, if it requires other raw materials or different operation methods). Marketing management has to launch a campaign to inform the consumer of the "new" product. Decisions on the price might include incentives such as an introductory discount for one month. The old labels will be useless, and new ones providing information on the "improved new" product have to be designed and printed.

- **Step 12: Implementation of management's decisions.** This is the final step, and, hopefully, leads to finding a solution to the problem of declining sales.

A further research project will have to be undertaken after a certain period to determine if the decisions taken and implemented were indeed correct.

The examples we discussed entailed a survey of consumer demands and preferences. Marketing research can be done in more or less the same way to investigate problems with dealers, competitors and suppliers. An internal survey can be conducted to determine the opinions of staff members of the business. Sales representatives, for example, could be chosen as respondents.

13.5.3 *Market forecasting*

When a marketing opportunity has been identified, its extent has to be measured in some way in order to determine expected future profits. Measuring an opportunity entails an estimate of future sales (sales forecasting) as well as an estimate of the contribution to profit.

13.5.3.1 Sales forecasting

The following types of forecasting are often used:

- Estimates made by a panel of experts from within the business and from outside – judgement and intuition are important in this type of forecasting.
- Estimates based on market research results. The number of potential consumers serves as a basis for the sales forecast of the next period.
- Estimates based on consumers' reactions in test marketing situations.
- Estimates based on historical figures (the previous year's sales figures serve as the point of departure).
- Estimates based on mathematical and statistical models (for example, probability models).

A combination of sales forecasting methods is often employed in practice. Obviously, it is difficult to make a reliable forecast, because nobody can see into the future. It is nevertheless the task of the marketing manager to make a reliable estimate not only of sales but also of the uncontrollable environment variables that may impede the attainment of those sales. If reliable sales figures are available, financing, purchasing, operation and inventory decisions can be taken in good time. If this is not possible, the growth, market share or profit position of the business may be harmed. There is even a very real danger that the business may not be able to survive.

13.5.3.2 Forecasting of the profit contribution

Forecasts of the profit contribution are made for much longer periods than the sales forecast, which is made every year. Forecasts of the profit contribution are often made for a full payback period (the time taken to recoup capital expenses incurred in producing a product, for example, five years). During a payback period, the sum of money invested in utilising an opportunity has to be recovered through the earnings generated by sales. Included in the payback amounts is, of course, the rate of return top management decided on at the outset. The financial aspects of forecasting the profit contribution are discussed in detail in the chapters on financial management.

Because not all consumers are the same, and they are unpredictable, it is important to study consumer behaviour.

Applying the concept: marketing research

Companies constantly engage in market research. Before deciding to invest vast sums of money in a new motor vehicle, a company such as BMW will do market research on every aspect of the proposed vehicle. The shape, engine size, features, styling and so on will all be researched in the market to ensure that it meets consumer demands. Various methods will be employed to obtain information, and various reference groups consulted.

13.6 Consumer behaviour

Consumer behaviour refers to the behaviour patterns of decision-making units (families or individuals) directly involved in the purchase and use of

products, including the decision-making processes preceding and determining these behaviour patterns. From this definition it is clear that consumer behaviour consists of overt acts, that is, acts that can be observed by people. A consumer can be seen buying a product, enjoying it, looking at it, placing it back on the shelf or throwing it away unused. Consumer behaviour also includes **covert processes**, however, which cannot be observed. A consumer cannot be seen considering his or her financial position, weighing the merits of different branded products, or doubting the promises made in advertising appeals. Marketers need to know why consumers behave as they do, because consumer behaviour can then be **explained, influenced and predicted**. Knowledge of the factors that determine consumer behaviour provides a sound basis for consumer-oriented marketing strategies.

Attention will now be given to the determinants of consumer behaviour, that is, those factors that may explain consumer behaviour. We will also look at the consumer decision-making process and the continual changes in behavioural patterns of consumers.

Figure 13.2 illustrates a model that can be used to explain consumer behaviour. Individual and group factors influence consumer decision making that may lead to repeat purchasing of a specific market offering.

Figure 13.2: Determinants of consumer behaviour

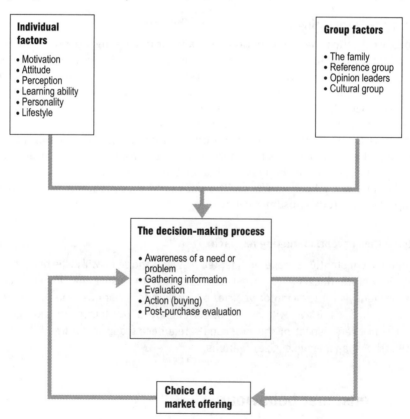

13.6.1 Determinants of consumer behaviour

There are two main groups of factors (determinants) that direct the behaviour of consumers: individual factors peculiar to a particular person, and group factors.

13.6.1.1 Individual factors

Needs, attitudes, perceptions, learning abilities and personality traits are individual factors that determine what a consumer will or will not buy. Needs (also called motives) are the driving force behind all human behaviour patterns. Maslow's **needs hierarchy** is discussed in chapter 10, where it is shown that people's behavioural patterns are directed at the satisfaction of basic survival, security, social and ego needs.

Consumers purchase bread, for instance, to satisfy a basic **survival** need, which is hunger. They take out insurance to satisfy the need for **security.** Flowers are bought and given in an attempt to satisfy a **social** need for love, and an expensive new motorcar is obtained as a status symbol to provide some measure of **ego** satisfaction. Time is spent enjoying a hobby or devoted to charity work to satisfy the need for **self-realisation.** Maslow maintains that people attempt to satisfy needs in a specific hierarchical sequence – the basic needs have to be satisfied before others can be attended to.

People's needs are unlimited, and they never reach a point where all needs are met. This is why consumers continue to purchase products even if they already have more possessions than they can use. Advertisements attempt to draw people's attention to unsatisfied needs that can be met by purchasing a specific product. Although needs are universal (that is, they apply to all people), need patterns differ from person to person. An asocial person does not have as many social needs, for example, as a very social person. People's needs determine what they decide to purchase and what not.

Attitudes also determine purchasing patterns. A consumer with a positive attitude towards a certain product can perhaps be persuaded to purchase it, whereas a consumer with a negative attitude will not buy. A negative attitude is virtually impossible to change. A mother who is health conscious may have a positive attitude towards margarine enriched with vitamins, and can perhaps be persuaded to purchase the product for her children. Conversely, a non-smoker maintains a negative attitude towards cigarettes, and therefore ignores all cigarette advertisements. It follows that marketers must make every effort to prevent the development of negative attitudes towards their market offering. Once consumers have decided to avoid a certain product because it is faulty, or bad quality, too expensive, or has the wrong taste, their negative attitudes towards the product cannot easily be changed. Marketers can, however, try to reinforce existing positive attitudes, or to change neutral attitudes to favour their products. This is done through marketing communication messages.

Consumer **perceptions** determine what they pay attention to and what excites their interest. Consumers hear only those things that the want to hear and see only what captures their interest. This means that they subconsciously choose whether to pay attention to a marketing message or not. Furthermore, consumers' perceptions cause them to attach their own interpretation to a message, which may not quite be what the marketer intended. Consumers seem able to defend or protect themselves against the content of communication. For this reason marketers often have difficulty in conveying a message in such a way that the person receiving it understands it and reacts in the required way. Marketers should keep this in mind when creating marketing messages. An advertisement must therefore be simple to ensure complete understanding of the message, it should have some impact to attract attention, and it must contain a promise of need satisfaction, or else consumers could distort the message or ignore it completely.

The **learning ability** of consumers determines whether they are able to learn the marketer's "lesson" about the benefits of a particular product that make it worth paying for. In addition, the marketer should "teach" consumers the product's name in such a way that they remember it. Sometimes consumers forget the name of the product they intend to purchase, but are still able to recognise the distinctive package among others on the shelf. This points to the importance of packaging. Reminder advertising, in which only the name of a product in distinctive lettering appears on a billboard, helps to remind consumers of what they have learned from the marketer.

Personality traits also influence purchasing patterns. People are described by means of these traits, for example, as cheerful, optimistic, or aggressive. It is difficult to relate personality traits to product choice. Normally people's traits, in conjunction with other characteristics, determine what they buy and use. As a rule, a combination of people's personality traits and other characteristics determines their **lifestyle**. Different groups have different lifestyles. The lifestyle of students, for example, differs drastically from that of newly-weds, and the lifestyle of farmers differs from that of urban dwellers. The lifestyles of the well-to-do and the less well-to-do differ completely, while those of academics are not the same as those of politicians. Lifestyle classification can therefore be used to segment the consumer market. A discussion on market segmentation follows in section 13.7.

13.6.1.2 Group factors

Group factors refer to the influence of various groups on consumer purchasing patterns. These groups include the following:

- **The family.** A child learns its consumption function in the family. At the age of seven, a child already understands that its needs can be satisfied by a process of purchasing and consumption. The family is also a decision-making unit whose members decide about purchasing products that will provide the greatest degree of need satisfaction for the family as a whole. Family members have certain roles. One member may be the buyer (perhaps the mother), another the decision maker (the father, possibly), while yet another (the baby) may be the consumer. Marketers have to know the role structure of families in their target market, because the marketing message must be based on such knowledge. The marketer of breakfast cereal, for example, appeals to the child who could be the decision maker for this product. Children also play a role in family decision making by acting as initiators, and making suggestions about products of which their parents may know very little: boys know, for example, how to operate a video recorder, while teenage girls are knowledgeable about the cosmetics their mothers might use.
- **Reference groups.** A reference group is any group against which people

can evaluate their behaviour (and purchasing patterns). Normally, people want to be members of some group or other and in order to gain acceptance maintain the habits and purchasing patterns of the group. A circle of friends, a social club and a work group are all examples of reference groups. Often, people who do not conform to group norms are either ignored, or held in contempt and ridiculed. A teenage boy who does not own a motorcycle, for example, cannot become a member of a motorcycle club. A person who wants to become a member of a tennis club should not only be able to play the game, but also needs to purchase several tennis outfits, as well as a racquet, tennis balls, tennis shoes and socks, sweatbands, and so on. Advertisements often portray group approval to attract the attention of those striving to gain acceptance and group membership. An advertisement for a motorcar could show friends and neighbours admiring the car, with the house in the background reflecting an upmarket neighbourhood. The implication is that the owner of such a motorcar will automatically gain the acceptance of higher social classes. There are, however, also negative groups, with whom association is undesirable, and consumers tend not to buy typical products purchased by such groups. Conservative, older and cultured people see skinheads and bikers as negative groups, and therefore disapprove of everything they may do or purchase. Choosing a typical reference group to portray in an advertisement is difficult, because what one person may regard as a positive group with which to be associated may well be regarded by another as something to be avoided at all costs.

There is a strong relationship between reference group influence and the choice of luxury products, but the relationship is rather weak in the case of necessities. However, if the necessity is highly visible, the relationship is stronger. A good example is detergents. As many advertisements suggest, housewives are easily led by the "expert" advice of other, more "experienced" housewives.

- **Opinion leaders.** They have an important function in the marketing communication process, acting as a go-between in what is known as the two-step flow of communication. Research results have indicated that information does not flow directly from the mass media to individual consumers in the target market, but is channelled through a person, the opinion leader, who interprets and evaluates the information, and then relays acceptance or rejection of the message to other consumers in the target market.

  The role of the opinion leader is especially important in purchasing high-risk new products. In the case of a new fashion, for example, a fashion opinion leader will accept the risk of ridicule or financial loss, which the ordinary consumer is usually anxious to avoid. The latter will only become interested after the new fashion has been vetted and approved by the opinion leader. Sports stars often act as opinion leaders in advertisements for sports equipment, reducing the risk of a poor decision when an ordinary consumer makes a similar purchase.

  Every consumer is a member of different reference groups and could be an opinion leader for a certain product while being a follower for another. Marketing management must endeavour to identify a suitable reference group and opinion leader for its product to ensure its acceptance in a specific market segment.

- **Cultural groups.** The cultural group to which people belong also strongly influences their purchasing and consumption patterns. Culture comprises a complex system of values, norms and symbols, which have developed in society over time and in which all its members share. Cultural values, norms and symbols are created by people and are transmitted from parents to children through the generations to ensure survival and to facilitate adaptation to circumstances. In this process schools, churches and other social institutions also play an important role (this process is referred to as socialisation).

  Each cultural group comprises several subcultures, each with its own norms, values and symbols. There are four main subcultures, categorised according to nationality, religion, race and geographical area. Besides the four main groups, smaller subcultures can also develop, perhaps according to language, age, interests or occupation.

  South African society is fragmented into many cultural groups and subgroups. Although whites are not numerically dominant, their norms, values and symbols exert great influence on economic activity. Most advertisements therefore reflect Western culture.

13.6.2 Consumer decision making

Every decision a consumer takes involves risks. These risks are often functional. If products are deficient or do not work as consumers expected them to, they feel that they have wasted money. There are also social risks involved in decision making. If the reference group does not approve of the purchase, the consumer may be ridiculed. To reduce the risks inherent in decision making, consumers may wait a long time before taking a decision, thereby extending the decision-making process. During this time, and during all the phases of decision making, marketers attempt on more than one occasion to influence consumers to decide in favour of their market offering.

Applying the concept: consumer decision making

When buying any product, consumers move through various steps in their decision making. People do not wake up one morning and suddenly decide to buy a new house. There must be a need or reason to do so. It may be that their house is too small or the neighbourhood has declined, for example.

Once the need has been identified, information must be gathered. This may be done by talking to friends, to estate agents from various estate agencies, and looking through newspapers. As soon as all the necessary information has been gathered, it is evaluated according to criteria that are important to the buyer. Price, area (location), distance from schools or shops, and so on, may be of importance.

The consumer may decide, for example, on a security estate, as this offers more protection, and then proceed to buy such a property. It is possible that after the house has been bought, the buyer may wonder if it was the right thing to do (post-purchase evaluation). Marketers must be aware of the steps a buyer goes through, and address them in their marketing campaign.

Marketing management must know how consumer decisions are reached, because consumer behaviour almost always entails a choice between alternatives. Marketers obviously want the consumer to give preference to their product. Consumer decisions are not made suddenly – the process of decision making progresses systematically through different phases. Figure 13.2 (see p. 292) depicts the five phases.

- **Phase 1: Awareness of an unsatisfied need or a problem.** An empty container or something broken indicates a consumer need. A pen that continually leaks or dries out may indicate a need to buy a new one. Marketers try, by means of advertising, to make consumers aware of problems and unsatisfied needs.
- **Phase 2: Gathering information on how best to solve the problem.** Consumers consult friends, look around in shops, or read the information contained in advertisements and on labels. Of course, marketers should see to it that the necessary information is available.
- **Phase 3: Evaluation of all the possible solutions.** This is done in the light of criteria such as price, quality, performance standards and aesthetic qualities, as consumers gauge the contribution the product will make to need satisfaction and their lifestyle. Conflict is caused by conflicting or unsuitable criteria or criteria that cannot easily be compared. Advertisements therefore have to stress product utility and benefits. For example, many pen advertisements reflect neatness, continuous writing, and style – all things that are important to consumers. Providing samples that can be used to test the product, a money-back guarantee, or a quality mark (such as that provided by the South African Bureau of Standards (SABS)) can help consumers resolve the conflict.
- **Phase 4: Decision on a course of action.** Although consumers may show intent to purchase a product, this does not mean that they will in fact do so. Therefore advertisements should encourage them to act, for example, with an injunction such as BUY NOW! When consumers act and buy the product, this entails a sacrifice (money must be paid). The transaction should therefore be concluded as "painlessly" as possible. Consumers forced to queue while waiting to pay, or confronted with uninterested sales staff, could quite easily reverse their decision to buy. When consumers are ready to pay, marketers should make a special effort to ensure their goodwill. Efficient sales staff, credit facilities and point of purchase promotions all help to encourage the buying action.
- **Phase 5: Post-purchase evaluation.** Consumers may not be quite sure that they have made the right decision. If the product is deficient or does not provide need satisfaction, they may decide never to buy it again and may influence friends to avoid the product. Advertisements are often directed at those who have already bought a product in order to reassure them that they have indeed made the correct decision.

In the case of expensive or important products (such as a house), decision making can sometimes be a long and arduous process. A person could take months to decide what type of washing machine to purchase. However, in the case of impulse buying, the actual decision-making process, through all its phases, could be over in the wink of an eye. Habitual purchasing is the result of previous decisions. For consumers loyal to a particular brand, it may become a habit to purchase the product consistently without having to make the decision again every time. The conclusion to be drawn is that the theory of consumer behaviour, even though discussed only very briefly here, is **explanatory** to a certain extent. It provides guidelines for **influencing** consumers, for example, through striking advertising. However, because of many influencing factors, **it is virtually impossible to predict the behaviour of consumers.** The marketer nevertheless attempts to do so, because market forecasting depends largely on such prediction.

Marketing management will probably never be able to satisfy all the needs, demands and preferences of the market, and therefore the marketing strategy should be directed only at those groups (market segments) that are profitable and accessible.

13.7 Market segmentation

The term market means different things to different people. In brief, a market consists of a relatively large number of people (or organisations) who:
- Have a need for a specific product
- Are able to buy it
- Are willing to spend money on it
- Are allowed to do so

All these requirements must be met before the word "market" can be used. For example, teenagers under the age of eighteen may have a need for liquor. They may even have enough money to purchase it, but because legislation forbids it, teenagers are not allowed to purchase alcoholic beverages. Hence, teenagers cannot be considered as a distinct "market" for alcoholic products.

The total market in a country can be subdivided into consumer, industrial, reseller and government markets. The **consumer market** consists of individuals or households purchasing products for their own consumption. The **industrial market** consists of individuals, groups of persons, or businesses purchasing materials and products to be used in production processes. **Resellers** such as wholesalers and retailers purchase a variety of products to be resold to financial consumers. The **government market** consists of state institutions and departments that purchase products needed to supply services to the public.

In the discussion of the marketing function in this book, attention is focused mainly on the **consumer market**. However, the principles of marketing are also applicable to all other markets. In industrial marketing, though, personal selling is more important than advertising, which is the most effective way of communicating with the consumer market, but one that is seldom used in the government market.

The consumer market can be subdivided into many different types of markets, such as a market for vehicles, a market for baby products, and a market for food. Consumers are, according to their needs, members of many different markets. A family consisting of parents and teenagers probably forms no part of the potential furniture market, because it already owns furniture, and family members would rather spend their available purchasing power on products such as clothing, education, books, sporting equipment, musical instruments and videos. Similarly, young couples with toddlers and young school-going children are not part of the overseas tourist market, because their responsibilities at home probably prevent them from spending money on travel. Each separate market for a specific product can further be subdivided into segments. Obviously, not all people desire the same type of clothing, vehicles or books. The different approaches to subdividing the market will now be discussed.

13.7.1 *The total market approach (market aggregation)*

In this approach marketing management assumes that all potential consumers have relatively uniform preferences and needs with regard to the market offering, which may therefore be the same for all consumers. A uniform approach is followed in the market for staples such as salt, sugar and flour, because virtually everyone requires these products and wants them in more or less standard packaging.

Market aggregation, however, is more the exception than the rule – even in the case of the staples mentioned above it is not always applicable. Flour, for instance, is not marketed as an undifferentiated product. Premier Milling markets different kinds of Snowflake flour in packs with different colours. The slogan "Too fresh to flop" makes a promise that differentiates Snowflake from competing products. Even if it is cost effective to have one product, one type of packaging, one price, one distribution channel, and identical marketing messages directed at the mass market, it is seldom possible to do so, because the market is not homogeneous. People, after all, are not the same, and not everyone has the same needs.

It is therefore to the advantage of the marketer to try and satisfy the divergent needs of specific market segments rather than providing only some measure of need satisfaction to everyone in the total market.

13.7.2 *The market segmentation approach*

Market segmentation, as stated previously, refers to the process in which the total heterogeneous market is subdivided into smaller, relatively homogeneous groups of consumers with relatively uniform characteristics and needs. Attempts are then made to satisfy the needs of different homogeneous groups by developing different market offerings. Marketing management can, on the one hand, follow a multisegment approach in which many different segments are served with the same basic product or with small product modifications; it can also, on the other hand, select only one segment and concentrate its marketing effort on that.

Figure 13.3 overleaf illustrates the three approaches to the market, namely:
- Market aggregation
- A single-segment approach
- A multisegment approach

Approach (1) in figure 13.3 indicates that marketing management has only one market offering aimed at the total market. Approach (2) shows that marketing management has selected a specific target market and aims its market offering only at it, and no attention is paid to other segments in the market. Approach (3) shows that three separate market offerings are made to three different target markets. One should bear in mind that any change – however small – in the product itself (for example, in the packaging), in the price, in the distribution channel, or in the marketing communication methods or messages, means that a different market offering is being made.

Figure 13.3: Approaches to market segmentation

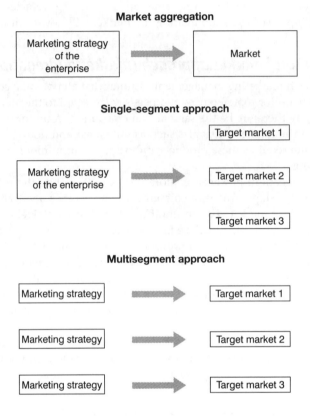

Source: Adapted from Strydom, J.W., Jooste, C.J. & Cant, M. C., *Marketing management*, 4th edition, Juta, Cape Town, 1999, p. 102.

The marketer of Johnson's baby products identified, in addition to babies, women and sportsmen as separate market segments. Even though the baby talcum powder is offered in the same package and at the same price to all three market segments, the marketing messages differ drastically. In reality this means that three separate market offerings are being made to three separate market segments. When the talc is intended for babies, the advertisement shows a mother lovingly caring for a baby. When it is intended for sportsmen or women, the advertisements show models with whom other adults can identify. In these cases the models act as opinion leaders.

Even when marketing management has succeeded in identifying a promising market segment, it does not necessarily follow that a market offering will be developed for that segment. Certain requirements have to be satisfied before marketing management can claim a segment as its target market.

13.7.3 Requirements for meaningful market segmentation

To be useful, a segment must meet the following criteria:

- **Identifiability and measurability.** It must be possible to identify the segments and measure their size. Data about provinces, sex, age, etc., are easily available, but data on people who are prepared to test a new medical product are not.

- **Substantialness.** The segment should be big enough to make profitable exploitation possible. In South Africa, because of our fragmented population, many different small market segments can be distinguished. Some of these segments, however, are so small that it would not be profitable to develop separate market offerings for them all.
- **Accessibility.** It should be possible for marketing management to reach its chosen segment. How, for example, can black women in rural areas, who do not read magazines or listen to the radio, be reached, or older people with hearing and vision problems?
- **Responsiveness.** For a segment to be cultivated, it must be receptive to a separate approach. If all consumers are equally conscious about a product, there is no need to offer high, medium and low priced versions to different segments.

When marketing management is satisfied that these requirements have been met with regard to a particular market segment, it can select this segment as a target market. A target market is a specific segment for which marketing management can develop and implement a marketing strategy. The question to be answered now is how to isolate the factors or criteria according to which homogeneous groups in the total consumer market are to be distinguished. Several of these criteria have already been mentioned – for example, age and language.

13.7.4 Criteria (bases) for market segmentation

The total market can be subdivided into different groups according to a variety of criteria as indicated in table 13.2 (see p. 303).

Segmenting the market according to socio-demographic and geographic criteria usually gives a good indication of the potential of particular market segments, that is, the number of consumers in each segment. Segmentation according to psychographic and product usage criteria gives an indication of the reasons why consumers select and purchase certain products. Each of these criteria merits further scrutiny.

13.7.4.1 Demographic criteria

Marketers often segment the market according to demographic criteria, as the information is easily obtainable. For example, it is easy to determine how many students are registered for this course, and therefore how large the potential market is for this book.

The other demographic variables in table 13.2 are self-explanatory and are therefore not discussed individually.

13.7.4.2 Geographic criteria

Geographic criteria relate to place of residence. Geographic factors result in the development of different need patterns, thereby affording marketers opportunities they can utilise.

13.7.4.3 Psychographic criteria

Table 13.2 shows the main psychographic variables according to which markets can be segmented. The main variables in this group are personality factors and lifestyles.

Personality traits are difficult to quantify, but they nevertheless offer opportunities to marketing management for market segmentation. Aggressiveness, conservatism, optimism, progressiveness and materialism are all examples of personality traits of individuals. Marketers know that these traits are related to product and brand selection. Many advertisements aimed at men, for example, contain elements of aggressiveness to capture their attention, because they tend to be more aggressive than women. Lifestyle segmentation comprises a group of characteristics known as the AIO classification (Activities, Interests and Opinions of the consumers).

13.7.4.4 Behavioural criteria

Table 13.2 lists the behavioural criteria according to which the consumer market can be segmented. **Product usage** refers to the way in which products are used by different consumers. Consumers can either be light, medium or heavy users of a product, or they can be existing or potential consumers. Teetotallers are non-users of liquor, and all attempts by a marketer to persuade this group to become heavy users will be to no avail. However, marketers often attempt to persuade light to medium users of a specific product to step up their consumption. A good example is potato chips; consumers are now encouraged to enjoy them at any time, even during ordinary meals, and not only as a snack on special occasions.

Brand loyalty is a behavioural criterion that must be encouraged, because when consumers are loyal to a particular brand, the competitive position of the marketer is strengthened. Brand-loyal consumers purchase products that have provided need satisfaction previously, and they do not think twice about doing so. It is well known that black consumers tend to be more loyal than their white counterparts. Iwisa, Lion, Jordan shoes and Castle Lager are examples of brands enjoying the loyalty of many black consumers. Brand loyalty develops only if a product provides such complete need satisfaction that competing products are never even considered.

Some consumers are extremely **price sensitive**, and can be persuaded to purchase by means of small price decreases. These consumers like to bargain, and prefer to shop at discount stores. Most well-to-do consumers purchase what they need, paying very little attention to price. They are usually averse to shopping around for bargains, and are also not much interested in sales.

Reverse price sensitivity means that consumers react negatively when a price is perceived to be too low. They immediately conclude that the cheap product lacks quality, and they therefore associate a high price with good quality and a low price with poor quality. If prices are lowered, these consumers buy less instead of more. Consumers can also be sensitive to service, quality and even advertisements. The advertisement promising "You are Number 1" is directed at consumers sensitive to service quality, while the "Quest for Zero Defect" points to quality excellence for quality-sensitive buyers. Some people are sensitive to advertising, and react immediately when an advertising message attracts their attention. They are ready to buy if they perceive the message as promising.

Table 13.2: Bases (criteria) for segmenting consumer markets

Bases	Possible variables
1. Geographic	
Region	Gauteng, Durban-Pinetown, Cape Peninsula, KwaZulu/Natal, Northern Province
Size of city or town	Under 10 000, 10 000 – 20 000, 20 000 – 25 000, over 25 000 inhabitants
Density	Urban, suburban, rural
Climate	Summer rainfall, winter rainfall, very hot and humid, very hot and dry
2. Demographic	
Age	Under 7, 7–13, 14–19, 20–34, 35–49, 50–65, above 65 years
Gender	Male, female
Family size	1 and 2, 3 and 4, more than 4 members
Family life cycle	Young, married without children; young, married with children; older, married with children; married couples without children living at home; singles
Income	Under R20 000, R20 001 – R50 000, R50 001 – R80 000, R80 001 – R110 000, R110 001 – R140 000, R14 001 – R170 000, over R170 000.
Occupation	Professional and technical, managerial, clerical, sales and related services, farmers, students, housewives, unemployed, retired
Religion	Protestant, Catholic, Muslim, Hindu, Jewish
Race	White, black, coloured, Asian
Education	Gr. 8, matric, diploma, degree, postgraduate
3. Psychographic	
Lifestyle	Conservative, liberal
Personality	Gregarious, authoritarian, impulsive, ambitious
Social class	Upper class, middle class, lower class
4. Behavioural	
Purchase occasion	Regular use, special occasion
Benefits sought	Economy, convenience, prestige, speed, service
User status	Non-user, ex-user, potential user, regular user
Usage rate	Heavy user, medium user, light user
Loyalty status	None, medium, strong, absolute
Readiness stage	Unaware, aware, informed, interested, desirous, intending to buy
Attitude to product	Enthusiastic, positive, indifferent, negative, hostile

Source: Strydom, J.W., Jooste, C.J. & Cant, M.C., *Marketing management,* 4th edition, Juta, Cape Town, 1999, p. 107.

The total potential market for a product can also be subdivided into segments according to the benefits a product is thought to offer, as shown in the accompanying box.

Product benefits of deodorant

The product benefits consumers expect from deodorant might include:
- Fresh smell
- Long lasting
- Social acceptance
- Safety (does not irritate skin)
- Ease of use
- Effective
- Dryness

The market for margarine is also segmented according to **product benefits**. Some people use margarine for a healthier life, others for its low cholesterol content, its vitamins, as a slimmer, or as a substitute for butter. Some marketers follow a multisegment approach and promise all the benefits listed above. According to their advertisements, their margarine not only prevents cholesterol, it also slims, as well as being pleasant tasting. Criteria are often combined to outline and define a particular segment profile.

13.7.5 Segment profiles

Demographic, geographic and usage criteria provide the profile of a specific segment, as shown in the accompanying box.

Profile of Exact! customer

LSM (Living Standards Measurement) groups 4 to 8, men, women and children. Focus is on adults aged 29 to 35 years, and children 2 to 10 years. Customers are price conscious, aspiring fashion followers, modern, young, with contemporary tastes, and a smart-casual preference in clothing.

Source: Cant, M.C. & Machado, R., *Marketing success stories*, 4th edition, Oxford University Press Southern Africa, 2002, p. 169.

Applying the concept: market segmentation

Volkswagen SA has segmented the market for its passenger vehicles into various categories. The CitiGolf is aimed at the small economy car segment, while the Playa is aimed at the medium-sized car market, as is the Jetta. The Audi A3 is aimed at the exotic or sports car market. The larger Audi is aimed at the family or luxury car segment. Different strategies are required to market these cars.

13.8 Target market selection and positioning

Once the heterogeneous total mass market has been subdivided into smaller homogeneous segments, the marketer has to identify a segment that looks promising as a target market. The objectives and resources of the business have to be carefully considered before a target market can be selected. When selecting target markets, the abilities and expertise of the business have to be linked to the characteristics of consumers in different market segments. A market offering is developed for each target market chosen in this manner. It is clear that target-market selection does not necessarily involve only one target market – numerous individual target markets can be selected.

The fact that marketing management has analysed the market and decided to target a specific market does not mean that the business now owns that market. On the contrary, an extensive survey of the market would probably have indicated the presence of competitors. Marketing management has to consider the competitive situation in the market carefully, and decide if it wishes to confront competitors directly or if it should rather seek and occupy a gap (or niche) in the market. A positioning guide is often used to show the competitive position confronting marketing management. This guide makes it easier to identify gaps in the market. Figure 13.4 depicts such a positioning guide.

According to figure 13.4, the total beer market can be subdivided into a demographic variable of gender (men/women) and a product benefit variable (strong/weak). The guide also shows three competitors (A, B, C) in the area of strong beer intended exclusively for men, while only one competitor (D) currently markets strong beer aimed at women, and one (E) markets weak beer, also for women. In the quarter bordered by the variables of "men" and "weak beer" there are no competitors, and a gap can be identified in this area. Before the marketer decides to fill this gap and claim the unexploited segment as a target market, it should of course be determined (by means of market research) if there are men who want to drink weak beer. The marketer who decides to confront competitors A, B and C directly should have some competitive advantage – the beer may be of a darker colour, or better tasting, or it may be sold in differently shaped bottles. Many other variables can, of course, be used when drawing positioning guides.

Figure 13.4: Positioning guide: the beer market

Source: Sinclair, R., *Make the other half work too*, Southern, Halfway House, 1985, p. 158.

Successful market segmentation, target market selection and product positioning obviously demand intensive market studies. Marketing research is central to this, as discussed in section 13.5.

13.9 Summary

This chapter focused on the marketing process, on the gradual change in management's approach to the market, and on the definition of marketing.

It was shown that a market-driven business is essentially consumer oriented, takes strategic decisions based on pertinent information, and maintains close relationships, with a view to long-term profitability.

Marketing is indeed a key function of the business, as is shown in the next two chapters, which deal with the four marketing instruments that are combined in a marketing strategy. Opportunities in the environment must be met, and threats dealt with within the framework of an ethical code of conduct, the marketing concept.

To conclude, marketing is a paradox. While it is a simple process, it can, at the same time, be extremely complex. It is at once a philosophy and a dynamic function of a business. It is new, but it is also as old as time itself.

Reference

1. This chapter is largely based on the explanations and discussions in chapter 1 (A market-driven approach), chapter 3 (Consumer behaviour), chapter 4 (Market segmentation, target market selection and product positioning) and chapter 5 (Information for marketing management) in Strydom, J.W., Jooste, C.J. & Cant, M.C., *Marketing management*, 4th edition, Juta, Cape Town, 2000.

14 The marketing instruments

The purpose of this chapter

The marketing instruments consist of what are known as the four Ps, namely the product or service that the organisation sells, the price charged for the product or service, the promotion or marketing communication decisions needed to promote the product, and the place decision (distribution decision), which relates to the inter-mediaries used to distribute the product. This chapter deals with these four instru-ments and how they may be used to develop a unique marketing mix aimed at the target market. The process of identifying the target market and selecting the right marketing mix results in the development of the organisation's marketing strategy.

Learning outcomes

The content of this chapter will enable learners to:
- Explain the use of the marketing strategy as an important part of the task of marketing management
- Demonstrate how the product or service of the business is used in the development of the marketing strategy
- Show how the price decision is used by the enterprise in formulating the marketing strategy
- Understand how distribution decisions are used by the business in the development of the marketing strategy
- Show how the marketing communication instrument is used by the organisation in the formulation of the marketing strategy of the business

14.1 Introduction

The previous chapter provided a firm foundation for the development of a marketing strategy for a target market. The marketing strategy discussed in this chapter entails the following:
- An integration of the product decision
- Price decisions for the product or service
- Decisions about distribution channels that will be used to get the product to the target market
- Decisions about marketing communication to be directed at the chosen target market(s)

The marketing strategy is directly related to the market offering and comprises the decisions that have to be made about the four marketing instruments. It is the task of marketing management to combine the four marketing instruments (that is, product, price distribution and marketing communication) correctly for a specific target market.

The decisions that have to be made by marketing management about the four instruments are constantly modified as circumstances change and consumers' acceptance of the product gradually increases. For instance, consumers first have to be educated to accept an innovation, that is, an original new product. At the same time, an existing product that is in a later phase of its life cycle should be actively promoted to prevent consumers from possibly buying a competing product.

In chapter 15 it will be pointed out that the marketing strategy is, in fact, a key to unlocking marketing opportunities. This concept will now be briefly elucidated.

14.2 The key to the market

Figure 14.1 below is a symbolic representation of the marketing strategy in the form of a key that has to unlock the target market in a specific environment.

Figure 14.1: The key to the market

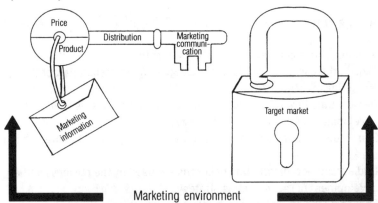

Source: Adapted from Murphy, P.E. & Enis, B.N., *Marketing. Series in marketing*, Pearson Education Inc, 1985, p. 197.

In figure 14.1 the key is made up of all four marketing instruments, which are directed at the target market in a specific environment. To bring key and lock together, relevant marketing information, provided on a continual basis, is required, bearing in mind the business's objectives and resources. We shall now discuss the four marketing instruments, starting with product decisions.[1]

14.3 Product decisions

14.3.1 The product offering

The product offering of a business may comprise a single product item or a number of product items and product ranges. This product offering changes according to the demands of time, and the situation in which the market finds itself.

Product decisions entail decision making about the product itself (for example, the type of packaging and the brand), as well as about the composition of the product offering. Before these decisions can be discussed, the concept "product" should be described in greater detail.

The differences between the concepts of product offering, product range, and product item

A product offering consists of various product ranges. The product ranges of Toyota SA consist of the following, namely:

- Passenger cars
- Bakkies (also called light delivery vehicles)
- SUVs (also called sport utility vehicles)
- Heavy transport vehicles (also called lorries)

The product range consists of various product lines. The passenger car product range consists of four product lines:

- Tazz – the top selling car in South Africa
- Corolla – new model introduced in 2002, also exported to Australia
- Camry – fully imported from Australia
- Lexus – fully imported

In the Tazz product line, there are four product items, of which the Tazz 130 Sport is an example.

14.3.2 What is a product?

A product may be described as **a composition of tangible and intangible need-satisfying utilities offered to consumers by a business, so that they can take note of them, procure them, and use them**. The need-satisfying utilities may include consumer products, services (for example, those provided by a hairdresser), personalities (such as a film star), places (such as the local cinema), institutions (such as the SPCA) and ideas (such as the "Red Nose Day" campaign). As indicated in chapter 13, this book focuses on consumer products. However, product decisions also apply to the other types of "products" or utilities mentioned above.

A **consumer product** consists of:

- A **core product** that can be described in terms of technical and physical qualities (for example, a crystal wine glass consisting of a round base, a long stem and a bell-shaped container, all made of glass)
- A **formal product** which, in addition to the core product, may also include specific features such as style, quality, brand and packaging (for example, a wineglass with a Vitro trademark, packaged in a red fabric-lined carton)
- A **need-satisfying product** comprising further need-satisfying utilities, such as guarantees, installation, repair services and free delivery (for example, the glasses are guaranteed to have been manufactured by the best artisans)
- The **product image** that gives the product symbolic value by means of the type of marketing message, price and choice of distribution outlet (Vitro glasses, for example, are sold only at exclusive shops and at a price 50% higher than ordinary wine glasses)

- The **total product** comprising all the above-mentioned components (that is, an expensive wine glass made by the best artisans which is sold only at exclusive shops)

When the concept of the total product is considered, it immediately becomes clear that there are large differences between different consumer products. Consumer products differ in respect of their particular features, their production and marketing methods, and the purposes for which they are used. Marketing management consequently has to classify products in more or less homogeneous categories, according to their different qualities.

14.3.3 Classification of consumer products

Consumer products are intended for immediate use by households or consumers. A distinction can be drawn between durable and non-durable consumer products. **Durable consumer products**, such as fridges, cars and furniture, are utilised over a longer period, whereas **non-durable consumer products**, such as cigarettes, chocolate and milk, have a relatively short lifespan. Consumer products can also be classified, on the basis of consumer buying habits, into convenience products, shopping products and speciality products:

- **Convenience products** are products such as sweets, cigarettes, milk, bread and newspapers, which should be within easy reach of the consumer. The qualities and prices of competing convenience products are reasonably homogeneous, and the products do not require much explaining to be sold. Furthermore, the retailer does not receive much incentive to "push" one brand in favour of another.
- **Shopping products** are those products in respect of which the consumer wants to compare suitability, quality, price and style before buying. He or she does not have sufficient knowledge of the range of shopping products available, and will "shop around" to acquire information. Examples of shopping products are clothing and jewellery. The consumer rarely has enough information and knowledge to visit just one store to buy the product. He or she therefore shops around to obtain information about the trademark before buying the product.
- **Speciality products** are those products with unique characteristics for which consumers will make a special purchasing effort. A purchaser will often insist on a specific brand. Examples of such products are cars (for example, a BMW Z3 sports car), television sets (such as Panasonic) and hi-fi equipment (such as Marantz).

It is important to note that the above classification is based on the purchasing habits of consumers. As consumer purchasing habits differ, the same product (for example, cigars) may be a convenience product for one consumer, a shopping product for another, and a speciality product for yet another.

The marketer has to make various **product decisions** based on the nature of the product to be marketed. One of the most important product decisions to be made is the choice of brand. Almost all the consumer products classified into homogeneous groups have brands that distinguish them from competing products.

14.3.4 Brand decisions

14.3.4.1 The meaning of brands

The brand is a mark that is unique to the product items or ranges produced and marketed by a particular business, which is chosen to distinguish them from similar competing products. The brand of a product includes the brand name and a specially designed trademark. The brand name is a word, a letter or a group of words (such as Mercedes Benz). Consumers use this name when they intend to buy the product. The concept of a brand name is therefore a much narrower concept than that of a brand (in this case, the three-point star within the circle which typifies the Mercedes Benz trademark).

Brands can be registered under the Trade Marks Act 194 of 1993. Such registration protects the exclusive right to use a particular brand for a period of ten years.

Figure 14.2 below shows a number of well-known brands. Some brands consist only of a brand name written in distinctive lettering. Pick 'n Pay is a good example. Some trade marks are so familiar that the names are almost unnecessary. The distinctive names and trade marks are often used in reminder advertising, such as that on the large billboards surrounding the field in soccer stadiums (usually positioned right in front of the television cameras).

Figure 14.2 has the names of products in their characteristic lettering as well as their trade marks: the reader knows what kind of product it is and, in most cases, what the marketing message is, although these are not mentioned.

Figure 14.2: Well-known South African brands

14.3.4.2 Advantages offered by the use of brands

Well-known brands offer the following advantages to **consumers**:
- They facilitate the identification of products when purchasing.
- They assure consumers of a quality standard they can count on.
- They offer a certain degree of protection to consumers, because branded products can be identified with a specific manufacturer.
- They facilitate decision making, because consumers easily recognise the brands they usually buy.
- They serve as a warning against products that do not meet requirements set by consumers.

For the **marketer**, the use of brands has the following advantages:
- Brands are the foundation stone of the marketing communication strategy, where the message indicates precisely which product should be purchased.

- Brands promote brand loyalty among consumers, and make product substitution by the retailer or consumer more difficult. An example is where the consumer insists on buying a Defy oven and no other brand is perceived to be good enough.
- Brands make price comparison with competing products more difficult and, to a certain extent, protect the retailer against self-destructive price wars. If the consumer wants only a Whirlpool brand, for example, he or she will not easily buy a cheaper substitute. Price competition is therefore obviated.
- Brands are an inseparable part of the product image and offer the marketer the opportunity of creating the product image. Consider, for example, what the connotation is of the brand name Mercedes Benz and the three-pointed star, in the mind of the ordinary consumer.
- Brands make product differentiation possible and enable the marketer to distinguish his or her product from competing products.
- Brands facilitate the expansion of existing product ranges, because consumers tend to accept new additions to an existing range more readily than an unknown product item that is not part of a range. A case in point is the success of Mercedes Benz's smaller car (the A-series) in the market.

In fact, in a competitive market it is almost impossible to market a consumer product successfully if it has no brand identification. These days attempts are increasingly being made to brand products that have traditionally not had brand names, such as milk (Clover) and bread (Albany), to reap the benefits of brand identification.

Closely related to the advantages offered by the use of brands is the manifestation of brand loyalty.

14.3.4.3 Brand loyalty

Brand loyalty, which occurs when consumers show loyalty to certain brands, is the result of good product quality, proven usefulness, and repeated marketing communication. A brand that does not meet consumer demands runs the risk of losing the battle against competing brands, and one not properly introduced will remain unknown, and therefore unloved. There are three phases of loyalty through which the consumer gradually moves, namely:

- **Brand recognition.** Consumers recognise the brand and know what it stands for.
- **Brand preference.** Consumers prefer the brand to other competing brands.
- **Brand insistence.** Consumers insist on the specific brand and refuse to accept a substitute.

Marketers naturally aim at achieving the third phase, because this gives the product speciality value in the eyes of consumers. The consumer will shop around until he or she finds the branded product. In such a situation a competitor will find it difficult to gain a foothold in the market. The marketer, however, still has to advertise the brand and bring it to the attention of consumers, even at this stage.

In the discussion of strategic marketing in chapter 15, reference will be made to the need for maintaining long-term relationships with consumers and clients. Brand loyalty is the result of such a long-term relationship, but brand loyalty is possible only if the marketing concept is strictly adhered to. The values of Avis, for example, in the execution of the marketing task all point to the principles of the marketing concept and show that Avis strives to attain a long-term relationship with customers.

The values held by Avis

- The customer is king
- Service quality has to be consistent
- Detail is important
- Do it right the first time
- Customer loyalty is not given, it is gained

14.3.4.4 Manufacturer, dealer or generic brands

Manufacturers usually give their own brands to the products they market, for instance, Levi's jeans. Large retailers (or dealers) also often buy unmarked products from producers and give these products their own brands, for example, Elements for small children, Free to B for teens and young adults (hip fashion wear), and Merien Hall for elderly adults, all of which are used by Edgars for different ranges for different market segments. Then there are the generic brands, the so-called "no-name" brands. The branded products of manufacturers compete directly with dealer and generic brands in what is referred to as the "battle of the brands". It remains to be seen which type of brand will become the most popular. In table 14.1 (see p. 314) marketing strategies for the three brand types are compared. A manufacturer should decide whether it wants to market its products bearing its own brands, or rather market unbranded products directly to dealers. Sometimes large manufacturers have excess manufacturing capacity that they utilise to produce unmarked products for dealers. In such cases there should be clearly distinguishable market segments at which the market offering can be directed – otherwise the dealer brand will only aggravate the competitive situation by making inroads into the market share of the manufacturer. Compare the divergent characteristics of the three types of brands mentioned in table 14.1.

SABMiller's range of brands

SABMiller is now one of the dominant players in the world beer market, with SAB having acquired the Miller group in the USA. Some of the brands of beer that are sold in South Africa are:
- Castle Lager
- Lion Lager
- Carling Black Label
- Amstel
- Hansa Pilsener
- Miller Lite

Table 14.1: Manufacturer, dealer and generic brands

Characteristic	Manufacturer brand	Dealer brand	Generic brand
Target market	Quality conscious buyer, brand loyal	Price conscious, loyal	Price consious, discriminating buyer, large family, accepts lower quality
Marketing Mix			
• Product	Well known product, strict quality control, clearly distinguishable brands, wide product ranges	Largely the same as for producer brands, but generally less known, limited number of product ranges	Poorer quality, less emphasis on packaging and labelling, few product items
• Price	High price, controlled by manufacturer	Price controlled by retailer	Lower price, controlled by retailer
• Distribution	Generally available at all large retail shops	Generally only available at branches of a specific retailer	The same as for dealer brands
• Marketing communication	Marketing communication campaigns launched by manufacturer	Campaigns launched by relevant retailer, most favourable shelf arrangement	Sales promotion at point of sales

Source: Griffin, R.W., *Management*, Houghton Mifflin Company, 1999, p. 663.

14.3.4.5 Individual/family brands

Marketing management also have to decide whether they are going to choose an individual brand for each product item (for example, Amstel, Carling Black Label and Hansa Pilsener Beer from SABMiller) or whether they are going to use a family brand (such as Kellogg's Rice Crispies, Kellogg's All Bran and Kellogg's Corn Flakes) for the whole range of products. Both decisions have advantages as well as disadvantages.

If a family brand is chosen, the costs of introducing a new product in the range into the market are lower. Spending on marketing communication usually decreases, because consumers are already familiar with the name of the products in the range. The new product can also benefit from the popularity of the others. The reverse is also true: if one product in such a range performs poorly, the reputation of the others bearing the same name is damaged. Individual brands are expensive to market, because separate marketing communication attempts have to be made for each individual product. An individual brand requires another name, offering the opportunity for originality and aggressive marketing attempts aimed at specific target markets.

14.3.5 Packaging decisions

Packaging can be described as **the group of activities concerned with the design, production and filling of a container or wrapper with the product item in such a way that it can be effectively protected, stored, transported and identified, as well as successfully marketed.**

Packaging should be designed in such a way that the product can be handled without damaging the quality of the contents. Even more important is the fact that packaging should promote product sales. The consumer should be able to identify the packaging standing on the shelf and distinguish it from that of numerous other competing products. The packaging therefore usually has a label bearing the characteristic brand and other important information. Bright colours and striking designs are used on packaging to attract the consumer's attention. The brand-loyal consumer, for instance, will recognise from a distance the characteristic packaging of the detergent he or she buys regularly.

> **Lion Lager in a new packaging**
>
> Beer aficionados were shocked when SABMiller decided to change the packaging of old favourite, Lion Lager. Gone were the traditional colours of cream and red, and in their place was a more modern silver colour with blue lettering. The target market was also changed to include younger adults (18-24 years) and the hip-generation of South Africa. The change in packaging and the repositioning were not successful, however, and the brand Lion Lager was discontinued in 2003.

14.3.5.1 Different kinds of packaging

Marketing management usually devotes a great deal of attention to choosing packaging and a packaging design that will show off the contents in the best possible way. The different kinds of packaging that can be chosen are the following:

- **Family packaging.** All the products in the range are more or less identically packed – the same packaging material is used, and the size of the packaging is more or less the same. Family packaging is usually related to family brands. (There are, however, exceptions, as in the case of beer, where each kind has an individual brand but all have more or less similar packaging.) All Koo jams are sold in identical packaging – obviously with different labels to indicate the contents. Family brands can facilitate consumer decision making, because the packaging is easily recognisable. It can, however, also be a source of irritation – the consumer may purchase a product that he or she did not really want if the labels and colours resemble each other too closely.
- **Speciality packaging.** This gives an image of exclusivity of the product. Perfume, jewellery and expensive liquor (like Chivas Regal whisky in its silver tin box) are often sold in speciality packaging. Such products are popular gifts.
- **Re-usable packaging.** This creates the impression that the consumer receives a "free" container if he or she buys the product. The container can be re-used for something else later. (An example is the metal container in which Bakers Tennis Biscuits used to be sold. The container could be used to store cookies or future packets of Tennis Biscuits). Re-usable packaging leads to repeat purchases because consumers tend to collect the containers. The danger is that consumers may stop buying when they have purchased enough containers and if they are reluctant to throw them away when empty.

4.3.5.2 Choice of packaging design

Regarding the choice of the packaging design, marketing management has to decide on the kind of packaging material, the shape and size of the packaging, and the graphic design on the label.

The **packaging materials** (glass bottles, cans, cardboard boxes, plastic tubs) best suited to the product itself are chosen. Glass bottles containing bottled fruit are, for example, more attractive than cans, but they are impractical to transport and usually more expensive. Marketers often choose different and better types of packaging material than their competitors in an attempt to differentiate their products from those of competitors. An example is the variety of packaging that is used for selling toothpaste. The traditional metal tubes have been replaced by plastic tubes, and there are also stand-alone toothpaste dispensers.

The **shape** of the packaging (or container) may have a specific functional value, such as margarine in re-usable plastic tubs. The shape may also have a symbolic value, which may subconsciously influence buyers. A square shape is supposed to have male connotations, whereas female consumers prefer flowing and round shapes. These types of "male" and "female" packaging shapes are especially noticeable in the case of toiletries.

Packaging: the silent salesperson

The average supermarket in South Africa stocks thousands of products. All these products compete for the attention of the consumer. One way of drawing attention to a product is to use packaging to add value to the product. The use of striking colours and unique packaging helps the consumer to identify the product and distinguish it from competing products. Unique packaging, like the Toblerone chocolate package (triangular packaging) and Toilet Duck (S-shaped spout to facilitate dispensing the liquid under the toilet rim) are examples. Red is also a colour that attracts attention, and it is especially used by national brand name products.

Characteristic packaging helps consumers to recognise the product on the shelf – even from a distance. This explains why it is not desirable to change the packaging without properly informing consumers. This does not mean that packaging should never be modified. Changes are often made in the shapes of the packaging and the printed matter or labels for the sake of improvements or for functional or aesthetic reasons. Just think how many times the word "new" is used in combination with a new kind of packaging. The product is then advertised in its new packaging to educate consumers about the new look of the packaging.

Packaging sizes are important in that marketing management have to retain the sizes that are traditionally used in the industry in order to save money, but in doing so they forego the competitive advantage of unusual sizes. Products packaged in unusual sizes draw the consumer's attention, and at the same time make price comparisons difficult. The **label** differentiates the product from other similar products, especially if containers have been standardised. The label also serves as the carrier of the marketing message. The colours used on the label, as well as the graphic design (letter-types and illustration), help to attract and hold the consumer's attention.

14.3.6 Product differentiation

Marketing management also has to decide on the way in which the product should be differentiated from other competing products. **Product differentiation means that a business distinguishes its product, whether physically and/or psychologically, from what are essentially identical competing products, so that it is regarded as a different product by consumers in a specific target market.** Physical and psychological differentiation can take place on the basis of design, quality, colour, taste, size, brand, packaging, or any other distinguishing feature such as the price of the product, the marketing communication message used to bring it to the attention of consumers, and the type of distribution outlet where it is offered for sale. One of the best examples of differentiation is found in the car market, where new models are added to a range to differentiate the product from competitors' products.

Different kinds of differentiation

- **Differentiation by means of packaging and brand.** The various types of margarine on the market are distinguished by the use of different types of packaging, such as plastic, foil or waxed paper, the brands, the designs on the labels, and the colours used.
- **Differentiation by advertising appeals.** Advertising appeals for one brand of detergent emphasise the "enzyme active ingredients", for another, the "stain removing power", and for yet another, the "clean fresh smell".
- **Differentiation on the basis of price.** There are big differences in the pricing of cosmetic products, for example, Revlon products vs Estee Lauder products.
- **Differentiation on the basis of distribution outlet.** Rolex watches are available only at the biggest and best-known jewellers.

14.3.7 Product obsolescence

An important product decision concerns obsolescence. A product may intentionally, and in a planned way, be made technically and/or psychologically obsolete in order to compel the consumer to make repeat purchases. At the technical level, products can be designed to have a specific life-span, for example, a light bulb. Psychological obsolescence points to the introduction of a new model or style, resulting in the consumer rejecting the "old" product, which may still be completely effective technically. New car models and new fashions are well-known examples of planned psychological obsolescence.

The strategy of planned obsolescence is often criticised because it leads to the wastage of scarce resources and aggravates the pollution problem. The fact remains, however, that new models are usually technically better than earlier ones, thereby contributing to greater consumer satisfaction. Planned obsolescence also contributes to economic progress and job creation. An interesting example of planned obsolescence is the Volkswagen Beetle, which made a dramatic comeback a few years ago. The new Beetle does not have the traditional air-cooled engine at the back, however, but rather a two-litre water-cooled engine in the front of the car. Not much of the old Beetle design was incorporated into the new version.

Examples of product obsolescence in ordinary life

When some of us were babies, our mothers used cotton fabric diapers. On average, ten to fourteen diapers were used every day – only to be disinfected, washed, and dried to be ready the next day for the next round of service to baby's bottom. Then, suddenly, a technological miracle happened! – the disposable nappy was invented, made of paper and plastic. Brand names such as Huggies and Pampers are today widely advertised, and many affluent parents spend hundreds of rand a month on disposable nappies. The demand for cotton diapers has declined dramatically, and they are barely used today.

Long ago, a telegram delivered by a messenger from the Post Office was usually the bearer of important news, a new job, a family member's death, someone coming to visit, etc. A new technological innovation called a fax machine replaced the telegram, and today the Postal Service uses fax machines to send important messages and documentation to places all over the world. E-mail is also extensively used.

14.3.8 Multi-product decisions

Marketing management also has to make decisions on the composition of the product offering (see section 14.3.1). A business seldom manufactures and markets one specific product item only. The product offering usually consists of a product range or even a diversified variety of product items and ranges. The total product offering of a business changes continually. Profitable opportunities occurring in the market are utilised in the development of new products or by take-overs of existing businesses with, naturally, the product items and ranges marketed by those businesses.

Multi-product items in the total product offering reduce the risk of failure and financial loss, because the success and profit of one product item can compensate for the poor performance of another.

Decisions on multi-product items include product range extensions, product diversification and product withdrawals.

14.3.8.1 Product range extension

Product ranges can be extended by making additions to existing ranges of products marketed by the business. A product range is a group of products related to one another in one way or another – for example, a range of cosmetics for different skin types, and a range of baby-care items such as baby oil, soap and talcum powder. A range may also include complementary items such as razors and blades, cameras and films. Through new additions to a range, new market segments can be exploited, possibly offering more consumer satisfaction to specific consumers than a single item would. An example of this is the extension of the Vicks product line. The traditional Vicks blue bottle balsam was extended with the introduction of Vicks Medi-Nite, a medicine for the treatment of flu and colds.

14.3.8.2 Product diversification

Diversification points to the search for unknown products or markets, and usually leads to the expansion of the business into areas previously unknown to it. Diversification requires knowledge and expertise, as well as processes that differ from those to which marketing management are accustomed. Therefore, a great deal of risk is attached to the decision to diversify.

Diversification in the South African car market

The Colt bakkie, previously sold in South Africa by the American company, Chrysler, is now assembled by Daimler-Benz SA. Daimler-Benz has no light delivery vehicle of its own in South Africa and was losing out on sales to this very lucrative market in Southern Africa. The addition of the Colt bakkie to its existing product range therefore makes good sense.

14.3.8.3 Product withdrawal

Product items or ranges that do not meet requirements or are no longer profitable can be withdrawn. The decision to withdraw a product or range from the market is a very difficult one, because withdrawal implies failure. This may be negative for the image of a business and may also cause employee problems (workers could be laid off because there are no more jobs available). Marketing management usually do everything in their power to prevent having to make the decision to withdraw.

The product offering changes continually as some products are withdrawn and new ones added.

14.3.9 New product decisions

Product decisions also have to be made about the development of new products. Each product starts its life as a mere idea, conjured up by someone. A sales representative, a dealer, a technician in the manufacturing division or a certain consumer may suddenly get an idea about a product which will meet specific consumer needs and which the business should be able to manufacture and market. Successful large businesses often have new product venture teams, consisting of various functional experts who actively and constantly seek new ideas for new products. In such businesses top management usually encourage staff to come forward with product ideas. The idea for a new product may be unique and original (an innovation). The product may also be "new" only in the sense that it is an improvement on or a modification of an existing product. The risk of failure and financial loss is usually greater with the marketing of an innovation – a unique, original product – but the possibility of releasing higher profits is also greater. Consider, for example, the introduction of the digital camera, and the price that is charged for this new innovative product.

New product development is planned and executed step by step, and the new product idea goes through various phases until the product is eventually introduced into the market. The phases of new product development are as follows:
- **Phase 1: Development of product ideas**
- **Phase 2: Screening of product ideas** according to financial criteria, for example, sales projection and profitability analysis

- **Phase 3: Elimination of product ideas** that do not appear to be viable (profitable)
- **Phase 4: Physical product development** by the production division, during which a prototype is manufactured
- **Phase 5: Development of the marketing strategy**, which entails the following:
  - Positioning of the product in the market
  - Choice of brand
  - Design of packaging
  - Compilation of the marketing communication message
  - Decision on price
  - Choice of a distribution outlet
- **Phase 6: Test marketing** in a specific small segment of the market, for example, in Cape Town only, to test the market's reaction
- **Phase 7: Introduction into the market**

Each of these phases is preceded by intensive research, and several factors can lead to the demise of the product idea. Nonetheless, the continual generation of product ideas remains a priority, for the survival and progress of a business are closely linked to the success achieved by the business in this field.

Applying the concept: product decisions

McDonalds, the American franchise chain that operates in many countries, including South Africa, is renowned for its delivery of hamburgers, the flagship item it sells. The hamburger is a product in the maturity phase of its life cycle, because, among other reasons, of health concerns among the public, and the way in which the burger is pre- pared. McDonalds as a global corporation is therefore looking at diversifying into other foodstuffs. Some of the new products are introduced on a regional basis, for example, such as Mexican sandwiches in Mexico. In South Africa McFlurry ice cream is the big hit at the moment that has increased sales for McDonalds.

14.4 Price decisions

14.4.1 The meaning of price

Price may be regarded as the exchange value of a product or service, and it is closely linked to concepts such as benefit and value. The value of a product or service is determined by its benefit to the consumer and the sacrifice required in terms of money and effort to obtain the product.

Owing to the following factors, it is difficult to describe the concept of "price" and its meaning:

- The marketer and the consumer attach different meanings to the price concept. Marketing management regards price as one of the marketing instruments used to achieve a business's objective. For the consumer, the price he or she pays for a product entails a sacrifice of disposable income. The final price usually represents a compromise between the seller (marketer), who wants to receive as much as possible, and the consumer, who wants to pay as little as possible.

- Because of the large number of products, the geographical distribution of consumers, and segmentation of the market, it is often not possible to specify a single price for a product.
- Price is but one of the four marketing instruments (or four Ps). Should any modification be made to any of the other marketing instruments, costs also change, necessitating a price adjustment. The product price cannot therefore be fixed without considering the influence of the other marketing instruments.

The question now arises as to how the problems mentioned above can be solved, thus making it possible to determine the final price of a product in such a way that both the marketer and the consumer are satisfied. To find an answer, we will now discuss the process of price determination.

14.4.2 The price determination process

The price determination process consists of the following four phases, namely:
- **Determination of the cost price.** The first step in determining the price of a product is the responsibility of the cost accounting department, and not of marketing management. The unit costs to produce and market the product are calculated. The product price cannot be lower than cost, because this would entail financial loss, which could ruin the business.
- **Determination of the market price.** The market price is the price the consumer is prepared to pay, or the current market price at which competing products are sold. It is marketing management's task to determine the market price. This can be done by launching a market-research project, involving consumers or dealers. A survey of the prices of competitors' products can also be undertaken. If the cost price is much higher than the market price, it means a cost reduction adjustment has to be made – or else marketing management have to make a special attempt to convince consumers that the particular product warrants a higher price.
- **Determination of target price.** The target price is the price that will realise the target rate of return, taking into consideration the cost structure, the business's capital needs, and the potential sales volume of the product. One way of calculating the target price is the cost-plus method. This is done by adding the profit margin to the unit costs of the product. The accepted rate of return determines how large the profit margin will be.
- **Determination of the final price.** The final price is the price at which the product is offered to consumers. This price is determined through a reconciliation of the market price and the target price. The final price therefore lies somewhere between the market price and the target price. Should the market price for an article be, say, R5,00, and the target price R3,50, then the final price may be set at different levels between R3,50 and R5,00. The final selling price can, for various reasons, be still further adjusted.

Determining the price of a can of bottled mineral water

Manufacturer's **cost price** to deliver a 500 ml bottle of mineral water = R2,00
→ Manufacturer sells to Shoprite supermarket group at a 50% mark up =R3,00
→ Shoprite is aware that the general **market price** for bottled mineral water is
R6,00 → Shoprite adds a 100% mark up on R3,00 to sell the product to the
customer (**target price**) → The **selling price** is therefore also.

14.4.3 Adaptations of the final price

14.4.3.1 Skimming prices

If the product is an innovation, and therefore a unique new product, the final
price may have a much higher profit margin. There are consumers who would
be prepared to pay the high price, because such new inventions usually have
prestige value. In fact, if the price is set too low, consumers could possibly
doubt the new product's usefulness. Electric shavers were priced too low when
they were first put on the market, and they started to sell only once the price
had been almost doubled. Yet another reason for an innovation having a high
initial price is that marketing management have to recover development costs
before a profit can be made. It has already been pointed out that the development of a new invention is an expensive process with great attendant risks. As
the product gains popularity, however, the high initial price can gradually be
reduced. The more units produced and sold, the lower the costs will be, with
the result that the price drops. Of course, competitors find high profits tempt-
ing, which means that marketing management cannot maintain a skimming
price for a long time in the face of new competitive products.

14.4.3.2 Market penetration prices

Marketing management may decide against setting a high skimming price and
rather set a market penetration price. Here, the initial price of a new product
is lower, and the marketer hopes to penetrate the market rapidly, discouraging
competitors in the process. Competitors may decide that the small profit margin is not worth the effort of marketing a competing product themselves.

14.4.3.3 Market price level

This strategy is followed if there is keen competition and numerous similar
products have to compete against one another. In such a situation the marketer
has to maintain the market price. If he or she sets the price of the product
higher than those of competitors, consumers will tend to avoid the product. If
the price is lower than those of competing products, consumers will think there
is something wrong with the product. Marketing management can escape the
limitations of the market price strategy only if their product is successfully
differentiated and is therefore regarded as unique. (Refer to section 14.3.6.)

14.4.3.4 Leader prices

Leader pricing concerns special offers widely used by retailers – the so-called
"specials". A very small profit is made on leader price products. These products
are sold at lower than the current market price for a limited period only. The

retailer uses this method to lure consumers to his or her shop. These purchasers buy the low-priced "specials", as well as many other products with a higher profit margin. Manufacturers do not usually like leader pricing. Even though they can sell more products, the profit margin is inadequate and, later, when competitors' products are selected as a leader price item, sales figures drop. If the manufacturer is not prepared to lower his or her profit margin so that the products can be sold as a special offer, the retailer refuses to give the manufacturer shelf space, giving preference instead to competing products. The producer is in an unenviable position if the retailer is so large that, as channel captain, he or she can enforce leader prices (the question of channel leadership is discussed in greater detail in section 14.5.3).

14.4.3.5 Odd prices

Odd prices indicate that the final prices of products have odd numbers. The even prices, for example, R2, R4, R10 are avoided, and products are rather marked R1,99, R3,79 and R9,95. It is thought that consumers are more likely to accept odd prices, and that an odd price appears lower than an even price.

14.4.3.6 Bait prices

Bait prices are unethical and are therefore avoided by honest retailers. A bait price item has a particularly low price and is widely advertised. On arriving to

Price wars are a lose-lose situation for all the role players

Price wars between competitors are to their general detriment. The net effect is that customer loyalty declines because customers will now buy the product that is the cheapest, and profits diminish because the margins are very slim. The best way to escape a crippling price war is to differentiate a product or service so that it is not directly comparable with those of its competitors.

Applying the concept: price decisions

The CitiGolf was introduced in 1984 after the withdrawal of the famous Beetle and when the Golf 1 production run came to an end (it was replaced by the Golf 2, called the jumbo Golf). The re-introduction of the Golf 1 in the form of the CitiGolf created a lot of interest. The reasons for the success of this old-model car are:

- There was a trading-down process by consumers with a lack of discretionary income. They traded in their large-engined cars for this smaller, more fuel-efficient smaller model.
- A general improvement in productivity at Volkswagen resulted in cost savings in the manufacturing process.

- The presses and moulds necessary for its manufacture were already paid for.
- Economies of scale were realised because the Volkswagen pick-up truck used the same manufacturing line as the CitiGolf.

After nearly twenty years, the CitiGolf is still strong and remains one of the cheapest cars on the market. Other manufacturers who followed the same route include the Mazda Midge and the Ford Laser, as well as the Toyota Tazz. The Tazz was the top-selling sedan car in South Africa by the end of 2002.

buy it, purchasers are then encouraged to buy a far more expensive item. The retailer does not really intend to sell the bait price item – most of the time it is not even in stock or only one is available at the low price.

14.5 Distribution decisions

14.5.1 Description of distribution

In chapter 13 **marketing is defined as those activities that have to be carried out to direct the flow of products and services from the business to the consumer in such a way that it satisfies the primary objective of the business and meets the needs of the consumer.** It is clear from this definition that **a flow or transfer process takes place, and distribution plays an important role here.** The transfer takes place along specific distribution channels, which consist of middlemen (wholesalers and retailers) who are involved in the transfer of products from the manufacturer to the consumer. It is the task of marketing management to link the manufacturer and the various middlemen in such a way that the product is made available to the consumer in the right place and at the right time.

Distribution entails decision making about the type of distribution channel and about the performance of certain activities, for example, physical distribution (also called logistical activities), such as transport scheduling and stock-keeping.

Distribution as a marketing instrument is represented as the shaft of the key to the market in figure 14.1 (see p. 308).

Later in this chapter we will examine the various types of distribution channels, the question of channel leadership, and the various types of market coverage. The channel leader or captain is the channel member who decides which type of channel should be used to achieve the most effective transfer of the product. Distribution decisions also demand that a choice be made regarding the degree of market coverage required.

14.5.2 The choice of distribution channel

The first decision to be made in respect of distribution strategy entails the choice of middlemen. Five different distribution channels are distinguished, namely:

- **Manufacturer → consumer.** Direct distribution takes place through this channel. Although the middleman is eliminated, physical distribution activities involved in the transfer of products still have to be performed, in this case by the producer – for example, a farmer, of the vegetables that he is selling at a farm stall.

  Manufacturers usually sell industrial products directly to other businesses such as factories, which use the products in their manufacturing processes. Door-to-door sales, like selling vacuum cleaners, are also an example of direct distribution.

- **Manufacturer → retailer → consumer.** This indirect distribution channel is found especially in large retail businesses that buy from manufacturers. Pick 'n Pay, for example, is a large retailer that buys directly from manufacturers.

- **Manufacturer** → **wholesaler** → **consumer.** This indirect distribution channel is common nowadays. Wholesalers may sell directly to the final consumer, provided these sales constitute less than 50% of their total sales. Examples include Makro and Metro wholesalers.
- **Manufacturer** → **wholesaler** → **retailer** → **consumer.** This is the classic indirect distribution channel that is still regarded as the most effective by a large number of manufacturers. An example is where wholesalers supply stock to the informal retailing sector, such as the spaza shop in more disadvantaged areas.
- **Manufacturer** → **wholesaler** → **wholesaler** → **retailer** → **consumer.** In this case, the first wholesaler is usually a speciality wholesaler who obtains a specific product from numerous manufacturers and then sells it to the second wholesaler, who sells it to the retail trade, which in turn sells it to the consumer. An example is where the first wholesaler is located in a foreign country. He or she buys the manufacturer's products in that country and delivers them to a wholesaler in South Africa. This wholesaler delivers these products to a retailer, who sells them to the consumer.

The type of product, the type of market, and the existing distribution structure determine which of the channels will offer the greatest advantages. If the product is perishable and the market localised, direct distribution is the ideal method. A stall next to the road where a farmer sells fresh garden vegetables and milk is an example of a situation where advantages offered by a direct distribution channel (producer → consumer) are utilised. If the product has to be handled and transported in bulk, and the market is such that consumers are widespread, the manufacturer probably has to depend on the specialised knowledge and facilities of middlemen (such as the wholesaler and retailer) to make the product(s) available to consumers. The indirect channel is the ideal choice in such a case.

14.5.3 Channel leadership

Traditionally, it is the marketing division of a manufacturer of consumer products that makes distribution channel decisions and consequently decides which retail outlets should market the business's products. More recently, however, it is often the retailer – for example, Pick 'n Pay – that makes the decisions and therefore controls/dominates the channel. The business that controls/dominates the channel is known as the **channel captain**.

14.5.3.1 The manufacturer as channel captain

If the manufacturer is the channel captain, specific middlemen often have to be persuaded to distribute his or her product. The manufacturer may persuade the middlemen to create a demand for the product by directing intensive marketing communication messages at consumers. This is known as "pull" because the product is "pulled" through the channel by means of consumer demand (the middleman is obliged to stock the product because the consumer demands it). An example of this is Shell Helix oil, which was launched by means of advertisements aimed directly at the consumer, who then asked the retailer to stock the product.

South African retailers

There are various types of retailers in South Africa. Below are some examples:

- **General dealers** are one of the oldest forms of retailers in South Africa. They offer a wide range of products and operate mostly in rural areas. They sell everything from coal stoves to bicycles to clothing to groceries.
- **Departmental stores** are large stores that sell products in different departments, for example, women's clothing, haberdashery, children's clothing, etc. An example is Stuttafords. This retailing format is, however, on the decline in South Africa, mainly because of the introduction of category killer stores (that is, a retailer who wants to achieve merchandise dominance by creating narrowly focused jumbo-sized stores, for example, Mr Price).
- **Speciality stores** have a narrow but deep product range, for example, jewellery stores.
- **Chain stores** are similar shops that are centrally controlled by a head-office. Woolworths is a chain store group.
- **Supermarkets** operate on a self-service basis and sell mostly fast moving consumer goods (FMCG). An example is Shoprite.
- **Convenience stores** are found all over South Africa. Some of the typical examples include the corner café, which sells typical convenience products such as bread, milk, newspapers and cigarettes. They are open for extended periods and provide a service to the customer. Another form of convenience store is the forecourt store at petrol filling stations.
- **Discount stores** have a high stock turnover and low prices. Examples include Dion's and Game.
- **Hypermarkets** are larger in size than supermarkets, and, in addition to FMCGs, they sell more durable products such as lawnmowers, furniture, etc. They attract people from a large geographical area, and an example is the Pick 'n Pay hypermarket.
- **Shopping centres** are usually found on the periphery of large cities or in the suburbs outside the city centre. These centres are large buildings that house independent retailers as well as some anchor stores that draw people to the shopping centre. Anchor stores may include a supermarket, discount store and/or departmental store. South African examples are Menlyn Retail Park in Pretoria's eastern suburbs, Cavendish Square to the south of Cape Town's city centre, and East Gate in Johannesburg.
- **Mail order stores** such as Leading Concepts market by means of catalogues, and people then order by mail.
- There are also a number of **informal retailers** that operate in South Africa. One of the best-known forms of such retailers is the spaza shop. The spaza is a form of a convenience store that is usually found in townships. Basic commodities such as bread, milk, cool drinks and cigarettes are sold through these stores, which are, typically, located in the home of the entrepreneur.

Intermediaries may also be persuaded to "push" a product by actively encouraging sales of products in a store. They may be persuaded to do this, for example, by offering a high profit margin on sales. Demonstration material, shop competitions, and special display shelves may also be supplied by the channel captain to encourage the push strategy. Most consumer products, such as soft drinks and coffee, are marketed in this way. In the marketing of groceries, where competition between different manufacturers is particularly keen, there is often a battle for shelf space. A combination of push and pull is used by the manufacturer as channel captain to persuade the retailer to find shelf space for a particular item between other competing products. It is especially difficult to obtain shelf space for a new competing product. In such a case the manufacturer should create a demand for the new item (pull) by thoroughly informing the consumer about it through advertising. It should then be expected of the retailer to apply the required push strategy.

14.5.3.2 The retailer as channel captain

If the retailer has a network of branches, enjoys store loyalty, and has adequate financial resources, he or she can take over the channel leadership and lay down conditions to the manufacturer. An example of this is the Pick 'n Pay store group which can be seen as a channel leader. In such cases, the retailer can pull as well as push the product. The retailer advertises the manufacturer's products, actively promoting its sales by granting a price discount to consumers, or by means of special exhibits to attract consumers' attention. Special shelf space is also allocated to such products. Understandably, however, manufacturers are not very happy with this state of affairs, and would rather retain the leadership themselves. If the manufacturer succeeds in obtaining brand loyalty for his or her products, it is not easy for a retailer to take over the channel leadership. Consumers then look for the specific brand products and tend to avoid stores that do not stock them. This means that a retailer can only be the channel captain for some of the products in his or her store.

14.5.4 *Market coverage*

The number of intermediaries in the channel is directly linked to the type of market coverage being aimed at. These include intensive, exclusive and selective market coverage.

- **Intensive market coverage** indicates a situation where as many suitable and available middlemen as possible are utilised, especially by convenience product manufacturers such as Coca-Cola, whose products are distributed through cafés, liquor stores, supermarkets, spaza shops and forecourts.
- **Exclusive market coverage** results when a manufacturer purposely limits the number of people handling his or her product to only a few intermediaries who obtain exclusive rights to sell the product in a specific geographical area. The intermediaries undertake not to stock other competing products. This type of market coverage is found particularly in speciality products such as men's evening clothing and cars.
- **Selective market coverage** refers to the selection of only those intermediaries who will distribute the product efficiently. Selective market coverage lies somewhere between intensive and exclusive market coverage and can be used by manufacturers of convenience, shopping and speciality products. Medicine, for example, is distributed by pharmacies, because chemists are the ideal people to do this efficiently.

14.5.5 *Physical distribution*

A further aspect of the distribution strategy is decision making about the physical distribution activities that have to take place to make a product available to the final consumer. These activities – in order of relative importance from a cost point of view – include:
- Transportation
- Storage
- Inventory holding
- Receipt and despatch
- Packaging
- Administration
- Ordering

The purpose of the physical distribution function is to maintain a specific satisfactory level of service to clients at the lowest possible distribution costs. The optimal service level is that level above which an increase in costs incurred in respect of physical distribution activities will not result in a corresponding increase in sales.

Physical distribution is becoming increasingly important. In earlier times, management were under the impression that physical distribution consisted of transport scheduling only. However, after it became apparent that the effective performance of the physical distribution activities could mean large cost savings for the business, and could also ensure that the product was in the right place at the right time for the convenience of consumers, more attention was paid to this function. The three main components of physical distribution are:
- Selecting warehouses
- Selecting the most suitable mode of transport
- Selecting optimal inventory holding levels

A compromise between cost and service must be reached in all three components. The most effective performance of physical distribution activities ensures the following:
- The timeous and reliable delivery of orders
- Adequate inventory, so that shortages do not occur
- Careful handling of stocks to eliminate damage, perishing and breakage, as far as possible

Physical distribution activities are discussed in greater detail in the chapters dealing with purchasing management. As far as marketing is concerned, close liaison between the marketing manager and the purchasing manager is required, and the marketing manager has to be involved in planning and decision making. If this is not the case, the flow of products from manufacturer to final consumer could be seriously hampered.

Applying the concept: distribution decisions

A dynamic development in distribution decision making is the use of the Internet to market a product or service to the customer. Among the success stories in South Africa are the retailer Pick 'n Pay with its website http://www.picknpay.co.za and Kalahari.net. The Pick 'n Pay website makes it possible for the customer to sit in the comfort of his or her home and order products on the Internet, pay by credit card, and arrange for a delivery period that suits him or her. The customer pays a R35 delivery fee and the products are delivered to his or her home at the agreed time. Kalahari.net enables the purchase of books, CDs and DVDs on the Internet, and these items are delivered to the customer's doorstep.

14.6 Marketing communication decisions

14.6.1 The nature of marketing communication

The consumer is removed from the manufacturer, intermediaries and point of sale in terms both of time and space. It is therefore obvious that it is the task of marketing management to communicate with the consumer, to inform him or her, and to make the customer aware of the variety of products offered on the market. The consumer should also be persuaded by the marketing message to select and buy the producer's product time and again.

Marketing communication can be regarded as the process of informing, persuading and reminding the consumer. It comprises four elements that can be used in a specific combination to communicate with consumers. These four elements are:

- Advertising
- Personal selling
- Sales promotion
- Publicity

Figure 14.3 (see p. 330) shows the elements of marketing communication. All four elements have to work together to convey the marketing message to the target audience.

It is the task of marketing management to decide about the best combination of the four elements. A marketing communication budget allocates funds to each of the four marketing communication elements. Within the restrictions of this budget, consumers have to be made aware of the business's market offering. They should be persuaded to select and buy product(s), and reminded constantly to buy the product(s) again. A discussion of the four marketing communication elements follows.

14.6.2 Advertising

Advertising is a controlled and paid non-personal marketing communication related to a need-satisfying product and directed by a marketer at a specific target audience.

Figure 14.3: Elements of marketing communication

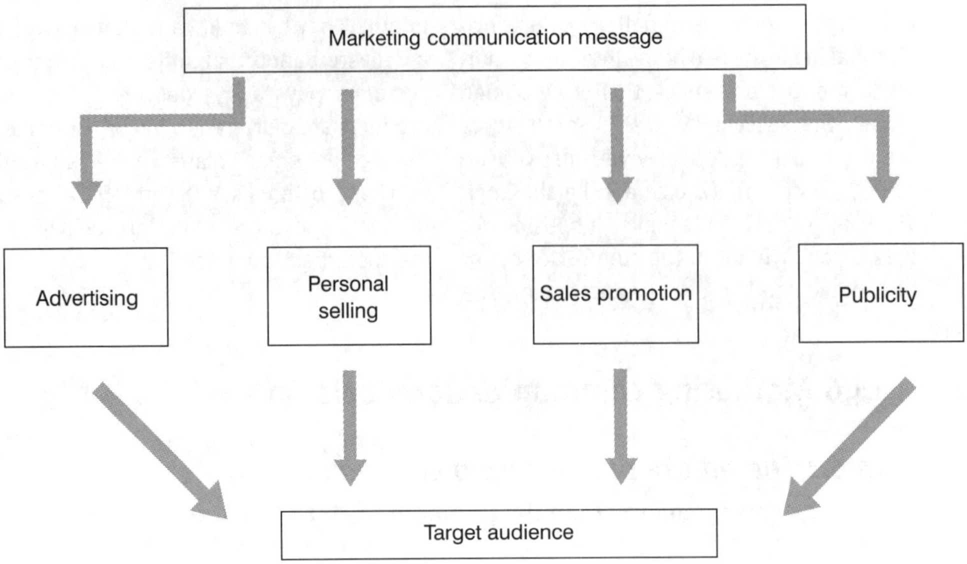

14.6.2.1 Advertising media

The advertisements shown on **television** or in the **movies**, broadcast on the **radio**, or placed in **magazines and newspapers**, are examples of advertising. A single placement of such an advertisement is very expensive – hence the need to pay careful attention to the choice of the media used, as well as to the marketing communication message. The marketing manager should be very sure that his or her message will reach the target market (or target audience in this case), and that this audience will notice the message, understand it, accept it, and react to it by repeatedly buying the same product.

Outdoor advertising on billboards, posters, bus stops and public transport vehicles reaches consumers at a time when they are busy with other activities. This is also a good way of reaching a target market that does not read regularly or does not have access to television or the movies. An advertising budget, as part of the marketing communication budget, is prepared in order to indicate the percentages of the budgeted amount that should be allocated to the various media. Obviously, market research is done to establish the way in which the target market can be reached most effectively.

14.6.2.2 The advertising message

The formulation of the marketing message in advertisements in the different media requires careful consideration. An advertisement in the print media usually consists of three main components, namely the heading, the illustration and the copy. The **heading** should attract the consumer's attention and deliver the main or most important appeal, or the reason why the product should be bought. The most important message is often repeated at the bottom of the copy. The headline and sub-headline are printed in big bold letters to attract attention. The **illustration** may be a drawing or a photograph, in black and white or colour. The illustration stimulates interest and invites the reader to actually read the copy, which contains information about the product and the need satisfaction that it can provide. Rational reasons (for example, petrol consumption of ten kilometres per litre in city traffic for the Honda Ballade) as well as emotional reasons (like claiming that a certain toothpaste will have the effect of all the girls swooning over you) for purchasing the product are given.

The product itself and the package and label should also appear in the illustration. All the components of the illustration itself are chosen to transmit a symbolic message. The models are carefully selected to play a specific role. A housewife is chosen to transmit a message about the excellence of a new detergent, while Miss South Africa is portrayed as a successful user of cosmetics. The intended target audience must be able to relate to or identify with the model in the illustration. (For example, it is likely to be ineffective to use a male as a role model for buying washing powder.) It is important, also, to achieve coherence in all three components. The headline, illustration and copy should not tell conflicting stories.

In radio advertisements, only words and sounds can be used to transmit the advertising message. Music is often used to reinforce the message or to create a specific mood. Jingles and slogans are especially effective in teaching the brand name to potential consumers.

Television advertisements are effective because the spoken and written word can be used to spell out the message clearly. Pictorial material, music, jingles and other sounds can be used to reinforce the message. For this reason, television commercials are very expensive and every second counts. Advertisers cannot afford to waste time on irrelevant material. Sometimes television advertisers get so caught up in the entertaining story line of the television advertisement that they forget what the most important message is – namely the brand name.

The success of the Red Bull advertising campaign

Red Bull is an energy drink that was launched in South Africa in 1997. The marketing mix is based on the following:

- The product as an energy drink was new to the market, and it worked.
- The packaging was eye-catching.
- The distribution channel was good, that is, the product was in the right place at the right time.
- The pricing strategy used was effective (a price-skimming premium strategy, implying that if it is expensive it must be working).
- A marketing communications strategy that was highly visible was employed, for example, cartoon characters on TV that provided humour and entertainment value with the slogan "Red Bull gives you wings!"

14.6.3 Personal selling

Personal selling is a **verbal presentation of a product, service or idea to one or more potential purchasers in order to conclude a transaction.** Sales representatives are used to inform buyers about a business's product(s) and to persuade buyers, through face-to-face communication, to buy the business's products time and again.

Sales representatives of manufacturers visit other businesses and dealers, communicating the marketing message directly. In the same way, wholesalers' sales representatives can be used to visit retailers to try to sell the variety of products handled by the wholesaler. Personal selling between sales representatives and final consumers also takes place: this is known as door-to-door selling (for example, selling Tupperware utility plastic containers and cosmetics from Avroy Shlain). Over-the-counter sales by shop assistants may also be regarded as personal selling, but normally the retailer does not see it in this light – the shop assistant is regarded merely as someone who helps with the physical distribution of the product, that is, a person who therefore does not have to be trained in the art of selling.

Example

Cosmetic products are often sold on a door-to-door basis. Avroy Shlain, for example, succeeded in building his extremely successful business by training (and motivating) his sales representatives to sell his cosmetic products, which bear his own brand name, by means of personal communication.

14.6.4 Sales promotion

Sales promotion consists of those **marketing communication methods not normally classified as advertising, personal selling, or publicity, but that complement these in trying to influence consumer behaviour.** Examples of such methods are diaries, calendars and T-shirts displaying the brand name and a short sales message. Competitions, demonstrations, and the handing out of samples (such as a sachet of Handy Andy Micro floor cleaning liquid) are also examples of sales promotions. Sales promotions often have short-term objectives only, for example, to introduce a new product to the market.

However, they are valuable methods, because they reinforce the effects of the other marketing communication elements. If, for example, a consumer has seen a supermarket demonstration of a new pan that browns meat without oil needing to being added (sales promotion), she would possibly understand the television advertisement (advertising) better and find it easier to accept the message, especially if she has also read an article in the women's column of the newspaper (publicity) in which the columnist explains the new cooking method.

14.6.5 Publicity

Publicity is the **non-personal stimulation of the demand for a product or service of a business by making its actual current news value available to the mass media to obtain a favourable and "free" review of the business and its product in the media.**

Publicity also interfaces with the business's public relations function, discussed in chapter 16. Should the business or its product receive favourable coverage in the press or on the radio or television, the publicity (created by the activities of the public relations division) has a specific marketing communication value for the business.

The distinguishing feature of publicity is that the message to be conveyed should have a certain degree of news value for the audience. Publicity is also more credible than advertising, because the audience is more receptive to the message. A further feature of publicity is that marketing management has no direct say in formulating the message, because the editor of a publication, for example, decides what he or she wants to publish. It is therefore clear that publicity can also have a negative effect (consider, for example, the negative publicity that a motor journalist would give a test car that breaks down on a rural road!).

However, publicity is not always "free", as is suggested in the definition. A business often has to spend large sums of money on favourable mentions in the press or on radio or television. Businesses often sponsor sports events or donate large amounts to charity. By doing this, a business effectively shows its responsibility towards the community – in addition getting free mention of its name or product in the media. Consumers who notice the hidden message are then more inclined to accept the marketing messages of such a "good" business.

Marketing management should decide which sponsorships or donations could be of benefit to the product(s) to be marketed. Top management some-times decide on sponsorships that are of interest to them personally, notwith-standing the nature of the product or market. In this way, funds are often wasted on events or causes that do not have sufficient positive marketing com-munication value and hence will not succeed in demonstrating social respon-sibility. Specific marketing communication objectives should also be set in respect of sponsorships.

Applying the concept: marketing communication decisions

One of the most interesting ways in which new products are marketed is stealth mar-keting. The effectiveness of this method was seen with the introduction of the new Mini that was launched by BMW. The car was introduced at a price of R160 000 and was marketed as a lifestyle product. One of the company's first marketing activities was to run a Mini-related competition. The e-mail reaction was followed up with a new compe-tition where the respondents were asked to develop a dream itinerary for a trip in the new Mini. There were 15 000 entrants. From the itineraries submitted the advertising agency could determine the lifestyle of the contestants. From this information they could deduce which of the entrants were potential buyers of the new car. The success of the campaign resulted in BMW deciding to change its advertising campaign to more below-the-line advertising.

14.7 Summary

In this chapter, the marketing strategy was represented as a key and the target market as a lock. All four parts of the key have to work together to open the lock. The various product decisions – including the product range, the brand, the packaging, the method used to differentiate the product from other prod-ucts, and new product development – were discussed. Product decisions con-sist of decisions regarding branding, packaging and aspects such as product differentiation and product obsolescence. Distribution decisions entail considering the various distribution channels and the market coverage. It was shown that a channel captain is able to dominate an entire channel, and that large retailers, rather than manufacturers, can act as channel captains. In addition, price decisions are important, because too low a price may lead to financial loss, perhaps giving the impression that the product is of inferior quality. Prices should be determined in such a way that they stimulate a demand for products. The marketer communicates with consumers through advertising, as well as personal selling and publicity, thus endeavouring to inform, persuade, and remind them to buy a specific brand repeatedly. Large sums of money are spent on effective messages to reach consumers.

Reference

1. This section is largely based on Strydom, J.W., Jooste, C.J., & Cant, M.C., *Marketing management*, 4th edition, Juta, Cape Town, 2000, pp. 179–268.
2. Brand logos reproduced by permission of Toyota (SA) Pty Ltd, Telkom (SA) Pty Ltd, and Pick 'n Pay (SA) Pty Ltd (p. 311).

15 The integrated marketing strategy

The purpose of this chapter

The integrated marketing strategy shows how all the marketing activities discussed in the previous two chapters are integrated. It provides an overall picture of the decision-making process required of the marketing manager. It commences by looking at the marketing concept, which is the philosophy upon which marketing is based, and indicates how the marketing objectives tie in with the organisational objectives. It also shows how the marketing strategy must adapt over the product life cycle. In addition, it examines the marketing planning and control process that is followed by the marketing manager.

Learning outcomes

The content of this chapter will enable learners to:
- Explain the role of the marketing concept and marketing objectives in the running of the business
- Demonstrate how changes in the product life cycle will influence the marketing strategy formulation of the business
- Show how marketing planning and control are exercised in the business

15.1 Introduction

In the previous chapter the four marketing instruments were discussed. As already explained, decisions pertaining to the four marketing instruments that are under the direct control of marketing management must be combined in an integrated marketing strategy that is aimed at a specific target market.

One of the dangers of being involved in a study of marketing is that one becomes so immersed in the details of marketing research, segmentation and the marketing instruments, that the overall picture becomes blurred. The focus of an integrated marketing strategy is therefore to put all the pieces together so that a marketing strategy can be developed – one that can best satisfy the needs of the target market. In this process, the marketing concept guides the enterprise. Changes in the life cycle and marketing strategy also form part of an integrated marketing strategy formulation.

In this chapter, the integrated marketing strategy is discussed in terms of the marketing concept, decision making during the different phases of the life cycle, as well as the marketing warfare that occurs. Finally, the question of the role of marketing planning and control is also addressed.

15.2 The marketing concept

Four principles are contained in the marketing concept, which is the ethical code according to which the marketing task (as described in this book) is performed. All four principles are equally important, and each one invariably influences the application of the others. The marketing concept directs all marketing decisions about products, distribution methods, marketing communication and price determination. In chapter 13 we pointed out that the evolution in marketing thought has led to the development of the following four principles of an ethical code known as the marketing concept, namely:

- Profitability
- Consumer orientation
- Social responsibility
- Organisational integration

15.2.1 *The principle of profitability*

The first principle of the marketing concept, in a profit-seeking business, is the long-term maximisation of profitability. This is the primary objective of the business in a free-market system and is therefore also the main objective of marketing management. The principle of profitability is fundamental to the marketing concept, and emphasises profitability instead of sales, which do not necessarily maximise profits.

> **Large food retailing: high turnover – low profits per unit**
>
> Pick 'n Pay is viewed as South Africa's leading large food retailer. In the 2001-2002 financial year the group had a turnover of R18,8 billion and an operating profit of R627,9 million. The profit margin per unit is, clearly, very low and it is therefore imperative for this large food retailer to realise a high stock turnover – the higher the turnover, the larger the profit.

Source: Pick 'n Pay Annual Report, 2002.

15.2.2 *The principle of consumer orientation*

The satisfaction of consumer needs, demands and preferences constitutes a consumer-oriented approach to marketing where emphasis is placed on what the consumer needs. Marketing decision making is based on what the consumer wants, but even though the consumer is regarded as "the king", complete need satisfaction can never be achieved.

Satisfaction can only be given within the constraints of the profit objective and the resources of a business. If the consumer is neglected and his or her wishes are ignored, this can have serious financial implications for the enterprise. Competitors are especially keen to note and turn such opportunities to their own advantage. Consumer orientation also means that the consumer has to be supplied with adequate and correct information about the business's market offering. This information is usually incorporated into marketing communication messages.

15.2.3 The principle of social responsibility

Besides their responsibility towards the consumers of their products, marketing management also have a responsibility towards the community in which the marketing task is performed. Business often discharges this responsibility by spending money on projects such as housing, education, job creation and health. The objective of these projects is to create a stable economic, social and political environment in which future profits can be optimised. Responsibility in this regard enhances the corporate image in the eyes of employees, consumers and the general public. It has long-term dimensions that might well have a positive influence on the profit position in future. Sporting events and educational institutions such as schools are also often sponsored by large businesses.

The other dimension of social responsibility hinges on the authority (legislation) under which the business operates. Should the business act irresponsibly or fail to abide by the laws of the land, reaction in terms of punitive legislation or even prosecution could result, as in the case of Leisurenet.

If a business were to disregard the norms of society, consumer resistance could result, thereby harming the primary objective of the business. Nothing should be done to violate the current norms or general moral and ethical standards of the community.

A sponsorship or a social responsibility project must have a certain marketing benefit for the sponsor. Usually top management must decide on the merits of alternative projects but it is the responsibility of marketing management to initiate projects, because of their close relationship with the public and their ability to evaluate projects in terms of marketing benefits. A sponsorship must be supported by marketing communication to ensure a large audience. A sponsored event must also be well organised and managed, which usually requires the help of the public relations department. An imaginative and successful social responsibility project may mean publicity value for the business enterprise. Because such projects are newsworthy, coverage in the mass media (newspapers, radio, television) is ensured. In sporting events, players usually display the name of the sponsor on equipment and clothing, while the sporting event itself offers opportunities to display brand names and marketing messages on billboards, flags, etc.

Marketing management should ensure that nothing is done that could be detrimental to the community. A case in point is the trouble taken to ensure that containers of harmful substances cannot easily be opened by children (tamper-free packaging). Also, an advertisement that mocks religion, for example, offends the prevalent moral or ethical values of the community. This may provoke consumer resistance. Consumers may decide to avoid the product in future.

15.2.4 The principle of organisational integration

This principle expresses the need for close cooperation between all the functions of the business. All the functional decision-making activities should be coordinated in a way that will eventually lead to the successful marketing of the products of the business. Organisational integration entails close coopera-

Corporate review of SABMiller

One South African company that has crossed the divide between an international company and a real global company is SABMiller. It is found in Africa, Europe (including Eastern Europe), and in the East (including China). South African Breweries recently bought Miller Breweries in the USA and SABMiller are now rated as the second largest beer brewer in the world. In their 2002 Financial Report SABMiller state the following regarding their social responsibility towards their employees:

- **Fair remuneration.** They seek to offer their employees a fair and rewarding pay based on industry comparisons and country norms.
- **Focus on health and safety of all their workers.** The SABMiller Alrode Brewery launched a new HIV/Aids programme by using industrial theatre to gain the attention and inform the employees.
- **Developing all employees.** The commitment of the SABMiller group is to develop employees to their full potential. To this end, on average of 3,9 days' training per employee was done in the 2001-2002 financial year.
- **Seeking to enhance diversity.** The South African sector of SABMiller is dedicated to offering equality of opportunity in employment and extending diversity.
- **Supporting local economic development.** In the majority of countries in which SABMiller operates, the average income is less than $4,00 per day. The creation and maintenance of jobs is therefore of the utmost importance for SABMiller. SABMiller invested $7 million in the local communities worldwide which represents 1,2% of group pre-tax profits. Some of the community projects are:
1. Poland, where Kompania Piwowarska supports local charity organisations.
2. Mozambique, where SABMiller has a long-term commitment to the Graca Machel Education Trust of $600 000 to build schools.
3. Kgalagadi Breweries in Botswana contributes one per cent of profits after tax to the KMS Trust yielding $148,900 a year. Major projects include Conservation International Okavango, Environmental Heritage Foundation and the Moremogolo Trust for financial assistance to set up a school for primary school dropouts.
4. The Kick Start Competition South Africa. This competition started in 1995 and encourages entrepreneurial activity among young people in South Africa. Total investment of SABMiller is more than R19 million.

Source: South African Breweries plc Corporate Accountability Report, 2002, pp. 36-44.

tion between the marketing, operational, purchasing, and all other functions of the business in pursuit of the business's mission and objectives. Organisational integration is a prerequisite for success – the primary objective can never be achieved without it.

15.2.5 *Merits of the marketing concept*

The criticism often levelled at marketing – that it purposely exploits consumers, "robbing" them of hard-earned money to be wasted on useless articles, is refuted by the principles of the marketing concept. The true marketer is proud of his or her product and of the way it satisfies the needs of consumers. The marketer jealously guards the product's name, paying meticulous attention to complaints and criticism, even though his or her main purpose is continually to improve profit position.

According to the first principle of the marketing concept, long-term maximisation of profitability is the primary objective of the business and also that of marketing management. The business is entitled to this profit to offset the risks involved in developing products for the market. It is necessary to discuss this primary objective in more detail because it is the guideline for activities and the criterion for success. The other secondary objectives of marketing management are also discussed in the following section.

Figure 15.1 illustrates the four principles of the marketing concept, the philosophy according to which all marketing tasks are performed.

Figure 15.1: The marketing concept

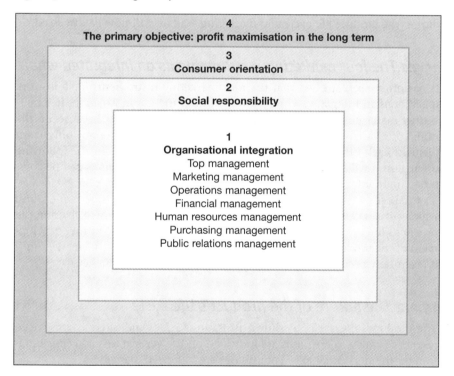

15.3 Marketing strategy during the product life cycle

The management of an integrated marketing strategy also requires that attention be focused on the specific phase in which the business's products are at a specific moment in time. There is a close relationship between the management of the four marketing instruments (as discussed in chapter 14) and the management of the product range during its life cycle. Marketing warfare, which uses the four marketing instruments as weapons in the attack on com-

Applying the concept: the marketing concept

Many global organisations stand accused that they answer to their shareholders rather than their conscience (in some instances they do not even answer to their shareholders, as in the case of Worldcom and Enron in the USA, and Leisurenet in South Africa). Worldwide, they are seen as plunderers and robber barons, taking from countries minerals and precious stones while the wealth created is never returned to those countries (an example is the "blood-diamonds" of Angola). In the last decade, however there has been a turnaround, and today we see organisations investing millions to uplift populations, with aspects such as the preservation of eco-sensitive areas and historical sites also receiving attention. The social conscience of global organisations has grown dramatically in this decade, and will hopefully improve even further in the future. The accountability reports of these global organisations reveal their attempts at adhering to the basic tenets of the marketing concept.

petitors, ties in with this. Aspects of the adaptation of the marketing strategy during the product life cycle and marketing warfare will now be discussed.

15.3.1 The four marketing instruments as an integrated whole

It has often been stressed that the four marketing instruments have to work together as an integrated whole – they cannot function in isolation. It is marketing management's responsibility to achieve this unity because of the numerous variables, and because the marketing instruments not only complement each other, but are also mutually interchangeable. In the following discussion it will be shown how the four marketing instruments can be combined in an integrated marketing strategy during the product's life cycle.

Chapter 14 (section 14.3.9) showed how a new product is developed, and which phases can be distinguished in new product development. During the product's life cycle (as indicated in figure 15.2 on p. 341) the further development of the product can be sketched, from its introduction to the market until it eventually becomes obsolete and is withdrawn from the market.

15.3.2 The nature of the product's life cycle

The product's life cycle, as shown in figure 15.2, is indicated as a curve in respect of which sales/profits are indicated on the vertical axis and time duration on the horizontal axis. Four phases are indicated, namely:

- The introductory phase
- The growth phase
- The maturity phase
- The declining phase

Figure 15.2 also illustrates the sales and profit curves during the four phases of the product's life cycle. The sales curve ascends during the introductory and growth phases, reaching a peak in the maturity phase and levelling off (stagnating) and descending during the declining phase. The profit curve looks

Figure 15.2: Phases in the product's life cycle

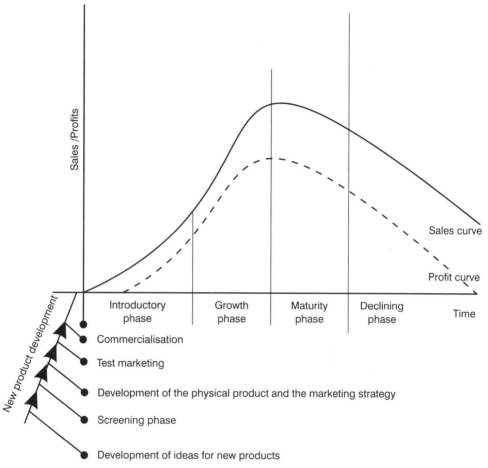

similar, but starts rising only later in the development phase. The reason is the high costs related to new product development. Costs first have to be recovered before any profit can be made.

The profit curve starts to decline earlier than the sales curve. This is because the product meets keen competition in the maturity phase, causing a price cut (thereby lowering profits).

The marketing communication costs normally rise in this phase, since competition necessitates stimulation of demand. The increased costs naturally affect profits. Marketing management's objective is to sustain the profitable phase of the life cycle for as long as possible. This can be done by constantly modifying the integrated marketing strategy. The declining phase should, at all costs, be avoided.

The curve in figure 15.2 illustrates the traditional life cycle of a product. Obviously, not all products have identical life cycles. Where an enterprise, for example, markets a whole range of products, each product has its own life cycle. Figure 15.3 (on p. 342) illustrates the different life cycles. Although the seven cycles differ, each one reflects a rise, a peak, a stagnation and, in most cases, inevitably a decline. In each of the life cycle phases the decisions regarding the price, product, distribution and marketing communication are adjusted.

Figure 15.3: Different product life cycle patterns

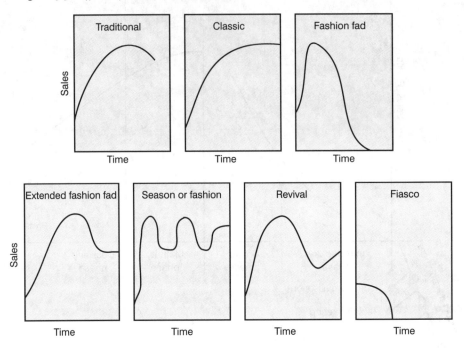

Source: Van der Walt, A., Strydom, J.W., Marx, S. & Jooste, C.J., *Marketing management*, Juta, Cape Town, 1999, chapter 15.

A discussion of the integrated marketing strategy in each phase now follows.

15.3.3 *Integrated marketing strategy in the introductory phase*

The integrated marketing strategy entails the following:

- **Objective.** The objective is to create a demand. A demand for the product has to be created in the first place, because at this stage consumers are not aware of such a new product (for example, the demand for DVD systems).
- **Target market.** The target market consists of consumers who are adventurous and prepared to try out new things and run risks, for it is possible that the new product may be a great failure.
- **Product decisions.** The product decisions taken during product development are implemented (for example, dimensions, colour of the product, etc.).
- **Distribution decisions:** These involve exclusive or selective market coverage. Only a few shops will be prepared to allocate shelf space to the new product (see chapter 14, section 14.5.4).
- **Price decisions.** A high initial price (skimming price) is fixed, since a new product (innovation) usually has a certain degree of prestige value.

- **Marketing communication decisions.** Initially, the business relies heavily on personal selling to dealers. Full-page colour advertisements appear in the more prestigious speciality periodicals. The sales message may contain highly technical information. Publicity is obtained fairly easily, because the product usually has news value. Sales promotion techniques can be used to attract attention to the product.

15.3.4 Integrated marketing strategy in the growth phase

This entails the following:
- **Objective.** The objective is to develop a demand. The demand for the specific brand has to be created. At this stage there are several competing products on the market and the target market is no longer unfamiliar with the product.
- **Target market.** The target market consists of consumers who are less receptive to new things and new ideas. They first want to establish whether the innovators approve of the product.
- **Product decisions.** Minor product modifications are made. The brand is emphasised.
- **Distribution decisions.** Selective market coverage.
- **Price decision.** The price declines because of competition.
- **Marketing communication decisions.** Advertising occurs through the mass media, such as newspapers, radio and television. Sales promotion methods are utilised. All of this is done to promote the specific product and the brand name.

15.3.5 Integrated marketing strategy in the maturity phase

This entails the following:
- **Objective.** The objective is to counteract competition and prolong the life cycle of the product.
- **Target market.** New target markets are sought and exploited because marketing management is aiming at a large market share. Most consumers are aware of the product and its benefits.
- **Product decisions.** Modifications or improvements have to be introduced to differentiate the product from numerous similar products on the market. (Product differentiation is discussed in chapter 14, section 14.3.6.) All four marketing instruments should help to achieve product differentiation. If this is successful, the product will be perceived as unique by a specific target market. In such a favourable situation little direct competition will be encountered, even though the product is in the maturity phase. Other product decisions that should receive attention in this phase are the development of new products, extending the product range, and product obsolescence. A new product or model starts its life cycle again in the introductory phase.
- **Distribution decision.** Intensive market coverage. All suitable dealers with the required facilities are allowed to stock and sell products.
- **Price decisions.** The current market price or market price level should be adhered to, unless marketing management have succeeded in differentiat-

ing the product successfully. The product is then accepted as unique. Marketing management have price discretion, because the consumer perceives the product as unique and does not mind paying more for it.

- **Marketing communication decisions.** Persuasive advertising through the mass media. The sales message is less technical and more emotional than during the introductory phase. In a television advertisement, for example, children might be depicted as expressing love for their father because he has bought them a specific brand of DVD player. This type of emotional appeal is often the most important way of differentiating a product from competing products in a highly competitive market.

15.3.6 Integrated marketing strategy in the declining phase

This entails the following:

- **Objective.** The objective is either to maintain the market share or to withdraw the product.
- **Target market.** The target market consists of an older, more conservative group of consumers who resist change and avoid innovation.
- **Product decisions.** No modification of the product is considered. Attention is paid to the development of substitute new products or models. The obsolete product is eventually withdrawn from the market.
- **Distribution decisions.** Limited market coverage, and this only in areas where the product is still in demand.
- **Price decisions.** Prices are reduced and the product is offered on sales.
- **Marketing communication decisions.** Personal selling and advertising only in areas where the product is still in demand.

Applying the concept: marketing strategy and the product life cycle

The success of the CitiGolf was mentioned in chapter 14. Another Volkswagen that had an exceptional life cycle was the Beetle. It was first manufactured in Germany in the late 1940s and had a life cycle that ended in 1981 in South Africa. During this time various changes were made to the car, including a larger engine, sporty colours and trimmings, etc., all of which illustrate how the marketing strategy changed over the intervening years. The old Beetle was eventually discontinued in Mexico in 2003, showing how long the life cycle of a car can be. Today the new Beetle is a huge success in the USA and Europe, and also in South Africa. The Mini Cooper followed the same life cycle, and was introduced into South Africa in 2002 by BMW.

15.4 Marketing warfare during the product life cycle

The different phases in the product life cycle were discussed above. During the progression of the product through its life cycle, adaptations must be made to the marketing strategy to obtain the optimum sales of the product and to keep the competition off balance.

15.4.1 Marketing warfare over the product life cycle

In all the phases of the product life cycle, marketing management are constantly involved in a struggle against direct and potential competitors. In this struggle the marketing strategy is implemented and the four marketing instruments are used as "weapons". The word "strategy" has a military connotation: "The art of war or the art of planning and directing large military movements" (Oxford English Dictionary). Emery says: "Marketing is merely a civilized form of warfare in which most battles are won with words, ideas and disciplined thinking."[1]

In the introductory phase, the product's future success in the battle must be carefully considered. While there are few direct competitors during this phase, the danger of future competition lurks if the product should prove successful in the market.[2] In this phase it is important for the business to identify a lucrative niche in the market, a position that can be defended at all costs. This is obtained by making it difficult for potential entrants to enter the market. Examples of how entry can be made more difficult are: by the registering of patent rights on new products, by obtaining the source of raw material and thus ensuring that nobody else can obtain this resource, and by delivering such excellent after-sales service that potential competitors will find it difficult to profitably compete in this market.

In the growth and maturity phases, when competition intensifies, the business must launch **attacks** against competitors and **defend** its position against counterattacks.

15.4.2 Attack alternatives

There are four main forms of attack:
- In a **frontal attack**, a competitor is threatened on all fronts, and especially on its strong points. Products are matched against products, prices against prices, and advertisements against advertisements. The strongest opponent in terms of resources and skills wins this attack.
- A **flanking attack** is a surprise attack on the opponent's weak points. A good example is the attack launched by Japanese and German automobile manufacturers who succeeded with small economical cars in the traditional, luxury automobile market in America. The American manufacturers were not even aware that a gap existed in their market.
- In **encirclement**, attacks are launched on many different fronts. Similar products are launched in the same target markets using the same distribution outlets and "me-too" marketing messages. The opponent must defend on all these fronts. The worldwide success of Seiko (a Japanese watch manufacturer) can be ascribed to encirclement. Seiko used all possible distributor outlets and overwhelmed competitors (especially Swiss watch manufacturers – at the time the world's leading watch manufacturers) and consumers with an enormous variety of models (about 2 300) that were constantly changed according to fashion and consumer preferences.[3]
- A **guerrilla attack** is used to launch surprise attacks at the opponent's weak points while a frontal attack is being planned. One example is when a retailer cuts the price of a well-known range of products for a limited time

and advertises it for a while, and then returns to the normal price. All this is done before the large competitor can react to the price decrease. This is usually a tactic that is used by a small business in its fight against a larger business.

15.4.3 Defence alternatives

A business that has been attacked should carefully select an appropriate defence method:

- It can launch a **counterattack** by concentrating mainly on the weaknesses of the attack that is launched against it.
- In **offensive defence** the business can pre-empt the attack if it discovers the plans of the attackers (market intelligence).[4] A business may decide to pre-empt a decrease in the price by a competitor. It can cut the price of the same product – before the announcement by the competitor – by a few cents more, thus creating confusion in the mind of the competitor.
- In **mobile defence** the business can move away from current markets and products by focusing on other expansion methods. However, research is essential here. Shell Oil's mission, for example, states that it wants to satisfy the energy needs of customers worldwide.[5] Shell succeeded in moving away from providing only petrol.
- In **strategic withdrawal** the business vacates the war zone until a later date when winning the war may be easier. The Apple computer group of the USA, for example, withdrew from South Africa in the early 1980s because of political pressure. After the introduction of a freely elected democratic government, Apple returned, however, to win back the lost market share and to engage with IBM in a fight for market leadership. In the decline phase of the product life cycle, the enterprise is often compelled to decide on strategic withdrawal.

Applying the concept: marketing warfare

Small businesses are seen as the key to the creation of jobs in South Africa, and will hopefully in the future create between 60% and 80% of GDP in South Africa. These small businesses are usually under pressure when competing against large (and sometimes even global) businesses. The advantages enjoyed by large businesses, for example, unlimited capital, the best know-how, and sufficient personnel, have led to the demise of many small businesses. There are, however, many success stories where a small "David" has taken on the "Goliaths'" of the business world and succeeded. Most small business success can be attributed to the use of marketing warfare tactics, such as "hit-and-run". The biggest advantage of a small business is its flexibility to adapt to changing circumstances. It can offer a special price with added services for a short time period, thereby attracting customers from some of its larger competitors, before changing back to the original price. Large businesses usually see a small competitor as a nuisance factor that they are forced to tolerate because of the time, money and effort needed to act against it.

15.5 Marketing planning and control[6]

Marketing planning firstly entails the analysis of the marketing environment in order to identify and evaluate certain marketing opportunities and threats so that realistic objectives can be set. The task of marketing management includes the implementation and control of all the activities that form part of the integrated marketing strategy.

15.5.1 Planning

15.5.1.1 Strategic market planning

The business must firstly develop strategic plans that are generated at top management level. The input of marketing management at this level centres around two basic decisions, namely the **competitive decision** and the **investment decision**. The competitive decision answers the question how the business is going to compete in the market. There are three basic options, namely:

- **Differentiation.** The business competes in the market in such a way that consumers perceive its range of products as different. Toyota, for example, decided to introduce an entry model car that can compete at the cheap end of the car market (in 2002 the average price in this segment was between R60 000 and R65 000). This market segment has shown sharp growth with the Fiat Mia, Daewoo Matiz, the Volkswagen CitiGolf, and Mazda's Sting as the main competitors. Toyota's answer was to add more value to its Tazz. The cheapest car in the Toyota range in 2002 was the Toyota Tazz at R68 990.
- **Focus (or niche) strategy.** The business tries to attain a small section of the large market by focusing solely on this section. This is probably the best strategy for a small business. The small business does not want to compete against a large competitor, but rather to concentrate on a geographic area in which a large competitor is not well represented.
- **Low cost strategy.** The business tries to obtain savings by mass manufacturing products, thereby attaining economies of scale. Thus lower prices are asked for its products.

The **investment decision** (or growth decision) centres round the following four options that exist for the business:
- Growth of the business unit and its products
- Maintaining the present position (status quo)
- Harvesting
- Divesting

If the enterprise decides on **growth**, it has the following options:
- Growth in existing markets (for example, by increasing market share, as Pick 'n Pay has done over the past few years)
- Growth by means of product development (such as adding new products to the existing product range), for example, Pick 'n Pay developed the retail market by introducing franchise operations
- Growth by means of market development (such as by entering new geographic areas and by selling the existing product in markets where the

consumers had not previously bought the product). Again, by way of example, Pick 'n Pay bought the Franklins stores in Australia.

- Growth by means of diversification (such as adding totally new products to the existing product range). For example, Pick 'n Pay opened five HealthPharm stores (a franchised pharmacy) where pharmacists serve their community.

The **status quo strategy** implies that funds are allocated so that the current position can be maintained. The current market share is maintained and no further growth is sought.

Harvesting implies that no further money is spent in the business unit or on the specific product. The cash that would have been invested is reallocated to other business units or products where there is a better chance of attaining future profits.

Divesting occurs when the business unit or products show losses. All activities are then shelved.

15.5.1.2 Functional marketing planning

After strategic marketing planning, the marketing plans must be formulated so that the activities for every business unit or product can be planned to attain the stated marketing objectives. This is known as the formulation of a marketing strategy at functional level. A detailed marketing plan must be developed for every product or brand name. The first part of the marketing plan forms part of the planning process. This is followed by the development of the action programme and the preparation of the budget, which both form part of the implementation phase. Control is the third leg of the management task. Figure 15.4 depicts the marketing plan.

Figure 15.4: Components of a marketing plan

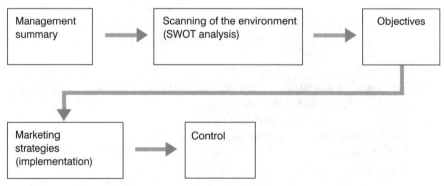

Source: Adapted from Kotler, P. & Armstrong, G., *Marketing: an introduction*, Pearson Education Inc, 1993, p. 3.

The marketing plan entails the following:

- A management summary providing the highlights of the marketing plan
- A discussion of market conditions
- An outline of the opportunities and threats that exist

The next step is the formulation of the marketing objectives. As mentioned previously, the marketing objective relates directly to the primary objective of the business. The primary objective of the business is long-term profit maximisation within the constraints imposed by the environment.

The marketing department, more than the other departments in the business, is closely involved in the achievement of profit, for by selling the business's products, it generates income. It can further contribute to profits by attempting to reduce marketing costs.

Attaining marketing objectives may contribute to the achievement of the primary objective either by effecting cost savings or by generating income. The following are the most important of these objectives:

- **Consumer orientation.** This marketing objective has been discussed as the second principle of the marketing concept. Thus far, we have emphasised repeatedly that the marketing strategy must be based on consumer needs, demands and preferences – for if not, the primary objective cannot be attained.
- **Survival and growth.** This marketing objective is, by implication, part of the long-term dimension of the primary objective. Marketing management must continually strive to survive, even in difficult circumstances. They should also encourage growth by timeously adapting to the ever-changing environment. Environmental scanning and realistic projections of sales may contribute to the attainment of the primary objective.
- **Increase in sales.** An increase in sales is often regarded as a relevant marketing objective because it is easy to monitor changes in sales figures. However, a high sales volume does not necessarily lead to high profits, because the cost of maintaining a high sales volume may be exorbitant, thus eroding profits. Consider, for example, the high costs of intensive distribution, aggressive marketing communication, and the maintenance of low prices.
- **The highest possible market share.** A large market share relative to that of competitors ensures a high sales volume as well as lower unit costs with regard to production and marketing – thereby contributing to profits. Marketers therefore continually strive to increase their market share.
- **Efficiency motive.** Non-profit-seeking businesses strive to maximise efficiency, instead of maximising profitability. However, this motive also applies to profit-seeking businesses, especially in times of economic decline. The efficiency motive has a beneficial effect on the profit position on account of cost savings.
- **Marketing instrument objectives.** Depending on environmental circumstances, other marketing instrument objectives can be set for different target markets, for example:
  - Introducing a new product to consumers
  - Promoting cooperation in the distribution channel
  - Launching a new advertising campaign
  - Creating an image for the product
  - Discouraging competitors from entering the market

It is important to realise that all marketing objectives eventually have to contribute to profit, even if only indirectly.

The next step in the marketing plan entails the formulation of the marketing strategy aimed at an identified target market (discussed in chapter 13), which entails combining the four marketing instruments (product, price, marketing communication and distribution).

15.5.2 Control

A changing environment demands that the implementation of the marketing strategy be controlled on a continuous basis, to ensure that the formulated objectives are attained and, if necessary, to effect changes in the objectives and the marketing strategy. The marketing control process is shown in figure 15.5.

Figure 15.5: The marketing control process

Set objectives	Measure performance	Evaluate performance	Take corrective action
What is our aim?	What is happening at the moment?	Why is this happening?	What can we do to attain the objectives?
• Increase turnover by R1 million	• Turnover decreased by R500 000	• Consumers regard our products as unreliable	• Product modification • TV advertising • Personal selling

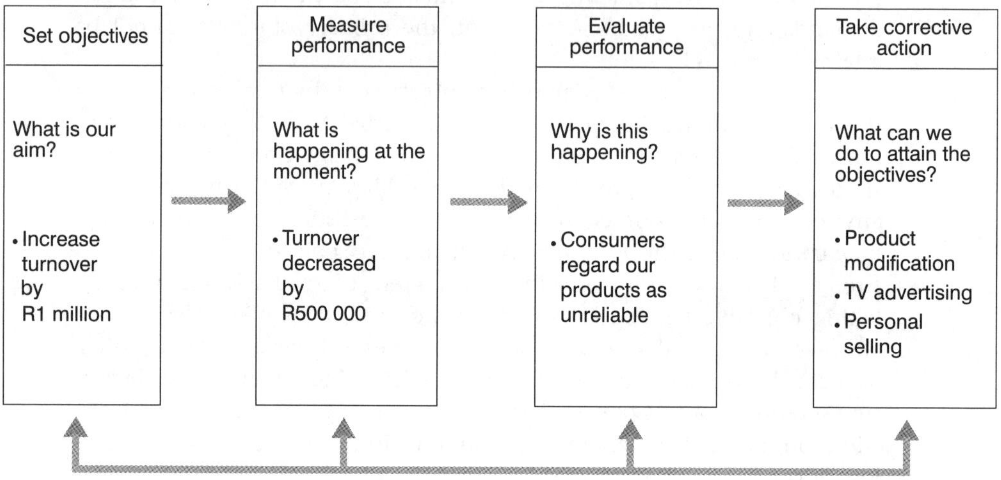

Source: Adapted from Kotler, P. & Armstrong, G., *Marketing: an introduction*, Pearson Education Inc, 1993, p. 52.

Figure 15.5 shows that there is in fact a difference between the set objective (increase sales by R1 million) and what is actually happening in the market (turnover decreased by R500 000. This means that the enterprise is R1,5 million below expected turnover. By conducting marketing research, it is found that the main reason for the sales decline is because of a consumer perception that the product is unreliable. Corrective action implies that minor product modifications are necessary, and that a marketing communication campaign should be implemented to bring the "new improved" product to the attention of consumers.

Applying the concept: marketing planning and control

Differentiation is one of the most profitable business options to use in the marketplace. By differentiating its product or service, a business is effectively saying to the target market that it is not the same as the run-of-the-mill competitors. Because the product or service is perceived to be different, consumers will, hopefully, be prepared to pay more for it. Differentiation is therefore an excellent management technique to counteract price competition and to realise long-term profitability for the business.

15.6 Summary

This chapter focused on the integrated marketing strategy and the management task of marketing. The primary task of marketing management is to plan and carry out the marketing activities and then control them. A specific philosophy underscores the marketing task. Marketing management should adhere to the principles of this philosophy, namely profit maximisation, the satisfaction of consumer needs and preferences, social responsibility and integration. This, rather than misusing the consumer in the short term, should be seen as the long-term objective of marketing management. Marketing management are also closely involved in the process of strategic decision making during the different life cycle phases of the product.

References

1. Kotler, P. & Singh, R, "Marketing warfare in the 1980s", *Journal of Business Strategy*, Vol. 8, No. 3, 1981, p. 30.
2. Durö, R. & Sandström, B., *The basic principles of marketing warfare*, Wiley, Chichester, 1987, p. 143.
3. Seiko's smash, *Business Week*, 5 June 1978, p. 89.
4. Thompson, A.A., & Strickland, A. J., *Strategy formulation and implementation*, 5th edition, Irwin, Homewood, Illinois, 1992, p. 116.
5. Busch, P.S. & Houston, M.J., *Marketing strategic foundations*, Irwin, Homewood, Illinois, 1985, p. 47.
6. Based on Kotler, P. & Armstrong, G., *Principles of marketing*, 9th edition, Prentice Hall, Englewood Cliffs, New Jersey, 2001, p. 73.

16 Public Relations

The purpose of this chapter

Every business has to interact with its environment, and included in this environment are role players that could have a significant influence on the fortunes of the business. This influence could be either to the benefit or the detriment of the business. Some of the role players, such as customers and employees, could have a direct impact. Others, on the other hand, such as the press and government, might have an indirect impact. A well run business will not leave the interactions with these role players up to chance, but will manage them so as to be able ensure the long term success of the business. However, this does not imply that all the interactions with the role players will always be positive, since many businesses have to deal with crises that arise from time to time. The objective is to be proactive in managing the interactions with the role players so as to help the business attain its long term objectives

This chapter introduces the concept of public relations and examines the process of managing the relations with the stakeholders (or publics) of a business. It will also investigate the communications task of the public relations function. Finally, the important topics of social responsibility and business ethics, which are critical in their interactions with the public relations function, will be discussed.

Learning outcomes

The content of this chapter will enable learners to:
- Explain the nature of the functional management area of public relations
- Describe the management process in public relations
- Explain the communications task of public relations
- Identify and describe the issues pertaining to social responsibility and business ethics

16.1 Introduction

In chapter 4 the interaction between a business and the environment within which it operates was discussed, including the numerous relations between the business and such variables in the environment as consumers, competitors, suppliers, the government, and the community. These variables and their relation to the business are examined and analysed to identify potential **opportunities** and **threats** that could affect the profitability of the business.

A business is described as an open system that influences the environment, on the one hand, and is influenced by it, on the other. As an open system in a specific environment, a business maintains close relationships with consumers, shareholders, suppliers, government institutions, several other target audiences (publics) as well as its own employees. The relationship between the business and its publics must be managed so that a favourable corporate image is created. To do this, purposeful communication is essential, and therefore a large part of this chapter is devoted to the communication process, that is, how a business communicates with its employees and its external publics.

In managing public relations, social responsibility and business ethics are of considerable importance. All the functional areas of management are involved in maintaining an ethical code of conduct. The public relations section is closely involved in formulating such a code of conduct, in which practices that are good and correct and others that are wrong and dishonest are spelled out. The way in which the code of conduct is maintained is reflected in the corporate image.

16.2 The nature of public relations

16.2.1 The approach to public relations

One of the tasks of public relations is to create and maintain a favourable public opinion of the business (or a positive image of it). Bringing about good relations requires the performance of numerous activities. There is no agreement in the literature or in practice as to what these activities are or should be. Some experts hold that the management of public relations is a matter of communicating with the external environment and getting publicity; it deals with the manipulation of perception, and with the influencing of opinion inside as well as outside the business. Others say that public relations is a form of propaganda, that it is an attempt to obtain media coverage, or even that public relations operates in the same area as marketing communication. These different approaches to public relations management account for the many and divergent definitions in the literature.

To explain the nature of public relations against the background of these different approaches, one must understand that everything revolves around creating a positive image of the business. To do this, public relations management must help to create a favourable corporate culture, that is, one in which a code of business ethics plays a role. Only then can the public relations practitioner communicate with consumers to reinforce customer loyalty, with suppliers to clear up misunderstandings, or with the public to counter negative perceptions. Employees must also be motivated to demonstrate loyalty as well as enthusiasm for their work. Links with the media are important because the media (newspapers, radio, television) relay communication messages to the various publics.

Public relations management is therefore an interface between a business and its environment: it interprets the mission, programmes and operations of management to its publics; it monitors trends in the business environment and the public perception of the business for management; it gives support to the marketing and other functions of the business; it helps management in its endeavour to satisfy the need for social responsibility.

A favourable corporate image has many advantages, which ultimately influence the business's profitability, survival and growth. These include the following:

- Consumers more readily support a friendly or responsible business that shows some respect for the interests of its community.
- Suppliers more readily give credit for longer periods to reliable businesses.
- Banks more readily lend money to "businesses that don't need it" that is, to reliable borrowers.
- Investors more readily invest in a "good" or "safe" business.
- Governments are more likely to give favourable consideration to requests from "responsible" businesses.
- People like to work for such a business.

16.2.2 Defining public relations

In the light of the discussion on the nature of public relations, the following definition[1] is acceptable because it includes the main elements of the function:

Definition

Public relations is a deliberate, planned and sustained process of communication between a business and its publics for the purpose of obtaining, maintaining or improving good strategic relations and mutual understanding between the organisation and its various publics – both internal and external.

The most important elements of this definition of public relations are the following:

- It is a **deliberate activity**. An analysis of the above definition shows that public relations is a conscious, purposeful activity of business management. Every programme is geared to realising clearly formulated objectives.
- It is a **planned activity**. It is not an incidental process, but an operation that anticipates events, and is prepared for problems and contingencies. It includes a conscious evaluation of all business activities and their influence on the business's image. The management of public relations should act proactively – it should be oriented to the future and always ready for any difficulty or emergency.
- It is a **sustained activity**. It takes account of the fact that the public is in a constant process of change, that people have short memories, and that amid all the numerous matters competing for their attention, consumers easily forget a business unless they are continually kept informed about it. It therefore has a long-term dimension.
- It is a **communication process**. The term public relations presupposes communication between individuals and businesses. Establishing communication channels, especially through the mass media, is therefore a responsibility of public relations. Public relations management needs to have the necessary communication skills to convey information to the business's various publics so that the members will grasp and accept the message and ultimately respond as management wishes them to. This

means that public relations management should include communications experts who, in addition to their knowledge of the principles of communication, should also be familiar with the policy and activities of all the functional areas of the business. Public relations should therefore be part of top management.

- It **deals with publics – both internal and external**. A public is any group that influences the organisation or its operations. Internal publics exist within the organisation, for example, employees and management. External publics exist outside the organisation. Examples of external stakeholders include unions, the media, the community, government, financial institutions, and the general public.

Public relations is pre-eminently – but not exclusively – concerned with the external environment. Of course, all business functions interact with the external environment. The difference between public relations and, for example, marketing, human resources management, finance, and purchasing is that their interaction is confined to a particular segment of the external environment. For example, marketing management concentrates on the consumer market, human resources management on the labour market, financial management on the money market, and purchasing management on the materials market. No restrictions apply to the public relations function, and, in principle, it interacts with the total internal and external environment. In other business functions, the nature of their interaction is based on their separate fundamental objectives. The same is true of the public relations function.

Public relations entails creating and maintaining goodwill towards a business. It is clear from the definition that goodwill is the decisive factor. Ill will is something that everyone prefers to avoid, and this applies in business too. The matter of goodwill and ill will occurs in all environmental markets: consumer, labour and financial. Public relations management concentrates on obtaining goodwill and avoiding ill will in all these markets. It is also important to maintain and improve goodwill once it has been obtained.

Mutual understanding has to be created, fostered and extended. This means that a business needs to understand change in its external environment and constantly endeavour to keep abreast of current opinions, demands, preferences and dislikes in it, so that it can adjust its activities in accordance with them. The converse is also true: a business should try to promote understanding of its actions (and problems). Hence public relations is concerned with obtaining, maintaining and extending mutual understanding.

Profitable growth and survival should be the ultimate objective for all businesses. The overall objective of a business is to maximise profits in the long term. It is clear that public relations is closely involved in this endeavour because it strives to maintain and reinforce public goodwill toward the business.

From another perspective, public relations is defined according to its managerial functions. Public relations evaluates public opinion and identifies the procedures for the planning and implementation of a programme of action directed at achieving goodwill. The Public Relations Institute of South Africa has a very clear code of conduct to ensure that public relations practitioners attempt to attain their objectives in a moral and ethical manner.

16.2.3 The development of public relations as a functional management area

16.2.3.1 The phases in the development process

Public relations, like other business functions, has progressed through a series of developmental phases to the point where it can now be regarded as a fully fledged functional management area. Three such phases can be distinguished, namely:

- The manipulation phase
- The information phase
- The mutual influence phase

During the first phase, public relations was concerned mainly with manipulation. It was a typical technique used by press agents in the 18th century to launch and direct political campaigns. In order to drum up political support for candidates, supporters were not always over-fastidious about telling the truth – something that has caused, and still causes, much damage to the reputation of public relations.

The public became antagonistic, and, in response to its resistance to such methods, public relations management changed tactics, and adopted a policy of providing information about the business. This change began at about the beginning of the twentieth century. By 1910 it had become apparent that businesses did not communicate with the public merely by means of words in newspapers, but also through their policies and actions.

This led to the third phase, that of mutual influence, in which an endeavour was made to win the approval of the public for the actions of the business. It is interesting to note that public relations developed in essentially negative conditions, for example, in a threatening situation or when public support was needed. A good example is the situation in which the image of a business has been harmed among consumers and a specific public relations campaign is launched to improve this image.

In South Africa today, many businesses have a fully-fledged public relations function, with a manager or director at the helm who is a member of top management. SABMiller, for example, has a Public Affairs Manager who becomes the "voice" of the organisation in communicating to the public. This is the angle from which public relations is approached in this book.

In other cases where an appreciation of the importance of public relations has filtered through, the managing director or general manager will often be responsible for the function. A general manager is familiar with the activities of all functional departments, and by virtue of his or her position, comes into direct contact with opinion formers among the external publics and business community. He or she is therefore able to project and establish a favourable image of the business. The question then arises whether he or she has the time to do the job properly.

In a situation where the general manager is responsible for the public relations function, there is usually a special section that assists with image-creation activities. The general manager decides what should be done and acts as the appointed spokesperson to the media. Where a separate public relations manager has senior status, he or she is a member of the top management team and shares in decision making. This manager is then responsible for liaison with the media. In virtually all businesses, media interviews with ordinary employees are frowned upon and often even prohibited. The Springbok rugby team and Bafana Bafana, for example, appoint a senior manager to handle liaison with the media.

PR in non-profit organisations

Increasingly, companies and organisations – right up to the top levels of government – are having to explain the value of what they do, the products, services and jobs they provide, and their contribution to society. Even the President has a spokesperson whose job it is to explain the aim of legislation and presidential actions, as well as liase with media representatives. Many of the different levels of government, from regional to municipal, are finding that good relations with stakeholders is critical to the performance of their tasks.

Source: Marketing Mix, November 1985, p.38.

McDonald's in Moscow: a marketing public relations (MPR) success story

Before opening a branch in Moscow, McDonald's launched a communication campaign which received the broadest publicity any company in the world had ever received at the time, from TV, radio and print coverage in North America to front pages and newscasts in Japan, Europe and the rest of the world. The communication campaign, (The McDonald's magic), was in the form of four stories which introduced McDonald's as a company having fun while running a successful business. The topics of the stories created media interest. The stories were the following:

- The **McDonald's free enterprise story** showed the dramatic contrast between the free enterprise system and the Soviet system.
- The **Crew story** explained the training and work ethic of the McDonald's crew.
- The **Quality story** told how Russian farmers grew potatoes and raised cattle to supply McDonald's and how the food was prepared.
- The **McDonald's leadership story** dealt with McDonald's perseverance and insistence on doing things the McDonald's way.

The campaign proceeded as follows:

- Two and a half years before the opening day in Moscow, a press conference was called to announce the signing of the agreement (the result of negotiations lasting fourteen years).
- The next newsworthy event was the sign-raising ceremony marking the beginning of construction.
- The laying of the cornerstone of the food-production plant, the largest in Eastern Europe, made news and gave McDonald's the opportunity to tell the Quality story.
- The first Russian managers arriving at McDonald's in Oak Brook, Illinois, to be trained at the "Hamburger University", created worldwide interest.

- Just before the opening of the restaurant in Moscow, it was announced that 27 000 Russians had applied for the 6 000 jobs at McDonald's. This really was NEWS!
- Approximately 400 journalists attended the opening day and the event was the main news item on television and on front pages worldwide. British television showed thousands of Russians queuing for the "ultimate happiness symbol and their first taste of glasnost – a hamburger!"
- A month after the opening, McDonald's Moscow sold their millionth hamburger and served about 50 000 people daily. Nobody knows how many extra hamburgers were sold worldwide as a direct result of the publicity.
- McDonald's launched a television advertisement in the USA, "Magic in Moscow", showing scenes of the opening day. The advertisement received wide publicity.

Source: Adapted from Harris, T.L., *The marketer's guide to public relations: how today's top companies are using new PR to gain a competitive edge*, © Thomas Harris, Thomas L. Harris & Co., 1991, pp. 165-169.

Many non-profit organisations and even government organisations have realised that the public demands accountability for what they do. Many of these organisations have a public relations department. A spokesperson will often participate in high-level talks on television and release statements on public affairs. The emphasis is usually on transparency and honesty. Non-profit organisations such as the SPCA and the Red Cross have senior representatives of management who appear in the media on a regular basis.

With increasing emphasis on the necessity for strategic planning in a changing and turbulent environment, maintaining close cooperation between the public relations department and the marketing department is imperative. Kotler refers to this cooperation as megamarketing.[2] Advertising agencies that previously handled only clients' advertising campaigns now also offer PR services in a total package. They are thus involved in the total communication campaigns of clients, including media advertising, displays, publicity, and sponsorships. In this way, synergy between communication media is obtained, reinforcing the message while avoiding conflicting communication contents.

The importance of effective public relations

Effective public relations contributes to the marketing effort by maintaining a hospitable social and political environment. Likewise, successful marketing and satisfied customers make good relations with others easier to build and maintain.

It has been estimated that brand-related public relations is the fastest growing segment in the public relations industry in the United States. The estimate is that up to 70% of the revenue of public relations firms comes from marketing-related business. In fact, thirteen of the fifteen largest public relations firms in the United States have been acquired by advertising agency conglomerates.

Source: Adapted from Duncan,T., *IMC: using advertising and promotions to build brands*, McGraw-Hill, New York, 2002, p. 544.

Writers refer to this development as the MPR function. In addition, the most recent development in marketing thought emphasises the need for close relations between management and the internal and external groups with which it should communicate (see the example of McDonald's in the box on pp. 357–358).

16.2.3.2 Reasons for the development of public relations

Some reasons have already been touched on in the previous section. The following changes have, to a greater or lesser extent, influenced the rate of development:

- The development of trade unionism all over the world, as well as increasing labour disputes and strikes, show the need to forge links with labour markets.
- The image of consumerism in the West, and also pressure from consumer groups, demonstrate the need for establishing links with consumer markets.
- Increasing competition has emphasised the benefits of a positive corporate image.
- There has been increasing hostility, particularly among young people, towards large businesses, the profit motive, and indeed the whole free-market system. This demands a new frankness about the activities of profit-seeking businesses.
- There is a continued awareness of the social responsibilities of businesses (in contrast to the effort to make a profit at all costs). This has led to acceptance that a business should make some contribution to the well-being of the community in which it makes its profits.
- A theory of public relations has been developed, and textbooks by acknowledged authorities have appeared, focusing the attention of management on the public relations function and what it can achieve.
- The development of communication media such as newspapers, magazines, radio stations and television channels has emphasised the need for competence in communications, and at the same time created opportunities for more and better communications with the world at large. The Internet has revolutionised the way a business communicates with its public.
- There have been developments at international level regarding multinational corporations, and these have shown how essential it is to promote goodwill and a favourable image.
- The need for economic growth and the creation of new jobs means businesses must be more sensitive to public disapproval.
- South Africa's continued bad reputation for poor service creates an opportunity for responsible businesses with an image of reliability.

> "Communication is the lubricant that makes it possible for change to take place in an atmosphere of understanding and acceptance. The need for effective communication has never been more pressing."
>
> *MARKETING MIX, NOVEMBER 1995, P. 38.*

16.2.3.3 What public relations is not

One should always consider what falls outside the scope of public relations:

- Public relations is not part of marketing communication, although the tasks of the two departments sometimes overlap in the areas of advertising and publicity.

Applying the concept: public relations

Thomas Madibane is the proprietor of a small business that provides a tour service to tourists who want to visit the Pilanesberg Game Reserve. He is talking to his friend, Valusela, about his business. Valusela asks, "Thomas, do you use public relations in your business at all? I hear it can be effective in helping you create a good image." "Oh yes," replies Thomas, "I use it a lot. I always answer the tourist's questions when they ask me things. Of course, this only happens when I'm on tour with them."

"Is that all you do?" asks Valusela. "Don't you do other things to communicate with those who might be interested?"

"No," replies Thomas, "Besides, I'm too busy to go around doing too many other things. If there are any requests for information I let my clerk, Thandi, answer the query."

Is Thomas really practising public relations in his business? Refer to the definition of public relations (see section 16.2.2) in answering this question.

Let us now consider the above in relation to the following key elements of public relations:

• **A deliberate activity.** Public relations is a purposeful activity, with every action geared towards achieving clearly formulated objectives. Thomas is not adhering to this, as he only responds to requests.

• **A planned activity.** The public relations process means that managers have prepared and are acting proactively. The approach of Thomas is ad hoc and purely responsive.

• **A sustained activity.** A business must continually interact with and inform its publics, as public relations is a long-term process. Thomas only responds to questions when he is "on tour", which means very little happens when he is not on tour. This is clearly not a sustained activity, but something that happens only once in a while.

• **A communication process.** This implies that communication channels have been established and that the staff responsible for public relations activities have the necessary communication skills. It is highly unlikely that Thandi has been properly trained in public relations and communication skills. In fact, it appears that Thomas himself is sadly lacking in the necessary skills and knowledge to use effective public relations correctly in his business!

- The public relations department is not a charitable organisation, even if charity often contributes to an image of involvement and responsibility.
- Public relations is not part of the human resources department, although the labour relations and human resources department and the public relations department are both interested in conditions in the labour market.
- Public relations does not necessarily mean currying favour through entertainment and parties, although these are often necessary to show goodwill toward certain groups.
- Public relations is not intended to put up a false front behind which the defects of a business can be hidden.
- Public relations does not mean employing attractive young women to put guests in a good mood, although attractive and agreeable people are always an asset when dealing with important people.
- Public relations is not there to think up foolish and expensive ways of wasting money.

- Public relations is not there exclusively to put out fires and save a business from difficult situations, although it may sometimes be called upon to do so.

16.3 Public relations management

16.3.1 The management task

Against the above background regarding the nature and development of the public relations function, it is clear that the management of public relations is indeed important for the profitable survival and growth of a business and therefore needs careful consideration. Planning, organising, leading and controlling public relations activities are discussed separately in the following sections, keeping in mind, however, that the management of public relations is a continuous process. Control over public relations activities provides, for example, new inputs to further planning, as indicated in figure 16.1.

Figure 16.1: Steps in public relations management

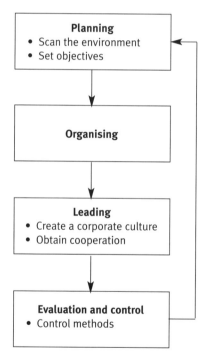

Every project or action programme undertaken by the public relations department should be managed. When a special event (for example, a reception) is planned, information must be gathered, objectives set, responsible people appointed to perform specific tasks, and a budget established. Control is also important to ensure that nothing happens during the reception to harm the image of the business.

Figure 16.1 shows the steps in managing public relations activities. The arrow shows that control methods lead to a new planning phase. The steps in figure 16.1 are discussed in the following sections.

16.3.2 Planning public relations activities

16.3.2.1 Scanning the environment

Information on environmental variables is crucial for planning. Scanning involves secondary and primary, as well as internal and external research.

Secondary information that may be used in planning can be obtained from government and professional publications, libraries, newspapers, trade periodicals, the Internet and reports. There is, however, also internal information available, such as sales reports and the annual financial report. Information files can also be useful in preparing speeches, reports and brochures, and, prior to embarking on advertising campaigns, exhibitions and special projects. The public relations practitioner should also be aware of new products launched by the business, any planned big expansions, and threatened strikes by employees. It often happens in practice that questions that cannot be answered by other departments are referred to the public relations division. Editors of newspapers and compilers of radio and TV programmes make use of the public relations information service as a source. The public relations department should therefore be up to date not only with changing external environmental variables, but also with internal developments.

The Foundation for Human Rights campaign

Research conducted during 1999 on behalf of the Foundation for Human Rights showed that at grass roots level at least half of all South Africans did not know their rights under the new Constitution. They were aware of the Bill of Rights, but had a poor understanding of its contents and implications. Awareness of institutions to help citizens, such as the Public Protector, was non-existent, and there was also low awareness of issues such as disability, immigrants, and rights of people living with HIV/Aids.

On the basis of this, emphasis was placed on informing the target publics on three aspects: the role of the Foundation, the basic rights of every South African, and the rights to redress where human rights abuses are suffered. Media liaison was critical in drawing attention to and coverage of human rights days, and the publication of features on human rights. The corporate identity of the Foundation was redesigned and emphasis was placed on human rights events of the Foundation and also non-governmental organisations (NGOs).

Source: Adapted from Rensburg, R. & Cant, M., *Public relations: South African perspectives*, Heinemann, Johannesburg, 2002, pp. 87-96.

Ad hoc research is conducted internally to obtain primary information on employees' opinions on specific issues, or externally to determine public opinion and the perception of the business's image. All information thus gathered must be systematised and processed, and be readily available to assist management in decision making.

Intensive analysis of publics, both external and internal, will indicate the special characteristics of various publics as well as their opinion makers. This information is necessary for the correct formulation of the message to be addressed to a particular public. The question to be answered is: Who are the people most important to our organisation? From this may follow a wide-ranging classification, such as employees, shareholders, dealers, suppliers, educational institutions, government, consumers, competitors, communications media, financial institutions, welfare organisations, and business and professional associations.

Figure 16.2 shows key publics for a multinational corporation such as Anglo American Corporation or SABMiller.

Figure 16.2: Twenty key publics of a typical multinational corporation

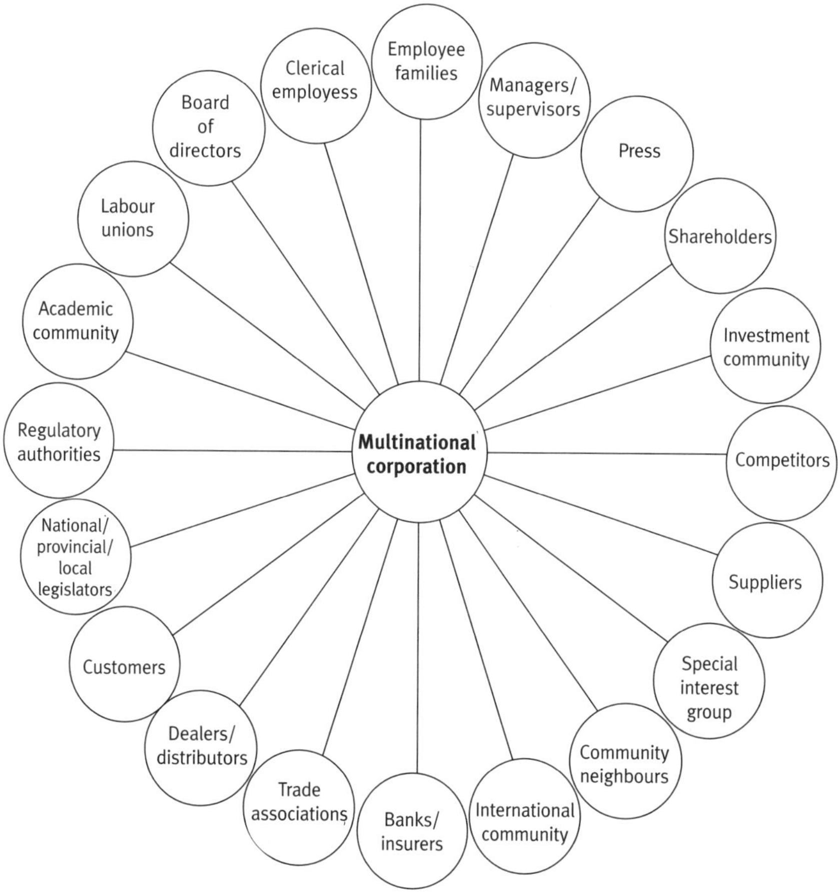

Source: Adapted from Seitel, F.P., *The practice of public relations*, Pearson Education Inc, 2001, p. 12.

The public relations function is aimed at specific publics, and the complexity of external groups points to the necessity for deliberate and planned research. Each group has a certain relationship with the business, and has an interest in it. For example, employees want employment and wages; shareholders, dividends; consumers, good products and services; the government, taxes; distributors and dealers, profits; suppliers, orders; educators and the community, financial support. The diverse interests of external groups must be identified.

Every business has to decide which of the publics is important to it. Few businesses have enough time or resources to keep in touch with all the possible publics. Nor is it always necessary for the public relations department to do so. For example, information about consumers can be obtained from the marketing department, about suppliers from the purchasing department, and about financial institutions from the finance department. Public relations should cooperate with all functional departments, taking care not to trespass on specialised areas.

16.3.2.2 Setting objectives for public relations

The objectives of public relations have already been partly explained in the definition and include the following:
- Demonstrating the social involvement of the business in an effective way
- Promoting a positive image of the business
- Bringing about mutual esteem and understanding between the business and external groups through effective communication
- Ensuring that the goodwill of external groups is obtained and preserved
- Preventing the image of the business from being harmed, and its operations from being impaired by dissatisfaction

Specific communication objectives are determined by whatever public relations programme is being launched as well as by the situation. Such objectives might be:
- To bring new ventures of the business to the attention of the publics
- To correct negative publicity
- To get "free" publicity for the business through press releases about newsworthy events
- To try to gain the goodwill of a certain public by means of sponsorship
- To counteract public resentment of certain actions taken by the business by showing willingness to listen to accusations and complaints
- To promote the image of the business in the eyes of potential employees

---

Richard's Bay Minerals and St Lucia

In responding to the crisis facing Richard's Bay Minerals (RBM) over its controversial plans for mining at St Lucia, the firm set out a few simple objectives:
- Create effective internal and external communication
- Position RBM as an organisation able to create a balance between conservation and essential economic development
- Communicate the facts about St Lucia

Source: Adapted from Lubbe, B.A. & Puth, G.E., *Public relations in South Africa*, Butterworth, Durban, 1994, p. 89.

16.3.3 Organising

16.3.3.1 Public relations as part of top management

The approach in this book is that public relations is a fully fledged functional management area and that the public relations manager is on an equal footing with top managers, such as in marketing, purchasing and human resources departments. Top management takes the strategic decisions that must be implemented at functional level. Where public relations is regarded as a fully fledged functional management area, it follows that an organisational structure must be designed for it, with the various public relations activities grouped together under the leadership of a public relations manager. Precisely how the department is organised differs from one business to the next, and is influenced by factors such as the number of people, the clients or external groups to be served, and geographical position. Figure 16.3 shows a typical organisation chart for public relations.

Figure 16.3: The organisational structure in a typical public relations department

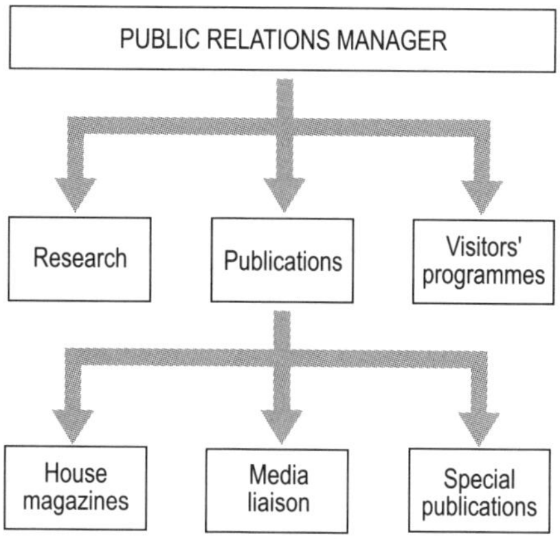

There are various advantages in a well-designed public relations department that functions at top management level. Here the public relations manager has personal and participative relations with other managers and subordinates; is familiar with the relationships between various departments and between employer and employees; is familiar with the undercurrents and knows key staff; knows the conservatives and the liberals, as well as those whose personal ambitions or convenience matter more to them than the welfare of the business. Because of his or her position in the business and commitment to it, the public relations officer is constantly available, and can carry out all manner of public relations duties. If something unexpected and potentially disastrous should happen, he or she is within easy reach for consultation with top management, will have established reliability and credibility with the press, and can save top management the embarrassment of communicating with the media by means of a consultant called in from outside.

The main disadvantage of a public relations department is the danger that the manager may simply come to agree with all the business's activities, and whose objectivity may be suspect because of loyalty to the business's products, its people and, most of all, its top management.

16.3.3.2 Public relations as a staff function

Public relations may also operate as a staff function. In this case the head of public relations is usually responsible only to the general manager, is not a member of the top management team, and has no line responsibility. All decisions are channelled through the general manager, and such a situation can make coordination between the various heads of departments difficult.

16.3.3.3 Public relations consultants from outside

Instead of a public relations department in the business, management sometimes prefers to use independent outside consultants. Consultants provide the necessary services to smaller businesses that do not have the expertise or resources. External consultants can act on the same level as top management and are more objective.

There are several public relations consulting firms in South Africa, mostly with their head offices in the big cities. Most consultants are members of the Public Relations Institute of South Africa (PRISA). One of the Institute's aims is the maintenance and improvement of professional standards and practices of external public relations consultants.

The reasons why the services of independent public relations consultants are used include the following:
- A business may lack the necessary knowledge and experience.
- The head office may be so far removed from communication and financial centres as to make liaison difficult.
- Public relations consultants usually have a wide range of useful contacts in the business sector and the mass media.
- Public relations consultants often offer the services of experienced specialists who earn salaries that a small business could not afford to pay.
- A business may have its own public relations department, but may occasionally need highly specialised advice.
- Critical matters concerning the general image of the business often require the independent, objective judgement of an outsider.
- An emergency situation can compel a business to call in public relations consultants from outside to help solve the problem.

Large consultancies are able to employ highly specialised staff, such as writers of "spots", editors of trade magazines, and compilers of radio and TV programmes. They also often employ trained researchers, education experts, legal advisers, sociologists, fund-raisers, economists, photographers and artists. The latest development is that advertising agencies provide this service. The result is that the marketing communication programme and the public relations programme are integrated and presented to the client as a package. An integrated programme has obvious advantages and virtually no disadvantages.

16.3.4 Leading the public relations activities

Public relations managers should play a leading role in all management decisions concerned with creating an image. They also have to make recommendations to top management concerning ways in which a positive image can be conveyed. They play an important role in establishing a positive corporate culture in which everyone will enthusiastically cooperate to achieve their objectives.

Creating a corporate culture

David Ogilvy, a well-known advertising expert and writer, described the corporate culture of his advertising agency as follows:

A nice place to work:
- Work is a happy experience for our personnel.
- We treat our people like human beings.
- We train people to make the best of their talents.
- We like people with good manners.
- We like people who are honest and free of prejudice.
- We admire people who work hard and are thorough.
- We despise office politicians, toadies, bullies and pompous asses.

Our attitude towards clients:
- The creative function is at the top of our list of priorities.
- We take pride in our work – but we are not neurotic.
- The client has the final say – after all, it is his money.
- We do not mislead consumers.

Our peculiarities:
- We have a habit of always being dissatisfied with our performance, and always try to improve.
- Our reports are well written and easy to read.
- We are revolted by complicated jargon.
- We take our Christmas get-togethers seriously.
- Our far-flung enterprise is held together by a network of personal friendships.
- Some of us write books.
- Most of our offices are decorated in white and red, our corporate colours.

Our *obiter dicta* (mottoes):
- "We sell – or else . . ."
- "The consumer is not an idiot. She is your wife."
- "We prefer the discipline of knowledge to the anarchy of ignorance."

A public relations department with strong leadership can develop into an undisputed competitive advantage, and an act that is hard to follow.

Source: Adapted from Ogilvy, D., *The unpublished David Ogilvy*, © 1968. The Ogilvy Group Inc.

By permission of Crown Publishers, a division of Random House USA.

Figure 16.4: Examples of public relations activities

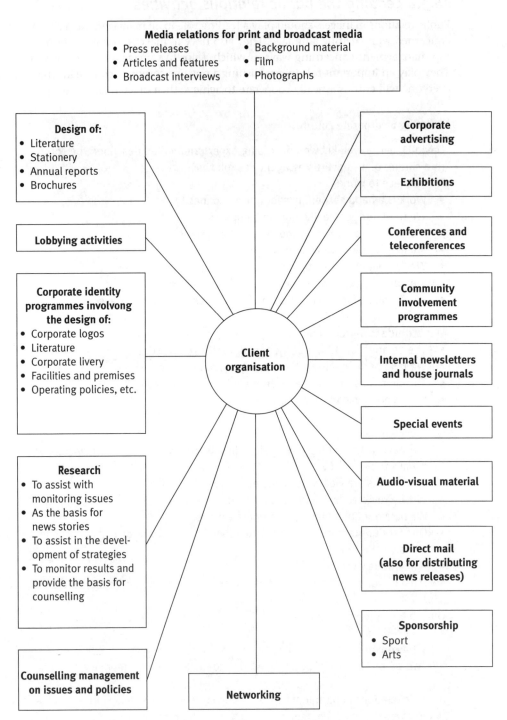

Media relations for print and broadcast media
- Press releases
- Articles and features
- Broadcast interviews
- Background material
- Film
- Photographs

Design of:
- Literature
- Stationery
- Annual reports
- Brochures

Lobbying activities

Corporate identity programmes involvong the design of:
- Corporate logos
- Literature
- Corporate livery
- Facilities and premises
- Operating policies, etc.

Research
- To assist with monitoring issues
- As the basis for news stories
- To assist in the development of strategies
- To monitor results and provide the basis for counselling

Counselling management on issues and policies

Client organisation

Corporate advertising

Exhibitions

Conferences and teleconferences

Community involvement programmes

Internal newsletters and house journals

Special events

Audio-visual material

Direct mail (also for distributing news releases)

Sponsorship
- Sport
- Arts

Networking

Source: Adapted from Skinner, J.C. & Von Essen, L.M., *The handbook of public relations*, Oxford University Press (SA), 1999, p. 12.

By making use of internal channels of communication such as a house journal, information concerning policy directives, management decisions, business decisions and other related messages can be conveyed to the functional departments.

Corporate culture is the sum total of the values, symbols and traditions of the business as well as the ways in which it is led, people are motivated, communication takes place, and conflict is handled. This is obviously not the responsibility of the public relations department only, but of the whole management team. It is, however, an area that requires much input from the public relations department. All the activities indicated in figure 16.4 (see p. 368) are aimed at creating and maintaining a positive corporate climate, as indicated in the example of the David Ogilvie agency (see p. 367).

16.3.5 Evaluation and control of the public relations programme

Although public relations managers, like all other managers, must exercise control over the activities of their personnel, their real task is to evaluate public relations programmes. One of the problem areas of public relations management is the absence of criteria by which to measure the total success or failure of a programme. The following are some methods that could measure the impact of a public relations programme:

- The sheer amount of publicity accepted by the media in itself gives some indication of the exposure obtained (for example, two 20-line exposures in newspapers, coverage in the main news on TV and radio, and an article with photographs in a financial journal on the opening of a new plant). Exposure does not, however, necessarily mean that all of the target audience has in fact been reached and has understood the message.
- Readability tests can be carried out to ascertain whether the reports were sufficiently readable and therefore intelligible. However, this does not necessarily mean that any of the publics have accepted the message.
- Listener research gives some indication of the number of people who watched or heard a particular radio or TV programme. Respondents can be asked to keep a daily record of their listening and watching times, or the times can be noted electronically.
- Attitudes can be gauged by surveys, using questionnaires, and rating scales, to determine people's responses to reports or programmes.

All these methods of evaluation are difficult, expensive and time-consuming, and the researchers need specialised knowledge, not only to carry out the research but also to interpret the results. The public relations manager should have a reasonable knowledge of research methods, and should apply them regularly, or else employ an agency, so that there is control over public relations activities.

A budget is used to plan and control the activities of the public relations department. The objective-and-task method is often used in budget allocations. A budget should be set for each separate programme of action. Deviations from these allocations must be investigated and corrected regularly.

Figure 16.5: Systematic evaluation of a communication message

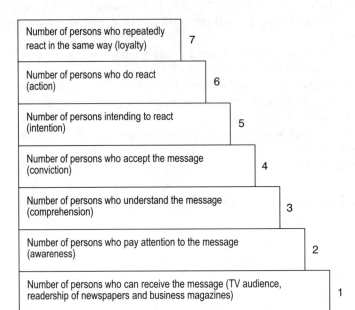

Source: Adapted from Cutlip, S.M., et al., *Effective public relations*, 6th edition, Pearson Education Inc, 1985, p. 196.

Large businesses tend not to reconsider budget allocations, but use the same budget each year, perhaps because it is easier to do so. Budget allocations should, however, be reconsidered for each new venture. The so-called "zero-based budget" is recommended, as it provides for the planning and launching of new programmes and campaigns called for by recent developments and problems.

Evaluation of a communication message is done systematically, as indicated in figure 16.5. The figure shows that even if the message succeeds in reaching many people, its impact decreases until only a few people react in the way the message intended.

Consider, for example, a communication message aimed at improving the image of business X, which received bad publicity because of fraud. The communication message is contained in a press release as well as a television advertisement in which someone from top management is the spokesperson. Although the message will reach many people, not all of them are likely to believe the message, and still fewer will demonstrate their loyalty by continuing to patronise business X.

Control therefore involves a great deal more than a mere survey or an audit – it is a continuous process that should enable managers of public relations to take corrective steps wherever necessary, and to bring about, maintain and improve relations between the business and its environment.

Applying the concept: publics and objectives to achieve

Assume you have been given a project to identify all the possible publics that a large retail chain-store group (such as Shoprite or Pick 'n Pay) should interact with. What would the important publics be, and what would you try to achieve with each of them? In order to answer these questions, we have to begin by identifying the important publics (see section 16.3.2.1). Some of the important publics are: employees, customers, the financial community, suppliers, government authorities, local communities, and the media.

What would be a good objective to achieve with each of these publics? We have to establish objectives that would improve the image of the group with each of these important publics. Possible objectives to consider include:

- **Employees.** Establish good internal communication channels, generate awareness of, and commitment to, being consumer oriented.
- **Customers.** Make sure they are aware of

the business's efforts to provide after-sales service, an environmentally friendly product range, as well as efforts to look after customers' interests.

- **The financial community.** Communicate the new growth and investment strategy and make them aware of the business's financial performance.
- **Suppliers.** Communicate that cooperation is required to meet the need for environmentally friendly products at a cost effective price.
- **Government authorities.** Try to influence legislation on recyclable packaging and the use of products bearing environmentally friendly logos or trademarks.
- **Local communities.** Communicate an anti-pollution strategy and the business's efforts at providing environmentally friendly products. Emphasise the extent of local community involvement.
- **Media.** Communicate overall group strategy and performance objectives to establish group as financially sound.

16.4 The communication programme

16.4.1 The nature of communication

The principles of communication are universal and applicable to all levels of life. Humans communicate by means of sounds and gestures. The most common communications methods in the business world are spoken and written words. The Internet, however, may change this. Non-verbal communication methods can also be used to convey certain messages. The purpose of communication is to convey a message in such a way that the receiver reacts as the sender intended.

Communication involves the transmission of ideas, attitudes and thoughts from one person to another. People can communicate through visible behaviour without uttering a word (non-verbal communication), for example, expressing anger or irritation by a shrug of their shoulders, the tap of heels as they walk away, the waving of arms, and so on. Other forms of non-verbal communication are pictures, graphs and statistical equations.

Communication is a process whereby one person – the communicator (or encoder) – conveys a particular message to another – the receiver (or decoder). Of course, the communicator has to formulate the message so that the receiver clearly understands its content and purpose. Furthermore, practically all communication is intended to produce a response in the receivers. It is not enough for them to grasp the content correctly – they must also perform the appropriate action. If a mother says to her child "Tidy up your room", it is not enough for the child to grasp the meaning – he or she also has to react physically and actually begin to tidy up. It is the task of the public relations department to act as a transmitter of messages aimed at many kinds of receivers. The public relations department tries to induce a particular group to respond in a specific way when a message is addressed to it.

Communication also involves feedback. The child communicates with his or her mother with a vigorous shake of the head. She interprets the signal as meaning that the child is unwilling to tidy up, and in turn makes an appropriate response.

The public relations department has to ensure that the audience correctly receives and interprets messages or signals sent to it, and that the proper response is made. Effective mutual communication is possible only if both parties – that is, sender and receiver – in turn correctly formulate and interpret messages. All the activities of the public relations department should be tested in accordance with the operation of the communication process.

16.4.2 The communication model

Figure 16.6 (see p. 373) shows the components of the communication model from the aspect of public relations management. Each of the components will now be discussed in greater detail (refer to figure 16.6 for clarification).

16.4.2.1 Communicator

Humans have a natural need to exchange ideas and opinions and, when they do so, they try to convey a message to someone who can understand it. Normally this means the structuring of an idea in the mind, and its transmission in the form of speech to somebody else. Speech, however, constitutes only a small proportion of communication. People also communicate by the manner in which they speak, how they sound, their appearance, or by whatever actions or gestures accompany their words. Conveying a message therefore includes both conscious and unconscious elements. "Conscious transmission" means the deliberate attempt to convey an idea, while "unconscious transmission" means the unintentional conveying of information.

The sender has to be a credible communicator – in other words, the receiver needs to have confidence in the sender and respect for his or her competence with regard to the subject matter. Interpersonal skills, as shown in figure 16.6, are particular skills that the communicator has to possess in interpersonal communication. We often say, "Unable to work with people", of someone who lacks interpersonal skills. Environmental factors (social climate) also influence the communication process (aggressive workers do not listen to the explanations of even a popular manager).

Figure 16.6: The communication model

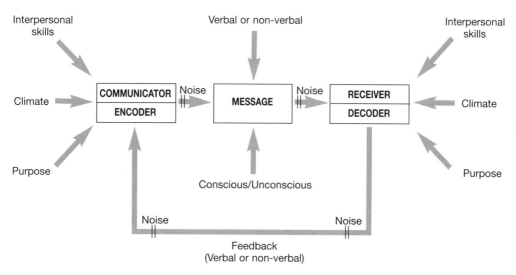

Source: Adapted from Lubbe, B.A. & Puth, C., *Public relations in South Africa: a management reader*, Heinemann (SA), 1995, p. 61.

16.4.2.2 Receiver

Communication occurs only if there is a receiver for the message transmitted. Messages are received not only through the sense of hearing, but also through the senses of sight, smell and touch. In the course of their daily routine, people continually receive both intentional and unintentional signals from all manner of sources about them. As with the communicator, the receiver's interpersonal skills and circumstances affect the process of communication. Messages should be composed to take all this into account.

Note that "noise" gets in the way of receiving the message. Noise is anything that interferes with the reception of the message. It may be something that distracts attention, or competitive actions (such as advertising) by other businesses.

The receiver is usually not a single person, and in the business world mainly comprises a group of people referred to as a target audience. The target audience can be employees, a specific group of consumers, shareholders, or the public at large.

16.4.2.3 Message

The message is the idea or information being transmitted. There are two kinds of messages: verbal (spoken or written) and non-verbal (that is, all other forms by which information can be conveyed, such as symbols). Figure 16.7 (see p. 374) provides examples of these.

The message has to make sense to the receiver, and must have reference to his or her situation and system of values. It must be simply composed, and carry the same meaning for both communicator and receiver. The message must be sent via suitable channels (for example, radio, television, the Internet or newspapers). The most effective channel for transmitting a message is face-

Figure 16.7: Non-verbal communication

A formula

$$\sigma = \frac{\sqrt{\Sigma x^2}}{N}$$

σ = the symbol for the standard deviation

$\sqrt{}$ = the symbol for the square root

Σ = the symbol meaning "the sum of"

x = scores

x^2 = scores squared ($x \times x$)

N = the number of scores

A warning sign

A graph

Source: Based on Perry, C. & Pendleton, W., *Successful small business management*, Pitman, Melbourne, 1987, p. 152.

A brand logo

Sanlam

© Sanlam (SA)

Body language

Source: Based on Perry, C. & Pendleton, W., *Successful small business management*, Pitman, Melbourne, 1987, p. 145.

Gestures

Source: Based on Adey, A.D. & Andrew, M.G., *Getting it right: the manager's guide to business communication*, Juta, Cape Town, 1990, p. 352.

to-face communication. Both words and gestures can be combined in the message. The receiver is virtually compelled to pay attention. This is why someone from top management in business X (see the example in section 16.4.1) appeared personally on television to make a statement about the bad publicity received as a result of fraud.

The message should be formulated in such a way that it engages the receivers' attention, arouses their interest and persuades them to respond. The composition of a message with persuasive impact is a task that requires specialised knowledge.

16.4.2.4 Feedback

For both participants to be fully involved in communication, the communicator of the message needs to know what effect it has on the receiver or target audience. Feedback is the response of the receiver to the information that he or she has received, and may be verbal or non-verbal. Feedback ensures that the cycle of communication is completed by linking the communicator and the receiver, thereby keeping the process dynamic. In face-to-face communication feedback is received immediately. The communicator can see the effect of the message and can then reformulate it if necessary. For example, the general manager of business organisation X does not know what the reaction of the audience is. Did they hear the message? Understand it? Believe it? These questions can only be answered after evaluation research has been conducted. Television viewers have to be questioned on their reactions, for only then can the message be reformulated.

It is interesting to test the activities of the public relations department through the operation of the communication model. What does the business propose to say to whom at a reception it is planning, in a news report sent out for publication, or when it sponsors a sporting event? What feedback is expected?

16.4.3 The communications media

Communications media are the channels used to convey the communication message. The spoken word, the printed word, sight and sound symbols, the electronic word, images on the Internet, and special events are examples of the communications media used by the public relations department to transmit messages.

16.4.3.1 The spoken word

The spoken word is used in face-to-face communication and is probably the most important method of communication in any business. Both communicator and receiver must speak the "same language" for the one to understand the other. In South Africa effective communication is difficult with so many languages, but even without a language problem misunderstandings frequently occur because people interpret communication messages differently.

The public relations department also uses the spoken word to communicate with external publics. This is usually done by means of news conferences, panel discussions and interviews, often on radio and television. In all these cases communicators must have the ability and fluency to deliver the message, even under pressure. They must give the right answers in arguments, and when confronted by difficult questions. In a news conference, a carefully prepared statement is read to reporters to ensure that the message is correctly conveyed. In question-and-answer sessions following the statement, the public relations officer must be diplomatic and able to talk "off the cuff". This makes it clear why the choice of a suitable spokesperson is so important, and why ordinary employees cannot be allowed to communicate freely with the media.

16.4.3.2 The printed media

Newspapers, magazines and company publications are important printed media for the written word. Receivers can read (and try to understand) the message, while carefully selected pictures (illustrations) are used to support and reinforce a non-verbal message.

- **Newspapers.** There are many morning, evening and Sunday papers available in urban and most rural areas. They appear in different languages and are read by a diverse audience. News reports are rigorously selected, and it is by no means easy for the public relations department to get its press releases accepted. Favourable mention of a business or its activities will be obtained only if the items are really newsworthy. Good relations with the press have to be cultivated, as it is the opinion of journalists and editors that will determine the placing of news items. The distribution of newspapers is well organised, and they are available in virtually every city and village on the day of publication.

    Besides numerous urban and national papers such as *The Star*, the *Sunday Times* and *Business Day*, there are also regional or local papers, for example, the *Pretoria News* and the *Sowetan*. Their purpose is to provide news about events and conditions in their immediate locality, and they are therefore generally very popular. Such publications are excellent media for public relations because they are usually willing to publish news items about the activities of local business entrepreneurs or notable personalities.

- **Magazines.** A great number and variety of magazines exist. The following types normally appear weekly, fortnightly or monthly, and are aimed at particular readers:
    - General magazines with articles on a variety of topics of general interest and a wide public readership
    - Magazines aimed at a particular section of the public, for example, men (*Men's Health*) or women (*Fair Lady, True Love*)
    - Specialised publications for those interested in particular sports, or with specific interests (health-conscious people like to read *Longevity*; outdoor-oriented people read *Getaway*)
    - Professional journals read by academics, doctors, lawyers, farmers, engineers, and so on (business people, for example, read the *Financial Mail*)

- **Company publications.** A wide range of publications are used: handbills, brochures, annual reports, news sheets, books, road maps, guides, directories, recipe books, posters, wall charts, photographs, pictures, pocketbooks, desk diaries and, in some cases, personal newsletters or circulars. Annual reports and newsletters constitute particularly effective means of conveying news about a business and its activities. It is the job of the public relations department to issue such publications, with the requisite input from other departments. The purpose of these publications is to obtain goodwill or to create a favourable corporate image.

The publication of annual financial statements is prescribed by law for public companies, and this has given rise to a highly competitive aspect of public relations, as companies vie with one another to bring out the most comprehensive and attractive report. Besides information about the year's activities, such a report contains photographs, diagrams and graphics, as well as information about notable achievements, difficulties, expectations, forecasts, expansions and developments. Its main purpose is to influence shareholders and investors positively.

The purpose of newsletters is to provide information about a business, its employees and its activities to various publics. Some newsletters are intended chiefly to promote a sense of solidarity among employees, and are therefore directed entirely at them. Such newsletters contain news about the employees themselves, their interests and achievements, and employees also learn about the business and its activities. Newsletters can also be used to reach other target audiences.

A good example is Eskom's use of its company newsletter to carry important information and to demonstrate its responsibility to its employees. The method used was newsworthy enough for newspapers to comment on, and thus publicity was obtained, as shown below.

Eskom employees receive a condom in the newsletter

Eskom employees were intrigued when, on a colourful cover page of the company's newsletter, a brightly coloured arrow led to a condom in a purple wrapper, pasted on the "I" of "AIDS". About 43 000 newsletters were distributed countrywide to Eskom employees.

Source: Translated from an article in *Beeld*, 18 November 1995, p. 4.

16.4.3.3 Sight and sound

The most effective method of conveying a message combines sight and sound, because receivers can see what is happening while sounds (like words and their sound effects) support and reinforce the message.

- **Radio and television.** Just as the public press is the most important medium for the written word, radio and television are the most important media for sound and picture communications. Today practically everybody owns a radio, and most households have a TV set too. The influence of these media is therefore as great as or even greater than that of printed media. The impact of TV is felt nationwide, while that of radio is both national and regional. The advent of television may have reduced the impact of radio to some extent, but it would be a mistake to underestimate its importance. Some people even prefer radio to TV, while others might be unable to watch TV because they are working or travelling.

    The public relations department can use radio and TV as communication media in three ways to transmit messages:

- It can present prestige advertisements, designed to build a business's image and to make its brands known to the public.
- It can provide news reports, for example, when there are notable achievements, or newsworthy events take place.
- A public relations officer might appear on news reviews or participate in discussion programmes in which newsworthy topics are discussed at length.

- **Films and videos.** Another way of bringing the activities of a business to the attention of the general public is to sponsor documentary films or videos, usually shown on TV, or in cinemas as a supporting feature. Sponsorship of films is not intended as direct sales promotion, but rather to create a positive and favourable attitude towards the business.

16.4.3.4 Special events

Visits, receptions, exhibitions and sponsorships are special occasions that present opportunities for communicating messages. The arrangements for such events are the responsibility of the public relations department. Crises that occur regularly and unexpectedly are also special events that make substantial demands on the expertise and communication skills of public relations practitioners. Special events include the following:

- **Press conferences.** Press conferences, usually organised and managed by the public relations department, are special events that afford the business an opportunity to communicate with the public through the mass media. Both the spoken and written word are used at these events. News reporters usually receive a copy of a specially formulated statement made by the spokesperson, after which questions are allowed. This is normally followed by a news report in the mass media. The public relations officer responsible for the organisation of the conference must show diplomacy in fielding difficult questions and an ability to encourage further questions by offering positive answers. A press conference on television often causes amusement when an inept spokesperson has to answer embarrassing questions.
- **Visits to the business.** Visits are usually encouraged because they create opportunities for the business to give out information that will foster goodwill. Of course, this is only done if there is nothing unfavourable to hide. There are usually set visiting times, when employees and members of the public are conducted through the premises by somebody with sufficient knowledge of the business to be able to answer any questions. Visitors or employees have an opportunity to see for themselves how products are manufactured, what working conditions are like, the facilities and amenities provided for employees, what safety regulations are taken, and how quality control methods are implemented. They are usually given pamphlets or brochures with additional information about the business. It is also common practice to treat visitors to refreshments at the end of the tour, which presents yet another opportunity of passing on more information.
- **Receptions.** Businesses often take advantage of a particular occasion to entertain a select group of people at a luncheon or cocktail party. This is usually accompanied by a speech informing those present about particular achievements or developments, and provides an opportunity for hosts and

guests to meet and mix informally. Again, the primary objective is to further the image of the business rather than to promote sales, although increased sales may in many cases result from a favourable image.

- **Exhibitions.** Most large businesses have places in their own buildings suitable for holding exhibitions. They may demonstrate the process a product undergoes through to completion, or what equipment or apparatus is used, or may provide information, accompanied by photographs, of performances achieved. Practical demonstrations can also be given. In 3M's head office in Minneapolis, for example, there is a Hall of Fame in which the products of the business, made over the years, are exhibited.
- **Crisis management.** Crises (and other unforeseen events) constitute threats to the continued survival of a business. The public relations department must have a crisis plan ready to manage these unfortunate events. A crisis can be caused by a strike, a fire, a big accident on the factory floor, fraud and theft, defective products which threaten danger and even loss of life to consumers, and a whole range of unexpected and unwelcome events. The purpose of a crisis plan is to limit as far as possible the physical and financial damage caused by the event, and to protect the corporate image.

A specially appointed crisis coordinator must also be responsible for the following, which relate to internal and external communications:
- Compiling a list of persons to be informed about the nature of the crisis
- Training of telephone operators to answer enquiries in the correct way
- Appointment of a spokesperson
- Informing and training employees to act correctly in emergencies. An emergency number should be readily available.
- Formulation of a message to prevent further possible damage caused by negative rumours

---

A bomb threat checklist

To handle bomb threats, large businesses distribute checklists to be used whenever a threatening phone call is received.

The checklist instructs the receiver to keep the caller talking by asking pertinent questions, while at the same time checking voice characteristics, accent, background noises, etc. The receiver is advised to remain calm and to call the emergency number as soon as possible.

After the crisis has passed, the public should be reassured that everything is back to normal. In handling a crisis, transparency and honesty should prevail.

Examples of the use of communication media by large businesses in South Africa are readily available. Students should study the news media for appropriate examples.

16.4.3.5 The Internet
There is no doubt that the interactive workplace (cyberspace, the Internet, the World Wide Web) has affected the way many businesses operate. One of the

most important developments is the use of public relations tools on these channels. Examples of this are the use of Web sales, intranet operations and using the Web to communicate with target publics. These electronic channels will become an increasingly powerful communications tool for public relations practitioners. Seitel[3] identifies three reasons for this:

- **An increasing consumer demand to be educated as opposed to merely being sold things.** Many consumers and target publics are better educated and know when someone is trying to oversell them. Communications programmes should respond by using more education-based information rather than blatant promotion. The Internet is a good example of the use of such information.
- **Time is of the essence.** The need to move quickly is well known in business, but there is an even greater pressure to operate in a real-time mode. The world has become a global village where immediate communication is possible. The Internet and the instantaneous access it provides can be used by public relations practitioners to respond instantly to any emerging issues or market changes.
- **An increasing need for customisation.** There are more and more choices available to consumers. Think of the number of television channels there used to be in South Africa and compare this with the current situation (satellite television has exponentially increased the number of possible channels available to consumers).

This increase in choice means that consumers today have increased expectations. They expect a more focused approach, catering to their specific needs and offering one-to-one communication. Businesses will have to focus on ever-narrower target segments or audiences, and the Internet offers the vehicle to do this.

Promoting "The Blair Witch Project" on the Internet

The 1999 film "The Blair Witch Project" was filmed on a budget of $35 000, but was one of the most successful films that year and helped to introduce Hollywood to the power of the Internet. A year before the release of the film the filmmakers launched a very realistic website and continued to add information to it over time. To build anticipation, the site reported a number of "events" surrounding the disappearance of the three students around which the plot of the movie revolved. Visitors to the site began to discuss the movie in chat rooms, and hypertext links were set up between the various chat sites, funnelling thousands of interested visitors to the site through the Blair Witch experience.

The production company kept placing new information on the site, and the updated site was tied to a number of promotions from books and TV specials to university campus events. The filmmakers even produced a soundtrack CD, which was unusual since the film did not have any music.

Source: Adapted from Seitel, F.P., *The practice of public relations*, Prentice Hall, Upper Saddle River, 2001, pp. 320-321.

In businesses, electronic mail or e-mail is an increasingly important channel for communication with internal publics or other employees. It is fast becoming the preferred choice over traditional print media or fax technology. The advantages of e-mail are that it is more immediate and more interactive. Employees can provide feedback immediately to what they read or hear, and businesses can respond quickly to this feedback.

Many businesses have created websites to profile their companies, promote their products and provide information to customers.

16.4.4 Publicity

16.4.4.1 The nature of publicity

Obtaining publicity is one of the most important communication tasks of the public relations department. Publicity is the free (hopefully positive) mention of the business, its products and activities in the mass media. The public relations department coordinates all efforts to gain positive publicity. This is no easy task and other departments should assist in the quest for publicity. In chapter 14 it was pointed out that the marketing department, which has direct contact with the market, also uses publicity to promote product sales.

All departments should be involved in the avoidance of harmful publicity, but the public relations department has the greatest responsibility in this regard. Firstly, it must help to create an ethical climate in which transparency and honesty prevail. Secondly, everybody should be made to realise that confidential information should not leak out, and that only the official spokesperson may talk to the media. And thirdly, the public relations department has the responsibility to reduce, as far as possible, the harmful effects of negative publicity. This can only be done if the corporate climate is positive and the spokesperson very diplomatic.

Negative publicity can lead to boycotts, ill-will and even legislation. The business consequently loses the goodwill of its employees and external publics, which could threaten its survival. If something unforeseen happens it is regarded as newsworthy by the media. Negative publicity is the result. If this happens, it serves no purpose to try to reduce its harmful effect by being dishonest. An acknowledgement and corrective action usually have positive results, especially as these actions also have news value. Sometimes even negative publicity can have positive results. There is a rather cynical view that says it is always a good thing to get one's name mentioned, no matter what is being said! An unacceptable advertisement that has received negative publicity can sometimes still have a positive effect. For example, Benetton, which received worldwide negative publicity for its unconventional advertisements, is still the biggest producer of children's clothing. A film that has received negative reviews also often attracts large audiences. However, it is better to avoid bad publicity by all ethical means.

16.4.4.2 Methods of obtaining publicity

There are four important methods that can be used in the quest for publicity, namely unique special events, unique communication messages, press releases and sponsorships.

- **Unique special events.** The more usual events are discussed in section 16.4.3.4, but to be really certain of publicity, the event must be unique and newsworthy. Media reporters are usually invited to special events, but only those that capture their interest are reported on. An ordinary event may merit a news item on the society page, but reports on a unique event reach the front page or the day's main news broadcast. The launch of a new model luxury motorcar is often a unique event where no expense is spared in treating reporters. Publicity is therefore not really free, but sometimes very expensive to obtain.

- **Unique communication messages.** The media often report on imaginative advertisements, unusual billboards or other communication methods. Sanlam succeeded in obtaining wide publicity some years ago with its entertaining advertisements featuring babies. A video report highlighted the difficulties encountered in making these advertisements. The value of such positive publicity to an innovative business cannot readily be determined. Innovation in any area usually merits positive mention in the mass media. BMW launched a unique communication campaign by offering 100 BMWs to the police to combat crime. In advertisements, public attention is drawn to this action, which in itself obtained wide publicity.

- **News releases.** The public relations department is responsible for carefully formulated news releases, which should be supplied on a regular basis to the media. This is done according to a prescribed method and is cleared by management beforehand. These news releases contain information regarded as newsworthy by the business, for example, information about new products, markets, appointments and promotions. The decision to give coverage to these releases depends on what the editor of the news medium regards as important. For newsworthy items, reporters are sent out to gather more information, for example, by visiting the business. An ordinary news release is perhaps given coverage in the business section of the newspaper, while something that is more newsworthy may merit placement on the front page.

    Media such as radio and television are informed in the same way as the print media. Many of their reports follow on original reports in the press, which can then be subjected to closer scrutiny. Press releases during and after a crisis situation are especially important. The news about the crisis should be handled diplomatically, and one should bear in mind that reporters will not be satisfied until they are absolutely convinced that they know all the details.

- **Sponsorships.** Sponsorships are possibly the most popular method used by businesses in the current quest for publicity. A sponsorship entails financial assistance to a deserving cause, with a view to obtaining goodwill, and to demonstrate social responsibility. Such projects are not launched simply because they have captured the interest of management. There should be definite reasons for some projects being undertaken and others rejected, and the main reason should be that the business will be likely to benefit. Hence, public relations management should have a specific policy on this, as well as a method of evaluation to differentiate between projects that will benefit the business and those that lack any advantages. Social responsibility does not consist of mere "bleeding-heart" charity – the business definitely expects something (goodwill) in return for what it gives.

Businesses are usually reluctant to publish details about the contributions they make to different sponsorships because there are always people who will object to them, and this creates ill-feeling. People who abhor boxing and wrestling, for example, will disapprove of a business that devotes large sums to such sponsorship, but of course the fans will feel differently. Shareholders are also apt to take exception to what they consider a "waste of money" – they naturally prefer a bigger dividend. Therefore, a budget for the control of contributions is necessary. A contributions committee usually assesses various proposals and requests. The public relations department is involved in the management of large sponsorships, on which thousands of rands are sometimes spent.

Planning a sponsorship

Sponsorship involves more than just financial support. The entire affair must be well planned, professionally executed and expertly marketed. A poorly planned sponsorship can damage the company's image. Nissan sponsors mainly cricket and motor sports, and may spend as much, if not more, on promotions, support services and publicity as on the event itself. Many sport sponsorships fail because of poor marketing. In 1987 R107 million was spent on sport sponsorships and about R92 million on related promotions.

SABMiller sponsors mainly sport because there is a high correlation between sports participants and beer drinkers. However, it only sponsors events where there is a clear link between their products and the sponsored event. For this reason, SABMiller would not consider motor sport and other high-risk activities, where the use of alcohol is inappropriate, for sponsorship.

A sponsorship must also be well marketed. The good deeds of the business should not go unnoticed. The sponsorship itself also offers the opportunity for marketing communication messages on T-shirts, stickers, flags, billboards, etc. Receptions, demonstrations and exhibitions are used extensively in sport sponsorships such as cricket, and also in cultural sponsorships, such as a music concert. The following types of sponsorship are popular:

- **Employee benefits**, for example, the funding of educational, cultural and scientific and social institutions serving the employees' community. Assistance with housing, and education assistance for the children of employees are usually also forthcoming, thus providing opportunities to attract and keep good workers.
- **Community development programmes**, for example, in education, health and charity
- **Nature conservation programmes**
- **Sports or cultural events**

Projects of social responsibility programmes

British American Tobacco South Africa (BATSA), although operating in a controversial business sector, has a number of programmes that illustrate its community involvement. These programmes include:

Education

The BATSA Scholarship Fund is located at eight of South Africa's major tertiary institutions and provides scholarships in the fields of engineering, information technology, commerce and business science.

Crime prevention

BATSA, in conjunction with the Stellenbosch Chamber of Commerce and Business, established the Stellenbosch Business Watch initiative designed to protect and enhance the central business district of Stellenbosch. Modelled on the successful camera surveillance scheme of Cape Town, and backed by a fully operational control room and SA Police reservists, the initiative has been successful in reducing crime in the central business district by 90%.

Economic development

BATSA has entered into an agreement with the Dysseldorp Community Trust's Liquorice Extraction Business in which it donated an analytical system to measure the critically important moisture content of the liquorice extract, and also committed to purchasing the extract from them for use in the manufacture of its blended cigarettes. Through their involvement the local community has been given infrastructure, technological, financial and administrative support, and a guaranteed market for its product. This has helped to create an economically viable community.

Source: Tsangwane, Y., Social reporting as a form of marketing, Unpublished Business Report for the Honours BCom. Degree, University of South Africa, Pretoria, 2003, pp. 8-9.

The examples below illustrate some aspects of the approach of big business to granting sponsorships.

Iscor's involvement in environmental protection

Iscor launched an intensive advertising campaign to create a positive image for the corporation and to draw attention to its efforts at protecting the environment. The advertising copy read as follows:

"One of the world's most exclusive reserves lies within a stone's throw of Iscor's Sishen iron ore mine. It is an archaeological reserve where giant buffalo, pygmy elephant, ancient zebra and other animals are protected forever amongst the fossils and stone-age artefacts. Thanks to Iscor's farsighted planning this area has not been blasted for ore but preserved for archaeological development and research. In fact, every Iscor mine has a blueprint for preservation of the environment and restoration of the total ecosystem in the area. It also requires that any historical or archaeological discoveries be protected and developed. It is the kind of responsibility expected of one of the leading steel producers in the world today."

An excellent sponsorship, or one that is successfully managed, is rewarded with broad, favourable publicity. That's real news!

The welfare of road users

BMW received wide publicity for its unique idea of using a variation on its award-winning advertisement of the white mouse "dancing" on the steering wheel of a BMW. In its more recent advertisement the white mouse – perhaps drunk, perhaps reckless – falls off the steering wheel. In this way, BMW builds its image as a responsible business that is concerned about the welfare of road users.

16.4.5 The communication campaign

All the different messages in all the different media should be combined in one communication campaign. The message in one medium must support another in another medium. The messages are designed to have the greatest possible effect, and the various communication media are therefore carefully considered. The media serve as channels through which the message reaches the target audience. The choice of media is often limited by the budget, however. Usually a business simply does not have enough money for all the available channels that might be used to get all its messages to all its possible target audiences. Obviously, "free" channels must be utilised as far as possible.

TV training for managers

The public relations department of a certain large South African company immediately reacted to the rather poor performance of its MD on television by buying expensive video equipment. They then proceeded to use it to train him and other senior managers to perform well during television interviews. According to the company, this investment will return quick dividends. A 30-second appearance on a discussion programme is worth thousands of rands to this company. It is therefore worthwhile to invest the money if, by doing so, a positive image for the company can be created.

Unfortunately, publicity is not easily obtainable if a business is reluctant to advertise. A newspaper or magazine will obviously not be disposed to give free publicity to a business that does not return the favour by purchasing advertising space. Through careful planning, public relations management has to devise a programme of action that will produce the greatest effect and convey its message to the greatest number of target audiences at the least possible expense. Unfortunately, there is no method of selecting an optimum programme. The choice of an optimum combination of advertisements, TV programmes, press handouts, entertainment, sponsorships, and so on, depends not only on a specialised knowledge of the activities of the business, the nature of the target audiences, and the principles of good communication, but also on experience and a good sense of interpersonal relations.

Cooperation between public relations and marketing is essential in formulating a communications campaign. The ultimate objective of both departments is to stimulate the business's sales or services to ensure survival and growth in a complex environment.

A business committed to the well-being of society will have an ethical code of conduct pertaining to all its activities, and directed at benefits to its own employees and the general public. The code of conduct will stipulate that legislation should be obeyed and that community welfare be emphasised in the pursuit of profit.

It is difficult to lay down universal rules on ethical and unethical conduct, because of individual differences and the varying norms and values of subcultures and communities. However, it is desirable for a business to have its own code of conduct, for such a code is directly reflected in the prevailing corporate culture and has an impact on the image of the business.

Applying the concept: publics and communication methods

Below are two lists: one identifying possible publics and the other identifying communication methods. Match the public (a-g) with the best communication method to effectively reach it (1-7).

PUBLICS	METHODS
a. Employees	1. Publicity
b. Shareholders	2. Press releases about the business
c. Local community	3. Annual financial reports
d. Customers	4. Participation in presentation to parliamentary committee
e. Government authorities	5. Internal company newsletter
f. Suppliers	6. Visits to manufacturing plants
g. Media	7. Sponsorship of local school plays

What are the possible matches?

a = 5 Businesses can communicate with their employees through the use of internal company newsletters.

b = 3 Annual financial reports are used to communicate a business's performance to its financial publics such as shareholders.

c = 7 Many businesses support the local community by sponsoring or making donations to local schools.

d = 1 Effective publicity is a good way of helping to create a good image for the business with its customers.

e = 4 The use of lobby groups and participating and supporting activities aimed at legislation is a good method of keeping communication channels open with government authorities.

f = 6 One way of communicating with suppliers is to go and visit their plants, to see how they produce their goods and services.

g = 2 A good method of supplying the media with newsworthy items is through the use of effective press releases.

16.5 Social responsibility and business ethics

In the present era, the spotlight in many quarters is on the social responsibility of business and the ethics of people in business. This trend is also evident in the news media and in the most recent literature on business management.

It is not possible to deal with social responsibility and business ethics in depth in this section, but the following are nevertheless dealt with, though briefly:

- A definition of the concepts of business ethics and social responsibility
- The areas in which issues pertaining to the social responsibility of business and business ethics are especially relevant

16.5.1 Definition of concepts

16.5.1.1 Business ethics

The term ethics refers to views or convictions about what is right and wrong, and good and bad. Therefore, ethical conduct is conduct or action that observes generally accepted social norms or values, while unethical conduct indicates action that is in conflict with generally accepted social norms and values. It follows that business ethics indicates generally accepted views on right and wrong behaviour in the business context. Ethical business behaviour is individual behaviour that corresponds with what is generally regarded as right (correct) business conduct, while unethical business practices refer to conduct that is in conflict with what is generally seen as right or correct business conduct.

Liebenberg[4] puts it as follows: "If I were to summarise the most popular definitions, I would define ethics (business ethics) as a person's judgement of what is inherently right or wrong in his or her interaction with others. Ethics is therefore primarily concerned with relationships between people."

It is clear from the above definition that what is regarded as ethical or unethical conduct is dependent on:

- The norms or values of a particular community or subculture
- The views of individuals in that community or subculture regarding what is right and wrong in certain circumstances

Within the general standards of a particular community or subculture, individuals develop their judgement of right and wrong behaviour. Their judgement stems from a variety of influences, such as parental upbringing, circles of friends, education, religious conviction, community involvement, and the work environment.

It is clear from the above discussion that it is impossible to have a universal set of rules on ethical and unethical conduct – different subcultures and communities, for example, have different social norms and values. Therefore, in a country such as South Africa, with its diverse ethnic and cultural groupings, it is out of the question to speak of generally accepted social norms and values.

Examples

- Some people feel that it is wrong to take a packet of sweets from the local café, but think nothing of taking home stationery from their office for their children's use.
- Some people do not think it is wrong to evade tax and inflate their insurance claims.
- Some people think nothing of taking sick leave, even though they are in good health.
- Some people who consider themselves law-abiding citizens do not feel it is wrong to use radar-detection devices to evade speed traps.

Because many businesses in South Africa employ people with divergent views on ethical and unethical conduct, it is imperative to draw up a code of conduct for employees if the business is to survive in the long term. Such a code should contain rules for employees on what is regarded as ethical or unethical business behaviour. In compiling such a code, the following points pertaining to ethical conduct should be taken into consideration:

- The general social norms and values of the community in which the business operates should provide the basis of the code of conduct.
- Vague generalisations about ethical conduct are meaningless. A code of ethics should be as specific as possible and contain details about ethical issues that employees might be confronted with, as well as their desired reaction to them.
- In the same way that management exercises control over the functional areas of a business, it should also ensure that employees adhere to the code of conduct at all times.
- Employees should be held accountable for their behaviour. Compliance with the code of conduct should be one of the conditions of service, and employees who transgress the code should be subjected to disciplinary action.
- When employees are remunerated according to the profitability of the business only, there is a tendency to ignore ethical questions. Remuneration should also be based on upholding ethical standards.

Ethical practice

Organisations that engage in dialogue with their publics, and that evaluate organisational performance on ethical standards developed in dialogue with publics, should gain in positive reputations with their publics. As we move further into the century, the role of public relations will need to change from that of merely wielding self-serving influence, crafting communications, and researching publics. Ethical practice for the field of public relations will require practitioners to be facilitators of dialogue, and listeners as well as speakers. Strong leadership will be needed from high-profile organisations that exemplify best practices in opening their own practices and decision making to public criticism.

Source: Adapted from Dougherty, E.L., Public relations and social responsibility, in Heath, R.L., *Handbook of public relations*, Sage, Thousand Oaks, 2001, p. 409.

- Employees may be unsure of what represents ethical behaviour in a particular situation, especially if they are suddenly confronted with it, for example, a supplier inviting one of the business's buyers to lunch at an upmarket restaurant. Employees should be encouraged to discuss such situations with management and co-workers so that consensus can be reached about suitable action.

16.5.1.2 Social responsibility

While business ethics is concerned with the behaviour of individuals (employees) at work, social responsibility has to do with the behaviour of a business towards stakeholders such as consumers, suppliers, competitors, employees, owners or shareholders, and the community at large. Being socially responsible essentially means that a business tries to reconcile the interests of its different stakeholders with each other. For example, profit maximisation is the primary concern of the owners or shareholders, while consumers are mainly interested in quality products at affordable prices. There is, clearly, a conflict of interests. In this case, one often finds that businesses act "irresponsibly" towards consumers in an effort to best serve the interests of their owners.

What are the factors that influence a business's approach to social responsibility? Firstly, businesses are dependent on the business ethics of their employees, and especially of top management. Secondly, social responsibility is often forced on businesses by the government (through legislation), and by consumer action (for example, boycotts). Thirdly, the approaches of competitors to this issue also influence the approach of a particular business.

16.5.2 Areas of social responsibility and business ethics

Issues concerning the social responsibility of businesses and business ethics are mainly prevalent in interactions with the following groups:
- Customers or clients (consumers)
- Suppliers
- Competitors
- Employees
- Owners and shareholders
- The community

Some of the issues that businesses are confronted with in these areas will now be examined.

16.5.2.1 Consumers

There are numerous ethical and social responsibility issues that confront businesses in their dealings with consumers, but these revolve mainly around marketing actions (product, price and marketing communication). Most countries have introduced legislation to protect consumers from exploitation and deceit in these areas, while many professional and industrial associations (pharmacists, attorneys, dentists, medical practitioners, builders, and the motor trade) have codes of ethical conduct. Besides these, businesses and business people have wide powers of discretion when it comes to considering whether the following, as examples, are ethical and socially responsible:

- The placing of tobacco, cigarette and alcohol advertisements
- Advertisements aimed at children
- The use of sex-oriented advertisements in media to which all people have access
- Keeping quiet about defects in products when selling them
- The extending of excessive credit to buyers
- A bank not informing a client about the interest rates charged on an overdrawn account
- Increasing interest rates without prior notice
- Basing price discrimination on gender and age
- Providing poor after-sales service or none at all
- Refusing to give customers credit for products they are dissatisfied with, or "forcing" them to buy other products in their place

16.5.2.2 Suppliers

In the interaction between a business and its suppliers, there are numerous cases of questionable ethics, for example:

- Where a supplier is in a strong position relative to that of a client, it is not unusual for the former to enforce unreasonably high prices or order quantities. This happens, for example, when the supplier is the sole source of a particular product or raw material.
- It is not unusual for a strong customer to compel suppliers to accept unreasonably low prices for their products or raw materials. Market gardeners, for example, often complain that retail groups (Shoprite, Pick 'n Pay, etc.) exploit them when they sign contracts to deliver vegetables.
- It is common knowledge that suppliers often invite purchasing personnel to luncheons, offer them trips abroad, and give them expensive Christmas gifts. Is this fair to competing suppliers who are not in a position – or simply do not wish – to make such offers?

16.5.2.3 Competitors

The following are examples of questionable actions in the interaction between a business and its competitors:

- Circulating rumours about the financial stability, product quality, service quality and business ethics of competitors
- Luring away a competitor's core personnel
- Attempting, in any conceivable way, to obtain confidential information about a competitor
- Waging price wars to eliminate competitors

16.5.2.4 Employees

The following are examples of issues that businesses have to cope with in their interaction with employees:

- A proper and fair general code of conduct for employees in their interaction with a business's other stakeholders, and the monitoring of such a code
- A policy on sexual harassment, smoking, drinking, drugs, and dress in the workplace
- A language policy

- Equity without discrimination on the basis of creed, race, gender, skin colour, age, and so forth
- The creation of a safe and healthy working environment
- The right of employees to privacy both inside and outside the workplace
- The replacement of permanent staff who enjoy pension and medical benefits with temporary, part-time staff who do not enjoy such benefits
- Health and child care in the workplace

16.5.2.5 Owners and shareholders

Issues of ethics and social responsibility that businesses have to deal with in their interaction with owners and shareholders include the following:

- **Choosing between short-term and long-term benefits.** The decision making of top management, boards of directors, and even shareholders of many businesses appears to revolve around the financial benefits (stemming from the business) that they can realise for themselves in the short term. In the process, the healthy continued existence of the business becomes a long-term, less important concern. This may happen, for example, if exceptionally high salaries are paid to top management, or profit is paid out in the form of dividends, rather than reserving it to create a healthy capital structure.
- **The tendency to make things seem rosier than they are to attract new investments.** Good profits, for example, are shown by writing off inadequate depreciation on fixed assets. For the same reason, there is often a tendency to make unrealistic sales or profit forecasts.
- **The investment of business capital in other businesses or projects.** This can include, for example, the manufacture of cigarettes and alcohol, pornographic magazines, the production of weapons, and projects that are a threat to nature and wildlife.

Opposing views on social responsibility

- **Proponents' view of social responsibility.** This view holds that corporations should contribute to worthy causes addressing social concerns. Corporations are viewed not only as economic institutions but also as social institutions, which, as such, have responsibilities to society. Thus, corporations have an obligation to solve some of society's most pressing social problems and to devote some of their resources to the solution of these societal problems.
- **Opponents' view of social responsibility.** Milton Friedman, a Nobel Prize-winning economist, believes that corporations have no responsibility to society besides adhering to the law and maximising profits for shareholders. Opponents of social responsibility say business makes its biggest contribution to society by producing useful products, providing jobs, and generating the wealth that makes a better standard of living possible. They caution that efforts to deal with social problems must not interfere with business's ability to perform its primary economic function.

Source: Adapted from Dougherty, E.I., Public relations and social responsibility, in Heath, R.L., *Handbook of public relations*, Sage, Thousand Oaks, 2001, p. 392.

16.5.2.6 The community

In its interaction with the community, the social responsibility of a business involves its views and actions on matters such as the following:

- **Conservation of the physical environment.** This is concerned with issues such as air, water and soil pollution, as well as nature conservation, wildlife conservation, and damage to the ozone layer.
- **Utilisation of scarce resources.** This is achieved through soil and water conservation and the recycling of waste matter and water.
- **Socio-economic issues.** These include community capacity development, health programmes (HIV/Aids, TB, etc.), crime prevention, education and training (bursaries, training facilities, etc.).

16.5.3 Final comments

This section discussed the concepts of business ethics and social responsibility. Thereafter, areas were identified in which these concepts are particularly relevant. The nature of the issues within each area was explained by means of examples.

16.6 Summary

The management of public relations entails the planning of a programme of action aimed at specific target audiences, the organisation of public relations activities, leading these activities, and controlling all programmes. The main objectives of public relations are to create a positive image of the business and to obtain the goodwill of specific target audiences. The public relations department is responsible for the communication campaign, where the spoken and written word, sight and sound media, and special events, exhibitions and sponsorships may be used to communicate with different publics. All the communication methods and media must be combined to have maximum impact and to obtain the required reaction. A budget must be prepared to give direction to all the different activities. Budget allocations are made for a variety of projects aimed at image building, obtaining goodwill and demonstrating social responsibility.

The manager of the public relations department should preferably be a member of the top management team and should have a say in the formulation of policy, the planning of strategy, and the taking of decisions. He or she must also be a communications expert and know how to direct messages to external groups; have insight into human behaviour; a gift for maintaining interpersonal relationships; and an ability to cooperate with managers of other functional departments so that the business is always presented in a positive light. Creating goodwill and avoiding antagonism are of prime importance to the survival and growth of a business.

References

1. Rensburg, R. & Cant, M., *Public relations: South African perspectives*, Heinemann, Johannesburg, 2002, p. 34.
2. Kotler, P., *Marketing management*, 11th edition, Prentice Hall, Upper Saddle River, 2003, p. 302.
3. Seitel, F.P., *The practice of public relations*, Prentice Hall, Upper Saddle River, 2001, p. 304.
4. Liebenberg, P.J., Etiese optrede noodsaaklik vir groei, *Finansies & Tegniek*, 11 August 1995, p. 35.

17 The financial function and financial management

The purpose of this chapter

This chapter explains financial analysis, planning and control as key elements of the financial function of a business organisation.

Learning outcomes

The content of this chapter will enable learners to:
- Describe and apply the fundamental principles of financial management
- Determine the break-even point of a business organisation
- Calculate the present and future value of amounts
- Analyse and interpret the financial statements of a business organisation

17.1 Introduction

In the introductory chapters of this book, the financial function was identified as one of the functional management areas in a business. In this chapter, the nature and meaning of the financial function and its management, that is, financial management, will be analysed. Thereafter, the relationship between financial management, the other functional management areas, related subject disciplines, and the environment will be shown, followed by an introduction to a few basic concepts and techniques used by financial management. The goal and fundamental principles of financial management will also be explained. In conclusion, we will discuss one of the tasks of financial management, namely that of financial analysis, planning and control.

17.2 The financial function and financial management

A business must have the necessary assets such as land, buildings, machinery, vehicles, equipment, raw materials and trade inventories at its disposal if it is to function efficiently. In addition, business organisations need further resources such as management acumen and labour, as well as services such as a power supply and communication facilities.

A business needs funds, also called capital, to obtain the required assets, resources and services. The people or institutions (which include the owners) that make funds available to the business lose the right to use those funds in the short or long term, and they also run the risk of losing those funds, or a portion thereof, should the business fail. As a result, suppliers of funds expect compensation for the funds they make available to the business (and also a repayment of funds lent to the business), when the business starts to generate funds through the sale of the products or services it produces. Hence, there is a continual flow of funds to and from the business – (see figure 17.15 on p. 417).

The **financial function** is concerned with this flow of funds, and in particular with the acquisition of funds (which is known as **financing**), the application of funds for the acquisition of assets (which is known as **investment**), as well as the administration of, and reporting on, financial matters.

Financial management is responsible for the efficient management of all facets of the financial function and, within the broad framework of the strategies and plans of the business, has as its objective making the highest possible contribution to the objectives through the performance of the following tasks:

- Efficient financial analysis, reporting, planning and control
- The management of the acquisition of funds, also known as the management of the financing or capital structure
- The management of the application of funds, also known as the management of the asset structure

(See section 17.3.1 for a further explanation of the concepts of financing or capital structure and asset structure, and chapters 18 and 19 for an exposition of the management of the asset and capital structures of a business.)

Figure 17.1: The relationship between financial management, other functional management areas, related disciplines and the environment

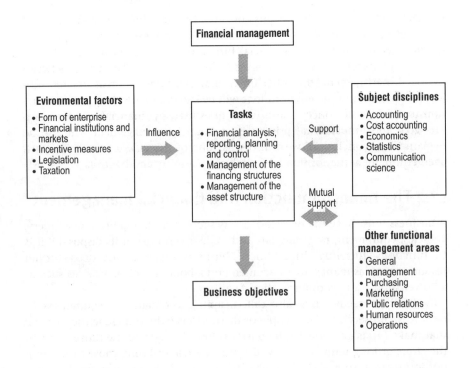

Financial management cannot function in isolation. Besides the interdependence between the functional management areas (without production, for example, there will be no funds, and vice versa), financial management should also depend on other related subject disciplines such as accounting and eonomics, if it wants to be efficient. As a subsystem of the business, the financial function, and therefore its management, is also influenced by environmental factors. The relationship between financial management, the other functional management areas, related subject disciplines, and the environment is illustrated in figure (see p. 394).

17.3 Concepts in financial management

As in any field of study, it is necessary to describe certain concepts in financial management to present the subject in a meaningful manner.

17.3.1 The balance sheet, asset and financing structure

The balance sheet is an "instant photo" of the financial position of a business and may be diagrammatically represented as in figure 17.2.

The information in figure 17.2 (see p. 396) is largely self-explanatory – hence a few comments will suffice.

The **asset side** reflects all the possessions of the business, together with their respective values as at the balance sheet date, and therefore shows the mutual coherence between these possessions. These assets represent the **asset structure** of the business. Assets are normally divided into two broad categories in the balance sheet, namely:

- **Fixed assets** (also called non-current assets) such as land, buildings, machinery, vehicles and other equipment
- **Current assets** such as cash in the bank, as well as other possessions of the business that will be converted into cash within one year during the normal course of business, such as marketable securities, debtors and all inventories

The values at which the assets are recorded in the balance sheet differ according to the objectives for drawing up the balance sheet. For this reason it is essential that the balance sheet should provide an indication of the values at which the assets have been recorded, for example, cost, cost less depreciation or cost plus appreciation.

The liability or claims side of the balance sheet reflects the nature and extent of the interests in the assets – in other words, the mutual coherence of the claims of the persons or institutions that provided funds (capital) for the "purchase" of the assets. Therefore the **liability** side of the balance sheet shows the **financing** or **capital structure** of the business as at the balance sheet date.

The liability side of the balance sheet is usually subdivided on the basis of two criteria, namely:

- The term for which the funds have been made available
- The source from which the funds have been obtained

Figure 17.2: A diagrammatic representation of a balance sheet

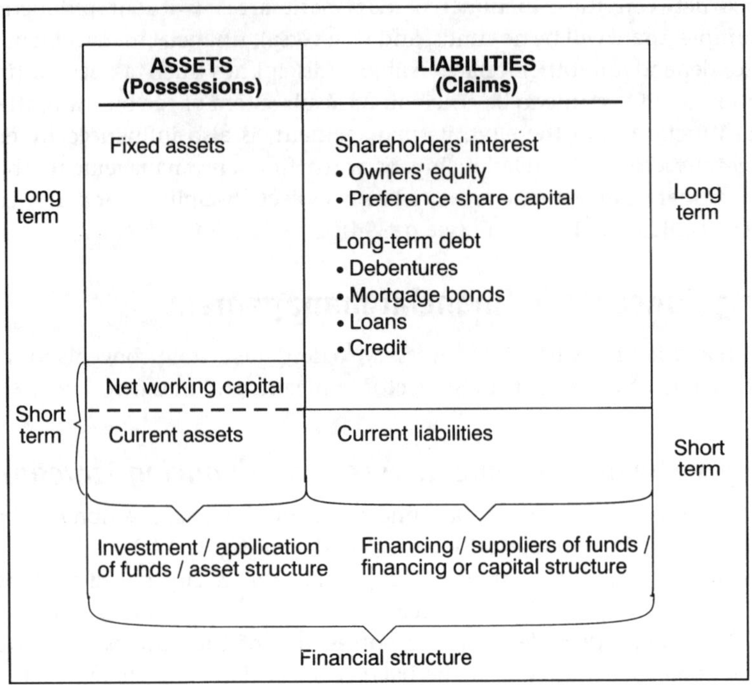

Therefore, the liability side of a company's balance sheet will contain the following details:

- **Long-term funds.** This is also known as non-current liabilities and comprises shareholders' interest and long-term debt.
- **Shareholders' interest** is further subdivided into owners' equity (made up of ordinary share capital, reserves, and undistributed, that is, retained profits) and preference share capital. **Long-term debt** is usually made up of debentures, mortgage bonds, secured loans, and long-term credit. The latter is often classified as medium-term funds.
- **Short-term funds.** These are also referred to as current liabilities, and represent all debts or credit that is normally repayable within one year. Examples of these funds are bank overdrafts and trade creditors. The favourable difference between the current assets and the current liabilities represents the net working capital or that portion of the current assets that has been financed from long-term funds.

The shareholders' interest on the liability side of the balance sheet of businesses that do not have ordinary or preference shareholders – for example, sole proprietorships, partnerships and close corporations – is replaced by a capital account that reflects the owners' interest in the business.

17.3.2 Capital

Capital can be described as the accrued power of disposal over the goods and services used by a business to generate a monetary return or profit. Stated differently, the capital of a business may briefly be described as the monetary value of the assets of the business at a specific time. The suppliers of capital are shown on the liability side of a balance sheet, as explained in section 17.3.1.

A business needs capital for investment in fixed assets – referred to as **the need for fixed capital** – and capital for investment in current assets – referred to as **the need for working capital**.

In a business of a given size, the need for fixed capital is permanent in that the business cannot carry on its current level of activities without such capital. For the same reason, a business has a permanent need for a certain minimum portion of working capital. The remaining need for working capital will vary according to factors such as seasonal influences and contingencies that result in an increase or decrease in production activities.

The capital needs of a business can therefore be depicted as in figure 17.3.

Figure 17.3:The capital requirements of a business

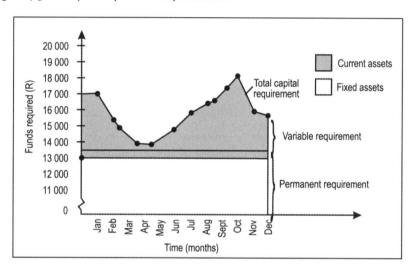

Source: Gitman, L.J., *Principles of managerial finance*, 6th edition, Pearson Education Inc, 1991, p. 675.

17.3.3 Income

The income of a business consists primarily of receipts resulting from the sale of its products and/or services. The extent of these receipts for a given period will depend on the quantity of goods and/or services sold within that period, and the unit price for which they were sold.

$$Income = Units\ sold \times unit\ price$$

The income of the business can also be obtained from other sources, such as interest earned on investments. However, this income will not be taken into account in the discussions that follow.

17.3.4 Costs

Different meanings are ascribed to the concept of costs. This often leads to confusion. Lynch and Williamson[1] offer the following useful definition of costs: "Essentially cost consists in value foregone for the purpose of achieving some economic benefit which will promote the profit making ability of the firm."

Costs can, therefore, be regarded as the monetary value sacrificed in the production of goods and/or services produced for the purpose of resale.

Example

Costs in a manufacturing business consist of materials used, rent paid for the premises and buildings, depreciation on equipment, wages and salaries of all workers, payments for electricity and communication services, and so on.

Costs are further subdivided according to certain criteria, and hence the business has direct costs, indirect costs, overhead expenses, fixed costs and variable costs.

The subdivision of total costs into fixed and variable costs is of particular importance for decision-making purposes. Hence, the remainder of this section will be devoted to this aspect. A further subdivision will be introduced in the discussion of the income statement in section 17.3.6.

Fixed costs is that portion of total costs that remains unchanged – within the boundaries of a fixed production capacity – regardless of an increase or decrease in the quantity of goods and/or services produced.

By way of illustration, we will now consider an accountancy practice with production capacity (that is, office space, equipment and permanent staff) to offer accounting services to 100 people. Office rent, depreciation on equipment, and staff salaries will not change as long as the clientele does not exceed 100. An increase in the number of clients will necessitate an increase in the staff required. The increase in staff will have an effect on office space and furniture requirements. In this way, a new production capacity is created, which gives rise to a new fixed cost component.

Total fixed costs as part of total costs for a particular period and capacity can be represented graphically as in figure 17.4.

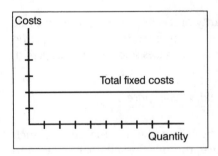

Figure 17.4: A graphical representation of total fixed costs

Total fixed costs are constant, irrespective of the volume produced. Therefore the fixed costs per unit produced will decrease with an increase in the quantity produced, as illustrated in figure 17.5.

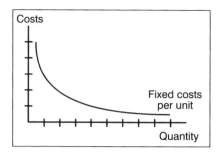

Figure 17.5: A graphical representation of fixed costs per unit produced

Variable costs is that portion of the total costs that changes according to a change in the volume produced. Some variable cost items, such as manufacturing material costs, can be regarded as pure variable costs because they change in direct proportion to a change in the volume produced. Other variable cost items contain a fixed cost component, such as the fixed telephone rental. In this instance, there is not a pure linear relationship between these variable cost items and the volume produced. Therefore, these costs are referred to as **semi-variable costs**. Since these semi-variable costs do not have any substantial effect on the principle of fixed and variable costs, a pure linear relationship can, for illustration purposes, be assumed between total variable costs and volume produced, as represented in figure 17.6.

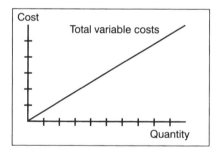

Figure 17.6: A graphical representation of total variable costs

The **variable costs per unit** produced remain more or less constant, irrespective of the quantity produced. This point is illustrated in figure 17.7.

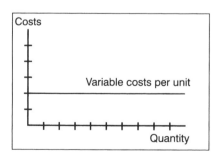

Figure 17.7: A graphical representation of variable costs per unit

The **total costs** involved in the production of a specific number of products produced in a particular period consist of the total fixed costs and the total variable costs incurred in the production of those products. Figure 17.8 graphically illustrates how total costs are arrived at.

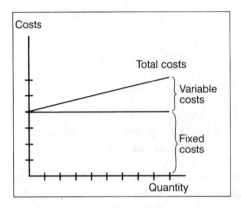

Figure 17.8: A graphical representation of total costs

To summarise, it may be stated that the total costs of the business comprise a fixed and a variable component, each of which has a specific relationship with the volume of production. These relationships have a specific influence on the profit made by businesses – as discussed in more detail in section 17.5.

17.3.5 Profit

Profit is regarded as the favourable difference between the income earned during a specific period and the cost incurred to earn that income. A loss results when the cost exceeds the income.

$$Profit\ or\ loss = Income - costs$$

or

$$Profit\ or\ loss = (Selling\ price \times sales\ quantity) - costs$$

Although the above comparison applies in general, various profit concepts in the different stages of the profit-determining process may be identified in the income statement.

17.3.6 The income statement

The income statement, one of the annual financial statements of a business, furnishes details about the manner in which the profit or loss for a particular period was arrived at, and how it has been distributed.

Figure 17.9 (see p. 401) represents, in diagram form, the income statement of a manufacturing business in company form. A numerical example of an income statement of such a business appears in section 17.7.1.1, while certain profit concepts are also further highlighted in figure 17.15 (see p. 417). Note that the income statement of a sole proprietorship, a partnership, and a close corporation will in essence differ solely in the division of the net profit.

The information in figure 17.9 is largely self-explanatory.

17.4 Objective and fundamental principles of financial management[2]

The long-term objective should be to increase the value of the business. This may be accomplished by:

Figure 17.9: A diagrammatic representation of an income statement

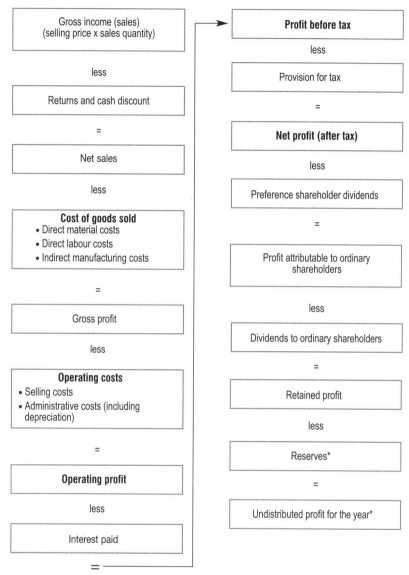

*Appears in the liability side of the balance sheet – see section 17.3.1

- Investing in assets that will add value to the business (as will be explained in chapter 18)
- Keeping the cost of capital of the business as low as possible (as will be explained in chapter 19)

The short-term financial objective should be to ensure the profitability, liquidity and solvency of the business. Profitability is the ability of the business to generate income that will exceed cost. Liquidity is the ability of the business to satisfy its short-term obligations as they become due – in other words, to be able to pay the trade creditors by the due dates. Solvency is the extent to which the assets of the business exceed its liabilities. Solvency differs from liquidity in that liquidity pertains to the settlement of short-term liabilities, while solvency pertains to long-term liabilities such as debentures and mortgage loans.

Financial management is based on three principles, namely the risk-return principle, the cost-benefit principle and the time value of money principle.

17.4.1 The risk-return principle

Risk is the probability that the actual result of a decision may deviate from the planned end result, with an associated financial loss or waste of funds. Risk differs from uncertainty in that in the case of the latter there is no probability or measure of the chances that an event will take place, whereas risk is measurable by means of statistical techniques.

Similar to the cost-benefit principle, the risk-return principle is a trade-off between risk and return. The greater the risk is, the greater the required rate of return will be.

17.4.2 The cost-benefit principle

Decision making, which is based on the cost of resources only, will not necessarily lead to the most economic utilisation of resources. Sound financial decision making requires making an analysis of the total cost and the total benefits, and ensuring that the benefits always exceed the cost. One application of the cost-benefit principle will be illustrated in section 17.5 when the cost-volume-profit relationship will be explained.

17.4.3 The time value of money principle

The time value of money principle means a person could increase the value of any amount of money by earning interest. If, however, the amount is invested in inventory, equipment, vehicles, etc., then the amount cannot earn interest. This ties up with the previous two principles. From a cost-benefit point of view, the investor will have to earn a greater return on the investment in inventory, equipment and vehicles than on the best alternative type of investment. Equally, from a risk-return point of view, the return must compensate adequately for any risk incurred. The time value of money principle will be illustrated in section 17.6.

Applying the concept: the principles of financial management

If a person invested R500 000 in a business, then he or she would forfeit the opportunity of earning interest on that amount, because he or she could have invested the amount in, say, a fixed deposit to earn 16% interest, and may have earned this return with less risk involved. The business would have to earn a return greater than 16% in order to increase the wealth of the owner.

17.5 Cost-volume-profit relationships

In section 17.3 the concepts of costs, fixed costs, variable costs, income, and profits, inter alia, were explained. In essence, the profitability of a business is determined by the unit selling price of its product, the costs (fixed and variable) of the product, and the level of the activity of the business (the volume of production and sales). A change in any one of the three components will result in a change in the total profit made by the business. The components therefore have to be viewed in conjunction with one another, and not in isolation. The underlying connection can be explained by means of a simplified numerical example in which only the volume of production and sales change.

The calculation in the example is referred to as break-even analysis, where the break-even point is reached when total costs are equal to total income. At the break-even point no profit or loss is realised.

The break-even point in a specific case can be calculated by using the following formula:

$$N = \frac{F}{(SP-V)}$$

N in the formula is the number of units (volume) where no profit or loss is made. The term (SP – V) is referred to as the marginal income or variable profit.

Example

Selling price (SP)	=	R12 per unit
Variable costs (V)	=	R8 per unit
Total fixed costs (F)	=	R100 000 per year

Number of units manufactured and sold:

N	=	30 000 (case 1)
N	=	40 000 (case 2)
Profit	=	P
From P	=	Income – cost
It follows that P	=	(N x SP) – [(N × V) + F]
Where N	=	30 000
P is	=	(30 000 × R12) – [(30 000 × R8) + R100 000]
	=	R360 000 – R340 000
	=	R20 000
Where N	=	40 000
P is	=	(40 000 × R12) – [(40 000 × R8) + R100 000]
	=	R480 000 – R420 000
	=	R60 000

The break-even analysis can also be done with the aid of a graph as in figure 17.10 (see p. 404).

Figure 17.10: A graphical representation of a breakeven analysis

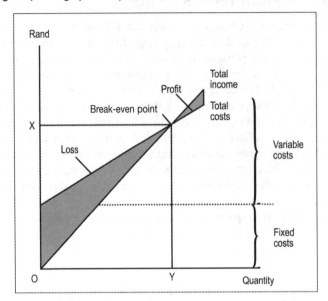

The break-even point is reached when the total income and total cost curves intersect – that is, at a sales and production volume of OY where the total costs and total income equal OX.

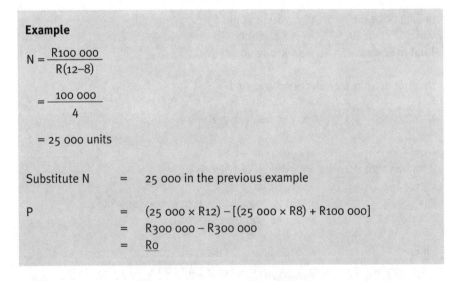

Example

$$N = \frac{R100\ 000}{R(12-8)}$$

$$= \frac{100\ 000}{4}$$

$$= 25\ 000\ \text{units}$$

Substitute N   =   25 000 in the previous example

P   =   (25 000 × R12) – [(25 000 × R8) + R100 000]

          =   R300 000 – R300 000

          =   R0

In the event of any change in the income as a result of a change in the selling price or a change in variable costs and/or fixed costs, the slope and point of intersection of the curves will change. The new break-even point is then to be obtained accordingly. The profit or loss at any sales volume can also be obtained. These values are the vertical differences between the total cost and the total income curves.

From the foregoing examples it is apparent that the production and sales volumes, the unit selling price and the fixed and variable costs together have an important effect on the profitability of a business. In practice, this type of analysis is carried out especially in the determination of the minimum size for a business at establishment, and also where the feasibility of potential expansion is concerned.

17.6 The time value of money

17.6.1 Introduction

In section 17.2 it was stated that all businesses require capital. As is evident from the following discussion, the payment or remuneration for the use of money or capital is fundamental to the financial structure of any free market society. In the investment and financing decisions of a business, it should be kept in mind that interest has to be paid for the use of capital. Also, funds or capital are normally required and used for either shorter or longer periods, and the use of capital therefore has a time implication.

Consequently, the purpose of this discussion is to explain the concept of the **time value of money** – the combined effect of both interest and time – in the context of financial decision making.

In principle, the time value of money bears a direct relation to the opportunity of earning interest on an investment. This is the opportunity rate of return on an investment. The opportunity to earn interest in the interim period is foregone if an amount is expected some time in future rather than received immediately.

The time value of money can be approached from two different perspectives. On the one hand, the calculation of the **future** value of some given present value or amount is possible, as is, on the other hand, the calculation of the **present** value of some expected future amount.

Applying the concept: the time value of money

If you were to choose between receiving a cash gift of R100 today or in a year's time, what would you prefer?

Naturally, you would prefer the R100 today. Why? The reasons are as follows:
- R100 received today is worth more than R100 expected one year from now, because it can be invested now to earn interest. This is the pure time value of money.
- There is the possibility that the person who wishes to make the gift will no longer wish to do so in a year's time, or may only give part of the money – there is therefore risk and uncertainty involved in waiting.
- The real purchasing power of the R100 may decline in the course of time under inflationary conditions.

The processes for the calculation of future values – **compounding** – and for the calculation of present values – **discounting** – proceed in opposite directions, as indicated in figure 17.11 (see p. 406).

Figure 17.11: The relationship between present value and future value

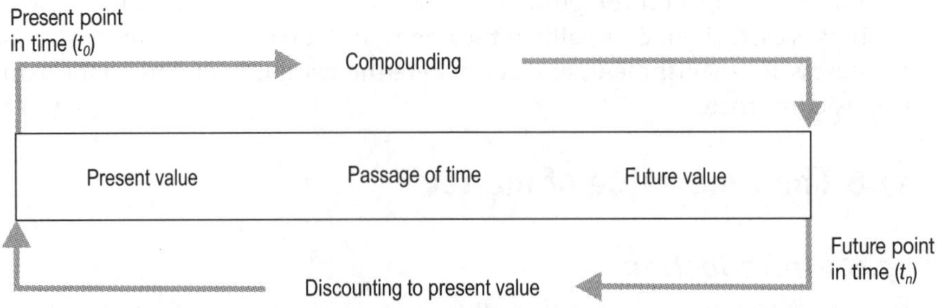

17.6.2 The approach to future value and present value

For the purpose of the following discussions on future values and present values a number of assumptions and principles underlying these concepts are mentioned briefly below.

- **The assumption of certainty.** It is assumed that all receipts and payments occur in the absence of risk and uncertainty.
- **The assumption of discrete periods.** It is assumed that the time periods over which future values or present values are calculated have been divided into discrete time periods – normally periods of one year.
- **The assumption concerning receipts and payments at the end of periods.** Unless stated otherwise, all payments and receipts are assumed to occur at the end of the specific time periods concerned. The initial investment, however, is normally assumed to occur at time t_0, the beginning of the investment period.
- **The assumption concerning inflation.** The effect of inflation is ignored, notwithstanding the direct though complex relationship between interest rates and inflation.
- **The assumption concerning taxation.** The effects of taxation are ignored.
- **The principle of the zero point in time.** The zero point in time refers to that specific point in time, in relation to a given time frame, where amounts – in terms of either future value or present value – are comparable. As will be explained in section 17.6.5, the zero point in time could be the beginning or the end of the investment period.

17.6.3 The future value of a single amount

The future value of an initial investment or principal is determined by means of **compounding**, which means that the amount of interest earned in each successive period is added to the amount of the investment at the end of the preceding period. Interest in the period immediately following is consequently calculated on a larger amount consisting of capital and interest. Interest is therefore earned on capital and interest in each successive period.

The formula for calculating the future value of an original investment is:

$$FV_n = PV (1 + i)^n$$

Where
- PV is the original investment or present value of the investment
- FV_n is the future value of the investment after n periods
- i is the interest rate per period expressed as a decimal number
- n is the number of discrete periods over which the investment extends

The factor $(1 + i)^n$ in the formula is known as the **future value factor** (FVF) or **compound interest factor** of a single amount.

Example

- What is the future value of an investment of R100 for one year at an interest rate of 5% per annum?

$$FV_1 = R100 \, (1 + 0{,}05)^1$$
$$= R100 \, (1{,}05)^1$$
$$= R105$$

- And if the investment is for three years?

$$FV_3 = R100 \, (1{,}05)^3$$
$$= R100 \, (1{,}1576)$$
$$= R115{,}76$$

The process for future value calculation is illustrated in figure 17.12.

Figure 17.12: Process for future value calculation

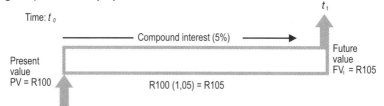

The future value of an original investment can also be calculated by using tables. An extract from these tables follows.

	Future value factors $(1 + i)^n$		
Periods (n)	**5%**	**10%**	**15%**
1	1, 0500	1, 1000	1, 1500
2	1, 1025	1, 2100	1, 3225
3	1, 1576	1, 3310	1, 5209
4	1, 2155	1, 4641	1, 7490
5	1, 2763	1, 6105	2, 0114
6	1, 3401	1, 7716	2, 3131
7	1, 4071	1, 9487	2, 6600
8	1, 4775	2, 1436	3, 0590
9	1, 5513	2, 3579	3, 5179
10	1, 6289	2, 5937	4, 0456

The example on page 407 for a three-year investment at an interest rate of 5% per annum is calculated as follows with the aid of the table on page 407:

$$FV^3 = R100\ (1,1576)$$
$$= R115,76$$

The result is identical to the one obtained by using the formula.

Bear in mind that the future value factor $(1 + i)^n$ is an exponential function, which means that the initial amount will grow exponentially over time.

The higher the interest rate, the faster the future value will grow for any given investment period as a result of the compounding effect and, consequently, interest is earned on interest in each successive period. The concept of the compound interest rate as a growth rate is of vital importance in financial management.

The values of any of the four variables in the equation for the calculation of the future value can be determined if the values of the remaining three are known, as shown below.

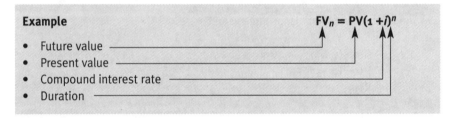

Example $FV_n = PV(1 + i)^n$

- Future value
- Present value
- Compound interest rate
- Duration

17.6.4 *Present value*

17.6.4.1 The present value of a single amount

The present value is also based on the principle that the value of money is, inter alia, affected by the timing of receipts or disbursements, as in the case of the future value.

If it is accepted that a rand today is worth more than a rand expected at some future date, what would the present value be now of an amount expected in future? The answer to this question revolves around the following:
- The investment opportunities available to the investor or recipient
- The future point in time at which the money is expected

An amount of R105 which is expected one year from now will have a present value of R100, provided the opportunity exists to invest the R100 today (time t_0) at an interest rate of 5% per annum.

This interest rate, which is used for discounting the future value of R105 one year from now to a present value of R100, reflects the time value of money and is the key to the present value approach. The interest rate or opportunity rate of return is the rate of interest that could be earned on alternative investments with similar risks if the money had been available for investment now. Stated differently, it is the rate of return that would be foregone by not utilising the investment opportunity. The process of discounting is explained by means of the time line in figure 17.13 (see p. 409).

Figure 17.13: Process for calculating the present value of a single amount

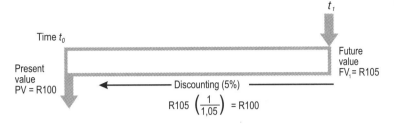

The **discounting process** is the reciprocal of the compounding process.

Consequently, the formula for the calculation of the present value of a future single amount is: $PV = FV_n \left[\frac{1}{(1 + i)}\right]^n$

The factor $\left[\frac{1}{(1 + i)}\right]^n$ is known as the **present value factor** or **discounting factor** for a future single amount.

Example

- What is the present value of R105 expected one year from now, if the investor's opportunity rate of return (discounting rate) is 5% per annum?

  $PV = FV_1 \left[\left(\frac{1}{(1 + 0,05)}\right)\right]^1$

  $\quad\quad R105 \left[\frac{1}{(1,05)}\right]^1$

  $\quad\quad \underline{R100}$

- What is the present value of R115,76 expected three years from now, if the discounting rate is 5% per annum?

  $PV = R115,76 \left[\frac{1}{(1,05)}\right]^3$

  $\quad\quad R105, 76 \ (0,8638)$

  $\quad\quad \underline{R100}$

Tables have also been compiled for the calculation of present values. An extract from these tables follows.

	Discounting factors $\left[\frac{1}{(1 + i)}\right]^n$		
Periods (n)	**5%**	**10%**	**15%**
1	0,9524	0, 9091	0, 8696
2	0, 9070	0, 8264	0, 7561
3	0, 8638	0, 7513	0, 6575
4	0, 8227	0, 6830	0, 5718
5	0, 7835	0, 6209	0, 4972
6	0, 7462	0, 5645	0, 4323
7	0, 7107	0, 5132	0, 3759
8	0, 6768	0, 4665	0, 3269
9	0, 6446	0, 4241	0, 2843
10	0, 6139	0, 3855	0, 2472

In the example on the previous page, the present value of R115,76 expected three years from now is calculated as follows, with the aid of the preceding table, at an opportunity rate of return or discounting rate of 5%.

$$PV = R115,76 \ (PVF_{5,3})$$
$$= R115,76 \ (0,8638)$$
$$= R100$$

The present value of a single amount is, accordingly, defined as follows:

> The **present value PV** of a future amount **FV$_n$** is the amount which, if invested today at a given interest rate of **i** per period, would grow to the same future amount **FV$_n$** at the end of **n** periods.

As illustrated in the example on p. 409, as long as the opportunity for investment at 5% per annum exists, the investor should be indifferent to a choice between R100 today or R115,76 in three years' time.

Closer investigation of the preceding discounting factors reveals that the values of these factors decrease progressively as i, or n, or both, increase. The exceptionally high decrease in the discounting factor with relatively high interest rates and long time periods means that:

- The higher the interest rate is, the smaller the present value of a given future amount will be
- The further in the future an amount is expected, the smaller its present value at a given interest rate will be

Interestingly, the present value factor $PVF_{10,10} = 0,3855$ implies that the present value of R1,00 expected in ten years is only 38,55 cents today, if the R1,00 could have been invested today at 10% for ten years. If an investment opportunity at 15% should exist – which is not unrealistic – the present value of R1,00 expected ten years from now is only 24,72 cents ($PVF_{15,10} = 0,2472$). Put differently, this also means that the value or purchasing power of R1,00 will decline to 24,72 cents over the next ten years if the average annual inflation rate is to be 15% a year over this period.

The present value factors and the future value factors (as well as the tables for these factors) are based on the assumption that any funds generated in any period over the total duration of the investment or project (such as annual interest receipts) are reinvested at the same interest rate for the remainder of the total investment period.

The values of any one of the four variables in the equation for the calculation of the future value can be determined, provided that the values of the three remaining variables are known.

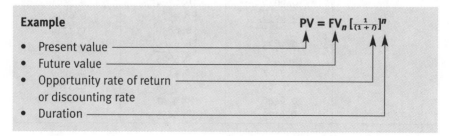

Example

$$PV = FV_n \ [\tfrac{1}{(1+i)}]^n$$

- Present value
- Future value
- Opportunity rate of return or discounting rate
- Duration

17.6.4.2 The present value of an uneven cash flow stream

The determination of the present value of a series of unequal cash flow amounts is approached in the same way as one would approach a single amount, irrespective of the total duration or the number of time periods involved. As in all applications of the time value of money, the timing of the cash receipts or disbursements is of crucial importance. This is evident from the following example of the calculation of the present value of an uneven cash flow stream at an interest rate or discounting rate of 10%.

Example

Year (t)	Annual cash flow (CF_t)
1	R 1 000
2	R 500
3	R 0
4	R 4 500
5	R 6 000
Total	R12 000

The appropriate discounting factors are found in the table on p. 409.

$$
\begin{aligned}
PV &= \text{R1 000 } (0{,}9091) + \text{R500 } (0{,}8264) + 0 + \text{R4 500 } (0{,}6830) + \text{R6 000} \\
&\quad (0{,}6209) \\
&= \text{R909,10} + \text{R413,20} + 0 + \text{R3 073,50} + \text{R3 725,40} \\
&= \text{R8 121,20}
\end{aligned}
$$

Note that no cash flow occurs at the end of the third period, and no contribution to the total present value at time t_0 therefore originates from that period. The cash flow amounts at the end of the first, second, fourth and fifth years respectively are multiplied by the respective discounting factors $PVF_{10,1}$, $PVF_{10,2}$, $PVF_{10,4}$ and $PVF_{10,5}$. The present values of the individual cash amounts are eventually added to obtain the total present value for the above uneven cash flow stream at time t_0. Capital investment decisions in particular require the calculation of the present value of uneven cash flow streams.

This brief overview of the present value approach is deemed sufficient for the purposes of this discussion. However, in practice, interest on savings accounts and deposits are often calculated biannually, quarterly, monthly, weekly and even daily. This could apply to both future value and present value applications, and is known as intra-year compounding and discounting.

17.6.5 The principles of equivalence and comparability

The **equivalence** of two different amounts at two given points in time is solely dependent on the investment opportunities available to the individual or business. If an amount of R100 today is invested for three years at a compound interest rate of 5% a year, this amount will grow to R115,76, as we have shown. The present value of R100 and the future value of R115,76 in three years is equivalent, if there are investment opportunities at 5%. The fact that these two amounts, at the specific points in time, reflect a time-adjusted equivalence only at an interest rate of 5% confirms the critical importance of the interest rate.

The comparison of the financial merits of two or more investment opportunities with different cash flow streams is meaningful only if the individual cash flow amounts for each investment alternative are adjusted to present values at a common point in time, normally t_0, using an appropriate discounting rate. However, the specific point in time selected for the comparison of alternative investments is not critical, as long as

- All the alternatives are compared at the same point in time
- The same interest rate or discounting rate is applied in the evaluation of all alternatives

The principles of equivalence and comparability are explained with reference to the three investment alternatives A, B and C, in table 17.1 , each requiring the same initial investment.

Table 17.1: Timing and the principles of equivalence and comparability

Timing of receipts (t)	Annual cash receipts		
	A	B	C
t_1	R100	R350	R 50
t_2	200	200	150
t_3	300	50	450
Total	R600	R600	R650

The total receipts for both investments A and B amount to R600. The only difference between A and B is found in the time patterns of their cash flow streams. Based on the time value of money, it is obvious that, as an investment, B is preferable to A, owing to B's larger cash flows in earlier years.

But is investment B also preferable to C? Although investment B has higher cash receipts in previous years than investment C, C has a larger total cash inflow than B. Hence, any choice merely on qualitative considerations on the basis of the time value of money, as in the case of A and B, is no longer straightforward. Investments B and C will now be compared with reference to the principle of comparability. All cash receipts for B and C are discounted to present values at time t_0 by means of an opportunity investment rate or discounting rate of 10% using the discounting factors $PVF_{i,n}$. The results are presented in table 17.2 on p. 413.

The present value of investment B at time t_0 (R521,04) is equivalent to the cash receipts of R350, R200 and R50 at times t_1, t_2 and t_3 respectively, provided that investment opportunities at an interest rate of 10% exist. Likewise, the present value of investment C at time t_0 (R507,51) is equivalent to the cash receipts of R50, R150 and R450 at times t_1, t_2 and t_3 respectively, provided that investment opportunities at an interest rate of 10% exist.

The time adjusted present value for investment B exceeds that for investment C, and investment B is, consequently, preferred. Despite the differences in the size as well as the timing of the individual annual receipts for investments B and C, their present values are, however, comparable at time t_0, provided that the same interest or discounting rate were used in evaluating both investments.

Table 17.2: Calculation of present values for investments B and C

Year	Timing	Investment B			Investment C		
		Receipts (1)	PVF (10%) (2)	Present value (1) x (2)	Receipts (1)	PVF (10%) (2)	Present value (1) x (2)
1	t_1	R350	0,9091	R318,19	R 50	0,9091	R 45,46
2	t_2	R200	0,8264	R165,28	R150	0,8264	R123,96
3	t_3	R50	0,7513	R 37,57	R450	0,7513	R338,09
Total present value (t_0)				R521,04			R507,51

Note: Because the present values for B and C are required at t_0, each individual cash receipt at the end of years 1, 2 and 3 has to be discounted to present values at t_0.

It has already been pointed out that the point in time at which investment alternatives are compared is not critical. This is illustrated in table 17.3 where it is shown that the end of the investment period at time t_3 could serve equally well for purposes of comparison, and that investment B is also preferable on the basis of future value.

Where cash flows differ with regard to the size of the cash flow amounts and the timing or occurrence of the cash flows, either the present value or the future value approach could be used for evaluation purposes in accordance with the principle of equivalence. This important relationship between present value and future value is illustrated in figure 17.14 with reference to investment B.

Figure 17.14: The equivalence of present and future values (10%)

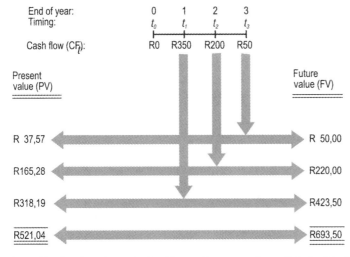

Note: The data have been obtained from tables 17.2 and 17.3. Note that the R50 at time t_3 is already a future value and requires no further adjustments.

It is evident from this figure that the cash flows of R350, R200 and R50 at times t_1, t_2 and t_3 respectively are equivalent to the present value of R521,04 at time t_0 and also to the future value of R693,50 at time t_3 at an interest rate of 10%.

Table 17.3: Calculation of the future values for investments B and C

Year	Timing	Investment B			Investment C		
		Receipts (1)	FVF (10%) (2)	Future value (1) x (2)	Receipts (1)	FVF (10%) (2)	Future value (1) x (2)
1	t_1	R350	1,2100	R423,50	R 50	1,2100	R 60,50
2	t_2	R200	1,1000	R220,00	R150	1,1000	R165,00
3	t_3	R50	1,0000	R 50,00	R450	1,0000	R450,00
Total future value (timing t_3)				R693,50			R675,50

Note: To determine the future values of B and C, each receipt has to be adjusted to a future value at time t_3, from the time of the receipt for the remainder of the investment period, by multiplying each individual cash receipt by the appropriate compound interest or future value factor, $FVFt_{i,n}$. Receipts at the end of the third year already constitute future values and do not require any further adjustment.

The following should be kept in mind with regard to the principle of equivalence and comparability:

- The "equivalence" of amounts at different points in time holds only for the same rate of interest.
- The comparison of alternative investments at any point in time – even earlier than t_0 or later than t_n – is acceptable, although t_0 and t_n are usually convenient points in time for comparison purposes.

The critical assumption that all interest or amounts generated by an investment are reinvested at the same rate for the remainder of the investment period applies to both present value and future value. All future value factors and present value factors in the respective tables have been developed on the basis of this assumption.

17.6.6 Conclusion

The principles and application of compounding and the time value of money as a basis for the determination of present values as well as future values have been explained in this section. The present value approach is an indispensable aid in financial management, particularly for a large business and listed company, where the majority of investment and financing decisions are taken in accordance with the goal of the maximisation of the value of the business. Even for small business organisations, a basic knowledge of compound interest methodology and unsophisticated discounted cash flow applications could be invaluable for capital investment decisions.

The most important implications of time value of money are as follows:

- Cash inflow must be accelerated (encourage debtors to pay their accounts as soon as possible)

- Cash outflow should be delayed without damaging the firm's credit record (pay creditors as late as possible)
- Manage inventory as optimally as possible

17.7 Financial analysis, planning and control[3]

In section 17.2, effective financial analysis, planning and control were identified as tasks of financial management. In this section, a short review of these related tasks is given.

17.7.1 Financial analysis

Financial analysis is necessary to monitor the general financial position of a business and, in the process, to limit the risk of financial failure of the business as far as possible. Financial analyses will reveal certain trends and also the financial strengths and weaknesses of the business so that corrective measures, if necessary, can be taken in time. To help it with its financial analyses, financial management have the following important aids at their disposal: the income statement, the balance sheet, the funds flow statement, and financial ratios. The following sections will focus on the various statements and the calculation of certain financial ratios.

Table 17.4: An example of an abridged income statement (rand values)

Abridged income statement of ABC Limited for the year ended 28 February 2003

Net sales (net income)		R3 000 000
Less cost of sales (cost of goods sold)		2 250 000
• Direct labour costs	1 000 000	
• Direct material costs	900 000	
• Indirect manufacturing costs	350 000	
Gross profit		750 000
Less operating costs		400 000
• Selling expenses	150 000	
• Depreciation	80 000	
• Administrative costs	170 000	
Operating profit		350 000
Less interest paid		30 000
Profit before tax		320 000
Tax (50%)		160 000
Net profit after tax		160 000
Less dividends to preference shareholders		5 000
Profit attributable to ordinary shareholders		155 000
Less dividends to ordinary shareholders		75 000
Retained profit (earnings)		80 000
Less reserves		–
Undistributed profit for the year		80 000

17.7.1.1 The income statement

The income statement has already been described in section 17.3.6, and diagrammatically represented in figure 17.9 (on p. 401). Consequently, a numerical example of a manufacturing company's abridged income statement (see table 17.4 on p. 415) will suffice for the purposes of this section.

17.7.1.2 The balance sheet

The balance sheet of a **company**, as well as the most important balance sheet items, have already been discussed in section 17.3.1, and diagrammatically represented in figure 17.2 (see p. 396). Thus, a numerical example of a company's balance sheet will suffice for the purposes of this section (table 17.5).

Table 17.5: An example of a company balance sheet (rand values)

Balance sheet of ABC Limited at 28 February 2003

Assets (Employment of capital)			R	Liabilities (Suppliers of capital)		R
Fixed assets			800 000	**Shareholders' capital**		
Land and buildings (cost price)		200 000		Authorised and issued – Ordinary shares (200 000 at R1 each)		200 000
Plant and equipment (cost price)	1 200 000					
Less				**Distributable reserves**		
Accumulated				Capital reserves	300 000	
depreciation	600 000	600 000		Undistributed profit	350 000	650 000
Other assets				*Owners' equity*		850 000
Investments			–	Preference share		
Total long-term assets			800 000	capital		50 000
				Shareholders' interest		900 000
Current assets			550 000			
Cash		60 000		**Long-term debt**		
Marketable securities		30 000		Debentures		200 000
Debtors (net)		220 000		*Total long-term*		
Inventory		200 000		*liabilities*		1 100 000
Prepaid expenses		40 000				
				Current liabilities		250 000
				Trade creditors	100 000	
				Bank overdraft	100 000	
				Arrear expenses	50 000	
			1 350 000			1 350 000

17.7.1.3 The flow of funds in a business

A business has to make optimum use of its limited funds to achieve its objectives. It is therefore necessary to conduct an analysis of how the capital of the business is employed and supplied. This analysis involves the flow of funds in the business.

The flow of funds of a firm is a continuous process and, following on the previous explanations of the balance sheet and income statement, can be represented as in figure 17.15 overleaf.

Figure 17.15: A simplified diagrammatical representation of the flow of funds of a business

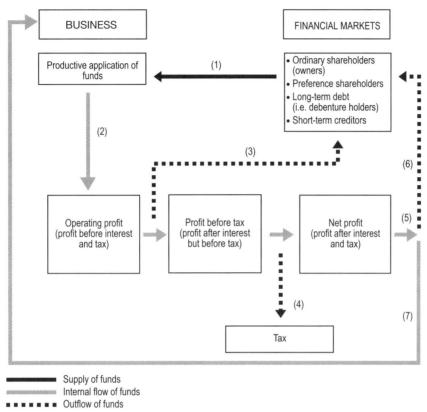

Supply of funds
Internal flow of funds
Outflow of funds

The following are apparent from figure 17.15:
- The business obtains funds in the financial market and applies these funds at a cost to produce goods and/or services.
- The business sells these goods and/or services at a price higher than the production costs and therefore shows an operating profit.
- Interest is paid to the suppliers of loan capital from the operating profit. This means an outflow of funds from the business.
- The profit remaining after the interest has been paid is taxable. This means a further outflow of funds from the business.
- The profit remaining after tax can be applied to preference and ordinary shareholders' dividends (outflow of funds), reserves and undistributed profits, resulting in a reinvestment in the production process.

It is clear from the above that there is a continuous flow of funds to and from the business. If the sales value of the goods and/or services produced by the business exceeds the costs incurred in the production of those goods and/or services, including the depreciation on equipment, the business will show a profit. A portion of the profit, after payment of interest and tax, is normally distributed among the preference and ordinary shareholders in the form of dividends. The remaining profit is reinvested in the business. The reinvestment leads to an increase in the available funds of the business.

17.7.1.4 The funds flow statement

The funds flow statement helps with the analysis of the changes in the financial position of the business between two consecutive balance sheet dates and, in the process, reflects the net effect of all transactions for a specific period on the financial position of the business. With this in mind, the balance sheets at the beginning and end of the period under review, as well as the income statement for the same period, are used.

The funds flow statement is based on the self-explanatory point of departure that the employment of funds depends on the availability of funds. In other words, before funds can be applied, they have to be obtained from some source.

There are two particular approaches to drawing up a funds flow statement, namely:

- According to changes in the net working capital
- According to changes in the cash position, including the current bank account

Table 17.6: A framework for a funds flow statement on cash use

Funds flow statement for the period 1 March 2002 to 28 February 2003

Source of funds	R	R	Application of funds	R	R
Profit before tax		......	*Loss*		......
			Decrease in share and preference share capital		......
Depreciation[1]		......	*Income tax paid*		......
Increase in share and preference share capital		......	*Cash dividends*		......
Increase in debt (Excluding bank overdraft and provisions			*Decrease in debt* (excluding bank overdraft and provisions		
• Trade creditors	......		• Trade creditors	......	
• Arrear expenses	......		• Arrear expenses	......	
• Long-term loans	......	......	• Long-term loans	......	......
			Increase in assets (Excluding cash in bank and on hand)		
Decrease in assets (Excluding cash in bank and on hand)			• Debtors	......	
• Debtors	......		• Stocks	......	
• Stocks	......		• Prepaid expenses	......	
• Prepaid expenses	......		• Sale of fixed assets[3]	......	......
• Sale of fixed assets[2]	......	......	Sub-total		
Sub-total		_____			
Balance (decrease in cash)[4]		(X) _____ XXX	Balance (decrease in cash)[4]		X _____ XXX

Notes:

1. Depreciation is deducted as a cost in order to calculate the profit (loss) before tax. Because it actually represents a non-cash cost, depreciation has to be added back to reflect the actual cash position.
2. Shown at net selling price.
3. At cost.
4. If the total source of funds exceeds the total application of funds, the difference will mean an increase in cash, and vice versa. These balances have to tally with the difference in cash between the opening and closing balance sheets.

Both approaches have their merits. However, the remainder of the discussion of the funds flow statement will be based on the second approach, simply because funds flow statements drawn up according to this method contain more information than those drawn up using the first approach.[4]

The funds flow statement that is drawn up on a cash basis contains a summary of the sources from which cash has been generated between two consecutive balance sheet dates, as well as a summary of the purposes for which cash has been used during the same period. If more cash has been generated than employed during the period under review, the cash available to the business will increase, and vice versa.

Funds flow statements drawn up according to this approach can be presented in various forms. Table 17.6 represents one of the forms that can be adopted.

An analysis of the funds flow statement offers many advantages, including the following:
- It gives an indication of whether the cash dividends are justified in terms of the cash generated by the business activities (profit).
- It gives an indication of how the growth in fixed assets has been financed.
- It gives an indication of possible imbalances in the application of funds.
- It helps financial management to analyse and evaluate the financing methods of the business.

17.7.1.5 Financial ratios

As mentioned earlier, financial ratios are one of the aids that financial management can employ in the process of effective financial analysis and control.

A financial ratio gives the relationship between two items (or groups of items) in the financial statements (especially the income statement and the balance sheet) and serves as a performance criterion to point out potential strengths and weaknesses of the business.

However, it must be emphasised that financial ratios do not identify the reasons for the strengths and weaknesses – they indicate only symptoms that need to be further diagnosed by financial management.

The financial ratios of a business are used by various interested parties, namely:
- **Financial management**, with a view to internal control, planning and decision making
- **The suppliers of borrowed capital**, to evaluate the ability of the business to pay its debt and interest
- **Potential owners**, to evaluate the business as an investment opportunity

Financial ratios as such have little, if any, usage value, and must be viewed against certain significant standards or norms to give them usage value. Three types of comparisons are significant in this regard:
- A comparison of the current financial ratios of the business with the corresponding ratios of the past and/or expected future ratios with a view to revealing a tendency
- A comparison of the financial ratios of the business with those of other similar businesses
- A comparison of the financial ratios of the business with the norms for the particular industry as a whole

There is a large variety of financial ratios as well as various classification methods. In this section only a few are mentioned, without paying attention to their respective merits. The calculations of the various ratios are explained by using the information given in the previous income statement and balance sheet.

(a) Liquidity ratios

Liquidity ratios provide an indication of the ability of a business to meet its short-term obligations as they become due, without curtailing or ceasing its normal activities. Providers of loan capital are interested in liquidity ratios because they give an indication of the degree to which a business can meet its debt obligations fully and punctually in the normal course of events.

Two liquidity ratios are of importance, namely:
- The current ratio
- The acid test ratio

The **current ratio** reflects the relationship between the value of the current assets and the extent of the current liabilities of a business.

$$\text{Current ratio} = \frac{\text{Current assets}}{\text{current liabilities}}$$

Using the figures of ABC Limited contained in table 17.5 results in a current ratio of 2,2:1, calculated as follows:

$$\text{Current ratio} = \frac{\text{Current assets}}{\text{current liabilities}}$$

$$= \frac{550\ 000}{250\ 000}$$

$$= 2,20:1$$

This means that the business had R2,20 of current assets available for each R1 of its current liabilities (short-term obligations). A larger ratio reflects a more favourable liquidity position than a smaller ratio. The smaller the ratio is, the greater the possibility that the business will not be able to meet its debt obligations fully and punctually, without curtailing or ceasing its normal activities. Traditionally a current ratio of 2:1 is recommended.

Since inventory cannot always be readily converted into cash in the short term, it may be misleading to evaluate the liquidity position of a business simply on the basis of the current ratio. The **acid test ratio** should therefore be used in combination with the current ratio as a criterion for evaluating liquidity.

$$\text{Acid test ratio} = \frac{\text{Current assets} - \text{inventory}}{\text{current liabilities}}$$

Using the figures of ABC Limited contained in table 17.5 (see p. 416) results in an acid test ratio of 1,4:1, calculated as follows:

$$\text{Acid test ratio} = \frac{\text{Current assets} - \text{inventory}}{\text{Current liabilities}}$$

$$= \frac{550\ 000 - 200\ 000}{250\ 000}$$

$$= \frac{350\ 000}{250\ 000}$$

$$= 1{,}40{:}1$$

This shows that for each rand's worth of current liabilities, the business had R1,40 of current assets, excluding inventory. As in the case of the current ratio, a larger ratio reflects a healthier liquidity position than a smaller ratio. Normally, a minimum acid test ratio of 1:1 is recommended.

Liquidity ratios should be evaluated with caution. The **nature** and **condition** of the current assets and the "correctness" of the **values** at which they were recorded in the balance sheet, can cause the actual liquidity position to differ radically from that which is reflected by the liquidity ratios.

Although it is important for a business to be liquid, it is also possible to be excessively liquid. In such a case funds are not being used optimally, but are confined to unproductive use in current assets. It is therefore important to realise that one should not strive unrestrictedly towards an improvement in the liquidity ratios.

(b) Solvency ratios

Solvency ratios indicate the ability of a business to repay its debts from the sale of the assets on cessation of its activities. Capital lenders usually show strong interest in solvency ratios because these indicate the risk level of an investment in the business. Seen from another angle, it gives the business an indication of the extent to which it will have access to additional loan capital, and the extent of its risk in its current financing.

There are two particularly important solvency ratios, namely:

• The debt ratio
• The gearing ratio

The **debt ratio** may be calculated using the following equation:

$$\textbf{Debt ratio} = \frac{\text{Debt}}{\text{Assets}} \times \frac{100}{1}$$

Using the figures of ABC Limited contained in table 17.5 (see p. 416) results in a debt ratio of 37%, calculated as follows:

$$\text{Debt ratio} = \frac{\text{Debt}}{\text{Assets}} \times \frac{100}{1}$$

$$= \frac{500\ 000}{1\ 350\ 000} \times \frac{100}{1}$$

$$= 37\%$$

This means that 37% of the assets were financed by debt (including preference shares). A lower percentage reflects a more favourable position than a higher percentage, and a maximum debt ratio of 50% is normally required.

The **gearing ratio** may be calculated using the following equation:

$$\text{Gearing ratio} = \frac{\text{Owners' equity}}{\text{Debt}}$$

Using the figures of ABC Limited contained in table 17.5 (see p. 416) results in a gearing ratio of 1,7:1, calculated as follows:

$$\begin{aligned}
\text{Gearing ratio} &= \frac{\text{Owners' equity}}{\text{Debt}} \\
&= \frac{850\ 000}{500\ 000} \\
&= 1,7{:}1
\end{aligned}$$

This indicates that for each R1 of debt (including preference shares), the business had R1,70 of owners' equity. A larger ratio once again reflects a more favourable situation than a smaller ratio, and a minimum gearing ratio of 1:1 is normally required.

The following aspects concerning solvency ratios need to be emphasised:

- The three solvency ratios illustrate the same situation as seen from different angles. To evaluate the solvency situation of a business it is therefore necessary to use only one of these ratios.
- Solvency ratios should not simply be accepted at face value. What constitutes a safe ratio for a particular business depends on various factors such as the risks to which it is subject, the nature of the assets and the degree to which creditors will be accommodating in emergency situations.

(c) Profitability, rate of return or yield ratios

- **Gross profit margin**

The gross profit margin may be found by:

$$\frac{\text{Gross profit}}{\text{sales}} \times \frac{100}{1}$$

The gross profit margin indicates how profitable sales have been. The gross profit also gives an indication of the mark-up percentage used by a firm. A firm with a gross profit margin of 50% uses (on average) a mark-up of 100%, as will be illustrated here. Assume sales equal R200 and the cost of goods sold equals R100. This yields a gross profit of R100 and a gross profit margin of 50%:

$$\text{Gross profit margin} = \frac{\text{R200} - \text{R100}}{\text{R200}} \times \frac{100}{1} = 50\%$$

- **Net profit margin**

Net profit margin may be found by:

$$\frac{\text{Net income}}{\text{sales}} \times \frac{100}{1}$$

The net profit margin gives an indication of the overall profitability of the firm and management's ability to control revenue and expenses. In order to improve profitability, management needs to increase revenue and/or decrease expenses.

- **Return on total capital**

This ratio may be computed as follows:

$$\text{Return on total capital} = \frac{\text{operating profit} - \text{tax}}{\text{total capital}} \times \frac{100}{1}$$

Using the figures of ABC Limited contained in tables 17.4 (see p. 415) and 17.5 (see p. 416) results in a return on total capital (after tax) of 14,1%, calculated as follows:

$$\text{Return on total capital} = \frac{350\,000 - 160\,000}{1\,350\,000} \times \frac{100}{1}$$
$$\text{(after tax)}$$
$$= 14,1\%$$

- **Return on shareholders' interest**

The return on shareholders' interest may be calculated using the following equation:

$$\frac{\text{Net profit after tax}}{\text{Shareholders' interest}}$$

Using the figures of ABC Limited contained in tables 17.4 and 17.5 results in a return on shareholders' interest of 21,1%, calculated as follows:

$$= \frac{190\,000}{900\,000} \times \frac{100}{1}$$

$$= 21,1\%$$

- **Return on owners' equity (ROE)**

The return on owners' equity may be calculated using the following equation:

$$\frac{\text{Net income}}{\text{sales}} \times \frac{\text{sales}}{\text{total assets}} \times \frac{\text{total assets}}{\text{owners' equity}}$$

which can be reduced to

$$\frac{\text{Net income}}{\text{owners' equity}} \times \frac{100}{1}$$

Using the figures of ABC Limited contained in tables 17.4 and 17.5 results in a return on owners' equity of 18,2%, calculated as follows:

$$\text{Return on owners' equity} = \frac{155\,000}{850\,000} \times \frac{100}{1}$$
$$= 18,2\%$$

A firm's return on equity (ROE) therefore depends on the firm's net profit margin, asset turnover and financial leverage. An increase in ROE can be achieved by increasing each of the aforementioned three variables.

The ROE, in turn, has an important influence on the sustainable growth rate (g) of a firm. The sustainable growth rate is found by:

g = ROE x retention ratio

where retention ratio = retained earnings ÷ net income

Example

Assume a firm achieved an ROE of 18,2% and paid out R62 000 of the net income as dividends. The retained earnings equal R155 000 – R62 000 = R93 000, which implies a payout ratio of 40% or a retention ratio of 60%:

$$\text{Retention ratio} = \frac{\text{R93 000}}{\text{R155 000}} \times \frac{100}{1} = 60\%$$

Given the ROE of 18,2% and a retention ratio of 60%, the firm's growth rate equals

g = 18,2% x 0,60 = 10,92%

So far liquidity, solvency and profitability ratios have been described. Since the long-term goal of the firm is to increase the value of the firm, management should focus on measures of economic value.

(d) Measures of economic value[5]

Measures of economic value are the economic value added (EVA®) and market value added (MVA). These measures can best be applied to public companies, in other words, companies listed on a securities exchange such as the Johannesburg Securities Exchange (JSE), the London Stock Exchange (LSE) and the New York Stock Exchange (NYSE).

EVA is defined as:

EVA = EBIT $(1 - T)$ – Cost of capital expressed in rand
where EBIT = earnings before interest and tax
         T = tax rate

Example

Assume a firm has achieved an EBIT of R2 400 000 and is subject to a tax rate of 35%. The firm's balance sheet shows equity at R8 000 000 and debt at R2 000 000. The firm's weighted average cost of capital (WACC) equals 16%.

EVA   = R2 400 000 $(1 - 0.35)$ – 0.16 (R800 000 + R200 000)
      = R2 400 000 (0.65) – 0.16 (R1 000 000)
      = R1 560 000 – R160 000
      = R1 400 000

A positive EVA is an additional contribution to shareholders' wealth made during the year.

The market value of a public company's equity is simply the number of shares which have been issued times the price of the share. If this market value is greater than the book value of the shares, then the value added is called market value added (MVA).[6]

Example

Assume the ordinary shares of Telkom Ltd were issued at R2 each (the so-called par value). A year later, a Telkom ordinary share trades at R6 each. The R4 difference is regarded as MVA.

17.7.1.6 Concluding remarks

The preceding explanation offered a brief survey of the financial analysis task of financial management. From the explanation it is apparent that the income statement, balance sheet, funds flow statement, and financial ratios are important aids in the performance of this task.

In the following section the focus is on financial planning and control on the basis of this planning.

17.7.2 Financial planning and control[7]

Financial planning and control are done in most business organisations by means of budgets.

A budget can be seen as a formal written plan of future action, expressed in monetary terms and sometimes also in physical terms, to achieve the objectives of the business with limited resources. As such, budgets are also used for control purposes. Control is carried out by comparing the actual results with the planned (budgeted) results periodically or on a continuous basis. In this way deviations are identified and corrective action can be taken in time.

This section provides a brief overview of the following:
- The focal points of budgets in the control system of a manufacturing business
- An integrated budgeting system for a manufacturing business
- Zero-based budgeting

17.7.2.1 The focal points of budgets in a control system

Control systems are devised to ensure that a specified strategic business function or activity (for example, manufacturing or sales) is carried out properly. Consequently, control systems should focus on, and budgets be devised, for various responsibility centres in a business. A responsibility centre can be described as any organisational or functional unit in a business that is headed by a manager responsible for the activities of that unit. All responsibility centres use resources (inputs or costs) to produce something (outputs or income). Typically, responsibility is assigned to income, cost (expense), profit and/or investment centres.
- In the case of an **income centre**, outputs are measured in monetary terms,

though the size of these outputs is not directly compared with the input costs. The sales department of a business is an example of such an income centre. The effectiveness of the centre is not measured in terms of how much the income (units sold x selling prices) exceeds the cost of the centre (for example, salaries and rent). Instead, budgets in the form of sales quotas are prepared, and the budgeted figures compared with actual sales. This provides a useful picture of the effectiveness of individual sales personnel or of the centre itself.

- In a **cost centre**, inputs are measured in monetary terms, though outputs are not. The reason for this is that the primary purpose of such a centre is not the generation of income. Good examples of cost centres are the maintenance, research and administrative departments of a business. Consequently, budgets should be developed only for the input portion of these centres' operations.
- In a **profit centre**, performance is measured by the monetary difference between income (outputs) and costs (inputs). A profit centre is created whenever an organisational unit is given the responsibility of earning a profit. In this case budgets should be developed in such a way that provision is made for the planning and control of inputs and outputs.
- In an **investment centre** the monetary value of inputs and outputs is again measured, but the profit is also assessed in terms of the assets (investment) employed to produce this profit.

It should be clear that any profit centre can also be considered as an investment centre because its activities require some form of capital investment. However, if the capital investment is relatively small or if its manager(s) have no control over the capital investment, it is more appropriate from a planning and control – and thus from a budgeting point of view – to treat it as a profit centre.

17.7.2.2 An integrated budgeting system for a manufacturing business

In essence, an integrated budgeting system for a manufacturing business consists of two main types of budgets, namely:
- Operating budgets
- Financial budgets

Figure 17.16 (see p. 427) diagrammatically shows the operating and financial components of an integrated budgeting system of a manufacturing business.

Operating budgets parallel three of the responsibility centres discussed earlier, namely cost, income and profit:
- **Cost budgets.** There are two types of cost budgets, namely manufacturing cost budgets and discretionary cost budgets. Manufacturing cost budgets are used where outputs can be accurately measured. These budgets usually describe the material and labour costs involved in each production item, as well as the estimated overhead costs. These budgets are designed to measure efficiency, and if the budget is exceeded it means that manufacturing costs were higher than they should have been. Discretionary cost budgets are used for cost centres in which output cannot be measured accurately (for example, administration and research). Discretionary cost budgets are

Figure 17.16: Diagrammatical representation of an integrated budgeting system of a manufacturing business

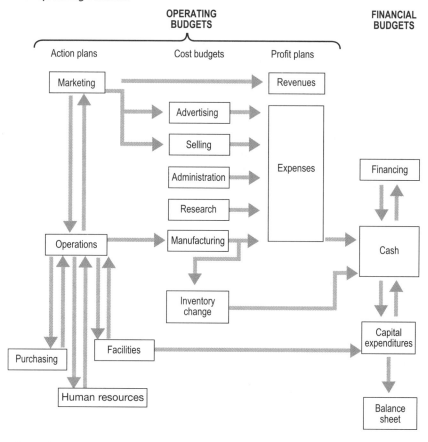

Source: Stoner, J.A.F. & Freeman, R.E., *Management*, 5th edition, Pearson Education (UK), 1992, p. 617.

not used to assess efficiency because performance standards for discretionary expenses are difficult to devise.

- **Income budgets.** These budgets are developed to measure marketing and sales effectiveness. They consist of the expected sales quantity multiplied by the expected unit selling price of each product. The income budget is the most critical part of a profit budget, yet it is also one of the most uncertain because it is based on projected future sales.

- **The profit plan or profit budget.** This budget combines cost and income budgets and is used by managers who have responsibility for both the expenses and income of their units. Such managers frequently head an entire division or business.

Financial budgets, which are used by financial management for the execution of the financial planning and control task, consist of capital expenditure, cash, financing and balance sheet budgets. These budgets, prepared from information contained in the operating budgets, integrate the financial planning of the business with its operational planning. Financial budgets serve three major purposes:

- They verify the viability of the operational planning (operating budgets).
- They reveal the financial actions that the business must take to make the execution of its operating budgets possible.
- They indicate how the operating plans of the business will affect its future financial actions and condition. If these future actions and conditions are undesirable (for example, over-borrowing to finance additional facilities) appropriate changes in the operating plans may be required.

The **capital expenditure budget** indicates the expected (budgeted) future capital investment in physical facilities (buildings, equipment, etc.) to maintain its present or expand the future productive capacity.

The **cash budget** indicates:

- The extent, time and sources of expected cash inflows
- The extent, time and purposes of expected cash outflows
- The expected availability of cash in comparison with the expected need for it

The **financing budget** is developed to assure the business of the availability of funds to meet the budgeted shortfalls of receipts (income) relative to payments (expenses) in the short term, and to schedule medium-term and long-term borrowing or financing. The financing budget is therefore developed in conjunction with the cash budget to provide the business with the funds it needs at the times it needs them.

The **balance sheet budget** brings together all the other budgets to project how the financial position of the business will look at the end of the budget period if actual results conform to planned results. An analysis of the balance sheet budget may suggest problems (for example, a poor solvency situation due to over-borrowing) or opportunities (for example, excessive liquidity, creating the opportunity to expand) that will require alterations to the other budgets.

17.7.2.3 Zero-based budgeting

In the normal budgeting process, the previous year's actual expenditure is used as the point of departure and is only adjusted to make provision for expected changing circumstances such as inflation. Such a process creates a built-in bias towards continuing the same activities year after year without critically re-evaluating priorities and possible changes in the external and internal environments.

In contrast, zero-based budgeting enables the business to look at its activities and priorities afresh on an annual basis. In this case, historical results are not automatically taken as a basis for the next budgeting period. Instead, each manager has to justify anew his or her entire budget request.

In theory, zero-based budgeting leads to a better prioritisation of resource allocations, and more efficient businesses. In practice, however, it may generate undue amounts of paperwork and demoralise managers and other employees who are expected to justify their activities, expenses, and in essence, therefore, their existence, on an annual basis. For these reasons, zero-based budgeting is less often used at present than in the past.

17.8 Summary

In this chapter we firstly examined the nature of the financial function and the tasks of financial management, as well as the relationship between financial management, the other functional management areas, related subject disciplines, and the environment. Thereafter, various concepts generally used in financial management, as well as certain techniques employed by financial management, were explained. The goal and fundamental principles of financial management were also explained. Finally, one of the tasks of financial management, namely financial analysis, planning and control, was outlined. The remaining tasks of financial management are dealt with, inter alia, in chapters 18 and 19.

References

1. Lynch, R.M. & Williamson, R.W., *Accounting for management, planning and control*, McGraw-Hill, New York, 1983, p. 8.
2. Marx, J., De Swardt, C.J. & Nortjé, A., *Financial management in Southern Africa*, Prentice Hall, Cape Town, 1999.
3. Partially based on Marx, F.W. & Van Aswegen, P.J. (eds.), *Business economics*, HAUM, Pretoria, 1983, and on Gitman, L.J., *Principles of managerial finance*, 10th edition, Addison Wesley, Boston, Massachusetts, 2003.
4. For example, Marx, F.W. & Van Aswegen, P.J. (eds.) and Gitman, L.J., *op. cit.*
5. Internet: www.eva.com
6. Marx, J., Mpofu, R.T. & Van de Venter, T.W.G., *Investment management*, J.L. van Schaik, Pretoria, 2003.
7. Based on Stoner, J.A.F. & Freeman, R.E., *Management*, 5th edition, Prentice Hall, Englewood Cliffs, New Jersey, 1992, pp. 613–621.

18 Asset management: the investment decision

The purpose of this chapter

This chapter gives an overview of the management of current assets, that is, cash and marketable securities, debtors and stock. It also explains the principles and the implementation of capital budgeting techniques in the management of fixed assets. Finally, it focuses on long-term investment decisions and capital budgeting, which includes the capital budgeting process, risk and return, and the evaluation of investment projects

Learning outcomes

The content of this chapter will enable learners to:
- Manage the current assets of a business by:
  - Identifying and describing the current asset categories
  - Describing the principles involved in managing each category
  - Applying the elementary techniques described in the text to manage each category of current assets
- Manage the fixed assets of a business to create wealth for stakeholders by:
  - Describing and justifying the principles of, and applying capital budgeting techniques such as the net present value (NPV) method
  - llustrating the ability to incorporate risk into the capital budgeting decision
- Manage assets optimally by combining short-term and long-term investment decisions

18.1 Introduction

In chapter 17 management of the asset structure is identified as one of the main tasks of financial management.

To successfully pursue the main objective, management of the asset structure requires that decisions regarding investment in current and fixed assets be taken as effectively as possible. These decisions have a direct influence on the scope of the investment in current assets and the acquisition of fixed assets that will maximise the wealth of stakeholders.[1]

Anglo American says:

Our corporation exists to create wealth and generate rewards for its key stake-holders – its shareholders and employees who, together with their dependants, account for 1,5 million South Africans. That is its first responsibility, to the community at large as much as to its stakeholders, for if it fails in that aim it will lack the means of discharging any broader social responsibilities.

Source: Relly, G., Supplement to *Financial Mail*, 28 September 1989, p. 41.

18.2 The management of current assets

18.2.1 *The cost and risk of investing in current assets*

In table 17.5 in chapter 17 (see p. 416) you will have seen that current assets include items such as cash, marketable securities, debtors and inventory. These items are needed to ensure the continuous and smooth functioning of the business. **Cash**, for example, is needed to pay bills that are not perfectly matched by current cash inflows, while an adequate supply of **raw materials** is required to sustain the manufacturing process. Sales may be influenced by the **credit** the business is prepared to allow.

Current assets are therefore a necessary and significant component of the total assets of the business. Figure 18.1 shows that the ratio of current to total assets may vary from company to company. A retailer such as Pick 'n Pay has a large ratio of current to total assets compared to, say, Sasol, which is listed under the JSE sector Oil and Gas Exploration and Production, and produces fuels and chemicals for the chemical industry. This is because most of the assets of retail stores are in the form of inventory (current assets). Their main business is trading in inventory, not manufacturing, while the chemical industry has large investments in plant and other fixed assets.

Figure 18.1:The ratio of current to total assets for Sasol and Pick 'n Pay (1998–2001)

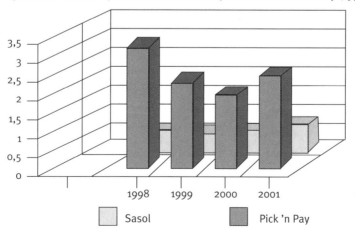

Source: Compiled from information supplied by *McGregor's securities exchange digest*, September–December 2002. © WhoOwnsWhom/McGregor's Digest.

In managing current assets, management should always keep in mind the consequences of having too much or too little invested in them. Two factors play a role, namely **cost** and **risk**.

An **over-investment** in current assets means a low degree of risk, in that more than adequate amounts of cash are available to pay bills when they come due, or sales are amply supported by more than sufficient levels of inventory.[2] However, over-investment causes profits to be less than the maximum, firstly because of the cost associated with the capital invested in additional current assets, and secondly because of income foregone which could have been earned elsewhere – the so-called "opportunity cost of capital". The funds invested in excess inventory could, for example, have been invested in a short-term deposit earning interest at the prevailing interest rate.

An **under-investment** in current assets, however, increases the risk of cash and inventory shortages and the costs associated with these shortages, but it also decreases the opportunity cost. For example, a business that is short of cash may have to pay high interest rates to obtain funds on short notice, while a shortage of inventory may result in a loss of sales, or even mean that the business has to buy inventory from competitors at high prices to keep customers satisfied.

The optimal level of investment in current assets is a trade-off between the costs and the risks involved.

Having made these general introductory remarks on investment in current assets, we will now discuss the management of the following current assets in more detail:

- Cash and marketable securities
- Debtors
- Inventory

18.2.2 The management of cash and marketable securities

Cash is the money (currency and coin) the business has on hand in petty cash drawers, in cash registers, and in current and savings accounts with financial institutions.

The costs of holding cash are:

- **Loss of interest.** Cash in the form of notes and coins, and even money in a current account at a bank, earns no interest.
- **Loss of purchasing power.** During a period of inflation there is an erosion in the value of money, which becomes even more serious if no interest is earned on that money.

The costs of little or no cash are:

- **Loss of goodwill.** Failure to meet financial obligations on time due to cash shortages will seriously affect the relationship between the company and its employees, creditors, and suppliers of raw materials and services.
- **Loss of opportunities.** Cash shortages will make it impossible to react quickly to a lucrative business opportunity.
- **Inability to claim discounts.** Discounts for prompt and early payment are very advantageous in percentage terms. Cash shortages may preclude the claiming of such discounts.

- **Cost of borrowing.** Shortages of cash may force a business to raise money at short notice at expensive rates.

Marketable securities are investment instruments on which the business earns a fixed interest income. They can easily be converted into cash, and are therefore also referred to as near-cash assets. An example of a marketable security is a short-term treasury bill issued by the government.

As shown in figure 17.2 in chapter 17 (see p. 396), cash and the investment in marketable securities (near-cash) are together referred to as the **liquid assets** of the business.

There are three reasons why a business should have a certain amount of cash available:
- The transaction motive
- The precautionary motive
- The speculative motive

The **transaction motive** exists primarily because receipts and disbursements are not fully synchronised. Expenses must often be paid before any cash income has been received. The business needs to have sufficient cash available to meet normal current expenditures such as the payment of wages, salaries, rent and creditors.

The **precautionary motive** entails the keeping of cash, in addition to that prompted by the transaction motive, for contingencies. Contingencies are unexpected events such as a large debtor defaulting on its account, or employees making an unexpected wage demand that may strain the financial position of the business. These funds are usually held in the form of marketable securities that can easily be converted into cash.

The **speculative motive** implies that the business must be able to capitalise on good opportunities such as unexpected bargains and bulk purchases. Additional funds for this purpose are usually also held in the form of marketable securities. A competitor may, for example, be declared insolvent and its inventory sold at bargain prices. The business can only capitalise on this opportunity if it has extra cash available to take advantage of it.

Cash management is essential to obtain the optimal trade-off between the liquidity risk and the cost of being too liquid. This is achieved by focusing on the **cash budget** and the **cash cycle**.

These two aspects of cash management will now be considered in more detail.

18.2.2.1 The cash budget

Determining the cash needs of a business is an important aspect of cash management. Unutilised cash surpluses or cash shortages result in the cost and risk of the cash investment increasing unnecessarily.

Cash-flow problems were advanced as the primary cause of the demise of several large real estate development companies, such as Corlett Drive Estates, in the early 1970s.

Applying the concept: risks and costs of investing in current assets

Assume there are two almost identical enterprises, A and B. Enterprise B differs from A only in an additional investment in current assets which is held in the form of marketable equities. The additional current assets were financed by shareholders' funds and the enterprise gets 6% interest on the marketable equities. The balance sheets and operating profit (after tax) of enterprises A and B is set out in table 18.1 below.

Table 18.1: Balance sheets and operating profit (after tax)

	Business	
	A	**B**
Cash	R1 000	R1 000
Marketable securities		R10 000
Debtors	19 000	19 000
Inventory	30 000	30 000
Current assets	R50 000	R60 000
Fixed assets	R100 000	R100 000
Total	R150 000	R160 000
Current liabilities	20 000	20 000
Debt (long term)	30 000	30 000
Shareholders' funds	100 000	110 000
Total	R150 000	R160 000
Operating income (after tax)	**15 000**	**15 300***

* B earns 6% on an investment of R10 000 in marketable securities. At a tax rate of 50% the income after tax is R300.

Current ratio = Current assets/Current liabilities	
Business A	**Business B**
50 000/20 000 = 2,5:1	60 000/20 000 = 3:1

Rate of return (after tax) = Operating income (after tax)/Total capital	
15 000/150 000 = 10%	15 300/160 000 = 9,6%

B is more liquid than A (current ratio of 3:1 compared to a ratio of 2,5:1 for A) and therefore also less risky than A. The rate of return of B, however, is less than that of A (a rate of return of 9,6% compared to that of A of 10%). See section 17.7.1.5 for a discussion and a definition of the current ratios and rate of return (after tax).

This example illustrates that cost and risk are of prime importance in the management of current assets.

The cash budget facilitates the planning and control of cash. Its purpose is to identify future cash shortages and cash surpluses. The cash budget is therefore a detailed plan of future cash flows for a specific period and is composed of the following three elements:

- **Cash receipts.** These originate from cash sales, collections from credit sales, and other sources such as cash injections in the form of, say, bank loans.

> **Quoth the banker, "Watch cash flow."**
>
> Though my bottom line is black, I am flat upon my back,
> My cash flows out and customers pay slow.
> The growth of my receivables is almost unbelievable;
> The result is certain unremitting woe!
> And I hear the banker utter an ominous low mutter,
> "Watch cash flow."

Source: Bailey, S.H., Quote the Banker: Watch cash flow, *Publishers' Weekly*, 13 January 1975.

- **Cash disbursements.** These are broadly categorised as cash paid for purchases of merchandise, raw materials, and operating expenses.
- **Net changes in cash.** These represent the difference between cash receipts and cash disbursements.

The cash budget serves as a basis for determining the cash needs of a business and indicates when bridging finance will be required. The following example (Save Retailers) shows how the cash budget is used to determine cash needs.

It is clear that the cash budget can be used to identify temporary cash shortages, and that this information can be used to arrange bridging finance timeously. It also indicates excess liquidity, and this information can again be used to plan temporary investments in marketable securities.

The cash budget for Save Retailers in the accompanying box shows, for example, that bridging finance will have to be arranged for April and May, and that arrangements will have to be made to invest the cash surplus that will arise during June. Although one assumes that profit equals an amount held in cash, this is almost never the case. The difference between profit and cash flow is illustrated in the accompanying box. This example shows that a profitable business may not be able to continue its operations due to a cash shortage. The shortage arises despite growing sales and the accumulation of profits.

Applying the concept: the cash budget

For Save Retailers there is a 30-day collection period on debtors, which means that there is a lag of 30 days between a credit sale and the receipt of cash. Consequently, cash collections in any month equal the credit sales one month prior. Purchases on credit must also be paid within 30 days.

Table 18.2: Save Retailers

		March	April	May	June
1.	CASH ON HAND (A)	0	20	(32)	(13)
2.	CASH RECEIPTS				
	(a) Cash sales	25	23	30	50
	(b) Collections from debtors	225	200	270	450
	TOTAL CASH RECEIPTS (B)	250	223	300	500
3.	CASH DISBURSEMENTS				
	(a) Creditors	144	144	144	144
	(b) Wages	60	60	66	66
	(c) Overheads	26	26	26	26
	(d) Owner's withdrawal	0	45	45	43
	TOTAL CASH DISBURSEMENTS (C)	230	275	281	277
4.	NET CASH POSITION (A + B – C)	20	(32)	(13)	210

Example: Profits and cash flow

Suppose we have a product that costs R75 to manufacture and is sold for R100. Payment is received within 30 days of sale. Production is based on the expected sales of the following month. Sales for the next three months, January to March, are expected to increase. Production costs are paid during the month in which production takes place. From December to April the course of events was as follows:

December   1 500 units were sold. Debtors on January 1 amount to R150 000 and 1 500 units were in stock.

January

1 January:	Cash	R75 000
	Inventory (1 500 @ R75)	112 500
	Debtors (1 500 @ R100)	150 000

During January, 2 000 units are sold and 2 500 are manufactured to keep one month's sales (1 500 + 2 500 − 2 000 = 2 000) in stock.

Profit for January: 2000 units × (R100 − 75)
= 2 000 × R25
= R50 000

February

1 February: Cash   R37 500

Opening balance	R75 000
Plus: Received from debtors	R150 000
Minus: Production costs (2 500 × R75)	R187 500

Inventory (2 000 @ 75)   R150 000

Opening balance	1 500
Plus: Manufactured	2 500
Minus: Sales	2 000

Debtors (2 000 @ R100)   R200 000

During February, sales increase to 2 500 units, and in preparation for sales expected in March, 3 000 units are produced.

Profit for February	2 500 units × (R100 − 75)
	= 2 500 × R25
	= R62 500
Cumulative Profit	= R50 000 + R62 500
	=R112 500

March

1 March: Cash   R12 500

Opening balance	R37 500
Plus: Received from debtors	R200 000
Minus: Production costs (2 500 × R75)	R225 000

                                        Inventory (2 500 @ R75)   R187 500

Opening balance	2 000
Plus: Manufactured	3 000
Minus: Sales	2 500

                                        Debtors (2 500 @ R100)   R250 000

During March, sales increase to 3 000 units, and in preparation for sales expected in April, 3 500 units are produced.

Profit for March   3 000 units × (R100 – 75)
                          = 3 000 × R25
                          = R75 000

Cumulative Profit   = R50 000 + R62 500 + R75 000
                          =R187 500

April

1 April: Cash   R0

Opening balance	R12 500
Plus: Received from debtors	R250 000
Minus: Production costs (3 500 × R75)	R262 500

                                        Inventory (3 000 @ R75)   R225 000

Opening balance	R2 500
Plus: Manufactured	R3 500
Minus: Sales	R3 000

                                        Debtors (3 000 @ R100)   R300 000

Notwithstanding a total profit of R187 500 after 3 months (on April 1) the business is without cash and production cannot be continued.

18.2.2.2 The cash cycle

The cash cycle in a manufacturing business, as illustrated in figure 18.2, indicates the time it takes to complete the following cycle:

- Investing cash in raw materials
- Converting the raw materials to finished products
- Selling the finished products on credit
- Ending the cycle by collecting cash

Figure 18.2: The cash cycle in a business

Wholesalers and retailers are not involved in the second step, but are rather concerned with directly converting cash into inventory. Businesses that offer no credit have no conversion from debtors to cash. As a rule, cash is available only after money has been collected from debtors.

The cash cycle is a continuous process, and it should be clear that the demand for cash can be greatly reduced if the cycle is speeded up. This is achieved by rapid cash collections and by proper management of debtors and stock (inventory).

18.2.3 The management of debtors

Debtors arise when a business **sells on credit** to its clients. Debtors have to settle their accounts in a given period (usually within 30 or 60 days after date of purchase). Credit may be extended to either an individual or a business. Credit granted to an individual is referred to as **consumer credit**. Credit extended to a business is known as **trade credit**. Debtor accounts represent a considerable portion of the investment in current assets in most businesses and obviously demand efficient management.

Credit sales increase total sales and income. As pointed out in the management of cash, debtor accounts have to be recovered as soon as feasible to keep the cash requirements of the business as low as possible. Once again, an optimal balance has to be struck between the amount of credit sales (the higher the credit sales, the higher the income and hopefully the profitability) and the size of debtor accounts (the greater the size of debtor accounts and the longer the **collection period**, the higher the investment and **cash needs** of the business will be, and the lower the profitability).

In any business, the three most important facets of the management of debtor accounts are the following:

- The credit policy
- The credit terms
- The collection policy

The **credit policy** contains directives according to which it is decided whether credit should be granted to clients and, if so, how much. Essentially, this involves an **evaluation of the creditworthiness** of debtors, based on realistic credit standards. The latter revolve around the "four Cs of credit":

- **Character** – the customer's willingness to pay
- **Capacity** – the customer's ability to pay
- **Capital** – the customer's financial resources
- **Conditions** – current economic or business conditions

These four general characteristics are assessed from sources such as financial statements, the customer's bank, and credit agencies. Credit agencies specialise in providing credit ratings and credit reports on individual businesses.

Credit terms define the credit period and any discount offered for early payment. They are usually stated as "net *t*" or "*d/t*1, *n/t*". The first (*t*) denotes that payment is due within *t* days from when the goods are received. The second (*d/t*1, *n/t*) allows a discount of *d*% if payment is made within *t*1 days; otherwise the full amount is due within *t* days. For example, "3/10, *n*/30" means that a 3% discount can be taken from the invoice amount if payment is made within ten days; otherwise, full payment is due within 30 days.

The **collection policy** concerns the guidelines for the collection of debtor accounts that have not been paid by due dates. The collection policy may be applied rigorously or less rigorously, depending on circumstances. The level of bad debts is often regarded as a criterion of the effectiveness of credit and collection policies.

> Saying "no" to a customer may be an easy answer, but your competitors may gain a profitable sale. This is not the way to increase turnover and profit.
>
> M. POSNER, SUCCESSFUL CREDIT CONTROL, BSP PROFESSIONAL BOOKS, NEW YORK, 1990, P. 1.

18.2.4 The management of stock (inventory)

The concept inventory stock includes raw and auxiliary materials, work in progress, semi-finished products, trading stock, and so forth, and, like debtors, represents a considerable portion of the investment in working capital. In inventory management there is once again a conflict between the **profit objective** (to keep the lowest possible supply of stock, and to keep stock turnover as high as possible, in order to minimise the investment in stock, as well as attendant cash needs) and the **operating objective** (to keep as much stock as possible to ensure that the business is never without, and to ensure that production interruptions and therefore loss of sales never occur).

It is once again the task of financial management to optimally combine the relevant variables in the framework of a sound purchasing and inventory policy, in order to increase profitability without subjecting the business to unnecessary risks.

The costs of holding inventory stock are:

- **Lost interest.** This refers to the interest that could have been earned on the money that is tied up in holding inventory stock.
- **Storage costs.** This cost includes the rent of space occupied by the inventory stock and the cost of employing people to guard and manage the stock
- **Insurance costs.** Holding inventory stock exposes the business to risk of fire and theft of the stock. Insurance will provide cover against these losses but this will involve an additional cost in the form of premiums that have to be paid to the insurance company

- **Obsolescence.** Stocks can become obsolete – for example, because they go out of fashion. Thus, apparently perfectly good inventory stock may be of little more value than scrap

The costs of holding little or no inventory stocks are:
- **The loss of customer goodwill.** Failure to be able to supply a customer due to insufficient stock may mean the loss of not only that particular order but of other orders as well.
- **Production interruption dislocation.** Running out of stock for certain types of companies can be very costly. A motor manufacturer running out of a major body section has no choice but to stop production.
- **Loss of flexibility.** Additional stock holding creates a safety margin whereby mishaps of various descriptions can be accommodated without major and costly repercussions. Without these buffer inventory levels, the company loses this flexibility.
- **Re-order costs.** A company existing on little or no stock will be forced to place a large number of small orders with short intervals between each order. Each order gives rise to costs, including the cost of placing the order and the cost of physically receiving the goods.

18.2.5 Final comments

In our discussion of the asset side of the balance sheet, we have only given a brief overview of the management of current assets, and only a few fundamental financial implications have been discussed to show how complex the management of current assets is.

18.3 Long-term investment decisions and capital budgeting

18.3.1 The nature of capital investments

Capital investment involves the use of funds of a business to acquire fixed assets such as land, buildings, and equipment, the benefits of which accrue over periods longer than one year.

Long-term investment decisions determine the **type, size, and composition** of the business's fixed assets, as well as the amount of permanent working capital required for the implementation and continued operation of capital investment projects.

The importance of capital investments and the capital investment decision-making process cannot be over-emphasised.

Table 18.3 (see p. 441) gives the five major capital expenditure projects in South Africa with estimated completion dates after 2005.

The success of large businesses ultimately depends on their ability to identify capital investment opportunities that will maximise stakeholders' wealth. Conversely, examples abound (see p. 441) of business failures because businesses failed to identify such opportunities, or invested in unprofitable projects.

Table 18.3: Five major capital expenditure projects

Project	Company	Value (Rm)	Estimated date
Amplats's Mining Expansion	Amplats	20 000	2006
Spoornet's capital renewal programme	Spoornet	15 000	2015
SA Airways fleet replacement	South African Airways	7 000	2010
Gautrain – Shilowa Express	Gauteng Provincial Government	7 000	2006
Coega Industrial Development Zone	Portnet	5 000	2006

Source: FM Top 100 companies – Capital expenditure (Information supplied by Nedbank).

Example

Danech Mining Supplies, a South African company, experienced a drop of 71% in its share price in 1988. Earnings per share dropped from 18,9c to 1,27c in 1988 and Danech had to write off R6,2m because of wrong investment decisions.

Source: Danech dropped the ball, *Financial Mail*, 6 January 1998, p 43.

The importance of capital-investment projects is reflected by the following three factors:

- **The relative magnitude of the amounts involved.** The amounts involved in capital investment are much larger than those relating to, say, decisions about the amount of credit to be extended, or purchasing inventory.

Examples

The decision of the Ford Motor Company during the 1950s to manufacture and market the Ford Edsel required an investment of US $250m. With losses amounting to US $200m in the first two-and-a-half years of the project, it was "in all, a $450m mistake".

Source: The Edsel dies and Ford regroups survivors, *Business Week*, 28 November 1959, p. 27.

Establishing a new platinum mine near Rustenburg by Goldfields of South Africa Limited was estimated to cost R599m in 1986.

Source: Plan for R559m platinum mine revealed, *Business Day*, 12 June 1986, p. 1.

Toyota SA invested R87m in an expansion programme in 1989, which created 1 000 new job opportunities and saved the country R120m in foreign exchange.

Source: Toyota, *Finansies & Tegniek*, 12 May 1989, p. 9.

- **The long-term nature of capital investment decisions.** The benefits from capital investment projects may accrue in periods varying from two or three years to as much as 30 or 40 years.

> **Example**
>
> Three of Eskom's power stations were closed down in 1988. Together they had given 153 years of service. They had burnt 144 million tons of coal and produced 140 000 million kilowatt hours of electricity.

Source: Three oldest power stations closed down, Eskom Annual Report 1988, p. 29.

- **The strategic nature of capital investment projects.** Investment decisions of a strategic nature, such as the development of an entirely new product, the application of a new technology, the decision to diversify internationally, or to embark on rendering a strategic service, could have a profound effect on the future development of a business. For example, Honda's decision to branch out from motorcycles to passenger vehicles entirely changed the strategic direction of the company.

18.3.2 The evaluation of investment projects

The basic principle underlying the evaluation of investment decision making is cost-benefit analysis, in which the cost of each project is compared to its benefits (see figure 18.3). Projects in which benefits exceed the costs add value to the business and increase stakeholders' wealth.

Two additional factors require further consideration when comparing benefits and costs. The first is that benefits and costs occur at different times. Any comparison of benefits and costs should therefore take the time value of money into account. The time value of money is discussed in chapter 17.

Figure 18.3: A cost-benefit representation of investment decision making

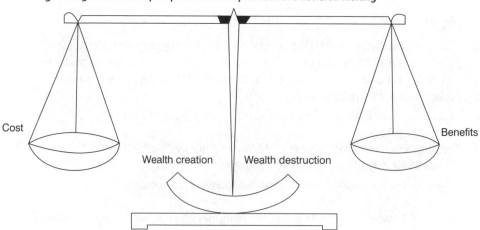

Source: Adapted from Kolb, B.A., *Principles of financial management*, Thomson Learning, 1983, p. 323.

Secondly, "cost" and "benefits" (income) are accounting concepts that do not necessarily reflect the timing and amounts of payments to the business. The concept "cash flow" is therefore used instead, which minimises accounting ambiguities associated with concepts relating to income and costs.

18.3.2.1 Cash-flow concepts

Cash flow represents cash transactions. The net effect of cash revenues (sources of cash) and cash expenses (uses of cash) is the net cash flow.

$$Net\ cash\ flow = cash\ revenues - cash\ expenses$$

Table 18.4 provides examples of transactions that result in cash inflows (sources of cash) and cash outflows (uses of cash).

Table 18.4:Examples of the sources and uses of cash

Sources of cash	Uses of cash
A decrease in assets	An increase in assets
An increase in liabilities	A decrease in liabilities
Cash sales	
Investment income	Dividend payments to shareholders

Cash flow differs from profit shown on the income statement in that the latter also includes non-cash costs such as depreciation.

Example

Assume that a printing business, ABC Litho Printing, buys a printing machine that will last for ten years. The business spends a large sum of money to acquire the machine but will not spend any significant amounts until the end of the tenth year, when the machine has to be replaced.

It does not make sense to assume that the business makes profits during years one to nine and then incurs a large loss in year ten when it has to replace the machine. The machine will be used for the entire period, and not only in year ten. The net profit of the business is adjusted for the use of the machine in years one to nine by deducting depreciation from income. The amount of depreciation is determined by depreciation rules laid down by the tax authorities, as tax is levied on profits after depreciation has been deducted.

However, the cash-flow amount the business has available for reinvestment is equal to the profit after tax plus the depreciation. This amount is the net cash flow into the business.

Figure 18.4 illustrates the concept of cash flow for ABC Litho Printers.

Figure 18.4: Profit and cash flow for ABC Litho Printers

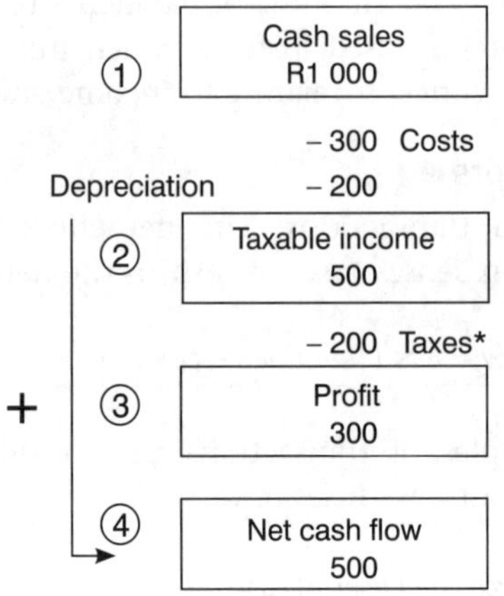

*Assume a tax rate of 40%

As shown in the graphical representation of the cash flow for ABC Litho, the net cash flow is the difference between cash income and cash expenditures. If the net cash flow is positive it means an inflow of cash and is referred to as a net cash inflow. However, cash expenditures can also exceed cash income. This results in a negative cash flow and is then referred to as net cash outflow.

The following three **cash-flow components** are distinguished for capital budgeting purposes:

- **The initial investment.** This is the money paid at the beginning of a project for the acquisition of equipment or the purchase of a production plant. The net cash flow during this phase is negative and represents a net cash outflow.
- **The expected annual cash flows over the life of the project.** The annual net cash flow can be positive or negative. The net cash flow is positive when cash income exceeds cash disbursements, and this represents a cash inflow for the business. The opposite is true when cash disbursements exceed income. This may happen, for example, when expensive refurbishing is required after a number of years of operation, and cash income is insufficient to cover these cash expenses.
- **The expected terminal cash flow, related to the termination of the project.** This terminal net cash flow is usually positive. The plant is sold and cash income exceeds cash expenses. It may happen, however, that the cost of cleaning up a site is so high that the terminal net cash flow is negative. Think, for example, of a nuclear power plant where the terminal value of the plant is low, because of its limited use, but where the cost of disposing of the enriched uranium is very high.

The **magnitude of the expected net cash flows** of a project, and the **timing of these cash flows**, are crucial in the evaluation of investment proposals on the basis of the present value or discounted cash-flow approach, **where the net cash flow (the cash inflow minus cash outflow) can occur during a specific period or at a specific time.**

For evaluation purposes it is therefore imperative to approach potential projects in a future-oriented time framework and to present the expected cash-flow stream of a potential project on a **time line**, as illustrated in figure 18.5 (see p. 446).

The **annual net cash flows** are normally calculated as the profit after interest and tax, plus any non-cash cost items such as depreciation minus the cash outflows for the particular year.

- The **initial investment** (Co) is the net cash outflow at the commencement of the project at time t_0, usually for the acquisition of fixed assets and required current assets.
- The **annual net cash flows** (operating cash flows) (CF_t) are the **net cash flows after tax** which occur at any point during the life of the project minus cash outflow for the year. A positive net cash flow means that the cash inflow exceeds the cash outflow. A negative net cash flow implies the opposite.
- The **life of the project** (*n* periods or years), also referred to as the economic life of the project, is determined by the effects of physical, technological and economic factors.
- The **terminal cash flow** (TCF) is the expected **net cash flow after tax**, which is related to the termination of the project, such as the sale of its assets and the recovery of the working capital that was initially required. Depending on circumstances, the terminal net cash flow can again be positive or negative, if it occurs only at the end of the final year of the life of the project life. This is indicated by TCF_n.

18.3.2.2 The net present value method (NPV)

Decision criteria that take the time value of money into account and are based on cash flow are called discounted cash-flow (DCF) methods. They involve discounting estimated future cash flows to their present values, and take the magnitude and timing of cash flows into account.

This discussion is limited to the net present value method. The application of NPV involves the following:[3]

- Forecasting the three components of project cash flows (the initial investment, the annual net cash flows, and the terminal cash flow) as accurately as possible
- Deciding on an appropriate discounting rate
- Calculating the present values of the above three project cash flow components for a project determining the NPV of the project (the difference between the present value of the net cash inflows and that of the net cash outflow), where the NPV may be positive or negative.
- Accepting all projects with a positive NPV and rejecting all those with a negative NPV, in accordance with NPV decision criteria

The NPV is the difference between the present value of all net cash inflows (after tax) and the present value of all cash outflows (usually the initial investment) directly related to the project.

The formula for the calculation of NPV is as follows:

NPV = Present value of net cash flows – initial investment

The NPV method is explained by a practical example and compared to investment proposals X and Y. The information regarding these projects appears in table 18.5.

Table 18.5: Information regarding potential projects X and Y

Relevant information: intial investment (C_0)		Project X	Project Y
		R10 000	R10 000
Year	Time	Net cash flow (CF_t)	Net cash flow (CF_t)
1	$t = 1$	R2 800	R6 500
2	$t = 2$	R2 800	R3 500
3	$t = 3$	R2 800	R3 000
4	$t = 4$	R2 800	R1 000
5	$t = 5$	R2 800	R1 000

Notes:

1. The initial investment C_0 at time t_0 is the same for both projects, namely R10 000.
2. In this example it is assumed that the net cash flow at the end of year 5 in both cases comprises only annual cash flows and not terminal cash flow.

Assuming that the business's cost of capital is given as 15%, determining the NPV, for example, for project Y, involves discounting the estimated net cash inflows at a discounting rate of 15% and subtracting the net cash outflow of R10 000 from the sum of the present value of the inflows.

To form a better idea of the cash flow at each point in time (year-end) over the entire project life, the total cash flows for project Y can be presented on a time line, as illustrated in figure 18.5.

Figure 18.5: A time-line for project Y

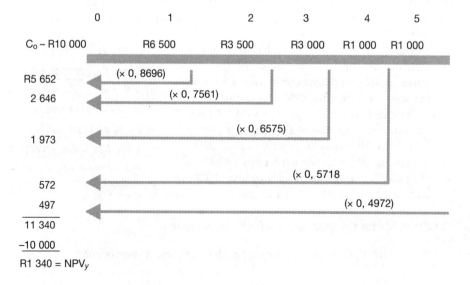

Table 18.6: Discounting factors

Period (n)	Discount rate	
	10%	15%
1	0,9091	0,8696
2	0,8264	0,7561
3	0,7513	0,6575
4	0.6830	0,5718
5	0,6209	0,4972

In addition to a **time line**, NPV_x and NPV_y can also be determined by using a **tabular format** as illustrated in table 18.7 (see p. 445) at a discount rate of 15%. (See table 18.6 for the discounting factors.)

Table 18.7: Calculation of the NPV for projects X and Y

Year (t)	Project X			Project Y		
	Net cash inflow (CF_t)	15% discounting factor $(PVT_{15,t})$	Present value (PV)	Net Cash inflow (Cf_t)	15% discounting factor $(PVT_{15,t})$	Present value (PV)
	(1)	(2)	(1) x (2)	(1)	(2)	(1) x (2)
1	R2 800	0,8696	R2 435	R6 500	0,8696	R5 652
2	2 800	0,7561	2 117	3 500	0,7561	2 646
3	2 800	0,6575	1 841	3 000	0,6575	1 973
4	2 800	0,5718	1 601	1 000	0,5718	572
5	2 800	0,4972	1 392	1 000	0,4972	497
		Total present value	9 386			11 340
		Minus: Investment (C_0)	− 10 000			− 10 000
		NPV_x =	− 614		NPV_y =	1 340

Notes:
- Since the initial investment C_0 occurs at time t_0, it represents a present value and requires no discounting
- The NPV's for projects X and Y are: NPV_x = − R614; NPV_y = R1 340

At a discount rate of 15%, NPV_x is negative and NPV_y is positive.

How should the NPV as a criterion for decisions on investment possibilities be interpreted? In short, what does NPV mean in this context?

- **NPV = 0.** For a project with NPV = 0, the given project net cash flow, discounted at the business's cost of capital, is just sufficient to repay both the financing costs of the project and the total amount of financing.
- **NPV > 0.** A positive NPV means that both the initial investment amount and all financing costs **as well as an addition to the value of the business – equal to the amount of the positive NPV** – are sustained by the net cash flow of the project. In the case of project Y in table 18.7, an investment of R10 000 will increase in value to R11 340 in present value terms.

- **NPV < 0.** The negative NPV of project X means that the project net cash flow at a discount rate of 15% is insufficient to redeem the initial investment amount and the related financing costs. **Such a project would consequently have an adverse effect on the value of the business** because additional funds (cash) would have to be found elsewhere to meet the shortfall. In the case of project X in table 18.7, an investment of R10 000 will decrease to R9 386 in present-day terms.

Applying the concept: the net present value method

Cola Company considers buying a new bottling machine at a cost of R45 000 that will increase bottling speed and save costs. The use of this machine will result in the following net cash flows:

Year 1: R15 000
Year 2: R20 000
Year 3: R25 000

The cost of the capital to be used to purchase the machine is 10%. It will have to be replaced after three years and will have no resale (terminal) value. (See table 18.6 on p.447) for the discounting factors.)

Should the machine be purchased?

The present values of the net cash inflows are:

Net cash inflow (R)	Discounting factor (10%)	Present value (R)
15 000	× 0,9091	= 13 636
20 000	× 0,8264	= 16 528
25 000	× 0,7513	= 18 783
Total present value of all net cash inflows		= R48 947
Minus: present value of the net cash outflow		= R45 000
Net present value		= R 3 947

The net present value is positive. This means that Cola Company should purchase the machine – it will add value to the business.

18.3.2.3 Risk and uncertainty

The limitation of the above analysis of new investments is that it does not take risk into account.

Risk is defined as any deviation from the expected outcome. These deviations may or may not occur. We are therefore not sure that they will occur, but we are able to identify the size of the deviations and even the likelihood that they will occur.

Example

Throwing the dice is an example of risk. We know that the outcome must be a number from 1 to 6. We also know that each number has the same chance of occurrence (1 in 6), but we do not know which number will come up in any particular throw.

Uncertainty, in contrast to risk, describes a situation where we are simply unable to identify the various deviations and, also, we are unable to assess the likelihood of their occurrence. Most business decisions have an element of uncertainty, but since there is no formal way of dealing with uncertainty we focus only on taking risk into account when making capital investment decisions.

We will now discuss **sensitivity analysis**[4] as one method for taking risk into account in capital investment decisions by referring to a practical example. Other methods will be discussed in later modules on finance.

Example

Assume that Khumbali Resources is considering investment in a mineral extraction process. The demand for the product is 5 000 tons for five years. The following data relates to this decision:
- The plant is expected to cost R500 000 and it has no resale value. The investment in the plant has to be paid immediately.
- The selling price is R100 per ton.
- The cost of producing one ton of the product is R70.
- The cost of capital for Khumbali resources is 10%.
- Tax is ignored.

Requirements:
- An assessment of the project by using the NPV method
- A sensitivity analysis of the project

Solution:
The cash flow of the project will be as follows:
Year 0   (500 000)
Year 1   5 000 × (100-70)= R150 000
Year 2   5 000 × (100-70)= R150 000
Year 3   5 000 × (100-70)= R150 000
Year 4   5 000 × (100-70)= R150 000
Year 5   5 000 × (100-70)= R150 000

The NPV is equal to -500 000 + (150 000 × PVF10,1) + (150 000 × PVF10,2) + (150 000 × PVF10,3) + (150 000 × PVF10,4) + (150 000 × PVF10,5)
= -500 000 + (150 000 × 0,909) + (150 000 × 0,826) +(150 000 × 0,751) + (150 000 × 0,683) +(150 000 × 0,621)
= -500 000 + 136 350 + 123 900 + 112 650 + 102 450 + 93 150
= 68 500

The project should therefore be accepted on the NPV. The NPV is positive. Sensitivity analysis requires that we determine how sensitive the project is to deviations in each of the cash flows. Our discussion of sensitivity analysis is limited to the sensitivity of the following factors whose estimates were used in calculating the NPV:
- Original investment (-I)
- Annual demand (V)
- Net cash flow per ton (C)

In terms of the above, the NPV of the project is given by:

$(-I) + (V \times C \times PVr,1) + (V \times C \times PVr,2) + (V \times C \times PVr,3)\ (V \times C \times PVr,4) + (V \times C \times PVr,5)$

$= (-I) + (5\ 000 \times 30 \times PV10,1) + (5\ 000 \times 30 \times PV10,2) + (5\ 000 \times 30 \times PV10,3) + (5\ 000 \times 30 \times PV10,4) + (5\ 000 \times 30 \times PV10,5)$

- **The original investment.** The present value of the cash inflows amounts to R568 500. This means that the original investment could increase by R68 500 before the project might become marginal.
- **Annual demand (V).** For the NPV to equal zero the annual demand has to decrease to:

  $(-I) + (V \times 30 \times 0,909) + (V \times 30 \times 0,826) + (V \times 30 \times 0,751) + (V \times 30 \times 0,683) + (V \times 30 \times 0,621) = 0$

  That is: $0 = -500\ 000 + 27,27V + 24,78V + 22,53V + 20,49V + 18,63V$

  $113,7V = 500\ 000$

  $V = 4\ 397,53$

This means that demand can decrease to 4 397 tons before the project becomes marginal.

- Net cash flow per ton. For the NPV to equal zero, the net cash flow has to decrease to:

  $(-I) + (5\ 000 \times C \times 0,909) + (5\ 000 \times C \times 0,826) + (5\ 000 \times C \times 0,751) + (5\ 000 \times C \times 0,683) + (5\ 000 \times C \times 0,621) = 0$

  That is: $0 = -500\ 000 + 4545C + 4\ 130C + 37\ 55C + 3\ 415C + 3\ 105C$

  $189\ 50C = 500\ 000$

  $C = 26,38$

The net cash flow can therefore decrease from R30 to R26,38 per ton before the project becomes marginal.

As indicated earlier, investment decisions based on the NPV criterion are made on the basis of "best" predictions of the various cash flows. Sensitivity analysis takes each cash flow and determines by how much the estimate of that factor could be incorrect before it would affect the decision.

We can now tabulate our results as follows:

Table 18.8 The sensitivity analysis of the Khumbali Resources project

Factor	Original estimate (R)	Value to give NPV of zero (R)	Difference as percentage of original estimate (%)
Original investment (I)	500 000	568 500	13,7
Annual demand (V)	5 000	4 397	12,1
Net cash flow (C)	30	26,38	12,1

From the results in table 18.8 we can see at a glance how sensitive the NPV is on the basis of the original estimates to changes in the variables used in the decision. This gives us some indication of the riskiness of the project.

18.3.2.4 Final comments

In this section we discussed the important facets of fixed asset management, namely the evaluation of potential capital investment projects, and decisions on the desirability of such projects. After briefly referring to the importance of capital investments, we described the net present value method (NPV) for the evaluation of capital investment proposals and the riskiness of projects.

The NPV is a discounted cash-flow method that takes the timing and the magnitude of cash flows into account. Investment decision making based on the NPV therefore maximises stakeholders' wealth.

Sensitivity analysis can be used to assess the riskiness of the factors that are used to determine the NPV.

18.4 Summary

In this chapter we explained the management of the asset structure of a business, namely short-term investment decisions as well as long-term capital investment decisions. Rational and purposeful decisions in these areas will to a large extent ensure that the goals of the business are pursued as effectively as possible. Some important guidelines and techniques for both types of investment decisions were presented in this chapter, bearing in mind that current and fixed asset management is totally integrated in practice.

References

1. Brigham, E.F. & Capenski, L.C., *Financial management: theory and practice*, 8th edition, Dryden, New York.
2. Damoran, A., *Corporate finance*, Wiley, New York, 1997.
3. Du Toit, G.S., Oost, E. & Neuland, E.W., *Investment decisions: principles and applications*, University of South Africa, Pretoria, 1997.
4. McLaney, M., *Business finance for decision makers*, Pitman Publishing, London, 1991.

19 Financing decisions

The purpose of this chapter

The purpose of this chapter is to introduce the reader to the financing structure of companies. This entails making decisions about the forms of financing (types of finance) and the sources of finance (the suppliers of finance) in order to minimise the cost and risk to the business. Firstly, financial markets and the sources and forms of short-term finance are examined. This is followed by a discussion of the sources and forms of long-term finance, the cost of long-term capital, and the establishment of an optimal capital structure. Finally, the role of financial markets in the pooling and efficient distribution of financing of businesses is examined.

Learning outcomes

The content of this chapter will enable learners to:
- Describe the money and capital markets as providers of finance
- Explain the types of short-term financing and the short-term financing decision (the financing of current assets)
- Describe the forms and sources of long-term financing
- Describe the forms and sources of finance for small businesses
- Explain the cost of capital
- Explain the long-term financing decision and the establishment of an optimal capital structure

19.1 Introduction

In chapter 17 we indicated that the management of the financing structure is one of the tasks of the financial manager. This entails making decisions about the forms of financing (types of finance) and the sources of finance (the suppliers of finance) to minimise the cost and risk to the business.

In this chapter we will first examine financial markets and the sources and forms of short-term finance. This will be followed by a discussion of the sources and forms of long-term finance, the cost of long-term capital and the establishment of an optimal capital structure.

19.2 Financial markets

Financial markets and financial institutions play an important role in the financing of businesses. The following section explains their role.

At a given point in time an economic system consists of individuals and institutions with surplus funds (the savers) and those with a shortage of funds. Growing businesses require funds for new investments or to expand their existing production capacity. These businesses have a shortage of funds, and to grow they must have access to the funds of individuals and institutions that do not have an immediate need for them.

- **Financial markets** are the channels through which holders of surplus funds (the savers) make their funds available to those who require additional finance.
- **Financial institutions** play an important role in this regard. They act as intermediaries on financial markets between the savers and those with a shortage of funds. This financial service is referred to as financial intermediation.
- **Financial intermediation**[1] is the process through which financial institutions pool funds from savers and make these funds available to those (for example, businesses) requiring finance.

Through financial intermediation the individual saver with relatively small savings is given the opportunity to invest in a large capital intensive business, such as a chemical plant. The saver who invests in a business is referred to as a financier. The business rewards the financier for the use of the funds, so that the financier shares in the wealth created by the business.

The financier receives an asset in the form of a financial claim in exchange for his or her money. Financial claims have different names and characteristics and include savings and cheque (call) accounts, fixed deposits, debentures and ordinary and preferred shares. In everyday usage, these financial claims are referred to as **securities** or **financial instruments**.

19.2.1 Primary and secondary markets

As indicated above, a saver receives an asset in the form of a financial claim against the institution to which money was made available. These claims are also referred to as securities. New issues of financial claims are referred to as issues on the **primary market**.

Some types of financial claims are negotiable and can be traded on financial markets. Trading in these securities after they have been issued takes place in the **secondary market**. This means that a saver who needs money can trade the claim on the secondary market to obtain cash. The Johannesburg Securities Exchange (JSE) is an example of a market where savers can virtually immediately convert their investments to cash. The tradability of securities ensures that savers with surplus funds continue to invest. Once issued, they can be traded on the market, and the holder may again obtain cash.

Company shares and debentures are examples of negotiable financial instruments, and savings and call accounts are non-negotiable claims.

19.2.2 Money and capital markets

The **money market** is the market for financial instruments with a short-term maturity. Funds are borrowed and lent in the money market for periods of one day (that is, overnight) or for months. The periods of the transactions depend on the particular needs of savers and institutions with a shortage of funds. The money market has no central physical location, and transactions are conducted from the premises of the various participants, for example, banks using telephones or on-line computer terminals.

Funds required for long-term investment are raised and traded by investors on the **capital market**. In South Africa, much of this trading takes place on the Johannesburg Securities Exchange. However, long-term investment transactions are also done privately. An investor may, for example, sell shares held in a private company directly to another investor, without channelling the transaction through a stock exchange.

19.2.3 Types of institutions

As indicated previously, financial institutions interpose themselves as intermediaries between savers and institutions with a shortage of funds by rendering a service to both. Financial institutions are divided into two broad categories, namely deposit-taking institutions and non-deposit-taking institutions.

19.2.3.1 Deposit-taking institutions

- The **South African Reserve Bank** is the country's central bank. It acts as a banker to the central government, keeps the banking accounts of government departments, and advances loans to the state. It also regulates private banks so that government monetary policy is adhered to, and has the sole right to issue bank notes. Its most important liability is the bank notes and coins in circulation. For example, a R50 note in circulation means that the Reserve Bank owes the holder an amount of R50.
- The **Land and Agricultural Bank (Land Bank)** grants loans to farmers and agricultural cooperatives.
- The **Corporation for Public Deposits (CPD)** accepts surplus funds from departments, institutions and organisations in the public sector, and is owned by the Reserve Bank. It accepts short-term deposits, pays interest on them and repays the deposits on demand
- **Private sector banks**, as a group, are the single largest type of financial intermediary in the financial system. Banks take deposits from individuals and organisations with surplus funds and lend them to others with a shortage of funds. In addition to this function they provide financial services such as insurance broking and administering estates. They also facilitate foreign trade.
- The **Post Office Savings Bank** accepts deposits from the public but does not grant credit or offer cheque facilities. The government is ultimately responsible for its solvency. In contrast to other banks, the Post Office Savings Bank is therefore not regulated by the Banks Act 94 of 1990.

19.2.3.2 Non-deposit-taking institutions

Non-deposit-taking institutions are considered in three categories: public sector, private sector and other.

- **Public sector institutions**
  - **Public Investment Commissioners (PIC).** The PIC operates as an investment intermediary for long-term public funds. It administers and invests the public sector's retirement and provident schemes and social security funds, for example, the Workmen's Compensation Fund. The funds it administers amount to approximately one third of the total administered by all private insurers and retirement funds.
- **Private sector institutions**
  - **Life assurers, pension and provident funds.** The main purpose of life assurers, pension and provident funds is the payment of lump sums to beneficiaries at death, on retirement or the attainment of a certain age. They provide people with income after retirement until death. To fulfil this function, life assurers collect premiums from policyholders, and pension and provident funds receive monthly contributions from employers and employees. The premiums and contributions received are made available to institutions until required by the insurance company or pension fund.
  - **Short-term insurers.** Short-term insurers provide cover against accidental losses caused by fire, theft, storms, etc. The premiums received are sufficient to cover the risk for a particular year. These premiums are also made available to borrowers by investing them on the money market.
  - **Unit trusts.** Unit trusts provide small investors with the opportunity to invest their surplus funds in large companies. The administrators of unit trusts invest funds received in, for example, a number of companies listed on the JSE. The fund is divided into small affordable units and each investor receives an allocation of units according to his or her investment. The funds are managed by professional investment managers.
- **Other institutions**
  - **Industrial Development Corporation (IDC).** The main purpose of the IDC is to promote industrial development by assisting the private sector in financing new businesses and expanding existing ones. It extends credit, takes up shares, and facilitates the financing of expansion of industrial businesses. For example, it helped to finance a business such as Sasol.
  - **Khula Enterprise Finance Limited (Khula).** Khula was established to provide wholesale finance for new small businesses and for the expansion of existing ones. For example, a person wishing to start a panel-beating business may approach Khula through its retail financial intermediaries (RFIs) for funds.
  - **Ntsika Enterprise Promotion Agency (Ntsika).** Ntsika's role is to render an efficient and effective promotion and support service to small, medium and micro enterprises (SMMEs) in order to contribute towards equitable economic growth in South Africa. Ntsika provides wholesale non-financial support services for SMME promotion and development. It also provides funding to organisations providing approved services.
  - **Development Bank of South Africa (DBSA).** The purpose of the DBSA is to promote development in areas not served by the private sector. It provides finance for projects such as roads, dams and telecommunications.

19.3 Short-term financing

Short-term financing means that repayment has to be made within one year.

The short-term financing decision requires finding the optimal combination of long-term and short-term financing to finance current assets.

As in the management of current assets, risks and costs must be weighed against each other when making this decision. This section introduces different forms of short-term financing, and this is followed by a discussion of the implications of a combination of long-term and short-term financing for the financing of current assets.

The following are the most common forms of short-term financing:

- Trade credit
- Accruals
- Bank overdrafts
- Factoring

Each of these forms of financing will now be discussed.

19.3.1 Trade credit

Trade credit is an important form of finance for businesses, and is mainly in the form of suppliers' credit. This means that a supplier does not take payment from the business when goods or services are purchased. The business is expected to pay only after 30, 60 or 90 days, depending on the credit terms.

When Pick 'n Pay, for example, purchases cereal on credit from Tiger Oats (the supplier) it implies that Tiger Oats finances the purchase for Pick 'n Pay for the period for which supplier's credit is granted, namely 30, 60 or 90 days.

As shown in figure 19.1, wholesalers and retailers such as Pick 'n Pay make extensive use of trade credit as a form of finance because of the nature of their business. Smaller businesses also rely on trade credit, because they find it more difficult to obtain funds on money and capital markets. As a rule, trade credit can be obtained quite readily by any business with a reasonable financial record.

Figure 19.1: The use of trade credit as a form of finance – selected listed companies

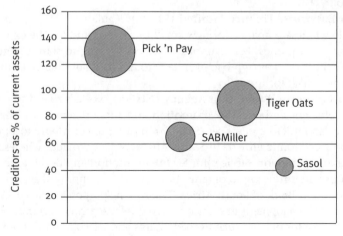

To ensure prompt payment, the supplier often offers a cash rebate for early payment. This rebate applies only if the buyer pays before a stated date, which precedes the due date of the account.

How do we calculate the advantage of the cash rebate? The following formula can be used:

Cost of not accepting the rebate

$$= \frac{(\% \text{ rebate})}{(100 - \% \text{ rebate})} \times \frac{365}{(\text{additional number of days after rebate period for which funds are available})}$$

Applying the concept: the cash rebate

Emex, a distributor of computers, buys components from a manufacturer, Camtron. Camtron's normal credit extension terms are 30 days, but it is prepared to allow a 3% rebate if Emex pays the account within ten days. Should Emex pay this account within 10 days and take advantage of the 3% discount, or should it only pay after 30 days?

According to our formula the cost of not accepting the rebate is:

Cost of not accepting the rebate

$$= \frac{3\%}{(100 - 3\%)} \times \frac{365}{(30 - 10)} = 56\% \text{ per annum}$$

Recommendation

Unless Emex can earn a return of at least 56% per annum elsewhere on its cash, it should take advantage of the cash rebate.

Management may also decide to delay payment within certain limits. Funds are consequently available to the business for a longer period, which decreases its additional cash needs. This is risky, as the consequence of such a decision could be that the creditworthiness of the business is jeopardised and suppliers may refuse to supply it in future.

Trade credit offers the following advantages as a source of short-term funds:[2]

- It is **readily available** to businesses that pay their suppliers regularly and is also a source of spontaneous financing, which is explained in the following example:

Example:

Simeka Retailers purchases an average of R5 000 a day on terms of "net 30" from Mega Wholesalers, that is, the goods must be paid for within 30 days of the invoice date. This means Mega Wholesalers provides R5 000 x 30 = R150 000 in short-term financing to Simeka. Now assume that Simeka's sales – and therefore purchases – double. The trade credit that Mega extends to Simeka also doubles to R300 000, and Simeka obtains this additional amount of financing virtually automatically, that is, it is obtained spontaneously.

- It is **informal**. If a business currently pays its bills within the discount period, additional credit can simply be obtained by delaying payment until the end of the net period at the cost of foregoing the discount.
- Trade credit is **more flexible** than other forms of short-term financing, because the business does not have to negotiate a loan agreement, provide security, or adhere to a rigid repayment schedule.

19.3.2 Accruals

As with trade credit, accruals are also a source of spontaneous finance. The most common expenses accrued are wages and taxes.

Accruals represent liabilities for services provided to the business which have not yet been paid for.

Accrued wages represent money that a business owes its employees. Employees provide part of the short-term financing for the business by waiting a month or a week to be paid, rather than being paid every day.

Accrued tax is also a form of financing. The level of financing from accrued taxes is determined by the amount of tax payable and the frequency with which it is paid.

Accruals have no associated cost. They are therefore a valuable source of finance because they are cost-free substitutes for otherwise costly short-term credit.

19.3.3 Bank overdrafts

An overdraft facility is an arrangement with a bank that allows a business to make payments from a cheque account in excess of the balance in the account. The purpose of an overdraft is to bridge the gap between cash income and cash expenses. An overdraft usually increases through to the month-end, when the business's clients pay their accounts.

An overdraft arrangement is reviewed annually, usually when the annual financial statements become available, so that the bank can evaluate the business's current financial position. The interest charged on an overdraft is negotiable and relates to the risk profile of the borrower.

Interest is charged daily on the outstanding balance. This means that the borrower only pays interest on that part of the overdraft that is being used. In contrast to other forms of financing, a bank overdraft is repayable on demand. This means that the bank may cancel the facility at any time.

An overdraft is a flexible form of short-term financing. It is cost-effective if used correctly.

19.3.4 Debtor finance

Debtor finance consists of factoring and invoice discounting. In contrast to a bank overdraft, debtor finance is, strictly speaking, not borrowing. It is not a loan secured by the book debts of the business. Instead, it involves the sale of debtors to a debtor financing company.

Invoice discounting is the sale of existing debtors and future credit sales to a debtor financing company. It then converts credit sales to cash sales and provides the business with a cash injection by releasing funds tied up in working capital. Invoice discounting is usually confidential, that is, debtors are not advised of the arrangement between the business and the finance company.

Factoring is similar to invoice discounting, but goes one step further. With factoring, the financier also undertakes to administer and control the collection of debt. In contrast to invoice discounting, debtors are aware of the agreement between the business and the financier.

The financier to whom the debtors are sold is known as the factor. The factor buys approved debtors from the business after carefully examining each account individually. The factor receives commission and interest on amounts paid to the business before the expiry date of the debt. The factor usually pays the business 70% to 80% of the amount outstanding from debtors immediately, and the remainder when the debtor pays.

Applying the concept: factoring

On the surface, Fun Toys looks like a healthy, growing business. Sales and turnover increase virtually every month. To cater for the increase in sales, Fun Toys purchased more stock.

But now, Fun Toys is experiencing problems. The nursery schools that buy from it are demanding trade credit of 60 days. Credit sales have therefore increased excessively. The bank overdraft is already fully utilised, and Fun Toys has just received letters from its three major suppliers demanding immediate payment of their accounts.

What can Fun Toys do about the situation?

The factoring of debt is one of the options to consider. Fun Toys has an average of R100 000 in accounts receivable on credit sales of R500 000. It may factor its debtors by discounting them at 3% in other words, by selling them for 97 cents in the rand.

By factoring, Fun Toys immediately receives R100 000 x 0,97 x 0,70 = R67 900 for its debtors, instead of having to wait for 60 days to collect R100 000.

Two common types of factoring practice are:
- **Non-recourse factoring.** The factor buys the debtors outright and bears the risk of bad debts. The factor accepts responsibility for credit control, debt collection and sales records. Customers pay the factor direct.
- **Recourse factoring.** In recourse factoring, the factor provides the same services as in non-recourse factoring, but the seller guarantees that debts are recoverable. The factor recovers any bad debt from the seller.

Factoring of debtor accounts has the following advantages:
- The cost of debtor administration is transferred to the factor.
- The turnover of current assets is increased and less capital is required to finance debtors.
- Liquidity ratios improve.
- More cash is available for other purposes.

The cost of factoring fluctuates according to the conditions laid down by the factor. In considering factoring, the cost should be compared to the savings achieved through not having the administrative liability of debt collection.

19.3.5 The short-term financing decision

> We use factoring now because we cannot beat the terms, either on the finance facility or on the debt administration.
>
> H. IRELAND, FINANCE WEEK, 16–22 OCTOBER 1986, P. 25.

The cost of short-term funds is generally lower than that of long-term funds. One reason is that trade credit does not really involve a cost. From a cost or profit point of view, it is advantageous for a business to make use of short-term funds for the financing of its current assets, but too heavy a dependence on them increases the risk of finance not being available when required.

Consider, for example, a financial manager who relies on having short-term debt rescheduled. There is an unforeseen economic downturn, the financial position of the business deteriorates, and the bank manager refuses to renew its overdraft. It is clear that the financial manager is faced with a liquidity crisis, and a plan will have to be devised to meet the crisis.

The more frequently a business has to refinance its debt, the greater the risk of becoming illiquid. This risk therefore increases as the period for which the debt is granted decreases.

Figure 19.2: Short-term financing plans

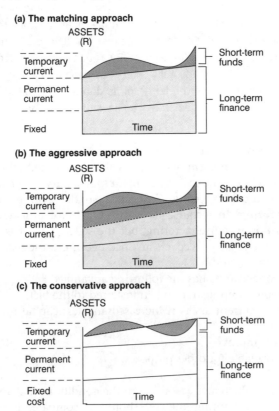

(a) The matching approach

ASSETS (R)

Temporary current — Short-term funds

Permanent current — Long-term finance

Fixed — Time

(b) The aggressive approach

ASSETS (R)

Temporary current — Short-term funds

Permanent current — Long-term finance

Fixed — Time

(c) The conservative approach

ASSETS (R)

Temporary current — Short-term funds

Permanent current — Long-term finance

Fixed cost — Time

Source: Adapted from Joy O.M., *Introduction to financial management*, McGraw-Hill Company, 1983, p. 378.

The use of **long-term funds** to satisfy working capital requirements has exactly the opposite implications for a business. From a **cost point of view** it is disadvantageous, because long-term funds are generally more expensive than short-term funds. They will also be underutilised because of the variable nature of portions of working capital requirements. On the other hand, by using more long-term funds there is less risk of funds not being available if and when required.

Figure 19.2 (see p. 460) illustrates the following three approaches to the short-term financing problem:

- The **matching approach** (also referred to as the hedging approach) involves matching the period for which finance is obtained with the expected life of the asset. Financing arranged for periods longer than the life of an asset is costly because it is not utilised for the entire period. However, if finance is arranged for a period shorter than the life of the asset, there will be additional transactional costs to repeatedly arrange for new short-term finance.

    According to this approach, fixed assets and permanent current assets are financed with long-term financing, and temporary current assets with short-term funds.

- In the **aggressive approach** the financial manager uses more short-term financing than is needed with the matching approach. Permanent current assets are partially financed with short-term funds, instead of using only long-term funds as in the case of the matching approach.

- In the **conservative approach**, the financial manager uses more long-term funds than is needed with the matching approach. The temporary current asset requirement is financed with long-term funds. This plan is conservative because it involves the use of a relatively large proportion of long-term funds, which is less risky.

19.3.6 Concluding remarks

The choice of a financing plan for a business's current assets entails a trade-off between risk and return. From a cost point of view, it is preferable to finance current assets needs with short-term funds, while risk considerations demand the use of long-term funds.

19.4 Long-term financing

In this section, we focus on the characteristics of the various forms of **long-term** financing and the implications of the various **sources of financing** for the business.

This is followed by a discussion of the cost of capital (section 19.4.5) and the establishment of an optimal capital structure (section 19.5), with specific reference to financial gearing.

19.4.1 Shareholders' interest

Shareholders' interest in a company is subdivided into owner's equity and preference shareholders' capital.

19.4.1.1 Owner's equity

Owner's equity is the funds made directly available by the legal owners (ordinary shareholders) in the form of share capital, as well as indirect contributions in the form of profit retention as reserves and undistributed profits.

- **The ordinary share.** Ordinary shareholders are the true owners of a business. An ordinary share therefore gives **right of ownership** (right of possession). Shareholders receive **share certificates** in exchange for the money they make available to the business.

Table 19.1: Sources and forms of long-term financing for a business in the form of a company

	Source	Balance sheet classification	Form
1	Owners or ordinary shareholders	Owner's equity or own capital	• Ordinary shares • Reserves • Undistributed profit
2	Preference shareholders	Preference shareholders' capital	• Preference shares
1 + 2	Share capital	Shareholders' interest	Total of the above
3	Suppliers of debt capital/ Credit suppliers	Long-term debt or borrowed capital over a long-term period	• Debentures • Bonds • Registered term loans • Financial leases
1 + 2 + 3		Total long-term capital	

Notes:
The sources and forms of long-term financing for other forms of businesses differ only in some respects to those for a company:
- Other forms of business do not have any preference shareholders and therefore there are no preference shares and no preference shareholders' capital.
- The own capital or owner's equity comprises funds that the owner(s) contribute to the business, as well as profits that are not withdrawn by the owners. The owners' equity is included in a capital account in the balance sheet.
- Other forms of business do not make use of debentures.

There are two types of ordinary shares, namely par value shares and non-par value shares. Par value shares all have the same value, while that of non-par value shares differs. A business can only issue one of the two types of shares, not both.

As a co-owner of the business, the ordinary shareholder has a claim to profits. The portion of profit paid to ordinary shareholders is known as a dividend and is paid out in proportion to the shareholding of each ordinary shareholder.

The following are **important characteristics** of the ordinary share:

- The liability of ordinary shareholders is limited to the amount of share capital they contributed to the business. This means that if the business is liquidated, shareholders may lose this money, but may otherwise not be held liable for its debts. That is why we add the word "Limited" to the name of a public or private company.

- Shareholders have no certainty that the money paid for the shares will be recouped, for this depends on the success of the business.
- Ordinary shares in a listed company (that is, a public company traded on the stock exchange) are tradable on a stock exchange.
- Ordinary shareholders are the owners of the business and usually have full control of it, in that they can vote at general meetings to appoint directors of the company, and on such matters as the amount of dividends to be paid to shareholders. Voting rights are usually in proportion to shareholdings.
- In contrast to interest payable on borrowed capital, a business has no legal obligation to reward ordinary shareholders in the form of dividends for their investment in shares.
- Share capital is available to the business for an unlimited period. Ordinary share capital does not have to be repaid. Shareholders may, however, convert their investments into cash by selling their shares to another investor. Currently, South African businesses are not allowed to buy back their own shares. This differs from the situation in other countries and this legislation may change in the near future.

The issue of additional ordinary shares by an existing company may have the following **disadvantages**:

- The earnings per share (profit attributable to ordinary shareholders divided by the number of issued shares) of existing shareholders may decrease, because the profit attributable to ordinary shareholders does not immediately increase in relation to the increase in the number of issued shares. This phenomenon is known as the dilution of existing shareholders' earnings.
- Existing shareholders may lose control, because voting rights are linked to shareholdings, and people other than existing shareholders may take up new shares and become majority shareholders. This danger applies not only to the issue of new shares, but generally also to a business whose shares are listed on a stock exchange and can therefore easily be obtained by others, including competitors.
- The cost of issuing new ordinary shares and the riskiness of an investment in ordinary shares may result in the cost of ordinary share capital being higher than that of other forms of financing.

Ordinary shares, however, hold some **advantages** for a business, the following being the most important:

- There is no risk involved for the business, because payment of dividends and redemption of capital are not compulsory.
- Additional ordinary shares serve as security for attracting additional borrowed capital, which provides greater flexibility for capital structure decisions. The base of shareholders' capital gives the financial manager the additional flexibility to use a combination of share capital and debt to finance the business.

- **Retained profit** consists of reserves and undistributed profit, and represents amounts that would otherwise have been paid out to shareholders as dividends. Retained profit is also referred to as self-financing or internal financing, and as a form of financing holds various **advantages** for a business:

- Because no issue costs are involved, it is cheaper than the issuing of additional ordinary shares.
- Capital is immediately available for use.
- It lends flexibility to the capital structure, because it serves as security for attracting additional borrowed capital.
- In contrast to the issue of new shares, there are no control implications for existing shareholders.
- It serves as an alternative form of financing, if conditions are unfavourable in the capital market as a result of, for example, high interest rates.
- It entails no interest or redemption obligations.

Internal financing is consequently an easy and inexpensive form of financing for a business. However, from the point of view of the owners (ordinary shareholders) it has a serious **short-term disadvantage**, because the retention of profit means the forfeiting of dividends.

19.4.1.2 Preference shareholders' capital

Preference shares fall somewhere between debentures (discussed later) and ordinary shares in terms of risk. They have some characteristics of both debentures and ordinary shares. If a business is doing poorly, it will first pay debenture holders their required interest and then pay dividends to preference shareholders. Anything left goes to ordinary shareholders.

Two forms of preference shares are distinguished, namely the **ordinary preference share** and the **cumulative preference share**. In the case of the ordinary preference share, shareholders forfeit a dividend if the directors decide not to declare one in a particular year. Cumulative preference shareholders retain the right to receive an arrear dividend in the following year.

A preference share has the following characteristics:

- It has a **preferential claim** over an ordinary share on profit after tax. In contrast to the dividend on an ordinary share, however, a preference share dividend is limited to a certain maximum. For example, the holders of a 10% preference share will never receive more than a 10% return on their investment, but could in bad times receive no dividend, or one of less than 10%.
- It has a **preferential claim** over ordinary shares on the assets of the business in the case of liquidation.
- The **term of availability** is unlimited.
- **Authority** can vary between full voting rights and no voting rights at all, but usually an ordinary preference share provides no voting rights.

From the viewpoint of the business, preference shares have an advantage over ordinary shares, in that their cost is usually lower. For the shareholder, ordinary shares are more risky, because preference shareholders have a priority claim on net profit after tax and on assets in the case of liquidation.

19.4.2 Long-term debt

Long-term debt generally refers to debt that will mature (has to be repaid) in a year or more, and can usually be obtained in two ways, namely:

- Through a loan
- Through credit

A **loan** is a contract in which the receiver of funds (the borrower) undertakes to make interest payments at specified times to the supplier of funds (the lender) and to redeem the total principal sum in payments over an agreed period or on a specific due date.

With **credit**, the supplier of credit (the supplier of capital) provides the business (receiver of capital) with power of disposal over an asset and receives extended payments in return, consisting of a principal sum and an interest component. Financial leasing, discussed later, is an example of credit financing.

Some debt instruments (such as debentures, which are discussed later) bear a fixed rate of interest for the period of the debt. In other cases, for example, mortgage bonds, the interest rate is not fixed but fluctuates with market forces. This is known as variable interest.

Debt that is secured on one or more assets of the business is known as secured debt. In the event of liquidation of the business, the proceeds from the secured assets would be used first to satisfy the claim of the secured supplier of credit. For example, the holder of a mortgage bond that is secured on any property must be repaid on liquidation before the proceeds from the sale of the property may be used to satisfy the claims of other creditors.

In the case of unsecured debt, a creditor does not have any preferential claim on the assets of a business.

In practice, there are various forms of long-term debt, and we now briefly discuss the most important ones.

19.4.2.1 Loans

The following types of loans are of special importance:

- **Debentures** are the most common form of long-term debt in the case of companies. The business (the borrower) issues a certificate to the lender showing the conditions of the loan. This certificate is negotiable, and means that it can be traded on financial markets. Payment of the loan, consisting of a principal sum plus interest, is made to the presenter of the certificate. A debenture has a fixed-interest charge, and the loan is available to the business over a specified term.

> AVI went to the market with a R388 million issue of debentures, as did Consol with debentures worth R300 million.
>
> *YEAR OF RECORD JSE RIGHTS ISSUES IN TOP COMPANIES, SUPPLEMENT TO THE FINANCIAL MAIL, 26 JUNE 1992, P. 53.*

- **Bonds** are secured loans and are issued with fixed assets such as fixed property as security (mortgage bonds). The amount that can be raised depends primarily on the value of the property. Typically a mortgage bond will not exceed 75% of the value of the property.

- **Registered term loans** are unsecured loans and, in contrast to debentures, are not freely negotiable. The name of the lender and the credit conditions are recorded in the books of the lender (business).

For a business, loans have the following **advantages**:
- Costs are limited in that they are determined by the loan interest rate.
- Interest payments are deductible for tax purposes.
- The control of the owners is usually not influenced by the issue of more loans.
- Loans do not dilute the earnings of ordinary shares.

A **disadvantage** is that the fixed interest obligations and the priority claims of loans in the case of liquidation increase the risks, inherent in the business, to its owners.

19.4.2.2 Financial leasing

A financial lease is a contract that provides the right to the use of an asset, legally owned by the lessor, in exchange for a specified rental paid by the lessee. The lessor is the party that promises to make the asset available for use by the lessee.

A **financial lease** is a form of credit financing that should not be confused with an operating lease. In contrast to an operating lease, financial leasing gives the lessee the opportunity of owning the asset at the end of the lease. An operating lease can be terminated by giving the required notice, but a financial lease is a non-terminative agreement between the lessee and the lessor. Hence it is a financing agreement (lease) and not an operating lease agreement.

Two basic forms of financial leasing are the following:[3]

- **Direct financial leasing** of operating equipment such as motor vehicles and computers. In direct leasing, the lease amount, which is repayable in regular instalments, is determined in such a way that the value of the asset, plus an interest charge, is paid back by the end of the term of the lease, which is usually related to the lifespan of the asset. Maintenance and insurance of the asset are normally the responsibility of the lessee. Financial leases are used to finance motor vehicles, equipment and plant.
- **Leaseback agreements**, in which more permanent assets are involved. In leaseback agreements, certain assets that the business owns are sold to the credit supplier and at the same time leased back by the business according to a long-term agreement. Leaseback agreements are usually entered into by businesses that need to raise funds. The assets are generally of a highly specialised nature and through leaseback arrangement the business obtains cash without losing the use of this equipment. For example, a dentist may decide to obtain additional funds by financing his or her equipment on a leaseback arrangement.

  The lease payments of a financial lease are deductible for tax purposes. When the advantages of financial leasing are weighed against ownership through purchase with loan capital, the after-tax costs have to be compared. One should therefore bear in mind that in the case of ownership through the use of loan capital, depreciation, investment rebates and interest payments contribute to tax savings.

19.4.3 Sources of financing for small businesses

It is always sad to see a new business with great profit potential fall by the wayside only because it was not properly financed from the beginning. And this happens too often among the thousands of new small businesses started in this country every year. The error comes from either not knowing the total financial needs of the business or failing to provide for those needs in the planning stage.

> "My banker advised me against placing a second mortgage on the house, selling my savings bonds, and selling our second car to raise funds to get started. But he wouldn't loan me any money. What was I to do?"
>
> *THE LATE LEARNER*

No business should ever be started without a clear and positive understanding of where its total capital needs are coming from. As we have seen in previous chapters, a very important phase of the entire planning process is to determine what assets will be needed and how they are to be provided. When the amount of the net ownership capital needed has been determined, the proprietors turn to the problem of making sure that the entire amount is available. The total sum should preferably be deposited in the company's bank account before any commitments are made by the new owners.

When several sources of capital are available, the planners must still bear in mind that all sources may not be equally desirable. Borrowed capital is shown on the balance sheet as a liability. It must be paid back at specific periods. These repayments of principal amounts are not operating expenses, which are deducted on the income statement before planned profits are produced. They are payments for the provision of investment capital, and are to be paid out of the profits shown on the income statement. Many researchers have found that failure to recognise this basic fact is the commonest cause of financial strain among small businesses. It is important, therefore, to consider the repayment schedules in choosing among sources of financing.

The various types of financing available to small businesses usually have a similar classification to those of a company, with a few differences and additions. We will discuss a few of these forms of financing a small business in the sections that follow.

Two things should be recognised when one is faced with the problem of obtaining outside capital assistance:

- An established business with a good record of operations usually has better access to available sources of capital than a new business.
- Some personal capital available for investment in the business by the owner is almost always essential to obtaining any type of outside assistance.

Against this background, we will now investigate the possibilities of each of the sources of funds listed.

19.4.3.1 Personal funds

Whenever potential creditors, partners, or shareholders are invited to invest in, or lend financial assistance to, a business, their first question is, "How much does the owner have invested?" Every business contains an element of risk, and outsiders who invest in a new business wish to be sure that such risk is shared by the owner. Trading on "too thin an equity base" means that the owner's investment is too small relative to the investment of outsiders. A financing plan that indicates that the business is starting out on this basis does not usually invite confidence from creditors. As we saw in the previous section on capital structure, this does not always mean that the new owners must have 50% of the total capital needs to invest, but it does mean that they should look to other ownership capital rather than only to creditor capital in their financial plan. In any event, it is important that the owners have assets of their own to invest in the business. The closer to 50% of the total capital needs that can be provided, the greater will be their independence and share of net profits.

19.4.3.2 Loans from relatives and friends

Although this type of borrowing to provide original investment capital is generally frowned upon by experienced business operators, it remains a prominent device used in the financial planning of small businesses. Many owners are encouraged in their enterprise by parents, relatives, or friends who offer to supply loans to the business to get it started. Quite often, no other sources are available after normal trade credit and supplier contracts have been utilised.

It is unfortunate, however, that many otherwise successful businesses have been beset by troubles because relatives or friends interfered with the operations. Mixing family or social relationships with business can be dangerous. Many such situations might have been averted if the terms of the loans had been more clearly specified, including the rights of the lenders to insist upon making operational policy. The best way to avoid subsequent problems is to make sure that loans are made on a businesslike basis. They should be viewed as business dealings. The right of the owner to make decisions should be respected by all parties involved. Arrangements for retiring such loans, including any options for early payment, and the procedure if loans become delinquent, should be clearly understood and set forth in writing. The owner should be sure such loans are properly presented on the balance sheet – payments due in one year are current liabilities; the others are fixed liabilities.

19.4.3.3 Trade credit

Trade credit is the financial assistance available from other businesses with whom the business has dealings. Most prominent are the suppliers of inventory that is constantly being replaced. We have previously noted that wholesalers who desire a retailer's business, for example, will offer generous terms for payment of invoices. Manufacturers will do the same for wholesalers whose business they desire. Financing the opening inventory usually represents one of the larger investments in a typical small business. If a R20 000 inventory can be purchased for a R10 000 down payment and the balance in 30 days, the wholesaler has virtually provided R10 000 of the required capital to open the business. The owner then has an opportunity to sell that inventory at a profit and thus to have the funds to pay off the original balance. As a record for successful operation is established, even more attractive terms may be offered on subsequent purchases. A grocer may have several such suppliers. Other businesses may have only one or two major suppliers. The inducement of a sales discount for prompt payment of invoices should always tempt the owner to pay within the maximum discount period.

19.4.3.4 Loans or credit from equipment sellers

This type of financial aid is often considered another form of trade credit. It does, however, have distinct characteristics. The small business may need counters, shelves, display cases, delivery trucks, and other equipment such as air conditioning, refrigeration units, and food counters. These, too, are a large investment for the new small business and are recognised as such by the major suppliers of items like these. The purchases, it is hoped, are not made on a regular basis, but represent a large part of the capital needed to get started. The suppliers usually offer good credit terms with a modest down payment and a contract for the balance spread over one, two, or three years.

This type of credit, when financing charges are reasonable, can be most helpful to the planner. The caution is in its overuse – remembering, again, that the principal payments must be paid out of profits anticipated. Any principal repayments of this type, too, are for the provision of capital and are not operating expenses. Too much of this type of financing can distort the current and quick ratios, and upset the business's financial liquidity. Many cases are on record where the monthly payments on such fixed assets exceed the profits earned from sales in the month.

19.4.3.5 Mortgage loans

If the small business owners own a commercial building, they can normally secure a mortgage on it with payments over as many as 20 years. This may, for example, be the building in which the new business will operate. In that case, the planners will be making mortgage payments instead of rental payments to a landlord. They may wish to risk a mortgage on their homes. Even second mortgages are sometimes used, although not recommended. When profits are uncertain, caution is advised in committing any assets to mortgage claims. As a clear profit pattern becomes more definitely established, the use of mortgage credit becomes less risky.

19.4.3.6 Commercial bank loans

Historically, a line of credit at a chartered bank was designed to enable a merchant to purchase an inventory of merchandise. When the merchandise was sold at a profit, the bank was paid its loan. This situation is still followed by many banks. This use of bank credit is still the best way to establish credit with a commercial bank. Since the relaxation of bank restrictions in recent years, however, many other types of loans and financing are now available to qualified applicants. In fact, we now have banks that advertise, "If you are planning to go into business, come see us." The cold, hard facts of economic reality will be faced in such a visit, but the prospective business owner with an otherwise sound financing plan, a reputation for integrity, and a business deemed likely to succeed, may still establish some bank credit in the planning stage. Long-term loans are less generally available than short-term loans. Short-term loans are usually considered those for not more than one year. If adequate collateral is available, longer-term loans may usually be obtained. Getting influential or wealthy friends to co-sign notes also may be helpful.

The policies of several of the chartered banks should always be checked in the planning stage. Many small business owners with experience have long described banks as "a place where you can borrow money when you prove that you don't need it." Some banks are earnestly trying to remove that image today. In keeping with our previously noted axiom that rewards must be commensurate with cost and risk, however, interest rates charged by banks to small businesses are significantly higher than the rates charged to large businesses.

Although commercial banks still dominate small business lending, credit unions and some trust companies are beginning to offer commercial loans to small business, and it is expected that in the 1980s these financial institutions will move very forcefully to compete for customers.

19.4.3.7 Small business loans

The proprietor of a small business enterprise, or one who is about to establish a new business, may borrow funds under this programme for the acquisition of fixed assets, modernisation of premises (leasehold improvements), or the purchase of land or buildings necessary for the operation of the business. The loans are usually provided and administered by the chartered banks and other designated lending institutions such as Khula Enterprise Finance Limited. The loans have fixed terms of repayments of the principal, typically five years, and the interest charged on these loans is fluctuating (floating), with the commercial bank's prime lending rate with an additional one or more percent above the prime rate.

19.4.3.8 Taking in partners

Despite all the necessary precautions, raising capital often necessitates taking one or more partners into the business. If more than one manager is not needed, the new partners may not be employed in the business, but may hold full partner status as a result of their investment in the business. The partnership agreement is important here. Inducements can be offered to such a finance partner, but the duties, responsibilities, and authority of each partner must be clearly understood. At this point we are looking at the partnership only from the standpoint of providing a source of investment funds.

19.4.3.9 Selling capital shares

Aside from the technical, legal, and operational advantages of the corporate form of legal organisation, its advantages are greater that the disadvantages as a device for raising capital. Many small business owners seem to believe that the corporate form was designed only for very large businesses. This is false, however. It is true that this legal form has not been as widely used as it might be, but this is believed to be due to lack of knowledge of its advantages.

Let us consider the new business planner who needs R100 000 in ownership capital, but has only R30 000 to invest. Would it not be desirable to go to a local investment dealer as a corporation and request the sale of R50 000 of 7% preference shares and R50 000 of common shares? The owner takes title to R30 000 of the voting common shares. The owner can hold the unsold shares in the business for possible future financing for expansion. The preference share is given a priority of dividends and may not have voting privilege.

Usually only the common share has voting power. The owner still owns a majority of the common shares outstanding, and has no problem of control. The investment dealer sells the shares to customers who are probably unknown. A detailed study of the plans of the business is contained in a prospectus, which the investment dealers will prepare. The business planner does not have to pursue relatives or to plead with friends for financial "favours", does not have to take in undesired partners to raise capital, has assured a financial plan for expansion, and has all the protections of the corporate form of organisation. The investment dealer will charge for this service. The charge will be higher if the dealer guarantees the sale of the full amount, and less if the shares are sold on a "best efforts" basis. The investment dealer's fee is chargeable to organisation expense and can be amortised over the succeeding five to ten years. This procedure is followed by the most informed new business planners who desire growth. It should be investigated for appropriateness by many more.

The raising of funds described above is called "private placement" of limited share distribution. When stock market conditions are depressed, this financing route can be an important alternative to the public distribution of the company's shares – that is, "going public".

19.4.3.10 Venture capital funding

Small businesses may sometimes (albeit not too often) qualify for investment funds from venture capital businesses. These companies provide equity and loan capital to potentially high-growth small companies. Examples of these are Khula Equity Scheme, whereby Khula has set up regional venture capital companies to invest a minimum of R1 million in small businesses needing significant equity investment.

When applying to a venture capital business, it is absolutely essential to provide it with a comprehensive business plan. If it passes the first screening, the venture capitalist will investigate further and examine "with due diligence" the product, the technology, potential market share, competitive situation, financial requirements and projections, and, most importantly, the competence of management. After the venture capitalist decides to make an investment, it will usually do so in return for part ownership in the business (common or preference shares) and/or by the provision of direct loan with share purchase options. Typically, a venture capital business will not seek controlling interest in the business. However, it will try to protect its investment by being able to assume control if the small business gets into financial trouble.

19.4.4 *Concluding remarks*

In the discussion above, the forms and sources of long-term financing available to a business were briefly analysed. The question that now arises is how the financial management of a business can combine the various forms of financing in the most efficient way. This consideration will now receive attention.

19.4.5 *The cost of capital*

Profitable and growing businesses continually need capital to finance expansion and new investment. Because of the costs involved in using capital, namely dividends to shareholders and interest paid to credit suppliers, financial management must ensure that only the necessary amount of capital is obtained, and that the cost and risk are kept to a minimum.

In attracting capital – one of the main tasks of financial management – the various forms of financing must be combined in a mix that results in the lowest possible cost and lowest risk for the business. We will now briefly discuss the concept cost of capital.

The cost of capital is the minimum compensation that must be offered to investors to persuade them to make their funds available to a business.

The cost of capital is of crucial importance in both **capital investment decisions** and **financing decisions:**

- In **capital investment decisions**, the cost of capital serves as a measure of profitability for investment proposals. In the discussions in chapter 18, the cost of capital was assumed as given, in the calculation of the net present value (NPV).
- In **financing decisions**, the various types of capital earmarked for financing the investments of a business should be combined so that the cost of capital to the business is kept to a minimum.

It is clear from the above that investment and financing decisions should be considered simultaneously because, in practice, they cannot really be separated.

Capital structure refers to the combination of forms of long-term financing, namely ordinary and preference shares and debt, to finance the business.

The **weighted average cost of capital**, k_a, is determined by weighting the component cost of each type of long-term capital in the capital structure by its proportion to the total. This involves the following three steps:

- Calculate the **after-tax cost of each individual form of capital** (for example, ordinary shares, preference shares and long-term debt).
- Calculate the **proportion** or **weight of each form of capital in the total capital structure.**
- Combine the costs of the individual forms of capital and the corresponding weights of each of these forms to determine the **weighted average cost of capital.**

Example: The calculation of weighted average cost of capital

Beta Limited has a marginal tax rate of 46%, and the following book values for its capital structure components:

Capital components			
Owners' equity	R500 000	0,5	50%
10% preference shares (P)	R300 000	0,3	30%
Long-term debt [13.5% debentures (D)]	R200 000	0,2	20%
Total	**R1 000 000**	**1,0**	**100%**

Assume that the after-tax cost of capital for long-term debt, k_d, is 7,29 % (the current after-tax interest rate on the 13,5% debentures in financial markets). The cost of owners' equity, k_e, is assumed to be 21%. The cost of the 10% preference shares, k_p, is 10% (the cost of preference shares is not tax-deductible).

Type of capital	Amount	Proportion (% of total)	Component cost of capital (after tax)	Weighted cost
(1)	(2)	(3)	(4)	(5) = (3) x (4)
Owners' equity	R500 000	0,5	$k_e = 0,21$	0,105
Preference shares	R300 000	0,3	$k_p = 0,10$	0,030
Long-term debt	R200 000	0,2	$k_d = 0,0729$	0,015
				$k_a = 0,150$

Notes:
(a) The weighted average cost of capital for Beta is $k_a = 15,0$
$$k_a = (0,5) (0,21) + (0,3) (0, 10) + (0,2) (0,0729) = 0,150 = 15,0\%$$
(b) The book values of the individual components of capital in the capital structure are used for the weighting process.

For privately-owned businesses as well as small businesses, it is extremely difficult to arrive at a reliable cost of capital figure, primarily because of a lack of information. The inherent uncertainty in small businesses has resulted in relatively high rates of return being required by those investing in such businesses.

19.4.6 Risk

For an investor, risk consists of two components, namely:
- The possible loss of the principal sum (the original amount invested)
- The possibility that no compensation will be paid for the use of the capital (no interest or dividend payments)

Any action that increases the possibility that the principal sum might be forfeited (as in the case of liquidation) or that compensation (in the form of dividends) will not be paid, increases the risk for the supplier of capital. The use of borrowed capital such as debentures increases the possibility that dividends might not be paid, and therefore increases the risk to ordinary shareholders.

With the cost of capital and risk in mind, capital structure will now be discussed.

19.5 The optimal capital structure

One of the chief facets of the management of the capital structure is effectively satisfying the planned capital requirements of a business by ensuring that funds are acquired at the lowest possible cost and on the most favourable conditions.

Financing decisions: the pecking order

Managers generally prefer using internal sources [of finance]; when they must turn to external financing, debt is the first choice because it is the cheapest. Managers also usually prefer short-term debt if interest rates are high, to avoid locking in long-term rates at the higher level. As a last resort, managers would elect to issue new equity (share capital). Thus, company leverage tends to increase over time.

Source: Myers, S.C., The capital structure puzzle, *Journal of Finance*, July 1989, pp. 575-92.

For the purposes of this discussion, let us assume that the capital structure consists of the following two components:
- Owners' equity
- Long-term debt

Decision making regarding the capital structure entails deciding on the ratio of debt to equity.

Long term financing decision

The purpose of the long-term financing decision is to combine owners' equity and long-term debt so that the risk and the cost of capital to the business will be at a minimum.

19.5.1 Capital structure and risk

As we have seen, there are good arguments for taking up as much debt as possible. However, this is impractical in the real world. As the level of debt increases, so does the risk of bankruptcy. The effect of debt is explained by referring to the functioning of the financial lever.

Financial risk and **financial leverage** come into being the moment a business introduces fixed interest-bearing capital, such as debentures, into its capital structure. The presence as well as the extent of financial risk is a direct result of the financing policy of the business. For example, the decision to finance the business equally with owners' equity and debt will result in a capital structure comprising 50% shareholders' funds and 50% loan capital. The presence of debt in the capital structure gives rise to financial risk and financial leverage.

Financial risk is reflected by the variability in profit income, which is attributable to the inclusion of fixed interest-bearing long-term debt in the capital structure.

The reason why debt results in financial risk is that variable financing costs (dividends payable out of after-tax profits) are in part replaced by fixed financing costs (fixed-interest payments out of profit before tax).

Example: Financial risk and the effect of financial leverage

Assume that there are three businesses in the same industrial sector, with similar operating characteristics and operating profits. The only difference between these companies is the way in which they have been financed. Company A is financed entirely with owners' equity, while companies B and C are financed by 40% and 70% long-term debt, respectively. In each case total assets amount to R1 000, the interest rate on long-term debt is 15%, the tax rate is 40%, and the value of issued shares is R10 per share.

Figure 19.3: Debt-equity ratios for selected sections

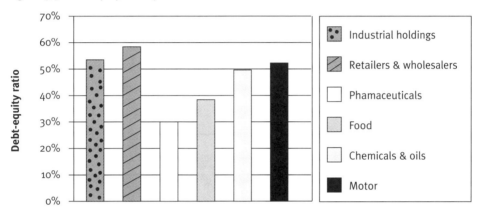

Source: Whitcutt, P.G., *The cost equity finance; an empirical study*, Unpublished MBA thesis, University of the Witwatersrand, Johannesburg, 1992.

Table 19.2: The effect of financial leverage at a 15% interest rate

Company	A	B	C
Number of issued shares	100	60	30
Owners' equity	R1 000	R600	R300
Long-term debt	–	R400	R700
Total assets	R1 000	R1 000	R1 000
Debt ratio (leverage factor)	0%	40%	70%
Operating profit (20% rate of return on total assets before tax)	R200	R200	R200
Minus: interest (15%)	–	R60	R105
Profit after interest before tax	R200	R140	R95
Minus: tax (40%)	R80	R56	R38
Net profit after tax	R120	R84	R57
Earnings per share (EPS)	R1,20	R1,40	R1,90
Rate of return on equity (ROE)	12%	14%	19%

The example (see p. 475) shows that long-term debt affects profit after interest and tax, and earnings per share, through the functioning of the financial lever. Table 19.2 illustrates that the positive effect of the financial lever for a given level of operating profit increases with an increase in the debt ratio or the leverage factor.

Table 19.3: The effect of financial leverage at a 25% interest rate

Company	A	B	C
Number of issued shares	100	60	30
Owners' equity	R1 000	R600	R300
Long-term debt	–	R400	R700
Total assets	R1 000	R1 000	R1 000
Debt ratio (leverage factor)	0%	40%	70%
Operating profit (20% rate of return on total assets before tax)	R200	R200	R200
Minus: interest (25%)	–	R100	R175
Profit after interest before tax	R200	R100	R25
Minus: tax (40%)	R80	R40	R10
Net profit after tax	R120	R60	R15
Earnings per share (EPS)	R1,20	R1,00	R0,50
Rate of return on equity (ROE)	12%	10%	5%

The positive effect of the lever is because funds are obtained at an interest rate of 15% and then used by the business to earn 20% before tax. The excess return of 5% goes to shareholders. This increases the rate of return on equity (ROE) for a given level of operating profit.

The financial lever may, however, also have a negative effect. This will happen when interest rates in this example increase above 20%. Let us see what happens if interest rates rise to 25% (see table 19.3 above).

From this table we see that the rate of return on owners' equity now decreases with an increasing debt ratio, and it may even become negative.

This illustrates the financial risk lever that the inclusion of debt in the capital structure causes.

The interest pincer tightens

We also have executives who have lived through the pain of the last recession. "It was a harsh lesson," says a broker, "and they were so traumatised that their financial risk tolerance is substantially lower than in the 1980s."

Source: The interest pincer tightens, *Financial Mail*, 21 April 1989, p. 29.

19.5.2 *Capital structure and the cost of capital*

In the previous section we indicated that the capital structure results in financial risk. The level of risk is reflected by the cost of capital. This means that investors expect a higher return on their investment as risk increases.

The financial manager has to take this into account when evaluating different financing proposals. The purpose is to identify the alternative with the lowest weighted average cost of capital. The alternative with the optimal ratio of debt to shareholders' equity will make the largest contribution to the wealth of shareholders.

Table 19.4: Summary of considerations in deciding on a form of finance

Consideration	Debt	Owners' equity
Return/cost	• Interest is tax deductible • Debt increases return on equity by leveraging profits	• Dividends not tax deductible
Risk	• As the level of debt increases, so does the risk of financial distress • Repayment of debt represents a fixed obligation that must be met	• Higher levels of equity reduce the risk of financial distress • No fixed obligations
Control	• Debt does not represent an ownership stake in the business • Owner retains full control	• Control may be diluted if the business issues new share

The factors to be considered in deciding on the most suitable form of finance and the mix between debt and equity are summarised in table 19.4 above.

19.5.3 *Concluding remarks*

The effects of financial risk and financial leverage on the total risk of the business were discussed in this section.

Knowledge of financial risk is valuable in planning the optimal capital structure for a business.

Businesses in industrial sectors characterised by a stable demand for products, and therefore subject to little variability or fluctuation in sales, as well as low fixed cost ratios, could accept a relatively high degree of debt financing. For example, the demand for electricity is relatively stable. Eskom therefore uses a large percentage of debt capital to finance its operations and has a high degree of financial leverage.

In contrast, businesses in predominantly capital-intensive sectors, characterised by a high fixed cost ratio and widely fluctuating sales, are obviously exposed to a high degree of risk. Because of the possibility of the negative effects of financial leverage, a financing policy requiring a minimal amount, or at most a moderate amount, of debt capital, based on accurate forecasting and sound financial planning, will probably be more acceptable. For example, a manufacturer of fashion goods, whose sales may fluctuate because of changing demand, will be well advised to restrict the amount of debt capital in the capital structure in order to limit the financial risk.

An optimal capital structure should also ensure that the business's cost of capital is kept to a minimum, and thus the profitability of the business is maximised for its owners.

19.6 Summary

In this chapter we described the various forms of short-term finance and indicated that the short-term financing decision is a trade-off between risk and return.

> Finance is a fun game to play, hard to win.
>
> E. Briys, Options, futures and exotic derivatives, Wiley, New York, 1998.

The nature and characteristics of the various forms of long-term capital were also discussed. This was followed by a discussion of the factors involved in establishing the cost of capital and determining the weighted average cost of capital. We then explained the long-term financing decision based both on the various forms of long-term capital and also on the risk involved.

The brief overview of financial management in chapters 17, 18 and 19 aimed to put into perspective not only the interesting and important facets, but also the challenges and complexities, of this functional area of management. Bear in mind, however, that the various aspects of financial management are all interrelated and integrated in the course of business operations, and that the function of financial management should be performed with full awareness and in the context of all other functions of the business.

References

1. Kohn, M., *Financial institutions and markets*, McGraw-Hill, New York, 1994.
2. Damadoran, A., *Corporate finance: theory and practice*, Wiley, New York, 1997.
3. ABSA Bank, *Principles of finance and your business*, ABSA, Johannesburg, 1996, p. 23.

Websites: www.finforum.co.za/markets
           www.BFA.co.za
           www.24.com
           www.khula.org.za

20 The operations management function

The purpose of this chapter

This chapter defines and examines the nature of operations management. It also depicts an operations management model and its components. Finally, the classification of operations processes for manufacturers and service providers is discussed.

Learning outcomes

The content of this chapter will enable learners to:
- Explain why operations management is important for a business
- Define operations management
- Identify and explain the components of an operations management model
- Explain how systems for classifying operations processes assist operations managers.

20.1 Introduction

Countries of the international community are regularly classified as **developed** or **developing** on the basis of different criteria. One of the criteria used is the extent and growth of a particular country's gross domestic product (GDP). The GDP represents the total value of all the final goods (referred to hereafter as **products**) and **services** produced in a country within a specific period of time (usually a year). The GDP per capita (or per person) is therefore a good indication of a country's economic wealth.

Developed countries such as the USA, Japan and Germany will therefore have a higher GDP per capita than developing countries such as Singapore, Taiwan – and also South Africa. In simple terms, the businesses of a developed country will jointly produce **more products and services** than those of a developing country. To increase the economic wealth of a country, businesses in that country must therefore provide more (and preferably better) products and services. Bearing in mind that the operations function is that function in a business directly responsible for manufacturing products and/or rendering services, its importance cannot be adequately emphasised – not only for the business concerned but also for the country in which it operates.

This chapter first looks at the nature and definitions of operations management and then depicts an operations management model. This model comprises operations management strategies and objectives, a basic transformation model, and a management component. The management strategies and objectives of operations management and the basic transformation model are discussed in this chapter, as is a classification system for different operations processes of both manufacturers and service providers. In chapter 21, the management component, which includes the principal activities of operations management, namely operations design, operations planning, and control and operations improvement, is examined more closely.

20.2 The nature and definition of operations management

In chapter 1 we indicated that a business transforms inputs **from** the environment into outputs **to** the environment. The operations function is that function of the business aimed at executing the transformation process. The operations function and the management thereof (operations management) are therefore directly concerned with creating products and providing services in order to realise the objectives of the business.

20.2.1 The importance of operations management

Operations management is important in the business for the following three reasons in particular:

- **It can improve productivity.** This will be to the benefit of the business as a whole.[1] Productivity, measured as the ratio of output to input, is a yardstick of the efficacy with which operations management transforms (or converts) the business's scarce resources into products and/or services. If a business such as Addis, which manufactures plastic products, produces more error- or defect-free outputs, say, plastic buckets, with less wastage of material inputs, or puts its manufacturing staff to better use, its overall productivity will improve. Higher productivity is directly related to an increase in the business's profitability.
- **It can help the business to satisfy the needs of its customers/clients more effectively.**[2] The customer/client is an important focal point in operations management, and the operations manager should see to it that quality products or services are provided for the consumer at a reasonable price. Satisfied customers/clients are of crucial importance to any business since its long-term survival or existence is dependent on this. Businesses will endeavour by means of their particular operations skills to satisfy the needs of their customers/clients more effectively than their competitors do.
- **It can be decisive for the general reputation of the business.** Certain businesses have, through their particular operations skills, built up outstanding reputations as far as high-quality products or services, low costs, or plain and simple "good value for money" are concerned. The operations skills of a business make (and also break) such reputations. Businesses like Woolworths and Panasonic have, over the years, built up exceptionally good reputations for high quality. For such businesses, quality is a competitive weapon (or competitive advantage) that can be used to protect and further expand their market position.

In the remaining part of this section, certain concepts generally used in operations management are defined.

20.2.2 Definitions

There are many definitions of operations management in the literature. A common characteristic of all these definitions is that operations management is concerned with the management of the **transformation process** (also referred to as the operations process) whereby products are manufactured and/or services rendered.

To further clarify what is meant by operations management, the following concepts are defined:[3]

- The **operations function** is that function in the business primarily aimed at the utilisation of resources to manufacture products and/or render services.
- **Operations managers** are the personnel in the business directly responsible for managing the operations function.
- **Operations management** (also referred to as the operations management function) involves all the activities, decisions and responsibilities of operations managers that tie in with the execution of the operations function. The operations management process includes operations planning, operations organising, operations scheduling and operations control.

20.3 An operations management model

An operations management model that can be used for the management of the operations function is depicted in figure 20.1 (see p. 482) and provides the basis of the discussion in chapters 20 and 21.

Three points stand out clearly in this operations management model, namely that operations management strategies and objectives, as well as management activities (see chapter 21), influence the transformation process to produce outputs.

20.3.1 Operations management strategies and objectives

All businesses formulate business objectives, and if a business intends surviving in the long term, consumers who are satisfied with the business's products or services should be a top priority objective. The operations management function should take cognisance of customers'/clients' needs and continually formulate its management strategies and objectives in such a way that the competitive position and customer/client base not only remain intact, but, where necessary, are also strengthened and expanded.

Although customer/client needs are numerous, they can be reduced to six main elements, namely:[4]

- High quality
- Low costs
- Shorter lead time (quicker manufacturing or provision of services)
- Greater adaptability (flexibility)
- Lower variability with regard to specifications (reliability)
- High level of service (better overall service)

Figure 20.1: An operations management model

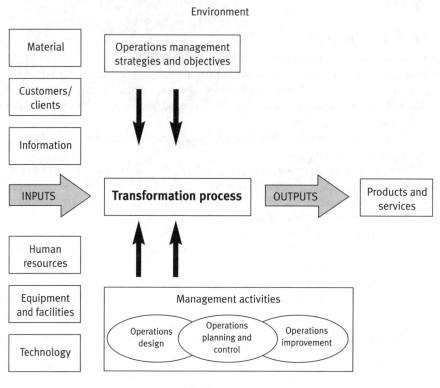

With these six customer/client requirements as a basis, operations management objectives can be formulated which give the business an "operations-based advantage"[5] over other businesses. For this reason, customer/client requirements are often referred to as "competitive priorities".[6] Operations management objectives therefore indicate the specific areas within the operations function which will be emphasised when products and/or services are produced or provided. The operations management objectives are formulated in such a way that they are applicable to both manufacturers and service providers. To acquire operations-based advantages, the following general guidelines (which incorporate the abovementioned customer/client needs) can be followed:

- **Do things right the first time.** This means that the operations function should not make mistakes. By providing error-free products and services that are ready and suitable for consumption by customers/clients, the business will gain a **quality advantage**. Higher quality not only means increased error-free outputs resulting in lower costs, but also an improved competitive position, which could lead to higher prices and a greater market share. Think again of Woolworths food products in this regard. This business is certainly one of the best-known providing top quality food products for which certain consumers are prepared to pay higher prices.

- **Do things cost effectively.** It is imperative that products and services be produced or provided at a cost that will enable the business to place them on the market at a price that will ensure an acceptable profit for the business. This also applies to non-profit organisations because taxpayers insist on good value, which they will only receive if the institution functions cost effectively. Hence, when the operations management function operates cost effectively, it can provide the business with a **cost advantage**. However, when this does not happen, say, in the case of a gold mine, where the cost per metric ton of mined gold-bearing ore is too high to run the mine profitably, drastic cost-saving measures, such as the large-scale retrenchment of miners, are necessary. In the case of Mossgas, for example, where the high procurement cost of the gas and oil made the project uneconomical, the state had to continuously subsidise the project at the expense of the taxpayer.
- **Do things fast.** This means that the period of time that elapses between the demand for a product or service and the delivery thereof should be as short as possible – or, put differently, the lead time should be shortened. This will increase the availability of the products and services and will give the business a **speed advantage**. Businesses that do not place their goods and services on the market quickly enough will not only initially have to accept lost sales, but will later on also have to overcome strong competition from established brands. Think, for example, of a paving construction business that promises to have your new driveway paved in three weeks, but then takes seven weeks to complete the job. Would you recommend this business to your friends? Businesses such as Boss Paving, which is reputed to complete paving faster than its competitors, acquires a speed advantage from which they will later build up a sound reputation in the market.
- **Change things quickly.** The operations management function should be able to adapt or change activities if unforeseen circumstances make it necessary to do so. This applies, for example, when more customers/clients demand a product or service, or if a customer/client requires the delivery of a wider variety of products or services within the agreed time. If the operations management function can change activities in this way to continuously satisfy customer/client demands both quickly and adequately, the business will have an **adaptability advantage**. During the 2002 World Summit on Sustainable Development in Johannesburg, South African businesses reacted quickly to the sharp increase in overseas visitors, and motor car rental companies such as Avis for example, were able to cope with the sudden increased demand for rental cars. Businesses like Toyota, in turn, are known for their ability to adapt their product line quickly to changing customer needs for cheaper, less luxurious motor vehicles such as the Toyota Tazz.
- **Do things right every time.** Error-free products and services that satisfy set specifications should regularly and continuously be provided to customers/clients. This gives the business a **high reliability** or **low variability advantage**. This guideline ties in with the customer/client requirement of high quality. However, it emphasises the ability of the business to continuously meet specifications in the long term. This is of particular impor-

tance to businesses that produce or provide products or services on a continuous (or mass) basis. Take the example of McDonald's Big Mac hamburgers. This international business claims that a Big Mac hamburger will taste the same in any place in the world where business is conducted. Thus, when you buy your second Big Mac, you will know exactly what you are getting! South African Airways (SAA) also strives for low variability in respect of scheduled departure times to various destinations. If SAA's flights over, say, a period of a year, depart on schedule and reach their destinations 90% of the time, one could say that the airline renders a reliable service.

- **Do things better.** With due regard for all the preceding operations management guidelines, the business will also endeavour to provide a better total product or service package compared to that of its competitors. This gives the business a **service advantage**. Think of businesses like M-Net (in South Africa) and BMW, which have gained reputations because they stand out above their rivals as far as service is concerned. This guideline is closely intertwined with the concept of Total Quality Management (TQM), which is today the focal point of many top businesses internationally. TQM's point of departure is that quality products or services cannot be produced or provided unless the whole business (all the different functional management areas) work together to achieve this goal. TQM will be discussed in more detail in chapter 21.

Figure 20.2 illustrates the positive results that can be obtained by each of the abovementioned operations management guidelines.

Figure 20.2: Positive results obtained by the application of operations management guidelines

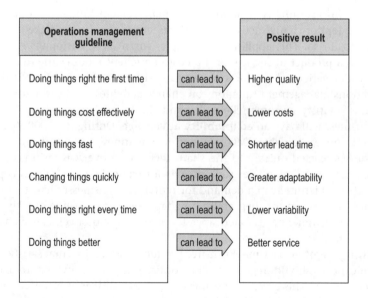

Source: Adapted from Slack, N., Chambers S., Harland, C., Harrison A. & Johnson, R., *Operations management*, Pearson Education (UK), 1995, p. 54.

Applying the concept: the priority of operations management objectives may vary

Some operations management objectives (also referred to as performance objectives) may become more or less important under different circumstances. One influence that is of particular importance to businesses in determining the relative priority that they will place on a specific objective is the **actions of competitors**.

Krüger[7] anticipated that this influence would be of special significance for South African manufacturers just after the historic 1994 democratic elections, when it was expected that most international sanctions against South Africa would be lifted. He empirically determined that the majority (more than 80% of those sampled) of so-called large South African manufacturers (that is, those employing more than 500 people in businesses located in any of the geographical regions in South Africa, and who undertook any kind of manufacturing activity in all of the standard industry code [SIC] categories) acknowledged that manufacturing-based strategies enhanced the competitive capabilities and advantages of their businesses, and that this contributed to long-term, superior business performance and success.

Furthermore, an even larger majority of the manufacturers (98% of those sampled) recognised that superior manufacturing capabilities would become a prerequisite for improving their national and international competitive positions in the future. In this regard, Krüger[8] later reported further findings showing that if

South African manufacturers were to better their positions against **national competitors**, the relative priority that had to be observed for the five selected performance objectives should be (1) low cost, (2) high quality, (3) high dependability (high reliability or low variability), (4) high speed (shorter lead times), and (5) high flexibility (greater adaptability). (Note: the terminology used for the equivalent operations management objectives used in this book are indicated in brackets. Also, this rank order is derived in a purely mathematical way, and is not necessarily statistically significant. With regard to better competitive positions against **international competitors**, a positional movement occurred between the relative priority of low cost and high quality, but this is not of statistical significance.

Finally, when the relative priority for the five operations management objectives for better competitive positions against both national and international competitors are considered together, it was found (this was confirmed statistically significant at a 0,05 level or with a 95% probability) that high quality, low cost and high dependability should all rank as priority number (1), high speed as priority number (2) and high flexibility as priority number (3).

The example in the box below illustrates how operations management objectives can be applied in practice to obtain a competitive advantage.

Applying the concept: a practical example of how operations management objectives can be used to gain competitive advantages

A manufacturer of television sets in South Africa recently effected several changes in its local production plant. The aim was to increase its share in the cheaper market segment, namely that for black and white television sets. The question that should be asked

here is which operations management objective(s) should be emphasised in this case to obtain an operations-based advantage for the business.

Part of the answer may be found if the business determines the most important customer requirements for this product. For example, do customers want low costs, high quality or short lead times? Were the business to determine the main customer requirements for this product, it would provide a good indication of what operations objectives should be focused on in this case, such as low costs and ready availability (or a shortened lead time).

Operations management objectives should therefore always be formulated in conjunction with the most important customer/client requirements for a particular product or service.

20.3.2 The transformation model

The operations function is primarily concerned with the application of resources (inputs) by means of a transformation process to provide outputs. A basic transformation model (also referred to as an input transformation-output model) is depicted in figure 20.3.

This model could apply to both manufacturers and service providers.

Figure 20.3: A basic transformation model

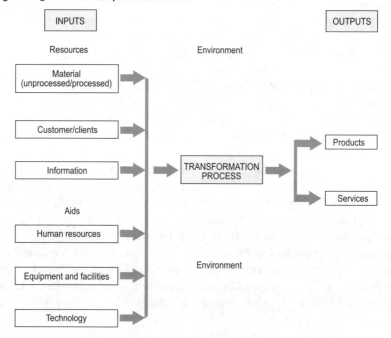

Source: Adapted from Schonberger, R.J. & Knod, E.M. (Jr), *Operations management: continuous improvement*, 4th edition, McGraw-Hill Company, 1994, p. 3.

The transformation model comprises three main components: inputs, the transformation process itself, and outputs. Each of these will now be discussed in more detail.

20.3.2.1 Inputs

Inputs used in the transformation process comprise both the **resources** that are processed, changed or converted (jointly known as transformation) and the **aids** required to make the transformation possible. The resources include the following:

- **Material.** A wide variety of material (both processed and unprocessed) can be used as inputs in the transformation process. For example, a motor manufacturer will use mainly processed material such as steel, glass and plastic, while a gold mine will use primarily unprocessed material (gold-ore). For a service provider such as a hairdresser, different hair products, for example, shampoo and tinting agents, will represent the material inputs.
- **Customers/Clients.** Clients can serve as the inputs in the transformation process when the client himself or herself is the subject who is "transformed or processed". In a dentist's rooms or hairdressing salon, the client who receives dental treatment or undergoes an improvement in his or her appearance is the primary input in the transformation process. The same applies to recreational facilities (cinemas or gymnasiums) and recreational events (symphony or rock concerts) because the client is the most important input who is "transformed" or entertained.
- **Information.** Information can either be the primary input that is processed or converted (for example, the information processed into news for a newspaper) or it can be used as the secondary input in a transformation process. Information about consumer preferences in respect of a particular product, such as a motor vehicle (colour, size and shape), is a case in point.

Aids include the following:

- **Human resources.** In most transformation processes some or other form of human involvement is necessary. This includes the workers who are physically involved in the transformation process and the people involved in a supervisory capacity. Some manufacturing processes are more labour intensive than others. A gold mine, for example, is more labour intensive than a motor vehicle manufacturer, where many of the processes have been automated. Service providers such as hotels are normally also labour intensive and the service sector is therefore seen as the sector with the most potential for job creation.
- **Equipment and facilities.** Equipment and facilities can assume many different forms. A few examples of specific facilities are highlighted:
  - A manufacturer will use factories, machinery and equipment.
  - Hospitals will use wards, examination rooms and operating theatres.
  - Banks, attorneys and auditing firms will make use of offices, computers and telephones.
  - Restaurants will make use of eating areas, tables and chairs, gridirons, serving tables and take-away counters.
  - Universities will use lecture halls, laboratories, theatres and sports fields.
  - Supermarkets and other retailers will use shopping areas, storage rooms, display areas, shelves, aisles and cash registers.
- **Technology.** The role of technology as an input in the transformation process is becoming increasingly important. Technology is generally used to enable the transformation process to function more efficiently. Thus, new knowledge and techniques (automation) can help a manufacturer to manufacture better, higher quality products faster. Service providers can also apply technology (for example, satellite communication) to render better services more quickly.

20.3.2.2 The transformation process

The inputs are converted to outputs in the transformation process. The nature of the process is determined by the type of input that is predominantly processed in the process itself. Three main types of resource inputs,[9] namely the transformation of materials, information and customers/clients, will now be discussed.

- **Transformation of materials.** The transformation process is primarily geared to processing materials by changing their physical characteristics (shape or composition). Most manufacturers, such as motor vehicle or furniture manufacturers, employ such transformation processes. Service providers that also fall into this category include those where the material changes location (a delivery business); there is a change of ownership (wholesalers and retailers); the material is primarily stored (warehouses).
- **Transformation of information.** Information is the primary source processed in this transformation process. It includes processes where information changes in composition or shape (an auditor's report); it changes ownership (a market research publication); it is disseminated and changes location (telecommunication); it is merely stored (a library).
- **Transformation of customers/clients.** Transformation processes that primarily process "clients" may also occur in a variety of ways. Some change the physical characteristics of clients (hairdressers), while others change their physiological condition (medical treatment at hospitals) or emotional condition (entertainment at cinemas). The location of clients can also be changed (airlines) or merely be "stored" (accommodated), for example, in hotels.

20.3.2.3 Outputs

The ultimate goal of any transformation process is to convert or process inputs into outputs. Outputs assume the form of products (goods) or services. Manufacturers normally produce some or other product (motor vehicles or furniture), while service providers render certain services (hairdressers or airlines). However, the characteristics of products manufactured and services provided, differ. It is important to note these differences because they have specific implications for the management of the various operations processes. Important differences between products and services are represented in table 20.1.

Table 20.1: Characteristics of products and services

Products (product manufacturer)	Services (service provider)
Physically tangible and durable	Intangible and perishable
Output kept in stock	Output not kept in stock
Low customer contact	High client contact
Manufactured before use	Provision and consumption simultaneous
Long response time	Short response time
Local and international markets	Mainly local markets
Large production facilities	Small service provision facility
Capital intensive	Labour intensive
Quality easily measurable	Quality difficult to measure

Source: Krajewski, L.J. & Ritzman, L.P., *Operations management*, 3rd edition, Pearson Education Inc, 1993, p. 5.

One should bear in mind that these differences represent two extreme positions on a continuum between pure product manufacturers and pure service providers. In practice, however, one finds that businesses are to a greater or lesser degree involved in both the manufacture of products and the provision of services.

The example in the box below illustrates such differences between the characteristics of products and services.

Applying the concept: a manufacturer of products versus a service provider

A product manufacturer. Toyota and Nissan manufacture motor vehicles. The product is physically tangible (the vehicle itself), durable (is not used up in one period of time) and can be kept in stock (where more vehicles are manufactured than the number in immediate demand). There is no customer contact while the vehicle is being manufactured and unless there are already a few vehicles in stock, it may take a while to deliver the vehicle to the customer. Motor vehicle manufacturers usually have large production facilities and expensive equipment, which make this a capital-intensive industry. Because of the tangible nature of vehicles, it is possible to set, monitor and ensure objec-

tive standards as far as quality is concerned.

A service provider. A dentist renders a professional service. The service itself is intangible (it cannot be held or touched) and can also not be kept in stock if it is not used immediately. The presence of the user of the service (the patient) is necessary while the service is being rendered, and the response time is usually short. Provision of the service takes place in a small service facility (a dental surgery), the service itself is labour intensive (the dentist is involved), and because the service is intangible, it is more difficult to set and maintain objective standards.

The transformation process, which comprises three main components of inputs, the transformation process, and outputs, has been explained. Table 20.2 (see p. 490) provides examples of the inputs, the nature of the transformation process, and outputs of a variety of businesses.

20.4 The classification of operations processes for manufacturers and service providers

In section 20.3 an operations management model applicable to both the manufacture of products and the provision of services was depicted. One should bear in mind, however, that the nature of the transformation processes (operations processes) will differ because of the different types of products and/or services manufactured and/or provided. Such differences are of special importance when considering the management of a particular operations process, because certain management techniques and methods are suitable for application only in certain types of operations processes.

In the following two sections, a classification system of the operations processes for both manufacturers and service providers is depicted.

Table 20.2: Inputs, transformation processes and outputs of a variety of businesses

Type of business	Inputs	Transformation process	Outputs
Rail transport	Locomotives Passenger coaches and trucks Locomotive drivers and personnel Railway tracks and sleepers Passengers and freight	Changes location of passengers and freight	Passengers and rail freight at new destinations
Banks	Bank tellers and financial advisers Safes and computers Bank notes and coins Clients	Receipt and payment of money (cash) Recordkeeping of accounts Safekeeping of valuable articles	Clients with financial peace of mind Accurate bank statements Financial earnings (interest)
Hairdressing salon	Hairdresser and assistants Combs, brushes and scissors Treatment agents Clients	Shampooing, tinting, treating, drying and cutting of hair	Clients with neat appearances
Gold mine	Gold-bearing ore Pneumatic drills and explosives Lifts and conveyer belts Miners and engineers	Mined gold-bearing ore and transport to processing plant Process ore and melt gold concentrates	Gold bars
Furniture manufacturer	Wood, steel and material Saw and planing equipment Factory workers	Design furniture Make furniture Sell furniture to wholesalers	Completed furniture such as lounge and dining-room suites
Printing works	Printing and binding machines Paper, cardboard and ink Design and printing personnel	Design, print and bind books, periodicals and reports	Designed and printed material
Construction firm	Sand, cement and other building material Construction equipment Construction workers Building plans	Plan and construct buildings according to plans	Office accommodation
Missile manufacturer	Electronic components Rocket launchers Engineers and technicians Computers	Design, assemble and test missiles	Air-to-air or ground-to-ground missiles

20.4.1 Classification of operations processes for manufacturers

In manufacturing, the most common classification system is one that classifies different operations processes according to scope (volume of output) and variety of products. Thus, a business that produces a product in large volumes with little variety (for example, a manufacturer of bricks), will be placed in a different category to a business that manufactures a small volume of a large variety of products (for example, a clothing manufacturer). According to such a classification system (see figure 20.4), three main categories with two additional combinations (hybrids) are identified. Each is discussed with the aid of practical examples.[10]

Figure 20.4: Classification of operations processes: manufacturers

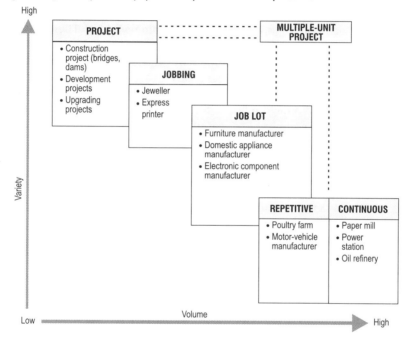

Source: Adapted from Slack, N., Chambers, S., Harland, C., Harrison, A. & Johnston, R., *Operations management*, Pearson Education (UK), 1995, p. 141.

- **Project systems.** Project systems represent operations processes that are highly individual, unique, and normally tackled on a large scale. It takes the project team months or even years to complete such projects. Examples of such project systems are construction projects (the building of an airport, bridge, highway, or office and shopping complex), a development programme for a new motorcar, or the upgrading of an assembly line.

  Each project produces an output volume of one (volume is therefore low), but as one can deduce from the above examples, a wide variety of type of projects can be undertaken (variety is therefore high). Projects are also not repeated in exactly the same way. When a tunnel has been completed, the construction company will construct the next tunnel somewhere else. The second tunnel would be of another design according to the requirements of the particular location. The Du Toit's Kloof tunnel in the Western Cape and the Lesotho Highland Water Scheme are good examples here.

- **Jobbing systems.** Jobbing systems normally represent operations processes conducted on a small scale with a low volume output. The nature of the work is the same throughout, but the specific requirements differ from one task to the next. Examples are a goldsmith who manufactures jewellery (each piece of jewellery is usually unique and takes the unique design preferences of the client into consideration) and the printing of wedding invitations at a printing works (two wedding invitations for two different couples are usually not exactly the same in all respects). Thus, an important feature of these types of systems is the great or wide variety, but small volumes of products supplied by the business.

- **Continuous or repetitive systems.** Continuous or repetitive systems represent operations systems in which the output volume is high. These systems provide the same product on a continuous basis, and here the variety is far less than in jobbing-systems. Examples are sugar mills, a power station, a cement manufacturer, a cattle-fodder kraal and a motorcar manufacturer. A distinction is, however, made between continuous systems (sugar mills, power stations and cement manufacturers) and repetitive systems[11] (cattle-fodder kraal and motor vehicle manufacturer). The difference lies in the way output is measured.

    In continuous systems, volume measures are used to give an indication of output. A sugar mill will measure its output in cubic metres of sugar (for example, 3 000 m^3), while a power station will measure its output in megawatts (2 000 mW). In contrast, a repetitive system will measure its output in terms of the number of completed units, say, 500 cattle in the case of a cattle-fodder kraal.

- **Multiple-unit project systems.** Multiple-unit projects are the first combination system (hybrid system) that can be identified. This type of system is a combination of a repetitive and a project system. The scope of the project is still large, but multiple units of the end-product are produced. Examples are found in aircraft and missile manufacturers.

- **Job-lot systems.** Job-lot systems are the second combination system (hybrid) that can be identified. This type of system is a combination of a repetitive and a jobbing system, and is also known as a lot production system. A limited range of products is manufactured by the business, and production occurs in lots or batches. Examples here are the manufacture of domestic appliances and sound equipment. A manufacturer of domestic appliances will alternate production of fridges, stoves and microwave ovens in batches, while a manufacturer of sound equipment will produce amplifiers, loudspeakers, CD players and tape recorders. The extent of repetition is determined by the type of product and the size of the demand.

20.4.2 *Classification of operations processes for service providers*

The same classification system can be used in service providers as depicted in manufacturers (one based on output volume and output variety).[12] Three main categories are identified according to such a classification system (see figure 20.5). Each will be further explained on the basis of practical examples.

Figure 20.5: Classification of operations processes: service providers

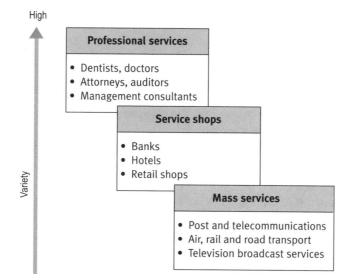

Source: Adapted from Slack, N., Chambers, S., Harland, C., Harrison. A. & Johnston, R., *Operations management*, Pearson Education (UK), 1995, p. 143.

- **Professional services.** Professional services represent operations processes provided on a high client-contact basis, where the client himself or herself is usually present in the service process for a considerable period of time. The nature of the service provided takes the specific needs of clients into consideration and is therefore more people-oriented than equipment-oriented. Because of the client-focused nature of these services, the extent (volume) of presentation is low, while the variety of services that can be provided is high. Examples of professional services (referred to as such because of the formal academic qualifications and registration that such professional practitioners need to obtain) include the services of dentists, attorneys, auditors, doctors and management consultants.
- **Service shops.** Service shops represent operations processes where the characteristics of service provision fall between those of professional services and mass services. Hence, there is a fair amount of client contact, services are standardised to a certain extent, but are also adapted to accommodate the unique needs of clients (although there is more variety than in mass services). The number of clients served is also greater (the volume is more than primarily the one-to-one basis of professional services). Examples of service shops are banks, hotels, beauty salons and retail stores.
- **Mass services.** Mass services represent operations processes in which many client transactions take place with limited client contact, and in which the

nature of the services provided is largely standardised (variety is therefore low). These services are usually equipment-oriented and are provided on a larger scale (volume is therefore high). Examples of mass services include post and telecommunication services, air and rail transport, and television broadcast services.

In the above discussion, a classification system based on the scope (or volume) and variety of products and/or services for both manufacturers and service providers was depicted. Bear in mind that it is sometimes difficult to place a specific operations process, encountered in practice, in one category, or even to make a clear distinction between manufacturing and service provision. The example in the box below illustrates such a case.

Applying the concept: classifying a restaurant

Pachalla is a restaurant serving á la carte meals. Is it a manufacturer or a service provider? Obviously, food is prepared, but clients are also served. The nature of the activities that have to be undertaken (for example, the labour intensity thereof, and the need for the client to be present) corresponds to that of a service provider (see the differences between the characteristics of products and services in table 20.1 on p. 488). On the strength of this, the restaurant is classified as a service provider. However, since there is a certain amount of standardisation (a fixed menu is normally used), it can also be placed in the category of a service shop.

20.5 Summary

The aim of this chapter was to introduce operations management. The nature and definitions of operations management were first examined, followed by the presentation of an operations management model. This model comprises three components, namely the operations management strategies and objectives (see section 20.3.1) as well as the management activities (see chapter 21) that influence the transformation process (see section 20.3.2) to produce outputs.

In conclusion, a classification system of the operations processes for both manufacturers and service providers was proposed. These systems are based on a classification of the operations processes on the basis of scope (volume) and the variety of products or services manufactured or provided. The classification system for manufacturers has three main categories (project, job-bing, and continuous or repetitive systems) and two additional combinations (multiple-unit project and job-lot systems), while the classification system for service providers contains only three main categories (professional services, service shops and mass services).

References

1. Stoner, J.A.F. & Freeman, R.E., *Management*, 5th edition, Prentice Hall, Englewood Cliffs, New Jersey, 1992, p. 634.
2. *Ibid.*, p. 634.
3. Slack, N., Chambers, S., Harland, C., Harrison, A. & Johnston, R., *Operations management*, 2nd edition, Pitman Publishing, London, 1998, p. 6.
4. Schonberger, R.J. & Knod, E.M. (Jr), *Meeting customers' demands*, 7th edition, McGraw-Hill, New York, 2001, pp. 17-18.

5. Slack, N., et al., *op cit.*, p. 51.
6. Krajewski, L.J. & Ritzman, L.P., *Operations management: strategy and analysis*, 3rd edition, Addison-Wesley, Reading, Massachusetts, 1996, p. 36.
7. Krüger, L.P., *Strategic manufacturing priorities for South African manufacturers*, Centre for Business Management, University of South Africa, Pretoria, Published research report, 1996, pp. 1-117.
8. Krüger, L.P., Strategic manufacturing priorities for South African manufacturers: the need to shift emphasis and improve on current performance levels, *South African Journal of Business Management*, Vol. 28, No. 4, 1997, pp. 138-146.
9. Slack, N., et al., *op cit.*, pp. 15–16.
10. De Wit, P.W.C. & Adendorff, S.A., *Production and operations management: a South African perspective*, 2nd edition, Thomson Publishing (Southern Africa), Johannesburg, 1997, pp. 9–10.
11. Schonberger, R.J., et al., *op cit.*, p. 16.
12. Slack, N., et al., *op cit.*, p. 125.

21 Operations management: activities, techniques and methods

The purpose of this chapter

This chapter deals with the three main activities of operations management, namely operations design, planning and control of the operations process, and operations improvement. Selected techniques and methods that can be used with these operational activities are also introduced.

Learning outcomes

The content of this chapter will enable learners to:
- Provide a broad framework of the different activities involved in the design of operations processes
- Outline the basic principles of planning and control of operations processes
- Outline a general strategy for the improvement of operations processes

21.1 Introduction

In chapter 20 an operations management model was put forward. This model comprises operations management strategies and objectives, as well as the management activities that influence the transformation process in order to provide outputs. The management activities (referred to hereafter only as activities) are the direct responsibility of operations managers.

This chapter deals in more detail with the three activities of operations managers, namely operations design, planning and control of the operations process, and operations improvement. Certain techniques and methods that operations managers can use to perform these activities "better" will also be discussed. In this context, "better" refers to **greater efficiency** and **greater effectiveness** in the performance of these operations activities.

21.2 Operations design

21.2.1 *The nature of operations design*

The design of a product, say, a motor vehicle, entails far more than merely determining its physical appearance in terms of shape, colour and finish. It also includes the design of the processes for manufacturing the different components of the motor vehicle itself, such as the body assembly, paintwork and composition of the chassis and engine. In the design of a service, too, for example, a 24-hour security monitoring and reaction service, the processes (or systems) should be designed to execute the particular service according to promise (or specification). This may include an alarm system, control room, security personnel, and reaction vehicles.

As stated above, operations design entails two interdependent aspects, namely the **design of products and services** (also referred to as product or service design) and the **design of processes** to manufacture or provide these products or services (also referred to as process design).

It stands to reason that operations management, as well as other functional managers, are actively involved in the design of the business's products and/or services. The design process will be briefly explained as a whole, followed by a more in-depth discussion of the operations manager's role.

Figure 21.1 provides a broad framework of the different activities involved in operations design.

Figure 21.1: The nature of operations design

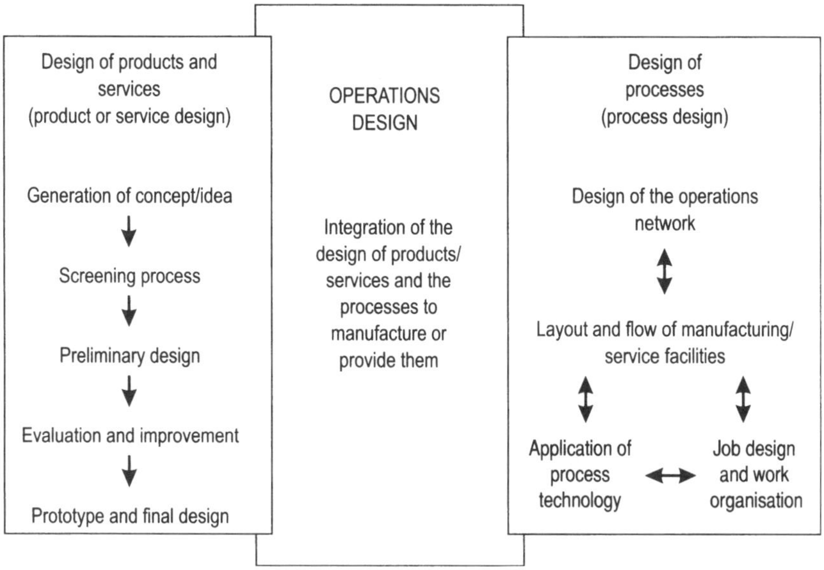

Source: Slack, N., Chambers, S., Harland, C., Harrison, A. & Johnston, R., *Operations management*, Pearson Education (UK), 1995, p. 152.

The primary aim of operations design is to establish products and/or services and the corresponding processes, so that the needs of customers/clients can always be satisfied in the best possible way.

Obviously, design, as an operations activity, helps to achieve the operations management objectives with regard to quality, cost, lead time, adaptability, variability and service (see section 20.3.1). The designers of a product such as a fridge, for example, will endeavour to design an aesthetically acceptable product that will satisfy customers' expectations in that it should function well, be reliable during its lifetime, and be quick and easy to manufacture. The design should also be such that errors in the manufacturing process are kept to a minimum so that manufacturing costs can be kept at a reasonable level. Designers of services (for example, a telephone service) are also expected to construct the service in such a way that clients' expectations are met; the service can be rendered within the operations ability of the business; and it is affordable.

Most, if not all, products or services encountered in the market today first have their origin as a vague idea or concept put forward as a suitable solution to a perceived need of a customer/client. The idea or concept is refined over a period of time, and in the process, more and more detailed information is attached to the idea or concept. Ultimately, there is sufficient information to put together a specification for the product or service, and the process for the manufacture or provision thereof.

21.2.2 *The design of products and services*

Although the operations manager is usually not solely (and directly) responsible for the design of a product or service, he or she is, however, indirectly responsible for providing the information and advice on which the ultimate success of the development and manufacture or provision of the product or service depends.

21.2.2.1 The competitive advantage of good design

The design of a product or service begins and ends with the customer/client. Initially, products and services are designed with a view to satisfying the needs of the customer/client in the best possible way. If products and services are well designed, produced and provided, so that the expectations of customers/clients are realised or even exceeded, the business's competitive position will be reinforced through increased sales of these products and services. The design and production of the famous Venter trailers is a good example of how a competitive advantage can be gained in the market. Other manufacturers have also entered the market, but Venter trailers are still the market leader.

21.2.2.2 The composition (or components) of products and services

A product or service is broadly defined as anything that can be offered to a customer/client in order to satisfy his or her needs. More specifically, however, all products or services consist of three interdependent components,[1] namely an idea or concept, a package, and a process. Each of these will now briefly be discussed:

- **Idea or concept**. In chapter 14 brief mention was made of the fact that when customers/clients buy a product or service, they do not buy only the physical product or intangible service – they in fact also buy a set of expected benefits which they deem will satisfy their needs. Hence, the product or service should meet all their expectations. For example, when someone buys a product such as a new motorcar, not only the car itself is bought but also all the expected benefits that go with it, such as safety, outstanding road-holding ability, good reliability, and a possible high resale value. The same applies when a service is purchased, for example, medical treatment at a hospital. The patient expects a set of benefits such as good medical care, the timeous receipt of prescribed medication, and a secure and peaceful environment so that he or she can recover from the illness. In both cases one refers to the set of expected benefits as the product or service concept. Thus, when the product or service is designed, the operations manager should understand exactly what the customer/client expects from the business. This knowledge and insight is of vital importance to ensure that the transformation process provides the "right" product or service concept.

- **Package composition of products and services.** Concepts involve a package of products or services. The concept of product usually refers to a tangible physical object like a motorcar, dishwasher or article of clothing, while the concept of service indicates an intangible object such as a visit to the theatre, a hairdressing salon or a night club. As mentioned in section 20.3.2.3, however, it is often difficult to make a clear distinction between these two concepts. Take, for example, a new motorcar. The physical vehicle is clearly a tangible object, but the other benefits such as a guarantee and the regular repairs at scheduled times are an intangible service. A meal in a restaurant comprises physical products such as food and drink, but also service in that food is prepared and served at the tables, and even the atmosphere in the restaurant plays a role here. Thus, regardless of whether a product or service is designed, the package comprises a combination of products and services. It is this package that the customer/client in fact purchases.

  Two further aspects should be kept in mind in the composition of a service package, namely the explicit versus the implicit advantages, and core versus peripheral services.[2] The explicit advantages indicate the physical benefits the client receives from the service package (for example, the short response time of a tow-in service after an accident). The implicit advantage, on the other hand, refers to the psychological advantage (for example, peace of mind, knowing that a tow-in service's reaction time will be short).

  The service package in many businesses comprises a core service and peripheral services. The core service is the principal product that the business offers, while peripheral services supplement the core service. A garage that repairs cars is a case in point. The core service is regarded as the repair of motor-vehicles, with a peripheral service such as the washing and polishing of cars after they have been repaired.

- **Process for creating the package.** A process is necessary to create the products and services. As stated earlier in section 21.2.1, it is almost unthinkable that the design of the products and/or services should not take place in conjunction with the design of the processes required to manufacture or provide them. The design of processes needed to manufacture products and/or provide services will be discussed in section 21.2.3. At this stage of the discussion, however, it is necessary to bear in mind that it is this operations process that creates the products and/or services, combines them into a product or service concept, and makes them available to customers/clients in order to satisfy their needs.

21.2.2.3 The stages in the design of products and services

The ultimate result of the design of products and services is a full detailed specification of the product or service. To compile this specification, detailed information must be obtained about the abovementioned three components of any product or service, namely information on the idea or concept (the form, function, aim and benefits of the design), the package (the composition of products and services required to support the idea or concept), and the process of creating the package (which determines the way in which the individual products and services of the package will be manufactured or provided).

To obtain this full detailed specification it is necessary to first follow certain consecutive steps. Figure 21.1 (see p. 497) illustrates the stages in the design of a product and/or service from the stage where the idea or concept is generated to the stage where the final specification for the product or service is compiled. These stages briefly entail the following:

- **Idea or concept generation.** The first step in designing a product or service starts when different ideas for new products or service concepts are generated. New ideas for products or services come from within the business itself (for example, the ideas of personnel, or from formal research and development programmes) or from outside the business (for example, the ideas of customers/clients or competitors). The example in the box below illustrates a case where customer needs for cheaper packaging materials led to the development of a new product.

Applying the concept: a new product idea is born

Until the late 1970s, wine was packaged and marketed in glass bottles only. However, following consumer demand for cheaper packaging, the well-known Cellar Cask range of wines began packaging and marketing wine in five-litre and two-litre cardboard containers. This concept took off overnight in South Africa, and wine sales reached unprecedented heights. Competitors were also compelled to package and market their wines in cardboard containers.

- **The screening process.** Not all ideas or concepts that are generated will necessarily develop into products and services. Ideas or concepts are evaluated by means of a screening process based on the design criteria of feasibility, acceptability and risk. In general, an endeavour is made to determine whether the idea or concept will make a significant contribution to the business's product and/or service range. Other functional management areas, such as marketing and finance, are also involved in this screening process of ideas and concepts, and each may use further criteria in this process. The operations manager is responsible for operations screening[3] to determine whether the business has both the ability (people, skills and technology) and the capacity to produce or provide the ideas and/or concepts.
- **Preliminary design.** Once the ideas and/or concepts generated by the particular functional management areas in the business are reduced to one or two potentially acceptable products or service concepts, the next step is the preliminary design of the product or service. The preliminary design is the first attempt to specify the composition of the components of the product or service to be included in the package and to identify the processes that will be necessary to produce or provide the product or service package.

- **Evaluation and improvement.** The aim of this step is to evaluate the preliminary design with a view to improving it and making the process of manufacturing and/or provision less expensive and easier. Various techniques and methods can be used as aids in this step. Two of these techniques and methods will be described at the end of this section.
- **Prototype and final design.** The last step in the design of products and services is the development of a prototype of the product, or simulation of the service, in order to test it in the market. If the prototype, which is based on the improved preliminary design, is favourably received in the market, the final design and specifications of the product or service can be compiled.

21.2.2.4 Techniques and methods that can be used during the product or service design

Various techniques and methods can be used during the design of products and services to better execute this design activity. While certain techniques and methods – such as process flow diagrams, quality function deployment (QFD), value engineering, and Taguchi methods – are regarded as advanced subjects and are therefore not included in this book, we will now consider the following two basic methods or techniques:

- **Basic product structures and bill of materials.** Basic product structures are used to determine precisely which components or parts are required for a specific product. Bills of material reflect the quantity of each component or part (also known as item). The example below illustrates a product structure and bill of material for a basic office chair.

Applying the concept: an example of a product structure and bill of material for a basic office chair

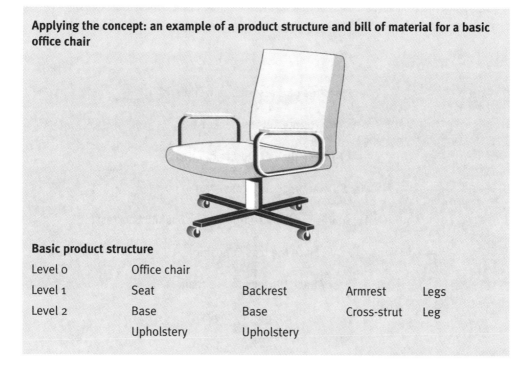

Basic product structure

Level 0	Office chair			
Level 1	Seat	Backrest	Armrest	Legs
Level 2	Base	Base	Cross-strut	Leg
	Upholstery	Upholstery		

Bill of material

Level 0	Level 1	Level 2	Quantity
Office chair			1
	Seat		1
		Base	0,25 m^2: 0,50 × 0,50; 10 mm thick
		Upholstery	0,90 m^2; 2/0.50 × 0,50 m + 4/0,50 × 0,20 m
	Back		1
		Base	0,25 m^2: 0,50 × 0,50 m: 10 mm thick
		Upholstery	0,70 m^2; 2/0.50 × 0,50 m + 4/0,50 × 0,10 m
	Armrest		2
		Cross-strut	1 support = 0,45 m: 60 × 40 mm
	Legs		4
		Leg	1 leg = 0,6 m: 60 × 40 mm
	Fastening	Screw	6 × 5 mm diameter × 50 mm long
		Liquid glue	20 ml

- **Simple flow charts.** Flow-charts are used to identify the main elements of a specific process. The example below illustrates a simple flow chart for manufacturing a basic office chair.

Applying the concept: a simple flow chart for manufacturing a basic office chair

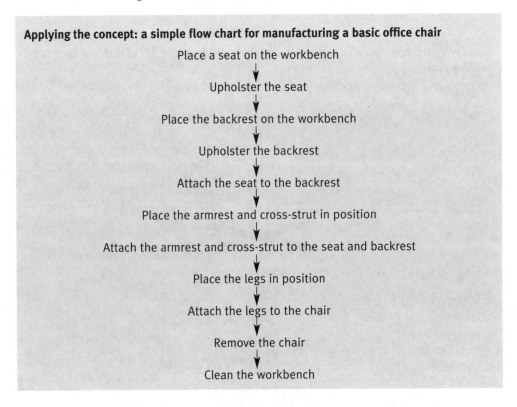

Place a seat on the workbench
↓
Upholster the seat
↓
Place the backrest on the workbench
↓
Upholster the backrest
↓
Attach the seat to the backrest
↓
Place the armrest and cross-strut in position
↓
Attach the armrest and cross-strut to the seat and backrest
↓
Place the legs in position
↓
Attach the legs to the chair
↓
Remove the chair
↓
Clean the workbench

21.2.3 The design of operations processes

The design of operations processes to manufacture products or provide services is just as important as the design of the products or services themselves. Without both good product and service design and a good process design, it is impossible to develop, manufacture or provide a successful product or service.

21.2.3.1 The design of the operations network

No operations process exists in isolation – it is part of a greater, integrated operations network.[4] Besides the specific operations process itself, the operations network also includes the suppliers of materials or services, as well as intermediaries and final customers/clients. The example in the accompanying box illustrates an operations network for a poultry farmer.

Applying the concept: an example of the operations network for a poultry farmer

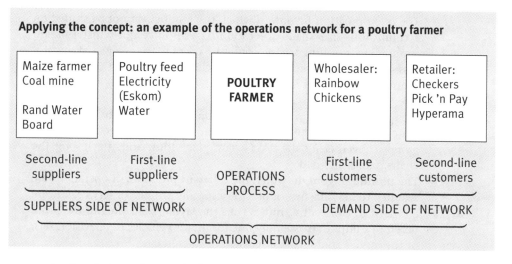

In the design of a particular operations process, it is important for the entire operations network to be taken into consideration. This enables the operations manager to determine precisely what the inputs for the specific process are, as well as the customer/client needs that have to be satisfied. Such a study also helps the business to determine its competitive position in the network, identify significant interfaces in the network, and reflect on its long-term involvement in the network.

21.2.3.2 Layout and flow of the manufacturing and/or service provision facility

The layout of the operations facility determines the physical arrangement of resources such as machines, equipment and personnel used in a particular transformation process. The layout of a manufacturing or service provision facility is usually the first characteristic of an operations process to be observed because it determines the physical form and appearance of the facility. At the same time, the layout determines the way in which resources such as material, information and customers/clients flow through the transformation process. Both the layout and flow of an operations facility are of particular importance since small changes in the placement of machines, the flow of material and people can greatly influence the operations process in terms of cost and efficiency.

The layout of a manufacturing/service facility entails the following three steps:

- **Step 1: Selecting the process type.** The first step in the layout of an operations facility involves selecting the appropriate process type. The different process types for both manufacturers and service providers were identified in section 20.4. The process types in manufacturers are project, job, continuous or repetitive, multiple-unit project, or job-lot processes. In service providers they are professional services, mass services and service shops.
- **Step 2: Selecting the basic layout type.** Once the appropriate process type has been selected, the next step involves selecting a basic layout type. Four basic layout types,[5] which depict the general form and arrangement of operations facilities, can be identified. These entail:
  - The **fixed position layout**, in which the product cannot be shifted on account of its size, shape or location. The resources for transformation (equipment, machinery and people) are taken to the receiver of the processing, which is static, for example, a construction site (Du Toit's Kloof tunnel) or a shipyard in Durban.
  - The **process layout**, in which similar processes (or operations) are grouped together into sections. If a business manufactures not only basic office chairs, but also tables and desks, such sections can be grouped together for the tasks – saw, plane, turn and attach – for the chairs, tables and desks.
  - The **product layout**, in which the different processes or operations are required to manufacture or provide a specific product or service, and are arranged in consecutive order. Thus the layout is adapted to the product, for example, an assembly line for motor vehicles or television sets, or the service counters in a self-service cafeteria.
  - The **cellular layout**, in which certain processes are placed in a cell, and the particular cell itself is then arranged according to either a process or a product layout. A good example here is a department store selling men's, ladies' and children's clothing. The men's department functions as an independent cell with its own layout, while the same applies to the ladies' and children's departments.

The example in the box (see p. 505) illustrates each of the four basic layout types.

- **Detailed design of the layout.** The selection of a basic layout type merely provides an indication of the broad layout of the operations facility. However, it does not determine the precise placement of the various machines and equipment. The final step in the layout of a manufacturing or service facility therefore entails the detailed design of the layout.

21.2.3.3 The application of process technology

All operations processes use some or other form of process technology. Process technology indicates the machines, equipment and apparatus used in the transformation process to transform materials, information and clients so that products and/or services can be manufactured or provided. Process technology

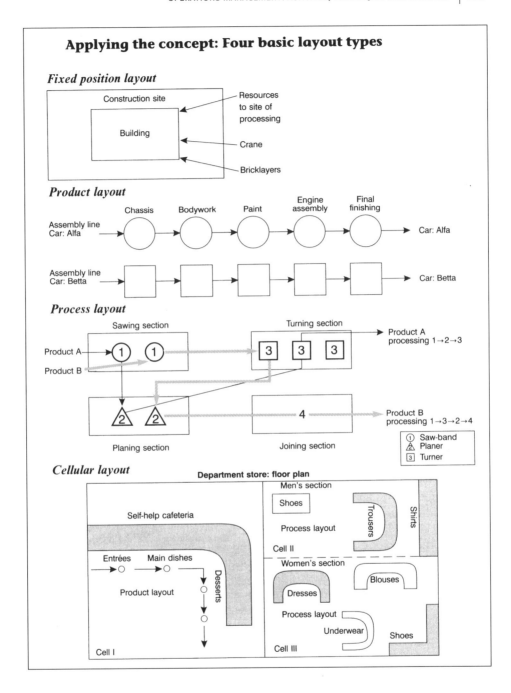

Applying the concept: Four basic layout types

Fixed position layout

Construction site — Resources to site of processing

Building — Crane

— Bricklayers

Product layout

Assembly line Car: Alfa → Chassis → Bodywork → Paint → Engine assembly → Final finishing → Car: Alfa

Assembly line Car: Betta → □ → □ → □ → □ → □ → Car: Betta

Process layout

Sawing section — ① ①

Product A →

Product B →

Turning section — ③ ③ ③ → Product A processing 1→2→3

Planing section — ② ②

Joining section — 4 → Product B processing 1→3→2→4

① Saw-band
② Planer
③ Turner

Cellular layout

Department store: floor plan

Self-help cafeteria

Entrées → ○ Main dishes → ○

Product layout

Desserts

Cell I

Men's section

Shoes

Process layout

Cell II

Trousers   Shirts

Women's section

Dresses   Blouses

Process layout

Underwear   Shoes

Cell III

---

may range from relatively simple processes, such as a word processor, to highly complex and sophisticated systems, such as automated (robot) manufacturing.

The operations manager has to be involved continuously in the management of all facets of process technology. To perform this task effectively, he or she needs to do the following:

- Foresee how technology can improve a specific operations process
- Decide which technology(ies) to use

- Integrate the new technology with existing operations activities
- Continually monitor the performance of the technology
- Upgrade or replace the technology when necessary

Although the operations manager is not necessarily a specialist in each technological field, he or she should still have an understanding of what a particular technology essentially entails, and how the technology performs the particular function, as well as being able to identify the advantages and limitations of a particular technology in the operations process.

A cotton farmer will have to decide whether to mechanise the harvesting process by using a cotton harvester, or to continue using manual labour. The advantages of mechanisation of the process include the speed at which the cotton is harvested, while limitations such as greater capital expenditure and losses in the quality of the cotton can also be prevented.

21.2.3.4 Job design and work organisation

Operations management focuses not only on the technologies, systems, procedures and facilities in a business (the so-called non-human component), but also on people's involvement in the operations activity itself. The way in which human resources are managed in a business has a fundamental effect on the effectiveness of the operations function.

Since most people who are appointed in a business are usually active in the operations function, this places a huge responsibility on the shoulders of the operations manager as far as leadership in the business and development of employees are concerned. The design of jobs (or job design) is of vital importance in operations management because it determines how workers perform their various daily tasks.

Work study is a scientific approach that can be used to great effect in job design and work organisation. It refers to the application of different techniques to systematically study all the factors influencing the people in the work environment in order to improve the execution of tasks, in terms both of efficiency and effectiveness. Two work study techniques often encountered in the literature are method study and work measurement.[6] **Method study** entails the systematic recording and critical investigation of the present and proposed work methods, with a view to the development and application of easier and more effective methods in an effort to reduce costs. **Work measurement** entails the application of techniques designed to determine how long it takes a trained and qualified worker to do a specific job at a fixed level of performance. The components of work study are illustrated diagrammatically in figure 21.2 (see p. 507).

21.2.3.5 Techniques and methods that can be used during process design

Various techniques and methods can be applied in the design of processes to better perform the design activity. The basic weighted-scoring method for alternative location decisions, the centre-of-gravity method for alternative location decisions, breakeven analysis, production flow analysis (PFA) and line-balancing techniques are examples hereof, but are regarded as advanced subjects and are therefore not included in this book.

Figure 21.2: Components of work study

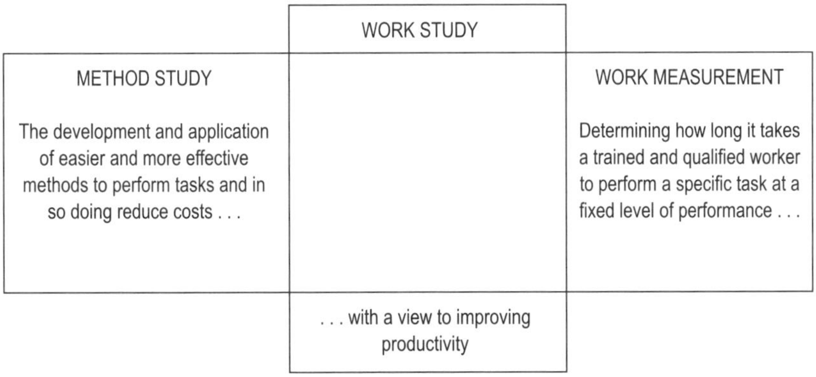

	WORK STUDY	
METHOD STUDY The development and application of easier and more effective methods to perform tasks and in so doing reduce costs . . .		WORK MEASUREMENT Determining how long it takes a trained and qualified worker to perform a specific task at a fixed level of performance . . .
	. . . with a view to improving productivity	

Source: Adapted from Adendorff, S.A. & De Wit, P.W.C., *Production and operations management: a South African perspective*, 2nd edition, Oxford Univesity Press (SA), 1997, p. 251.

21.3 Planning and control of the operations process

21.3.1 *The nature of planning and control of the operations process*

In section 21.2 design was examined as one of the activities of operations management. It should be clear that this design activity determines the physical form and structure of the operations process. Within the limits imposed by the design of the operations process, however, this process now has to be put into operation or be activated. This is done by means of the activity operations planning and control. Planning and control of the operations process focus on all the activities required to efficiently put the operations process into action on a continuous basis so that products can be manufactured and/or services provided to meet the needs of customers/clients.

In contrast to operations design, which may be regarded as a "passive" activity primarily aimed at determining the broad limits of the operations process, planning and control are an activating activity to "physically" start the operations process so that products can be manufactured and/or services rendered. In the activation of the operations process, the operations manager is responsible for ensuring that the operations management objectives of quality, cost, lead time, adaptability, variability and service (see chapter 20, section 20.2.3) are pursued and achieved.

The planning and control of the operations process broadly endeavour to reconcile two entities. Firstly, on the supply side, there are the products and/or services manufactured or provided in the operations process, and secondly, on the demand side, there are the specific needs of actual and potential customers/clients for products and/or services. Planning and control activities are aimed at reconciling the provision ability of the operations facility with the demand for specific products and/or services. Figure 21.3 (see p. 508) illustrates the nature of planning and control in this process of reconciliation.

Reconciling the supply of products and/or services with the demand for them by means of planning and control activities, occurs in terms of three dimensions, namely volume (or quantity), timing and quality. The dimensions of volume (quantity of products and/or services) and timing (when the products and/or services have to be manufactured or provided) will be briefly explained. The quality dimension will be discussed later in section 21.3.4.

Figure 21.3: The nature of planning and control of the operations process

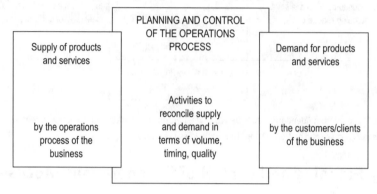

Source: Slack, N., Chambers, S., Harland, C., Harrison, A. & Johnston, R., *Operations management*, 2nd edition, Pearson Education (UK), 1998, p. 352.

To reconcile the volume and timing dimensions with each other, three different but integrated activities are performed. They entail the following:

- **Loading of tasks.** This refers to the volume or quantity of work allocated to a particular work centre. The available capacity of the operations process needs to be taken into consideration in the loading of work centres. A medical practitioner will examine only one patient at a time in his or her consulting rooms, while the other patients wait in the waiting room.
- **Sequencing of tasks.** This refers to the sequence in which the tasks are performed. The sequence in which tasks are performed can be determined beforehand by the use of certain priority rules such as earliest deadline first, or first in first out. A commercial bank, for example, will serve the client who is in front of the queue first.
- **Scheduling of tasks.** This refers to the use of a detailed roster which indicates when a specific task should start and when it should be completed. Gantt charts are especially popular for planning and scheduling projects, and also give an indication of which tasks are late and which are at a more advanced stage than anticipated.

In this section, the planning and control of the operations process were viewed from a general perspective. The operations manager, however, is responsible for the planning and control of specific operations activities, such as capacity and quality.

21.3.2 Capacity planning and control

Capacity planning and control focus on the provision of manufacturing and/or service capacity of a particular operations process. When a suitable balance is found between the available capacity and expected demand, the possibility exists of the business having both satisfied customers/clients as well as acceptable profits. However, if the balance is "wrong" – that is, too much capacity and too little demand, or too little capacity and too much demand – the business is faced with a potentially disastrous situation. Businesses in this position may either sit with costly surplus capacity or possible lost sales opportunities. Because of the far-reaching impact that capacity decisions may have on the business as a whole, capacity planning and control are of vital importance in operations management.

21.3.2.1 Definition of capacity

The term capacity, as it is used in everyday parlance, usually refers to the fixed volume of, say, a fuel tank (50 litres) or the space in a parking garage (parking bays for, say, 500 vehicles). From an operations point of view, these scale or size dimensions are not sufficient, since capacity also has a time dimension. The example in the box illustrates this point.

Applying the concept: determining the total capacity of a parking garage

If there are 500 parking bays in a parking garage at a supermarket, 500 vehicles can park there at a given time. However, this is not the total capacity. If the parking garage and supermarket are open ten hours a day, and customers take on average an hour to do their shopping, the total capacity of the parking garage is actually 5 000 motor vehicles (number of parking bays x number of hours the parking garage is open ÷ average time one car is parked).

Capacity in an operations process is defined as the maximum usable operations capacity of a particular operations process over a certain period of time under normal operating circumstances.[7]

21.3.2.2 The nature of capacity planning and control

While long-term capacity is already determined during the design of the operations process (see section 21.2.3) in the medium and short term, there is the possibility of adapting (or varying) the capacity of the operations process in accordance with changes in the demand for particular products and/or services. Thus, certain machinery or equipment can be used for longer periods each day, or workers can be asked to work overtime during peak periods.

Operations managers usually have to work with a demand forecast which is by no means completely accurate, and moreover, is sometimes subject to regular fluctuation. Quantitative data on the expected demand, and the required capacity to satisfy it, must be obtained by applying the following three steps:

- **Step 1: Determine the total demand and required capacity.** As a rule, the marketing function is responsible for determining the total demand by means of demand forecasting. Since this forecasting is an important input in determining the required capacity, the operations manager must at least have a knowledge of the basis of and rationale behind the demand forecasts. The way in which the required capacity will be determined depends on the nature of the products or services manufactured or provided. In standardised and repetitive products and services (high volume with little variety), capacity will be measured in terms of output; for example, the number of television sets to be produced per week or the number of flights to be provided (flown) to Cape Town each day. In the case of less standardised and repetitive products and/or services (lower volume and more variety), capacity will rather be measured in terms of input. Examples here are the number of working hours per week of a goldsmith making items of jewellery or the number of beds available in a hospital per day.

- **Step 2: Identify alternative capacity plans.** The operations manager is expected to have alternative capacity plans in order to accommodate possible changes in demand. Three options are available:[8]
  - A **level capacity plan** in which the capacity levels are kept constant and demand fluctuations are ignored
  - A **chase-demand plan** in which capacity levels are adjusted according to fluctuations in demand
  - A **demand management plan** in which demand as such is adjusted to tie in with available capacity

  In practice, it usually happens that operations managers use a mixture of the three alternatives, although one of them may be more dominant than the others.
- **Step 3: Choice of a particular capacity planning and control approach.** The final step entails choosing the most suitable capacity planning and control approach. Here an endeavour is made to choose an approach that will best reflect the business's specific circumstances. A fruit packing plant will, for example, employ more temporary workers during the harvesting season to help with the packing of the fruit. Supermarkets will also staff more checkout points at the end of the month when more customers tend to visit the supermarket.

21.3.2.3 Techniques and methods that can be used during capacity planning and control

Various techniques and methods can be applied during capacity planning and control to better execute this planning and control activity. Two of these methods that will be examined here are: the moving average demand forecasting technique, and the cumulative representations of demand and capacity. Other techniques and methods, such as exponential levelling, demand forecasting accuracy measures, and the application of the queuing theory are regarded as advanced topics and are therefore not included in this text.

- **Moving average demand forecasting technique.** Based on the availability of actual demand data over preceding periods, this technique can be used to forecast the demand for the following period. This technique is especially suitable in the demand for products or services that manifest a stable demand pattern over the short term. The example in the box (see p. 511) shows the application of the technique in forecasting the demand for washing machines for May 2003.

Applying the concept: three-month moving average forecast of the demand for washing machines

Month	Demand (Actual)	Demand (Forecast)	Three-month moving average (Calculation)
December 2002	480		
January 2003	530		
February 2003	520		
March 2003	540	510	480 + 530 + 520 = 1 530 ÷ 3 = 510
April 2003	590	530	530 + 520 + 540 = 1 590 ÷ 3 = 530
May 2003	–	550 ·	520 + 540 + 590 = 1 650 ÷ 3 = 550

Based on a three-month moving average, the demand forecast for May 2003 is therefore 550 units of washing machines

The disadvantage of this approach is that if the demand continues to grow, the predicted demand is always going to be too low. In the example above, the actual demand may be 610, but according to the moving average, only 550 washing machines will be manufactured and there will therefore be a shortage.

- **Cumulative representations of demand and capacity.** This method can be used to evaluate the effect of different capacity plans graphically. The example on p. 512 shows the application of the method for evaluating a capacity plan for a coalmine.

It would appear from the example that the production of coal during the months January to April was greater than the demand for it, and that there was a "surplus" production during this period. From April to July (autumn and winter) the demand for coal was greater than production – hence there was a period of "underproduction".

21.3.3 Inventory and purchasing planning and control

These days, inventory and purchasing planning and control are regarded as activities executed by a separate functional management area, namely purchasing management. However, since the inventory of materials and the purchase thereof have significant implications for the smooth functioning of the transformation process, for which the operations manager is mainly responsible, inventory is usually defined (from an operations management perspective) as all stored resources (material, information or clients) required for the smooth functioning of the operations process. The operations manager should therefore liaise closely with the purchasing manager in order to manage inventory levels optimally.

Since inventory and purchasing planning and control are discussed in chapters 22 and 23, it is not necessary to continue the discussion here.

Applying the concept: cumulative representation of demand and capacity for a coalmine

	Jan	Feb	March	April	May	June	July	Aug
Demand ('000 m³ coal)	50	75	75	200	200	100	100	100
Cumulative demand	50	125	200	400	600	700	800	900
Production ('000 m³ coal)	100	100	100	100	100	100	200	200
Cumulative production	100	200	300	400	500	600	800	1 000
Production surplus/ (shortfall)	50	75	100	0	(100)	(100)	0	100

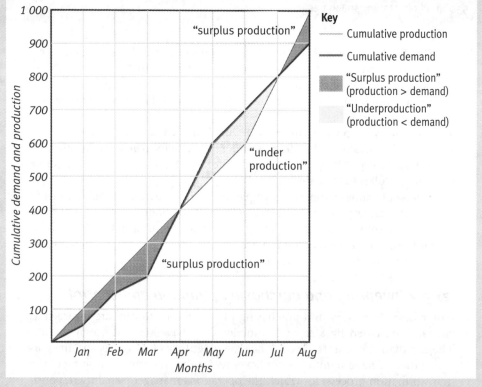

21.3.4 Quality planning and control

Nowadays, quality is regarded as being so important in many businesses that responsibility for it is not confined to the operations management function only. The basic premise of concepts such as **total quality management (TQM)** is that quality products and/or services can only be manufactured if the entire or total business contributes to the achievement of such an objective.

Quality is one of the main methods of adding value to products and/or services, and thereby to obtain a long-term competitive advantage over competitors. Better quality influences both factors that contribute to the business's profitability, namely income and cost. Income can be increased by more sales and greater market share, while costs can be reduced by lower repair and inspection costs, and reduced wastage and inventory as well as processing time.

21.3.4.1 Definition of quality

Different definitions of quality are often advanced. Each of them stems from another approach to or view of quality. Thus, quality can be defined as "the absolute best", "something flawless", "suitable for the purpose for which it was designed", "meeting a set of measurable characteristics" or "good value for money". From an operations management perspective, quality is defined as "continuous conformance to customers'/clients' expectations".[9]

Operations management therefore defines quality in terms of what a customer/client expects of a particular product or service, while the customer/client sees quality in terms of his or her own perception of the product or service. This difference between expected quality (operations management) and perceived quality (customer/client) is known as the quality gap. Operations management, in conjunction with the other functional management areas, should endeavour to eliminate any quality gaps.

21.3.4.2 The nature of quality planning and control

The aim of quality planning and control is to ensure that the products and/or services that are manufactured or provided, should conform to or satisfy design specifications. In the design of the products and/or services (see section 21.2.2) it was stated that the ultimate goal of this activity is to establish specifications for products and/or services that will satisfy the needs of customers/clients. Hence, what we have here is a customer/client-marketing-design-operations cycle. This design cycle (see figure 21.4 on p. 514) can be further extended to include quality planning and control activities to ensure that products and/or services do in fact meet the design specifications.

21.3.4.3 The steps in quality planning and control

Quality planning and control can be divided into six steps:
- **Step 1: Defining the quality characteristics of the product or service.** The design specifications for products/services are determined in the design activity. The design specifications as such are not monitored by quality planning and control, but rather by the operations process that manufactures and/or provides the products or services, to ensure that the specifications are met. For the purposes of quality planning and control, it is necessary to define certain quality characteristics that relate directly to the design specifications for products or services. Quality characteristics that are often used include:
  - Functionality (performance ability)
  - Appearance (aesthetic attractiveness)
  - Reliability (continuous performance capability)
  - Durability (total life expectancy)
  - Serviceability (repairability)
  - Contact (convenience of interaction)

Figure 21.4: Design cycle of products and services that includes planning and control

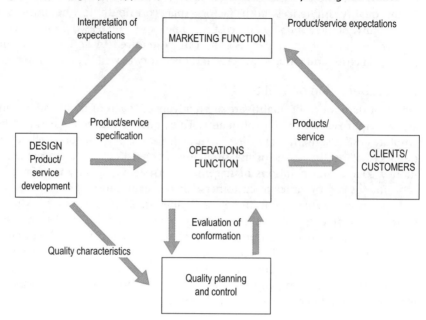

Source: Slack, N., Chambers, S., Harland, C., Harrison, A. & Johnston, R., *Operations management*, 2nd edition, Pearson Education (UK), 1998, p. 642.

Thus, for example, a customer will expect an expensive video recorder to record and replay TV programmes clearly, to be aesthetically pleasing, to have a long and reliable lifespan, and problem-free maintenance and repair.

- **Step 2: Measuring the quality characteristics of the product or service**. For each individual product or service, the quality characteristics should be defined in such a way that they can in fact be measured and controlled. The different quality characteristics should thus be further broken down to make such measurement possible. For example, if the quality characteristic "functionality" of a motor-vehicle is measured, it can be broken down into the measurable dimensions of speed, acceleration, fuel consumption and road-holding ability. However, it is sometimes difficult to measure certain quality characteristics, such as the "friendliness" of the cabin crew of an airline. Here, an effort will instead be made to gauge passengers' perceptions of the friendliness of staff, in order to measure this. Indeed, every few months, SAA conducts such a survey among its regular passengers (frequent flyers).

- **Step 3: Set standards for each quality characteristic of the product or service**. Once the operations manager has ascertained which, and how, quality characteristics are going to be measured, the next step is to set certain quality standards against which the achievement of, and conformance with, the quality characteristic can be measured. Although most businesses strive for "absolutely perfect" standards (for example, "the quest for zero defect"), it is generally too expensive or unrealistic to expect a motor vehicle, for example, to last forever. Instead, realistic achievable standards are set, for example, that the motor vehicle will have an effective lifespan of ten years.

- **Step 4: Control of quality against the set standards.** Once realistic standards for measuring the output of the operations process have been laid down, the next step is to determine whether or not the product or service does in fact measure up to them. Three questions in particular are of importance to the operations manager here:
  - Where in the operations process should one check to see if the standards have been satisfied? There are three possible positions, namely: at the beginning of the process (preventive control); during the process (in-time control); or after the process (reactive control).
  - Should each individual product or service that is provided be checked to determine whether the standards have been met? It is not always possible or desirable to fully inspect all products and/or services, and one could rather determine on the basis of samples whether the products and/or services do in fact meet the standards.
  - How should the inspection be conducted? In practice, one finds that most businesses use sampling to ascertain whether their products and/or services measure up to standards. Two methods that can be used here are statistical process control (SPC), where the inspection of a quality characteristic takes place **during** the process of manufacturing and/or service rendering, or acceptance sampling, where inspection occurs **after** the process of manufacturing and/or service rendering.
- **Step 5: Identifying and rectifying the causes of poor quality.** An important goal in quality planning and control is to identify and rectify the presence of poor quality and the reasons for it. This step will be discussed further in section 21.4.
- **Step 6: Continuous improvement of quality.** As mentioned earlier, quality is one of the most important ways of adding value to products and/or services in order to obtain a long-term competitive advantage over competitors – hence the importance of improving quality on a continuous basis. This aspect will be further discussed in section 21.4.

21.4 Operations improvement

21.4.1 The nature of operations improvement

In sections 21.2 and 21.3, the design, and planning and control of the operations process were examined. Even if both of these activities are successfully executed, the task of the operations manager is still not complete, however. Any operations process, regardless of how well it was initially designed, or how well it was planned and controlled, can certainly be improved. Nowadays, the improvement of the operations process of a business is seen as a further identifiable activity of the operations manager.

Figure 21.5 (see p. 516) provides a broad framework of the various activities that are pertinent in operations improvement.

Before any operations process can be improved, it is necessary to determine what its current performance is. Performance measurement is therefore a prerequisite for any improvement. In measuring performance, one must ascertain to what extent the present operations process satisfies the formulated opera-

Figure 21.5: Operations improvement

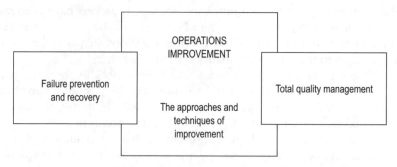

Source: Slack, N., Chambers, S., Harland, C., Harrison, A. & Johnston, R., *Operations management*, 2nd edition, Pearson Education (UK), 1998, p. 677.

tions management objectives as far as quality, service, adaptability, lead time, cost, and variability are concerned.

21.4.1.1 Different types of performance standards

Once it has been determined by means of performance measurement to what extent the present operations process satisfies the set operations management objectives, the overall performance of the process should be evaluated. This is done by comparing the present performance level with certain standards. Four kinds of standards are generally used:

- **Historical standards**, where present performance is compared to the particular business's own performance in previous years
- **Target performance standards**, where present performance is compared to predetermined standards which indicate an acceptable or reasonable level of performance
- **Competitors' performance standards**, where present performance is compared to that of one or more similar competitors. (Nowadays, benchmarking is a popular approach that businesses follow in evaluating their own operations function by comparing their product and/or service package with that of their competitors.)
- **Absolute performance standards**, where current performance is compared to the theoretical maximum achievable performance standards

21.4.1.2 Priorities for improvement

Once the performance of the present operations process has been measured and compared with one or more of the performance standards, it should be clear which areas need improvement. However, not all areas earmarked for improvement are equally important. Priorities for improvement therefore need to be determined, and this is done by taking into consideration the needs and preferences of customers/clients and the performance and activities of competitors.

The needs of customers/clients provide an indication of those performance area(s) of particular importance to them. Operations management objectives should reflect such preferences as high quality or low costs for the internal operation or functioning of a specific operations process.

However, the role of the performance and activities of competitors in establishing priorities for improvement are somewhat different. Of concern here is the performance of the business's operations process in relation to the performance of competitors. This comparison enables the business to identify its operations-based advantages as compared with those of its competitors.

21.4.1.3 Approaches to improvement

Once the priority areas for improvement have been determined, a specific approach or strategy for improvement must be decided upon. Two divergent approaches to improvement can be followed, namely breakthrough improvement and continuous improvement:

- In **breakthrough improvement** there is less regular, but large-scale dramatic change, which occurs in leaps and bounds in the functioning of an operations process. The major changes in respect of products and/or services, process technology, or methods of work will hopefully lead to improved performance. Business process re-engineering (BPR) is an example of a radical, breakthrough improvement approach that is today encountered in practice.
- In **continuous improvement**, also known as Kaizen improvement, more regular, but smaller incremental changes take place in the functioning of the operations process. The aim is to improve the process on a continuous basis. The PDCA cycle (plan-do-check-act) is an example of a continuous improvement approach that is used in practice. South African motor manufacturers make frequent use of this approach. Their staff are, accordingly, strongly encouraged to suggest continuous small changes in the work process.

21.4.2 Failure prevention and recovery

Regardless of how well a particular operations process is designed, and thereafter put into operation by means of planning and control, there is always the chance of failures or breakdowns occurring. No operations process is ever (or always) perfect. Acceptance of the fact that failures will occur, however, does not mean that such events should be ignored. Certain failures may have less serious consequences, while others may even be critical for the functioning of the operations process itself. Hence, a continuous endeavour should be made to limit the occurrence of failures. Operations managers have a particular responsibility to improve the reliability of the operations processes that manufacture or provide products or services on a continuous basis.

21.4.2.1 Types of failures that occur

Failures in operations processes may occur for one or more of the following reasons:

- **Design failures.** These occur when the design of the process is found to be wrong or inadequate, for example, all Pentium personal computers were withdrawn after it was established that there was a design error in the processors.
- **Facility failures.** This happens when one or more components of the facility itself, such as machines or equipment, breaks and causes parts of, or the

whole facility, to grind to a halt – for example, if lightning should strike out all the computers in a service provider.

- **Staff failures.** These happen when mistakes are made, or set procedures are not followed, for example, when workers are not properly trained, or where job performance comes to a standstill because of strikes.
- **Supplier failures.** These happen when suppliers do not provide products or services according to the agreement, for example, where supermarkets place advertisements for special offers, and the suppliers do not deliver the order on time.
- **Customer/client failures.** These occur when customers/clients use a product or service incorrectly, or do not use it for the purpose for which it was designed. An example of this failure is when a customer tows a caravan that specifies that the size of engine of the motor vehicle towing the caravan should be at least 3 000cc, but the person nevertheless tows the caravan with a 1 300cc car.

21.4.2.2 Failure detection and analysis

If one accepts that failures will occur, operations managers should have mechanisms in place to detect such failures, and then be able to put procedures into operation to determine the causes of the failures. Mechanisms to detect failures include process monitoring, complaints, and feedback questionnaires from customers/clients. In failure analysis, techniques such as cause-effect diagrams and analysis of customer/client complaints are used. Feedback questionnaires from clients are especially important to detect shortcomings in the rendering of services. This is one of the principal reasons why hotels ask their guests to fill in a form on the quality of service.

21.4.2.3 Systems reliability improvement

When there is clarity about the causes and consequences of failures, operations managers should endeavour to prevent them in the first place. This will increase the reliability of the entire operations process. This can be done by redesigning the products and/or services or processes that manufacture or provide them, using additional back-up systems or components in the case of a failure, or implementing regular maintenance and repairs. It may also be necessary to launch a training or motivation programme for the staff.

21.4.2.4 Recovery of failures

Operations managers attempt to reduce the occurrence of failures and the results thereof by means of failure detection and analysis and systems reliability improvement. However, when failures still occur, recovery procedures and contingency plans should already have been devised and put in place to minimise the potential detrimental effects on customers/clients.

21.4.3 Total quality management (TQM)

Mention was made in section 21.3.4 (in the discussion of the quality planning and control activities of operations management) of the concept of total quality management or what is generally referred to in practice as TQM. It was also stated that the quality of products or services today is not regarded as the responsibility of the operations manager only. The concept of TQM is far wider – hence, the entire business is responsible.

21.4.3.1 Definition of TQM

TQM as a concept did not develop overnight. Many so-called quality gurus, such as Feigenbaum, Deming, Juran, Ishikawa, Taguchi and Crosby, have contributed to what has today become known as TQM. The latter is a management philosophy, a method of "thinking and doing" with the primary aim of satisfying the needs and expectations of customers/clients by means of high quality products or services. It endeavours to shift the responsibility for quality from merely the operations management function to the entire business (that is, all other functional management areas and the employees therein). TQM is further primarily aimed at:[10]

- Making each and every employee in the business quality conscious and holding him or her responsible for his or her contribution to the achievement of TQM
- Identifying and accounting for all costs of quality (both prevention and failure costs)
- Doing things right the first time (proactive rather than reactive action)
- Developing and implementing systems and procedures for quality and the improvement thereof
- Establishing a continuous process for improvement

According to Oakland's TQM model (see figure 21.6), the focal point of total quality is the underlying processes that occur at each customer/client and supplier interface. To this should be added certain human or so-called soft management components (commitment, communication and culture) and hard management components (of quality systems, techniques and/or methods, and teams).

Figure 21.6: Total quality management model

Source: Oakland, J.S., *Total quality management: text with cases*, Butterworth-Heinemann, Oxford, 2000, p. 31.

21.4.3.2 The ISO 9000 quality standard for quality systems

Improving quality within a business requires a great deal more than good intentions. It also demands concrete action. One such action that should be taken is the development of a quality system. Such a system includes the organisational structure, the responsibilities, procedures, processes, and resources for implementing quality.

A quality standard used throughout the world today to lay down the requirements for the specific quality systems of businesses is the ISO 9000 series. This series provides comprehensive recommendations as to how a quality system should be compiled for a particular type of business. The ISO 9001: 2000 document,[11] under the four major headings of management responsibilities, resource management, process management, measurement, analysis and improvement, includes guidelines on the following:

- Customer/clients needs and requirements, quality policy, quality objectives and planning, management review, quality manual, control of documents, control of quality records
- Human resources
- Customer/client-related processes, design and development, purchasing, production and service delivery processes, control of non-conformities, post delivery services
- Measurement, analysis of data, and improvement[12]

21.4.3.3 The implementation of TQM

The way in which TQM is implemented in a business determines the ultimate successful application thereof. Factors that should be taken into account are listed below. (Note that the corresponding "hard" and "soft" management components of Oakland's (2000) TQM model (see figure 21.6) are also given for each factor.):[13]

- The integration of TQM in the overall business strategy (systems)
- Top management and employees' support and involvement (commitment)
- Teamwork in improvement initiatives (teams)
- Feedback on quality successes that have in fact been achieved (communication)
- The creation of a quality awareness (culture)
- Training of employees in quality techniques and methods (techniques/ methods)

21.5 Summary

In this chapter we examined in more detail three of the activities of operations managers, namely design, planning and control, and improvement.

Operations design is concerned with the design of products and/or services that will satisfy the needs of customers/clients and the design of processes to manufacture or provide them.

Once the design activities have been completed, the operations process must be put into action by means of operations planning and control. Specific responsibilities in this regard include:

- **Capacity planning and control**, in which the manufacturing or service providing ability should be reconciled with the demand for the business's products or services

- **Inventory and purchasing planning and control**, in which adequate inventory resources and the purchase thereof should be obtained and made available to enable the operations process to function smoothly (if this is not the responsibility of the purchasing manager)
- **Quality control and planning**, in which conformity with the design specifications of products or services should be ensured

However, once the foregoing activities have been executed, the task of the operations manager is still not over. Any operations process, regardless of how well it is initially designed and how well it has been planned and controlled, can still be improved. Operations improvement as an identifiable activity of operations management endeavours, firstly, to improve the reliability of the entire operations process on a continuous basis by failure prevention and recovery. Secondly, in applying the concept of TQM, an attempt is made to improve the operation of the entire or total business so that quality products or services can be manufactured or provided to optimally satisfy the needs of customers/clients.

References

1. Slack, N., Chambers, S., Harland, C., Harrison, A. & Johnston, R., *Operations management*, 2nd edition, Pitman Publishing, London, 1998, p. 136.
2. Adendorff, S.A. & De Wit, P.W.C., *Production and operations management: a South African perspective*, 2nd edition, Thomson Publishing (Southern Africa), Johannesburg, 1997, pp. 322-324.
3. Slack, N., et al., *op. cit.*, pp. 145-147.
4. Slack, N., et al., *op. cit.*, p. 176.
5. Krajewski, L.J. & Ritzman, L.P., *Operations management: strategy and analysis*, 4th edition, Addison-Wesley, Reading, Massachusetts, 1996, pp. 400–404.
6. Adendorff, S.A. & De Wit, P.W.C., *op. cit.*, p. 251.
7. Slack, N., et al., *op. cit.*, p. 390.
8. Schonberger, R.J. & Knod, E.M. (Jr), *Operations management: customer-focused principles*, 6th edition, Irwin, Illinois, 1997, p. 233.
9. Slack, N., et al., *op. cit.*, p. 636.
10. Slack, N., et al., *op. cit.*, p. 763.
11. SABS ISO 9001, South African Standard, Code of practice, Quality management systems – requirements, SABS, Pretoria, 2000.
12. Oakland, J.S., *Total quality management: text with cases*, 2nd edition, Butterworth-Heinemann, Oxford, 2000, pp. 81-91.
13. Slack, N., et al., *op. cit.*, pp. 778-781.

Purchasing and supply[1] management

The purpose of the chapter is to place the purchasing or sourcing function and its role into perspective, to elucidate new concepts, and to explain the management of the function.

The content of this chapter will enable learners to:
- Place the purchasing and supply function and the nature of purchasing and supply activities in a business perspective
- Elucidate new concepts or approaches to the provision of materials to a business
- Emphasise the role and importance of the purchasing and supply function in the success and efficiency of a business
- Explain the application of the management tasks of planning, organising and control in the purchasing and supply function
- Point out certain management aids at the disposal of the purchasing and supply manager

22.1 Introduction: purchasing and supply in perspective

Just as consumers need to make purchases almost on a daily basis to satisfy their normal needs, and large purchases, such as buying a motorcar, to satisfy their long-term needs, a business also has to make purchases to meet its daily and long-term needs. Because people make purchases almost every day, the value of the purchasing and supply function in business is often underestimated. There is a perception that anyone is capable of making purchases for a business.

However, purchasing and supply in a business entails far more than merely comparing the prices of two or more competitive bids and then buying material from the supplier that offers the best prices and service. Buyers in a manufacturing business buy a great variety of materials: from stationery, cleaning agents, cafeteria services and globes to bulk fuel, strategic material (which is sometimes difficult to obtain) for production processes, and equipment for office and production processes. They are also involved in the purchase of capital goods, for example, robot-controlled processing equipment and complicated computer systems.

Buyers are expected to keep abreast of better substitute materials, new developments and technology in the market. A buyer's expertise can improve the progressiveness, productivity and profitability of a business. Buyers often have to make trips abroad or develop local suppliers because of the lack of existing sources. They also have to ensure that materials purchased meet laid-down quality requirements, because this has a decisive effect on the quality of the business's final product (in the case of a manufacturer) and the quality of products resold (in a retail business). Buyers therefore need to be aware of market trends and the state of the market. They should, for example, know how many suppliers and how many buyers are present in a particular market, as this has a crucial effect on the purchase price of materials and how suppliers should be approached.

Purchasing and supply function

The purchasing and supply function is the function that satisfies the business's needs in the most effective way or at the lowest cost: for a manufacturer, firstly, its needs for equipment, materials and services to facilitate its normal activities, and secondly, processed, semi-processed or unprocessed materials to be assembled or transformed in the manufacturing process in order to provide the business's final product; for a retailer, this function satisfies the need to provide consumer goods to be displayed on shelves for sale to end-users.

The **purpose of the purchasing and supply function** is not only to provide the right materials, services and equipment, but also to ensure that they are purchased at a reasonable price, satisfy quality requirements, and are received at the right place and time, in the correct quantities. The **activities** of the purchasing and supply function are derived from this. The purchasing and supply function should:

- Select suppliers
- Purchase and arrange for the transport of materials to the business
- Decide what prices to accept
- Determine the quantity and quality of materials or services
- Expedite and receive materials
- Control warehousing and the inventory holding

To perform these activities optimally, the purchasing and supply function needs to be managed, that is, planned, organised and controlled.

Purchasing and supply management

Purchasing and supply management entails the planning, organising, leading and controlling of all activities relating to the purchase of materials and services from an external source, and is aimed at maintaining and increasing the business's profitability and efficiency of customer service.

To manage the purchasing and supply function optimally, purchasing and supply managers use certain management aids to facilitate their task, for example, benchmarking, purchasing budgets, and purchasing and supply policy. To execute purchasing and supply activities optimally, a buyer or purchasing and supply manager applies certain purchasing and supply techniques such as negotiation, purchasing and supply research, price analysis, and learning curves. This chapter deals with the **management** of the purchasing and supply function, and management aids. The principal purchasing and supply **activities** and techniques are covered in chapter 23.

22.2 Broadening the provision function

Today, one increasingly hears of concepts such as materials management, logistics management, and supply chain management in relation to the purchasing and supply function. These concepts or approaches (which is what they really are) mean a broadening of the purchasing or supply function. Although chapters 22 and 23 mainly focus on the purchasing and supply function, the broadening of this function needs elucidating. Materials management, logistics management and supply chain management approaches are often found in manufacturing and assembly industries, but the principles can also be applied in large retail and service organisations. Figure 22.1 (see p. 525) provides an exposition of the extent of the various concepts.

Materials management is an overarching organisational concept embracing purchasing management and warehousing, as well as certain operations functions such as the movement of materials through the transformation (production) process. It is an effort to combine all materials provision activities under one head, that is, the materials manager. The aim is to eliminate the often conflicting objectives of different materials provision activities by combining them under materials management. Materials management integrates all the provision activities up to final product stage. Figure 22.1 shows the activities included in the materials management approach.

Example

The different sub-functions involved in the provision of materials often have conflicting objectives. A buyer's aim, for example, is to purchase at the lowest possible price per unit. With this goal in mind, in the negotiation process the buyer may be persuaded by suppliers to purchase larger quantities in order to obtain lower unit prices. However, this is in direct conflict with the goal of inventory management, which strives to keep inventory levels as low as possible. If a materials management approach is adopted in a business, all materials provision activities are integrated under one head, and the goal is the pursuit of lowest total costs and optimal service provision in the whole materials provision chain, rather than a focus on individual activities.

Logistics management entails integrating all movements (transport) and warehousing activities, from the point where the materials are purchased, through the transformation process, to the final consumer. Some activities of purchasing, operations and materials managers are therefore integrated under the logistics manager, together with the physical distribution of final products, which traditionally fell under the control of the marketing manager. The movement of materials and products, and the flow of information, are vital to the provision of efficient and satisfactory customer service. The aim of logistics management is to provide the best customer service at the lowest possible logistics cost.

Supply chain management is an extension of the systems approach. According to the systems approach, the internal functions of the business (marketing, finance, purchasing and supply, production, human resources, etc.) are managed as an integrated whole. In the supply chain management approach, the integration extends beyond the individual business. The "system" in supply chain management consists of managing, in an integrated fashion, the **flow of materials** in all the linked organisations, from the raw material stage, through all the stages of transformation, to delivery of the final product to the end user (consumer). The intention is that businesses in the supply chain cooperate in networks with mutual long-term agreements to deliver the end product to the final consumer in the most effective way and at the lowest cost. This is achieved by sharing information and know-how (and even facilities), and by eliminating waste between the various stages of the transformation process. Figure 22.2 (see p. 526) shows a simplified supply chain – the supply chain of a milk processing plant.

Figure 22.1: The scope of materials supply approaches and activities

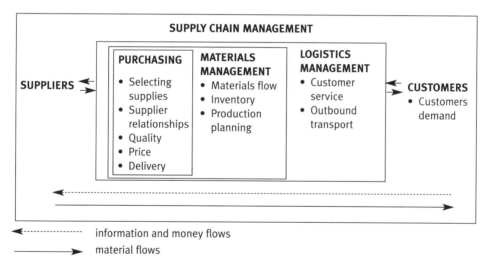

information and money flows
material flows

In conclusion, supply chains are a series of linked suppliers and customers. Each customer is in turn a supplier to another business lower down the supply chain, until the finished product reaches the end-user.

All businesses are part of one or more supply chains. The emphasis in supply chain management is to manage processes in the entire supply chain (instead of concentrating on internal functions and direct suppliers and direct customers). Naturally, this is a complex task, and strategic alliances, long-term contracts and shared information networks form an important component of supply chain management.

Figure 22.2: A milk processing plant's supply chain

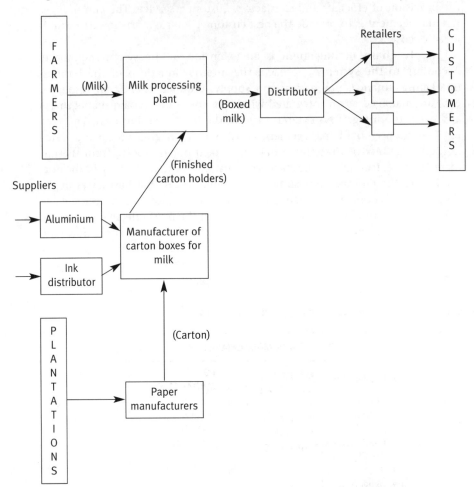

As seen in figure 22.2 and the example in the box (see p. 527), a supply chain represents a network of organisational relationships that tie firms together and may tie their success to the supply chain as a whole. A supply chain as a whole may have its own identity, and function like an independent firm. The network of organisation is a loose and flexible coalition, guided and managed from a **hub** (the strongest partner in the supply chain – such as the milk processing plant in figure 22.2 – for example, Bonnita or Clover; and Volkswagen SA in the example in the motor industry). This hub organisation takes the lead in managing the supply chain, and its key functions and activities include the following:

- The development and management of the alliances with other organisations/firms in the supply chain
- Coordination of financial resources and technology in the supply chain
- The definition and management of core competencies (the most important activities of each party) and strategies in the supply chain
- The development of relationships with customers and suppliers
- The management of information systems that bind the network

Applying the concept: the supply chain of a vehicle assembler

A vehicle assembler such as Volkswagen SA has a supply chain consisting of three main sections:

- Suppliers
- Assembly plant
- Car dealers

The supplier network consists of numerous businesses providing a wide range of parts or items to be assembled into a motor vehicle. These include engines, panels, chassis, lights, bulbs, seats, exhausts, windscreens, etc. All these parts at one time consisted of raw materials, and had to be converted (in the transformation process) by suppliers to render them useful so that Volkswagen SA can assemble them to create a vehicle. The vehicle is then supplied to the final consumer through the dealer network. The accompanying graphic shows the sections in the supply chain of a motor vehicle.

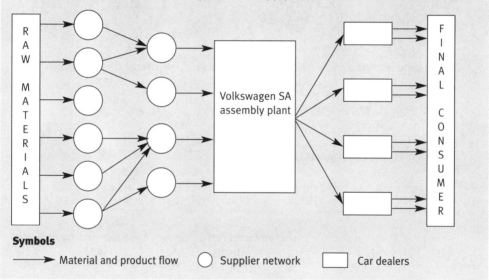

Symbols

→ Material and product flow   ◯ Supplier network   ▢ Car dealers

The current trend of broadening the supply function does not mean that the purchasing function is less important. On the contrary, at the core of all these concepts is the purchasing function, which has a direct influence on the profitability of the business, as shown in the next section.

22.3 The importance of the purchasing and supply function to the business

The importance of the purchasing and supply function differs from one business to the next, but in most, purchasing has a profound influence on profit and in the aspects discussed below.

22.3.1 Greatest expenditure for the business

It is a worldwide phenomenon that purchasing costs are a business's biggest expense, especially in businesses where final products are purchased and no actual value is added to the product. In retailing businesses, up to 90% of each rand may be spent on purchases, and as much as 60% in manufacturing businesses. It therefore stands to reason that purchasing costs is an area where cost savings can make a vital contribution to the business's profits, if one accepts that profit is the favourable difference between income and expenditure. Figure 22.3 illustrates the share of purchasing in the spending of each available rand in various businesses.

Figure 22.3: The share of purchasing in each rand spent in various businesses

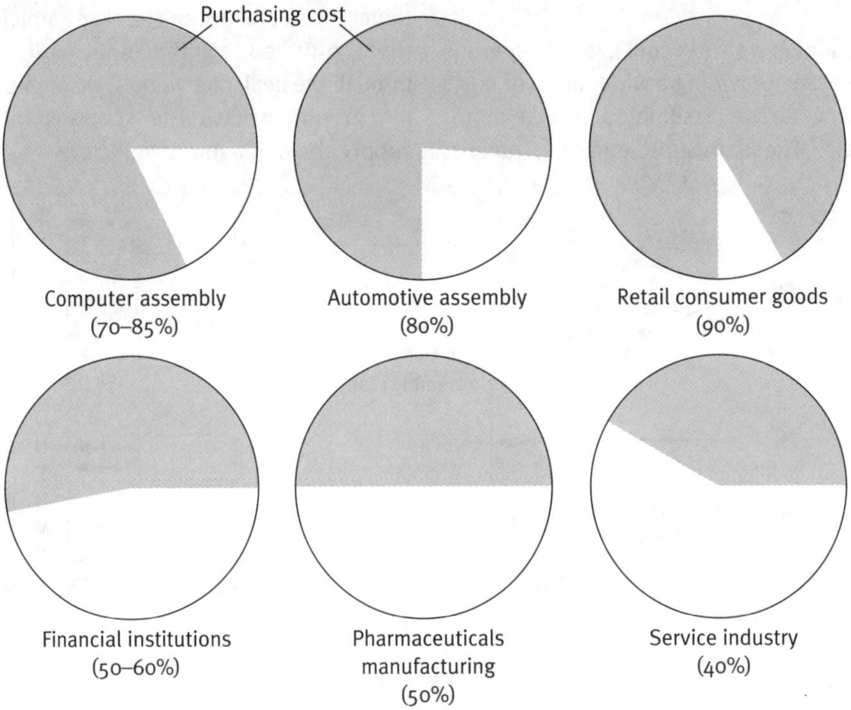

Purchasing cost

Computer assembly (70–85%)	Automotive assembly (80%)	Retail consumer goods (90%)
Financial institutions (50–60%)	Pharmaceuticals manufacturing (50%)	Service industry (40%)

Source: McKinsey Quarterly Report, 1996.

22.3.2 Inventory holding

Stock is held to prevent disruptions in the transformation process (production or operational) when there is an interruption in the flow of materials to a business. The aim of inventory management is to keep inventory levels as low as possible, without risking an interruption in the operational process (as a result of an out-of-stock situation). The reason for this is that large sums of operating capital are tied up in inventory, and these could be applied elsewhere to earn revenue. If too much capital is tied up in inventory, a business could encounter cash-flow problems (discussed in the chapters on financial management). Besides cash-flow problems, warehousing costs are a big cost element, usually ranging from 10% to 25% of total investment in inventory.[2] They include the costs of financing, warehousing, warehouse staff, insurance and obsolescence. Effective purchasing and supply management can reduce inventory holding by ensuring an uninterrupted flow of materials of the right quality to the production process. The more reliable the provision or purchase of materials is, the less inventory needs to be stored.

22.3.3 Profit leverage

The profit-leverage effect can be deduced from the preceding two sections on the contribution to profit of effective purchasing and supply. The profit-leverage effect means that if purchasing costs constitute a major portion of the total cost of a business, a saving in purchasing costs has greater profit potential than a similar increase in sales. For example, a 4% reduction in purchasing costs can make the same contribution to profitability as an increase of 20% in sales.

The contribution of the purchasing and supply function to profitability differs from business to business, and from sector to sector. Effective purchasing normally has a greater profit potential in a commercial organisation than in a manufacturing business, as can be inferred from section 22.3.1. In the pharmaceutical industry, where the value of patent medicine content is very low compared to the research and marketing costs of the product, saving on purchasing costs do not have such a profound effect on profit. However, in the motor assembly industry, any saving on purchasing costs, where material costs are very high, has a decisive effect on the business's profitability.

Purchasing as a factor in profitability is also more critical when a business frequently changes its suppliers, if the price of materials fluctuates continually, where fashion is concerned, and where markets for the final product are highly competitive, for example, in the case of everyday consumer articles. The contribution of purchasing to profitability is less critical but still important where prices and suppliers are relatively stable, and where the industry is not characterised by innovation.[3]

22.3.4 Contributions to the marketing of products

By purchasing materials of the right quality and price at the right time, a manufacturer can make final products available in the right quantities at a competitive price at the right time in its industry or market. A retail buyer has a greater and more direct influence on the marketing of merchandise (for example, clothing) where the availability of the right product (type, quality, style and brand) at the right time in the right quantities is an important consideration in successful marketing. Effective purchasing can therefore facilitate the marketing of a business's products, and indirectly contributes to profits through the marketing function.

22.4 The management task of the purchasing and supply manager

In part 2 of this book, you were introduced to the general management principles of planning, organising and control. As mentioned earlier, purchasing and supply, like all other functional areas (marketing, finance, operations, etc.), must be managed to ensure that the purchasing and supply function operates effectively and makes the best possible contribution to the profit of the business and efficient client service. In the following sections, without discussing the principles in detail, we look at the application of the main management elements of the purchasing and supply function: planning, organising and control.

22.4.1 Purchasing and supply planning

Essentially, the planning of the purchasing and supply function means "managing the purchasing and supply function for the future". Purchasing and supply planning entails formulating objectives, which the purchasing and supply function should strive to reach by a particular future period (purchasing and supply objectives), and the drawing up of plans to achieve the objectives (purchasing and supply plans), including the optimal application of resources (people, physical facilities and funds) to achieve the objectives.

Purchasing and supply is a service function in a business, and purchasing and supply planning is therefore subject to business planning; purchasing and supply objectives are similarly subordinate to business objectives. In other words, purchasing and supply planning should support business planning and purchasing, and supply objectives should help to realise the business's objectives which, in a profit-seeking business, are usually minimum costs, maximum efficiency, profitability, and customer value in the long term. Purchasing and supply planning should also be conducted in consultation with other functional management areas, because the plans of marketing, operational and financial functions affect the purchasing and supply function.

Applying the concept: the importance of purchasing and supply planning

The fact that purchasing and supply planning is subordinate to business planning does not mean that it is less important to the business. A pharmaceutical firm, for example, approved the development of a new product with superior therapeutic value on the strength of positive marketing research reports. After three years, and research investment amounting to millions of rand, it was ascertained by the purchasing and supply function that there was not a single supplier that could deliver the key components in the quantities required, or at a price to make the final product competitive in the market. Thus, three years' work and money were wasted. If purchasing and supply had featured in the initial planning and development of the product, this expensive and futile exercise could have been stopped in time.[4]

The planning of the purchasing and supply function, like planning in the business itself and other functional management areas, takes place at the following levels (see chapter 6):

- **Strategic level.** At this level, planning entails the purchasing and supply manager providing input to business planning. The elements of strategic purchasing and supply planning differ from one business to the next. Where the purchasing and supply function is deemed to be less important and merely involves a clerical function, the purchasing and supply function is not involved in strategic planning. When a business has accepted the supply chain management approach, purchasing and supply will be involved in strategic planning. Planning at strategic level is normally of a long-term nature and is aimed at safeguarding materials provision, developing supplier sources, and maintaining the business's competitive position. Typical strategic planning elements are: supplier alliances, supplier development, supply chain process integration, availability forecasting, and purchasing and supply policy.

- **Tactical or middle-management level.** This type of planning may cover the business's medium-term needs, budgeting, the purchasing and supply system and organisation, purchasing and supply methods, negotiation, development of human resources, interface development with other functions and suppliers (by means of cross-functional teams), contracting, and cost-reduction techniques.
- **Operations level.** At the lowest operations level, plans are formulated to allow the daily functioning of the purchasing and supply function to proceed as smoothly as possible, to the benefit of the business as a whole and other functions serviced by the purchasing and supply function. Planning at this level is short-term, and includes planning the tasks of expediting, keeping records, and maintaining the purchasing and supply system, invoice clearance, handling of requisitions, enquiries and quotations, and pricing decisions.[5]

The levels of purchasing and supply planning are depicted in figure 22.4.

Figure 22.4: Levels of purchasing and supply planning

STRATEGIC LEVEL
Supplier alliances
Supplier development
Supply chain integration
Long-term planning
Availability forecasting
Policy formulation
In/outsourcing decisions

TACTICAL MANAGEMENT LEVEL
Systems integration
Negotiation
Interface development
Human resources development
Total quality management
Contracting
Cost-reduction techniques

OPERATIONAL LEVEL
Communication with suppliers' operational staff
Expediting
File and system maintenance
Enquiries and quotations
Pricing
Returns and recycling

Source: Bailey et al, *Purchasing Principles and Management*, Pearson Education (UK).

The elements of planning cited as examples in the different planning levels may differ from one business to the next, and even from situation to situation. Planning regarding purchases can, for example, take place at middle-management level in one case (for example, the purchase and price of fleet vehicles) and in another case at operational level (for example, the purchase and price of pencils).

The formulation of objectives is one of the most important planning tasks. As mentioned earlier, purchasing and supply objectives can be derived from the business's objectives. Table 22.1 provides an indication of the purchasing and supply objectives that can be derived from the business's objectives.

Table 22.1: Purchasing and supply objectives derived from the business's objectives

Business objectives	Purchasing and supply objectives
• To retain the market share	• To search for more unique products in the supplier market
• To move from the speciality market to the general market	• To seek new and larger suppliers and develop a new materials flow system to handle larger quantities and a greater variety of items while keeping total inventory volume as low as possible
• To develop specific new products and services	• To seek or develop new suppliers
• To develop an overall production capacity plan, including an overall make-or-buy policy	• To develop systems that integrate capacity planning and purchasing and supply planning, together with a policy of make-or-buy
• To initiate a cost-reduction plan	• To standardise materials and reduce suppliers

The purchasing and supply function should also formulate specific objectives on how to realise the general objectives. **Specific objectives** should be formulated, if possible, in quantitative terms, for instance in periods of time and figures. A specific objective for cost reduction (the last objective in table 22.1) would be to standardise inventory items such as drills, screwdrivers, pliers, lubricants and batteries within a month, and to enter into a contract with only one supplier of the items, for delivery as and when they are needed. Thus, inventory holding is kept to a minimum and better prices can be negotiated because the total value of purchases per supplier is higher over a specific period.

Purchasing and supply budgets are also a significant element of purchasing and supply planning. (Refer to section 22.5.2).

22.4.2 Organising the purchasing and supply function

While chapter 7 has an in-depth discussion of organising as an element of management, the focus in this section is merely on the application of organising in the purchasing and supply function.

Purchasing and supply organisation

Purchasing and supply organisation involves the creation of a structure of responsibility and authority for the purchasing and supply function, and the organisation of purchasing and supply activities to realise purchasing and business objectives.

There are four main issues in organising the purchasing and supply function that need to be addressed:
• The place of the purchasing and supply function in the organisational structure
• The internal organisation of the purchasing and supply function

- Coordination with other functional management areas
- Cross-functional teams (organising the purchasing and supply function according to the supply chain management approach)

22.4.2.1 The place of the purchasing and supply function in the organisational structure

The place of the purchasing and supply function in the business is affected by three elements: centralisation or decentralisation; the hierarchical level of the purchasing and supply function in the organisational structure of the business; the approach to the integration of purchasing and materials flow activities under the materials management, logistics management or supply chain management approach.

- **Centralisation or decentralisation.**[6] In a business with a centralised purchasing and supply function, the purchasing and supply manager and his or her personnel are responsible for the purchasing and supply function. In an organisation with a single business unit, this is the obvious organisa-

Figure 22.5: Business with a centralised purchasing and supply structure

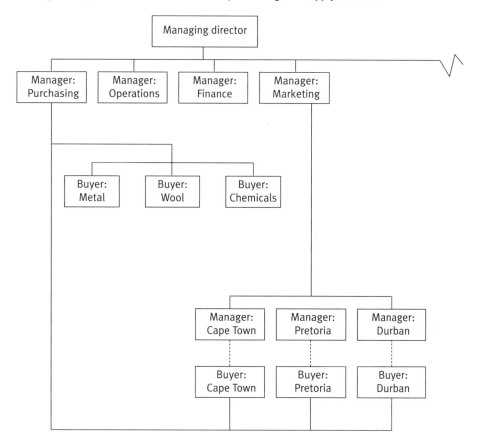

tional structure, but if an organisation has a head office with different business units, branches, or plants, there are various options.

One option is for a centralised purchasing and supply function, situated at head office, to be responsible for purchasing. Another option is for each plant to do its own purchasing, which means that the purchasing and supply function is organised on a decentralised basis. The final option is a combination of centralised and decentralised functions, where some materials and services are bought on a centralised basis and others on a decentralised basis.

A **centralised purchasing and supply structure** has certain advantages, one of them being that the standardisation of purchasing and supply procedures and materials purchased is possible. Standardisation has great cost-

Figure 22.6: Business with a decentralised purchasing and supply structure

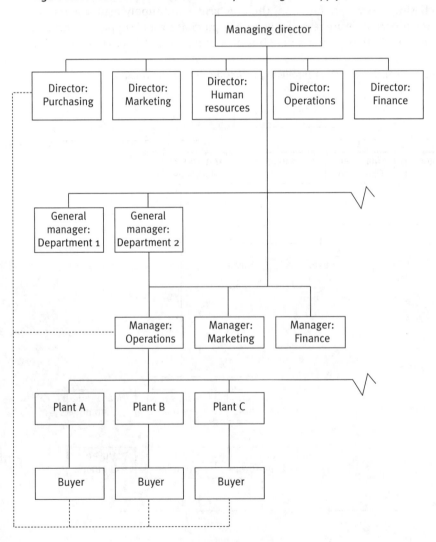

saving advantages, for example, a greater volume of materials of one kind being purchased from a supplier, resulting in lower inventory levels and lower prices because of better discounts for volume orders. Because of volumes, purchasing and supply personnel can concentrate on buying a specific commodity, which makes specialisation possible. A centralised purchasing and supply organisation is especially suitable if the needs of different business units are much the same, for example, all Pick 'n Pay hypermarkets. If the greatest proportion of a business's purchases is made from a single supplier or a few suppliers, and if the material is of strategic importance to the continuation of the business's activities, it is preferable to purchase on a centralised basis. Figure 22.5 (see p. 533) illustrates a centralised purchasing and supply structure for a multi-plant business.

A **decentralised purchasing and supply structure** is particularly suited to a business comprising geographically dispersed plants whose purchases are made from a number of their local suppliers. If the plants perform divergent activities and therefore have unique needs in terms of purchases, decentralisation is the obvious choice. Where the different decentralised plants are regarded as profit centres, it is necessary for each plant to have autonomy over its own expenditure, hence, in this case, decentralisation of purchasing and supply is the right option. A decentralised purchasing and supply structure has the advantage that buyers have closer contact with users (users of the purchased goods and services in the business) and local suppliers, and reaction times to the requests of users are quicker. Figure 22.6 (see p. 534) depicts a decentralised purchasing and supply structure in a business with various plants.

A **combination of centralisation and decentralisation** is a useful middle course. In this application the centralised purchasing office purchases collective requirements, enters into long-term contracts on behalf of the whole business, purchases capital equipment, formulates purchasing and supply policy and strategies, trains buyers, and evaluates decentralised purchasing and supply. Decentralised purchasing and supply provides for the specialised needs and small purchases of the plant, and the buyers report directly to the head of the plant, but operate within the parameters of policy laid down by the centralised purchasing and supply authority. Figure 22.7 (see p. 536) shows a centralised/decentralised purchasing and supply structure.

Applying the concept: a combination of centralised and decentralised purchasing and supply

At Telkom, the head office negotiates large contracts with suppliers of copper cable, optic fibre, and microwave dishes. Decentralised regional offices buy non-strategic items such as tools, maintenance materials and services from local suppliers.

- **The hierarchical level of the purchasing and supply function in the organisational structure.** The hierarchical level of the purchasing and supply function is primarily determined by the importance of the purchasing and supply function to the business. The importance of the function is determined, among others, by the following factors:[7]

Figure 22.7: Business with a centralised/decentralised purchasing and supply structure

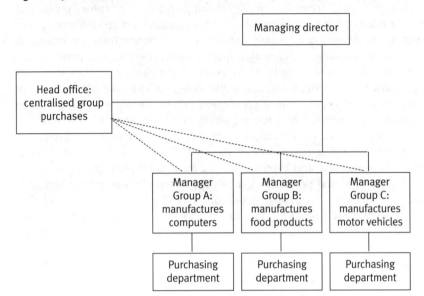

- **The value of the purchased materials in relation to the total expenditure of the business.** The greater purchasing's share of total expenditure, the more important the purchasing and supply function is. If solely this factor is taken into consideration, one could say that purchasing and supply is more important in a commercial organisation than in a manufacturing business. However, it is not the only factor that determines the importance of purchasing and supply.
- **The situation in the supplier market.** Where the market is a monopoly (only one supplier) or an oligopoly (only a few suppliers), as is the case in certain markets in South Africa, negotiation should take place at a high level to negotiate the best value for the business. Purchasing and supply is important here, and the head of the purchasing and supply function should put forward proposals and operate at a high level of the business.
- **The size of the business.** In larger businesses, the purchasing and supply manager is usually placed on the same level as other functional managers, such as the marketing manager, the financial manager, and the operations manager. In smaller businesses, the purchasing and supply function often falls under the financial manager or the marketing manager.
- **The nature of the materials purchased and the specialised knowledge and skills of buyers.** This determines the status of buyers and the purchasing and supply manager in the business. For example, in the purchase of technologically advanced custom-made materials, the buyer needs in-depth technical knowledge and also negotiating and commercial skills. However, when it comes to purchasing cleaning agents and stationery, no special knowledge or skills are required.
- **Top management's perception.** Top management's perception of its importance will determine the status of the purchasing and supply function.

- **The approach to the integration of activities.** The approach to the integration of activities of the total materials supply chain influences the position of purchasing and supply. In a materials management or logistics management approach, the purchasing and supply manager falls under the materials or logistics manager, and may be seen to have lower status than other functional managers. In the supply chain management approach hierarchical levels are reduced (disappear to some extent). The business is operated and managed by process or cross-functional teams. Purchasing staff form part of the process or cross-functional teams. (See section 22.4.2.4.)

- **Integration of purchasing and materials-flow activities.** The materials management and logistics management approaches were discussed in section 22.2. Acceptance of one of these two approaches will, as mentioned above, influence the hierarchical level and status of the purchasing and supply function. Because the principle of the approaches has already been discussed, it is sufficient here to give examples of how the provision activities in a typical materials management approach are organised (see figure 22.8). In figure 22.9 (see p. 538) the organisation is shown according to the logistics management approach.

Figure 22.8: Organisation of provision activities according to the materials management approach

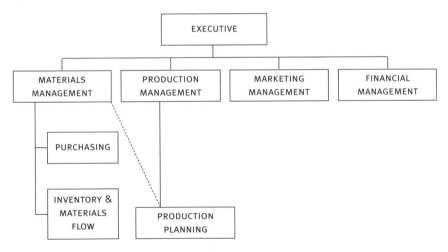

22.4.2.2 Internal organisation of the purchasing and supply function

The purchasing and supply function can be organised internally in a variety of ways. The organisation may comprise an informal structure in which buyers purchase any material or service, processing whatever requisitions or enquiries are placed on their desks. In such a case, the buyer is responsible for the whole spectrum of activities, from asking for quotations or calling for tenders to the expediting and receipt of the product. Conversely, the function can be divided into specialist groups in which each person takes responsibility for buying a specific material or service, or in a larger business, split so that a buyer is responsible for all the purchases from a specific supplier, especially in the case of strategic materials.

Figure 22.9: Organisation of provision activities according to the logistics management approach

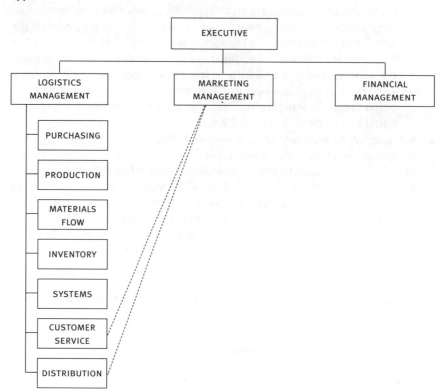

In the case of the purchase of a specific commodity or material, the buyers concerned may develop into specialists who come to know the product and supplier market extremely well, thus bringing large-scale cost benefits for the business. A buyer who is responsible for purchasing from a specific supplier can build up a long-term relationship with that supplier, with an open and personal relationship developing over time, which is especially important when procuring scarce or strategic materials.

The organisational structure can also be subdivided internally into activity groups in which specific people assume responsibility for executing specific activities such as the following:[8]

- **Purchasing and negotiation**, in which purchasing and supply staff are responsible for choosing and screening suppliers, pricing, drawing up specifications, and negotiating with suppliers
- **Follow-up and expediting**, which involve solving problems with suppliers concerning the services they render
- **Administration**, which concerns the preparation and dispatch of purchasing documents, keeping records, and compiling reports and procedure manuals
- **Purchasing and supply research**, which deals with the collection, analysis and classification of information on which effective purchasing and supply decisions are based

- **Inventory holding**, which deals with warehousing and the maintenance of inventory levels
- **Maintaining long-term relationships with suppliers**, which include joint problem solving, planning, and identification of cost opportunities

The disadvantage of this approach is that certain staff members have to do stereotyped work and do not have the opportunity for further development. Figure 22.10 (see p. 540) is a representation of internal organisation as discussed above.

22.4.2.3 Coordination with other functional management areas

Some management experts regard coordination as a management task. However, this book follows the latest trends and sees coordination as part of organising. Therefore, little mention is made here of coordination.

However, because the purchasing and supply function has a support role and function, coordination with other functions in the business and with suppliers is important. The purchasing and supply function cannot make an optimal contribution to the objectives of the business and the supply chain in isolation. Coordination of the purchasing and supply function occurs at three levels. Various purchasing and supply activities must be coordinated internally in the purchasing and supply function, the purchasing environment (suppliers) must be coordinated with purchasing and supply activities, and the purchasing and supply function must be coordinated with other functional management areas such as finance, marketing and production.

Purchasing and supply coordination

Purchasing and supply coordination may be regarded as the conscious effort to harmonise the activities of the purchasing and supply function, the activities of other functional areas, and those of suppliers in ways to ensure full cooperation in the pursuit of purchasing and supply objectives.

Budgets play a vital role in the internal coordination of the purchasing and supply function and coordination with other functions (see section 22.5.2 in this regard). Communication (including the use of information systems), motivation, standardisation of specifications, procedures and documentation are aids to improve coordination internally in the purchasing and supply function, in the business itself, and externally with suppliers. The so-called just-in-time (JIT), materials requirements planning (MRP), and other systems plan and control not only the inventory and materials flow process, as is generally accepted, but are also an important coordinating instrument within the purchasing and supply function and the business, and with suppliers.

22.4.2.4 Cross-functional sourcing teams

A new trend in organising the purchasing and supply function is the establishment of cross-functional sourcing teams. The use of cross-functional teams is an important practice in the supply chain management approach. The purchaser cooperates on a team with colleagues in other functional management

Figure 22.10: Internal organisation of the purchasing and supply function

(a) Internal organisation according to the specialisation approach

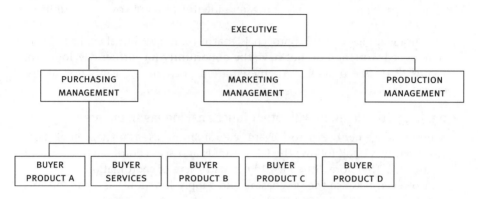

(b) Internal organisation according to activities

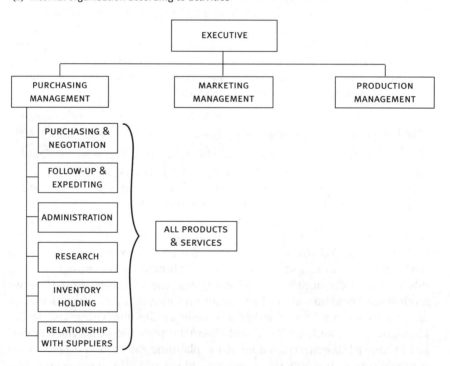

areas to perform numerous tasks, which include supplier selection, negotiation of prices and conditions, determination of supply levels, and the evaluation of suppliers' performance. In these tasks the purchaser heads the team,
but in other tasks, such as value analysis and the development of new products, a design engineer assumes leadership, although the purchaser remains a
member of the team.

The objective is to reach decisions that will be best for the business and customers, but not necessarily for performance in an individual functional man-

agement area (as mentioned earlier, individual fields of management may well have conflicting aims). The teams may be permanent, or else exist only for a specific period or until a specific task has been completed. It is important that team members retain close ties with their functional management area (for example, purchasing and supply management) and that the decisions of the cross-functional team should enjoy the support of individual functional areas. Suppliers can be included in a functional team for certain tasks, such as new product development or the establishment of quality standards. Personnel of various firms in the supply chain may also be included in a purchasing and supply team. Five applications for cross-functional teams have been identified:[9]

- Commodity sourcing strategy
- Sourcing
- Supplier evaluation
- Supplier certification
- New product development

To be a member of a cross-functional team, a buyer must have the ability to work with groups and display leadership qualities

22.4.3 *Control in the purchasing and supply function*

Purchasing and supply control, like control in other functional management areas of a business, is the measure adopted to ensure that purchasing and supply objectives are pursued within acceptable and accepted standards or norms and guidelines according to a specific policy established during purchasing and supply planning. Purchasing and supply planning, and, more specifically, formulating objectives, is therefore the first step in the control process. The steps comprise setting objectives, setting criteria and norms, measuring actual performance, comparing actual performance with the norms, studying deviations, and taking corrective measures (if necessary). The steps in the control process are discussed in detail and illustrated in chapter 12. Areas of control in the purchasing situation, however, require further investigation. The management task in the purchasing and supply function, and the performance of purchasing and supply activities, need to be evaluated (controlled).

22.4.3.1 The assessment of purchasing and supply management

The **management** performance of the purchasing and supply function should be evaluated just like other activities of the purchasing and supply function, because management can influence the overall job performance and achievement of the purchasing and supply function and, ultimately, the performance of the business. Management is intangible, and difficult to measure quantitatively. Therefore, there is a certain amount of subjectivity in measuring management. The performance of purchasing and supply management should be measured by the executive director responsible for the purchasing and supply function. The following questions cover the main areas of control of purchasing and supply management:[10]

- What are the scope and authority of purchasing and supply activities at supply chain, business, functional, and plant level, and are they clearly demarcated?

- Are purchasing and supply policies, procedures and practices up to date, written and effective?
- Does the purchasing and supply manager have adequate knowledge and skills to lead the purchasing and supply function in an increasingly complex purchasing environment?
- Is a programme in place for the development of purchasing and supply personnel, as well as training plans and procedures?
- What are the relationships like between the purchasing and supply function, suppliers, and other functions in the business, as well as cooperation and interfaces among them?
- How effective is the internal organisation of the purchasing and supply function?
- Are there adequate coordination measures in the purchasing and supply function?
- How do suppliers feel about the purchasing and supply function?
- Does the business make optimal use of its total purchasing leverage?
- Are there adequate performance appraisal and control systems in the purchasing and supply function?

22.4.3.2 Assessment of purchasing and supply activities

As mentioned earlier, the aim of the purchasing and supply function is to supply the business in the most effective way with the right materials, and of the desired quality, at the right place and time, in the right quantities, at the right price. To realise this objective, the purchasing and supply function has to perform certain **activities**. Control is necessary to ascertain whether these activities are being performed effectively. The following control points or criteria can be used to gauge the **effectiveness** of purchasing and supply activities:[11]

- **Price proficiency**, by, for example, comparing actual prices with planned or market prices, the number and value of discounts negotiated for a specific period, and determining which part of every rand turnover constitutes purchasing costs
- **Supplier performance**, by, for instance, noting rejected orders, orders received late, and the number of times it was necessary to expedite
- **Timeliness**, by, say, noting the number of orders indicated as urgent and the number of operations interruptions or operations rescheduling as a result of shortages
- **Cost saving**, by, for example comparing costs with those of previous periods
- **Work load**, by, for example, looking at the number of orders and requisitions
- **Purchasing costs**, by expressing administrative purchasing costs as a percentage of the monetary value of purchases
- **Inventory holding**, by calculating inventory turnover and making further enquiries into inventory losses and obsolescence of stock
- **Relationship performance** with suppliers, by means of a survey or scrutiny of supplier turnover, or number of alliances formed
- **Relationship with other functional management areas**, by monitoring the diligent execution of requests to the purchasing and supply function, and the contribution purchasers make in cross-functional teams

Once these measurement criteria have been laid down, the actual results can be measured and compared with a standard or norm, for example, past performance or that of similar businesses. A report on performance and problem areas should be compiled and submitted to top management with the necessary recommendations. (See again the elements of the control process in chapter 12.)

22.4.3.3 Concluding remarks

A brief overview of the important management task of control in the purchasing and supply function has been given. Only a few criteria were mentioned for the assessment of performance. However, every business should develop as many criteria for control as possible, and cooperate with other businesses to develop benchmarks.

22.5 Tools available to purchasing and supply management

Purchasing and supply managers have certain aids at their disposal to facilitate the execution of the management tasks of planning, organising and control. Each of these aids will now be briefly discussed.

22.5.1 Benchmarks

A new tool in laying down standards for setting objectives and measuring the performance of the purchasing and supply function is to obtain a benchmarking partner in a similar industry and then for both to compare the performance of various aspects of their two businesses. Thus, for example, Eskom, Transnet and Telkom could be benchmarking partners, because all three operate in the same environment, have the same background, and purchase a large quantity of materials in the same markets, for example, copper wire, wooden poles and fuel.

Such a partnership can help iron out problem areas, especially in respect of purchasing and supply processes and practices. Benchmarks are also frequently compiled by outside organisations such as the Centre for Advanced Purchasing Studies in the USA, the Institute for Purchasing and Supply SA, and by entrepreneurs who develop benchmarks to "sell" or use during consultations for businesses.

22.5.2 Purchasing and supply budgets

The chapters on financial management (chapters 17-19) deal with budgets. Clearly, a budget is, in essence, the financial plan for the allocation of the business's resources for a specific period. A purchasing and supply budget, like other budgets, is a planning aid as well as a financial standard for control. Besides planning and control, the purchasing and supply budget also has a role in coordinating the activities of the purchasing and supply function with the activities of other functional management areas in the business. In fact, it would be impossible to prepare the purchasing and supply budget without inputs from marketing, operations and financial budgets. The purchasing and supply budget mainly comprises two components, the materials and the administrative budget.

Applying the concept: benchmarks in the fuel industry

In the fuel industry, the following benchmarks have been laid down:

- Buyers spend 9% of their organisation's total sales turnover on the purchase of material from suppliers.
- The operating expenditure of the purchasing and supply function is eight-hundredths of a cent per rand of sales revenue.
- It costs less than a cent to buy a rand's worth of goods or services.
- There is one purchasing and supply employee per 171 other employees in the business.
- There is one purchasing and supply employee for every R104 million sales.
- Purchases from suppliers in disadvantaged groups amount to 2,8% of total purchases (in rand).
- Inventory purchases comprise 1% of sales income.
- For every buyer, a business has 102 active suppliers.

Source: Adapted from *Purchasing benchmarking in the petroleum industry*, Centre for Advanced Purchasing Studies, Tempe, Arizona, USA.

The **administrative budget** consists of budgeted cost components such as salaries for the purchasing and supply function, stationery, telephone costs, travelling and hotel costs, and the cost of renting offices and warehouse equipment. This budget is not as important as the materials budget, but still plays a major role in the control of costs in the purchasing and supply function.

The **materials budget** is especially important because of the broad use of the money involved and because it is an instrument for planning purchasing and supply quantities and inventory levels, timing of purchases, and purchase prices. The materials budget is closely related to the operations and marketing budget. The marketing budget forms the foundation of the operations budget, which, in turn, underpins the materials budget (see figure 22.11). The materials budget is therefore also an important instrument in the coordination of the purchasing and supply function with other functional management areas in the business.

Figure 22.11: The relationship of the purchasing and supply budgets with other budgets

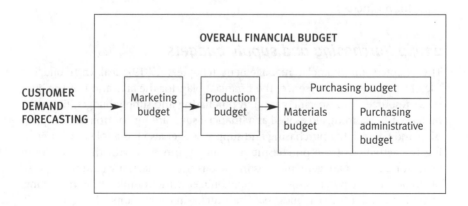

22.5.3 *Purchasing and supply policy and procedures manual*

The purchasing and supply policy is a written directive from top management (usually supported by the head of the purchasing and supply function) to the purchasing and supply function to act in a prescribed manner in handling specific purchasing and supply issues. The purchasing and supply policy is subordinate to the policy of the business, and in practice should support it. If the policy of the business is, say, to make affirmative action a priority, purchasing and supply policy should make provision for this, not only in respect of affirmative action within the purchasing and supply function, but also with regard to suppliers. The purchasing and supply policy gives direction and can be regarded as a framework within which buyers act. It reduces the need to refer too many matters back to higher authority. It also eliminates misunderstandings and concentrates purchasing efforts on the achievement of the agreed objectives.

The purchasing and supply policy comprises sub-policies, of which the following are the most important:

- **Policy in respect of ethical purchasing practices.** This policy usually contains guidelines on the actions of buyers in terms of loyalty and the protection of the interests of the employer in the purchasing situation; avoidance of conflict of interest; acceptance of gifts and samples; purchases by employees; selling to employees; and adhering to the law during buying transactions.
- **Policy in respect of internal purchasing and supply matters.** This policy usually contains guidelines on matters such as the organisation of the purchasing and supply function (for example, the extent of centralisation or decentralisation) and guidelines on the authority and responsibility of each of those subject to the policy; guidelines on the use or non-use of contracts; purchases by employees in other functions; administrative and operational guidelines that find expression in the purchasing and supply procedure manual.
- **Supplier policy.** This policy contains guidelines on action toward suppliers: one or more suppliers per item; the use of local or foreign suppliers or suppliers in far-off places; handling a selection of suppliers; evaluation of suppliers' performance; reciprocal purchasing and supply. The policy on purchasing from previously disadvantaged suppliers and small businesses is often included in this policy. However, the issue of disadvantaged purchasing and supply is sometimes regarded as too important, and a separate policy is therefore formulated in this regard.

22.6 Summary

The purchasing and supply function is an important one because:
- It has a significant influence on the profitability of the business.
- It is often the greatest spender of business revenue.
- The purchasing and supply function makes it possible for the business to sell its final products at competitive prices.

The purchasing and supply function, like all other functions in the business, should be planned, organised and controlled to ensure that it helps achieve the objectives of the business.

The main sourcing activities (activities of the purchasing and supply function) will be discussed in chapter 23.

References

1. Supply is added to the purchasing function because purchasing is no longer seen as a reactive, service function of organisations. Modern purchasing management also includes involvement in processes (both at suppliers and logistics providers) that ensure the efficient flow of supplies (materials and services) to the organisation.
2. Zenz, G. J., *Purchasing and the management of materials*, 7the edition, Wiley, New York, 1994, p. 153.
3. Lysons, C.K., *Purchasing*, 3rd edition, Pitman Publishing, London, 1993, p. 4.
4. *Ibid.*, p. 4.
5. *Ibid.*, p. 11.
6. Zenz, G.J., op. cit., p. 83.
7. Leenders, M. R. & Fearon, H.E., *Purchasing and supply management,* 11th edition, Irwin, Chicago, 1997, pp. 41-42.
8. *Ibid.*, pp. 44-46.
9. Dobler, D.W. & Burt, D.N., *Purchasing and supply management: text and cases*, McGraw-Hill, New York, 1996, p. 128.
10. Fearon, H.E., Dobler, D.W. & Killen, K.H. (eds), *The purchasing handbook*, McGraw-Hill, New York, 1993, pp. 324-325.
11. *Ibid.*, pp. 328-348 and Zenz, G. J., *op. cit.*, p. 305.

23 Sourcing activities

The purpose of this chapter

The purpose of this chapter is to explain the purchasing or sourcing process in organisations, and to provide an overview of the most important activities involved in the process.

Learning outcomes

The content of this chapter will enable learners to:
- Provide clarity on the logical steps to be followed in a purchasing and supply transaction
- Indicate the role of the purchasing and supply function in quality decisions
- Emphasise the role of quantity desicions in the purchasing and supply process
- Give an overview of the selection and management of suppliers
- Pinpoint certain aspects of pricing as purchasing and supply activity
- Place the right time for purchasing and supply in perspective
- Briefly explain the outsourcing strategy
- Give an overview of purchasing and supply research as an aid for decision making
- Briefly explain negotiation as an aid in concluding purchasing transactions

23.1 Introduction

Purchasing and supply activities are mentioned in chapter 22, section 22.1. The main activity groups of the purchasing and supply function emerge from the traditional definition of the purchasing function: the purchase and supply of a product of the right quality, at the right price, in the right quantities, at the right time, and from the right supplier.

Each purchasing and supply activity is discussed separately in this chapter, but this does not mean that purchasing and supply activities exist, and are performed, in isolation. In fact, purchasing and supply activities are interdependent. Therefore, for example, price and quality, price and time, price and choice of suppliers, time and quantity, are inseparably intertwined. The practical execution of purchasing and supply activities is clear from the discussion of the stages in the purchasing and supply process or cycle.

23.2 The purchasing and supply cycle

The discussion of the purchasing and supply cycle or process in this section provides a clear picture of the steps in the purchasing and supply transaction, how the steps follow each other logically, who in the business is involved in each step, and the documentation involved in each step. Not all the steps are necessarily taken in each purchasing and supply transaction, and some steps often take place simultaneously.

A large number of businesses in South Africa have computerised their purchasing and supply process. Computerised systems are also based on the purchasing and supply cycle discussed here. Computerisation expedites the process considerably and usually reduces the documentation involved. The steps in the purchasing and supply cycle can be divided into three main phases:

- **The notification phase**, when the purchasing and supply function is informed of the need
- **The order phase**, during which the purchasing and supply function checks the documentation, assesses the newness of the purchase, contacts suppliers, orders, receives and inspects the materials, and acknowledges their receipt
- **The post-order phase**, which primarily entails sorting out discrepancies, processing and handling documentation, paying suppliers, and keeping sound relations with suppliers

Figure 23.1 (see p. 549) reflects the basic steps in the purchasing and supply cycle, the functional management areas involved, and the documentation.

These steps are now explained in more detail:

- **The development and description of a need.** Because of the activities of other functional management areas (also called "users" or "consumers"), there is a need for materials and services. The need is conveyed by means of a requisition, order card, or materials and specification list to the purchasing and supply function. To ensure that the desired materials are purchased, the buyer must take careful note of the specification, which is actually a description of the need. The specification not only describes the material, but also the quality. The buyer should also look closely at the quantities specified and the date on which the materials are required. In a manufacturing business, the greatest need is for materials in the production or operational function (or functions), and in a commercial organisation, in the marketing function. (Note that operational and marketing functions are included as "Consumers" in figure 23.1.)
- **Choice of suppliers.** The choice of the right supplier is the principal activity of the purchasing and supply function, and is discussed in more detail later. The complexity of this decision will depend on various factors, for example, whether it is a new purchase or a repurchase, whether a contract needs to be entered into or whether a contract already exists, or whether standard or specialised materials are required. Depending on the factors, the buyer will use documents such as the register of suppliers, order forms, contracts, price lists, quotations, or tenders.

  In a new buying situation, especially where a contract has to be drawn up, determining the present and future availability of the materials is a vital consideration in the choice of suppliers. Determining the future availability of materials is no easy task. A study of the technical, managerial and financial abilities of suppliers, their progressiveness, idle capacity and past performance (if used in the past) is necessary. This is done by analysing the financial statements of suppliers, making personal visits and conducting interviews with their staff and management, and obtaining credit bureau reports. It is important to note that user functions (e.g. marketing or production) may make recommendations about a particular supplier, but the final choice rests with the purchasing and supply function.

Figure 23.1: Steps in the purchasing and supply cycle of a commercial business

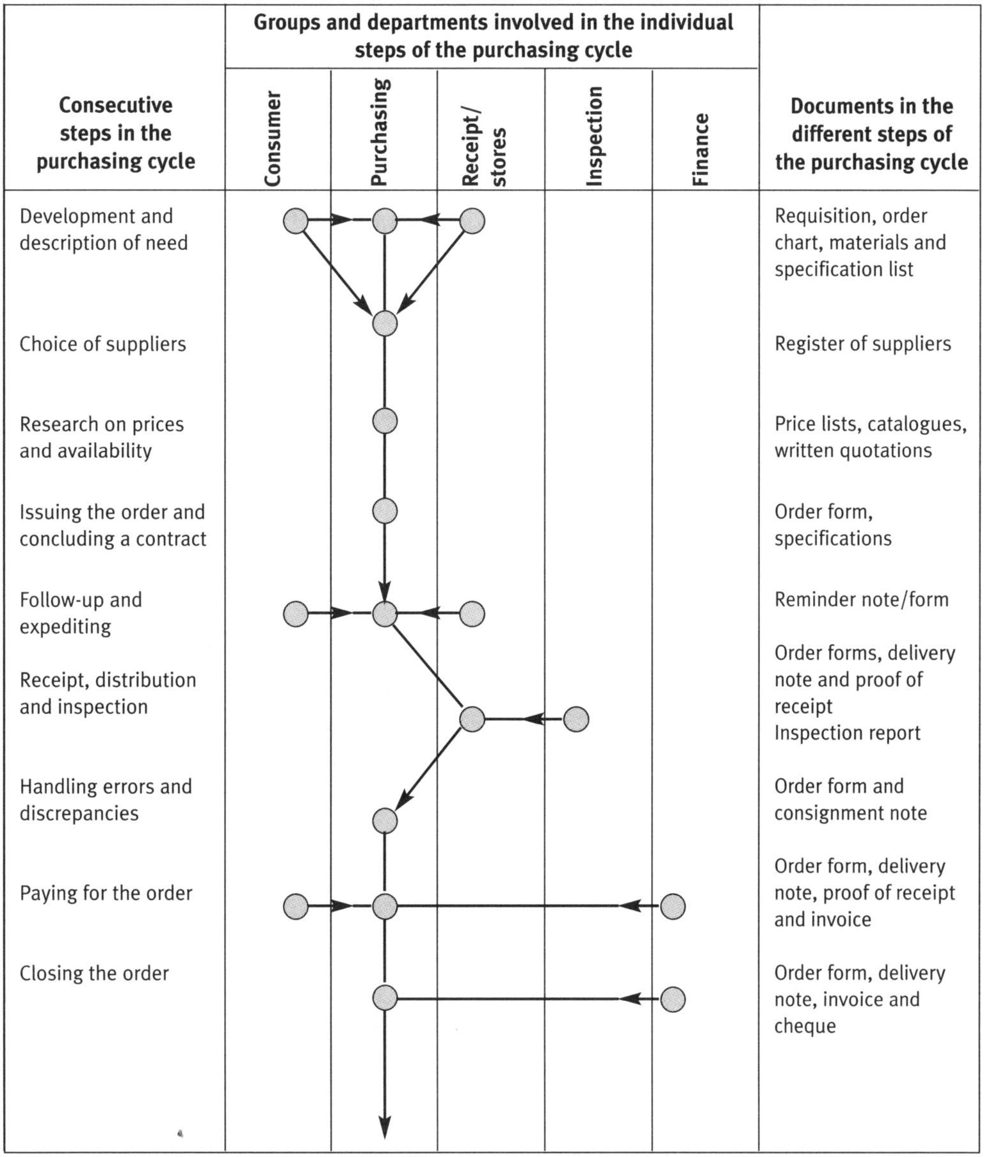

Consecutive steps in the purchasing cycle	Groups and departments involved in the individual steps of the purchasing cycle					Documents in the different steps of the purchasing cycle
	Consumer	Purchasing	Receipt/ stores	Inspection	Finance	
Development and description of need						Requisition, order chart, materials and specification list
Choice of suppliers						Register of suppliers
Research on prices and availability						Price lists, catalogues, written quotations
Issuing the order and concluding a contract						Order form, specifications
Follow-up and expediting						Reminder note/form
Receipt, distribution and inspection						Order forms, delivery note and proof of receipt Inspection report
Handling errors and discrepancies						Order form and consignment note
Paying for the order						Order form, delivery note, proof of receipt and invoice
Closing the order						Order form, delivery note, invoice and cheque

Source: Hugo, W.M.J., Badenhorst-Weiss, J.A. & Van Rooyen, D.C., *Purchasing and materials management*, 4th edition, J.L. van Schaik, Pretoria, 2002, p. 17.

- **Determining prices.** This is actually part of the previous step. The prices of standard materials and materials with a low monetary value are determined with the aid of price lists and telephonic, verbal or written quotations. Because standard materials are available everywhere, prices are in fact determined by competition. The prices of non-standard or specialised materials or custom-made items are often determined by tender or quotation in conjunction with negotiations.

- **Placing an order or concluding a contract.** The order and the contract are important documents because they spell out unequivocally to the supplier the needs of the business and the conditions of the purchasing transaction, and because they constitute a legally valid contract to which both parties are bound by law. The order or contract should contain specific conditions for the transaction in respect of quantities, quality, prices, discounts, delivery dates, customs clearances, and exchange rate clearances.

  An order and a contract should also refer to the clauses of the general conditions that apply to all buying transactions of the business. The general conditions are there to protect the purchasing organisation, and should be given to the supplier together with the contract, or be sent with the order. The general conditions relate to the business's payment policy (for example, 30 days after invoice), delivery and acceptance, transfer of risks, compliance with quality requirements, over-deliveries, under-deliveries, statutory regulations, patent rights, and exchange rate clearance.

- **Expediting and follow-up.** The purchasing and supply function's task is completed only when materials of the right quality have been received, in the right quantities, at the right place, and, most importantly, at the right time. One of the administrative tasks in the purchasing and supply function is to determine whether materials are received in good time. If not, or if they are overdue, the supplier should be reminded by letter, facsimile, telephone, or electronically if a computer system links the business and its suppliers, that it has not adhered to the clauses of the contract and that it should concentrate on the speedy delivery of required materials. The importance of this task is often underestimated. If a supplier is late with deliveries, this can interrupt the production or operational process in a manufacturing business, or leave a retailer with empty shelves. This can also have serious implications for supplier relations and the continued use of a specific supplier.

- **Receipt, inspection and distribution.** As mentioned previously, stores reception (as a sub-function of purchasing and supply) is responsible for checking the quantities and conditions of materials when they are received. The delivery note of the supplier is signed and is proof that the materials were received. Inspection (a sub-function of purchasing and supply) checks the quality of the materials and compiles an inspection report. The materials are sent to the users (that is, the functions that requested the products) with a copy of the order, or they are taken up as inventory in the stores.

- **Handling errors and discrepancies.** Communication and keeping good relations with suppliers are important tasks of the purchasing and supply function. If defective materials are received, the purchasing and supply function should communicate with the suppliers concerning these in a way that will prevent future defective consignments, but still ensure good relations.

- **Paying for the order.** It is the task of purchasing and supply to prepare authorisation for payment of the supplier. The purchasing and supply function checks the delivery note, the inspection report, the invoice, and the order, to confirm that the quantities, quality, price, and discounts are correct, and to verify the calculations. It then authorises the finance function to pay the supplier. The purchasing and supply function should execute this task carefully and quickly so that suppliers are paid in accordance with the payment policy of the business.
- **Closing of the order.** Once the supplier has been paid, the purchasing and supply function must file all documents pertaining to the particular transaction or incorporate them into a system for future reference. This is a crucial part of the evaluation of a supplier's performance, and also constitutes an assessment of the purchasing and supply function's performance.

In the discussion of the purchasing and supply cycle we placed in perspective the principal purchasing and supply activities, namely decisions regarding quality and quantities, choosing and managing suppliers, pricing, decisions regarding purchasing, and supply times. The next step is to examine these activities in greater depth.

23.3 Quality decisions as a purchasing and supply activity

23.3.1 The role of quality

The three main factors in each purchasing and supply decision are quality, supplier service, delivery and price. Quality is probably the most important of these factors. Even if the price and the service that a supplier offers are outstanding, material will not be bought from it if the quality is any way less than required, because the material will not perform the function for which it was purchased.

Quality is an inseparable part of other purchasing and supply activities. Top quality is normally associated with high prices and vice versa. Quality also determines the number of suppliers. The higher the quality requirements, the fewer suppliers there will be to satisfy such requirements. Quality also influences inventory holding or the quantity to be purchased. In the case of high quality requirements, a reliable supplier that can meet the specification and deliver on time will be chosen. Smaller volumes of materials can therefore be kept in stock, because fewer materials will be rejected during inspection. In fact, continuous high quality is an absolute necessity in stockless systems such as just-in-time (JIT) and materials requirements planning (MRP), which are discussed in section 23.4.3.

The quality of purchased products and services rests on the various considerations discussed in the following section, namely:

- Determining the right quality for a given goal
- Describing quality so that both the buyer and seller understand it clearly
- Controlling quality to ensure that requirements are met

23.3.2 Determining the right quality

A buyer has a different perspective to a technical person of the concept "the right quality". From a purchasing and supply perspective, the right quality can be defined as follows:

> **Definition**
>
> The right quality is that quality that is purchased at the lowest price, which satisfies a specific need and performs the function for which it was purchased.

For **engineers and designers**, technical considerations such as job performance and reliability are often the only factors that are important. It frequently happens that engineers and designers, without any commercial considerations, request the purchase of the highest or best quality materials, when lower quality materials would do the job just as well. **Buyers** are more attuned to commercial considerations such as the right quality, availability, price and delivery. A buyer should therefore have the right to question technical requirements, or to request that specifications be reconsidered on the strength of commercial considerations. A design engineer may, for example, ask for a specific brand of ball bearing. The purchasing and supply function should have the right to point out that a cheaper equivalent is available on the market, and to request that it be considered as a substitute.

The best quality is therefore not necessarily the right quality. The right quality for a specific purchase is determined by balancing suitability (technical requirements), availability and cost (commercial requirements).

The **end-user** and/or the **marketing function** also often provide input on suitable quality, since the right quality materials not only increase the productivity of the user, but also influence the quality and price of the final product to be marketed. The quality of products is not only important for marketing, but also for public relations, because this influences the image the business wants to project, and will be decisive in determining which customers wish to associate with the business and its products. After-sales service, a policy on taking back materials of a poor quality, and the provision of guarantees by the supplier are important considerations that tie in closely with decisions pertaining to quality. Suppliers also play a vital role in determining suitable quality, because they are often in a position to recommend alternative materials.

23.3.3 Description of quality

Quality refers to measurable qualities, a condition or characteristics of materials, usually expressed according to grade, class, brand or specifications. It should be possible to describe the desired quality, otherwise there is no way the person requisitioning can communicate clearly with a buyer, and a buyer with a supplier, about what exactly is required. (For communication purposes, the description of quality is entered on the requisition and order.) The description of quality is also important because it serves as a measure for judging the quality of incoming materials by means of inspection. The following methods and forms should be noted:

- **Specifications** are the most general method of describing quality. A specification is a description of non-standard materials that are able to perform a certain function. Specifications can be drawn up according to dimensions or physical features such as tolerance, work ability, uniformity and chemical composition. The purchasing and supply function should endeavour to prevent specifications being drawn up that are to the advantage of only one supplier, and eliminate competition. A supplier can, for example, change an unimportant feature of material (for example, the colour or name) to distinguish it from competing materials. If the user or buyer specifies the unique name or colour of the specific material, all competition (which is essential in the purchasing and supply process) is eliminated, even though the material performs exactly the same function as others competing in the market.
- **Standardisation** is a further aid in describing quality. It is, in effect, the process of making materials, methods, practices and techniques uniform. Standardisation can be set by a business or organisation, or nationally or internationally by an industry, and it has several advantages. If a business or organisation standardises, total inventory can be reduced, because fewer kinds and qualities are kept. Standardisation also improves collaboration between the user and buyer in a business, and communication between the buyer and supplier. Industrial and international standards make possible the mass production of products. Because many suppliers manufacture standard products, and standard materials can be bought everywhere, competition in the market is increased, and the purchasing and supply price of the product is reduced.
- **Other forms** of quality description are market grades, brands, SABS (South African Bureau of Standards) standards, engineering drawings and samples.

23.3.4 Control over quality

It is imperative to control the quality of incoming materials. Poor quality materials interrupt the manufacturing process, expose workers to danger, have a detrimental effect on the final product, and ultimately reduce the satisfaction of end-users and alter the perception they have of the business and its products.

Inspection is the normal process used to control quality. It is a method that ensures that the measurement, design, job performance and quality of materials received, satisfy the standards or specifications on the order, and that goods are suitable for the purpose for which they have been ordered. Inspection is a technical process, and is not the task of purchasers, but that of the quality control function (a sub-function of purchasing and supply).

During inspection by quality controllers, samples of delivered materials are subjected to tests. However, inspection per se is not enough to guarantee the quality of incoming materials. If the purchasing and supply function buys from a supplier that has maintained top quality standards for years, it is actually unnecessary to inspect its products. In such a case, the business can negotiate a **supplier certification agreement** with the supplier. Based on agreed terms, the supplier and the buyer's quality control functions work together for a specific time, and the materials and operation processes are subject to intensive inspection for a certain period. After this, the supplier is certified, and it becomes responsible for quality.

Another proactive approach to quality control is **quality assurance**. A complete quality assurance programme commences with the compilation of specifications, and continues with the determining of standards and ongoing testing of suppliers' products and processes. The SABS has a certification scheme whereby manufacturers are encouraged and supported in endeavours to establish and operate quality control systems, or quality assurance programmes. Part of the certification scheme of the SABS is the well-known ISO 9000 to 9004 and ISO 14 000 international standards. Because the establishment and operation of such programmes is extremely costly, and the quality of materials is assured, buyers must be prepared to pay high prices.

23.4 Deciding on purchasing and supply quantities

23.4.1 *The need for inventory holding*

If the operations function is 100% certain of the quantity of material to be used in the manufacturing process, the marketing function is 100% certain about how many products are going to be sold, there are no supply problems in the supplier market, and the incoming materials completely satisfy quality requirements, then the purchasing and supply function can buy the exact quantity of materials required. Unfortunately, such a situation simply does not exist in practice. Because marketing and production or operations budgets are based solely on estimates, and the supplier market in South Africa tends often to be unreliable with regard to delivery and quality, the buyer has to purchase more materials than required, with the result that inventory holding becomes necessary. Inventory holding is therefore inextricably intertwined with the task of a buyer.

Pre-1994, during the sanctions era, it was normal practice for South African businesses to keep large stocks, especially those importing materials from abroad. After South Africa's readmission to normal world trade, however, the worldwide trend of keeping minimum inventory also took root here. The reason for this trend is that inventory holding generates considerable costs, and large amounts of operating capital are tied up in inventory. One of the main aims of new approaches to the supply of materials, such as supply chain management and the concomitant enablers such as supplier alliances, e-procurement, JIT, MRP, ERP (Efficient consumer response), AR (Automatic replenishment) and QR (Quick response) is to limit inventory holding to the minimum.

If the holding of inventory is so unpopular, why should it be held? There are two major reasons for this:

- Inventory is held to ensure that the operations process (or the marketing process in a retailing organisation) can continue without interruptions resulting from shortages of materials.
- Inventory is held to utilise cost savings through longer production runs and volume discounts.

It is therefore clear that too little or too much inventory is undesirable, and that both have certain cost implications or disadvantages. Table 23.1 (see p. 555) provides a succinct summary of some of the implications of too little or too much inventory.

Table 23.1: Implications of inventory positions

Disadvantages of too much inventory	Disadvantages of too little inventory
• Operating capital is tied up with the resultant opportunity and interest costs • Losses in terms of depreciation, obsolescence, damage and theft • Costs in terms of storage space (rental or interest), more warehouse staff and equipment, and bigger insurance premiums	• Higher unit prices as a result of smaller orders • More urgent orders with concomitant higher order and transport costs, and strained relations with suppliers • Cost of production or job interruptions and the accompanying strained relations with users or marketers in the business • Lost sales because of empty shelves in the retail organisation and the resultant negative influence on its image

23.4.2 Inventory costs

Certain costs increase when large quantities of stock are purchased, while others increase with the purchase of small quantities. It is necessary to categorise these cost elements and examine them more closely to determine optimal inventory quantity, that is, the inventory quantity that results in the lowest total cost of inventory.

Inventory-carrying costs are those involved in keeping inventory. They include the cost of storage, salaries of warehouse staff, insurance, property tax, obsolescence, wear and tear, theft, interest charges (for the financing of inventory), and opportunity costs (loss of income from investment in alternative profit-bearing projects, as capital has been invested in inventory). Larger order quantities cause larger inventory levels and therefore higher inventory-carrying costs. The opposite applies to small quantities and lower inventory levels.

Inventory ordering costs are the costs of placing an order. Ordering costs include the salaries of purchasing and supply and expediting personnel, stationery, telephone and telefax costs, on-line (e-procurement) costs, and postage. Larger purchasing and supply quantities result in fewer orders being placed, and a decline in ordering costs.

Total inventory costs comprise the sum total of inventory-carrying costs and inventory ordering costs. Ordering costs decline and carrying costs increase as order quantities increase, and ordering costs increase (because more orders have to be made) and carrying costs decrease as order quantities decrease. The influence of quantity on the two cost categories is indicated clearly in figure 23.2 (see p. 556). The lowest total inventory cost is achieved where the two curves (carrying cost and ordering cost curves) intersect, in other words, when ordering costs are equal to carrying costs. The number of units opposite the lowest total inventory cost on the graph is the most economic order quantity (EOQ).

23.4.3 Inventory control systems

Inventory should be managed and controlled so that optimal inventory levels can be maintained. This means that inventory should be kept at such a level that the best service can be rendered to the user or customer at the lowest pos-

Figure 23.2: The economic ordering quantity

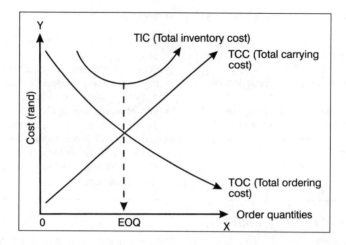

sible cost, and the quantities ordered each time should keep inventory at this level. Most inventory control systems are based on the principles of one of the following systems:

Figure 23.3: The system of fixed order quantities

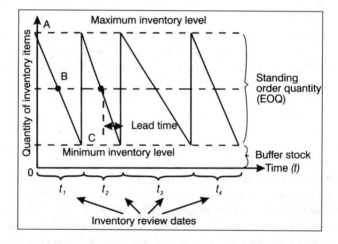

- **The system of fixed order quantities.** This system is based on the principle that each time new inventory is required, a fixed quantity (the economic order quantity) is ordered. The system is represented visually in figure 23.3.

  The economic order quantity is ordered once inventory reaches a certain level (order point B) as a result of the use (or selling) of inventory items (A to B). Inventory is then replenished by ordering the economic order quantity to reach the maximum inventory level. The order level is determined in such a way that inventory does not become depleted during the delivery period of the order.

The system is advantageous because attention is focused only on a specific item when the inventory level reaches the ordering point, and the same quantity is ordered every time. However, the system is unsuitable for items whose consumption or lead times are unreliable.

Figure 23.4: The cyclical ordering system

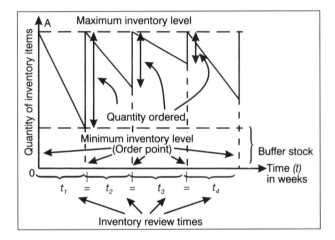

- **The cyclical ordering system.** Each item in the inventory is checked or reviewed at fixed intervals and is supplemented by an order to bring the inventory level to its maximum level again. Thus the ordering times are fixed, but the order quantity varies, as shown in figure 23.4. The system is suitable for seasonal materials or materials used on an irregular basis, but where the acquisition of such materials can be planned far in advance on the basis of sales forecasts, for example, in a clothing store. This system is used in grocery stores where, at the end of every month, stocktaking is done for each product on the shelves, and the order quantities adjusted to the quantity on the shelves. Thus, for example, more cold-drinks are ordered every month during summer than in winter.
- **The materials requirements planning system (MRP).** MRP is a computer-assisted system whose aim is to maintain minimum inventory levels. The system uses a computer to calculate the total need for materials that may be required by a manufacturing process in a given period. The planned quantity of final products to be manufactured during the production process in the given period is broken down into components and materials by the computer. It then determines the total need for each type of material and component, with due consideration for lead times, so that

materials or components are received when the production process needs them. The advantage of the system is that inventory levels are low. However, the system only works if suppliers are extremely reliable with their delivery and quality. Contracts with suppliers are usually needed to keep this system going.

- **Just-in-time (JIT).** This is in fact a production scheduling system and not an inventory system. It virtually eliminates the holding of inventory. Its operation is based on requiring suppliers to deliver materials of the right quality to the business on the day they are needed – in other words, just in time. The system requires regular deliveries, and quantities should correspond exactly to needs. In other words, it is not the inventory system that determines the quantities to be purchased or to be delivered, but the operations (or production) system. Therefore, purchasing and supply has little or no influence on the quantities to be purchased. It is imperative for purchasing and supply to work closely with operations management, because the purchasing and supply function needs to be fully conversant with the changing needs of the operations system.

  The JIT system only works properly if the supplier is extremely reliable and is integrated into the business's production system. Supplier alliances are needed to make JIT work. The JIT system cannot satisfy all the needs of the business. Usually materials used in the production process are purchased according to the JIT approach. Requirements that do not relate to the manufacture of the business's final product, for example, office equipment and cleaning materials, obviously cannot be purchased according to the JIT approach.

- **Quick response (QR) and Automatic replenishment (AR).** QR is defined as a vertical strategy (in the supply chain) in which the manufacturer strives to provide products and services to its retail customers in exact quantities on a continuous basis with minimal lead times, resulting in minimum inventory levels throughout the retail apparel supply chain.[1] QR is based on the manufacturing JIT concept – to deliver materials to production areas in the exact required amount at the precise time they are needed. The use of raw materials pulls raw materials into the production process. QR developed as an attempt to reduce the amount of inventory held within the apparel supply chain. It requires of retailers to share point-of-sale-scanned data with manufacturers to improve the flow of products through the supply chain.[2]

  AR is an integral part of any QR programme. AR can be defined as an exchange relationship in which the supplier replenishes or restocks inventory, based upon actual product usage and stock level information provided by the retail buyer. AR therefore provides the final customer (consumer) with the desired product and service in a timely fashion. The goal of AR is to effectively manage inventory levels. With AR, information is substituted for inventory.

- **Efficient consumer response (ECR).** ECR is developed for the grocery industry and is based on the same principles as QR. ECR calls for the creation of a timely, accurate and paperless flow of information – relying heavily on EDI (electronic data interchange) and strategic alliances between supply chain members. The goal of ECR is to eliminate costs, such as inventory holding and ordering costs in an entire supply chain. The underlying objectives are to reduce cycle time (time from placing the order to receiving the goods) in the supply chain, reduce inventories, avoid duplications in logistics costs and to increase customer service.[3]

23.5 The selection and management of suppliers

23.5.1 The importance of selecting the right suppliers

Selecting the right suppliers is one of the most vital tasks of the purchasing and supply function, since effective purchasing and supply rely mainly on this. Competitive prices, reliable quality, timely deliveries, technical support, and good after-sales service are determined primarily by the choice of the right supplier. Hence, it is essential for the purchasing and supply function to make the effort and proceed systematically and objectively in selecting suppliers. An important consideration when making this choice is that a long-term relationship with suppliers is necessary to ensure effective purchasing and supply at all times. Important components of such a relationship are honesty, fairness and frankness.

23.5.2 The selection process

Supplier selection is an ongoing process, because existing suppliers have to be constantly reconsidered with each new purchase, especially in view of changing circumstances and needs. Past performance of an existing supplier obviously counts a great deal in the selection process. However, the care taken in the selection process will be determined by the scope of the transaction, the availability of materials, their strategic value, and whether they are standard or custom-made. The latter are items for a specific purpose and therefore not generally available in the market. Standard items, however, are freely available, and in this case the choice of suppliers is not that important.

The process starts with the compilation of a list of suppliers that may be able to satisfy the need. The list can be compiled from various sources, for example, own supplier register, industrial advertisements, the Yellow Pages, trade guides, open tenders, shows and exhibitions. It is then reduced to a short list, after taking into account factors such as location, progressiveness, general reputation, and financial and technical ability. Suppliers on the short list are then requested to give a quote, or negotiations are conducted with them, to obtain the best value (in respect of price, quality, service and delivery) for the business. The final choice of a supplier is based on considerations such as past performance, quality, price, delivery, technical support, progressiveness and reliability.

Once the choice has been made, the next steps are the continuous evaluation of the performance of the supplier to ensure that it conforms to expectations, and the elimination of unsatisfactory suppliers. This will now be discussed in more detail.

23.5.3 Evaluating supplier performance

The objective evaluation of supplier performance is important for the following reasons:

- Ineffective or unreliable suppliers are identified.
- It leads to an improvement in supplier performance.
- It serves as a guideline for the development of suppliers.

Various methods can be used to evaluate the performance of suppliers, the most common being the weighted-point method.

Table 23.2: Supplier performance evaluation by the weighted-point method

Assessment of (weight)	Quality (4)		Delivery (3)		Price (2)		Service (1)		Total
Supplier	Rating	Perfor-mance	Rating	Perfor-mance	Rating	Perfor-mance	Rating	Perfor-mance	
Supplier A	8	32	7	21	6	12	5	5	70
Supplier B	7	28	3	9	6	12	1	1	50
Supplier C	9	36	6	18	5	10	9	9	73

With this method, weights are allocated to each factor taken into consideration. The above table could be the supplier assessment by a manufacturer of measuring equipment. For this type of organisation, the **quality** of purchased materials is the most important consideration. Therefore, a weight of four is assigned to it. If **delivery** is also important, but less than quality, it is assigned a weight of three. Depending on importance, price may receive a two and **service** a one. Every supplier's performance is rated out of ten in the different categories (quality, delivery, price and service) and each rating is multiplied by the specific weight in order to obtain a total for each factor. By adding the factor totals, an overall total for each supplier is obtained. (For example, Supplier A got a total rating of 70. This is calculated as follows: (8×4) + (7×3) + (6×2) + (5×1).)

The supplier with the highest total has the best performance. This method is of particular importance in comparing suppliers. If only one supplier is evaluated, its total should be measured against a predetermined standard. When only one source is used for particular materials, a different method can be used to make an assessment. For example, it could be made by purchasing and supply staff, users of the materials and the inspection function, using, say, categories "good", "satisfactory" or "unsatisfactory" with regard to quality, delivery, price and service.

23.5.4 *Developing suppliers*

Purchasing and supply functions may become involved in the development of suppliers for various reasons. Suppliers may be developed for affirmative purchasing purposes or to improve their performance as a result of performance appraisals, or if materials or service do not exist in the market.

- **Affirmative purchasing.** In the spirit of reconstruction and development, and setting right apartheid inequalities, there is increasing pressure on South African businesses to give disadvantaged suppliers who show potential an opportunity to enter the market. Large organisations can help these suppliers develop, over time, into fully-fledged independent suppliers. Affirmative purchasing and supply may be done in the following ways:

- When comparing prices, a certain percentage (see section 23.6.3) is subtracted from the quoted prices of independent disadvantaged suppliers in order to benefit them.
- Purchase specific pre-identified materials and services from disadvantaged suppliers with potential, and support such suppliers in adhering to the contract and executing orders. Support given to disadvantaged suppliers may be in the form of managerial and technical assistance, making facilities available, staff training, and advancing operating capital.
- Subcontract or outsource to disadvantaged suppliers products and services that were formerly produced by the business. Products and services are often contracted out to employees who were previously responsible for manufacturing or providing products or services in the business. The specific process is therefore "privatised". Management of a business may, for example, decide to sell catering services to employees in the cafeteria, and it then functions as a separate business, rendering services on a contract basis.
- Accord a certain preference percentage, when comparing prices, to other suppliers who, in turn, commit to making a certain percentage of their purchases from suppliers (second-tier suppliers) from disadvantaged groups.

- **Materials or service not available.** If a purchaser has a need for a particular material or service, and such material or service is not available in the market, it can enter into a contract with a chosen supplier of another material or service to manufacture this material (product) or provide this service. Assistance to such a supplier may be in the form of staff training, the reconstruction or expansion of facilities, or the implementation of new facilities. A long-term agreement with such suppliers is a prerequisite.
- **Normal performance appraisal.** Normal performance appraisals can be used to indicate suppliers' weaknesses, and they can be encouraged to perform better. This is an important factor in establishing successful long-term ties with suppliers.

23.5.5 Long-term relationships with suppliers

During the 1990s many new strategies developed in the supply of products and services. One of the most important developments is closer cooperation with suppliers in the form of strategic alliances or partnerships. Organisations have a variety of relationships with different suppliers. Some relationships are at arms-length, while other relationships are more involved. Every organisation, therefore, has various kinds of relationships with suppliers – from no involvement with suppliers of standard-easy-to-get products or services, to high involvement with suppliers of strategic scarce materials or highly complicated, unique services. An alliance or a partnership is a high involvement relationship. Attributes of strategic supplier alliances are trust and cooperation, interdependence, joint quality improvement efforts, information (and systems) sharing, risk and benefit sharing, and joint problem solving.

23.6 Pricing decisions

23.6.1 The "best" price

Price has traditionally been regarded as the decisive factor in awarding orders. However, low prices go hand in hand with higher costs in other areas, such as the costs and risks attached to low quality, and high inventory when low prices (as a result of quantity discounts) are linked to quantity. The right price is not necessarily the lowest one. The total or final costs should rather be seen as the decisive factor in awarding orders. In other words, price should be regarded as only one of the components of value, together with quality, delivery and cost of use. A buyer should always strive to obtain the **highest value** for the business.

The price paid for materials must be **reasonable** and should enable the purchaser to make its own product competitive in the market. A reasonable price should be fair to ensure that a supplier sells its materials or service at a price that will ensure its profitability and survival. The price should therefore be in relation to the supplier's costs.

23.6.2 Price determination

The methods used to obtain prices depend on the nature of the materials and the value of the transaction. **Published price lists and available market information**, including catalogues, brochures and advertisements in trade journals, are most suitable for the purchase of standard materials and orders of a low monetary value, for example, when purchasing screws and stationery. Other methods of price determination are **quotations** and **tenders**. When using quotations and tenders, suppliers are asked to make an offer. The purchaser calls for **open tenders** where the invitation to tender is published, and any supplier can make an offer. The trend, however, is to issue a request to tender to a number of known suppliers. These are the so-called closed tenders, and are most suitable for purchasers with a complete list of suppliers.

Quotations are quick and informal and can be made by telephone, facsimiles or electronically. Quotations are used not only when standard materials are purchased, but are also suitable for non-standard or custom-made materials with a high monetary value, for example, equipment that performs a unique function. **Tenders** go hand in hand with a drawn-out procedure that has to be followed to the letter. The modern trend is to limit the use of tenders to the minimum. Tenders are usually suitable for the purchase of custom-made materials with a high monetary value, when there is plenty of time for the process, and when there are many suppliers in the market in active and serious competition with each other.

Tenders and quotations are also used as a basis for **post-tender negotiations**. Post-tender negotiations take place between purchaser and tenderer(s) once tenders have been considered and none of those received is acceptable, or where a supplier is chosen above another for certain reasons but the price or other conditions are unacceptable. Strong ethical conduct is a prerequisite in this type of negotiation. No information or any indication of any other tender should be made known during this type of negotiation.

Negotiation often gives a buyer the best results. However, it requires careful preparation by an experienced negotiation team if it is to be successful.

Negotiation entails a personal meeting between buyer and seller with a view to reaching a compromise and concluding a deal. It is an expensive method and only justified in transactions with a high monetary value, where contract conditions are complex, when the execution of the contract stretches over a long period, and when business is conducted with the only suppliers in the market (a monopoly) or suppliers in a strong market position.

Although the role of tenders and negotiations has been discussed as pricing methods, it is important to emphasise that they are also determinants of quality, service and delivery.

23.6.3 Preferences in price comparison

Purchasers often adopt a policy of allocating a specified preference percentage to certain suppliers. This means that for price comparison purposes the supplier's price is reduced by, say, 8%, because the material contains 80% local content (South African manufactured components). In other words, if a supplier enjoys preference because of local content, the price that it quotes is reduced by 8% before it is compared with the prices of other suppliers. Sometimes the preference is enforced **statutorily** (by legislation), as is the preference for local content in the example given above. Preference can also be given to suppliers according to the **purchasing and supply policy** of the business, for example, on the basis of affirmative purchasing and supply programmes or fixed price contracts.

23.7 Timing of purchases

23.7.1 The "right" time to buy

The time at which purchases are made often determines the price paid for materials. In the same way, time and price determine the quantity to be purchased.

The aims of buying at the right time are:
- To ensure that the business is supplied on an ongoing basis with the materials and services required for it to operate without interruptions
- To reduce the risk of price fluctuations
- To keep inventory holding at an optimal level

To realise these aims, a buyer should have a sound knowledge of the market and trends.

23.7.2 Factors influencing the scheduling of purchases

Various internal and external factors influence the time at which purchases (and obviously their quantity) should be made. **Internally**, business policy may prevent buyers from buying speculatively, so that they are unable to make use of bargain offers. Furthermore, the availability of funds in the business determines when products are purchased. Changes in the marketing and operations functions may influence the time at which purchases are made, because most purchases are made for these functions. Physical facilities, such as storage space, is another factor that influences the timing of purchases.

The first **external factors** to determine the time of purchases are market conditions and government regulations. During **recessions**, there is a favourable buyers' market, and materials can be bought at lower prices because of the decrease in demand for materials resulting from fewer economic activities. During these periods it is advisable to buy large quantities of materials. Obviously a business can only benefit from such market conditions if it has the necessary funds, and provided that its economic activities are expected to increase. In a **boom** period, economic activities are high and the demand for suppliers' products increases. Prices increase and service to the purchaser tapers off. During such periods it is wise to buy early at lower prices. Buyers should, as far as possible, avoid making purchases when prices are high. If the boom is expected to level out (prices are expected to decrease) it is wise to buy at the last minute (within the limits of lead times) and in small quantities.

Lead times and the reliability of suppliers are additional external factors that determine the timing of purchases. Government restrictions are another consideration, in that they place limitations in particular on those organisations conducting business with foreign suppliers. A buyer will, for example, have difficulty in obtaining permission to purchase materials overseas if the country's foreign money supply is limited.

23.7.3 Market structures and the scheduling of purchases

Buyers make purchases in stable, unstable and structured markets. In **stable markets**, such as for standard materials (for example, equipment, chemicals, nuts and bolts), buyers purchase materials as needed to maintain optimal inventory levels, because in the short term, prices are not sensitive to fluctuations in demand and supply, and the products are widely available at more or less the same price.

In **unstable markets** which are subject to major fluctuations in price and availability, as in the case of agricultural products, minerals and metals, the timing of purchases is a vital consideration. Here, buyers should purchase larger quantities during favourable periods and smaller quantities in less favourable times. Successful purchasing and supply requires an in-depth knowledge of the market, as well as perfect timing.

Structured markets or commodity exchanges are found throughout the world, their aim being to facilitate international trade in materials such as grain, coffee and wool. A commodity exchange is in fact a market where buyers and sellers meet and barter for a particular commodity (material). Commodity exchanges actually exist in two markets, namely the spot market and the futures market. Each commodity has two prices on a commodity exchange:

- A **cash price** determined by the existing market mechanism (supply and demand) and in practice, the prevailing market price
- A **futures price** based on market conditions

Skilled buyers, by scheduling purchases in these two markets, are able to hedge against risk associated with large price variations. This ensures that commodities and materials are bought at competitive prices.

23.7.4 Policies for purchasing and supply at the right time

There are four main policies that affect the scheduling of purchases:

- **Scheduling purchases according to needs.** This is the most common policy, and entails purchasing materials when the business needs them, regardless of the price and market conditions. It is ideal for purchasing standard materials, but is sometimes also adopted by businesses that buy within unstable markets.
- **Advance purchasing.** This involves the purchase of more materials than required, the aim being to ensure future availability. However, one disadvantage is that excessively high inventory levels lead to high inventory costs.
- **Speculative purchasing.** This entails purchasing materials that the business does not need in the near future, or may never need. Speculative buying is based on a knowledge of the market, and a buyer's anticipation that the price of materials is going to increase drastically in the future. The idea is to sell the purchased materials (which are not always part of the business's normal activities) at a profit when prices do rise. Another reason for speculative buying is the expectation that the business may develop a need for such materials sometime in the future.
- **Minimum purchases.** This entails scheduling purchases so that inventory is available only for the immediate needs of the business. Inventory is kept to a minimum and no buffer stocks are held. This policy is normally applied when prices of materials are in a downward phase. Of course, the business always runs the risk of running out of stock.

This concludes the discussion regarding the purchasing and supply activities, but it is important to emphasise once again that these activities should be executed in an integrated fashion. The next section deals with the strategy of outsourcing and two tools that buyers use to execute their task, namely purchasing and supply research, and negotiations.

23.8 The outsourcing decision

Outsourcing has recently become a popular strategy in the purchasing and supply of materials and services. It can be defined as the process of transferring a business activity, including the relevant assets, to a third party. Organisations outsource when they decide to buy something they had been making in-house. For example, many organisations outsource services such as cafeteria, cleaning and security services, previously provided by internal personnel. The basic philosophy behind outsourcing is that organisations concentrate all their efforts and resources on core activities or core competencies, and buy all non-core activities from outside institutions or experts specialising in the specific activity or function. Often these institutions or experts can provide a better product or service at a lower cost. Competencies are the skills, knowledge and technologies that an organisation possesses, on which its success depends. Only some activities performed by an organisation are core competencies. These core competencies underpin the ability of the organisation to outperform the competition, and they must therefore be defended and nurtured.[4]

Applying the concept: core competency or core activity

The core-competency of a university is its academic programmes. The competitive edge of a specific university depends on the quality, uniqueness and applicability of the academic programmes it offers. Other activities such as security services, logistics, purchasing, catering, marketing, public relations, human resources management, computer services, etc., are not core competencies and can be provided by outside organisations, and these may therefore be outsourced.

Management of organisations should be cautious with respect to decisions as to what the core competencies are, and what activities can be outsourced. Some organisations define core competencies and activities as "those things that we do best". Such an application has clear risks in that it may lead organisations to outsource activities with which they are having trouble. These activities may be of significant value to the organisation both currently and in the future – thus contributing to the organisation's competitive advantage.[5]

Insourcing is the opposite of outsourcing. Organisations can, for certain reasons – in particular, strategic reasons – decide to insource (provide internally) a function or activity rather than buy it from an outside supplier.

The insourcing/outsourcing decision requires a wide variety of knowledge and technical skills, ranging from strategic thinking to an in-depth cost analysis. The cost analysis consists of a comparison of the costs of buying the product or service, and the cost of making the product or performing the service in the organisation. The discussion of the insourcing/outsourcing strategy will be concluded with table 23.3, which clearly indicates the costs that have to be considered regarding the insourcing/outsourcing decision.

Table 23.3: Main cost elements that should be included in the insourcing/outsourcing analysis

Costs to be included with insourcing	Costs to be included with outsourcing
Operating expenses	Purchase cost
• Direct labour	Freight
• Fringe benefits	Inventory costs
• Direct materials	Administrative costs
Indirect labour	Relationship costs
Fringe benefits	
Equipment depreciation	
Fixed overheads	
Engineering/design/research	

23.9 Purchasing and supply research

Purchasing and supply research comprises the **systematic collection and processing of information** on the environment (internal and external) in which the purchasing and supply function operates, so that purchasing and supply decision making can be placed on an objective and scientific footing, and environmental risks kept to a minimum.

All research is costly, and purchasing and supply research is certainly no exception. Therefore, the benefits obtained from such research should be weighed up against the costs involved. Purchasing and supply research should only be undertaken in the areas of greatest risk to the effective performance of the purchasing and supply task. Also, such research is only undertaken in businesses that spend large sums of money on the purchasing of materials and services.

Purchasing and supply research can be organised in various ways. It may, for example, be undertaken by specialist researchers in an independent purchasing and supply research section. This is one of the more effective methods, but is also the most expensive. Another option is for buyers themselves to conduct the research. This method is less expensive, and buyers have first-hand knowledge of any problems being experienced. The disadvantage, however, is that buyers seldom have the time to do research over and above their daily purchasing and supply tasks.

The following are areas in which purchasing and supply research may be conducted:

- **Research on materials and services.** This type of research is mainly concerned with:
  - The supply and demand of materials used by the business
  - A forecast of the business's needs for materials, especially strategic materials
  - The availability of the most important materials in the supply market
  - Price trends in the supply market for the planning periods in question
  - The development of new materials and services
  - Substitute materials
  - Cost-reducing strategies

  This type of research is important because the needs of the market and technology are continually changing. The task of the purchaser is directly influenced by changes in the consumer market. The buyer may cooperate with marketing (in a cross-functional team) in conducting research in the **consumer market**. The areas to be investigated will be:
  - Trends in the consumer market
  - Supply and demand in the consumer market
  - Competitive products, etc.

- **Research on suppliers.** This is one of the most important fields of research. Information on financial stability, production capacity, and the progressiveness and performance of suppliers is indispensable in the choice of the right supplier.

- **Research on the purchasing and supply system.** This type of research is concerned with the effective functioning of the purchasing and supply system, both internally and externally, with suppliers. Areas that merit research are the design of documentation, development of price indexes, the application of computers, and performance appraisal of the purchasing and supply function. This type of research is important when organisations decide to implement the supply chain management approach, which means an integration of systems with suppliers.

The above discussion emphasises the dire need for purchasing and supply research for effective decision making and the efficient performance of the purchasing and supply function. Extensive research is needed in all three areas before organisations can adapt new approaches to the purchasing and supply of materials and services.

23.10 Negotiations in purchasing and supply

Price negotiations were dealt with in section 23.6.2. However, negotiation is a technique that can be used for other purposes as well. Negotiation is required for purchasers and suppliers to reach a common understanding about the assignment and execution of a contract, and includes considerations such as extent of cooperation, delivery, specifications, prices, and conditions of payment. Negotiation is a comprehensive process and demands careful preparation, intelligent manoeuvres, and compromises.

Negotiation is used mainly in cases where:
- Unique or complex materials are purchased for the first time
- The supplier is in a strong position in the market
- There are few suppliers in the market
- There is price collusion between suppliers
- A buying transaction is accompanied by a service or maintenance contract, for example, the purchase of a computer system
- Price increases are requested
- Long-term agreements and/or strategic alliances or partnerships are to be concluded with suppliers

The buyer should be part of the negotiating team and should therefore assist in preparing for negotiations. When making its preparations, the team should first collect information on the economy, conditions in the market, the legal considerations involved, and the financial position of the supplier. A sound knowledge of the materials required and possible substitute materials is also imperative. Secondly, the supplier's offer should be carefully considered and a cost analysis conducted. Thirdly, the strengths and weaknesses of the two negotiating teams should be weighed against each other and analysed prior to proceeding to the actual negotiations.

During the negotiating process, the two parties start at different levels and should move closer to each other through mutual concessions. Because various factors are involved in negotiations, one party may be more compliant about one aspect, and the other more compliant about another. The idea is not to obtain maximum concessions from the supplier, but to negotiate the maximum total value for the purchaser. In the process, the buyer should yield to some extent.

Negotiating tactics should not be used as a substitute for careful preparation or an experienced negotiating team. They can only be applied as a complementary psychological advantage and should not be overdone, otherwise there is no chance of a win-win situation. Also, negotiating tactics should be avoided when negotiating with long-term suppliers.

Other techniques, such as value analysis and the learning curve, can be applied during the preparatory phases and during negotiations to assist the buyer.

Applying the concept: negotiations

The buyer should consider the strengths and weaknesses of each party in the negotiating process, and not give the supplier the opportunity to weaken the buyer's position with guile. For years, a well-known telecommunications institution unconsciously allowed a supplier to weaken its bargaining position in this way. The supplier sold computer systems and offered the purchaser one year's free back-up service, after which a service contract for the following years would be negotiated. The moment the supplier's systems were purchased, the buyer's position weakened against the supplier in bargaining for the back-up service contract. Virtually any price could be asked for the back-up service, because by then the purchaser was dependent on the supplier. The contracts for the computer system and the back-up service should have been negotiated simultaneously. This is the only way that a purchaser can compare different quotations and gain some idea of what the operation of the system is going to cost during its economic life.

23.11 Summary

The discussion in this chapter concerned the purchasing and supply function. It was emphasised that the different purchasing and supply activities do not occur in isolation, but on an integrated basis.

In both chapter 22 and this chapter attention was focused on the integration of the purchasing and supply function with other functions of the business to enable the system to operate as a whole.

References

1. Fiorito, S., Giunipero, L. & Yan, H., Retail buyers' perceptions of Quick Response, *International Journal of Retail and Distribution Management*, Vol. 23, 1998, pp. 237-244.
2. Harris, J.K., Swatman, P.M.C. & Kurnia, S., Efficient consumer response (ECR): a survey of the Australian grocery industry, *Supply Chain Management: An International Journal*, Vol. 4, No. 1, 1999, pp. 35-42.
3. Kotzab, H., Improving supply chain performance by efficient consumer response? A critical comparison of existing ECR approaches, *Journal of Business and Industrial Marketing*, Vol. 14, Nos 5/6, 1999, pp. 364-377.
4. McIvor, R., A practical framework for understanding the outsourcing process, *Supply Chain Management: An International Journal*, Vol. 5, No. 1, 2000, p. 24.
5. Lonsdale, C. & Cox, A., Outsourcing risk and rewards, *Supply Management*, July, 1997, p. 33.

PART 4

Contemporary issues in business management

Contemporary management challenges in business management

This chapter includes a number of contemporary challenges and management problems peculiar to the South African business environment to illustrate the increasing importance of sound management principles in the efficient and effective functioning of businesses, and to demonstrate the comprehensive field of study of this science. Therefore, three contemporary challenges in South African business management, namely productivity issues and productivity improvement, globalisation, and knowledge management are briefly discussed.

Learning outcomes

The content of this chapter will enable learners to:
- Place productivity problems in South Africa in perspective
- Identify misconceptions about productivity and productivity improvement
- Explain the importance of productivity improvement and the level of productivity in South Africa
- Explain ways of improving productivity in South Africa
- Identify the components of globalisation
- Identify and explain the advantages and disadvantages of globalisation
- Understand the three building blocks of the knowledge hierarchy
- List the benefits of knowledge management
- Explain the benefits of knowledge management

24.1 Introduction

In the introductory chapters of this book we discussed in detail the close relationship between a business and its environment, as well as the role of the business in satisfying the needs of society. Because of the important role of business in a market economy, there is a need for a science that can study ways and means of improving its functioning. These were elaborated on in previous chapters of this book. From the discussion of general management and the environmental influences on it, it is clear that business management is not static but dynamic, because it has to deal with environmental change and management problems stemming from this change.

Business management is also multidisciplinary, and must continually keep track of developments in related disciplines that can be utilised to its advantage. The fact that different industries face different business and management problems further complicates this field of study. South African businesses, for example, increasingly need international management skills. At the same time, businesses constantly need to increase their productivity to remain competitive. Small businesses, which provide 95% of all jobs in the USA, have their own management problems relating to their scope and size. We need to be aware of these problems.

An introductory work of this kind can only provide a framework for examining the numerous problems confronting management in all spheres of business. In this context, it serves no purpose to complicate this framework by including too many additional and advanced aspects related to business management. However, a number of contemporary issues and management problems peculiar to the South African business environment are included here to illustrate the increasing importance of sound management principles in the efficient and effective functioning of businesses, and to demonstrate the comprehensive field of study of this science. Therefore, three contemporary issues in South African business management, namely productivity issues and productivity improvement, globalisation, and knowledge management are briefly discussed.

24.2 The problem of productivity in South Africa

24.2.1 Definition of concepts

Few concepts in business management are as frequently misinterpreted as those of productivity and productivity improvement. Any discussion of the problem of productivity in South Africa therefore requires one to have perfect clarity regarding the meaning of these two concepts.

Productivity[1] can be defined as the ratio between goods and services produced (output) and the resources (input) used to produce them, to indicate the productive efficiency with which labour, capital, material, and other inputs are combined and used to produce goods and services of a specific quality for the satisfaction of customer needs.

Example

$$\text{Productivity} = \frac{Q_u}{Q_i}$$

where Q_u = quantity of outputs of goods and services

and Q_i = quantity of inputs in resources (labour, capital, materials, etc.) needed to produce Q_u

---

Productivity improvement from one period to the next is represented by an increase in the output/input ratio in the second period compared to the first.

Example

$$\text{Productivity improvement} = \frac{Qu_t}{Qi_t} < \frac{Qu_t + 1}{Qi_i + 1}$$

where Qu_t = quantity of output of goods and services in period t

and Qi_t = quantity of inputs in resources in period t to produce Qu_t

---

There are five basic ways in which productivity improvements can be achieved:

- Increased output is accomplished with fewer inputs.
- Increased output is produced with the same inputs.
- The same output is produced with fewer inputs.
- A smaller output is produced with even fewer inputs.
- A larger output is produced with more inputs, but the marginal increase in output is larger than the marginal increase in inputs.

From our definition of the concept of productivity, it is clear that an improvement in quality also implies a productivity improvement, even if a particular output/input ratio remains unchanged.

From the viewpoint of the individual business, the objective of productivity improvement is the optimum combination or maximum utilisation of all production factors in a specific business so that only economically unavoidable costs remain. Thus the primary goal of the business, namely maximising the return on invested capital, can ultimately be achieved.[2]

With reference to the above explanation of the concepts of productivity and productivity improvement, one may ask why so much emphasis is currently placed on higher productivity and therefore productivity improvement in South Africa. Will higher productivity not result in larger business profits only, without any advantages for the rest of the community? Does productivity in South Africa really compare as poorly as claimed with that in other countries and, if so, what can be done, especially by management, to increase productivity?

After examining some of the misconceptions about productivity and productivity improvement, we will attempt to provide answers to the above questions.

24.2.2 Misconceptions about productivity and productivity improvement

In section 24.2.1 we mentioned that there are many misconceptions about productivity and productivity improvement. Included among these are the following:

- **Productivity improvement will result in a decrease in job opportunities.** This is obviously not true. The foregoing definition of productivity indicates that productivity improvement can be achieved without affecting the number of job opportunities, because productivity can be increased through improved utilisation of any of the production factors. Even if the number of workers is increased, but the productivity of, say, capital and materials increases at an even higher rate, total productivity will still increase.
- **A productivity improvement programme is a one-off occurrence.** Productivity improvement is, in fact, a lengthy, ongoing process requiring continuous attention if progress is to be achieved and maintained.
- **A productivity improvement programme is the responsibility of one person, institution or sector.** Such an approach can at most be only partly successful. The best results in a productivity improvement programme can

only be achieved with the full cooperation of the management team, workers, input suppliers, and even consumers.

- **Productivity is the same as production.** Production is merely the cumulative output of goods or services, while productivity is related to the input used to achieve the output.
- **Productivity and productivity improvement relate only to the manufacturing sector.** This is incorrect, because businesses in all sectors use inputs to produce outputs. By definition, the concept of productivity therefore applies to all organisations, and every organisation is more or less productive.
- **Productivity improvement is equated with harder work or longer working hours.** Productivity refers to the input/output ratio, while harder work and longer working hours relate only to inputs. Although all people should do a fair day's work, and idleness leads to low productivity, productivity in general does not mean harder work or longer working hours; it means working without wasting.
- **Productivity improvement benefits only employers.** There is a strong correlation between real remuneration and productivity, and therefore employers will pay employees more if they produce more. They cannot, however, pay them more than they are worth, because then they will eventually be forced out of business.
- **Productivity improvement increases work stress and reduces work satisfaction.** Research has proved this to be incorrect, because about two-thirds of both stress and dissatisfaction at work are linked to non-productive activities. Teaching stress management skills often merely teaches people to be happy with such non-productive activities. It is far better in such cases to remove the non-productive factors and the resultant stress and dissatisfaction, and replace them with satisfying, productive activities.

24.2.3 The importance of productivity improvement and the level of productivity in South Africa

Since it is impossible within the ambit of this section to give a full exposition of the importance of productivity improvement and the level of productivity in South Africa, we will focus on a few salient aspects only.

Economic growth can basically be obtained in two ways:

- Through an **increase in resources consumed** (capital, labour, material, energy)
- Through **more productive utilisation** of these resources

In South Africa, productivity makes a very small contribution to overall economic growth (in some years it has even made a negative contribution). However, the converse applies to many of South Africa's trading competitors, for whom productivity growth is responsible for as much as 80% of economic growth. South Africa could achieve a much higher economic growth rate if productivity growth could be enhanced.

Productivity improvement is, therefore, particularly important to the community because it plays a crucial role in economic growth. The better the productivity improvement, the higher the economic growth rate.

Figure 24.1: Economic growth: winners and losers

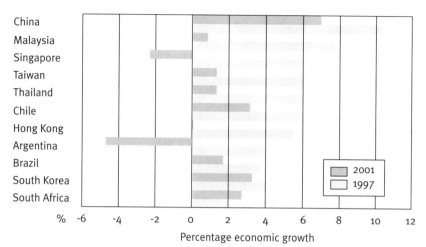

Percentage economic growth

Source: Print Media Association, 2002.

A high economic growth rate is essential to improving the **standard of living** of all South Africans, because it **entails more job opportunities**, combats unemployment, and allows more people to share in the economic prosperity being created.

"Productivity improvement is the single most important strategy for dealing with the most pressing priorities of any political entity, whether this is a city or village, a country or state, a nation or region."

TOR DAHL, PRODUCTIVITY FOCUS, 1991, P. 8.

Economic growth

It is however true that growth rather than redistribution of existing income and wealth offers the key to higher living standards for all. It is the only way to appreciably increase the portion of wealth going to the poorest groups, as it will not reduce the real income levels of the better off – those who often have the critical skills necessary for growth.

Source: NPI, *Productivity Focus*, 1991, p. 12.

It is theoretically possible to strip the rich of their wealth by decree. However, one cannot make the poor even moderately well-off by means of policies such as nationalisation. The emphasis should be on the improvement of South Africa's economic growth potential.

The standard of living can also not be permanently improved by means of salary and wage increases – these must be accompanied by increased productivity. Cost-push inflation can be effectively combated by productivity improvements, because productivity enhancement means better utilisation of resources with further cost savings, resulting in a lower cost structure and inflation rate. **It is also only through productivity improvement that South African manufacturing organisations can ensure that their products can compete in national and international markets.**

Any reduction in a business's cost structure will inevitably have a favourable effect on its profits. Hence, profitability and productivity enhancement have a positive correlation – the greater the productivity improvement, the higher the profits achieved.

To summarise the importance of productivity improvement, higher productivity creates the possibility of paying higher wages to employees, of declaring satisfactory dividends to shareholders, and of offering products and services at lower prices. Productivity improvement thus benefits the entire community and is hence also its responsibility.

24.2.4 Productivity improvement in South Africa

How can productivity improvement be stimulated in South Africa? In section 24.2.1 we mentioned five ways to increase productivity. Although theoretically correct, these methods are oversimplified and too vague to be of any real value, and therefore a summary of the most important factors and techniques of productivity improvement is provided in table 24.1 (see p. 579).

It is not possible, within the ambit of this section, to make a detailed analysis of all the different factors and techniques of productivity improvement provided in this table. Therefore a few comments must suffice.

24.2.4.1 Productivity awareness

Productivity is a state of mind. It is the spirit of progress, of the continuous improvement of what already exists. It is the determination to perform better today than yesterday. It is the desire to improve the existing situation, irrespective of how good it may already be. It is the continuous attempt to implement new techniques and methods.

Is this state of mind present among South Africans? Unfortunately, the answer is "no". In the past, South Africans never needed to maintain a high level of productivity. The economy grew by using more labour, capital, raw materials and energy, which were readily available. Growth was not dependent on the better utilisation of inputs – hence, productivity was not part of the national culture.

The National Productivity Institute (NPI) actively promotes productivity, but its promotion is the responsibility of the population as a whole, and of the economically active sector in particular. Productivity awareness should therefore form an integral part of education from an early age.

24.2.4.2 Training

Illiteracy does not promote productivity, and unfortunately, it takes many years to rectify the effects of poor schooling. Hence, management has a huge responsibility to train employees to meet the requirements of their jobs. In this regard, it has been claimed that insufficient investment in education and training is one of the major causes of low productivity.

Employees are increasingly realising that there is a positive correlation between training and remuneration, because trained workers are more productive and therefore better paid. However, it is common knowledge that in the past (and in some cases even today) remuneration bore no relation to productivity performance. This situation may be attributed mainly to the notion

Table 24.1: Summary of the most important factors and techniques of productivity improvement

A. External factors and techniques for enhancing productivity
1. The attitudes of workers and management towards productivity enhancement
2. Economic and environmental factors enhancing productivity:

(a) The size of the market
(b) Stability of the market
(c) The mobility of production factors
(d) The quality and availabilty of raw materials
(e) The availability of capital and credit

(f) The tax structure
(g) Available training facilities
(h) Research and exchange of information
(i) Technological innovation and mechanisation
(j) Locality advantages

B. Internal techniques for enhancing productivity
1. Factory layout, machinery and equipment:

(a) The amount of capital per worker
(b) Materials management

(c) The maintenance of machinery and equipment
(d) Factory layout

2. Costing and cost reducing techniques:

(a) Cost control
(b) Budgets and budgetary control
(c) Opportunity cost analysis
(d) Incremental cost analysis
(e) Break-even analysis

(f) Management by exception
(g) Organised cost-reducing programmes
(h) Discounted cash-flow computations

3. Organisation, planning and control of production:

(a) Production planning and control
(b) Classification, standardisation and specialisation
(c) Work study
(d) Organisation and method study

(e) Inventory control
(f) Value analysis
(g) Other techniques such as performance research, random sampling, simulation, PERT.

4. Personnel policy

(a) Cooperation between management and workers
(b) Selection and placement of workers
(c) Vocational training
(d) Job analysis, staff evaluation and promotion
(e) Supervision and discipline

(f) Wage incentives and profit-sharing schemes
(g) Work environment and welfare services
(h) Work methods
(i) Length of working day
(j) Number of shifts worked

Source: Van Niekerk, W.P., *Produktiwiteit en werkstudie,* © W.P. van Niekerk, 1978, p. 32.

that workers could easily switch between different types of jobs – hence there was little specialisation. It is only now that South Africa is reaping the bitter fruits both of indifference in the selection, training and placing of workers, as well as bad planning for the country's future needs.

It is of critical importance that management implement training to stimulate productivity. Management has to realise that there are four main factors in training that will increase the performance and resultant productivity of employees.[3]

- Employees require an adequate knowledge of tasks.
- Employees require skills to perform tasks.
- Employees need to be motivated.
- Management should create opportunities to effectively utilise other production resources.

One of the most important issues in training is the motivation of employees towards higher performance. Unfortunately, many organisations in South Africa do not have productivity standards – the point of departure for productivity improvement – and, as a result, employees usually do not know what is expected of them in terms of increased performance. Even if they sometimes do know, the encouragement to live up to expectations is often lacking.

Today, trainers quantify the advantages of training in terms of higher productivity, which, although no easy task, is essential. The idea is to evaluate training (to measure its influence on productivity) rather than to confirm it (to determine whether it has taken place).

24.2.4.3 The implementation of new technology

Technological development and its successful implementation are significant factors that can contribute to productivity improvement. However, South African organisations do not make sufficient use of the advantages offered by improved technology – in many instances, South African organisations are still struggling with its complexity.

In South Africa, there is a large gap between the technology available and its utilisation in trading and manufacturing industries. There is therefore a pressing need for the selection of well-chosen technology and its appropriate implementation in order to bring about clear productivity advantages.

24.2.4.4 Government action

From the information provided in table 24.1, and the discussion of productivity improvement thus far, it is clear that government can, in various direct and indirect ways, influence the productivity performance of a country.

In order to be a positive influence on productivity improvement in South Africa, government should take the following actions:
- **Generally lower tax rates.** Excessively high tax rates have a negative impact on entrepreneurship and efficiency in the production of goods and services, and productivity is therefore reduced.
- **Create training facilities.** Training can make employers and employees more aware of the importance of higher productivity.
- **Link wage and salary increases.** Productivity improvements should accompany wage and salary increases in the public as well as related sectors.
- **Make training subsidies available.** Such action would help to establish a better trained labour force.

If the above were attended to, the country would be assured of productivity enhancement.

24.2.4.5 Business management

In the final instance, the responsibility for productivity improvement lies with an organisation's management, which should follow a holistic approach that includes all resources and activities (see table 24.1, p. 579) in this regard. A major stumbling block, however, is the general shortage of properly trained managers.

To increase productivity in South Africa to desired levels, more and better managers are needed. The existing management echelon is too small to satisfy this need, and the solution is for all workers to be properly utilised. Development and promotion on merit should be accepted as healthy competition, because it is becoming increasingly necessary for management positions to be filled by candidates whose abilities fit the job description, and who will not be chosen on the basis of skin colour. The philosophy, outlook and form of management should be aimed at the optimal utilisation and exploitation of knowledge, ability and experience. Such an approach will assist productivity improvement, because then the most suitable person will be appointed to the right post.

24.2.5 Final comments

A high real economic growth rate is essential to ensure a satisfactory standard of living for all South Africans, and this can come about only through sustained productivity improvement. The latter is the responsibility of every member of the community, but it probably applies all the more to business management, which has the power to realise it through the application of healthy management principles.

24.3 Globalisation

24.3.1 Introduction

Globalisation is a term that is widely used, but it defies precise definition. From an economic perspective, it may be described as the increasing interaction and integration of national economic systems through the growth of international trade, investment and capital flows – but globalisation also has social and cultural implications, which are not captured in this description.

Description

Globalisation involves the growing interdependence among countries as reflected by increasing cross-border flows of goods, services, capital and know-how, thereby creating a whole new world order for firms around the world.

24.3.2 The components of globalisation

Globalisation has two components:
- The globalisation of markets
- The globalisation of production

24.3.2.1 The globalisation of markets

The globalisation of markets refers to the merging of historically distinct and separate markets into one integrated marketplace. Thus, it is argued that the tastes and preferences of consumers in different countries are beginning to converge in accordance with some global norm, thereby helping to create a global marketplace. Consumer products such as Coca-Cola, Levi's jeans, Sony walkmans and McDonalds hamburgers are examples of this trend.

Lifestyle

We are not just connected with the rest of the world, we have assimilated parts or more of their culture and values, whether it was forced upon us or embraced willingly in the name of "lifestyle". As we look around us today, at the clothes and shoes we are wearing, the brands of make-up and perfume, and the fact that we use make-up and perfume, speaks volumes for the close-likeness of lifestyle, globalisation, westernisation and colonisation, all seemingly very much the same animal, evolving over time.

Source: The effects of globalization on women worldwide, in *Women's International Network News,* Winter 2001, Vol. 2, Issue 1, p. 20.

Although consumer products are gaining importance on global markets, industrial products still form the basis for world trade. Commodities such as aluminium, gold, oil, and wheat are traded in huge quantities on world markets. Rivalry between suppliers of these goods as well as certain consumer goods occurs on a global basis. Coca-Cola's rivalry with Pepsi is, for example, not limited to the American or the European market – the competition is global.

24.3.2.2 The globalisation of production

The globalisation of production refers to the tendency of companies to source goods and services from locations all over the world to take advantage of national differences in the cost and quality of factors of production. In so doing, companies attempt to lower their overall cost structure and to improve the quality of their product offering.

24.3.3 Causes of globalisation

Economies were previously isolated (and protected) from each other by barriers to cross-border trade, long distances, different time zones, language and cultural differences, and government regulation.

The majority of these economies are now actively involved in cross-border trade as a result of the following developments:[4]

- **Trade liberalisation and the easing of barriers to trade and investment by governments worldwide**. After World War II, nations committed themselves to removing barriers to the free flow of goods, services and capital. This goal was enshrined in a treaty known as the General Agreement on Tariffs and Trade (GATT). In 1995, GATT was replaced by the World Trade Organisation (WTO). The WTO is, similarly, a multinational institution with the goal of lowering trade and investment barriers. It also polices the global trading system and allows member nations to impose retaliatory tariffs on countries that do not abide by WTO rules. The WTO has 135 member countries, and it attempts to resolve trade disputes between member nations.

> World trade increased by almost 2000% between 1950 and 1998.
>
> *WORLD TRADE ORGANISATION 1999 ANNUAL REPORT, GENEVA, WTO.*

- **Rapid technological advances in communications and transportation.** Over the past 30 years, global communications have been revolutionised by developments in satellite, optical fibre and wireless technologies, the Internet and the World Wide Web. Lower communication costs, quicker response time, and the establishment of Web-based electronic commerce (e-commerce) make it possible for businesses to expand their global presence at a lower cost than ever before. The Web makes it easier for buyers and sellers to find each other, wherever they are located and whatever their size.

  Advances in transportation also contributed to globalisation. Commercial jet aircraft reduced the time it takes to get from one location to another in different countries, thus making it easier for business people to operate in locations all over the world. Containerisation, on the other hand, significantly contributed to the lowering of costs of shipping goods over long distances, thus making it cheaper and easier to export goods to other countries.

- **The change from formerly centrally-planned economies to freer market economies.** Today, many of the former communist nations of Europe and Asia share a commitment to democratic politics and free market economics. Having been largely closed to western trade for many years, these countries now trade actively with other countries. The huge potential for trade with a country like China has not been exploited fully, even though trade with China has increased over 15% per annum over the past twenty years.

- **The increasing importance of multinational enterprises worldwide.** During the 1960s global activity was dominated by large US multinational businesses. This has, however, changed quite remarkably, and Japanese, German, French and British companies currently compete actively in the global market. South African companies such as Billiton, Anglo-American and SABMiller have invested in other countries, while a number of companies such as Sappi, Old Mutual, Liberty and Didata have exploited international capital markets through listings on foreign stock exchanges. Multinational companies have a pronounced effect on world trade.

The extent of the increase in world trade compared to growth in Gross Domestic Product (GDP) is depicted in figure 24.2 (see p. 584).

24.3.4 Measuring globalisation

One of the ways in which globalisation can be measured is in terms of the rising ratio of world trade to output (GDP). Figure 24.2 shows that world output expanded by 27% for the period 1990 to 2001, while world trade expanded by 83% over this same period.

Another measure of globalisation is foreign direct investment (FDI). According to Hill,[5] FDI occurs when a firm invests directly in productive facilities in a foreign country where an equity interest of at least 10% is regarded as a direct investment. In some countries, this minimum requirement could be as high as 25% or even 30% .

Compared to that in other developing countries, FDI in South Africa is small in value terms. The cumulative FDI in South Africa between 1994 and

1998 amounted to almost US$5 billion. In comparison, China, for example, received US$203 billion in the same period, while India received US$12 billion. Between 1994 and 1998, 17,5% of FDI in South Africa went to telecommunications, 15,2% to "other sectors", 11,4% to energy and oil, 10,7% to motor and components, and 10,4% to food and beverages.

The sources of FDI for this period are given in figure 24.3.

Figure 24.2: The growth of world trade and world output (GDP) 1990–2001

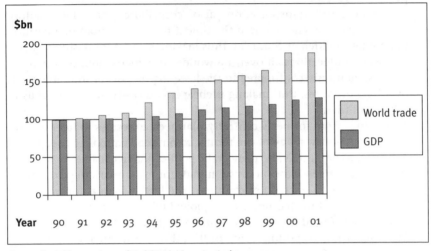

Source: http://www.wto.org (World Trade Organisation).

Figure 24.3: The sources of FDI in South Africa by country for the period 1995-1998

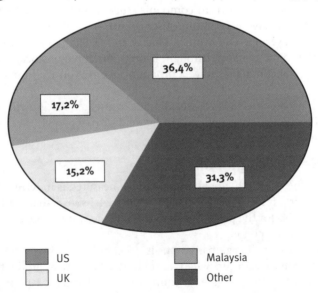

Source: du Mhango, D., Industrial Development Corporation – Foreign Direct Investment in South Africa: How has the policy towards FDI worked and how can it be strengthened? http://www.tips.org.za/events/proceedings/fdi.html

As indicated in figure 24.3, of the FDI received, 36% came from the USA, 17% from Malaysia, and 15% from the UK. Other notable investors included Germany, Japan, Switzerland and Italy.

24.3.5 The advantages and disadvantages of globalisation

The **advantages** of globalisation include the following:

- The lowering of trade barriers allows businesses to market and sell their products internationally. The world as a whole becomes the market for a specific product or service – the market is not limited to a specific region or country.
- The lowering of investment barriers allows companies to base production in the optimal location from where world markets can be served.
- Many supporters of globalisation believe that increased cross-border trade and investments result in greater efficiency and therefore lower prices for goods and services. Because its proponents believe that globalisation stimulates economic growth, they argue that globalisation raises the income of consumers and that it creates jobs in countries that participate in the global system.

Example

The Boeing Company's 777 jet airliner contains 132 500 major component parts that are produced all over the world by 545 suppliers in Singapore, Japan, Italy and other countries.

Source: Hill, C.W.H., *International business*, McGraw-Hill, New York, 2001, p. 6.

The **disadvantages** of global trade are as follows:

- Globalisation confronts companies with the challenge of having to compete internationally, whereas previously they had only to compete with local rivals. In addition, it raises questions as to how to invest, produce and compete in foreign markets while dealing with differences in culture, language and government regulations.
- Falling trade barriers often destroy jobs instead of creating jobs. Globalisation allows countries to move their production facilities to locations where wage rates are lower, thereby destroying jobs in the country of origin. People in developing countries, on the other hand, argue that jobs are destroyed because smaller local companies cannot compete with large international organisations. International competition eventually forces them to close down, with an accompanying loss of job opportunities.

The counter arguments to these concerns is that the benefits of free trade exceed the costs, that free trade will eventually result in a more efficient system, and that the advantages of economies of scale, increased productivity, and the increased level of skills required to compete in a global economy should have a positive net effect.

24.3.6 Conclusion

Since World War II there has been a significant lowering of trade and investment barriers, which has resulted in a freer flow of products, services and capital. This has in turn resulted in a more integrated and interdependent world economy, referred to as globalisation. Globalisation has two components, markets and production, and is measured by world trade in relation to world output and foreign direct investment.

Although severe criticism is often directed at globalisation, its proponents believe that it results in greater efficiency, with a net benefit to the entire world.

24.4 Knowledge management

24.4.1 Introduction

Knowledge management emerged in the 1990s as an attempt by companies to harness the wealth of under-utilised data, information and knowledge in their organisations. Traditionally, certain individuals and departments have secured their positions and status within the corporate hierarchy by hoarding information and knowledge. However, the demands of a post-industrial economy, with its fast changing and more competitive environment, has forced organisations to intelligently manage and use the existing information and knowledge. Knowledge is today regarded as a new form of capital in what is referred to as the "knowledge economy". Organisations need to share and manage knowledge as a valuable resource in order to survive in this economy.

24.4.2 What is knowledge management?

Applying the concept: knowledge management

Imagine being able to extract specific information about your business and its processes from filing cabinets, computer hard drives, websites, and people's minds. Now imagine depositing that information in a system that automatically organises it into logical subject areas, is easily able to be searched, and is accessible to whoever has approved access to it. Imagine that the information is centralised, easy to understand, and can also be added to.

Imagine, also, improving your workplace environment by removing physical obstacles between people (partitions and filing cabinets) so that informal knowledge-sharing becomes the norm. Finally, imagine employees so encouraged by having the right information at their fingertips, that they are more than happy to follow set procedures and help collect, update and store your intellectual property.

Knowledge management is the process of identifying, collecting, storing, and transforming data and information into an intellectual asset that is available to all staff members. It aims to develop a solid base of intellectual capital by gathering and sharing the knowledge of individual staff members.

Companies introduce knowledge management in order to:
* Increase workplace efficiency
* Save time

- Reduce costs
- Retain, re-use and exchange knowledge

24.4.3 *The knowledge hierarchy*

Knowledge consists of the following three building blocks:

- **Data.** This is the most elementary building block in the knowledge hierarchy. Data has the following characteristics:
  - It represents facts, events or uncoded source-data.
  - It has no meaning in itself.
  - It simply exists, and has no significance beyond its existence.
  - As a result of the lack of context, data requires human intervention and interpretation in order to extract even a minimal amount of usefulness from it.

Examples of data

- Student lists
- Statistics of population trends
- Bank statements
- List of share prices

- **Information.** Data becomes information when it is categorised in a logical manner. In information, units of measure – such as time, distance, and magnitude – provide additional context not found in data alone. This is data that has been given meaning by way of a relational connection. Information embodies the understanding of a relationship of some sort, possibly cause and effect.

Examples of information

- The temperature dropped 15 degrees and then it started raining.
- The increase in earnings per share of 10% resulted in an increase in the share price.

- **Knowledge.** This is an organised body of information that forms the basis of insights or judgements. Information becomes knowledge when people use the information to make decisions or predictions. The human contribution therefore distinguishes knowledge from data and information. Nonaka and Takeuchi[6] make three observations in describing the similarities and differences between knowledge and information:
  - Knowledge, unlike information, is about beliefs and commitment.
  - Knowledge is a function of a particular stance, perspective, or intention.
  - Knowledge, unlike information, is about action. It is always knowledge "to some end".
  - Knowledge, like information, is about meaning. It is context-specific and relational.

> **Examples of knowledge**
>
> - If the humidity is very high and the temperature drops substantially, it is unlikely that the atmosphere will be able to hold the moisture, so it rains.
> - Given that general market conditions remain the same, an increase in earnings will most probably result in an increase in the share price.

Source: Adapted from *Jakarta Post*, 8 June, 2002.

24.4.4 *The knowledge management process*

The knowledge management process consists of four steps:[7]

- **Step 1: Identify existing knowledge.** Knowledge management starts by identifying what you already know. This includes the knowledge that resides in the minds of staff members, in reports, in data sets held throughout the organisation, or among regular suppliers and customers. The start of any knowledge management strategy is to be clear about where you will begin.
- **Step 2: Reflect on existing knowledge.** Once you have identified where the existing knowledge resides in the organisation, the next step is to take stock of the knowledge. What is it that the people in the organisation know? How useful is that knowledge? Reflecting on current knowledge provides the opportunity of summarising the existing knowledge into a form that can be easily shared with others. This also makes it possible to identify the gaps in the existing knowledge, and to focus future knowledge-gathering efforts.

> "If only Hewlett Packard (HP) knew what HP knows, it could be three times more productive."
>
> *LEW PLATT (FORMER CEO OF HEWLETT-PACKARD)*

- **Step 3: Redistribute the knowledge.** A critical component of knowledge management is creating a system that ensures knowledge is shared with those who need it. The aim is to make the knowledge available everywhere it is needed in the organisation.
- **Step 4: Apply the knowledge.** The most important reason why organisations initiate a knowledge management system is to improve their performance. Hence, the ultimate goal of identifying, reflecting upon, and sharing what an organisation knows, is to apply that knowledge.

24.4.5 *The benefits of knowledge management*

The following benefits of knowledge management have been reported by companies of varying sizes:

- **Less frustration.** Staff members can access information themselves and do not need to rely on the availability of other people.
- **Better customer service.** Staff members know where to find the information that the customer needs.
- **Decreased vulnerability when staff leave.** Their work processes are documented so that others can pick up those tasks without confusion arising.
- **Increased competitiveness.** Management can see at a glance where the business is weaker or stronger.

- **Improved productivity.** Access to the right knowledge saves time that might have been wasted in looking for it.
- **Improved internal communication and teamwork.**
- **Some tasks may be able to be automated.** This could occur when enough information about them has been gathered.
- **Improved market forecasting.** Knowledge management systems can provide forecasts on supply or economic problems, and companies can, accordingly, adjust inventory and other expensive processes to cope with these.

24.5 Summary

This chapter dealt with three contemporary issues in South African business management, namely productivity issues and productivity improvement, globalisation, and knowledge management.

References

1. Mainly based on Republic of South Africa, Presidentís Council, *Report of the committee for economic affairs on a strategy and action plan to improve productivity in the RSA*, Report PC 1/1989, Government Printer, Cape Town: National Productivity Institute, *Productivity Focus*, National Productivity Institute, Pretoria, 1991.
2. Van Niekerk, W. P., *Produktiwiteit en werkstudie*, Butterworth, Durban, 1978, p. 6.
3. Botha, F., Verhoogde produktiwiteit deur motivering, in *Volkshandel*, October, 1980, p. 26.
4. Ball D.A., McCulloch, W.H., Frantz, P., Geringer, J.M. & Minor, M.S., *International business*, 8th edition, McGraw-Hill Irwin, New York, 2002.
5. Hill, C.W.L., *International business*, 4th edition, McGraw-Hill Irwin, New York, 2003.
6. Nonaka, I. & Takeuchi, H., *The knowledge-creating company: how Japanese companies create the dynamics of innovation*, Oxford University Press (USA), 1995, pp. 57–58.
7. Sterndale-Bennett, B., Defining knowledge management, *British Journal of Administrative Management (AMT)*, July 2001, p. 26.

Index

Page numbers in italics refer to tables and figures.